contemporary
american thought

a college reader

Edited by **E. W. Johnson**

Western Illinois University

THE FREE PRESS, NEW YORK

Second Printing June 1968

Stacy, Shane, and Leigh

This textbook assumes that life is not a mortal sin. The esoteric dead is not buried in these pages under a drab-brown tombstone of laborious prose. Instead, I have attempted to collect a group of stories, poems, essays, and plays which someone might conceivably *want* to read — selections which cut at the flesh of contemporary America — lay bare the anatomy of a nation in transition.

Assassination, civil strife, isolation, parched emotions, glittering lights. Cultural Disorientation and Depersonalization. Alienation, Fear and Anxiety. Affirmative Re-orientation. America since World War One. And the literature which reflects the culture: an omnibus of sixty-three readings; all alive, intense.

OH DAD, POOR DAD, MAMA'S HUNG YOU IN THE CLOSET AND I'M FEELIN' SO SAD. LAS VEGAS (WHAT?) LAS VEGAS (CAN'T HEAR YOU! TOO NOISY) LAS VEGAS!!!! GOOD NEWS! GOD IS LOVE! UNDERWEAR. Norman Mailer, E. E. Cummings, Tennessee Williams, Theodore H. White. John Hawkes, William Faulkner, Pete Seeger, Nathanial West. Contemporary American thought, contemporary American thinkers. A contemporary American textbook. With, incidentally, no comments, no interpretation, no discussion — critical analysis left to student discourse, student thought.

— E. W. J.

Contents

SECTION 1:
cultural disorientation and depersonalization

affirmative re-orientation

nonfiction

section **1** cultural

disorientation

and

depersonalization

fiction

soldier's home

Ernest Hemingway

Krebs went to the war from a Methodist college in Kansas. There is a picture which shows him among his fraternity brothers, all of them wearing exactly the same height and style collar. He enlisted in the Marines in 1917 and did not return to the United States until the second division returned from the Rhine in the summer of 1919.

There is a picture which shows him on the Rhine with two German girls and another corporal. Krebs and the corporal look too big for their uniforms. The German girls are not beautiful. The Rhine does not show in the picture.

By the time Krebs returned to his home town in Oklahoma the greeting of heroes was over. He came back much too late. The men from the town who had been drafted had all been welcomed elaborately on their return. There had been a great deal of hysteria. Now the reaction had set in. People seemed to think it was rather ridiculous for Krebs to be getting back so late, years after the war was over.

At first Krebs, who had been at Belleau Wood, Soissons, the Champagne, St. Mihiel and the Argonne did not want to talk about the war at all. Later he felt the need to talk but no one wanted to hear about it. His town had heard too many atrocity stories to be thrilled by actualities. Krebs found that to be listened to at all he had to lie, and after he had done this twice he, too, had a reaction against the war and against talking about it. (A distaste for everything that had happened to him in the war set in because of the lies he had told.) All of the times that had been able to make him feel cool and clear inside himself when he thought of them; the times so long back when he had done the one thing, the only thing for a man to do, easily and naturally, when he might have done something else, now lost their cool, valuable quality and then were lost themselves.

His lies were quite unimportant lies and consisted in attributing to himself things other men had seen, done or heard of, and stating as facts certain apocryphal incidents familiar to all soldiers. Even his lies were not sensational at the pool room. His acquaintances, who had heard detailed accounts of German women found chained to machine guns in the Argonne forest and who could not comprehend, or were barred by their patriotism from interest in, any German machine gunners who were not chained, were not thrilled by his stories.

Krebs acquired the nausea in regard to experience that is the result of untruth or exaggeration, and when he occasionally met another man who had really been a soldier and they talked a few minutes in the dressing room at a dance he fell into the easy pose of the old soldier among other soldiers: that he had been badly, sickeningly frightened all the time. In this way he lost everything.

During this time, it was late summer, he was sleeping late in bed, getting up to walk down town to the library to get a book, eating lunch at home, reading on the front porch until he became bored and then walking down through the town to spend the hottest hours of the day in the cool dark of the pool room. He loved to play pool.

In the evening he practised on his clarinet, strolled down town, read and went to bed. He was still a hero to his two young sisters. His mother would have given him breakfast in bed if he had wanted it. She often came in when he was in bed and asked him to tell her about the war, but her attention always wandered. His father was non-committal.

Before Krebs went away to the war he had never been allowed to drive the family motor car. His father was in the real estate business and always wanted the car to be at his command when he required it to take clients out into the country to show them a piece of farm property. The car always stood outside the First National Bank building where his father had an office on the second floor. Now, after the war, it was still the same car.

Nothing was changed in the town except that the young girls had grown up. But they lived in such a complicated world of already defined alliance and shifting feuds that Krebs did not feel the energy or the courage to break into it. He liked to look at them, though. There were so many good-looking young girls. Most of them had their hair cut short. When he went away only little girls wore their hair like that or girls that were fast. They all wore sweaters and shirt waists with round Dutch collars. It was a pattern. He liked to look at them from the front porch as they walked on the other side of the street. He liked to watch them walking under the shade of the trees. He liked the round Dutch collars above their sweaters. He liked their silk stockings and flat shoes. He liked their bobbed hair and the way they walked.

When he was in town their appeal to him was not very strong. He did not like them when he saw them in the Greek's ice cream parlor. He did not want them themselves really. They were too complicated. There was something else. Vaguely he wanted a girl but he did not want to have to work to get her. He would have liked to have a girl but he did not want to have to spend a long time getting her. He did not want to get into the intrigue and the politics. He did not want to have to do any courting. He did not want to tell any more lies. It wasn't worth it.

He did not want any consequences. He did not want any consequences ever again. He wanted to live along without consequences. Besides he did not really need a girl. The army had taught him that. It was all right to pose as though you had to have a girl. Nearly everybody did that. But it wasn't true. You did not need a girl. That was the funny thing. First a fellow boasted how girls meant nothing to him, that he never thought of them, that they could not touch him. Then a fellow boasted that he could not get along without girls, that he had to have them all the time, that he could not go to sleep without them.

That was all a lie. It was all a lie both ways. You did not need a girl unless you thought about them. He learned that in the army. Then sooner or later you always got one. When you were really ripe for a girl you always got one. You did not have to think about it. Sooner or later it would come. He had learned that in the army.

Now he would have liked a girl if she had come to him and not wanted to talk. But here at home it was all too complicated. He knew he could never get through it all again. It was not worth the trouble. That was the thing about French girls and German girls. There was not all this talking. You couldn't talk much and you did not need to talk. It was simple and you were friends. He thought about France and then he began to think about Germany. On the whole he had liked Germany better. He did not want to leave Germany. He did not want to come home. Still, he had come home. He sat on the front porch.

He liked the girls that were walking along the other side of the street. He liked the look of them much better than the French girls or the German girls. But the world they were in was not the world he was in. He would like to have one of them. But it was not worth it. They were such a nice pattern. He liked the pattern. It was exciting. But he would not go through all the talking. He did not want one badly enough. He liked to look at them all, though. It was not worth it. Not now when things were getting good again.

He sat there on the porch reading a book on the war. It was a history and he was reading about all the engagements he had been in. It was the most interesting reading he had ever done. He wished there were more maps. He looked forward with a good feeling to reading all the really good histories when they would come out with good detail maps. Now he was really learning about the war. He had been a good soldier. That made a difference.

One morning after he had been home about a month his mother came into his bedroom and sat on the bed. She smoothed her apron.

"I had a talk with your father last night, Harold," she said, "and he is willing for you to take the car out in the evenings."

"Yeah?" said Krebs, who was not fully awake. "Take the car out? Yeah?"

"Yes. Your father has felt for some time that you should be able to take the car out in the evenings whenever you wished but we only talked it over last night."

"I'll bet you made him," Krebs said.

"No. It was your father's suggestion that we talk the matter over."

"Yeah. I'll bet you made him," Krebs sat up in bed.

"Will you come down to breakfast, Harold?" his mother said.

"As soon as I get my clothes on," Krebs said.

His mother went out of the room and he could hear her frying something downstairs while he washed, shaved and dressed to go down into the dining-room for breakfast. While he was eating breakfast his sister brought in the mail.

"Well, Hare," she said. "You old sleepy-head. What do you ever get up for?"

Krebs looked at her. He liked her. She was his best sister.

"Have you got the paper?" he asked.

She handed him *The Kansas City Star* and he shucked off its brown wrapper and opened it to the sporting page. He folded *The Star* open and propped it against the water pitcher with his cereal dish to steady it, so he could read while he ate.

"Harold," his mother stood in the kitchen doorway, "Harold, please don't muss up the paper. Your father can't read his *Star* if it's been mussed."

"I won't muss it," Kreb said.

His sister sat down at the table and watched him while he read.

"We're playing indoor over at school this afternoon," she said. "I'm going to pitch."

"Good, said Krebs. "How's the old wing?"

"I can pitch better than lots of the boys. I tell them all you taught me. The other girls aren't much good."

"Yeah?" said Krebs.

"I tell them all you're my beau. Aren't you my beau, Hare?"

"You bet."

"Couldn't your brother really be your beau just because he's your brother?"

"I don't know."

"Sure you know. Couldn't you be my beau, Hare, if I was old enough and if you wanted to?"

"Sure. You're my girl now."

"Am I really your girl?"

"Sure."

"Do you love me?"

"Uh, huh."

"Will you love me always?"

"Sure."

"Will you come over and watch me play indoor?"

"Maybe."

"Aw, Hare, you don't love me. If you loved me, you'd want to come over and watch me play indoor."

Kreb's mother came into the dining-room from the kitchen. She carried a plate with two fried eggs and some crisp bacon on it and a plate of buckwheat cakes.

"You run along, Helen," she said. "I want to talk to Harold."

She put the eggs and bacon down in front of him and brought in a jug of maple syrup for the buckwheat cakes. Then she sat down across the table from Krebs.

"I wish you'd put down the paper a minute, Harold," she said.

Krebs took down the paper and folded it.

"Have you decided what you are going to do yet, Harold?" his mother said, taking off her glasses.

"No," said Krebs.

"Don't you think it's about time?" His mother did not say this in a mean way. She seemed worried.

"I hadn't thought about it," Krebs said.

"God has some work for every one to do," his mother said. "There can be no idle hands in His Kingdom."

"I'm not in His Kingdom," Krebs said.

"We are all of us in His Kingdom."

Krebs felt embarrassed and resentful as always.

"I've worried about you so much, Harold," his mother went on. "I know the temptations you must have been exposed to. I know how weak men are. I know what your own dear grandfather, my own father, told us about the Civil War and I have prayed for you. I pray for you all day long, Harold."

Krebs looked at the bacon fat hardening on his plate.

"Your father is worried, too," his mother went on. "He thinks you have lost your ambition, that you haven't got a definite aim in life. Charley Simmons, who is just your age, has a good job and is going to be married. The boys are all settling down; they're all determined to get somewhere; you can see that boys like Charley Simmons are on their way to being really a credit to the community."

Krebs said nothing.

"Don't look that way, Harold," his mother said. "You know we love you and I want to tell you for your own good how matters stand. Your father does not want to hamper your freedom. He thinks you should be allowed to drive the car. If you want to take some of the nice girls out riding with you, we are only too pleased. We want you to enjoy yourself. But you are going to have to settle down to work, Harold. Your father doesn't care what you start in at. All work is honorable as he says. But you've got to make a start at something.

He asked me to speak to you this morning and then you can stop in and see him at his office."

"Is that all?" Krebs said.

"Yes. Don't you love your mother, dear boy?"

"No," Krebs said.

His mother looked at him across the table. Her eyes were shiny. She started crying.

"I don't love anybody," Krebs said.

It wasn't any good. He couldn't tell her, he couldn't make her see it. It was silly to have said it. He had only hurt her. He went over and took hold of her arm. She was crying with her head in her hands.

"I didn't mean it," he said. "I was just angry at something. I didn't mean I didn't love you."

His mother went on crying. Krebs put his arm on her shoulder.

"Can't you you believe me, mother?"

His mother shook her head.

"Please, please, mother. Please believe me."

"All right," his mother said chokily. She looked up at him. "I believe you, Harold."

Krebs kissed her hair. She put her face up to him.

"I'm your mother," she said. "I held you next to my heart when you were a tiny baby."

Krebs felt sick and vaguely nauseated.

"I know, Mummy," he said. "I'll try and be a good boy for you."

"Would you kneel and pray with me, Harold?" his mother asked.

They knelt down beside the dining-room table and Krebs's mother prayed.

"Now, you pray, Harold," she said.

"I can't," Krebs said.

"Try, Harold."

"I can't."

"Do you want me to pray for you?"

"Yes."

So his mother prayed for him and then they stood up and Krebs kissed his mother and went out of the house. He had tried so to keep his life from being complicated. Still, none of it had touched him. He had felt sorry for his mother and she had made him lie. He would go to Kansas City and get a job and she would feel all right about it. There would be one more scene maybe before he got away. He would not go down to his father's office. He would miss that one. He wanted

his life to go smoothly. It had just gotten going that way. Well, that
was all over now, anyway. He would go over to the schoolyard and
watch Helen play indoor baseball.

the man who studied yoga

Norman Mailer

1.

I would introduce myself if it were not useless. The name I had last
night will not be the same as the name I have tonight. For the
moment, then, let me say that I am thinking of Sam Slovoda. Obligatorily, I study him, Sam Slovoda who is neither ordinary nor
extraordinary, who is not young nor yet old, not tall nor short. He is
sleeping, and it is fit to describe him now, for like most humans he
prefers sleeping to not sleeping. He is a mild pleasant-looking man
who has just turned forty. If the crown of his head reveals a little
bald spot, he has nourished in compensation the vanity of a mustache.
He has generally when he is awake an agreeable manner, at least
with strangers; he appears friendly, tolerant, and genial. The fact is
that like most of us, he is full of envy, full of spite, a gossip, a man
who is pleased to find others are as unhappy as he, and yet — this is
the worst to be said — he is a decent man. He is better than most. He
would prefer to see a more equitable world, he scorns prejudice and
privilege, he tries to hurt no one, he wishes to be liked. I will go even
further. He has one serious virtue — he is not fond of himself, he
wishes he were better. He would like to free himself of envy, of the
annoying necessity to talk about his friends, he would like to love
people more; specifically, he would like to love his wife more, and
to love his two daughters without the tormenting if nonetheless ir-
remediable vexation that they closet his life in the dusty web of domestic responsibilities and drudging for money.

How often he tells himself with contempt that he has the cruelty of a kind weak man.

May I state that I do not dislike Sam Slovoda; it is just that I am disappointed in him. He has tried too many things and never with a whole heart. He has wanted to be a serious novelist and now merely indulges the ambition; he wished to be of consequence in the world, and has ended, temporarily perhaps, as an overworked writer of continuity for comic magazines; when he was young he tried to be a bohemian and instead acquired a wife and family. Of his appetite for a variety of new experience I may say that it is matched only by his fear of new people and novel situations.

I will give an instance. Yesterday, Sam was walking along the street and a bum approached him for money. Sam did not see the man until too late; lost in some inconsequential thought, he looked up only in time to see a huge wretch of a fellow with a red twisted face and an outstretched hand. Sam is like so many; each time a derelict asks for a dime, he feels a coward if he pays the money, and is ashamed of himself if he doesn't. This once, Sam happened to think, I will not be bullied, and hurried past. But the bum was not to be lost so easily. "Have a heart, Jack," he called after in a whisky voice, "I need a drink bad." Sam stopped, Sam began to laugh. "Just so it isn't for coffee, here's a quarter," he said; and he laughed, and the bum laughed. "You're a man's man," the bum said. Sam went away pleased with himself, thinking about such things as the community which existed between all people. It was cheap of Sam. He should know better. He should know he was merely relieved the situation had turned out so well. Although he thinks he is sorry for bums, Sam really hates them. Who knows what violence they can offer?

At this time, there is a powerful interest in Sam's life, but many would ridicule it. He is in the process of being psychoanalyzed. Myself, I do not jeer. It has created the most unusual situation between Sam and me. I could go into details but they are perhaps premature. It would be better to watch Sam awaken.

His wife, Eleanor, has been up for an hour, and she has shut the window and neglected to turn off the radiator. The room is stifling. Sam groans in a stupor which is neither sleep nor refreshment, opens one eye, yawns, groans again, and lies twisted, strangled and trussed in pajamas which are too large for him. How painful it is for him to rise. Last night there was a party, and this morning, Sunday morning, he is awakening with a hangover, Invariably, he is depressed in the morning, and it is no different today. He finds himself in the flat and familiar dispirit of nearly all days.

It is snowing outside. Sam finally lurches to the window, and opens it for air. With the oxygen of a winter morning clearing his brain, he looks down six stories into the giant quadrangle of the Queens housing development in which he lives, staring morosely at the inch of slush which covers the monotonous artificial park that separates his apartment building from an identical structure not two hundred feet away. The walks are black where the snow has melted, and in the children's playground, all but deserted, one swing oscillates back and forth, pushed by an irritable little boy who plays by himself among the empty benches, swaddled in galoshes, muffler, and over-coat. The snow falls sluggishly, a wet snow which probably will turn to rain. The little boy in the playground gives one last disgusted shove to the swing and trudges away gloomily, his overshoes leaving a small animal track behind him. Back of Sam, in the four-room apartment he knows like a blind man, there is only the sound of Eleanor making breakfast.

Well, thinks Sam, depression in the morning is a stage of his analysis, Dr. Sergius has said.

This is the way Sam often phrases his thoughts. It is not altogether his fault. Most of the people he knows think that way and talk that way, and Sam is not the strongest of men. His language is doomed to the fashion of the moment. I have heard him remark mildly, almost apologetically, about his daughters: "My relation with them still suffers because I haven't worked through all my feminine identifica-tions." The saddest thing is that the sentence has meaning to Sam even if it will not have meaning to you. A great many ruminations, discoveries, and memories contribute their connotation to Sam. It has the significance of a cherished line of poetry to him.

Although Eleanor is not being analyzed, she talks in a similar way. I have heard her remark in company, "Oh, you know Sam, he not only thinks I'm his mother, he blames me for being born." Like most women. Eleanor can be depended upon to employ the idiom of her husband.

What amuses me is that Sam is critical of the way others speak. At the party last night he was talking to a Hollywood writer, a young man with a great deal of energy and enthusiasm. The young man spoke something like this: "You see, boychick, I can spike any script with yaks, but the thing I can't do is heartbreak. My wife says she's gonna give me heartbreak. The trouble is I've had a real solid-type

life. I mean I've had my ups and downs like all of humanity, but
there's never been a shriek in my life. I don't know how to write
shrieks."

On the trip home, Sam had said to Eleanor, "It was disgraceful. A
writer should have some respect for language."

Eleanor answered with a burlesque of Sam's indignation. "Listen,
I'm a real artist-type. Culture is for comic-strip writers."

Generally, I find Eleanor attractive. In the ten years they have been
married she has grown plump, and her dark hair which once was
long is now cropped in a mannish cut of the prevailing mode. But,
this is quibbling. She still possesses her best quality, a healthy exuber-
ance which glows in her dark eyes and beams in her smile. She has
beautiful teeth. She seems aware of her body and pleased with it.
Sam tells himself he would do well to realize how much he needs
her. Since he has been in analysis he has come to discover that he
remains with Eleanor for more essential reasons than mere responsibility. Even if there were no children, he would probably cleave to
her.

Unhappily, it is more complicated than that. She is always — to use
their phrase — competing with him. At those times when I do not like
Eleanor, I am irritated by her lack of honesty. She is too sharp-
tongued, and she does not often give Sam what he needs most, a
steady flow of uncritical encouragement to counteract the harshness
with which he views himself. Like so many who are articulate on the
subject, Eleanor will tell you that she resents being a woman. As Sam
is disappointed in life, so is Eleanor. She feels Sam has cheated her
from a proper development of her potentialities and talent, even as
Sam feels cheated. I call her dishonest because she is not so ready as
Sam to put the blame on herself.

Sam, of course, can say all this himself. It is just that he experiences
it in a somewhat different way. Like most men who have been married
for ten years, Eleanor is not quite real to him. Last night at the party,
there were perhaps half a dozen people whom he met for the first
time, and he talked animatedly with them, sensing their reactions,
feeling their responses, aware of the life in them, as they were aware
of the life in him. Eleanor, however, exists in his nerves. She is a
rather vague embodiment, he thinks of her as "she" most of the time,
someone to conceal things from. Invariably, he feels uneasy with her.
It is too bad. No matter how inevitable, I am always sorry when love
melts into that pomade of affection, resentment, boredom and occasional compassion which is the best we may expect of a man and

woman who have lived together a long time. So often, it is worse, so often no more than hatred.

They are eating breakfast now, and Eleanor is chatting about the party. She is pretending to be jealous about a young girl in a strapless evening gown, and indeed, she does not have to pretend altogether. Sam, with liquor inside him, had been leaning over the girl; obviously he had coveted her. Yet, this morning, when Eleanor begins to talk about her, Sam tries to be puzzled.

"Which girl was it now?" he asks a second time.

"Oh, you know, the hysteric," Eleanor says, "the one who was parading her bazooms in your face." Eleanor has ways of impressing certain notions upon Sam. "She's Charlie's new girl."

"I didn't know that," Sam mutters. "He didn't seem to be near her all evening."

Eleanor spreads marmalade over her toast and takes a bite with evident enjoyment. "Apparently, they're all involved. Charles was funny about it. He said he's come to the conclusion that the great affairs of history are between hysterical women and detached men."

"Charles hates women," Sam says smugly. "If you notice, almost everything he says about them is a discharge of aggression." Sam has the best of reasons for not liking Charles. It takes more than ordinary character for a middle-aged husband to approve of a friend who moves easily from woman to woman.

"At least Charles discharges his aggression," Eleanor remarks.

"He's almost a classic example of the Don Juan complex. You notice how masochistic his women are?"

"I know a man or two who's just as masochistic."

Sam sips his coffee. "What made you say the girl was an hysteric?"

Eleanor shrugs. "She's an actress. And I could see she was a tease."

"You can't jump to conclusions," Sam lectures. "I had the impression she was a compulsive. Don't forget you've got to distinguish between the outer defenses, and the more deeply rooted conflicts."

I must confess that this conversation bores me. As a sample it is representative of the way Sam and Eleanor talk to each other. In Sam's defense I can say nothing; he has always been too partial to jargon.

I am often struck by how eager we are to reveal all sorts of supposedly ugly secrets about ourselves. We can explain the hatred we feel for our parents, we are rather pleased with the perversions to which we are prone. We seem determinedly proud to be superior to ourselves. No motive is too terrible for our inspection. Let someone hint, however, that we have bad table manners and we fly into a rage. Sam will agree to anything you may say about him, provided it is sufficiently serious — he will be the first to agree he has fantasies of murdering his wife. But tell him that he is afraid of waiters, or imply to Eleanor that she is a nag, and they will be quite annoyed.

Sam has noticed this himself. There are times when he can hear the jargon in his voice, and it offends him. Yet, he seems powerless to change his habits.

An example: He is sitting in an armchair now, brooding upon his breakfast, while Eleanor does the dishes. The two daughters are not home; they have gone to visit their grandmother for the week-end. Same had encouraged the visit. He had looked forward to the liberty Eleanor and himself would enjoy. For the past few weeks the children had seemed to make the most impossible demands upon his attention. Yet now they are gone and he misses them, he even misses their noise. Sam, however, cannot accept the notion that many people are dissatisfied with the present, and either dream of the past or anticipate the future. Sam must call this "ambivalence over possessions." Once he even felt obliged to ask his analyst, Dr. Sergius, if ambivalence over possessions did not characterize him almost perfectly, and Sergius whom I always picture with the flat precision of a coin's head — bald skull and horn-rimmed glasses — answered in his German accent, "But, my dear Mr. Slovoda, as I have told you, it would make me happiest if you did not include in your reading, these psychoanalytical text-works."

At such rebukes, Sam can only wince. It is so right, he tells himself, he is exactly the sort of ambitious fool who uses big words when small ones would do.

2

While Sam sits in the armchair, gray winter light is entering the windows, snow falls outside. He sits alone in a modern seat, staring at the gray, green, and beige décor of their living room. Eleanor was a painter before they were married, and she has arranged this room. It is very pleasant, but like many husbands, Sam resents it, resents the reproductions of modern painters upon the wall, the slender coffee table, a free-form poised like a spider on wire legs, its feet set onto a straw rug. In the corner, most odious of all, is the playmate of his children, a hippopotamus of a television-radio-and-phonograph cabinet with the blind monstrous snout of the video tube.

Eleanor has set the Sunday paper near his hand. Soon, Sam intends to go to work. For a year, he has been giving a day once or twice a month to a bit of thought and a little writing on a novel he hopes to begin sometime. Last night, he told himself he would work today. But he has little enthusiasm now. He is tired, he is too depressed. Writing for the comic strips seems to exhaust his imagination.

Sam reads the paper as if he were peeling an enormous banana. Flap after flap of newsprint is stripped away and cast upon the straw rug until only the Magazine Section is left. Sam glances through it with restless irritability. A biography of a political figure runs its flatulent prose into the giant crossword puzzle at the back. An account of a picturesque corner of the city becomes lost in statistics and exhortations on juvenile delinquency, finally to emerge with photographs about the new style of living which desert architecture provides. Sam looks at a wall of windows in rotogravure with a yucca tree framing the pool.

There is an article about a workingman. His wife and his family are described, his apartment, his salary and his budget. Sam reads a description of what the worker has every evening for dinner, and how he spends each night of the week. The essay makes its point; the typical American workingman must watch his pennies, but he is nonetheless secure and serene. He would not exchange his life for another.

Sam is indignant. A year ago he had written a similar article in an attempt to earn some extra money. Subtly, or so he thought, he had suggested that the average workingman was raddled with unsecurity. Naturally, the article had been rejected.

Sam throws the Magazine Section away. Moments of such anger torment him frequently. Despite himself, Sam is enraged at editorial dishonesty, at the smooth strifeless world which such articles present. How angry he is — how angry and how helpless. "It is the actions of men and not their sentiments which make history," he thinks to himself, and smiles wryly. In his living room he would go out to tilt the windmills of a vast, powerful, and hypocritical society; in his week of work he labors in an editorial cubicle to create spaceships, violent death, women with golden tresses and wanton breasts, men who act with their fists and speak with patriotic slogans.

I know what Sam feels. As he sits in the armchair, the Sunday papers are strewn around him, carrying their war news, their murders, their parleys, their entertainments, mummery of a real world which no one can grasp. It is terribly frustrating. One does not know where to begin.

Today, Sam considers himself half a fool for having been a radical. There is no longer much consolation in the thought that the majority of men who succeed in a corrupt and acquisitive society are themselves obligatorily corrupt, and one's failure is therefore the price of one's idealism. Sam cannot recapture the pleasurable bitterness which resides in the notion that one has suffered for one's principles. Sergius is too hard on him for that.

They have done a lot of work on the subject. Sergius feels that Sam's concern with world affairs has always been spurious. For example, they have uncovered in analysis that Sam wrote his article about the worker in such a way as to make certain it would be refused. Sam, after all, hates editors; to have such a piece accepted would mean he is no better than they, that he is a mediocrity. So long as he fails he is not obliged to measure himself. Sam, therefore, is being unrealistic. He rejects the world with his intellect, and this enables him not to face the more direct realities of his present life.

Sam will argue with Sergius but it is very difficult. He will say, "Perhaps you sneer at radicals because it is more comfortable to ignore such ideas. Once you became interested it might introduce certain unpleasant changes in your life."

"Why," says Sergius, "do you feel it so necessary to assume that I am a bourgeois interested only in my comfort?"

"How can I discuss these things," says Sam, "if you insist that my opinions are the expression of neurotic needs, and your opinions are merely dispassionate medical advice?"

"You are so anxious to defeat me in an argument," Sergius will reply. "Would you admit it is painful to relinquish the sense of importance which intellectual discussion provides you?"

I believe Sergius has his effect. Sam often has thoughts these days which would have been repellent to him years ago. For instance, at the moment, Sam is thinking it might be better to live the life of a worker, a simple life, to be completely absorbed with such necessities as food and money. Then one could believe that to be happy it was necessary only to have more money, more goods, less worries. It would be nice, Sam thinks wistfully, to believe that the source of one's unhappiness comes not from oneself, but from the fault of the boss, or the world, or bad luck.

Sam has these casual daydreams frequently. He likes to think about other lives he might have led, and he envies the most astonishing variety of occupations. It is easy enough to see why he should wish for the life of an executive with the power and sense of command it may offer, but virtually from the same impulse Sam will wish himself a bohemian living in an unheated loft, his life a catch-as-catch-can from day to day. Once, after reading an article, Sam even wished himself a priest. For about ten minutes it seemed beautiful to him to surrrender his life to God. Such fancies are common, I know. It is just that I, far better than Sam, know how serious he really is, how fanciful, how elaborate, his imagination can be.

The phone is ringing. Sam can hear Eleanor shouting at him to answer. He picks up the receiver with a start. It is Marvin Rossman who is an old friend, and Marvin has an unusual request. They talk for several minutes, and Sam squirms a little in his seat. As he is about to hang up, he laughs. "Why, no, Marvin, it gives me a sense of adventure," he says.

Eleanor has come into the room toward the end of this conversation. "What is it all about?" she asks.

Sam is obviously a bit agitated. Whenever he attempts to be most casual, Eleanor can well suspect him. "It seems," he says slowly, "that Marvin has acquired a pornographic movie."

"From whom?" Eleanor asks.

"He said something about an old boy friend of Louise's."

Eleanor laughs. "I can't imagine Louise having an old boy friend with a dirty movie."

"Well, people are full of surprises," Sam says mildly.

"Look, here," says Eleanor suddenly. "Why did he call us?"

"It was about our projector."

"They want to use it?" Eleanor asks.

"That's right." Sam hesitates. "I invited them over."

"Did it ever occur to you I might want to spend my Sunday some other way?" Eleanor asks crossly.

"We're not doing anything," Sam mumbles. Like most men, he feels obliged to act quite nonchalantly about pornography. "I'll tell you, I am sort of curious about the film. I've never seen one, you know."

"Try anything once, is that it?"

"Something of the sort." Sam is trying to conceal his excitement. The truth is that in common with most of us, he is fascinated by pornography. It is a minor preoccupation, but more from lack of opportunity than anything else. Once or twice, Sam has bought the sets of nude photographs which are sold in marginal bookstores, and with guilty excitement has hidden them in the apartment.

"Oh, this is silly," Eleanor says. "You were going to work today."

"I'm just not in the mood."

"I'll have to feed them," Eleanor complains. "Do we have enough liquor?"

"We can get beer." Sam pauses. "Alan Sperber and his wife are coming too."

"Sam, you're a child."

"Look, Eleanor," says Sam, controlling his voice, "if it's too much trouble, I can take the projector over there."

"I ought to make you do that."

"Am I such an idiot that I must consult you before I invite friends to the house?"

Eleanor has the intuition that Sam, if he allowed himself, could well drown in pornography. She is quite annoyed at him, but she would never dream of allowing Sam to take the projector over to Marvin Rossman's where he could view the movie without her — that seems indefinably dangerous. Besides she would like to see it, too. The mother in Eleanor is certain it cannot hurt her.

"All right, Sam," she says, "but you are a child."

More exactly, an adolescent, Sam decides. Ever since Marvin phoned, Sam has felt the nervous glee of an adolescent locking himself in the bathroom. Anal fixation, Sam thinks automatically.

While Eleanor goes down to buy beer and cold cuts in a delicatessen, Sam gets out the projector and begins to clean it. He is far from methodical in this. He knows the machine is all right, he has shown movies of Eleanor and his daughters only a few weeks ago, but from the moment Eleanor left the apartment, Sam has been consumed by an anxiety that the projection bulb is burned out. Once he has examined it, he begins to fret about the motor. He wonders if it needs oiling, he blunders through a drawer of household tools looking for an oilcan. It is ridiculous. Sam knows that what he is trying to keep out of his mind are the reactions Sergius will have. Sergius will want to "work through" all of Sam's reasons for seeing the movie. Well, Sam tells himself, he knows in advance what will be discovered: detachment, not wanting to accept Eleanor as a sexual partner, evasion of responsibility, etc. etc. The devil with Sergius. Sam has never seen a dirty movie, and he certainly wants to.

He feels obliged to laugh at himself. He could not be more nervous, he knows, if he were about to make love to a woman he had never touched before. It is really disgraceful.

When Eleanor comes back, Sam hovers about her. He is uncomfortable with her silence. "I suppose they'll be here soon," Sam says.

"Probably."

Sam does not know if he is angry at Eleanor or apprehensive that she is angry at him. Much to his surprise he catches her by the waist and hears himself saying, "You know, maybe tonight when they're gone . . . I mean, we do have the apartment, to ourselves." Eleanor moves neither toward him nor away from him. "Darling, it's not because of the movie," Sam goes on, "I swear. Don't you think maybe we could . . ."

"Maybe," says Eleanor.

3

The company has arrived, and it may be well to say a word or two about them. Marvin Rossman who has brought the film is a dentist, although it might be more accurate to describe him as a frustrated doctor. Rossman is full of statistics and items of odd information about the malpractice of physicians, and he will tell these things in his habitually gloomy voice, a voice so slow, so sad, that it almost conceals the humor of his remarks. Or, perhaps, that is what creates his humor. In his spare time, he is a sculptor, and if Eleanor may be trusted, he is not without talent. I often picture him working in the studio loft he has rented, his tall bony frame the image of dejection. He will pat a piece of clay to the armature, he will rub it sadly with his thumb, he will shrug, he does not believe that anything of merit could come from him. When he talked to Sam over the phone, he was pessimistic about the film they were to see. "It can't be any good," he said in his melancholy voice. "I know it'll be a disappointment." Like Sam, he has a mustache, but Rossman's will droop at the corners.

Alan Sperber who has come with Rossman is the subject of some curiosity for the Slovodas. He is not precisely womanish; in fact, he is a large plump man, but his voice is too soft, his manners too precise. He is genial, yet he is finicky; waspish, yet bland; he is fond of telling long rather affected stories, he is always prepared with a new one, but to general conversation he contributes little. As a lawyer, he seems miscast. One cannot imagine him inspiring a client to confidence. He is the sort of heavy florid man who seems boyish at forty, and the bow ties and gray flannel suits he wears do not make him appear more mature.

Roslyn Sperber, his wife, used to be a schoolteacher, and she is a quiet nervous woman who talks a great deal when she is drunk. She is normally quite pleasant, and has only one habit which is annoying to any degree. It is a little flaw, but social life is not unlike marriage in that habit determines far more than vice or virtue. This mannerism which has become so offensive to the friends of the Sperbers is Ros-

lyn's social pretension. Perhaps I should say intellectual pretension.
She entertains people as if she were conducting a salon, and in her
birdlike voice is forever forcing her guests to accept still another intellectual canapé. "You must hear Sam's view of the world market,"
she will say, or "Has Louise told you her statistics on divorce?" It is
quite pathetic for she is so eager to please. I have seen her eyes fill
with tears at a sharp word from Alan.

Marvin Rossman's wife, Louise, is a touch grim and definite in her
opinions. She is a social welfare worker, and will declare herself with
force whenever conversation impinges on those matters where she is
expert. She is quite opposed to psychoanalysis, and will say without
quarter, "It's all very well for people in the upper-middle area" —
she is referring to the upper middle class — "but, it takes more than a
couch to solve the problems of . . ." and she will list narcotics, juvenile delinquency, psychosis, relief distribution, slum housing, and other
descriptions of our period. She recites these categories with an odd
anticipation. One would guess she was ordering a meal.

Sam is fond of Marvin but he cannot abide Louise. "You'd think
she discovered poverty," he will complain to Eleanor.

The Slovodas do feel superior to the Rossmans and the Sperbers.
If pressed, they could not offer the most convincing explanation why.
I suppose what it comes down to is that Sam and Eleanor do not think
of themselves as really belonging to a class, and they feel that the
Sperbers and Rossmans are petit-bourgeois. I find it hard to explain
their attitude. Their company feels as much discomfort and will apologize as often as the Slovodas for the money they have, and the money
they hope to earn. They are all of them equally concerned with progressive education and the methods of raising children to be well
adjusted — indeed, they are discussing that now — they consider themselves relatively free of sexual taboo, or put more properly, Sam and
Eleanor are no less possessive than the others. The Slovodas' culture
is not more profound; I should be hard put to say that Sam is more
widely read, more seriously informed, than Marvin or Alan, or for
that matter, Louise. Probably, it comes to this: Sam, in his heart,
thinks himself a rebel, and there are few rebels who do not claim an
original mind. Eleanor has been a bohemian and considers herself
more sophisticated than her friends who merely went to college and
got married. Louise Rossman could express it most soundly. "Artists,
writers, and people of the creative layer have in their occupational
ideology the belief that they are classless."

One thing I might remark about the company. They are all being

the most unconscionable hypocrites. They have rushed across half the
city of New York to see a pornogarphic film, and they are not at all
interested in each other at the moment. The women are giggling like
tickled children at remarks which cannot possibly be so funny. Yet,
they are all determined to talk for a respectable period of time. No
less, it must be serious talk. Roslyn has said once, "I feel so funny at
the thought of seeing such a movie," and the others have passed her
statement by.

At the moment, Sam is talking about value. I might note that Sam
loves conversation and thrives when he can expound an idea.

"What are our values today?" he asks. "It's really fantastic when
you stop to think of it. Take any bright talented kid who's getting
out of college now."

"My kid brother, for example," Marvin interposes morosely. He
passes his bony hand over his sad mustache, and somehow the remark
has become amusing, much as if Marvin had said, "Oh, yes, you have
reminded me of the trials, the worries, and the cares which my fabulous younger brother heaps upon me."

"All right, take him," Sam says. "What does he want to be?"

"He doesn't want to be anything," says Marvin.

"That's my point," Sam says excitedly. "Rather than work at certain occupations, the best of these kids would rather do nothing at all."

"Alan has a cousin," Roslyn says, "who swears he'll wash dishes
before he becomes a businessman."

"I wish that were true," Eleanor interrupts. "It seems to me everybody is conforming more and more these days."

They argue about this. Sam and Eleanor claim the country is suffering from hysteria; Alan Sperber disagrees and says it's merely a reflection of the headlines; Louise says no adequate criteria exist to
measure hysteria; Marvin says he doesn't know anything at all.

"More solid liberal gains are being made in this period," says Alan,
"than you would believe. Consider the Negro — "

"Is the Negro any less maladjusted?" Eleanor shouts with passion.

Sam maneuvers the conversation back to his thesis. "The values of
the young today, and by the young I mean the cream of the kids, the
ones with ideas, are a reaction of indifference to the culture crisis. It
really is despair. All they know is what they don't want to do."

"That is easier," Alan says genially.

"It's not altogether unhealthy," Sam says. "It's a corrective for
smugness and the false value of the past, but it has created new false

value." He thinks it worth emphasizing. "False value seems always to beget further false value."

"Define your terms," says Louise, the scientist.

"No, look," Sam says, "there's no revolt, there's no acceptance. Kids today don't want to get married, and — "

Eleanor interrupts. "Why should a girl rush to get married? She loses all chance for developing herself."

Sam shrugs. They are all talking at once. "Kids don't want to get married," he repeats, "and they don't want not to get married. They merely drift."

"It's a problem we'll all have to face with our own kids in ten years," Alan says, "although I think you make too much of it, Sam."

"My daughter," Marvin states. "She's embarrassed I'm a dentist. Even more embarrassed than I am." They laugh.

Sam tells a story about his youngest, Carol Ann. It seems he had a fight with her, and she went to her room. Sam followed, he called through the door.

"No answer," Sam says. "I called her again, 'Carol Ann.' I was a little worried you understand, because she seemed so upset, so I said to her, 'Carol Ann, you know I love you.' What do you think she answered?"

"What?" asks Roslyn.

"She said, 'Daddie, why are you so anxious?' "

They all laugh again. There are murmurs about what a clever thing it was to say. In the silence which follows, Roslyn leans forward and says quickly in her high voice, "You must get Alan to tell you his wonderful story about the man who studied yogi."

"Yoga," Alan corrects. "It's too long to tell."

The company prevails on him.

"Well," says Alan, in his genial courtroom voice, "it concerns a friend of mine named Cassius O'Shaugnessy."

"You don't mean Jerry O'Shaugnessy, do you?" asks Sam.

Alan does not know Jerry O'Shaugnessy. "No, no, this is Cassius O'Shaugnessy," he says. "He's really quite an extraordinary fellow." Alan sits plumply in his chair, fingering his bow tie. They are all used to his stories, which are told in a formal style and exhibit the attempt to recapture a certain note of urbanity, wit, and *élan* which Alan has probably copied from someone else. Sam and Eleanor respect his ability to tell these stories, but they resent the fact that he talks *at* them.

"You'd think we were a jury of his inferiors," Eleanor has said.

"I hate being talked down to." What she resents is Alan's quiet implication that his antecedents, his social position, in total his life outside the room is superior to the life within. Eleanor now takes the promise from Alan's story by remarking, "Yes, and let's see the movie when Alan has finished."

"Ssh," Roslyn says.

"Cassius was at college a good while before me," says Alan, "but I knew him while I was an undergraduate. He would drop in and visit from time to time. An absolutely extraordinary fellow. The most amazing career. You see, he's done about everything."

"I love the way Alan tells it," Roslyn pipes nervously.

"Cassius was in France with Dos Passos and Cummings, he was even arrested with e.e. After the war, he was one of the founders of the Dadaist school, and for a while I understand he was Fitzgerald's guide to the gold of the Côte D' Azur. He knew everybody, he did everything. Do you realize that before the twenties had ended, Cassius had managed his father's business and then entered the monastery? It is said he influenced T. S. Eliot."

"Today, we'd call Cassius a psychopath," Marvin observes.

"Cassius called himself a great dilettante," Alan answers, "although perhaps the nineteenth-century Russian conception of the great sinner would be more appropriate. What do you say if I tell you this was only the beginning of his career?"

"What's the point?" Louise asks.

"Not yet," says Alan, holding up a hand. His manner seems to say that if his audience cannot appreciate the story, he does not feel obliged to continue. "Cassius studied Marx in the monastery. He broke his vows, quite the Church, and became a Communist. All through the thirties he was a figure in the Party, going to Moscow, involved in all the Party struggles. He left only during the Moscow trials."

Alan's manner while he relates such stories is somewhat effeminate. He talks with little caresses of his hand, he mentions names and places with a lingering ease as if to suggest that his audience and he are aware, above all, of nuance. The story as Alan tells it is drawn overlong. Suffice it that the man about whom he is talking, Cassius O'Shaugnessy, becomes a Trotskyist, becomes an anarchist, is a pacifist during the second World War, and suffers it from a prison cell.

"I may say," Alan goes on, "that I worked for his defense, and was successful in getting him acquitted. Imagine my dolor when I learned that he had turned his back on his anarchist friends and was living with gangsters."

"This is weird," Eleanor says.

"Weird, it is," Alan agrees. "Cassius got into some scrape, and disappeared. What could you do with him? I learned only recently that he had gone to India and was studying yoga. In fact, I learned it from Cassius himself. I asked him of his experiences at Brahna-puth-thar, and he told me the following story."

Now Alan's voice alters, he assumes the part of Cassius and speaks in a tone weary of experience, wise and sad in its knowledge. " 'I was sitting on my haunches contemplating my navel,' Cassius said to me, 'when of a sudden I discovered my navel under a different aspect. It seemed to me that if I were to give a counter-clockwise twist, my navel would unscrew.' "

Alan looks up, he surveys his audience which is now rapt and uneasy, not certain as yet whether a joke is to come. Alan's thumb and forefinger pluck at the middle of his ample belly, his feet are crossed upon the carpet in symbolic suggestion of Cassius upon his haunches.

" 'Taking a deep breath, I turned and the abysses of Vishtarni loomed beneath. My navel had begun to unscrew. I knew I was about to accept the reward of three years of contemplation. So,' said Cassius, 'I turned again, and my navel unscrewed a little more. I turned and I turned,' " Alan's fingers now revolving upon his belly, " 'and after a period I knew that with one more turn my navel would unscrew itself forever. At the edge of revelation, I took one sweet breath, and turned my navel free.' "

Alan looks up at his audience.

" 'Damn,' said Cassius, "if my ass didn't fall off.' "

4

The story has left the audience in an exasperated mood. It has been a most untypical story for Alan to tell, a little out of place, not offensive exactly, but irritating and inconsequential. Sam is the only one to laugh with more than bewildered courtesy, and his mirth seems excessive to everyone but Alan, and of course, Roslyn, who feels as if she has been the producer. I suppose what it reduces to, is a lack of taste. Perhaps that is why Alan is not the lawyer one would expect. He does not have that appreciation — as necessary in his trade as for an actor — of what is desired at any moment, of that which will encourage as opposed to that which does not encourage a stimulating

but smooth progression of logic and sentiment. Only a fool would
tell so long a story when everyone is awaiting the movie.

Now, they are preparing. The men shift armchairs to correspond
with the couch, the projector is set up, the screen is unfolded. Sam
attempts to talk while he is threading the film, but no one listens.
They seem to realize suddenly that a frightful demand has been placed
upon them. One does not study pornography in a living room with a
beer glass in one's hand, and friends at the elbow. It is the most unsatisfactory of compromises; one can draw neither the benefits of
solitary contemplation nor of social exchange. There is, at bottom,
the same exasperated fright which one experiences in turning the
shower tap and receiving cold water when the flesh has been prepared
for heat. Perhaps that is why they are laughing so much now that the
movie is begun.

A title, *The Evil Act,* twitches on the screen, shot with scars, holes,
and the dust lines of age. A man and woman are sitting on a couch,
they are having coffee. They chat. What they say is conveyed by
printed words upon an ornately flowered card, interjected between
glimpses of their casual gestures, a cup to the mouth, a smile, a cigarette being lit. The man's name, it seems, is Frankie Idell; he is talking to his wife, Magnolia. Frankie is dark, he is sinister, he confides
in Magnolia, his dark counterpart, with a grimance of his brows,
black from make-up pencil.

This is what the titles read:

FRANKIE: She will be here soon.
MAGNOLIA: This time the little vixen will not escape.
FRANKIE: No, my dear, this time we are prepared.
(*He looks at his watch.*)
FRANKIE: Listen, she knocks!

There is a shot of a tall blond woman knocking on the door. She
is probably over thirty, but by her short dress and ribboned hat it is
suggested that she is a girl of fifteen.

FRANKIE: Come in, Eleanor.

As may be expected, the audience laughs hysterically at this. It is
so wonderful a coincidence. "How I remember Frankie," says Eleanor
Slovoda, and Roslyn Sperber is the only one not amused. In the
midst of the others' laughter, she says in a worried tone, obviously
adrift upon her own concerns, "Do you think we'll have to stop the
film in the middle to let the bulb cool off?" The others hoot, they

giggle, they are weak from the combination of their own remarks and
the action of the plot.

Frankie and Magnolia have sat down on either side of the heroine,
Eleanor. A moment passes. Suddenly, stiffly, they attack. Magnolia
from her side kisses Eleanor, and Frankie commits an indecent caress.

ELEANOR: How dare you? Stop!
MAGNOLIA: Scream, my little one. It will do you no good. The walls
   are soundproofed.
FRANKIE: We've fixed a way to make you come across.
ELEANOR: This is hideous. I am hitherto undefiled. Do not touch
   me!

The captions fade away. A new title takes their place. It says, *But
There Is No Escape From The Determined Pair.* On the fade-in, we
discover Eleanor in the most distressing situation. Her hands are
tied to loops running from the ceiling, and she can only writhe in
helpless perturbation before the deliberate and progressive advances
of Frankie and Magnolia. Slowly they humiliate her, with relish they
probe her.

The audience laughs no longer. A hush has come upon them. Eyes
unblinking they devour the images upon Sam Slovoda's screen.

Eleanor is without clothing. As the last piece is pulled away,
Frankie and Magnolia circle about her in a grotesque of pantomime,
a leering of lips, limbs in a distortion of desire. Eleanor faints.
Adroitly, Magnolia cuts her bonds. We see Frankie carrying her
inert body.

Now, Eleanor is trussed to a bed, and the husband and wife are
tormenting her with feathers. Bodies curl upon the bed in postures
so complicated, in combinations so advanced, that the audience leans
forward, Sperbers, Rossmans, and Slovadas, as if tempted to embrace
the moving images. The hands trace abstract circles upon the screen,
passes and recoveries upon a white background so illumined that
hollows and swells, limb to belly and mouth to undescribables, tip
of a nipple, orb of a navel, swim in giant magnification, flow and
slide in a lurching yawing fall, blotting out the camera eye.

A little murmur, all unconscious, passes from their lips. The audience sways, each now finally lost in himself, communing hungrily
with shadows, violated or violating, fantasy triumphant.

At picture's end, Eleanor the virgin whore is released from the bed.
She kisses Frankie, she kisses Magnolia. "You dears," she says, "let's
do it again." The projector lamp burns empty light, the machine keeps

turning, the tag of film goes *slap-tap, slap-tap, slap-tap, slap-tap, slap-tap, slap-tap.*

"Sam, turn it off," says Eleanor.

But when the room lights are on, they cannot look at one another. "Can we see it again?" someone mutters. So, again, Eleanor knocks on the door, is tied, defiled, ravished, and made rapturous. They watch it soberly now, the room hot with the heat of their bodies, the darkness a balm for orgiastic vision. To the Deer Park, Sam is thinking, to the Deer Park of Louis XV were brought the most beautiful maidens of France, and there they stayed, dressed in fabulous silks, perfumed and wigged, the mole drawn upon their cheek, ladies of pleasure awaiting the pleasure of the king. So Louis had stripped an empire, bankrupt a treasury, prepared a deluge, while in his garden on summer evenings the maidens performed their pageants, eighteenth-century tableaux of the evil act, beauteous instruments of one man's desire, lewd translation of a king's power. That century men sought wealth so they might use its fruits; this epoch men lusted for power in order to amass more power, a compounding of power into pyramids of abstraction whose yield are cannon and wire enclosure, pillars of statistics to the men who are the kings of this century and do no more in power's leisure time than go to church, claim to love their wives, and eat vegetables.

Is it possible, Sam wonders, that each of them here, two Rossmans, two Sperbers, two Slovodas, will cast off their clothes when the movie is done and perform the orgy which tickles at the heart of their desire? They will not, he knows, they will make jokes when the projector is put away, they will gorge the plate of delicatessen Eleanor provides, and swallow more beer, he among them. He will be the first to make jokes.

Sam is right. The movie has made him extraordinarily alive to the limits of them all. While they sit with red faces, eyes bugged, glutting sandwiches of ham, salami, and tongue, he begins the teasing.

"Roslyn," he calls out, "is the bulb cooled off yet?"

She cannot answer him. She chokes on beer, her face glazes, she is helpless with self-protecting laughter.

"Why are you so anxious, Daddie?" Eleanor says quickly.

They begin to discuss the film. As intelligent people they must dominate it. Someone wonders about the actors in the piece, and discussion begins afresh. "I fail to see," says Louise, "why they should be hard to classify. Pornography is a job to the criminal and prostitute element."

"No, you won't find an ordinary prostitute doing this," Sam insists. "It requires a particular kind of personality."

"They have to be exhibitionists," says Eleanor.

"It's all economic," Louise maintains.

"I wonder what those girls felt?" Roslyn asks. "I feel sorry for them."

"I'd like to be the cameraman," says Alan.

"I'd like to be Frankie," says Marvin sadly.

There is a limit to how long such a conversation may continue. The jokes lapse into silence. They are all busy eating. When they begin to talk again, it is of other things. Each dollop of food sops the agitation which the movie has spilled. They gossip about the party the night before, they discuss which single men were interested in which women, who got drunk, who got sick, who said the wrong thing, who went home with someone else's date. When this is exhausted, one of them mentions a play the others have not seen. Soon they are talking about books, a concert, a one-man show by an artist who is a friend. Dependably, conversation will voyage its orbit. While the men talk of politics, the women are discussing fashions, progressive schools, and recipes they have attempted. Sam is uncomfortable with the division; he knows Eleanor will resent it, he knows she will complain later of the insularity of men and the basic contempt they feel for women's intelligence.

"But you collaborated," Sam will argue. "No one forced you to be with the women."

"Was I to leave them alone?" Eleanor will answer.

"Well, why do the women always have to go off by themselves?"

"Because the men aren't interested in what we have to say."

Sam sighs. He has been talking with interest, but really he is bored. These are nice pleasant people, he thinks, but they are ordinary people, exactly the sort he has spent so many years with, making little jokes, little gossip, living little everyday events, a close circle where everyone mothers the other by his presence. The womb of middle-class life, Sam decides heavily. He is in a bad mood indeed. Everything is laden with dissatisfaction.

Alan has joined the women. He delights in preparing odd dishes when friends visit the Sperbers, and he is describing to Eleanor how he makes blueberry pancakes. Marvin draws closer to Sam.

"I wanted to tell you," he says, "Alan's story reminded me. I saw Jerry O'Shaugnessy the other day."

"Where was he?"

Marvin is hesitant. "It was a shock, Sam. He's on the Bowery. I guess he's become a wino."

"He always drank a lot," says Sam.

"Yeah." Marvin cracks his bony knuckles. "What a stinking time this is, Sam."

"It's probably like the years after 1905 in Russia," Sam says.

"No revolutionary party will come out of this."

"No," Sam says, "nothing will come."

He is thinking of Jerry O'Shaugnessy. What did he look like? what did he say? Sam asks Marvin, and clucks his tongue at the dispiriting answer. It is a shock to him. He draws closer to Marvin, he feels a bond. They have, after all, been through some years together. In the thirties they have been in the Communist Party, they have quit together, they are both weary of politics today, still radicals out of habit, but without enthusiasm and without a cause. "Jerry was a hero to me," Sam says.

"To all of us," says Marvin.

The fabulous Jerry O'Shaugnessy, thinks Sam. In the old days, in the Party, they had made a legend of him. All of them with their middle-class origins and their desire to know a worker-hero.

I may say that I was never as fond of Jerry O'Shaugnessy as was Sam. I thought him a showman and too pleased with himself. Sam, however, with his timidity, his desire to travel, to have adventure and know many women, was obliged to adore O'Shaugnessy. At least he was enraptured with his career.

Poor Jerry who ends as a bum. He has been everything else. He has been a trapper in Alaska, a chauffer for gangsters, an officer in the Foreign Legion, a labor organizer. His nose was broken, there were scars on his chin. When he would talk about his years at sea or his experiences in Spain, the stenographers and garment workers, the radio writers and unemployed actors would listen to his speeches as if he were the prophet of new romance, and their blood would be charged with the magic of revolutionary vision. A man with tremendous charm. In those days it had been easy to confuse his love for himself with his love for all underprivileged workingmen.

"I thought he was still in the Party," Sam says.

"No," says Marvin, "I remember they kicked him out a couple of years ago. He was supposed to have piddled some funds, that's what they say."

"I wish he'd taken the treasury," Sam remarks bitterly. "The Party used him for years."

Marvin shrugs. "They used each other." His mustache droops. "Let me tell you about Sonderson. You know he's still in the Party. The most progressive dentist in New York." They laugh.

While Marvin tells the story, Sam is thinking of other things. Since he has quit Party work, he has studied a great deal. He can tell you about prison camps and the secret police, political murders, the Moscow trials, the exploitation of Soviet labor, the privileges of the bureaucracy; it is all painful to him. He is straddled between the loss of a country he has never seen, and his repudiation of the country in which he lives. "Doesn't the Party seem a horror now?" he burst out.

Marvin nods. They are trying to comprehend the distance between Party members they have known, people by turn pathetic, likable, or annoying — people not unlike themselves — and in contrast the immensity of historic logic which deploys along statistics of the dead.

"It's all schizoid," Sam says. "Modern life is schizoid."

Marvin agrees. They have agreed on this many times, bored with the petulance of their small voices, yet needing the comfort of such complaints. Marvin asks Sam if he has given up his novel, and Sam says, "Temporarily." He cannot find a form, he explains. He does not want to write a realistic novel, because reality is no longer realistic. "I don't know what it is," says Sam. "To tell you the truth, I think I'm kidding myself. I'll never finish this book. I just like to entertain the idea I'll do something good some day." They sit there in friendly depression. Conversation has cooled. Alan and the women are no longer talking.

"Marvin," asks Louise, "what time is it?"

They are ready to go. Sam must say directly what he had hoped to approach by suggestion. "I was wondering," he whispers to Rossman, "would you mind if I held onto the film for a day or two?"

Marvin looks at him. "Oh, why of course, Sam," he says in his morose voice. "I know how it is." He pats Sam on the shoulder as if, symbolically, to convey the exchange of ownership. They are fellow conspirators.

"If you ever want to borrow the projector," Sam suggests.

"Nah," says Marvin, "I don't know that it would make much difference."

It has been, when all is said, a most annoying day. As Sam and Eleanor tidy the apartment, emptying ash trays and washing the few dishes, they are fond neither of themselves nor each other. "What a waste today has been," Eleanor remarks, and Sam can only agree. He has done no writing, he has not been outdoors, and still it is late in the evening, and he has talked too much, eaten too much, is nervous from the movie they have seen. He knows that he will watch it again with Eleanor before they go to sleep; she has given her assent to that. But as is so often the case with Sam these days, he cannot await their embrace with any sure anticipation. Eleanor may be in the mood or Eleanor may not; there is no way he can control the issue. It is depressing; Sam knows that he circles about Eleanor at such times with the guilty maneuvers of a sad hound. Resent her as he must, be furious with himself as he will, there is not very much he can do about it. Often, after they have made love, they will lie beside each other in silence; each offended, each certain the other is to blame. At such times, memory tickles them with a cruel feather. Not always has it been like this. When they were first married, and indeed for the six months they lived together before marriage, everything was quite different. Their affair was very exciting to them; each told the other with some hyperbole but no real mistruth that no one in the past had ever been comparable as lover.

I suppose I am a romantic. I always feel that this is the best time in people's lives. There is, after all, so little we accomplish, and that short period when we are beloved and triumph as lovers is sweet with power. Rarely are we concerned then with our lack of importance; we are too important. In Sam's case, disillusion means even more. Like so many young men, he entertained the secret conceit that he was an extraordinary lover. One cannot really believe this without supporting at the same time the equally secret conviction that one is fundamentally inept. It is — no matter what Sergius would say — a more dramatic and therefore more attractive view of oneself than the sober notion which Sam now accepts with grudging wisdom, that the man as lover is dependent upon the bounty of the woman. As I say, he accepts the notion, it is one of the lineaments of maturity, but there is a part of him which, no matter how harried by analysis, cannot relinquish the antagonism he feels that Eleanor has respected his private talent so poorly, and has not allowed him to confer its benefits upon more women. I mock Sam, but he would mock himself on this. It hardly matters; mockery cannot accomplish everything, and Sam seeths with that most private and tender pain: even worse than being unattractive to the world is to be unattractive to one's mate; or, what is the same and describes Sam's case more accurately, never to know in advance when he shall be undesirable to Eleanor.

I make perhaps too much of the subject, but that is only because it is so important to Sam. Relations between Eleanor and him are not really that bad — I know other couples who have much less or

nothing at all. But comparisons are poor comfort to Sam; his standards are so high. So are Eleanor's. I am convinced the most unfortunate people are those who would make an art of love. It sours other
effort. Of all artists, they are certainly the most wretched.

Shall I furnish a model? Sam and Eleanor are on the couch and
the projector, adjusted to its slowest speed, is retracing the elaborate
pantomime of the three principals. If one could allow these shadows
a life . . . but indeed such life has been given them. Sam and Eleanor
are no more than an itch, a smart, a threshold of satisfaction; the important share of themselves has steeped itself in Frankie-, Magnolia-,
and Eleanor-of-the-film. Indeed the variations are beyond telling. It is
the most outrageous orgy performed by five ghosts.

Self-critical Sam! He makes love in front of a movie, and one cannot say that it is unsatisfactory any more than one can say it is pleasant.
It is dirty, downright porno dirty, it is a lewd slop-brush slapped
through the middle of domestic exasperations and breakfast eggs. It
is so dirty that only half of Sam — he is quite divisible into fractions —
can be exercised at all. The part that is his brain worries along like
a cuckolded burgher. He is taking the pulse of his anxiety. Will
he last long enough to satisfy Eleanor? Will the children come back
tonight? He cannot help it. In the midst of the circus, he is suddenly
convinced the children will walk through the door. "Why are you so
anxious, Daddie?"

So it goes. Sam the lover is conscious of exertion. One moment he
is Frankie Idell, destroyer of virgins — take that! you whore! — the
next, body moving, hands caressing, he is no more than some lines
from a psychoanalytical text. He is thinking about the sensitivity of
his scrotum. He has read that this is a portent of femininity in a male.
How strong is his latent homosexuality worries Sam, thrusting stiffly,
warm sweat running cold. Does he identify with Eleanor-of-the-film?

Technically, the climax is satisfactory. They lie together in the dark,
the film ended, the projector humming its lonely revolutions in the
quiet room. Sam gets up to turn it off; he comes back and kisses
Eleanor upon the mouth. Apparently, she has enjoyed herself more
than he; she is tender and fondles the tip of his nose.

"You know, Sam," she says from her space beside him, "I think I
saw this picture before."

"When?"

"Oh, you know when. That time."

Sam thinks dully that women are always most loving when they
can reminisce about infidelity.

"That time!" he repeats.

"I think so."

Racing forward from memory like the approaching star which begins as a point on the mind and swells to explode the eyeball with its odious image, Sam remembers, and is weak in the dark. It is ten years, eleven perhaps, before they were married, yet after they were lovers. Eleanor has told him, but she has always been vague about details. There had been two men it seemed, and another girl, and all had been drunk. They had seen movie after movie. With reluctant fascination, Sam can conceive the rest. How it had pained him, how excited him. It is years now since he has remembered, but he remembers. In the darkness he wonders at the unreasonableness of jealous pain. That night was impossible to imagine any longer — therefore it is more real; Eleanor his plump wife who presses a pigeon's shape against her housecoat, forgotten heroine of black orgies. It had been meaningless, Eleanor claimed; it was Sam she loved, and the other had been no more than a fancy of which she wished to rid herself. Would it be the same today, thinks Sam, or had Eleanor been loved by Frankie, by Frankie of the other movies, by Frankie of the two men she never saw again on that night so long ago?

The pleasure I get from this pain, Sam thinks furiously.

It is not altogether perverse. If Eleanor causes him pain, it means after all that she is alive for him. I have often observed that the reality of a person depends upon his ability to hurt us; Eleanor as the vague accusing embodiment of the wife is different, altogether different, from Eleanor who lies warmly in Sam's bed, an attractive Eleanor who many wound his flesh. Thus, brother to the pleasure of pain, is the sweeter pleasure which follows pain. Sam, tired, lies in Eleanor's arms, and they talk with the cozy trade words of old professionals, agreeing that they will not make love again before a movie, that it was exciting but also not without detachment, that all in all it has been good but not quite right, that she had loved this action he had done, and was uncertain about another. It is their old familiar critique, a sign that they are intimate and well disposed. They do not talk about the act when it has failed to fire; then they go silently to sleep. But now, Eleanor's enjoyment having mollified Sam's sense of no enjoyment, they talk with the apologetics and encomiums of familiar mates. Eleanor falls asleep, and Sam falls almost asleep, curling next to her warm body, his hand over her round belly with the satisfaction of a sculptor. He is drowsy, and he thinks drowsily that these few moments of creature-pleasure, this brief compassion he can feel for the body that trusts itself to sleep beside him, his comfort in its warmth, is perhaps all the meaning he may ask for his life. That out of disappointment, frustration, and the passage of dreary years come these few moments when he is close to her, and their years together possess a connotation more rewarding than the sum of all which has gone into them.

But then he thinks of the novel he wants to write, and he is wide-awake again. Like the sleeping pill which fails to work and leaves one warped in an exaggeration of the ills which sought the drug, Sam passes through the promise of sexemptied sleep, and is left with nervous loins, swollen jealousy of an act ten years dead, and sweating irritable resentment of the woman's body which hinders his limbs. He has wasted the day, he tells himself, he has wasted the day as he has wasted so many days of his life, and tomorrow in the office he will be no more than his ten fingers typing plot and words for Bramba the Venusian and Lee-Lee Deeds, Hollywood Star, while that huge work with which he has cheated himself, holding it before him as a covenant of his worth, that enormous novel which would lift him at a bound from the impasse in which he stifles, whose dozens of characters would develop a vision of life in bountiful complexity, lies foundered, rotting on a beach of purposeless effort. Notes here, pages there, it sprawls through a formless wreck of incidental ideas and half-episodes, utterly without shape. He has not even a hero for it.

One could not have a hero today, Sam thinks, a man of action and contemplation, capable of sin, large enough for good, a man immense. There is only a modern hero damned by no more than the ugliness of wishes whose satisfaction he will never know. One needs a man who could walk the stage, someone who — no matter who, not himself. Someone, Sam thinks, who reasonably could not exist.

The novelist, thinks Sam, perspiring beneath blankets, must live in paranoia and seek to be one with the world; he must be terrified of experience and hungry for it; he must think himself nothing and believe he is superior to all. The feminine in his nature cries for proof he is a man; he dreams of power and is without capacity to gain it; he loves himself above all and therefore despises all that he is.

He is that, thinks Sam, he is part of the perfect prescription, and yet he is not a novelist. He lacks energy and belief. It is left for him to write an article some day about the temperament of the ideal novelist.

In the darkness, memories rise, yeast-swells of apprehension. Out of bohemian days so long ago, comes the friend of Eleanor, a girl who had been sick and was committed to an institution. They visited her, Sam and Eleanor, they took the suburban train and sat on the lawn of the asylum grounds while patients circled about intoning a private litany, or shuddering in boob-blundering fright from an insect that crossed their skin. The friend had been silent. She had smiled, she had answered their questions with the fewest words, and had returned again to her study of sunlight and blue sky. As they were about to leave, the girl had taken Sam aside. "They violate me," she said in a whisper. "Every night when the doors are locked, they come to my room and they make the movie. I am the heroine and am subjected to all variety of sexual viciousness. Tell them to leave me alone so I may enter the convent." And while she talked, in a horror of her body, one arm scrubbed the other. Poor tortured friend. They had seen her again, and she babbled, her face had coarsened into an idiot leer.

Sam sweats. There is so little he knows, and so much to know. Youth of the depression with its economic terms, what can he know of madness or religion? They are both so alien to him. He is the mongrel, Sam thinks, brought up without religion from a mother half Protestant and half Catholic, and a father half Catholic and half Jew. He is the quarter-Jew, and yet he is a Jew, or so he feels himself, knowing nothing of Gospel, tabernacle, or Mass, the Jew through accident, through state of mind. What . . . whatever did he know of penance? self-sacrifice? mortification of the flesh? the love of his fellow man? Am I concerned with my relation to God? ponders Sam, and smiles sourly in the darkness. No, that has never concerned him, he thinks, not for better nor for worse. "They are making the movie," says the girl into the ear of memory, "and so I cannot enter the convent."

How hideous was the mental hospital. A concentration camp, decides Sam. Perhaps it would be the world some day, or was that only his projection of feelings of hopelessness? "Do not try to solve the problems of the world," he hears from Sergius, and pounds a lumpy pillow.

However could he organize his novel? What form to give it? It is so complex. Too loose, thinks Sam, too scattered. Will he ever fall asleep? Wearily, limbs tense, his stomach too keen, he plays again the game of putting himself to sleep. "I do not feel my toes," Sam says to himself, "my toes are dead, my calves are asleep, my calves are sleeping . . ."

In the middle from wakefulness to slumber, in the torpor which floats beneath blankets, I give an idea to Sam. "Destroy time, and chaos may be ordered," I say to him.

"Destroy time, and chaos may be ordered," he repeats after me, and in desperation to seek his coma, mutters back, "I do not feel my nose, my nose is numb, my eyes are heavy, my eyes are heavy."

So Sam enters the universe of sleep, a man who seeks to live in such a way as to avoid pain, and succeeds merely in avoiding pleasure. What a dreary compromise is life!

[handwritten annotations: "Gray is associated with" and "Black is associated with the father in Barn Burning"]

color of darkness

James Purdy

Sometimes he thought about his wife, but a thing had begun of late, usually after the boy went to bed, a thing which *should* have been terrifying but which was not: he could not remember now what she had looked like. The specific thing he could not remember was the color of her eyes. It was one of the most obsessive things in his thought. It was also a thing he could not quite speak of with anybody. There were people in the town who would have remembered, of course, what color her eyes were, but gradually he began to forget the general structure of her face also. All he seemed to remember was her voice, her warm hearty comforting voice.

Then there was the boy, Baxter, of course. What did he know and what did he not know. Sometimes Baxter seemed to know everything. As he hung on the edge of the chair looking at his father, examining him closely (the boy never seemed to be able to get close enough to his father), the father felt that Baxter might know everything.

"Bax," the father would say at such a moment, and stare into his own son's eyes. The son looked exactly like the father. There was no trace in the boy's face of anything of his mother.

"Soon you will be all grown up," the father said one night, without ever knowing why he had said this, saying it without his having even thought about it.

"I don't think so," the boy replied.

"Why don't you think so," the father wondered, as surprised by the boy's answer as he had been by his own question.

The boy thought over his own remark also.

"How long does it take?" the boy asked.

"Oh a long time yet," the father said.

"Will I stay with you, Daddy," the boy wondered.

The father nodded. "You can stay with me always," the father said.

The boy said *Oh* and began running around the room. He fell over one of his engines and began to cry.

Mrs. Zilke came into the room and said something comforting to the boy.

The father got up and went over to pick up the son. Then sitting down, he put the boy in his lap, and flushed from the exertion, he said to Mrs. Zilke: "You know, I am old!"

Mrs. Zilke laughed. "If you're old, I'm dead," she said. "You must keep your youth," she said almost harshly to the father, after a pause.

He looked up at her, and the boy suddenly moved in his father's arms, looking questioningly at his father. He kissed his father on his face.

"He's young yet," the boy said to Mrs. Zilke.

"Why, of course. He's a young man," she said. "They don't come no younger for fathers."

The father laughed and the boy got up to go with Mrs. Zilke to his bed.

The father thought about Mrs. Zilke's remark and he listened as he heard her reading to the boy from a story-book. He found the story she read quite dry, and he wondered if the boy found anything in it at all.

It was odd, he knew, that he could not remember the color of his wife's eyes. He knew, of course, that he must remember them, and that he was perhaps unconsciously trying to forget. Then he began to think that he could not remember the color of his son's eyes, and he had just looked at them!

"What does he know?" he said to Mrs. Zilke when she came downstairs and sat down for a moment with the newspaper. She lit a cigarette and blew out some smoke before she replied to him. By then he was looking out the window as though he had forgotten her presence and his question.

"He knows everything," Mrs. Zilke said.

The father came to himself now and looked at her gently.

"They all do now, don't they," the father said, meaning children.

"It seems so," the woman said. "Yes," she said, thinking. "They know everything."

"Everybody seems forty years old to me," the father said. "Even children maybe. Except they are complete mysteries to me. I don't know what to say to any of them. I don't know what they know, I guess."

"Oh, I understand that. I raised eight kids and I was always thinking the same thing."

"Well, that relieves me," he told Mrs. Zilke.

She smiled, but in her smile he thought he saw some thought reserved, as though she had not told everything.

"Of course we never know any other human being, do we?" he told Mrs. Zilke, hesitating as though to get the quotation right.

She nodded, enjoying her cigarette.

"Your son is lonely," she said suddenly.

The father did not look at her now.

"I mean by that," she went on, "it's too bad he's an only child."

"Doesn't he have other children over here, though. I thought — "

"Oh, it's not the same," Mrs. Zilke said. "Having in other youngsters like he does on Saturday and all. It's not enough."

"Of course I am gone a good deal."

"You're gone all the time," she said.

"That part can't be helped, of course. You see," he laughed, "I'm a success."

Mrs. Zilke did not return his laughter, he noticed, and he had noticed this before in plain strong old working women of her kind. He admired Mrs. Zilke tremendously. He was glad she had not laughed with him.

"No one should have just one child," she told him.

"You know," he said, confidentially, "when you have just your work, as I do, people get away from you."

He looked at the bottle of brandy on the bookshelf.

"Would you have a pony of brandy with me, Mrs. Zilke."

She began to say no because she really didn't like it, but there was such a pleading look on his young face, she nodded rather regally, and he got up and poured two shots.

"Thank you for drinking with me," he said suddenly, as though to brush away something that had come between his words and his memory.

"Quite a bouquet," she said, whiffing first.

"You are really very intelligent," he told Mrs. Zilke.

"Because I know the bouquet," she said coldly.

"Oh that and a lot of other things."

"Well, I don't know anything," Mrs. Zilke said.

"You know everything," he remarked. "All I have is my work."

"That's a lot. They need you," she said.

He sat down now, but he did not touch the brandy, and Mrs. Zilke having smelled the bouquet put her tiny glass down too.

They both sat there for a moment in silence as though they were perhaps at communion.

"I can't remember the color of my wife's eyes," he said, and he looked sick.

Mrs. Zilke sat there as though considering whether this had importance, or whether she might go on to the next topic of their talk.

"And tonight, would you believe it, I couldn't remember the color of his!"

"They're blue as the sea," Mrs. Zilke said rather gruffly, but with a kind of heavy sad tone also in her voice.

"But what does it matter about those little things," she said. "You're an important man!"

He laughed very loud at this, and Mrs. Zilke suddenly laughed too. A cord of tension had been snapped that had existed between them earlier.

The father lifted his glass and said the usual words and Mrs. Zilke took her glass with a slight bored look and sipped.

"I can taste the grapes in that, all right," she said.

"Well, it's the grapes of course I buy it for," he replied in the tone of voice he might have used in a men's bar.

"You shouldn't care what color their eyes are or were," Mrs. Zilke said.

"Well, it's my memory about people," he told her. "I don't know people."

"I know you don't," she said. "But you have other things!"

"No, I don't. Not really. I could remember people if I wanted to."

"If you wanted to," Mrs. Zilke said.

"Well, why can't I remember my wife's eyes," he brought the whole thing out. "Can you remember," he wanted to know, "the color of eyes of all those in your family."

"All forty-two of them," she laughed.

"Well, your husband and your sons and daughters."

"Oh, I expect I can," she was rather evasive.

"But you do, Mrs. Zilke, you know you do!"

"All right, but I'm just a woman about the house. You're out in the world. Why should you know the color of people's eyes! Good grief, yes!"

She put her glass down, and picked up some socks she had been darning before she had put the boy to bed.

"I'm going to work while we talk," she said with a firmness that seemed to mean she would be talking less now and that she would probably not drink the brandy.

Then suddenly closing his own eyes tight he realized that he did not know the color of Mrs. Zilke's eyes. But suddenly he could not be afraid anymore. He didn't care, and he was sure that Mrs. Zilke would not care if he knew or not. She would tell him not to care. And he remembered her, which was, he was sure, more important. He remembered her kindness to him and his son, and how important they both were to him.

"How old *are* you?" Baxter asked him when he was sitting in his big chair with his drink.

"Twenty-eight, I think," the father said vaguely.

"Is that old enough to be dead?" the son wondered.

"Yes and no," the father replied.

"Am I old enough to be dead?"

"I don't think so," the father replied slowly, and his mind was on something else.

"Why aren't we all dead then?" the son said, sailing a tiny paper airplane he had made. Then he picked up a bird he had made out of brown paper and sailed this through the air. It hit a philodendron plant and stuck there in it, as though it were a conscious addition.

"You always think about something else, don't you?" the boy said, and he went up and stared at his father.

"You have blue eyes," the father said. "Blue as the sea."

The son suddenly kissed his father, and the father looked at him for a long time.

"Don't look funny like that," the boy said, embarrassed.

"Like what?" the father said, and lowered his gaze.

The son moved awkwardly, grinding his tiny shoes into the carpet.

"Like you didn't know anything," the boy said, and he ran out into the kitchen to be with Mrs. Zilke.

After Mrs. Zilke went to bed, which was nearly four hours after the boy had gone, the father was accustomed to sit on downstairs thinking about the problems in his work, but when he was at home like this he often thought about *her,* his wife of long ago. She had run off (this was almost the only term he used for her departure) so long ago and his marriage to her had been so brief that it was almost as though Baxter were a gift somebody had awarded him, and that as the gift increased in value and liability, his own relation to it was more and more ambiguous and obscure. Somehow Mrs. Zilke seemed more real to him than almost anybody else. He could not remember the color of her eyes either, of course, but she was quite real. She was his "mother," he supposed. And the boy was an infant "brother" he did not know too well, and who asked hard questions, and his "wife," who had run off, was just any girl he had gone out with. He could not remember her now at all.

He envied in a way Mrs. Zilke's command over everything. She understood, it seemed, everything she dealt with, and she remembered and could identify all the things which came into her view and under her jurisdiction. The world for her, he was sure, was round, firm, and perfectly illuminated.

For him only his work (and he remembered she had called him a man of importance) had any real meaning, but its meaning to everything else was tenuous.

As he went upstairs that night he looked into his son's room. He was surprised to see that the boy was sleeping with an enormous toy crocodile. The sight of the toy rather shocked him. For a moment he hesitated whether or not to remove the toy and then deciding not to disturb him, he went to his room, took off all his clothes, and stood naked, breathing in front of the open window. Then he went quickly to bed.

"It's his favorite doll," Mrs. Zilke said at breakfast. "He wouldn't part with it for the world." She referred to the toy crocodile.

"I would think it would give him nightmares," the father said.

"He don't have nightmares," Mrs. Zilke said, buttering the toast. "There you are, sir!" and she brought him his breakfast.

The father ate silently for a while.

"I was shocked to see that crocodile in his bed," he told Mrs. Zilke again.

"Well, that's something in you, is all," she said.

"I expect. But why couldn't it have been a teddy bear or a girl doll."

"He has those too. It just happened to be crocodile night last night," Mrs. Zilke said, restless now in the kitchen.

"All right," the father said, and he opened the newspaper and began to read about Egypt.

"Your boy needs a dog," Mrs. Zilke said without warning, coming in and sitting down at the table with him. Her hands still showed the traces of soap suds.

"What kind?" the father said.

"You're not opposed to it, then?" Mrs. Zilke replied.

"Why would I oppose a dog." He continued to look at the newspaper.

"He's got to have something," Mrs. Zilke told him.

"Of course," the father said, swallowing some coffee. Then, having swallowed, he stared at her.

"You mean he doesn't have anything?"

"As long as a parent is living, any parent, a child has something. No, I didn't mean *that*," she said without any real apology, and he expected, of course, none.

"I'd rather have him sleeping with a dog now than that crocodile."

"Oh, that," Mrs. Zilke said, impatient.

Then: "All right, then," he said.

He kept nodding after she had gone out of the room. He sat there looking at his old wedding ring which he still wore. Suddenly he took the ring off his finger for the first time since he had had it put on there by the priest. He had left it on all these years simply because, well, he wanted men to think he was married, he supposed. Everybody was married, and he had to be married somehow, anyhow, he knew.

But he left the wedding ring lying on the table, and he went into the front room.

"Sir," Mrs. Zilke called after him.

"Just leave the ring there," he said, thinking she had found it.

But on her face he saw something else. "You'll have to take the boy to buy the dog, you know. I can't walk on hard pavements any more, remember."

"That will be fine, Mrs. Zilke," he said, somehow relieved at what she said.

The dog they bought at the shop was a small mongrel with a pitifully long tail, and — the father looked very close: brown eyes. Almost the first thing he did was to make a puddle near the father's desk. The father insisted on cleaning it up, and Baxter watched, while Mrs. Zilke muttered to herself in the kitchen. She came in finally and poured something white on the spot.

The dog watched them too from its corner, but it did not seem to want to come out to them.

"You must make up to your new little friend," the father said.

Baxter stared but did not do anything.

"Go to him," the father said, and the son went over into the corner and looked at the pup.

The father sat down at his desk and began to go through his papers.

"Did you have a dog?" Baxter asked his father.

The father thought there at the desk. He did not answer for a long time.

"Yes," the father finally said.

"What color was it," the son asked, and the father stirred in his chair.

"That was so long ago," he said almost as though quoting himself.

"Was it gray then?" the boy wanted to know.

The father nodded.

"A gray dog," the son said, and he began to play with his new pet. The dog lifted its wet paw and bit the boy mildly, and the boy cried a little.

"That's just in fun," the father said absentmindedly.

Baxter ran out into the kitchen, crying a little, and the small dog sat in the corner.

"Don't be afraid of the little fellow now," Mrs. Zilke said. "Go right back and make up to him again."

Baxter and Mrs. Zilke came out of the kitchen and went up to the dog.

"You'll have to name him too," Mrs. Zilke said.

"Will I have to name him, Daddy?" the boy said.

The father nodded.

After supper all three sat in the front room. Baxter nodded a little. The father sat in the easy chair smoking his pipe, the pony of brandy near him. They had gathered here to decide what name to choose for the dog, but nobody had any ideas, it seemed, and the father, hidden from them in a halo of expensive pipe smoke, seemed as far away as if he had gone to the capital again.

Baxter nodded some more and Mrs. Zilke said, "Why, it still isn't bedtime and the little man is asleep!"

From below in the basement where they had put the pup they could all hear the animal's crying, but they pretended not to notice.

Finally, Mrs. Zilke said, "When he is housebroken you can sleep with him, Baxter."

Baxter opened his eyes and looked at her. "What is that?" he said.

"When he learns to take care of himself, not make puddles, you can have him in bed with you."

"I don't want to," the boy said.

Mrs. Zilke looked stoically at the father.

"Why don't you want to, sweetheart," she said, but her words showed no emotion.

"I don't want anything," the boy said.

Mrs. Zilke looked at the father again, but he was even more lost to them.

"What's that hanging loose in your mouth." Mrs. Zilke suddenly sprang to attention, adjusting her spectacles, and looking at the boy's mouth.

"This." The boy pointed to his lips, and blushed slightly. "Gum," he said.

"Oh," Mrs. Zilke said.

The clock struck eight.

"I guess it *is* your bedtime," Mrs. Zilke said.

She watched the boy.

"Do you want to go to bed, Baxter," she said, abstractedly.

The boy nodded.

"Say goodnight to daddy and kiss him," she told him perfunctorily.

The boy got up and went over to his father, but stopped in front of the rings of smoke.

"Goodnight," the boy lisped.

"What's that in his mouth," the father addressed his remark to Mrs. Zilke and his head came out of the clouds of smoke.

Mrs. Zilke got up painfully now and putting on her other glasses looked at the boy.

"What are you sucking?" Mrs. Zilke said, and both of them now stared at him.

Baxter looked at them as though they had put a net about him. From his long indifference to these two people a sudden new feeling came slowly into his dazed, slowly moving mind. He moved back a step, as though he wanted to incite them.

"Baxter, sweetheart," the old woman said, and both she and the father stared at him as though they had found out perhaps who he was.

"What do you have in your mouth, son," the father said, and the word *son* sounded queer in the air, moving toward the boy with the heaviness and suggestion of nausea that the dog puddle had given him earlier in the afternoon.

"What is it, son," the father said, and Mrs. Zilke watched him, her new understanding of the boy written on her old red face.

"I'm chewing gum," the boy told them.

"No, you're not now, Baxter. Why don't you tell us," Mrs. Zilke whined.

Baxter went over into the corner where the dog had been.

"That dog is bad, isn't he," Baxter giggled, and then he suddenly laughed loudly when he thought what the dog had done.

Meanwhile Mrs. Zilke and the father were whispering in the cloud of tobacco smoke.

Baxter sat down on the floor talking to himself, and playing with a broken piece of Tinker Toy. From his mouth still came sounds of something vaguely metallic.

Then Mrs. Zilke came up stealthily, a kind of sadness and kindness both in her face, like that of a trained nurse.

"You can't go to sleep with that in your mouth, sweetheart."

"It's gum," the boy said.

Mrs. Zilke's bad legs would not let her kneel down beside the boy on the floor as she wished to do. She wanted to have a close talk with him, as she did sitting by his bed in the nursery, but instead now, standing over him, so far away, her short heavy breathing sounding obnoxiously in the room, she said only, "You've never lied to me before, Baxter."

"Oh yes I have," Baxter said. "Anyhow this is gum," and he made the sounds again in his mouth.

"I'll have to tell your father," she said, as though *he* were already away in Washington.

"It's gum," the boy said in a bored voice.

"It's metal, I think," she said looking worriedly at the boy.

"It's just gum." The boy hummed now and played with the Tinker Toy.

"You'll have to speak to him," Mrs. Zilke said.

The father squatted down with the son, and the boy vaguely realized this was the first time the father had ever made the motion of playing with him. He stared at his father, but did not listen to what he was talking about.

"If I put my finger in your mouth will you give it to me?" the father said.

"No," the boy replied.

"You wouldn't want to swallow the thing in your mouth," the father said.

"Why not," the boy wondered.

"It would hurt you," the father told him.

"You would have to go to the hospital," Mrs. Zilke said.

"I don't care where I go," the boy said. "It's a toy I have in my mouth."

"What sort of toy," the father wondered, and he and Mrs. Zilke suddenly became absorbed in the curiosity of what Baxter had there.

"A golden toy," the boy laughed, but his eyes looked glassy and strange.

"Please," the father said, and he put his finger gently on the boy's lips.

"Don't touch me!" the son called out suddenly. "I hate you!"

The father drew back softly as though now he would return to his work and his papers, and it was Mrs. Zilke who cried out instead: "Shame!"

"I do hate him," the boy said. "He's never here anyhow."

"Baxter," the father said.

"Give your father what's in your mouth or you will swallow it and something terrible will happen to you."

"I want it right where it is," the boy said, and he threw the Tinker Toy at Mrs. Zilke.

"Look here now, Baxter," the father said, but still sleepily and with no expression.

"Shut your goddamn face," the boy spat out at his father.

The father suddenly seized the boy's chin and jaw and forced him to spit out what he had.

His wedding ring fell on the carpet there, and they all stared at it a second.

Without warning the son kicked the father vigorously in the groin and escaped, running up the stairs.

Baxter stopped deliberately from the safety of the upper staircase and pronounced the obscene word for his father as though this was what he had been keeping for him for a long time.

Mrs. Zilke let out a low cry.

The father writhing in pain from the place where the boy had kicked him, managed to say with great effort: "Tell me where he learned a word like that."

Mrs. Zilke went over to where the ring lay now near the Tinker Toy.

"I don't know what's happening to people," she said, putting the ring on the table.

Then, a weary concern in her voice, she said, "Sir, are you hurt?"

The tears fell from the father's eyes for having been hit in such a delicate place, and he could not say anything more for a moment.

"Can I do anything for you, sir?" Mrs. Zilke said.

"I don't think right now, thank you," he said. "Thank you." He grunted with the exquisite pain.

"I've put your ring up here for safekeeping," she informed him.

The father nodded from the floor where he twisted in his pain.

the enormous radio

John Cheever

Jim and Irene Westcott were the kind of people who seem to strike that satisfactory average of income, endeavor, and respectability that is reached by the statistical reports in college alumni bulletins. They were the parents of two young children, they had been married nine years, they lived on the twelfth floor of an apartment house near Sutton Place, they went to the theatre on an average of 10.3 times a year, and they hoped someday to live in Westchester. Irene Westcott was a pleasant, rather plain girl with soft brown hair and a wide, fine forehead upon which nothing at all had been written, and in the cold weather she wore a coat of fitch skins dyed to resemble mink. You could not say that Jim Westcott looked younger than he was, but you could at least say of him that he seemed to feel younger. He wore his graying hair cut very short, he dressed in the kind of clothes his class had worn at Andover, and his manner was earnest, vehement, and intentionally naïve. The Westcotts differed from their friends, their classmates, and their neighbors only in an interest they shared in serious music. They went to a great many concerts — although they seldom mentioned this to anyone — and they spent a good deal of time listening to music on the radio.

Their radio was an old instrument, sensitive, unpredictable, and beyond repair. Neither of them understood the mechanics of radio — or of any of the other appliances that surrounded them — and when the instrument faltered, Jim would strike the side of the cabinet with his hand. This sometimes helped. One Sunday afternoon, in the middle of a Schubert quartet, the music faded away altogether. Jim struck the cabinet repeatedly, but there was no response; the Schubert was lost to them forever. He promised to buy Irene a new radio, and on Monday when he came home from work he told her that he had got one. He refused to describe it, and said it would be a surprise for her when it came.

The radio was delivered at the kitchen door the following afternoon, and with the assistance of her maid and the handyman Irene uncrated it and brought it into the living room. She was struck at once with the physical ugliness of the large gumwood cabinet. Irene was proud of her living room, she had chosen its furnishings and colors as carefully as she chose her clothes, and now it seemed to her that the new radio stood among her intimate possessions like an aggressive intruder. She was confounded by the number of dials and switches on the instrument panel, and she studied them thoroughly before she put the plug into a wall socket and turned the radio on. The dials flooded with a malevolent green light, and in the distance she heard the music of a piano quintet. The quintet was in the distance for only an instant; it bore down upon her with a speed greater than light and filled the apartment with the noise of music amplified so mightily that it knocked a china ornament from a table to the floor. She rushed to the instrument and reduced the volume. The violent forces that were snared in the ugly gumwood cabinet made her uneasy. Her children came home from school then, and she took them to the Park. It was not until later in the afternoon that she was able to return to the radio.

The maid had given the children their suppers and was supervising their baths when Irene turned on the radio, reduced the volume, and sat down to listen to a Mozart quintet that she knew and enjoyed. The music came through clearly. The new instrument had a much purer tone, she thought, than the old one. She decided that tone was most important and that she could conceal the cabinet behind a sofa. But as soon as she had made her peace with the radio, the interference began. A crackling sound like the noise of a burning powder fuse began to accompany the singing of the strings. Beyond the music, there was a rustling that reminded Irene unpleasantly of the sea, and as the quintet progressed, these noises were joined by many others. She tried all the dials and switches but nothing dimmed the interference, and she sat down, disappointed and bewildered, and tried to trace the flight of the melody. The elevator shaft in her building ran beside the living-room wall, and it was the noise of the elevator that gave her a clue to the character of the static. The rattling of the elevator cables and the opening and closing of the elevator doors were reproduced in her loudspeaker, and, realizing that the radio was sensitive to electrical currents of all sorts, she began to discern through the Mozart the ringing of telephone bells, the dialing of phones, and the lamentation of a vacuum cleaner. By listening more carefully, she was able to distinguish doorbells, elevator bells, electric razors, and Waring mixers, whose sounds had been picked up from the apartments that surrounded hers and transmitted through her loudspeaker. The powerful and ugly instrument, with its mistaken sensitivity to discord, was more than she could hope to master, so she turned the thing off and went into the nursery to see her children.

When Jim Westcott came home that night, he went to the radio confidently and worked the controls. He had the same sort of experience Irene had had. A man was speaking on the station Jim had chosen, and his voice swung instantly from the distance into a force so powerful that it shook the apartment. Jim turned the volume control and reduced the voice. Then, a minute or two later, the interference began. The ringing of telephones and doorbells set in, joined by the rasp of the elevator doors and the whir of cooking appliances. The character of the noise had changed since Irene had tried the radio earlier; the last of the electric razors was being unplugged, the vacuum cleaners had all been returned to their closets, and the static reflected that change in pace that overtakes the city after the sun goes down. He fiddled with the knobs but couldn't get rid of the noises, so he turned the radio off and told Irene that in the morning he'd call the people who had sold it to him and give them hell.

The following afternoon, when Irene returned to the apartment from a luncheon date, the maid told her that a man had come and fixed the radio. Irene went into the living room before she took off her hat or her furs and tried the instrument. From the loudspeaker came a recording of the "Missouri Waltz." It reminded her of the thin, scratchy music from an old-fashioned phonograph that she sometimes heard across the lake where she spent her summers. She waited until the waltz had finished, expecting an explanation of the recording, but there was none. The music was followed by silence, and then the plaintive and scratchy record was repeated. She turned the dial and got a satisfactory burst of Caucasian music — the thump of bare feet in the dust and the rattle of coin jewelry — but in the background she could hear the ringing of bells and a confusion of voices. Her children came home from school then, and she turned off the radio and went to the nursery.

When Jim came home that night, he was tired, and he took a bath and changed his clothes. Then he joined Irene in the living room. He had just turned on the radio when the maid announced dinner, so he left it on, and he and Irene went to the table.

Jim was too tired to make even a pretense of sociability, and there was nothing about the dinner to hold Irene's interest, so her attention wandered from the food to the deposits of silver polish on the candlesticks and from there to the music in the other room. She listened for a few moments to a Chopin prelude and then was surprised to hear a man's voice break in. "For Christ's sake, Kathy," he said, "do you always have to play the piano when I get home?" The music stopped abruptly. "It's the only chance I have," a woman said. "I'm at the office all day." "So am I," the man said. He added something obscene about an upright piano, and slammed a door. The passionate and melancholy music began again.

"Did you hear that?" Irene asked.

"What?" Jim was eating his dessert.

"The radio. A man said something while the music was still going on—something dirty."

"It's probably a play."

"I don't think it *is* a play," Irene said.

They left the table and took their coffee into the living room. Irene asked Jim to try another station. He turned the knob. "Have you seen my garters?" a man asked. "Button me up," a woman said. "Have you seen my garters?" the man said again. "Just button me up and I'll find your garters," the woman said. Jim shifted to another station. "I wish you wouldn't leave apple cores in the ashtrays," a man said. "I hate the smell."

"This is strange," Jim said.

"Isn't it?" Irene said.

Jim turned the knob again. "'On the coast of Coromandel where the early pumpkins blow,'" a woman with a pronounced English accent said, "'in the middle of the woods lived the Yonghy-Bonghy-Bò. Two old chairs, and half a candle, one old jug without a handle . . .'"

"My God!" Irene cried. "That's the Sweeneys' nurse."

" 'These were all his worldly goods,' " the British voice continued.

"Turn that thing off," Irene said. "Maybe they can hear *us*." Jim switched the radio off. "That was Miss Armstrong, the Sweeneys' nurse," Irene said. "She must be reading to the little girl. They live in 17-B. I've talked with Miss Armstrong in the Park. I know her voice very well. We must be getting other people's apartments."

"That's impossible," Jim said.

"Well, that was the Sweeneys' nurse," Irene said hotly. "I know her voice. I know it very well. I'm wondering if they can hear us."

Jim turned the switch. First from a distance and then nearer, nearer, as if borne on the wind, came the pure accents of the Sweeneys' nurse again: " '*Lady Jingly! Lady Jingly!*' " she said, " '*Sitting where the pumpkins blow, will you come and be my wife,* said the Yonghy-Bonghy-Bò . . .' "

Jim went over to the radio and said "Hello" loudly into the speaker.

" '*I am tired of living singly,*' " the nurse went on, " '*on this coast so wild and shingly, I'm a-weary of my life; if you'll come and be my wife, quite serene would be my life . . .*' "

"I guess she can't hear us," Irene said. "Try something else."

Jim turned to another station, and the living room was filled with the uproar of a cocktail party that had overshot its mark. Someone was playing the piano and singing the Whiffenpoof Song, and the voices that surrounded the piano were vehement and happy. "Eat some more sandwiches," a woman shrieked. There were screams of laughter and a dish of some sort crashed to the floor.

"Those must be the Fullers, in 11-E," Irene said. "I knew they were giving a party this afternoon. I saw her in the liquor store. Isn't this too divine? Try something else. See if you can get those people in 18-C."

The Westcotts overheard that evening a monologue on salmon fishing in Canada, a bridge game, running comments on home movies of what had apparently been a fortnight at Sea Island, and a bitter family quarrel about an overdraft at the bank. They turned off their radio at midnight and went to bed, weak with laughter. Sometime in the night, their son began to call for a glass of water and Irene got one and took it to his room. It was very early. All the lights in the neighborhood were extinguished, and from the boy's window she could see the empty street. She went into the living room and tried the radio. There was some faint coughing, a moan, and then a man spoke. "Are you all right, darling?" he asked. "Yes," a woman said wearily. "Yes, I'm all right, I guess," and then she added with great feeling, "but, you know, Charlie, I don't feel like myself any more. Sometimes there are about fifteen or twenty minutes in the week when I feel like myself. I don't like to go to another doctor, because the doctor's bills are so awful already, but I just don't feel like myself, Charlie. I just never feel like myself." They were not young, Irene thought. She guessed from the timbre of their voices that they were middle-aged. The restrained melancholy of the dialogue and the draft from the bedroom window made her shiver, and she went back to bed.

The following morning, Irene cooked breakfast for the family — the maid didn't come up from her room in the basement until ten — braided her daughter's hair, and waited at the door until her children and her husband had been carried away in the elevator. Then she went into the living room and tried the radio. "I don't want to go to school," a child screamed. "I hate school. I won't go to school. I hate school." "You will go to school," an enraged woman said. "We paid eight hundred dollars to get you into that school and you'll go if it kills you." The next number on the dial produced the worn record of the "Missouri Waltz." Irene shifted the control and invaded the privacy of several breakfast tables. She overheard demonstrations of indigestion, carnal love, abysmal vanity, faith, and despair. Irene's life was nearly as simple and sheltered as it appeared to be, and the forthright and sometimes brutal language that came from the loudspeaker that morning astonished and troubled her. She continued to listen until her maid came in. Then she turned off the radio quickly, since this insight, she realized, was a furtive one.

Irene had a luncheon date with a friend that day, and she left her apartment at a little after twelve. There were a number of women in the elevator when it stopped at her floor. She stared at their handsome and impassive faces, their furs, and the cloth flowers in their hats. Which one of them had been to Sea Island, she wondered. Which one had overdrawn her bank account? The elevator stopped at the tenth floor and a woman with a pair of Skye terriers joined them. Her hair was rigged high on her head and she wore a mink cape. She was humming the "Missouri Waltz."

Irene had two Martinis at lunch, and she looked searchingly at her friend and wondered what her secrets were. They had intended to go shopping after lunch, but Irene excused herself and went home. She told the maid that she was not to be disturbed; then she went into the living room, closed the doors, and switched on the radio. She heard, in the course of the afternoon, the halting conversation of a woman entertaining her aunt, the hysterical conclusion of a luncheon party, and a hostess briefing her maid about some cocktail guests. "Don't give the best Scotch to anyone who hasn't white hair," the hostess said. "See if you can get rid of that liver paste before you pass those hot things, and could you lend me five dollars? I want to tip the elevator man."

As the afternoon waned, the conversations increased in intensity. From where Irene sat, she could see the open sky above the East River. There were hundreds of clouds in the sky, as though the south wind had broken the winter into pieces and were blowing it north, and on her radio she could hear the arrival of cocktail guests and the return of children and businessmen from their schools and offices. "I found a good-sized diamond on the bathroom floor this morning," a woman said. "It must have fallen out of that bracelet Mrs. Dunston was wearing last night." "We'll sell it," a man said. "Take it down to the jeweller on Madison Avenue and sell it. Mrs. Dunston won't know the difference, and we could use a couple of hundred bucks . . ." " 'Oranges and lemons, say the bells of St. Clement's,' " the Sweeneys' nurse sang. " 'Half-pence and farthings, say the bells of St. Martin's. When will you pay me? say the bells at old Bailey . . .' " "It's not a hat," a woman cried, and at her back roared a cocktail party. "It's not a hat, it's a love affair. That's what Walter Florell said. He said it's not a hat, it's a love affair," and then, in a lower voice, the same woman added, "Talk to somebody, for Christ's sake, honey, talk to somebody. If she catches you standing here not talking to anybody, she'll take us off her invitation list, and I love these parties."

The Westcotts were going out for dinner that night, and when Jim came home, Irene was dressing. She seemed sad and vague, and he brought her a drink. They were dining with friends in the neighborhood, and they walked to where they were going. The sky was broad and filled with light. It was one of those splendid spring evenings that excite memory and desire, and the air that touched their hands and faces felt very soft. A Salvation Army band was on the corner playing "Jesus Is Sweeter." Irene drew on her husband's arm and held him there for a minute, to hear the music. "They're really such nice people, aren't they?" she said. "They have such nice faces. Actually, they're so much nicer than a lot of the people we know." She took a bill from her purse and walked over and dropped it into the tambourine. There was in her face, when she returned to her husband, a look of radiant melancholy that he was not familiar with. And her conduct at the dinner party that night seemed strange to him, too. She interrupted her hostess rudely and stared at the people across the table from her with an intensity for which she would have punished her children.

It was still mild when they walked home from the party, and Irene looked up at the spring stars. " 'How far that little candle throws its beams,' " she exclaimed. " 'So shines a good deed in a naughty world.' " She waited that night until Jim had fallen asleep, and then went into the living room and turned on the radio.

Jim came home at about six the next night. Emma, the maid, let him in, and he had taken off his hat and was taking off his coat when Irene ran into the hall. Her face was shining with tears and her hair was disordered. "Go up to 16-C, Jim!" she screamed. "Don't take off your coat. Go up to 16-C. Mr. Osborn's beating his wife. They've been quarrelling since four o'clock, and now he's hitting her. Go up there and stop him."

From the radio in the living room, Jim heard screams, obscenities, and thuds. "You know you don't have to listen to this sort of thing," he said. He strode into the living room and turned the switch. "It's indecent," he said. "It's like looking in windows. You know you don't have to listen to this sort of thing. You can turn it off."

"Oh, it's so horrible, it's so dreadful," Irene was sobbing. "I've been listening all day, and it's so depressing."

"Well, if it's so depressing, why do you listen to it? I bought this damned radio to give you some pleasure," he said. "I paid a great deal of money for it. I thought it might make you happy. I wanted to make you happy."

"Don't, don't, don't, don't quarrel with me," she moaned, and laid her head on his shoulder. "All the others have been quarrelling all day. Everybody's been quarrelling. They're all worried about money. Mrs. Hutchinson's mother is dying of cancer in Florida and they don't have enough money to send her to the Mayo Clinic. At least, Mr. Hutchinson says they don't have enough money. And some woman in this building is having an affair with the handyman — with that hideous handyman. It's too disgusting. And Mrs. Melville has heart trouble and Mr. Hendricks is going to lose his job in April and Mrs. Hendricks is horrid about the whole thing and that girl who plays the 'Missouri Waltz' is a whore, a common whore, and the elevator man has tuberculosis and Mr. Osborn has been beating Mrs. Osborn." She wailed, she trembled with grief and checked the stream of tears down her face with the heel of her palm.

"Well, why do you have to listen?" Jim asked again. "Why do you have to listen to this stuff if it makes you so miserable?"

"Oh, don't, don't, don't," she cried. "Life is too terrible, too sordid and awful. But we've never been like that, have we, darling? Have we? I mean we've always been good and decent and loving to one another, haven't we? And we have two children, two beautiful children. Our lives aren't sordid, are they, darling? Are they?" She flung her arms around his neck and drew his face down to hers. "We're happy, aren't we, darling? We are happy, aren't we?"

"Of course we're happy," he said tiredly. He began to surrender his resentment. "Of course we're happy. I'll have that damned radio fixed or taken away tomorrow." He stroked her soft hair. "My poor girl," he said.

"You love me, don't you?" she asked. "And we're not hypercritical or worried about money or dishonest, are we?"

"No, darling," he said.

A man came in the morning and fixed the radio. Irene turned it on cautiously and was happy to hear a California-wine commercial and a recording of Beethoven's Ninth Symphony, including Schiller's "Ode to Joy." She kept the radio on all day and nothing untoward came from the speaker.

A Spanish suite was being played when Jim came home. "Is everything all right?" he asked. His face was pale, she thought. They had some cocktails and went in to dinner to the "Anvil Chorus" from "Il Trovatore." This was followed by Debussy's "La Mer."

"I paid the bill for the radio today," Jim said. "It cost four hundred dollars. I hope you'll get some enjoyment out of it."

"Oh, I'm sure I will," Irene said.

"Four hundred dollars is a good deal more than I can afford," he went on. "I wanted to get something that you'd enjoy. It's the last extravagance we'll be able to indulge in this year. I see that you haven't paid your clothing bills yet. I saw them on your dressing table." He looked directly at her. "Why did you tell me you'd paid them? Why did you lie to me?"

"I just didn't want you to worry, Jim," she said. She drank some water. "I'll be able to pay my bills out of this month's allowance. There were the slipcovers last month, and that party."

"You've got to learn to handle the money I give you a little more intelligently, Irene," he said. "You've got to understand that we won't have as much money this year as we had last. I had a very sobering talk with Mitchell today. No one is buying anything. We're spending all our time promoting new issues, and you know how long that takes. I'm not getting any younger, you know. I'm thirty-seven. My hair will be gray next year. I haven't done as well as I'd hoped to do. And I don't suppose things will get any better."

"Yes, dear," she said.

"We've got to start cutting down," Jim said. "We've got to think of the children. To be perfectly frank with you, I worry about money a great deal. I'm not at all sure of the future. No one is. If anything should happen to me, there's the insurance, but that wouldn't go very far today. I've worked awfully hard to give you and the children a comfortable life," he said bitterly. "I don't like to see all of my energies, all of my youth, wasted in fur coats and radios and slipcovers and — "

"Please, Jim," she said. "Please. They'll hear us."

"*Who'll hear us?* Emma can't hear us."

"The radio."

"Oh, I'm sick!" he shouted. "I'm sick to death of your apprehensiveness. The radio can't hear us. Nobody can hear us. And what if they can hear us? Who cares?"

Irene got up from the table and went into the living room. Jim went to the door and shouted at her from there. "Why are you so Christly all of a sudden? What's turned you overnight into a convent girl? You stole your mother's jewelry before they probated her will. You never gave your sister a cent of that money that was intended for her — not even when she needed it. You made Grace Howland's life miserable, and where was all your piety and your virtue when you went to that abortionist? I'll never forget how cool you were. You packed your bag and went off to have that child murdered as if you were going to Nassau. If you'd had any reasons, if you'd had any good reasons — "

Irene stood for a minute before the hideous cabinet, disgraced and sickened, but she held her hand on the switch before she extinguished the music and the voices, hoping that the instrument might speak to her kindly, that she might hear the Sweeneys' nurse. Jim continued to shout at her from the door. The voice on the radio was suave and noncommittal. "An early-morning railroad disaster in Tokyo," the loudspeaker said, "killed twenty-nine people. A fire in a Catholic hospital near Buffalo for the care of blind children was extinguished early this morning by nuns. The temperature is forty-seven. The humidity is eighty-nine."

drama

blood money

a play in one act on the value of money stretching

Dennis Jasudowicz

CHARACTERS
> D.H., *a Negro man*
> LADY C., *a Negro woman*
> OIL MAGNATE, *a very fat white man, over-, overfat man*

SCENE: A highly grotesque set of a cabin in the mountains.

(D.H. *and* LADY C. *are standing by the fireplace.*)
D.H. (*cross*): Where's he now?
LADY C. (*calm*): Chopping wood.
D.H.: We must tell him.
LADY C.: Of —
D.H.: Our love for each other.

LADY C.: There isn't anything else we can do?

D.H.: Are we to hide it? Are we ashamed of it?

LADY C.: No — it's too beautiful. Yet I thought we might spare him. We're New England blacks, aren't we? Be polite.

D.H.: For what? Hasn't he been the cause of our troubles? (*With pride.*) Look, I'm proud of it, maybe you aren't?

LADY C. (*shocked*): But I am, I am proud of it, D. H. Before you came, I had nothing, and now I have everything. With him I was Lady C., married to the oil magnate, an old fat man. With you I'm a woman of fire, burning with passion, living with desire, flaming with blood. When your naked body's against my naked body, the world is majestic.

D.H.: Never will I forget the first time I saw you without having on any clothes whatsoever; the picture of your nude body is always in my eyes, the feeling of your bare skin in my hands, and the splendor of your breast in my heart.

LADY C.: We're one and the same, our blood drives us together; when you stick it in, it's the final movement of two becoming one — nothing else matters.

D.H.: I tell you, dearest Lady C., our bodies are holy. When we're nude, and in each other's arms, we're spiritual, our natures are spiritual, our bodies are spiritual. (*Looks at the fireplace and he laughs.*) There's a fire — and why? Because it's cold outside, because there's snow on the ground, yet why have a fire when we're flame itself! And that's the reason he has to know! He must know it! From now on, we won't hide it from him no longer. We — who are spiritual and holy — should be ashamed before him, the unspiritual, the unholy? I should say not! Let us be open before the bastard! Show our blood to his face! Who does he think he is? God? Since he's an oil magnate, he believes he's God almighty!

LADY C.: That's why he's here in the mountains, he's trying to discover some precious material — he's out there now searching for it — it's nearly time for him to be back, then he'll sit in his rocking chair, and he'll rock all night.

D.H.: Why did he marry you? He never touches you.

LADY C. (*puzzled*): My family was poor, we lived in the slums, and we didn't have a thing. One day he sent a man to all the slum families, inquiring if there was a poor family with a beautiful daughter. The man he sent offered my family riches if I would marry the oil magnate — I had to do it, we were so financially unstable.

D.H.: Yes, he also sent a man for me — to come out here in the mountains, far away from any civilization, far away from any people, to paint the cabin black, to put in black window shutters — two days' work.

LADY C.: Therefore you couldn't leave for a week. There are no cars here, the man whom he employs brings food from the city once a week, he lives in the city, he'll be here tomorrow, then you'll leave.

D.H.: But with you in my arms. Your family has money now, and there's no need for you to stay here. In fact, there was no need for you to ever stay here, your brain brought you here, and your body will take you away.

LADY C.: You, D.H., are completely body, you are brainless.

D.H.: Pretty soon you'll be brainless, too; a woman should never have a brain, it's unheard of. A woman should be her body and not anything else. A woman should allow a man to be her only movement, the master of her body, her sole master. Actually you never had to marry him, you thought of your family, a woman mustn't ever use her brains. (*His hands on her face.*) Oh, I want your face — (*Drops his hands to her arms.*) I want your arms — (*Stares hard at her figure, as if he's reaching for it.*) But mostly, I want your body — (*Reaches more.*)

LADY C. (*retreats*): No, don't — he might walk in.

D.H. (*raging*): Too bad! It doesn't matter what he does! Hear! When he comes in, I'll inform him about everything! We'll do it right before his eyes!

LADY C. (*stunned*): No!

D.H.: Then we'll go outside to nature, and do it on his mountains in the raw.

LADY C.: That would be lovely.

D.H.: You'll do it?

LADY C.: With my body and heart — yes.

(*Enter the* OIL MAGNATE. *Through the entire play, he seems quite frightened, and whenever he speaks, he glances around quickly.*)

D.H.: Here he is.

OIL MAGNATE: Gosh! Gosh!

(*He moves to the rocking chair and he sits on it.*)

D.H.: So you returned.

OIL MAGNATE: Gosh! Gosh!

D.H.: For the past few days, we've been wanting to tell you the truth, oil magnate.

OIL MAGNATE (*chair squeaking loudly*): Gosh! Gosh!

D.H. (*pointing at* LADY C.): Take an eyeful of the woman you married — go on! Because she is a woman with a body, and that body lives.

OIL MAGNATE: Gosh! Gosh!

D.H.: And did you ever do anything to make it alive, did you! Why, man, she's got blood in her and I made that blood a flame — I made her a woman!

OIL MAGNATE: Gosh! Gosh!

D.H.: Listen to this carefully. I screwed her good, I took her nude body into my arms and made it breathe.

OIL MAGNATE: Gosh! Gosh!

D.H. (*to* LADY C.): Didn't I give you a good screw?

LADY C.: The best.

OIL MAGNATE: Gosh! Gosh!

D.H.: Didn't I make every inch of you a woman of fruitful bliss?

LADY C.: Every inch.

OIL MAGNATE: Gosh! Gosh!

D.H.: Tomorrow I take her away from here. And right now she's mine — we're one.

OIL MAGNATE: Gosh! Gosh!

D.H.: Outside is nature, and we're part of it. I'm a man, and she's a woman, we're blood, and we're blood together.

OIL MAGNATE (*pulls two one-dollar bills from his pocket, and he pushes them in his nostrils — half of them are hanging out*): Gosh! Gosh!

D.H. (*exploding*): Why don't you shove them up your ass instead!

LADY C. (*afraid*): Please ——

D.H.: Since he's got dollars in his nostrils he thinks he's it! As if dollars in the nostrils are something to brag about!

LADY C.: Oh, forget his dollars in his nostrils.

D.H.: How can I forget his dollars in his nostrils when they're hanging out!

LADY C.: Pretend you don't see the dollars in his nostrils.

OIL MAGNATE: Gosh! Gosh!

D.H.: All right, keep your dollars in your nostrils. Her and I are going outside, and I'll strip her naked and lay her down in the snow, and we'll do it right there. And I'll feel her bare skin under my hands, I'll slide them over her — all over her — even under the toes! (*To* LADY C.) Come on, we'll show him.

(*They exit.*)

OIL MAGNATE: Gosh! Gosh! (*He paces to the door, and he locks it. Every once in a while he utters, "Gosh! Gosh!" He bolts the shutters on the windows, he places objects against the door and windows, he goes into the other rooms — much noise is heard — he returns, and he builds up the fire in the fireplace, then he seats himself on the rocker and rocks.*) Gosh! Gosh!

(*Someone is trying to open the door. A knock. More knocking.*)

VOICE OF D.H. (*laughing*): Hey, open the door! God, laying in that snow, it's cold. Though a lot of fun — eh? (*Laughter.*) Wow, it's freezing! Say, open this door, will yeh!

OIL MAGNATE: Gosh! Gosh!

(*Pounding on door.*)

VOICE OF D.H.: Stop blowing farts, and unlock this door! We could hear you in there!

OIL MAGNATE: Gosh! Gosh!

VOICE OF D.H.: Say, quit your stalling, unclose this door! Damn bastard, open this rotten door! (*Pounding again.*) It's an icebox out here, open up, before we freeze to — to —— (*Louder pounding on door.*) Man, for god's s'sake, let us in!

OIL MAGNATE: Gosh! Gosh!

(*Much pounding on shutters.*)

VOICE OF D.H.: Look here, you got to open up some time, you can't keep the doors locked forever —— Son of a bitch, you must think you're God! What if we froze to — to ——

(*Pounding on door.*)

VOICE OF LADY C.: Why, you old fat bastard, if you don't open the door, you'll be sorry!

OIL MAGNATE: Gosh! Gosh!

VOICE OF D.H.: Sure, he believes he's the Lord Himself! Since he's got dollars in his nostrils he thinks he can do anything!

VOICE OF LADY C.: Oh, he burns me up with his dollars hanging from his nostrils!

VOICE OF D.H.: Shit, it's colder than hell out here! (*Banging at door.*) Open up!

OIL MAGNATE: Gosh! Gosh!

VOICE OF LADY C.: My women's clothes are so thin, why don't you offer me your jacket, darling.

VOICE OF D.H.: Unlock this door, you dirty moron!

(*Banging at door.*)

VOICE OF LADY C.: I asked you for your jacket, D.H.

VOICE OF D.H.: Hear me, unlock this door!
(*More banging.*)

OIL MAGNATE: Gosh! Gosh!

VOICE OF LADY C.: D.H., you're not allowing him —— (*A long pause.*) Jesus Christ, you didn't have to strike me!

VOICE OF D.H.: Then cease complaining, I'm freezing, too!
(*Banging at door and shutters.*)

OIL MAGNATE: Gosh! Gosh!

VOICE OF D.H.: When I lay my hands on you, I'll kill you for this! Slimy chump! Unbolt the goddam door!

VOICE OF LADY C.: Tell him his dollars are nice hanging from his nostrils, maybe he'll leave us in.

VOICE OF D.H.: No, I won't tell him that, his dollars hanging from his nostrils are terrible!

OIL MAGNATE: Gosh! Gosh!

VOICE OF LADY C.: Oil magnate, the dollars hanging in your nostrils are cute.

VOICE OF D.H.: What did you pronounce that for?

VOICE OF LADY C.: Perhaps he'll open the door; I'm cold.

VOICE OF D.H.: Well, you didn't have to tell him his dollars are cute hanging from his nostrils!

OIL MAGNATE: Gosh! Gosh! (*Quite a bit of pounding on the door and shutters.*) Gosh! Gosh!

VOICE OF D.H.: Come on, will you open this door or not! We can't stay out here all night, we'll —— (*Banging at door.*) There's no use keeping us out here, you won't gain a thing by it! It won't help you none! Could it be, you suppose you'll have avenged yourself by not allowing us to enter? (*Laughter.*) Face the facts, you can't have any revenge, since you never had anything in the first place, you never touched her, you never even looked at her, she never cooked for you, she never even did a thing for you or you for her, then you couldn't actually have anything — you can't kill nothing, you can't obtain revenge on nothing, because there's nothing to obtain from nothing.

VOICE OF LADY C.: Yes, if I'm nothing, there's nothing to revenge.

OIL MAGNATE: Gosh! Gosh!

VOICE OF D.H.: But you are something, not nothing!

VOICE OF LADY C.: To you I'm something, but to him I'm nothing. So together I'm something, yet nothing.

VOICE OF D.H.: True, to me you're always something and to him you're never nothing.

VOICE OF LADY C.: Then together, I'm an always something and a never nothing.

OIL MAGNATE: Gosh! Gosh!

(*Much banging on door.*)

VOICE OF D.H.: I'm warning you, you don't open this door, I'll pull your dollars out of your nostrils!

VOICE OF LADY C.: Be calm.

VOICE OF D.H.: Why should I? He's asking for his dollars to be pulled out of his nostrils!

VOICE OF LADY C.: Perhaps his dollars aren't in his nostrils now?

VOICE OF D.H.: Of course they are, where else would his dollars be if they weren't in his nostrils!

OIL MAGNATE: Gosh! Gosh!

(*Banging on door and shutters.*)

VOICE OF D.H.: What if he doesn't open up?

VOICE OF LADY C.: Don't say that — please.

VOICE OF D.H.: But what if he doesn't open up?

VOICE OF LADY C.: Oh, he must, nobody could be that mean.

VOICE OF D.H.: With his dollars in his nostrils he might never open up!

OIL MAGNATE: Gosh! Gosh! (*Banging on door and shutters; then, for a considerable time, banging all around the cabin.*) Gosh! Gosh!

VOICE OF D.H.: Everything's locked! (*A pause.*) See, the smoke coming from the chimney! Loads of it! We can't go in through it! God, he's thought of everything with his dollars in his nostrils!

VOICE OF LADY C.: It would seem rather difficult to think with dollars in your nostrils!

VOICE OF D.H.: Not him, he loves his dollars in his nostrils!

(*From now on,* D.H. *and* LADY C. *are speaking from outside.*)

(*More banging on door and shutters.*)

LADY C.: D.H., it's so cold! Do something! I'm afraid!

D.H.: Well, it's your own fault we're out here!

LADY C.: Me!

D.H.: Yes, you!

LADY C.: It was your idea ——

D.H.: Dirty bitch! Shut up!

LADY C.: Don't have to hit me!

D.H.: Didn't I tell you to shut up!

LADY C.: Stop that, it hurts!

D.H.: Then shut up, it was all your fault!

OIL MAGNATE: Gosh! Gosh!
  (*Much pounding on door.*)
D.H.: Rotten slut!
LADY C.: That's enough!
D.H.: Crossing your husband — eh!
LADY C.: Please, that's enough, I'm bleeding!
D.H.: Goddammit, I'll teach you to double-time your husband! You
  won't run away!
  (*A loud moan from* LADY C.)
LADY C.: In the name of God ——
D.H.: Two-timing whore!
OIL MAGNATE: Gosh! Gosh!
  (*Pounding on door and shutters.*)
D.H.: Listen, oil magnate, I hate her, every damn inch of her, except
  that hole in the middle, that's all I was after from the very be-
  ginning! I swear it, that's all! And hers isn't anything to brag
  about, I've seen better on old bags! In fact, an old paper bag is
  better! Man, believe me, I didn't have a chance, she climbed all
  over me—I didn't even want to do it!
LADY C.: That's not true ——
D.H.: Close that trap! Hear me, close that trap!
OIL MAGNATE: Gosh! Gosh!
LADY C.: D.H., it's not in your nature to act like that — you were
  always gentle and kind.
D.H.: Gentle — eh! Kind, eh!
LADY C.: You don't have to kick me!
D.H.: Maybe you deserve it — two-timing your husband — I'll teach
  you to play around behind his back!
LADY C.: Not that! No, don't ——
D.H.: Can't lay off other men—eh! Somebody's gotta learn you
  women a lesson, and I guess I'm the one! Because your husband
  got dollars in his nostrils, you chase after every pair of pants that
  comes along!
LADY C.: No ——
D.H.: What you got against his dollars in his nostrils!
LADY C.: Nothing.
D.H.: What you got against his dollars in his nostrils!
LADY C.: Not a thing.
D.H.: In this day and age, a husband can't even put his dollars in his
  nostrils without his wife running for another man!
OIL MAGNATE: Gosh! Gosh!

D.H.: The least little thing, such as dollars in the nostrils, and you women want a different man!

LADY C.: My ear's coming off!

D.H.: And you were claiming you were spiritual ——

LADY C.: My ear's coming off!

D.H.: Besides, you were holy, too ——

LADY C.: It fell off! God, it fell off!

D.H.: Well, he's the one who's holy, he's the one who's spiritual, with his dollars in his nostrils, and you're unholy, unspiritual ——

LADY C.: Look, it fell off! It fell off!

D.H.: No wonder it fell off; you ain't got any dollars in your nostrils!

LADY C.: But it's my ear! My ear!

D.H.: Quit staring at me, I don't have no paste! For Christ sake, I ain't even a peppermint king!

OIL MAGNATE: Gosh! Gosh!

(*Banging on door and shutters.*)

LADY C.: Where you going?

D.H.: On the roof — by the chimney — stay warm there.

LADY C.: Help me up.

D.H.: If you crawl up there, your ——

LADY C.: Don't worry yourself with my clothes —— What are you gazing at me like that for? —— What you doing! Don't! You can't ——

(*A moan from* LADY C., *then a lengthy silence.*)

OIL MAGNATE: Gosh! Gosh! (*More silence.*) Gosh! Gosh! (*More silence.*) Gosh! Gosh!

(*A pause.*)

D.H.: Ha! Ha! Listen, oil magnate, I'm wearing her clothes — they don't fit — she's dead. I pushed her face in the snow, that stuff came out of her mouth — red stuff — blood! Wiped some on my face, it's warm, I always thought she had warm blood — yeah, she's a real flame! Bet it came from her stomach! — Stomach —— Stomach ——

(*A long silence.*)

OIL MAGNATE: Gosh! Gosh!

(*A pause.*)

D.H.: Has she got the guts! They're warm, too! Didn't I always tell her, she was a girl with guts! Man, they're so soft; now I could see why doctors love their work!

(*Banging at door.*)

OIL MAGNATE: Gosh! Gosh!

D.H.: Oil magnate, let me in. I ain't mad with your dollars in your nostrils no more! (*More banging at door.*) Oil magnate, I'm just blood and guts like her, don't leave me out here to perish! —— Come on, don't be that cruel, allow me to pass through the door —— I'm sorry I killed her —— But her clothes looked warm, and I'm freezing, and she was so hot, well, when we did it — she was hot, all right — man, she was hot! Then why don't you permit me to enter? Why!

(*Pounding on door and shutters.*)

OIL MAGNATE: Gosh! Gosh!

D.H.: O.K. I'm climbing on the roof — to the very top!

(*Noise is heard against the cabin and above.*)

OIL MAGNATE: Gosh! Gosh!

D.H. (*from the chimney above*): Oil magnate, I'm here, sitting on the chimney. Lot a snow and ice on this roof, dear Lord! Just sitting here with her clothes on. Gee, I wish this chimney wasn't so hot, I have to be constantly moving. Please, oil magnate, can I have some dollars for my nostrils and some dollars for my ear drums — I can see myself now taking a bath with a dollar in each nostril, and a dollar in each ear drum; crawl in the warm water in the bath tub, then I'll pick up a roll of dollars and dip them in the water, nice, soft, soggy dollars, first I'll begin washing my neck, wiping it with the nice, soft, soggy dollars — it'll be a grand time —— God, I'm slipping — help! Oh, help! — God!

(*Rolling is heard on the roof, and something gigantic smashes to the ground outside. A long pause.*)

OIL MAGNATE: Gosh! Gosh!

(OIL MAGNATE *rises, goes to the cupboard, uncloses it, takes out a sign, and pins it to the wall. Sign states:* "HOMECOMING, I HAVE ARRIVED." *He takes out another sign and he pins it on his shirt. The sign has written on it:* "MESSIAH." *Lastly he takes out a box of Cheerios, unwraps it; then he paces to the record machine and he turns it on. He steps to the rocker and sits on it, he eats the Cheerios without milk or cream — plain — as if he's fearful somebody will steal them from him, he makes as much noise as possible with them — he rocks.*)

RECORD MACHINE:

> I'm sitting on top of the world,
> Just rolling along,
> Just singing a song ——

(*Curtain.*)

oh dad, poor dad, mamma's hung you in the closet and I'm feelin' so sad

a pseudoclassical tragifarce in a bastard french tradition

Arthur L. Kopit

CHARACTERS

MADAME ROSEPETTLE
JONATHAN ROSEPETTLE
ROSALIE
COMMODORE ROSEABOVE

ROSALINDA THE FISH
TWO VENUS'-FLYTRAPS
A CUCKOO CLOCK
VARIOUS BELLBOYS

The play is in three scenes, without intermission.
The setting is a hotel in Havana, Cuba.

SCENE ONE: *A lavish hotel room in Havana, Cuba. Downstage center French windows open onto a large balcony that juts out over the audience. Upstage center are the doors to the master bedroom. At stage left is the door to another bedroom, while at stage right is the door to the suite itself. On one of the walls is hung a glass case with a red fire axe inside it and a sign over it that reads, "*IN CASE OF EMERGENCY, BREAK."

(*The door to the suite opens and* BELLBOYS NUMBER ONE AND TWO *enter carrying a coffin.*)

WOMAN'S VOICE (*from off stage*): Put it in the bedroom!
BELLBOYS NUMBER ONE AND TWO (*together*): The bedroom.
      (BELLBOY NUMBER ONE *starts toward the bedroom at stage left.* BELLBOY NUMBER TWO *starts toward the bedroom at upstage center. The handles come off the coffin. It falls to the floor. The* BELLBOYS *freeze with horror.*)

WOMAN'S VOICE (*still off stage*): Fools!

> (*Enter* MADAME ROSEPETTLE, *dressed in black, a veil hiding her face.* JONATHAN, *a boy seventeen years old but dressed like a child of ten, enters directly behind her. He follows her about the room like a small helpless puppy trailing his master.*)

MADAME ROSEPETTLE: Morons! Imbeciles!

BELLBOY NUMBER ONE: Uh . . . which bedroom, madame?

BELLBOY NUMBER TWO: Yes. Which bedroom?

MADAME ROSEPETTLE: Which bedroom!? They have the nerve to ask, which bedroom? The master bedroom, of course. Which bedroom did you think? (*The* BELLBOYS *smile ashamedly, bow, pick up the coffin and carry it toward the master bedroom.*) Gently! (*They open the bedroom doors.* MADAME ROSEPETTLE *lowers her face as blindingly bright sunlight pours out from the room.*) People have no respect for coffins nowadays. They think nothing of the dead. (*Short pause.*) I wonder what the dead think of them? Agh! The world is growing dismal.

> (*The* BELLBOYS *reappear in the doorway, the coffin in their hands.*)

BELLBOY NUMBER ONE: Uh . . . begging your pardon, madame, but . . . but . . .

MADAME ROSEPETTLE: Speak up! Speak up!

BELLBOY NUMBER ONE: Well, you see . . .

BELLBOY NUMBER TWO: You see . . . we were curious.

BELLBOY NUMBER ONE: Yes. Curious. That is . . .

BELLBOY NUMBER TWO: What we mean to say is . . .

BELLBOY NUMBER ONE: Just where in your bedroom would you like us to put it?

MADAME ROSEPETTLE: Next to the bed of course!

BELLBOYS NUMBER ONE AND TWO: Of course.

> (*Exit,* BELLBOYS NUMBER ONE *and* TWO.)

MADAME ROSEPETTLE: Fools.

> (*There is a rap on the door to the suite.*)

BELLBOY NUMBER THREE (*Off stage*): The dictaphone, madame.

MADAME ROSEPETTLE: Ah, splendid.

> (BELLBOY NUMBER THREE *enters carrying a dictaphone on a silver tray and black drapes under his arm.* BELLBOYS NUMBER ONE *and* TWO *leave the bedroom and exit from the suite, bowing fearfully to Madame Rosepettle as they leave.*)

BELLBOY NUMBER THREE: Where would you like it placed?

MADAME ROSEPETTLE: Great gods! Are you all the same? The

center table, naturally! One never dictates one's memoirs from anywhere but the middle of a room. Any nincompoop knows that.

BELLBOY NUMBER THREE: It must have slipped my mind.

MADAME ROSEPETTLE: You flatter yourself. (*He puts the dictaphone and drapes down on the table.*)

BELLBOY NUMBER THREE: Will there be anything else?

MADAME ROSEPETTLE: Will there be anything else, he asks!? Will there be anything else? Of course there'll be something else. There's always something else. That's one of the troubles with Life.

BELLBOY NUMBER THREE: Sorry, madame.

MADAME ROSEPETTLE: So am I. (*Pause.*) Oh, this talk is getting us nowhere. Words are precious. On bellboys they're a waste. And so far you have thoroughly wasted my time.

BELLBOY NUMBER THREE: Madame, this must end. I can take no more. I will have you know I am not a common bellboy. I am a lieutenant. Notice, if you will, the finely embroidered stripes on my hand-tailored sleeve. I am a lieutenant, madame, and being a lieutenant am in charge of other bellboys and thereby entitled to a little more respect from you.

MADAME ROSEPETTLE: Well, you may consider yourself a lieutenant, lieutenant, but I consider you a bore! If you're going to insist upon pulling rank, however, I'll have you know that I am a tourist. Notice, if you will, the money. And being a tourist I am in charge of you. Remember that and I'll mail you another stripe when I leave. As for "respect," we'll have none of that around here. We've got too many important things to do. Right, Albert? (JONATHAN *tries to speak but cannot.*) Rrrright, Albert?

JONATHAN: Ra . . . ra . . . ra . . . ra-right.

MADAME ROSEPETTLE: You may begin by picking up the drapes you so ingeniously dropped in a lump on my table, carrying them to the master bedroom and tacking them over the windowpanes. I don't wear black in the tropics for my health, my boy. I'm in mourning. And since the problems confronting civilization are ultimately moral ones, while I'm here in Havana no single speck of sunlight shall enter and brighten the mournful gloom of my heart. (*Short pause.*) At least, not while I'm in my bedroom. Well, go on, lieutenant, go on. Forward to the field of battle, head high. Tack the drapes across my windows, and when my room is black, call me in.

BELLBOY NUMBER THREE: Yes, madame.

(*He picks up the drapes and walks into the master bedroom.*)

MADAME ROSEPETTLE: In Buenos Aires the lieutenant clicked his heels when leaving. That's the trouble with these revolutionaries. No regard for the duties of rank. Remind me, Edward, to decrease my usual tip. (JONATHAN *takes a pad of paper out of his pocket and writes with a pencil he has tied on a cord about his neck. To the hallway.*) Well, come in, come in. Don't just stand there with your mouths hanging open.

(BELLBOYS NUMBER ONE *and* TWO *and* FOUR *enter pushing heavy trunks before them.*)

BELLBOY NUMBER ONE: Where would you like the stamp collection, madame?

MADAME ROSEPETTLE: Ah, your fantastic stamp collection, Robinson. Where should it be put?

JONATHAN: Uh . . . uh . . . uh . . .

MADAME ROSEPETTLE: Oh, stop stammering and speak up! They're only bellboys.

JONATHAN: Uh . . . um . . . um . . . ma . . . ma . . . ma-ma-ma-ma-ma . . . ma—maybe . . . in . . . in . . . in . . .

MADAME ROSEPETTLE: Will you stop this infernal stammering? You know what I think about it! I said, where would you like your fantastic stamp collection put? God knows it's a simple enough question. If you can't muster the nerve to answer, at least point. (*He points to a bureau in the room.*) The bottom drawer of the bureau. And be careful not to get your fingers on them. They stick. (*The* BELLBOYS *go to the bureau, open the drawer, and dump hundreds of loose stamps that had been in the trunk into the drawer.* MADAME ROSEPETTLE *dips her hand into the drawer and plucks out three stamps. She offers one to each of the* BELLBOYS.) Here, for your trouble: 1903 Borneo, limited edition. Very rare. Almost priceless.

(*The* BELLBOYS *look disappointedly at their tips.* BELLBOY NUMBER THREE *returns from the master bedroom.*)

BELLBOY NUMBER THREE: I'm terribly sorry, madame, but I find that —

MADAME ROSEPETTLE: I wondered when you'd ask. (*She takes a huge hammer from her purse and hands it to him.*)

BELLBOY NUMBER THREE: Thank you, madame. Thank you. (*He turns nervously and starts to leave.*)

MADAME ROSEPETTLE: Bellboy? (*He stops.*) The nails.

BELLBOY NUMBER THREE (*flustered by his forgetfulness*): Yes, of course. How foolish of me. (*She reaches into her purse again and takes out a fistful of nails which she promptly dumps into his hands.*)

MADAME ROSEPETTLE: Keep the extras. (*He exits into the master bedroom.*) (*To* JONATHAN.) In Buenos Aires the lieutenant came equipped with a pneumatic drill. Remind me, Albert dearest, to cut this man's tip entirely. (JONATHAN *scribbles on his pad. To the other* BELLBOYS.) Well?

BELLBOY NUMBER TWO: The . . . uh . . . coin collection, madame. Where would you like it put?

MADAME ROSEPETTLE: Your fabulous coin collection, Edward. Where should they put it?

JONATHAN: Uh . . . uh . . . I . . . I . . . I tha . . . tha . . . tha-think —

MADAME ROSEPETTLE: What is wrong with your tongue? Can't you talk like a normal human being without showering this room with your inarticulate spit!?

JONATHAN (*completely flustered*): I-I-I-I-I . . . I . . . da . . . da . . . don't . . .

MADAME ROSEPETTLE: Oh, all right, stick out your paw and point. (*He thrusts out his trembling hand and points again to the bureau.*)

JONATHAN: If . . . if . . . if . . . if they . . . if they would . . . be so . . . kind

MADAME ROSEPETTLE: Of course they would! They're bellboys. Remember that. It's your first lesson in Life for the day. (*To the* BELLBOYS.) Next to the bottom drawer, bellboys. And make sure none of them gets in with his fantastic collection of stamps. (*From the master bedroom can be heard the sound of* BELLBOY NUMBER THREE *smashing nails into the wall. While the other* BELLBOYS *are busy dumping hundreds of loose coins into the bureau,* MADAME ROSEPETTLE *walks to the bedroom door and opens it, shielding her eyes from the blinding light.*) Don't bang, my boy. Don't bang. That's not the way. Just tap. It takes longer, I will admit, but the effect is far more satisfactory on one's auditory nerves—and my ears, you see, are extremely sensitive. (*To* JONATHAN.) The lieutenant in Buenos Aires had a muffler on his drill. Remind me, Robinson darling, to have this man fired first thing in the morning. He'll never do. (JONATHAN *scratches a large "X" on his pad. The* BELLBOYS, *having finished dumping the coins, stand awaiting a tip.* MADAME ROSEPETTLE *goes to the drawer and takes out three coins. To* BELLBOY NUMBER ONE.) Here, for your trouble: a little something. It's a Turkish piaster . . . 1876. Good year for piasters. (*To*

BELLBOY NUMBER TWO.) And for you an . . . an 1889 Danzig gulden. Worth a fortune, my boy. A small fortune, I will admit, but nevertheless, a fortune. (*To* BELLBOY NUMBER FOUR.) And for you we have a . . . a . . . a 1959 DIME!! *Edward* . . . what is a dime doing in here? Fegh! (*She flings the dime to the ground as if it had been handled by lepers. The* BELLBOYS *leap to get it.*)

JONATHAN (*sadly*): Some . . . some . . . someday it will be . . . as rare as the others.

MADAME ROSEPETTLE: Someday! Someday! That's the trouble with you, Edward. Always an optimist. I trust you have no more such currency contaminating your fabulous collection. H'm, Albert? Do I assume correctly? H'm Do I? H'm? Do I? H'm Do I?

JONATHAN: Ya . . . yes.

MADAME ROSEPETTLE: Splendid. Then I'll give you your surprise for the day.

JONATHAN: Na . . . now?

MADAME ROSEPETTLE: Yes, now.

JONATHAN: In . . . in . . . front of . . . them?

MADAME ROSEPETTLE: Turn your backs, bellboys. (*She digs into her handbag and picks out a coin in a velvet box.*) Here, Edward, my sweet. The rarest of all coins for your rarest of all collections. A 1372 Javanese Yen-Sen.

JONATHAN (*excitedly*): How . . . how . . . how ma-many were . . . ma-minted?

MADAME ROSEPETTLE: None.

JONATHAN: Na-none?

MADAME ROSEPETTLE: I made it myself. (*She squeezes his hand.*) So glad you like it. (*She turns to the* BELLBOYS.) You may turn around now. (*They turn around as a unit.*) Well, who has the—? (*She stares in horror at the door to the master bedroom. The tapping can clearly be heard. She goes to the door, shielding her eyes from the now less powerful glare.*) You are tapping and not banging, which is good, but when you tap please tap with some sort of rhythm, which is, you see, much better. (*She smiles acidly and closes the door.*) The lieutenant in Buenos Aires, Robinson. The lieutenant in Buenos Aires. Do you remember him? Do you remember the rhythm he had? Oh, the way he shook when he drilled. I fairly danced that day. (*Reminiscent pause.*) Make note, Robinson. This man must be barred from all hotels, everywhere. Everywhere! (JONATHAN *retraces his "X" with a hard, firm stroke as if he were carving a figure on stone.*) Now where was I?

Oh, yes. Forgive me, but my mind, of late, has been wandering. The books, bellboys. The books! (*The* BELLBOYS *push a large trunk forward.*)

JONATHAN: Ca . . . ca . . . could they . . . open it . . . I . . . I-I wonder?

MADAME ROSEPETTLE: You want to see them, eh Albert? You really want to see them again? That badly? You really want to see them again, that badly?

JONATHAN (*trying very hard not to stutter*): Yyyyesssssss,

MADAME ROSEPETTLE (*very dramatically*): Then let the trunk be opened! (*They open the trunk. Hundreds of books fall onto the floor in a cloud of dust.* JONATHAN *falls on top of them like a starved man upon food.*)

JONATHAN (*emotionally*): Tra-Tra . . . Trollope . . . Ha-Haggard . . . Dau-Dau-Daudet . . . Gautier . . . Tur-Tur-Turgenev . . . ma-ma-my old fra-fra . . . friends. (*He collapses over them like a lover over his loved one.*)

MADAME ROSEPETTLE: Enough, Albert. Come. Off your knees. Rise from your books and sing of love.

JONATHAN: But I . . . I ca-can't . . . sing.

MADAME ROSEPETTLE: Well, stand up anyway. (*He rises sadly.*) Now, where are my plants?

BELLBOY NUMBER TWO: Plants?

MADAME ROSEPETTLE: Yes. My plants. Where are they? (BELLBOY NUMBER FOUR *whispers something in* BELLBOY NUMBER TWO'S *ear.*)

BELLBOY NUMBER TWO (*laughing nervously*): Oh. I . . . I . . . (*He laughs again, more nervously.*) I didn't realize . . . they were . . . plants.

MADAME ROSEPETTLE: What did you think they were?

BELLBOY NUMBER FOUR: We have them, madame. Outside.

BELLBOY NUMBER TWO: Yes. Outside.

BELLBOY NUMBER FOUR: Should we . . . bring them in?

MADAME ROSEPETTLE: Of course you should bring them in! Do you think they enjoy waiting out there in the hall? Fools.

BELLBOYS NUMBER TWO AND FOUR (*together, weakly*): Yes . . . madame.

(*They exit and return immediately carrying two large black-draped "things" before them at arm's length.*)

MADAME ROSEPETTLE: Ah, splendid. Splendid. Set them on the porch, if you will. (*They go out to the porch and set them down.*)

Uh . . . not so close together. They fight (*The* BELLBOYS *move the* PLANTS *apart.*)

BELLBOY NUMBER FOUR (*weakly*): Should we . . . uncover them?

MADAME ROSEPETTLE: No. That will be fine. Let the poor things rest awhile.

BELLBOYS NUMBER TWO AND FOUR (*together, weakly*): Yes . . . madame.

MADAME ROSEPETTLE: Now . . . who has my fish? (*All* BELLBOYS *look toward the door.*)

A VOICE (*from outside the door*): I have it, madame.

(*Enter* BELLBOY NUMBER FIVE *carrying, at arm's length, an object covered by a black cloth. He wears large, thick, well-padded gloves — the sort a snake trainer might wear when handling a newly caught cobra.*)

MADAME ROSEPETTLE (*with love in her voice*): Ah, bring it here. Put it here, by the dictaphone. Near my memoirs. Bring it here, bellboy. Set it gently, then lift the shawl.

JONATHAN (*staring sadly at his books*): Sho-Sho-Sholo-Sholokhov . . . Alain-Fournier . . . Alighieri . . . ma-my ffffriends. (*The* BELLBOY *sets the object down.*)

MADAME ROSEPETTLE: The black shawl of mourning, bellboy. Remove it, if you will. Lift it off and drape it near its side. But gently. Gently. Gently as she goes. (*The* BELLBOY *lifts off the shawl. Revealed is a fish bowl with a* FISH *and a cat's skeleton inside.*) Ah, I see you fed it today. (*She reaches into her handbag and extracts a pair of long tongs. She plucks the skeleton from the fish bowl.*) Siamese, I presume.

BELLBOY NUMBER FOUR: No, madame. Alley.

MADAME ROSEPETTLE: WHAT!? A common alley cat? Just who do you think I am? What kind of fish do you think I have? Alley cat! Alley cat! The idea! In Buenos Aires, I'll have you know, Rosalinda was fed nothing but Siamese kittens, which are even more tender than Siamese cats. That's what I call consideration! Edward, make note: we will dismiss this creature from the bellboy squad first thing in the morning! (JONATHAN *scribbles on his pad.*)

BELLBOY NUMBER FOUR: Madame, please, there were no Siamese cats.

MADAME ROSEPETTLE: There are always Siamese cats!

BELLBOY NUMBER FOUR: Not in Havana.

MADAME ROSEPETTLE: Then you should have flown to Buenos Aires.

I would have paid the way. Give me back your 1903 Borneo, limited. (I'll bet you've made it sticky.) (*He hands back the stamp.*) You can keep your Danzig gulden. It's not worth a thing except in Danzig, and hardly a soul uses anything but traveler's checks there anyhow! Shows you should never trust me.

BELLBOY NUMBER FOUR: Madame, please. I have a wife.

MADAME ROSEPETTLE: And *I* have a fish. I dare say there are half a million men in Cuba with wives. But show me another woman in Cuba with a silver piranha fish and then you'll be showing me something. Your marital status does not impress me, sir. You are common, do you hear? Common! While my piranha fish is rare. Now green piranhas can eat alley cats if they like; and red piranhas, I've been told, will often eat alley cats, tomcats, and even dogs; but my silver piranha has been weaned on Siamese, and Siamese it will be, sir. Siamese it will be. Now get out. All of you. There is much to do. Right, Albert?

JONATHAN: Ra . . . ra . . . ra . . . ra . . .

MADAME ROSEPETTLE: Right, Albert?

JONATHAN: Ra-right.

ROSALINDA THE FISH (*sadly*): Glump.

MADAME ROSEPETTLE: Oh, dear thing. You can just tell she's not feeling up to snuff. Someone will pay for this!

(*Enter* LIEUTENANT *of the bellboys from the bedroom.*)

BELLBOY NUMBER THREE: Well I'm finished.

MADAME ROSEPETTLE: You certainly are, monsieur lieutenant. You certainly are.

BELLBOY NUMBER THREE: I beg your pardon?

MADAME ROSEPETTLE: Make note, Edward. First thing in the morning we speak to the chef. Subject: Siamese cats — kittens if possible, though I seriously doubt it here. And make a further note, Albert, my darling. Let's see if we can't get our cats on the American Plan, while we're at it. (JONATHAN *scribbles on his pad of paper.*)

BELLBOY NUMBER THREE: Madame, is there something I can — ?

MADAME ROSEPETTLE: QUIET! And put that hammer down. (*He puts it down. She puts it back in her purse.*) You have all behaved rudely. If the sunset over Guanabacoa Bay were not so full of magenta and wisteria blue I'd leave this place tonight. But the sunset is full of magenta and wisteria blue, to say nothing of cadmium orange and cerise, and so I think I'll stay. Therefore beware, bellboys. Madame Rosepettle will have much to do. Right, Robinson? (JONATHAN *opens his mouth to speak but no words come out.*) I said, right Robinson? (*Again he tries to speak, and again no words come out.*) RIGHT, ROBINSON!? (*He nods.*) There's your answer. Now get out and leave us alone. (*They start to exit.*) No wait. (*They stop.*) A question before you go. The yacht in the harbor. The pink one with the lilacs draped about the railing. One hundred and eighty-seven feet long, I'd judge. Who owns it?

BELLBOY NUMBER ONE: Commodore Roseabove, madame. It's a pretty sloop.

MADAME ROSEPETTLE (*distantly*): Roseabove. I like that name.

BELLBOY NUMBER ONE: He's a strange man, madame. A man who knows no master but the sea.

MADAME ROSEPETTLE (*with a slight smile*): Roseabove . . .

BELLBOY NUMBER ONE: A wealthy man but a gentleman, too. Why I've seen him with my own eyes toss real silver dollars to the native boats as he sailed into port. And when some poor diver came to the surface without a coin glimmering in his hand, Commodore Roseabove, without the slightest hesitation, dropped a dollar bill instead. Oh he's a well-loved, man madame. A true, true gentleman with a big, big heart. A man who knows no master but the sea. And even the sea, they say, is no match for the commodore and his yacht, which, as you know, is the largest yacht in Cuba.

MADAME ROSEPETTLE: And also the largest yacht in Haiti, Puerto Rico, Bermuda, the Dominican Republic, and West Palm Beach. I haven't checked the Virgin Islands yet. I thought I'd leave them till last. But I doubt if I'll find a larger one there. (*She laughs to herself.*) I take great pleasure, you see, in measuring yachts. My hobby, you might say.

BELLBOY NUMBER ONE: Your hubby, did you say?

MADAME ROSEPETTLE (*viciously*): Get out! Get out before I lose my temper! Imbeciles! FOOLS! (*They exit, running.*) Edward, make note. First thing in the morning, we restaff this hotel. (JONA-THAN *scribbles on his pad of paper.* MADAME ROSEPETTLE *walks over to the French windows and stares wistfully out. There is a short silence before she speaks. Dreamily, with a slight smile.*) Roseabove. I like that name.

ROSALINDA THE FISH (*gleefully*): Gleep.

MADAME ROSEPETTLE (*fondly*): Ah, listen. My lovely little fish. She, too, is feeling better already.

Curtain

SCENE TWO: *The place is the same. The time, two weeks later.* JONA-
THAN *is in the room with* ROSALIE, *a girl some two years older than
he and dressed in sweet girlish pink.*

ROSALIE: But if you've been here two weeks, why haven't I seen
you?

JONATHAN: I've . . . I've been in my room.

ROSALIE: All the time?

JONATHAN: Yes. . . . All the time.

ROSALIE: Well, you must get out sometimes. I mean, sometimes you
simply must get out. You just couldn't stay inside all the time . . .
could you?

JONATHAN: Yyyyyes.

ROSALIE: You never get out at all? I mean, never at all?

JONATHAN: Some-sometimes I do go out on the porch. M-Ma-Mother
has some . . . Venus'-flytraps which she bra-brought back from the
rain forests of Va-Va-Venezuela. They're va-very rrrrrare and need
a . . . a lot of sunshine. Well sir, she ka-keeps them on the porch
and I . . . I feed them. Twice a day, too.

ROSALIE: Oh.

JONATHAN: Ma-Ma-Mother says everyone must have a vocation in
life. (*With a slight nervous laugh.*) I ga-guess that's . . . my job.

ROSALIE: I don't think I've ever met anyone before who's fed . . .
uh . . . Venus'-flytraps.

JONATHAN: Ma-Ma-Mother says I'm va-very good at it. That's what
she . . . says. I'm va-very good at it. I . . . don't know . . . if . . .
I am, but . . . that's . . . what she says so I . . . guess I am.

ROSALIE: Well, uh, what . . . what do you . . . feed them? You see,
I've never met anyone before who's fed Venus'-flytraps so . . .
that's why I don't know what . . . you're supposed to feed them.

JONATHAN (*happy that she asked*): I fa-feed them . . . l-l-lots of
things. Ga-ga-green peas, chicken feathers, rubber bands. They're
. . . not very fussy. They're . . . nice, that way. Ma-Ma-Mother says
it it it ga-gives me a feeling of a-co-co-complishment. Iffffff you
would . . . like to see them I . . . could show them to you. It's . . .
almost fa-feeding time. It is, and . . . and I could show them to
you.

ROSALIE: No. That's all right. (JONATHAN *looks away, hurt.*)
Well, how about later?

JONATHAN: Do-do-do you ra-really wwwwwwant to see them?

ROSALIE: Yes. Yes I really think I would like to see them . . . later.

If you'll show them to me then, I'd really like that. (JONATHAN *looks at her and smiles. There is an awkward silence while he stares at her thankfully.*) I still don't understand why you never go out. How can you just sit in———?

JONATHAN: Sometimes, when I'm on the porch . . . I do other things.

ROSALIE: What?

JONATHAN: Sa-sa-sometimes, when I'm . . . on the porch, you know, when I'm on the porch. Sssssssome-times I . . . do other things, too.

ROSALIE: What sort of things? (JONATHAN *giggles.*) What sort of things do you do?

JONATHAN: Other things.

ROSALIE (*coyly*): What do you mean, "Other things"?

JONATHAN: Other things besides feeding my mother's plants. Other things besides that. That's what I mean. Other things besides that.

ROSALIE: What kind of things . . . in particular?

JONATHAN: Oh, watching.

ROSALIE: Watching?

JONATHAN: Yes. Like . . . watching.

ROSALIE: Watching what? (*He giggles.*) Watching what!?

JONATHAN: You. (*Short pause. She inches closer to him on the couch.*)

ROSALIE: What do you mean . . . watching me?

JONATHAN: I . . . watch you from the porch. That's what I mean. I watch you from the porch. I watch you a lot, too. Every day. It's . . . it's the truth. I . . . I swear it . . . is. I watch you ev-ry day. Do you believe me?

ROSALIE: Of course I believe you, Albert. Why—

JONATHAN: Jonathan!

ROSALIE: What?

JONATHAN: Jonathan. Ca-ca-call me Ja-Jonathan. That's my na-na-na——

ROSALIE: But your mother said your name was—

JONATHAN: Nooooo! Call . . . me Jonathan. Pa-pa-please?

ROSALIE: All right . . . Jonathan.

JONATHAN (*excitedly*): You do believe me! You rrrrreally do believe me. I-I-I can tell!

ROSALIE: Of course I believe you. Why shouldn't — ?

JONATHAN: You want me to tell you how I watch you? You want me to tell you? I'll bet you'll na-never guess.

ROSALIE: How?

JONATHAN: Guess.

ROSALIE (*ponders*): Through a telescope?

JONATHAN: How did you guess?   •

ROSALIE: I . . . I don't know. I was just joking. I didn't really think that was—

JONATHAN: I'll bet everyone watches you through a telescope. I'll bet everyone you go out with watches you through a telescope. That's what I'll bet.

ROSALIE: No. Not at all.

JONATHAN: Well, that's how I watch you. Through a telescope.

ROSALIE: I never would have guessed that —

JONATHAN: I thought you were . . . ga-going to say I . . . I watch you with . . . with love in my eyes or some . . . thing like that. I didn't think you were going to guess that I . . . watch you through a telescope. I didn't think you were going to guess that I wa-watch you through a telescope on the fa-first guess, anyway. Not on the first guess.

ROSALIE: Well, it was just a guess.

JONATHAN (*hopefully*): Do you watch me through a telescope?

ROSALIE: I never knew where your room was.

JONATHAN: Now you know. Now will you watch me?

ROSALIE: Well I . . . don't have a telescope.

JONATHAN (*getting more elated and excited*): You can make one. That's how I got mine. I made it. Out of lenses and tubing. That's all you need. Lenses and tubing. Do you have any lenses?

ROSALIE: No.

JONATHAN: Do you have any tubing?

ROSALIE: No.

JONATHAN: Oh. (*Pause.*) Well, would you like me to tell you how I made mine in case you find some lenses and tubing? Would you like that?

ROSALIE (*disinterestedly*): Sure, Jonathan. I think that would be nice.

JONATHAN: Well, I made it out of lenses and tubing. The lenses I had because Ma-Ma-Mother gave me a set of lenses so I could see my stamps better. I have a fabulous collection of stamps, as well as a fantastic collection of coins and a simply unbelievable collection of books. Well sir, Ma-Ma-Mother gave me these lenses so I could see my stamps better. She suspected that some were fake so she gave me the lenses so I might be . . . able to see. You see?

Well sir, I happen to have nearly a billion sta-stamps. So far I've looked closely at 1,352,769. I've discovered three actual fakes! Number 1,352,767 was a fake. Number 1,352,768 was a fake, and number 1,352,769 was a fake. They were stuck together. Ma-Mother made me feed them im-mediately to her flytraps. Well . . . (*He whispers.*) one day, when Mother wasn't looking . . . that is, when she was out, I heard an airplane flying. An airplane . . . somewhere . . . far away. It wasn't very loud, but still I heard it. An airplane. Flying . . . somewhere, far away. And I ran outside to the porch so that I might see what it looked like. The airplane. With hundreds of people inside it. Hundreds and hundreds and hundreds of people. And I thought to myself, if I could just see . . . if I could just see what they looked like, the people, sitting at their windows looking out . . . and flying. If I could see . . . just once . . . if I could see just once what they looked like . . . then I might . . . know what I . . . what I . . . (*Slight pause.*) So I . . . built a telescope in case the plane ever . . . came back again. The tubing came from an old blowgun (*He reaches behind the bureau and produces a huge blowgun, easily a foot larger than he.*) Mother brought back from her last hunting trip to Zanzibar. The lenses were the lenses she had given me for my stamps. So I built it. My telescope. A telescope so I might be able to see. And . . . (*He walks out to the porch.*) and . . . and I could see! I could! I COULD! I really could. For miles and miles I could see. For miles and miles and miles! (*He begins to lift it up to look through but stops, for some reason, before he's brought it up to his eye.*) Only . . . (*He hands it to* ROSALIE. *She takes it eagerly and scans the horizon and the sky. She hands it back to him.*)

ROSALIE (*with annoyance*): There's nothing out there to see.

JONATHAN (*sadly*): I know. That's the trouble. You take the time to build a telescope that can sa-see for miles, then there's nothing out there to see. Ma-Mother says it's a lesson in Life. (*Pause.*) But I'm not sorry I built my telescope. And you know why? Because I saw you. Even if I didn't see anything else, I did see you. And . . . and I'm . . . very glad. (ROSALIE *moves slightly closer to him on the couch. She moistens her lips.*) I . . . I remember, you were standing across the way in your penthouse garden playing blind man's buff with ten little children. (*After a short pause, fearfully.*) Are . . . are they by any chance . . . yours?

ROSALIE (*sweetly*): Oh, I'm not married.

JONATHAN: Oh!

ROSALIE: I'm a baby sitter.

JONATHAN (*with obvious relief*): Oh.

ROSALIE: I work for the people who own the penthouse.

JONATHAN: I've never seen them around.

ROSALIE: I've never seen them either. They're never home. They just mail me a check every week and tell me to make sure I keep the children's names straight.

JONATHAN: If you could tell me which way they went I could find them with my telescope. It can see for miles.

ROSALIE: They must love children very much. I'll bet she's a marvelous woman. (*Pause.*) There's going to be another one, too! Another child is coming! I got a night letter last night.

JONATHAN: By airplane?

ROSALIE: I don't know.

JONATHAN: I bet it was. I can't see at night. Ma-Mother can but I can't. I'll bet that's when the planes fly.

ROSALIE (*coyly*): If you like, I'll read you the letter. I have it with me. (*She unbuttons the top of her blouse and turns around in a coquettish manner to take the letter from her brassiere. Reading.*) "Have had another child. Sent it yesterday. Will arrive tomorrow. Call it Cynthia."

JONATHAN: That will make eleven. That's an awful lot of children to take care of. I'll bet it must be wonderful.

ROSALIE: They do pay very well.

JONATHAN: They pay you?

ROSALIE: Of course . . . What did you think? (*Pause. Softly, seductively.*) Jonathan? (*He does not answer but seems lost in thought. With a feline purr.*) Jonathan?

JONATHAN: Yyyyyes?

ROSALIE: It gets very lonesome over there. The children go to sleep early and the parents are never home so I'm always alone. Perhaps . . . well Jonathan, I thought that perhaps you might . . . visit me.

JONATHAN: Well . . . well . . . well, you . . . you see . . . I . . . I . . .

ROSALIE: We could spend the evenings together . . . at my place. It gets so lonesome there, you know what I mean? I mean, I don't know what to do. I get so lonesome there.

JONATHAN: Ma-ma-ma-maybe you . . . you can . . . come over . . . here? Maybe you you can do . . . that.

ROSALIE: Why are you trembling so?

JONATHAN: I'm . . . I'm . . . I'm . . . I'm . . .

ROSALIE: Are you afraid?

JONATHAN: Nnnnnnnnnnnnnnnnnnnnno. Whaaaaaaaaaa-why . . . should I . . . be . . . afraid?

ROSALIE: Then why won't you come visit me?

JONATHAN: I . . . I . . . I . . . I . . .

ROSALIE: I don't think you're allowed to go out. That's what I think.

JONATHAN: Nnnn-o. I . . . I can . . . can . . . can . . .

ROSALIE: Why can't you go out, Jonathan? I want to know.

JONATHAN: Nnnnnnnnn-

ROSALIE: Tell me, Jonathan!

JONATHAN: I . . . I . . .

ROSALIE: I said I want to know! Tell me.

JONATHAN: I . . . I don't . . . know. I don't know why. I mean, I've . . . nnnnnnnever really thought . . . about going out. I . . . guess it's . . . just natural for me to . . . stay inside. (*He laughs nervously as if that explained everything.*) You see . . . I've got so much to do. I mean, all my sssssstamps and . . . ca-coins and books. The pa-pa-plane might fffffly overhead while I was going downstairs. And then thhhhere are . . . the plants ta-to feeeeeeed. And I enjoy vvvery much wa . . . watching you and all yyyyyyour chil-dren. I've . . . really got so ma-many things . . . to . . . do. Like my future, for instance. Ma-Mother says I'm going to be great. That's . . . that's . . . that's what she . . . says. I'm going to be great. I sssswear. Of course, she doesn't know ex-actly what I'm . . . going to be great in . . . so she sits every afternoon for . . . for two hours and thinks about it. Na-na-naturally I've . . . got to be here when she's thinking in case she . . . thinks of the answer. Otherwise she might forget and I'd never know . . . what I'm ga-going to be great in. You . . . see what I mean? I mean, I've . . . I've ggggggot so many things to do I . . . just couldn't possibly get *anything* done if I ever . . . went . . . out-side. (*There is a silence.* JONATHAN *stares at* ROSALIE *as if he were hoping that might answer her question sufficiently. She stares back at him as if she knows there is more.*) Besides, Mother locks the front door.

ROSALIE: I thought so.

JONATHAN: No! You-you don't understand. It's not what you think. She doesn't lock the door to kaka-keep me in, which would be malicious. She . . . locks the door so I can't get out, which is for my own good and therefore . . . beneficent.

CUCKOO CLOCK (*from the master bedroom*): Cuckoo! Cuckoo! Cuckoo!

ROSALIE: What's that?

JONATHAN (*fearfully*): A warning.

ROSALIE: What do you mean, a warning?

JONATHAN: A warning that you have to go. Your time is up.

ROSALIE: My time is what?

JONATHAN: Your time is up. You have to go. Now. At once. Right away. You can't stay any longer. You've got to go!

ROSALIE: Why?

JONATHAN (*puzzled: as if this were the first time the question had ever occurred to him*): I don't really know.

CUCKOO CLOCK (*louder*): Cuckoo! Cuckoo! Cuckoo! (JONATHAN *freezes in terror.* ROSALIE *looks at him calmly.*)

ROSALIE: Why did your mother ask me to come up here?

JONATHAN: What?

ROSALIE: Why did your mother ask me — ?

JONATHAN: So I . . . I could meet you.

ROSALIE: Then why didn't you ask me yourself? Something's wrong around here, Jonathan. I don't understand why you didn't ask me yourself.

JONATHAN: Ma-Mother's so much better at those things.

CUCKOO CLOCK (*very loudly*): CUCKOO! CUCKOO! CUCKOO!

JONATHAN: You've got to get out of here! That's the third warning. (*He starts to push her toward the door.*)

ROSALIE: Will you call me on the phone?

JONATHAN: Please, you've got to go!

ROSALIE: Instead of your mother telling me to come, will you come and get me yourself? Will you at least call me? Wave to me?

JONATHAN: Yes-yes — I'll do that. Now get out of here!

ROSALIE: I want you to promise to come and see me again.

JONATHAN: Get out!

ROSALIE (*coyly*): Promise me.

JONATHAN: GET OUT! (*He pushes her toward the door.*)

ROSALIE: Why do you keep looking at that door?

JONATHAN (*almost in tears*): *Please.*

ROSALIE: Why do you keep looking at that door?

JONATHAN: *Please!* You've got to go before it's too late!

ROSALIE: There's something very wrong here. I want to see what's behind that door. (*She starts toward the master bedroom.* JONATHAN *throws his arms about her legs and collapses at her feet, his face buried against her thighs.*)

JONATHAN (*sobbing uncontrollably*): I love you. (ROSALIE *stops dead in her tracks and stares down at Jonathan.*)

ROSALIE: What did you say?

JONATHAN: I-I-I llllllllove you. I love you, I love you, I love you I — (*The* CUCKOO CLOCK *screams, cackles, and goes out of its mind, its call ending in a crazed, strident rasp as if it had broken all its springs, screws, and innards. The door to the master bedroom opens.* MADAME ROSEPETTLE *appears.*)

JONATHAN (*weakly*): *Too late.*

MADAME ROSEPETTLE: Two warnings are enough for any man. Three are enough for any woman. The cuckoo struck three times and then a fourth and still she's here. May I ask why?

ROSALIE: You've been listening at the keyhole, haven't you!

MADAME ROSEPETTLE: I'm talking to my son, harlot!

ROSALIE: What did you say!

MADAME ROSEPETTLE: Harlot, I called you! Slut, scum, sleazy prostitute catching and caressing children and men. Stroking their hearts. I've seen you.

ROSALIE: What are you talking about?

MADAME ROSEPETTLE: Blind man's buff with the children in the garden. The redheaded one — fifteen, I think. Behind the bush while the others cover their eyes. Up with the skirt, one-two-three and it's done. Don't try to deny it. I've seen you in action. I know your kind.

ROSALIE: That's a lie!

MADAME ROSEPETTLE: Life is a lie, my sweet. Not words but Life itself. Life in all its ugliness. It builds green trees that tease your eyes and draw you under them. Then when you're there in the shade and you breathe in and say, "Oh God, how beautiful," that's when the bird on the branch lets go his droppings and hits you on the head. Life, my sweet, beware. It isn't what it seems. I've seen what it can do. I've watched you dance.

ROSALIE: What do you mean by that?

MADAME ROSEPETTLE: Don't try to deny it. I've watched you closely and I know what I see. You danced too near him and you let him do too much. I saw you rub your hand across the back of his neck. I saw you laugh and look closely in his eyes. I'll bet you even told him he was the only one. How many, I wonder, have you told that to? I saw you let him stroke you with his hairy paw and saw you smile. I fancy your thighs must have fairly trembled. It was, my dear, obscene, lewd, disgusting, and quite disgraceful. Everyone was staring at you and yet you went right on. Don't try to deny it.

Words will only make it worse. It would be best for all concerned if you left at once and never came again. I will keep the story of your dancing quiet. Good day. (MADAME ROSEPETTLE *turns to leave.* ROSALIE *does not move.*)

ROSALIE: Why don't you let Jonathan out of his room?

MADAME ROSEPETTLE (*sharply*): Who!?

ROSALIE: Jonathan.

MADAME ROSEPETTLE: Who!?

ROSALIE: Your son.

MADAME ROSEPETTLE: You mean Albert? Is that who you mean? Albert?

JONATHAN: Pa-pa-please do-don't.

MADAME ROSEPETTLE: Is that who you mean, slut? H'm? Speak up? Is that who you mean?

ROSALIE: I mean your son.

MADAME ROSEPETTLE: I don't let him out because he is my son. I don't let him out because his skin is as white as fresh snow and he would burn if the sun struck him. I don't let him out because outside there are trees with birds sitting on their branches waiting for him to walk beneath. I don't let him out because you're there, waiting behind the bushes with your skirt up. I don't let him out because he is susceptible. That's why. Because he is susceptible. Susceptible to trees and to sluts and to sunstroke.

ROSALIE: Then why did you come and get me?

MADAME ROSEPETTLE: Because, my dear, my stupid son has been watching you through that stupid telescope he made. Because, in short, he wanted to meet you and I, in short, wanted him to know what you were really like. Now that he's seen, you may go.

ROSALIE: And if I choose to stay? (*Pause.*)

MADAME ROSEPETTLE (*softly: slyly*): Can you cook?

ROSALIE: Yes.

MADAME ROSEPETTLE: How well?

ROSALIE: Fairly well.

MADAME ROSEPETTLE: Not good enough! My son is a connoisseur. A connoisseur, do you hear? I cook him the finest foods in the world. Recipes no one knows exist. Food, my sweet, is the finest of arts. And since you can't cook you are artless. You nauseate my son's aesthetic taste. Do you like cats?

ROSALIE: Yes.

MADAME ROSEPETTLE: What kind of cats?

ROSALIE: Any kind of cats.

MADAME ROSEPETTLE: Alley cats?

ROSALIE: Especially alley cats.

MADAME ROSEPETTLE: I thought so. Go, my dear. Find yourself some weeping willow and set yourself beneath it. Cry of your lust for my son and wait, for a mocking bird waits above to deposit his verdict on your whorish head. My son is as white as fresh snow and you are tainted with sin. You are garnished with garlic and turn our tender stomachs in disgust.

ROSALIE: What did you come to Havana for?

MADAME ROSEPETTLE: To find you!

ROSALIE: And now that you've found me . . . ?

MADAME ROSEPETTLE: I throw you out! I toss you into the garbage can! If you'd have left on time I'd have told the sordid details of your dance when you were gone instead of to your face. But it makes no difference. I heard everything, you know. So don't try to call. The phone is in my room . . . and no one goes into my room but me. (*She stares at* ROSALIE *for a moment, then exits with a flourish.* ROSALIE *and* JONATHAN *moves slowly toward each other. When they are almost together* MADAME ROSEPETTLE *reappears.*) One more thing, If, by some chance, the eleventh child named Cynthia turns out to be a Siamese cat, give it to me. I too pay well. (MADAME ROSEPETTLE *turns toward her room.* ROSALIE *starts toward the door.* JONATHAN *grabs her hand in desperation.*)

JONATHAN (*in a whisper*): Come back again. Pa-please . . . come back again. (*For a moment* ROSALIE *stops and looks at* JONATHAN. *But* MADAME ROSEPETTLE *stops too, and turning, looks back at both of them, a slight smile on her lips.* ROSALIE, *sensing her glance, walks toward the door, slipping from* JONATHAN'S *outstretched hands as she does. The lights fade about* JONATHAN, *alone in the center of the room.*)

Curtain.

SCENE THREE: *The hotel room at night, one week later* JONATHAN *is alone in the living room. He is sitting in a chair near the fish bowl, staring at nothing in particular with a particularly blank expression on his face. A clock is heard ticking softly in the distance. For an interminably long time it continues to tick while* JONATHAN *sits in his chair, motionless. After a while the ticking speeds up almost imperceptibly and soon after, laughter is heard. At first it is a giggle from the rear of the theater, then a cough from the side, then a self-conscious laugh from the other side, then a full gusty belly-roar*

*from all corners of the theater. Soon the entire world is hysterical.
Cuban drums begin to beat. Fireworks explode. Orgiastic music is
heard.*

JONATHAN *continues to sit, motionless. Only his eyes have begun
to move. The clock continues to tick. The laughter grows louder: the
laughter of the insane. Suddenly* JONATHAN *leaps up and rushes to
the French windows, his fingers pressed against his ears. He slams
the French windows shut. The noises stop.* JONATHAN *closes his eyes
and sighs with relief. The French windows sway unsteadily on their
hinges. They tip forward. They fall to the floor. They shatter. The
laughter returns.*

JONATHAN *stares down at them in horror. The* VENUS'-FLYTRAPS
grow larger and growl.

VENUS'-FLYTRAPS (*viciously*): *Grrrrrr.* (*The* PIRANHA FISH *stares
hungrily from its bowl.*)

ROSALINDA THE FISH (*more viciously*): Grarrgh! (*The* FLYTRAPS
*lunge at Jonathan but he walks dazedly past, unaware of their
snapping petals, and goes out to the edge of the balcony. He stares
out in complete bewilderment. The laughter and music of a carnival, the sounds of people dancing in the streets fill the air. He looks
down at them sadly. Meekly he waves. The sounds immediately
grow softer and the people begin to drift away. He watches as they
leave. Behind him the* FLYTRAPS *keep growing and reaching out
for him, but of this he is unaware. He only stands at the railing,
looking down. A last lingering laugh is heard somewhere in the
distance, echoing.*)

(*The door to the suite opens.*)

FIRST VOICE (*from outside the door*): Are you sure this is the room?

SECOND VOICE (*also outside*): This is the room, all right. (JONA-
THAN *hides behind one of the* FLYTRAPS *and watches.*)

THIRD VOICE: And she wants all this stuff in here?

FOURTH VOICE: That's what she said.

FIFTH VOICE: Seems strange to me.

SECOND VOICE: Well don't worry about it. Just do it. After all . . .
she tips very well.

THIRD VOICE: If you do what she wants.

FOURTH VOICE: Yes. If you do what she wants.

ALL TOGETHER: Well . . . shall we?

(*They enter. The voices, we discover, belong to the* BELLBOYS,
now dressed as waiters. They enter in order.)

BELLBOY NUMBER ONE (*carrying a small, round table*): She said to put it here, I think. (*He sets the table down in the center of the room. The lights slowly begin to fade as an overhead spot begins to illuminate the table.*)

BELLBOYS NUMBER TWO AND THREE (*carrying chairs in their arms*): And these here. (*They set one chair on either side of the table.*)

BELLBOY NUMBER FOUR (*carrying an ice bucket with a huge bottle of champagne in it*): And the champagne here. (*He sets the ice bucket on the floor between the two chairs at the rear of the table.*)

BELLBOY NUMBER TWO: But what about the candles?

BELLBOY NUMBER THREE: And the glasses?

BELLBOY NUMBER FOUR: And the one wilting rose?

(*Enter* BELLBOY NUMBER FIVE *carrying a tray with two champagne glasses on it, two flickering candles, and a flower vase with one wilting rose protruding.*)

BELLBOY NUMBER FIVE: I've got them here.

BELLBOY NUMBER ONE (*placing a tablecloth on the table*): Then everything is set.

BELLBOY NUMBER TWO: Just the way she wanted it.

BELLBOY NUMBER THREE: Exactly the way she wanted it.

BELLBOY NUMBER FIVE: *Specifically* wanted it. (*He finishes setting the glasses, candles, and flower vase.*)

BELLBOY NUMBER ONE: Yes. Everything is set.

BELLBOY NUMBER FOUR: No. Something is missing.

OTHERS: What!

BELLBOY NUMBER FOUR: We have forgotten something.

OTHERS: Forgotten what?

BELLBOY NUMBER FOUR: Well, it seems that we have forgotten the —(*He is interrupted by the sound of a Viennese waltz playing softly, romantically in the background.*)

BELLBOY NUMBER ONE: Oh, I'm sorry. I guess I didn't tell you. She said she'd take care of the music herself.

(*The lights fade in the room and only the table is lit. The* BELLBOYS *disappear into the shadows. The music grows in brilliance.* THE COMMODORE *and* MADAME ROSEPETTLE *waltz into the room. A spot of light follows them about the floor.*)

THE COMMODORE: How lovely it was this evening, madame, don't you think? (*She laughs softly and demurely and discreetly lowers her eyes. They waltz about the floor.*) How gentle the wind was, madame. And the stars, how clear and bright they were, don't you think? (*She blushes with innocence. They dance on.*) And the moon, madame, shining across the water, lighting the yachts, anchored, so silent and white and clean, waiting for the wind to come and fill their great, clean, white sails again. How poetic it was. How pure, madame. How innocent . . . don't you think? (*She turns her face away and smiles softly. They begin to whirl about the floor.*) Ah, the waltz. How exquisite it is, madame, don't you think? One-two-three, one-two-three, one-two three. Ahhhhh, madame, how classically simple. How mathematically simple. How stark; how strong . . . how romantic . . . how sublime. (*She giggles girlishly. They whirl madly about the floor.*) Oh, if only Madame knew how I've waited for this moment. If only Madame knew how long. How this week, these nights, the nights we shared together on my yacht; the warm, wonderful nights, the almost-perfect nights, the would-have-been-perfect nights had it not been for the crew peeking through the portholes. Ah, those nights, madame, those nights; almost alone but never quite; but now, tonight, at last, we are alone. And now, madame, now we are ready for romance. For the night was made for Love. And tonight, madame . . . we will love.

MADAME ROSEPETTLE (*with the blush of innocence*): Oh, Commodore, how you do talk. (*They whirl about the room as the lilting rhythm of the waltz grows and sweeps on and on.*)

THE COMMODORE (*suavely*): Madame, may I kiss you?

MADAME ROSEPETTLE: Why?

THE COMMODORE (*after recovering from the abruptness of the question; with forced suaveness*): Your lips . . . are a thing of beauty.

MADAME ROSEPETTLE: My lips, Commodore, are the color of blood. (*She smiles at him. He stares blankly ahead. They dance on.*) I must say, you dance exceptionally well . . . for a man your age.

THE COMMODORE (*bristling*): I dance with you, madame. That is why I dance well. For to dance with you, madame—is to hold you.

MADAME ROSEPETTLE: Well, I don't mind your holding me, Commodore, but at the moment you happen to be holding me too tight.

THE COMMODORE: I hold you too dear to hold you too tight, madame. I hold you close, that is all. And I hold you close in the hope that my heart may feel your heart beating.

MADAME ROSEPETTLE: One-two-three, one-two-three. You're not paying enough attention to the music, Commodore. I'm afraid you've fallen out of step.

THE COMMODORE: Then lead me, madame. Take my hand and lead me wherever you wish. For I would much rather think of my words than my feet.

MADAME ROSEPETTLE (*with great sweetness*): Why certainly Commodore. Certainly. If that is what you want . . . it will be my pleasure to oblige. (*They switch hands and she begins to lead him about the floor. They whirl wildly about, spinning faster than they had when* THE COMMODORE *led.*)

MADAME ROSEPETTLE: Beautiful, isn't it, Commodore? The waltz. The Dance of Lovers. I'm so glad you enjoy it so much. (*With a gay laugh she whirls him around the floor. Suddenly he puts his arms about her shoulders and leans close to kiss her. She pulls back.*) Commodore! You were supposed to spin just then. When I squeeze you in the side it means spin!

THE COMMODORE (*flustered*): I . . . I thought it was a sign of affection. (*She laughs.*)

MADAME ROSEPETTLE: You'll learn. (*She squeezes him in the side. He spins about under her arm.*) Ah, you're learning. (*He continues to spin around and around, faster and faster like a runaway top while* MADAME ROSEPETTLE, *not spinning at all, leads him about the floor, a wild smile of ecstasy spreading over her face.*)

THE COMMODORE: Ho-ho, ho-ho. Stop. I'm dizzy. Dizzy. Stop, please. Stop. Ho-ho. Stop. Dizzy. Ho-ho. Stop. Too fast. Slow. Slower. Stop. Ho-ho. Dizzy. Too dizzy. Weeeeeee! (*And then, without any warning at all, she grabs him in the middle of a spin and kisses him. Her back is to the audience, so* THE COMMODORE'S *face is visible. At first he is too dizzy to realize that his motion has been stopped. But shortly he does, and his first expression is that of shock. But the kiss is long and the shock turns into perplexity and then, finally, into panic; into fear. He struggles desperately and breaks free from her arms, gasping wildly for air. He points weakly to his chest.*)

THE COMMODORE (*gasping*): *Asthma.* (*His chest heaves as he gulps in air.*) Couldn't breathe. Lungs bad. Asthmatic. Nose stuffed, too. Sinus condition. Couldn't get any air. (*He gasps for air. She starts to walk toward him, slowly.*) Couldn't get any . . . air. (*She nears him. Instinctively he backs away.*) You . . . you surprised me . . . you know. Out . . . of breath. Wasn't . . . ready for that. Didn't . . . expect you to kiss me.

MADAME ROSEPETTLE: I know. That's why I did it. (*She laughs and puts her arm tenderly about his waist.*) Perhaps you'd prefer to sit down for a while, Commodore. Catch your breath, so to speak. Dancing can be so terribly tiring . . . when you're growing old.

Well, if you like, Commodore, we could just sit and talk. And
perhaps . . . sip some pink champagne, eh? Champagne?

THE COMMODORE: Ah, champagne. (*She begings to walk with him
toward the table.*)

MADAME ROSEPETTLE: And just for the two of us.

THE COMMODORE: Yes. The two of us. Alone.

MADAME ROSEPETTLE (*with a laugh*): Yes. All alone.

THE COMMODORE: At last.

MADAME ROSEPETTLE: With music in the distance.

THE COMMODORE: A waltz.

MADAME ROSEPETTLE: A Viennese waltz.

THE COMMODORE: The Dance of Lovers. (*She takes his hand,
tenderly.*)

MADAME ROSEPETTLE: Yes, Commodore. The Dance of Lovers.
(*They look at each other in silence.*)

THE COMMODORE: Madame, you have won my heart. And easily.

MADAME ROSEPETTLE: No, Commodore. You have lost it. Easily.
(*She smiles seductively. The room darkens till only a single spot
of light falls upon the table set in the middle of the room. The
waltz plays on.* MADAME ROSEPETTLE *nods to* THE COMMODORE
*and he goes to sit. But before he can pull his chair out, it slides
out under its own power. He places himself and the chair slides
back in, as if some invisible waiter had been holding it in his invisible hands.* MADAME ROSEPETTLE *smiles sweetly and, pulling out
her chair herself, sits. They stare at each other in silence. The waltz
plays softly.* THE COMMODORE *reaches across the table and touches
her hand. A thin smile spreads across her lips. When finally they
speak, their words are soft: the whispered thoughts of lovers.*)

MADAME ROSEPETTLE: Champagne?

THE COMMODORE: Champagne.

MADAME ROSEPETTLE: Pour?

THE COMMODORE: Please. (*She lifts the bottle out of the ice bucket
and pours with her right hand, her left being clasped firmly in*
THE COMMODORE'*s passionate hands. They smile serenely at each
other. She lifts her glass. He lifts his. The music swells.*)

MADAME ROSEPETTLE: A toast?

THE COMMODORE: To you.

MADAME ROSEPETTLE: No, Commodore, to you.

THE COMMODORE: No, madame. To us.

MADAME ROSEPETTLE, THE COMMODORE (*together*): To us. (*They
raise their glasses. They gaze wistfully into each other's eyes. The*

music builds to brilliance. THE COMMODORE *clinks his glass against* MADAME ROSEPETTLE's *glass. The glasses break.*)

THE COMMODORE (*furiously mopping up the mess*): Pardon madame! Pardon!

MADAME ROSEPETTLE (*flicking some glass off her bodice*): Pas de quoi, monsieur.

THE COMMODORE: J'étais emporté par l'enthousiasme du moment.

MADAME ROSEPETTLE (*extracting pieces of glass from her lap*): Pas de quoi. (*The* COMMODORE *suddenly stretches across the table in order to stop the puddle of champagne from spilling over onto* MADAME ROSEPETTLE'S *glass-spattered lap. His elbow knocks over the flower vase. The table is inundated with water.*)

THE COMMODORE (*gasping*): Mon dieu!

MADAME ROSEPETTLE (*watching with a serenely inane grin, as the water pours over the edge of the table and onto her dress*): Pas de quoi, monsieur. Pas de quoi.

> *She snaps her fingers gaily. Immediately a* WAITER *appears from the shadow with a table in his hands. It is already covered with a tablecloth, two champagne glasses, two candelabra (the candles already flickering in them), and a vase with one wilting rose protruding. Another* WAITER *whisks the wet table away. The new table is placed. The* WAITERS *disappear into the shadows.*)

MADAME ROSEPETTLE (*lifting the bottle of champagne out of the ice bucket*): Encore?

THE COMMODORE: S'il vous plaît. (*She pours. They lift their glasses in a toast. The music swells again.*) To us.

MADAME ROSEPETTLE: To us, monsieur . . . Commodore. (*They clink their glasses lightly.* THE COMMODORE *closes his eyes and sips.* MADAME ROSEPETTLE *holds her glass before her lips, poised but not touching, waiting. She watches him. Then she speaks softly.*) Tell me about yourself.

THE COMMODORE: My heart is speaking, madame. Doesn't it tell you enough?

MADAME ROSEPETTLE: Your heart, monsieur, is growing old. It speaks with a murmur. Its words are too weak to understand.

THE COMMODORE: But the feeling, madame, is still strong.

MADAME ROSEPETTLE: Feelings are for animals, monsieur. Words are the specialty of Man. Tell me what your heart has to say.

THE COMMODORE: My heart says it loves you.

MADAME ROSEPETTLE: And how many others, monsieur, has your heart said this to?

THE COMMODORE: None but you, madame. None but you.

MADAME ROSEPETTLE: And you, monsieur, with all your money and your worldly ways, how many have loved you?

THE COMMODORE: Many, madame.

MADAME ROSEPETTLE: How many, monsieur?

THE COMMODORE: Too many, madame.

MADAME ROSEPETTLE: So I, alone, am different?

THE COMMODORE: You alone . . . do I love.

MADAME ROSEPETTLE: And pray, monsieur, just what is it that I've done to make you love me so?

THE COMMODORE: Nothing, madame. And that is why. You are a strange woman, you see. You go out with me and you know how I feel. Yet, I know nothing of you. You disregard me, madame, but never discourage. You treat my love with indifference . . . but never disdain. You've led me on, madame. That is what I mean to say.

MADAME ROSEPETTLE: I've led you to my room, monsieur. That is all.

THE COMMODORE: To me, that is enough.

MADAME ROSEPETTLE: I know. That's why I did it. (*The music swells. She smiles distantly. There is a momentary silence.*)

THE COMMODORE (*with desperation*): Madame, I must ask you something. Now. Because in all the days I've been with you there's been something I've wanted to know, but you've never told me so now, right now, I must ask. Madame, why are you here?

MADAME ROSEPETTLE (*she pauses before answering*): I have to be somewhere, don't I?

THE COMMODORE: But why here, where I am? Why in Havana?

MADAME ROSEPETTLE: You flatter yourself, monsieur. I am in Havana only because Havana was in my way. . . . I think I'll move on tomorrow.

THE COMMODORE: For . . . home?

MADAME ROSEPETTLE (*laughing slightly*): Only the very young and the very old have homes. I am neither. And I have none.

THE COMMODORE: But . . . surely you must come from somewhere.

MADAME ROSEPETTLE: Nowhere you've ever been.

THE COMMODORE: I've been many places.

MADAME ROSEPETTLE (*softly*): But not many enough. (*She picks up her glass of champagne and sips, a distant smile on her lips.*)

THE COMMODORE (*with sudden, overwhelming, and soul-rendering passion*): Madame, don't go tomorrow. Stay. My heart is yours.

MADAME ROSEPETTLE: How much is it worth?

THE COMMODORE: A fortune, madame.

MADAME ROSEPETTLE: Good. I'll take it in cash.

THE COMMODORE: But the heart goes with it, madame.

MADAME ROSEPETTLE: And you with the heart, I suppose?

THE COMMODORE: Forever.

MADAME ROSEPETTLE: Sorry, monsieur. The money's enticing and the heart would have been nice, but you, I'm afraid, are a bit too bulky to make it all worth while.

THE COMMODORE: You jest, madame.

MADAME ROSEPETTLE: I never jest, monsieur. There isn't enough time.

THE COMMODORE: Then you make fun of my passion, madame, which is just as bad.

MADAME ROSEPETTLE: But monsieur, I've never taken your passion seriously enough to make fun of it. (*There is a short pause.* THE COMMODORE *sinks slowly back in his seat.*)

THE COMMODORE (*weakly, sadly*): Then why have you gone out with me?

MADAME ROSEPETTLE: So that I might drink champagne with you tonight.

THE COMMODORE: That makes no sense.

MADAME ROSEPETTLE: It makes perfect sense.

THE COMMODORE: Not to me.

MADAME ROSEPETTLE: It does to me.

THE COMMODORE: But *I* don't understand. And I want to understand.

MADAME ROSEPETTLE: Don't worry, Commodore. You will.

THE COMMODORE: When?

MADAME ROSEPETTLE: Soon.

THE COMMODORE: How soon?

MADAME ROSEPETTLE: Very soon. (*He stares at her in submissive confusion. Suddenly, with final desperation, he grabs her hands in his and, leaning across the table, kisses them passionately, sobbingly. Then in a scarcely audible whisper she says.*) Now.

THE COMMODORE: Madame . . . I love you. Forever. Don't you understand? (*He kisses her hand again. A smile of triumph spreads across her face.*) Oh, your husband . . . He must have been . . . a wonderful man . . . to deserve a woman such as you. (*He sobs and kisses her hands again.*)

MADAME ROSEPETTLE (*nonchalantly*): Would you like to see him?

THE COMMODORE: A snapshot?

MADAME ROSEPETTLE: No. My husband. He's inside in the closet. I had him stuffed. Wonderful taxidermist I know. H'm? What do you say, Commodore? Wanna peek? He's my very favorite trophy. I take him with me wherever I go.

THE COMMODORE (*shaken; not knowing what to make of it*): Hah-hah, hah-hah. Yes. Very good. Very funny. Sort of a . . . um . . . white elephant, you might say.

MADAME ROSEPETTLE: You might say.

THE COMMODORE: Well, it's . . . certainly very . . . courageous of you, a . . . a woman still in mourning, to . . . to be able to laugh at what most other women wouldn't find . . . well, shall we say . . . funny.

MADAME ROSEPETTLE: Life, my dear Commodore, is *never* funny. It's grim! It's there every morning breathing in your face the moment you open your red baggy eyes. Worst of all, it follows you wherever you go. Life, Mr. Roseabove, is a husband hanging from a hook in the closet. Open the door without your customary cup of coffee and your whole day's shot to hell. But open the door just a little ways, sneak your hand in, pull out your dress, and your day is made. Yet he's still there, and waiting—your husband, hanging by his collar from a hook, and sooner or later the moth balls are gone and you've got to clean house. It's a bad day, Commodore, when you have to stare Life in the face, and you find he doesn't smile at all; just hangs there . . . with his tongue sticking out.

THE COMMODORE: I . . . don't find this . . . very funny.

MADAME ROSEPETTLE: Sorry. I was hoping it would give you a laugh.

THE COMMODORE: I don't think it's funny at all. And the reason that I don't think it's funny at all is that it's not my kind of joke. One must respect the dead.

MADAME ROSEPETTLE: Then tell me Commodore . . . why not the living, too? (*Pause. She lifts the bottle of champagne and pours herself some more.*)

THE COMMODORE (*weakly, with a trace of fear*): How . . . how did he die?

MADAME ROSEPETTLE: Why, I killed him of course. Champagne? (*She smiles sweetly and fills his glass. She raises hers in a toast.*) To your continued good health. (*He stares at her blankly. The music swells in the background.*) Ah, the waltz, monsieur. Listen. The waltz. The Dance of Lovers. Beautiful . . . *don't you think?*

(*She laughs and sips some more champagne. The music grows to brilliance.* THE COMMODORE *starts to rise from his chair.*)

THE COMMODORE: Forgive me, madame. But . . . I find I must leave. Urgent business calls. Good evening. (*He tries to push his chair back, but for some reason it will not move. He looks about in panic. He pushes frantically. It does not move. It is as if the invisible waiter who had come and slid the chair out when he went to sit down now stood behind the chair and held it in so he could not get up. And as there are arms on the chair,* THE COMMODORE *cannot slide out the side.* MADAME ROSEPETTLE *smiles.*)

MADAME ROSEPETTLE: Now you don't really want to leave . . . do you, Commodore? After all, the night is still so young . . . and you haven't even seen my husband yet. We shared such love for so many years, Commodore, I would so regret if you had to leave without seeing him. And believe me, Commodore, the expression on his face is easily worth the price of admission. So please, Commodore, won't you reconsider? Won't you stay? . . . just for a little while? (*He stares at her in horror. He tries once more to push his chair back. But the chair does not move. He sinks down into it weakly. She leans across the table and tenderly touches his hand.*) Good. I knew you'd see it my way. It would have been such a shame if you'd have had to leave. For you see, Commodore, we are in a way united. We share something in common . . . you and I. . . . We share desire. For you desire me, with love in your heart. While I, my dear Commodore . . . desire your heart. (*She smiles sweetly and sips some more champagne.*) How simple it all is, in the end. (*She rises slowly from her chair and walks over to him. She runs her hand lovingly through his hair and down the back of his neck.*) Tell me, Commodore, how would you like to hear a little story? A bedtime story? A fairy tale full of handsome princes and enchanted maidens; full of love and joy and music; tenderness and charm? Would you like to hear it, Commodore? Eh? It's my very favorite story, you see . . . and since you're my very favorite commodore, it seems only appropriate that I tell it to you . . . don't you think?

THE COMMODORE: No. I . . . I don't think so.

MADAME ROSEPPETTLE: Good. Then I'll tell it. I never leave a place without telling it to at least one person. How very lucky you are. How very lucky. (*The light on the table dims slightly.* MADAME ROSEPETTLE *walks slowly away. A spot of light follows her as she goes. The light on the table fades more.* THE COMMODORE *sits, motionless.*) His name was Albert Edward Robinson Rosepettle III. How strange and sad he was. All the others who had come to see me had been tall, but he was short. They had been rich, while he was poor. The others had been handsome, but Albert, poor Albert, he was as ugly as a humid day . . . (*She laughs sadly, distantly.*) and just about as wet, too. Oh, he was a fat bundle of sweat, Mr. Roseabove. He was nothing but one great torrent of perspiration. Winter and summer, spring and fall, Albert was dripping wet. And he wasn't very good-looking either. He had a large green wart on the very tip of his nose and he talked with a lisp and walked with a limp and his left ear, which was slightly larger than his right, was as red as a bright red beet. He was round and wet and hideous and I never could figure out how he ever got such a name as Albert Edward Robinson Rosepettle III.

Oh, I must have been very susceptible indeed to have married Albert. I was twenty-eight and that is a susceptible year in a woman's life. And of course I was a virgin, but still I — Oh, stop blushing, Mr. Roseabove. I'm not lying. It's all true. Part of the cause of my condition, I will admit, was due to the fact that I still hadn't gone out with a man. But I am certain, Mr. Roseabove, I am certain that despite your naughty glances my virtue would have remained unsoiled, no matter what. Oh, I had spoken to men. (*Their voices are gruff.*) And in crowded streets I had often brushed against them. (*Their bodies, I found, are tough and bony.*) I had observed their ways and habits, Mr. Roseabove. Even at that tender age I had the foresight to realize I must know what I was up against. So I watched them huddled in hallways, talking in nervous whispers and laughing when little girls passed by. I watched their hands in crowded buses and even felt their feeling elbows on crowded streets. And then, one night, when I walked home I saw a man standing in a window. I saw him take his contact lenses out and his hearing aid out of his ear. I saw him take his teeth out of his thin-lipped mouth and drop them into a smiling glass of water. I saw him lift his snow-white hair off of his wrinkled white head and place it on a gnarled wooden hat tree. And then I saw him take his clothes off. And when he was done and didn't move but stood and stared at a full-length mirror whose glass he had covered with towels, then I went home and wept.

And so one day I bolted the door to my room. I locked myself inside, bought a small revolver just in case, then sat at my window and watched what went on below. It was not a pretty sight. Some

men came up to see me. I don't know how they got my name. But
I have heard that once a woman reaches womanhood her fragrance
wanders out into the world and her name becomes the common
property of Men. Just as a single drop of blood will attract a distant
school of sharks, so Man, without any introduction, can catch the
scent of any woman anywhere and find her home. That is what I've
heard. No place then is safe from them. You cannot hide. Your
name is known and there is nothing left that can be done. I
suppose if you like you can lock your door. It doesn't keep them
away; just keeps them out. I locked my door. They came and
knocked. I did not let them in.

> "Hello in there," they said.
> "Hello in there,
> My name is Steven
> Steven S. (for Steven) Steven.
> One is odd
> But two is even.
> I know you're hot
> So I'm not leavin'."
> . . . or something like that.

(*Short pause.*) But they all soon left anyway. I think they caught
the scent of a younger woman down the hall. And so I stayed inside my room and listened to the constant sound of feet disappear-
ing down the stairs. I watched a world walk by my window; a
world of lechery and lies and greed. I watched a world walk by and
I decided not to leave my room until this world came to me, exactly
as I wanted it.

One day Albert came toddling up the stairs. He waddled over
to my room, scratched on the door and said, in a frail and very
frightened voice, "Will you please marry me?" And so I did. It was
as simple as that. (*Pause. Then distantly.*) I still wonder why I
did it though. I still wonder why. (*Short pause. Then with a laugh
of resignation.*) I don't really know why. I guess it just seemed like
the right thing to do. Maybe it's because he was the first one who
ever asked me. No, that's not right. . . . Perhaps it's because he was
so ugly and fat; so unlike everything I'd ever heard a husband
should be. No, that doesn't make much sense either. . . . Perhaps
it's . . . yes, perhaps it's because one look at Albert's round, sad face
and I knew he could be mine . . . that no matter where he went, or
whom he saw, or what he did, Albert would be mine, all mine —

mine to love, mine to live with, mine to kill; my husband, my lover, my own . . . my very own.

And so we were wed. That night I went to bed with a man for the first time in my life. The next morning I picked up my mattress and moved myself into another room. Not that there was something wrong with Albert. Oh, no! He was quite the picture of health. His pudgy, pink flesh bouncing with glee. Oh, how easily is Man satisfied. How easily is his porous body saturated with "fun." All he asks is a little sex and a little food and there he is, asleep with a smile and snoring. Never the slightest regard for you, lying in bed next to him, your eyes open wide. No, he stretches his legs and kicks you in the shins; stretches his arms and smacks you in the eye. Lean over to kiss him good night and he'll belch in your face till all your romantic dreams are dissolved in an image of onions, garlic, and baked Boston beans. Oh, how considerate is Man when he's had his fill of sex. How noble, how magical, how marvelous is Love.

And so, I picked up my mattress and left his room. For as long as I stayed in his room I was not safe. After all, he was a total stranger to me. We'd only met the day before and I knew far too little. But now that we were married I had time to find out more. His life was a mystery and his mind contained too many secrets. In short, I was in danger. So I decided to find out certain things. A few of these were: what had he done before we'd ever met, what had he wanted to do, what did he still want to do, what was he doing about it? What did he dream about while he slept? What did he think about when he stared out the window? What did he think about when I wasn't near?

These were the things that concerned me most. And so I began to watch him closely.

My plan worked best at night, for that was when he slept. . . . I would listen at my door until I heard his door close. Then I'd tiptoe out and watch him through his keyhole. When his lights went out I'd open up his door and creep across the floor to his bed. And that, Mr. Roseabove, is where I stayed, every night — next to him; my husband, my "Love." I never left his side, never took my eyes from his sleeping face. I dare you to find me a wife who's as devoted as that. (*She laughs.*) And so I watched. I listened to him breathe. My ear was a stethoscope that recorded the fluctuations of his dream life. I put my ear next to his mouth so I might hear the slightest word that he might say, the slightest word that would betray his sleeping secret thoughts. I listened for my name upon his lips. I listened for a word of "love." I listened for anything, but he only snored, and smiled, and slept on and on. So every night I waited and listened, and every morning when the dawn came I left, knowing no more than when I'd come.

A month later I found that I was pregnant. It had happened that first horrible night. How like Albert to do something like that. I fancy he knew it was going to happen all the time, too. I do believe he planned it that way. One night, one shot, one chance in a lifetime and bham! you've had it. It takes an imaginative man to miss. It takes someone like Albert to do something like that. But yet, I never let on. Oh, no. Let him think I'm simply getting fat, I said. And that's the way I did it, too. I, nonchalantly putting on weight; Albert nonchalantly watching my belly grow. If he knew what was happening to me he never let me know it. He was as silent as before. It was only at night that he changed. Only at night while he slept that something strange suddenly occurred. I found that the smile on his face had become a grin. (*Pause.*)

Twelve months later my son was born. He was so overdue that when he came out he was already teething. He bit the index finger off the poor doctor's hand and snapped at the nurse till she fainted. I took him home and put him in a cage in the darkest corner of my room. But still I —

THE COMMODORE: Was it a large cage?

MADAME ROSEPETTLE: What?

THE COMMODORE: Was his cage large? I hope it was. Otherwise it wouldn't be very comfortable.

MADAME ROSEPETTLE: I'm sorry. Did I say cage? I meant crib. I put him in a crib and set the crib in a corner of my room where my husband would not see him. For until I found out exactly why he'd married me, until I understood his dreams, until that time I was not safe, and until that time I would not tell him that his son had been born. And so I went on as if nothing had happened. At night I'd slip into his room and watch him while he slept. He still refused to say a word. And yet, somehow, his grin seemed broader. And then, one night, he made that noise. At first I thought it just some . . . sort of snore. But then I listened closely. I was wrong. I know it sounds peculiar, Mr. Roseabove, but I swear it's true. While I looked on, Albert slept . . . and giggled. (*Pause.*)

Shortly after that, Rosalinda came. She was one of Albert's many secretaries. Since I'd married him, you see, he'd become a multibillionaire. My influence, of course. We'd moved from a four-room flat to a four-acre mansion. Albert had taken the north wing, my son and I the south. But when Rosalinda came, things changed. I've always felt there was something star-crossed about those two, for she was the only person I ever met who was equally as ugly as he. It seems her mother had once owned a laundromat and, at the tender age of five, Rosalinda, a curious child, had taken an exploratory trip through the mangler. The result of the trip being that her figure took on an uncanny resemblance to nothing less than a question mark.

Well, naturally I never let on that I knew she had come. When she walked in front of me I looked straight through her. When she spoke I looked away. I flatly refused to recognize her presence. I simply set an extra place at the table and cooked a little bit more. Though Albert watched me like a naughty boy anxious to see his mother's reaction to a mischievous deed, I disregarded his indiscretions and continued my life as if nothing had changed. If he were searching for some sign of annoyance, I never showed it. If he were waiting to be scolded *I* was waiting for him to give up. So at night, instead of preparing one, I prepared two beds. Instead of fluffing one pillow I fluffed up two and straightened an extra pair of sheets. I said good night as politely as I could and left them alone—the hunchback and my husband, two soulmates expressing their souls through sin. And while they lay in bed I listened at the keyhole. And when they slept I crept in and listened more. Albert had begun to speak!

After months of listening for some meager clue he suddenly began to talk in torrents. Words poured forth and I, like some listening sponge, soaked them up and stayed for more. At last he was talking in his sleep and I was there, sinking farther and farther into his brain, gaining more and more control. He told her things he never told to me. Words of passion and love. He told her how he worshipped the way she cooked; how he worshiped the way she talked; how he'd worshiped the way she'd looked when he'd first met her; even the way she looked now. And this to a hunchback. A hunchback! To a hideous, twisted slut sleeping in sin with him! Words he never told to me. I ask you, Mr. Roseabove, how much is a woman supposed to take?

But the signs of regret were beginning to show. And oh, how I laughed when I found out: when I saw how tired he'd begun to look, when I noticed how little he ate; how little he spoke; how slowly he seemed to move. It's funny, but he never slept any more. I could tell by his breathing. And through the keyhole at night I could see his large, round, empty eyes shining sadly in the dark. (*Pause.*)

Then one night he died. One year after she had come he passed on. The doctors don't know why. His heart, they said, seemed fine. It was as large a heart as they'd ever seen. And yet he died. At one o'clock in the morning his heart stopped beating. (*She laughs softly.*) But it wasn't till dawn that she discovered he was dead. (*She starts to laugh louder.*)

Well, don't you get it? Don't you catch the irony, the joke? What's wrong with you!? He died at one. At ONE O'CLOCK IN THE MORNING!! DEAD!!! Yet she didn't know he was dead till dawn. (*She laughs again, loudly.*)

Well don't you get the point? The point of the whole story. What is wrong with you? He was lying with her in bed for nearly six hours, dead, and she never knew it! What a lover he must have been! WHAT A LOVER! (*She laughs uproariously but stops when she realizes he's not laughing with her.*)

Well don't you see? Their affair, their sinfulness — it never even existed! He tried to make me jealous but there was nothing to be jealous of. His love was sterile! He was a child. He was weak. He was impotent. He was mine! Mine all the time, even when he was in bed with another, even in death . . . he was mine! (THE COMMODORE *climbs up in his chair and crawls over his arm rest. He begins to walk weakly toward the door.*) Don't tell me you're leaving, Commodore. Is there something wrong? (THE COMMODORE *walks weakly toward the door, then runs the last part of the way. In panic he twists the doorknob. The doorknob comes off. He falls to the ground.*) Why Commodore, you're on your knees! How romantic. Don't tell me you're going to ask me to marry you again? Commodore, you're trembling. What's wrong? Don't tell me you're afraid that I'll accept?

THE COMMODORE (*weakly*): I . . . I-I . . . feel . . . sa-sorry for your . . . sssssson . . . that's . . . all I can . . . sssssay.

MADAME ROSEPETTLE: And I feel sorrier for you! For you are nothing! While my son is mine. His skin is the color of fresh snow, his voice is like the music of angels, and his mind is pure. For he is safe, Mr. Rosabove, and it is *I* who have saved him. Saved him from the world beyond that door. The world of you. The world of his father. A world waiting to devour those who trust in it;

those who love. A world vicious under the hypocrisy of kindness, ruthless under the falseness of a smile. Well, go on, Mr. Roseabove. Leave my room and enter your world again — your sex-driven, dirt-washed waste of cannibals eating each other up while they pretend they're kissing. Go, Mr. Roseabove, enter your blind world of darkness. My son shall have only light! (*She turns with a flourish and enters her bedroom.* THE COMMODORE *stares helplessly at the doorknob in his hand. Suddenly the door swings open, under its own power.* THE COMMODORE *crawls out. The door closes behind him, under its own power. From outside can be heard the sound of a church bell chiming. The bedroom door reopens and* MADAME ROSEPETTLE *emerges wearing an immense straw hat, sunglasses, tight toreador pants, and a short beach robe. She carries a huge flashlight. She is barefoot. She tiptoes across the floor and exits through the main door. The church bell chimes thirteen times.*)

(JONATHAN *emerges from behind the* VENUS'-FLYTRAPS. *He runs to the door, puts his ear to it, then races back to the balcony and stares down at the street below. Carnival lights flash weirdly against the night sky and laughter drifts up. The* VENUS' FLYTRAPS *reach out to grab him but somehow he senses their presence and leaps away in time.*)

VENUS'-FLYTRAPS (*gruffly*): Grrrrrrr! (*He walks dazedly into the living room.*)

ROSALINDA THE FISH (*snarlingly*): Snarrrrrrrl! (*The* VENUS'-FLY-TRAPS *have grown enormous. Their monstrous petals wave hungrily in the air while they growl.* JONATHAN *stairs at them fearfully, the laughter below growing stronger all the while. Suddenly he runs to the wall and smashes the glass case that covers the fire axe. He takes out the axe. He advances cautiously toward the* FLYTRAPS. *He feints an attack, they follow his movements. He bobs, they weave. It is a cat-and-mouse game of death. Suddenly* JONATHAN *leaps upon them and hacks them apart till they fall to the floor, writhing, then dead.* JONATHAN *stands above them, victorious, panting, but somehow seeming to breathe easier. Slowly he turns and looks at the fish bowl. His eyes seem glazed, his expression insanely determined. He walks slowly toward the fish bowl. . . . There are three knocks on the door. He does not hear them. He raises his axe.*)

(*The door opens.* ROSALIE *enters. She is dressed in an absurdly childish pink dress with crinolines and frills — the picture of innocence, the picture of a girl ten years old. Her shoes are black leather pumps and she wears short girlish-pink socks. Her cheeks have round circles of rouge on them — like a young girl might have who had never put on make-up before.*)

ROSALIE: Jonathan! Jonathan! What have you done? (JONATHAN *stops. He does not look at her but stares at the fish bowl.*) Jonathan! Put down that silly axe. You might hurt yourself. (*He still does not answer but stares at the bowl. He does not lower the axe.*) Jonathan! (*Slowly he turns and faces her.*)

JONATHAN: I killed it.

ROSALIE: Ssh. Not so loudly. Where'd you put her body?

JONATHAN (*pointing to the* PLANTS): There.

ROSALIE: Where? I don't see a body. Where is she?

JONATHAN: Who?

ROSALIE: Your mother.

JONATHAN: I haven't killed my mother. I've killed her plants. The ones I used to feed. I've chopped their hearts out.

ROSALIE (*with an apologetic laugh*): I thought you'd . . . killed your mother. (*The* PIRANHA FISH *giggles.* JONATHAN *turns and stares at it again. He starts to move toward it, slowly.*)

ROSALIE: Jonathan, stop. (*He hesitates, as if he is uncertain what to do. Slowly he raises the axe.*) Jonathan! (*He smashes the axe against the fish bowl. It breaks. The fish screams.*)

ROSALINDA THE FISH (*Fearfully*): AAIEEEEEEEEEEEEEEE!

ROSALIE: Now look at the mess you've made.

JONATHAN: Do you think it can live without water?

ROSALIE: What will your mother say when she gets back?

JONATHAN: Maybe I should hit it again. Just in case. (*He strikes it again.*)

ROSALINDA THE FISH (*mournfully*): UGHHHHHHH (JONATHAN *stares in horror at the dead* FISH. *He drops the axe and turns away, sickened and weak.* ROSALIE *walks over and touches him gently, consolingly, on the arm.*)

ROSALIE: There's something bothering you, isn't there? (*Pause — coyly.*) What's-a matter, Jonathan? (JONATHAN *does not answer at first but stares off into space frightened, bewildered.*)

JONATHAN (*weakly*): I never thought I'd see you again. I never thought I'd talk to you again. I never thought you'd come.

ROSALIE: Did you really think that?

JONATHAN: She told me she'd never let you visit me again. She said no one would *ever* visit me again. She told me I had seen enough.

ROSALIE: But I had a key made.

JONATHAN: She . . . she hates me.

ROSALIE: What?

JONATHAN: She doesn't let me do anything. She doesn't let me listen to the radio. She took the tube out of the television set. She doesn't let me use her phone. She makes me show her all my letters before I seal them. She doesn't —

ROSALIE: Letters? What letters are you talking about?

JONATHAN: Just . . . letters I write.

ROSALIE: To whom?

JONATHAN: To people.

ROSALIE: What people?

JONATHAN: Oh . . . various people.

ROSALIE: Other girls? Could they be to other girls, by any chance?

JONATHAN: No. They're just to people. No people in particular. Just people in the phone book. Just names. I do it alphabetically. That way, someday, I'll be able to cover everyone. So far I've covered all the "A's" and "B's" up to Barrera.

ROSALIE: What is it you say to them? Can you tell me what you say to them . . . or is it private? Jonathan, just what do you say to them!?

JONATHAN: Mostly I just ask them what they look like. (*Pause. Suddenly he starts to sob in a curious combination of laughter and tears.*) But I don't think she ever mails them. She reads them, then takes them out to mail. But I don't think she ever does. I'll bet she just throws them away. Well if she's not going to mail them, why does she say she will? I . . . I could save the stamps. Why must she lie to me? Why doesn't she just say she's not going to mail them? Then I wouldn't have to wait for letters every day.

ROSALIE: Guess why I had this key made.

JONATHAN: I'll bet she's never even mailed one. From Abandono to Barrera, not one.

ROSALIE: Do you know why I had this key made? Do you know why I'm wearing this new dress?

JONATHAN: She doesn't let me stand in the window at noon because the sun is too strong. She doesn't let me stand in the window at night when the wind is blowing because the air is too cold. And today she told me she's going to nail shutters over the windows so I'll never have to worry about being bothered by the sun or the wind again.

ROSALIE: Try and guess why I'm all dressed up.

JONATHAN: She tells me I'm brilliant. She makes me read and re-read books no one's ever read. She smothers me with blankets at night in case of a storm. She tucks me in so tight I can't even get out till she comes and takes my blankets off.

ROSALIE: Stop talking about that and pay attention to me!

JONATHAN: She says she loves me. Every morning, before I even have a chance to open my eyes, there she is, leaning over my bed, breathing in my face and saying, "I love you, I love you."

ROSALIE: Jonathan, isn't my dress pretty?

JONATHAN: But I heard everything tonight. I heard it all when she didn't know I was here. (*He stares off into space, bewildered.*)

ROSALIE: What's the matter? (*He does not answer.*) Jonathan, what's the matter?

JONATHAN: But she must have known I was here. She *must* have known! I mean . . . where could I have gone? (*Pause.*) But . . . if that's the case . . . *why did she let me hear?*

ROSALIE: Jonathan, I do wish you'd pay more attention to me. Here, look at my dress. You can even touch it if you like. Guess how many crinolines I have on. Guess why I'm wearing such a pretty, new dress. Jonathan!

JONATHAN (*distantly*): Maybe . . . it didn't make any difference to her . . . whether I heard or not. (*He turns suddenly to her and hugs her closely. She lets him hold her, then she steps back and away from him. Her face looks strangely old and determined under her girlish powder and pinkness.*)

ROSALIE: Come with me.

JONATHAN: What?

ROSALIE: Leave and come with me.

JONATHAN (*fearfully*): Where?

ROSALIE: Anywhere.

JONATHAN: What . . . wha . . . what do you mean?

ROSALIE: I mean, let's leave. Let's run away. Far away. Tonight. Both of us, together. Let's run and run. Far, far away.

JONATHAN: You . . . mean, leave?

ROSALIE: Yes. Leave.

JONATHAN: Just like that?

ROSALIE: Just like that.

JONATHAN: But . . . but . . . but . . .

ROSALIE: You want to leave, don't you?

JONATHAN: I . . . I don't . . . don't know. I . . . I . . .

ROSALIE: What about the time you told me how much you'd like to go outside, how you'd love to walk by yourself, anywhere you wanted?

JONATHAN: I . . . I don't . . . know.

ROSALIE: Yes you do. Come. Give me your hand. Stop trembling so. Everything will be all right. Give me your hand and come with me. Just through the door. Then we're safe. Then we can run far away, somewhere where she'll never find us. Come, Jonathan. It's time to go. I've put on a new dress just for the occasion. I even had a key made so I could come and get you.

JONATHAN: There are others you could take.

ROSALIE: But I don't love them. (*Pause.*)

JONATHAN: You . . . you love me?

ROSALIE: Yes, Jonathan. I love you.

JONATHAN: Wha-wha-why?

ROSALIE (*softly*): Because you watch me every night.

JONATHAN: Well . . . can't we stay here?

ROSALIE: No.

JONATHAN: Wha-wha-whhhy?

ROSALIE: Because I want you alone. (JONATHAN *turns from her and begins to walk about the room in confusion.*) I want you, Jonathan. Do you understand what I said? I want you for my husband.

JONATHAN: I . . . I . . . can't, I mean, I . . . I want to . . . go with you very much but I . . . I don't think . . . I can. I'm . . . sorry. (*He sits down and holds his head in his hands, sobbing quietly.*)

ROSALIE: What time will your mother be back?

JONATHAN: Na — not for a while.

ROSALIE: Are you sure?

JONATHAN: Ya-yes.

ROSALIE: Where is she?

JONATHAN: The usual place.

ROSALIE: What do you mean, "The usual place"?

JONATHAN (*With a sad laugh*): The beach. (ROSALIE *looks at* JONATHAN *quizzically.*) She likes to look for people making love. Every night at midnight she walks down to the beach searching for people lying on blankets and making love. When she finds them she kicks sand in their faces and walks on. Sometimes it takes her as much as three hours to chase everyone away. (ROSALIE *smiles slightly and walks toward the master bedroom.* JONATHAN *freezes in fear. She puts her hand on the doorknob.*)

JONATHAN: WHAT ARE YOU DOING!? (*She smiles at him*

over her shoulder. She opens the door.) STOP! You can't go in there! STOP! (*She opens the door completely and beckons to him.*)

ROSALIE: Come.

JONATHAN: Close it. Quickly!

ROSALIE: Come, Jonathan. Let's go inside.

JONATHAN: Close the door!

ROSALIE (*with a laugh*): You've never been in here, have you?

JONATHAN: No. And you can't go in, either. No one can go in there but Mother. It's her room. Now close the door! (*She flicks on the light switch. No lights go on.*)

ROSALIE: What's wrong with the lights?

JONATHAN: There are none. . . . Mother's in mourning. (ROSALIE *walks into the room and pulls the drapes off the windows. Weird colored lights stream in and illuminate the bedroom in wild, distorted, nightmarish shadows and lights. They blink on and off, on and off. It's all like some strange, macabre fun house in an insane amusement park. Even the furniture in the room seems grotesque and distorted. The closet next to the bed seems peculiarly prominent. It almost seems to tilt over the bed.*)

JONATHAN (*still in the main room*): What have you done!? ROSALIE *walks back to the door and smiles to him from within the master bedroom.*) What have you done?

ROSALIE: Come in, Jonathan.

JONATHAN: GET OUT OF THERE!

ROSALIE: Will you leave with me?

JONATHAN: I can't!

ROSALIE: But you want to, don't you?

JONATHAN: Yes, yes, I want to, but I told you . . . I . . . I . . . I can't. I can't! Do you understand? I can't! Now come out of there.

ROSALIE: Come in and get me.

JONATHAN: Rosalie, please.

ROSALIE (*bouncing on the bed*): My, what a comfortable bed.

JONATHAN (*horrified*): GET OFF THE BED!

ROSALIE: What soft, fluffy pillows. I think I'll take a nap.

JONATHAN: Rosalie, please listen to me. Come out of there. You're not supposed to be in that room. Please come out. Rosalie, *please.*

ROSALIE: Will you leave with me if I do?

JONATHAN: Rosalie . . . ? I'll . . . I'll show you my stamp collection if you'll promise to come out.

ROSALIE: Bring it in here.

JONATHAN: Will you come out then?

ROSALIE: Only if you bring it in here.

JONATHAN: But I'm not allowed to go in there.

ROSALIE (*poutingly*): Then I shan't come out!

JONATHAN: You've got to!

ROSALIE: Why?

JONATHAN: Mother will be back.

ROSALIE: She can sleep out there. (ROSALIE *yawns.*) I think I'll take a little nap. This bed is so comfortable. Really, Jonathan, you should come in and try it.

JONATHAN: MOTHER WILL BE BACK SOON!

ROSALIE: Give her your room, then, if you don't want her to sleep on the couch. I find it very nice in here. Good night. (*Pause.*)

JONATHAN: If I come in, will you come out?

ROSALIE: If you don't come in I'll never come out.

JONATHAN: And if I do?

ROSALIE: Then I may.

JONATHAN: What if I bring my stamps in?

ROSALIE: Bring them and find out. (*He goes to the dresser and takes out the drawer of stamps. Then he takes out the drawer of coins.*)

JONATHAN: I'm bringing the coins, too.

ROSALIE: How good you are, Jonathan. (*He takes a shelf full of books.*)

JONATHAN: My books, too. How's that? I'll show you my books and my coins and my stamps. I'll show you them all. Then will you leave?

ROSALIE: Perhaps. (*He carries them all into the bedroom and sets them down next to the bed. He looks about fearfully.*)

ROSALIE: What's wrong?

JONATHAN: I've never been in here before.

ROSALIE: It's nothing but a room. There's nothing to be afraid of. (*He looks about doubtfully.*)

JONATHAN: Well, let me show you my stamps. I have one billion, five —

ROSALIE: Later, Jonathan. We'll have time. Let me show you something first.

JONATHAN: What's that?

ROSALIE: You're trembling.

JONATHAN: What do you want to show me?

ROSALIE: There's nothing to be nervous about. Come. Sit down.

JONATHAN: What do you want to show me?

ROSALIE: I can't show you if you won't sit down.

JONATHAN: I don't want to sit down! (*She takes hold of his hand. He pulls it away.*)

ROSALIE: Jonathan!

JONATHAN: You're sitting on Mother's bed.

ROSALIE: Then let's pretend it's my bed.

JONATHAN: It's not your bed!

ROSALIE: Come, Jonathan. Sit down here next to me.

JONATHAN: We've got to get out of here. Mother might come.

ROSALIE: Don't worry. We've got plenty of time. The beach is full of lovers.

JONATHAN: How do you know?

ROSALIE: I checked before I came. (*Pause.*)

JONATHAN: Let . . . let me show you my coins.

ROSALIE: Why are you trembling so?

JONATHAN: Look, we've got to get out! Something terrible will happen if we don't.

ROSALIE: Then leave with me.

JONATHAN: The bedroom?

ROSALIE: The hotel. The island. Your mother. Leave with me, Jonathan. Leave with me now, before it's too late.

JONATHAN: I . . . I . . . I . . .

ROSALIE: I love you, Jonathan, and I won't give you up. I want you . . . all for myself. Not to share with your mother, but for me, alone . . . to love, to live with, to have children by. I want you, Jonathan. You, whose skin is softer and whiter than anyone's I've ever known; whose voice is quiet and whose love is in every look of his eye. I want you, Jonathan, and I won't give you up. (*Short pause.*)

JONATHAN (*softly, weakly*): What do you want me to do?

ROSALIE: Forget about your mother. Pretend she never existed and look at me. Look at my eyes, Jonathan; my mouth, my hands, my skirt, my legs. Look at me, Jonathan. Are you still afraid?

JONATHAN: I'm not afraid. (*She smiles and starts to unbutton her dress.*) What are you doing!? No! (*She continues to unbutton her dress.*)

ROSALIE: Your mother is strong, but I am stronger. (*She rises and her skirt falls about her feet. She stands in a slip and crinolines.*)

I don't look so pink and girlish any more, do I? (*She laughs.*)
But you want me anyhow. You're ashamed but you want me anyhow. It's written on your face. And I'm very glad. Because I want
you. (*She takes off a crinoline.*)

JONATHAN: PUT IT ON! *Please,* put it back on!

ROSALIE: Come, Jonathan. (*She takes off another crinoline.*) Lie
down. Let me loosen your shirt.

JONATHAN: No . . . No . . . No! STOP! *Please,* stop! (*She takes
her last crinoline off and reaches down to take off her socks. The
lights outside blink weirdly. Wild, jagged music with a drum beating in the background is heard.*)

ROSALIE: Don't be afraid, Jonathan. Come, Lie down. Everything
will be wonderful. (*She takes her socks off and lies down in her
slip. She drops a strap over one shoulder and smiles.*)

JONATHAN: Get off my mother's bed!

ROSALIE: I want you, Jonathan, all for my own. Come. The bed is
soft. Lie here by my side.

> (*She reaches up and takes his hand. Meekly he sits down on the
> edge of the bed. The closet door swings open suddenly and the
> corpse of Albert Edward Robinson Rosepettle III tumbles for-
> ward stiffly and onto the bed, his stone-stiff arms falling across
> ROSALIE'S legs, his head against her side. JONATHAN, too ter-
> rified to scream, puts his hand across his mouth and sinks down
> onto the bed, almost in a state of collapse. Outside the music
> screams.*)

ROSALIE: Who the hell is this!?

JONATHAN: It-it-it-it . . . it . . . it's . . .

ROSALIE: What a stupid place to keep a corpse. (*She pushes him
back in the closet and shuts the door.*) Forget it, Jonathan. I put
him back in the closet. Everything's fine again.

JONATHAN: It's . . . it's . . . it's my . . . my . . . my . . .

ROSALIE (*kneeling next to him on the bed and starting to unbotton
his shirt.*) It's all right, Jonathan. It's all right. Sshh. Come. Let
me take off your clothes.

JONATHAN (*still staring dumbly into space*): It's . . . it's my . . .
ffffather.

> (*The closet door swings open again and the corpse falls out, this
> time his arms falling about ROSALIE'S neck. JONATHAN almost
> swoons.*)

ROSALIE: Oh, for God's sake. (*She pushes the corpse off the bed and
onto the floor.*) Jonathan . . . ? LISTEN TO ME, JONATHAN!

STOP LOOKING AT HIM AND LOOK AT ME! (*He looks away from his father, fearfully, his mouth open in terror.*) I love you, Jonathan, and I want you now. Not later and not as partner with your mother but now and by myself. I want you, Jonathan, as my husband. I want you to lie with me, to sleep with me, to be with me, to kiss me and touch me, to live with me, forever. Stop looking at him! He's dead! Listen to me. I'm alive. I want you for my husband! Now help me take my slip off. Then you can look at my body and touch me. Come, Jonathan. Lie down. I want you forever.

JONATHAN: Ma-Mother was right! You *do* let men do anything they want to you.

ROSALIE: Of course she was right! Did you really think I was that sweet and pure? Everything she said was right. (*She laughs.*) Behind the bushes and it's done. One-two-three and it's done. Here's the money. Thanks. Come again. Hah-hah! Come again! (*Short pause.*) So what!? It's only you I love. They make no difference.

JONATHAN: You're dirty! (*He tries to get up but can't, for his father is lying in front of his feet.*)

ROSALIE: No, I'm not dirty. I'm full of love and womanly feelings. I want children. Tons of them. I want a husband. Is that dirty?

JONATHAN: You're dirty!

ROSALIE: No. I'm pure. I want no one but you. I renounce all past lovers. They were mistakes. I confess my indiscretions. Now you know all so I'm pure again. Take off your clothes.

JONATHAN: NO!

ROSALIE: Forget about your father. Drop your pants on top of him, then you won't see his face. Forget about your mother. She's gone. Forget them both and look at me. Love is so beautiful, Jonathan. Come and let me love you; tonight and forever. Come and let me keep you mine. Mine to love when I want, mine to kiss when I want, mine to have when I want. Mine. All mine. So come, Jonathan. Come and close your eyes. It's better that way. Close your eyes so you can't see. Close your eyes and let me lie with you. Let me show you how beautiful it is . . . love.

(*She lies back in bed and slowly starts to raise her slip. JONATHAN stares at her legs in horror. Then, suddenly, he seizes her crumpled skirt and throws it over her face. He smothers her to death. . . . At last he rises and, picking up his box of stamps, dumps the stamps over her limp body. He does the same with his coins and finally his books, until at last she is buried. Then, done, he throws his hands over his eyes and turns to run. But as he staggers past the corpse of his father, his father's lifeless arms somehow come to life for an instant and, reaching out, grab Jonathan by the feet.* JONATHAN *falls to the floor. For a moment he lies there, stretched across his father's body, too terrified to move. But a soft, ethereal-green light begins to suffuse the room and heavenly harp music is heard in the air. As if his body had suddenly become immortal and weightless,* JONATHAN *rises up from the floor and with long, slow, dreamlike steps (like someone walking under water), he floats through the bedroom door and drifts across the living room, picking up his telescope on the way. He floats out to the balcony and begins to scan the sky. The harp music grows louder and more paradisiacal: Debussy in Heaven. While under the harp music, soft, muffled laughter can be heard; within the bedroom, within the living room, from the rear of the theater, laughter all about.) (His mother tiptoes into the living room. Her hair is awry, her hat is on crooked, her blouse hangs wrinkled and out of her pants. Her legs are covered with sand.)*

MADAME ROSEPETTLE: Twenty-three couples. I annoyed twenty-three couples, all of them coupled in various positions, all equally distasteful. It's a record, that's what it is. It's a record! (*Breathing heavily from excitement she begins to tuck in her blouse and straighten her hair. She notices the chaotic state of the room. She shrieks slightly.*) What has happened!? (*She notices the* PLANTS.) My plants! (*She notices the* FISH.) Rosalinda! Great gods, my fish has lost her water! Albert! Albert! (*She searches about the room for her son. She sees him standing on the porch.*) Ah, there you are. Edward, what has been going on during my brief absence? What are you doing out here when Rosalinda is lying in there dead? Dead!? Oh God, dead. Robinson, answer me. What are you looking for? I've told you there's nothing out there. This place is a madhouse. That's what it is. A madhouse. (*She turns and walks into her bedroom. An airplane is heard flying in the distance.* JONATHAN *scans the horizon frantically. The plane grows nearer.* JONATHAN *follows it with his telescope. It flies overhead. It begins to circle about. Wildly, desperately, Jonathan waves his arms to the plane. . . . It flies away.*) (MADAME ROSEPETTLE *re-enters the room.*) Robinson! I went to lie down and I stepped on your father! I lay down and I lay on some girl. Robinson, there is a woman on my bed and I do believe she's stopped breathing. What is more, you've buried her under your fabulous collection of stamps, coins, and books. I ask you, Robinson. As a mother to a son I ask you. What is the meaning of this?

(Blackout and Curtain.)

alienated man searching for love or substitute of love, askes ~~it~~ for it in disguised terms, the woman agrees, knowing he is false, takes him in and then disguises the

poetry

poem

James Jones

Once a young man, wandering beneath the bleary
Streetlamps of a town that is all towns,
Stopped at the door of a young unmarried woman.
"I am hungry," the young man said.
"For what do you hunger?" the woman smiled.
"I do not know," he said.
"Come," she smiled, "and I will feed you."
And she took him to her bed where she poured ashes upon
His head and laughed at his surprise.
"Ashes are good for you," she said;
"They are full of minerals."

From *Some Came Running* by James Jones, Charles Scribner's Sons.

second skin

John Hawkes

I will tell you in a few words who I am: lover of hummingbird that darts to the flower beyond the rotten sill where my feet are propped; lover of bright needlepoint and the bright stitching fingers of humorless old ladies bent to their sweet and infamous designs; lover of a parasols made from the same puffy stuff as young girl's underdrawers; still lover of that small naval boat which somehow survived the distressing years of my life between her decks or in her pilothouse; and also lover of poor dear black Sonny, my mess boy, fellow victim and confidant, and of my wife and child. But most of all, lover of my harmless and sanguine self.

lie down in darkness

William Styron

The door of the room where they stood, he and Peyton together, her hand in his, confronted the edge of darkness, like a shore at night facing on the sea. Beyond them in the shadows arose swollen, mysterious scents, powders and perfumes which, though familiar to both of them, never lost the odor of strangeness and secrecy — to him, because they stung his senses with memories of dances and parties in the distant past, and of love, always the scent of gardenias. In Peyton they aroused wicked excitement, a promise, too, of dances and parties, and — since she was still nine years old — hope that when the Prince came finally with love and a joyful rattling of spurs, the day would smell like this, a heartbreaking scent, always of roses. A breeze stirred somewhere in the room, shook a piece of paper with a tiny clattering noise, like toy hooves echoing down a tiny road. He and Peyton stood still, listening; the paper clattered endlessly, small hooves galloping across the silence: the breeze died with a whisper and the paper, hooves, horse and rider, vanished without a sound, tumbled into some toy abyss. They listened, hesitant, somehow afraid, for now beyond them, floating up like crickets from the darkness, an alarm clock went click-cluckclick, a broken-down soliloquy, promising terrible things.

down in dallas

X. J. Kennedy

Down in Dallas, down in Dallas
Where the shadow of blood lies black
Lee Oswald nailed Jack Kennedy up
With the nail of a rifle crack.

Every big bright Cadillac stompled its brakes,
Every face in the street fell still,
While the slithering gun like a tooth of sin
Recoiled from the window sill.

In a white chrome room on a table top,
Oh, they tried all a scalpel knows
But they couldn't spell stop to that drop-by-drop
Till it bloomed to a rigid rose.

Down on the altar, down on the altar
Christ is broken to bread and wine
But each asphalt stone where the blood dropped down
Prickled into a cactus spine.

"Down in Dallas," by X. J. Kennedy, is reprinted by permission of the author & Messrs. Erwin A. Glikes and Paul Schwaber, editors of *Of Poetry and Power: Poems Occasioned by the Presidency and by the Death of John F. Kennedy* (Basic Books Inc., Publishers, New York, 1964).

Oh down in Dallas, down in Dallas
Where the wind has to cringe tonight
Lee Oswald nailed Jack Kennedy up
On the cross of a rifle sight.

this little bride & groom are

E. E. Cummings

this little bride & groom are
standing)in a kind
of crown,he dressed
in black candy,she

veiled with candy white,
carrying a bouquet of
pretend flowers,this
candy crown with this candy

little bride & little
groom,in it kind of stands on
a thin ring which stands on a much
less thin,very much more

big & kinder of ring &,which
kinder of stands on a
much more than very much
biggest & thickest & kindest

of ring & all,one two three rings
are cake & everything is protected by
cellophane against anything(because
nothing really exists.

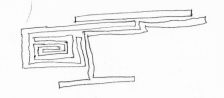
i know a man

Robert Creeley

> As I sd to my
> friend, because I am
> always talking, — John, I
>
> sd, which was not his
> name, the darkness sur-
> rounds us, what
>
> can we do against
> it, or else, shall we &
> why not, buy a goddamn big car,
>
> drive, he sd, for
> christ's sake, look
> out where yr going.

america

Allen Ginsberg

America I've given you all and now I'm nothing.
America two dollars and twentyseven cents January 17, 1956.
I can't stand my own mind.
America when will we end the human war?
Go fuck yourself with your atom bomb.
I don't feel good don't bother me.
I won't write my poem till I'm in my right mind.

America when will you be angelic?

When will you take off your clothes?

When will you look at yourself through the grave?

When will you be worthy of your million Trotskyites?

America why are your libraries full of tears?

America when will you send your eggs to India?

I'm sick of your insane demands.

When can I go into the supermarket and buy what I need with my good looks?

America after all it is you and I who are perfect not the next world.

Your machinery is too much for me.

You made me want to be a saint.

There must be some other way to settle this argument.

Burroughs is in Tangiers I don't think he'll come back it's sinister.

Are you being sinister or is this some form of practical joke?

I'm trying to come to the point.

I refuse to give up my obsession.

America stop pushing I know what I'm doing.

America the plum blossoms are falling.

I haven't read the newspapers for months, everyday somebody goes on trial for murder.

America I feel sentimental about the Wobblies.

America I used to be a communist when I was a kid I'm not sorry.

I smoke marijuana every chance I get.

I sit in my house for days on end and stare at the roses in the closet.

When I go to Chinatown I get drunk and never get laid.

My mind is made up there's going to be trouble.

You should have seen me reading Marx.

My psychoanalyst thinks I'm perfectly right.

I won't say the Lord's Prayer.

I have mystical visions and cosmic vibrations.

America I still haven't told you what you did to Uncle Max after he came over from Russia.

I'm addressing you.

Are you going to let your emotional life be run by Time Magazine?

I'm obsessed by Time Magazine.

I read it every week.

Its cover stares at me every time I slink past the corner candystore.

I read it in the basement of the Berkeley Public Library.

It's always telling me about responsibility. Businessmen are serious.
Movie producers are serious. Everybody's serious but me.
It occurs to me that I am America.
I am talking to myself again.

Asia is rising against me.
I haven't got a chinaman's chance.
I'd better consider my national resources.
My national resources consist of two joints of marijuana millions of
genitals an unpublishable private literature that goes 1400 miles
an hour and twentyfive-thousand mental institutions.
I say nothing about my prisons nor the millions of underprivileged
who live in my flowerpots under the light of five hundred suns.
I have abolished the whorehouses of France, Tangiers is the next to go.
My ambition is to be President despite the fact that I'm a Catholic.

America how can I write a holy litany in your silly mood?
I will continue like Henry Ford my strophes are as individual as his
automobiles more so they're all different sexes.
America I will sell you strophes $2500 apiece $500 down on your
old strophe.
America free Tom Mooney
America save the Spanish Loyalists
America Sacco & Vanzetti must not die
America I am the Scottsboro boys.
America when I was seven momma took me to Communist Cell meet-
ings they sold us garbanzos a handful per ticket a ticket costs a
nickel and the speeches were free everybody was angelic and senti-
mental about the workers it was all so sincere you have no idea
what a good thing the party was in 1835 Scott Nearing was a grand
old man a real mensch Mother Bloor made me cry I once saw Israel
Amter plain. Everybody must have been a spy.
America you don't really want to go to war.
America it's them bad Russians.
Them Russians them Russians and them Chinamen. And them Russians.
The Russia wants to eat us alive. The Russia's power mad. She wants
to take our cars from out our garages.
Her wants to grab Chicago. Her needs a Red Readers' Digest. Her
wants our auto plants in Siberia. Him big bureaucracy running our
fillingstations.

That no good. Ugh. Him make Indians learn read. Him need big
    black niggers. Hah. Her make us all work sixteen hours a day.
    Help.
America this is quite serious.
America this is the impression I get from looking in the television set.
America is this correct?
I'd better get right down to the job.
It's true I don't want to join the Army or turn lathes in precision parts
    factories, I'm nearsighted and psychopathic anyway.
America I'm putting my queer shoulder to the wheel.

sweeney among the nightingales

ὤμοι, πέπληγμαι χαιρίαν πληγὴν ἔσω

T. S. Eliot

> Apeneck Sweeney spreads his knees
> Letting his arms hang down to laugh,
> The zebra stripes along his jaw
> Swelling to maculate giraffe.
>
> The circles of the stormy moon
> Slide westward toward the River Plate,
> Death and the Raven drift above
> And Sweeney guards the hornèd gate.
>
> Gloomy Orion and the Dog
> Are veiled; and hushed the shrunken seas;
> The person in the Spanish cape
> Tries to sit on Sweeney's knees

Slips and pulls the table cloth
Overturns a coffee-cup,
Reorganized upon the floor
She yawns and draws a stocking up:

The silent man in mocha brown
Sprawls at the window-sill and gapes;
The waiter brings in oranges
Bananas figs and hothouse grapes;

The silent vertebrate in brown
Contracts and concentrates, withdraws;
Rachel *née* Rabinovitch
Tears at the grapes with murderous paws;

She and the lady in the cape
Are suspect, thought to be in league;
Therefore the man with heavy eyes
Declines the gambit, shows fatigue,

Leaves the room and reappears
Outside the window, leaning in,
Branches of wistaria
Circumscribe a golden grin;

The host with someone indistinct
Converses at the door apart,
The nightingales are singing near
The Convent of the Sacred Heart,

And sang within the bloody wood
When Agamemnon cried aloud,
And let their liquid siftings fall
To stain the stiff dishonoured shroud.

the bad children

Carl Bode

The children of light — mongoloid,
Hydrocephalic, crazed, awry —
Will build their glass houses
Out of shards of pale sky
Or brittle splinters of causes.

Their names will be biblical,
Esther, Naomi, Levi, Moses,
Or else cheap blue plastic,
Charlene, Joni, Sondra, Elvis.
Their minds will be lame or spastic,

Their hearts futile. While they
Play with their impossible toys
Their parents, aching, will stand
And watch them. Outside, the healthy noise
Of other children, playing Pretend,

Joyously aping the children of light,
Will meet the ears of the wordless
Parents. And they will stop and ponder
The rich health of the children of darkness,
Who deny God. And they will wonder

(The fathers turning to the mothers),
They will wonder as they try to measure
Sure causes against clumsy effects,
Which is worse, God's displeasure
In this world or the next?

suburban homecoming

John Ciardi

As far as most of what you call people, my darling, are
concerned, I don't care who or what gets into the phone. I
am not home and not expected and I even, considerably, doubt I live
   here.

I mean this town and its everlasting katzenjammer whenever whoever dials again, is going to hell, or to some other
perpetual buffet, in a wheelbarrowful of bad martinis: and you, my

legal sweet, forever in the act of putting your hat on
as I come in the door to be told I have exactly five —
or, on good days, ten — minutes to change in because here we go

again to some collection of never-quite-the-same-but-
always-no-different faces; you, my moth-brained flutter
from bright cup to cup, no matter what nothing is in them; you, my
   own

brand-named, laboratory-tested, fair-trade-priced, wedded
(as advertised in *Life*) feather-duster, may go jump into
twenty fathoms of Advice to the Lovelorn and pull it in after you —

but I have not arrived, am not it, the phone did not ring
and was not answered, we have not really, I believe, met, and
if we do and if I stay to be (I doubt it) introduced, I'm still not going.

Used by permission of the author and the Trustees of Rutgers, the State University of New Jersey.

drug store

Karl Shapiro

> *I do remember an apothecary*
> *And hereabouts 'a dwells*

It baffles the foreigner like an idiom,
And he is right to adopt it as a form
Less serious than the living-room or bar;
    For it disestablishes the cafe,
Is a collective, and on basic country.

Not that it praises hygiene and corrupts
The ice-cream parlor and the tobacconist's
Is it a center; but that the attractive symbols
    Watch over puberty and leer
Like rubber bottles waiting for sick-use.

Youth comes to jingle nickles and crack wise;
The baseball scores are his, the magazines,
Devoted to lust, the jazz, the Coca-Cola,
    The lending-library of love's latest.
He is the customer; he is heroized.

And every nook and cranny of the flesh
Is spoken to by packages with wiles.
"Buy me, buy me," they whimper and cajole;
    The hectic range of lipsticks pouts,
Revealing the wicked and the simple mouth.

With scarcely any evasion in their eye
They smoke, undress their girls, exact a stance;
But only for a moment. The clock goes round;
    Crude fellowships are made and lost;
They slump in booths like rags, not even drunk.

notes for a speech

Leroi Jones

African blues
does not know me. Their steps, in sands
of their own
land. A country
in black and white, newspapers
blown down pavements
of the world. Does
not feel
what I am.
                        Strength
in the dream, an oblique
suckling of nerve, the wind
throws up sand, eyes
are something locked in
hate, of hate, of hate, to
walk abroad, they conduct
their deaths apart
from my own. Those
heads, I call
my "people."
                        (And who are they. People. To concern
myself, ugly man. Who
you, to concern
the white flat stomachs
of maidens, inside houses
dying. Black. Peeled moon
light on my fingers
move under
her clothes. Where
is her husband. Black
words throw up sand
to eyes, fingers of
their private dead. Whose
soul, eyes, in sand. My color

is not theirs. Lighter, white man
talk. They shy away. My own
dead souls, my, so called
people. Africa
is a foreign place. You are
as any other sad man here
american.

the emperor of ice-cream

Wallace Stevens

Call the roller of big cigars,
The muscular one, and bid him whip
In kitchen cups concupiscent curds.
Let the wenches dawdle in such dress
As they are used to wear, and let the boys
Bring flowers in last month's newspapers.
Let be be finale of seem.
The only emperor is the emperor of ice-cream.

Take from the dresser of deal.
Lacking the three glass knobs, that sheet
On which she embroidered fantails once
And spread it so as to cover her face.
If her horny feet protrude, they come
To show how cold she is, and dumb.
Let the lamp affix its beam.
The only emperor is the emperor of ice-cream.

nonfiction

good news! god is love!

Henry Miller

It was in a hotel in Pittsburgh that I finished the book on Rama-krishna by Romain Rolland. Pittsburgh and Ramakrishna — could any more violent contrast be possible? The one the symbol of brutal power and wealth, the other the very incarnation of love and wisdom. We begin here then, in the very quick of the nightmare, in the crucible where all values are reduced to slag.

I am in a small, supposedly comfortable room of a modern hotel equipped with all the latest conveniences. The bed is clean and soft, the shower functions perfectly, the toilet seat has been sterilized since the last occupancy, if I am to believe what is printed on the paper band which garlands it; soap, towels, lights, stationery, everything is provided in abundance.

I am depressed, depressed beyond words. If I were to occupy this room for any length of time I would go mad — or commit suicide. The spirit of the place, the spirit of the men who made it the hideous city

it is, seeps through the walls. There is murder in the air. It suffo-
cates me.

A few moments ago I went out to get a breath of air. I was back
again in Czarist Russia. I saw Ivan the Terrible followed by a caval-
cade of snouted brutes. There they were, armed with clubs and
revolvers. They had the look of men who obey with zest, who shoot
to kill on the slightest provocation.

Never has the status quo seemed more hideous to me. This is not
the worst place, I know. But I am here and what I see hits me hard.

It was fortunate perhaps that I didn't begin my tour of America
via Pittsburgh, Youngstown, Detroit; fortunate that I didn't start out
by visiting Bayonne, Bethlehem, Scranton and such like. I might never
have gotten as far as Chicago. I might have turned into a human bomb
and exploded. By some canny instinct of self-preservation I turned
south first, to explore the so-called "backward" states of the union.
If I was bored for the most part I at least knew peace. Did I not see
suffering and misery in the South too? Of course I did. There is suffering and misery everywhere throughout this broad land. But there
are kinds and degrees of suffering; the worst, in my opinion, is the
sort one encounters in the very heart of progress.

At this moment we are talking about the defense of our country,
our institutions, our way of life. It is taken for granted that these *must*
be defended, whether we are invaded or not. But there are things
which ought not to be defended, which ought to be allowed to die;
there are things which we should destroy voluntarily, with our own
hands.

Let us make an imaginative recapitulation. Let us try to think back
to the days when our forefathers first came to these shores. To begin
with, they were running away from something; like the exiles and
expatriates whom we are in the habit of denigrating and reviling,
they too had abandoned the homeland in search of something nearer
to their heart's desire.

One of the curious things about these progenitors of ours is that
though avowedly searching for peace and happiness, for political and
religious freedom, they began by robbing, poisoning, murdering, almost exterminating the race to whom this vast continent belonged.
Later, when the gold rush started, they did the same to the Mexicans
as they had to the Indians. And when the Mormons sprang up they
practised the same cruelties, the same intolerance and persecution upon
their own white brothers.

I think of these ugly facts because as I was riding from Pittsburgh to Youngstown, through an Inferno which exceeds anything that Dante imagined, the idea suddenly came to me that I ought to have an American Indian by my side, that he ought to share this voyage with me, communicate to me silently or otherwise his emotions and reflections. By preference I would like to have had a descendant of one of the admittedly "civilized" Indian tribes, a Seminole, let us say, who had passed his life in the tangled swamps of Florida.

Imagine the two of us then standing in contemplation before the hideous grandeur of one of those steel mills which dot the railway line. I can almost hear him thinking — "So it was for this that you deprived us of our birthright, took away our slaves, burned our homes, massacred our women and children, poisoned our souls, broke every treaty which you made with us and left us to die in the swamps and jungles of the Everglades!"

Do you think it would be easy to get him to change places with one of our steady workers? What sort of persuasion would you use? What now could you promise him that would be truly seductive? A used car that he could drive to work in? A slap-board shack that he could, if he were ignorant enough, call a home? An education for his children which would lift them out of vice, ignorance and superstition but still keep them in slavery? A clean, healthy life in the midst of poverty, crime, filth, disease and fear? Wages that barely keep your head above water and often not? Radio, telephone, cinema, newspaper, pulp magazine, fountain pen, wrist watch, vacuum cleaner or other gadgets ad infinitum? Are these the baubles that make life worthwhile? Are these what make us happy, carefree, generous-hearted, sympathetic, kindly, peaceful and godly? Are we now prosperous and secure, as so many stupidly dream of being? Are any of us, even the richest and most powerful, certain that an adverse wind will not sweep away our possessions, our authority, the fear or the respect in which we are held?

This frenzied activity which has us all, rich and poor, weak and powerful, in its grip — where is it leading us? There are two things in life which it seems to me all men want and very few ever get (because both of them belong to the domain of the spiritual) and they are health and freedom. The druggist, the doctor, the surgeon are all powerless to give health; money, power, security, authority do not give freedom. Education can never provide wisdom, nor churches religion, nor wealth happiness, nor security peace. What is the meaning of our activity then? To what end?

We are not only as ignorant, as superstitious, as vicious in our con-

incurable romantic

duct as the "ignorant, bloodthirsty savages" whom we dispossessed and annihilated upon arriving here — we are worse than they by far. We have degenerated; we have degraded the life which we sought to establish on this continent. The most productive nation in the world, yet unable to properly feed, clothe and shelter over a third of its population. Vast areas of valuable soil turning to waste land because of neglect, indifference, greed and vandalism. Torn some eighty years ago by the bloodiest civil war in the history of man and yet to this day unable to convince the defeated section of our country of the righteousness of our cause nor able, as liberators and emancipators of the slaves, to give them true freedom and equality, but instead enslaving and degrading our own white brothers. Yes, the industrial North defeated the aristocratic South — the fruits of that victory are now apparent. Wherever there is industry there is ugliness, misery, oppression, gloom and despair. The banks which grew rich by piously teaching us to save, in order to swindle us with our own money, now beg us not to bring our savings to them, threatening to wipe out even that ridiculous interest rate they now offer should we disregard their advice. Three-quarters of the world's gold lies buried in Kentucky. Inventions which would throw millions more out of work, since by the queer irony of our system every potential boon to the human race is converted into an evil, lie idle on the shelves of the patent office or are bought up and destroyed by the powers that control our destiny. The land, thinly populated and producing in wasteful, haphazard way enormous surpluses of every kind, is deemed by its owners, a mere handful of men, unable to accommodate not only the starving millions of Europe but our own starving hordes. A country which makes itself ridiculous by sending out missionaries to the most remote parts of the globe, asking for pennies of the poor in order to maintain the Christian work of deluded devils who no more represent Christ than I do the Pope, and yet unable through its churches and missions at home to rescue the weak and defeated, the miserable and the oppressed. The hospitals, the insane asylums, the prisons filled to overflowing. Counties, some of them big as a European country, practically uninhabited, owned by an intangible corporation whose tentacles reach everywhere and whose responsibilities nobody can formulate or clarify. A man seated in a comfortable chair in New York, Chicago or San Francisco, a man surrounded by every luxury and yet paralyzed with fear and anxiety, controls the lives and destinies of thousands of men and women whom he has never seen, whom he never wishes to see and whose fate he is thoroughly uninterested in.

This is what is called progress in the year 1941 in these United
States of America. Since I am not of Indian, Negro or Mexican de-
scent I do not derive any vengeful joy in delineating this picture of
the white man's civilization. I am a descendant of two men who ran
away from their native land because they did not wish to become
soldiers. My descendants, ironically enough, will no longer be able
to escape that duty: the whole white world has at last been turned
into an armed camp.

Well, as I was saying, I was full of Ramakrishna on leaving Pittsburgh. Ramakrishna who never criticized, who never preached, who
accepted all religions, who saw God everywhere in everything: the
most ecstatic being, I imagine, that ever lived. Then came Coraopolis,
Aliquippa, Wampum. Then Niles, the birth-place of President McKinley, and Warren, the birth-place of Kenneth Patchen. Then Youngstown and two girls are descending the bluff beside the railroad tracks
in the most fantastic setting I have laid eyes on since I left Crete. Instantly I am back on that ancient Greek island, standing at the edge
of a crowd on the outskirts of Heraklion just a few miles from
Knossus. There is no railroad on the island, the sanitation is bad, the
dust is thick, the flies are everywhere, the food is lousy — but it is a
wonderful place, one of the most wonderful places in the whole world.
As at Youngstown by the railroad station there is a bluff here and a
Greek peasant woman is slowly descending, a basket on her head, her
feet bare, her body poised. *Here the resemblance ends. . . .*

As everybody knows, Ohio has given the country more Presidents
than any other State in the Union. Presidents like McKinley, Hayes,
Garfield, Grant, Harding — weak, characterless men. It has also given
us writers like Sherwood Anderson and Kenneth Patchen, the one
looking for poetry everywhere and the other driven almost mad by
the evil and ugliness everywhere. The one walks the streets at night
in solitude and tells us of the imaginary life going on behind closed
doors; the other is so stricken with pain and chagrin by what he sees
that he re-creates the cosmos in terms of blood and tears, stands it
upside down and walks out on it in loathing and disgust. I am glad
I had the chance to see these Ohio towns, this Mahoning River which
looks as if the poisonous bile of all humanity had poured into it,
though in truth it may contain nothing more evil than the chemicals
and waste products of the mills and factories. I am glad I had the
chance to see the color of the earth here in winter, a color not of
age and death but of disease and sorrow. Glad I could take in the
rhinoceros-skinned banks that rise from the river's edge and in the

pale light of a wintry afternoon reflect the lunacy of a planet given over to rivalry and hatred. Glad I caught a glimpse of those slag heaps which look like the accumulation droppings of sickly prehistoric monsters which passed in the night. It helps me to understand the black and monstrous poetry which the younger man distils in order to preserve his sanity; helps me to understand why the older writer had to pretend madness in order to escape the prison which he found himself in when he was working in the paint factory. It helps me to understand how prosperity built on this plane of life can make Ohio the mother of presidents and the persecutor of men of genius.

The saddest sight of all is the automobiles parked outside the mills and factories. The automobile stands out in my mind as the very symbol of falsity and illusion. There they are, thousands upon thousands of them, in such profusion that it would seem as if no man were too poor to own one. In Europe, Asia, Africa the toiling masses of humanity look with watery eyes towards this Paradise where the worker rides to work in his own car. What a magnificent world of opportunity it must be, they think to themselves. (At least we like to think that they think that way!) They never ask what one must do to have this great boon. They don't realize that when the American worker steps out of his shining tin chariot he delivers himself body and soul to the most stultifying labor a man can perform. They have no idea that it is possible, even when one works under the best possible conditions, to forfeit all rights as a human being. They don't know that the best possible conditions (in American lingo) means the biggest profits for the boss, the utmost servitude for the worker, the greatest confusion and disillusionment for the public in general. They see a beautiful, shining car which purrs like a cat; they see endless concrete roads so smooth and flawless that the driver has difficulty keeping awake; they see cinemas which look like palaces; they see department stores with mannikins dressed like princesses. They see the glitter and paint, the baubles, the gadgets, the luxuries; they don't see the bitterness in the heart, the skepticism, the cynicism, the emptiness, the sterility, the despair, the hopelessness which is eating up the American worker. They don't want to see this — they are full of misery themselves. They want a way out: they want the lethal comforts, conveniences, luxuries. And they follow in our footsteps — blindly, heedlessly, recklessly.

Of course not all American workers ride to work in automobiles. In Beaufort, S.C., only a few weeks ago I saw a man on a two-wheeled cart driving a bullock through the main street. He was a black man, to be sure, but from the look on his face I take it that he was far better off than the poor devil in the steel mill who drives his own car. In Tennessee I saw white men toiling like beasts of burden; I saw them struggling desperately to scratch a living from the thin soil on the mountainsides. I saw the shacks they live in and wondered if it were possible to put together anything more primitive. But I can't say that I felt sorry for them. No, they are not the sort of people to inspire pity. On the contrary, one has to admire them. If they represent the "backward" people of America then we need more backward people. In the subway in New York you can see the other type, the newspaper addict, who revels in social and political theories and lives the life of a drudge, foolishly flattering himself that because he is not working with his hands (nor with his brain either, for that matter) he is better off than the poor white trash of the South.

Those two girls in Youngstown coming down the slippery bluff — it was like a bad dream, I tell you. But we look at these bad dreams constantly with eyes open and when some one remarks about it we say, "Yes, that's right, that's how it is!" and we go about our business or we take to dope, the dope which is worse by far than opium or hashish — I mean the newspapers, the radio, the movies. Real dope gives you the freedom to dream your own dreams; the American kind forces you to swallow the perverted dreams of men whose only ambition is to hold their job regardless of what they are bidden to do.

The most terrible thing about America is that there is no escape from the treadmill which we have created. There isn't one fearless champion of truth in the publishing world, not one film company devoted to art instead of profits. We have no theatre worth the name, and what we have of theatre is practically concentrated in one city; we have no music worth talking about except what the Negro has given us, and scarcely a handful of writers who might be called creative. We have murals decorating our public buildings which are about on a par with the aesthetic development of high school students, and sometimes below that level in conception and execution. We have art museums that are crammed with lifeless junk for the most part. We have war memorials in our public squares that must make the dead in whose name they were erected squirm in their graves. We have an architectural taste which is about as near the vanishing point as it is possible to achieve. In the ten thousand miles I have travelled thus far I have come across two cities which have each of them a little section worth a second look — I mean Charleston and New Orleans. As for the other cities, towns and villages through which I passed

I hope never to see them again. Some of them have such marvelous names, too, which only makes the deception more cruel. Names like Chattanooga, Pensacola, Tallahassee, like Mantua, Phoebus, Bethlehem, Paoli, like Algiers, Mobile, Natchez, Savannah, like Baton Rouge, Saginaw, Poughkeepsie: names that revive glorious memories of the past or awaken dreams of the future. Visit them, I urge you. See for yourself. Try to think of Schubert or Shakespeare when you are in Phoebus, Virginia. Try to think of North Africa when you are in Algiers, Louisiana. Try to think of the life the Indians once led here when you are on a lake, a mountain or river bearing the names we borrowed from them. Try to think of the dreams of the Spaniards when you are motoring over the old Spanish Trail. Walk around in the old French Quarter of New Orleans and try to reconstruct the life that once this city knew. Less than a hundred years has elapsed since this jewel of America faded out. It seems more like a thousand. Everything that was of beauty, significance or promise has been destroyed and buried in the avalanche of false progress. In the thousand years of almost incessant war Europe has not lost what we have lost in a hundred years of "peace and progress." No foreign enemy ruined the South. No barbaric vandals devastated the great tracts of land which are as barren and hideous as the dead surface of the moon. We can't attribute to the Indians the transformation of a peaceful, slumbering island like Manhattan into the most hideous city in the world. Nor can we blame the collapse of our economic system on the hordes of peaceful, industrious immigrants whom we no longer want. No, the European nations may blame one another for their miseries, but we have no such excuse — we have only ourselves to blame.

Less than two hundred years ago a great social experiment was begun on this virgin continent. The Indians whom we dispossessed, decimated and reduced to the status of outcasts, just as the Aryans did with the Dravidians of India, had a reverent attitude towards the land. The forests were intact, the soil rich and fertile. They lived in communion with Nature on what we choose to call a low level of life. Though they possessed no written language they were poetic to the core and deeply religious. Our forefathers came along and, seeking refuge from their oppressors, began by poisoning the Indians with alcohol and venereal disease, by raping their women and murdering their children. The wisdom of life which the Indians possessed they scorned and denigrated. When they had finally completed their work of conquest and extermination they herded the miserable remnants of a great race into concentration camps and proceeded to break what spirit was left in them.

Not long ago I happened to pass through a tiny Indian reservation belonging to the Cherokees in the mountains of North Carolina. The contrast between this world and ours is almost unbelievable. The little Cherokee reservation is a virtual Paradise. A great peace and silence pervades the land, giving one the impression of being at last in the happy hunting grounds to which the brave Indian goes upon his death. In my journey thus far I have struck only one other community which had anything like this atmosphere, and that was in Lancaster County, Pennsylvania, among the Amish people. Here a small religious group, clinging stubbornly to the ways of their ancestors in comportment, dress, beliefs and customs, have converted the land into a veritable garden of peace and plenty. It is said of them that ever since they settled here they have never known a crop failure. They live a life in direct opposition to that of the majority of the American people — and the result is strikingly apparent. Only a few miles away are the hell-holes of America where, as if to prove to the world that no alien ideas, theories or isms will ever get a foothold here, the American flag is brazenly and tauntingly flown from roofs and smokestacks. And what sorry looking flags they are which the arrogant, bigoted owners of these plants display! You would think that such fervid patriotism would be inconsonant with the display of a torn, blackened, weatherbeaten emblem. You would think that out of the huge profits which they accumulate enough might be put aside to purchase a bright, new, gleaming emblem of liberty. But no, in the industrial world everything is soiled, degraded, vilified. It has become so to-day that when you see the flag boldly and proudly displayed you smell a rat somewhere. The flag has become a cloak to hide iniquity. We have two American flags always: one for the rich and one for the poor. When the rich fly it it means that things are under control; when the poor fly it it means danger, revolution, anarchy. In less than two hundred years the land of liberty, home of the free, refuge of the oppressed has so altered the meaning of the Stars and Stripes that to-day when a man or woman succeeds in escaping from the horrors of Europe, when he finally stands before the bar under our glorious national emblem, the first question put to him is: *"How much money have you?"* If you have no money but only a love of freedom, only a prayer for mercy on your lips, you are debarred, returned to the slaughter-house, shunned as a leper. This is the bitter caricature which the descendants of our liberty-loving forefathers have made of the national emblem.

Everything is caricatural here. I take a plane to see my father on his death-bed and up there in the clouds, in a raging storm, I overhear two men behind me discussing how to put over a big deal, the big deal involving paper boxes, no less. The stewardess, who has been trained to behave like a mother, a nurse, a mistress, a cook, a drudge, never to look untidy, never to lose her Marcel wave, never to show a sign of fatigue or disappointment or chagrin or loneliness, the stewardess puts her lily-white hand on the brow of one of the paper-box salesmen and in the voice of a ministering angel, says: "Do you feel tired this evening? Have you a headache? Would you like a little aspirin?" We are up in the clouds and she is going through this performance like a trained seal. When the plane lurches suddenly she falls and reveals a tempting pair of thighs. The two salesmen are now talking about buttons, where to get them cheaply, how to sell them dearly. Another man, a weary banker is reading the war news. There is a great strike going on somewhere—several of them, in fact. We are going to build a fleet of merchant vessels to help England — *next December*. The storm rages. The girl falls down again — she's full of black and blue marks. But she comes up smiling, dispensing coffee and chewing gum, putting her lily-white hand on someone else's forehead, inquiring if he is a little low, a little tired perhaps. I ask her if she likes her job. For answer she says, "It's better than being a trained nurse." The salesmen are going over her points; they talk about her like a commodity. They buy and sell, buy and sell. For that they have to have the best rooms in the best hotels, the fastest, smoothest planes, the thickest, warmest overcoats, the biggest, fattest purses. We need their paper boxes, their buttons, their synthetic furs, their rubber goods, their hosiery, their plastic this and that. We need the banker, his genius for taking our money and making himself rich. The insurance man, his policies, his talk of security, of dividends — we need him too. *Do we?* I don't see that we need any of these vultures. I don't see that we need any of these cities, these hell-holes I've been in. I don't think we need a two-ocean fleet either. I was in Detroit a few nights ago. I saw the Mannerheim Line in the movies. I saw how the Russians pulverized it. I learned the lesson. *Did you?* Tell me what it is that man can build, to protect himself, which other men cannot destroy? What are we trying to defend? Only what is old, useless, dead, indefensible. Every defense is a provocation to assault. Why not surrender? Why not give — give all? It's so damned practical, so thoroughly effective and disarming. Here we are, we the people of the United States: the greatest people on earth, so we think. We have everything—everything it takes to make people happy. We have land, water, sky and all that goes with it. We could become the great shining example of the world; we could radiate peace, joy, power, benevolence. But there are ghosts all about, ghosts whom we can't seem to lay hands on. We are not happy, not contented, not radiant, not fearless.

We bring miracles about and we sit in the sky taking aspirin and talking paper boxes. On the other side of the ocean they sit in the sky and deal out death and destruction indiscriminately. We're not doing that yet, *not yet,* but we are committed to furnishing the said instruments of destruction. Sometimes, in our greed, we furnish them to the wrong side. But that's nothing — everything will come out right in the end. Eventually we will have helped to wipe out or render prostrate a good part of the human race—not savages this time, but civilized "barbarians." Men like ourselves, in short, except that they have different views about the universe, different ideological principles, as we say. Of course, if we don't destroy them they will destroy us. That's logic — nobody can question it. That's political logic, and that's what we live and die by. A flourishing state of affairs. Really exciting, don't you know. "We live in such exciting times." Aren't you happy about it? The world changing so rapidly and all that — isn't it marvelous? Think what it was a hundred years ago. Time marches on. . . .

A man of genius whom I know would like to be spared the ordeal of indiscriminate killing which they are preparing him for. He is not interested in putting the world to rights. He is interested in putting his thoughts down on paper. But then he has a good set of teeth, he is not flat-footed, his heart and lungs are sound, he has no nervous disorders. He is thoroughly healthy and a genius to boot. He never talks about paper boxes or buttons or new-fangled gadgets. He talks poetry, talks about God. But he doesn't belong to some God sect and therefore is disqualified as a conscientious objector. The answer is that he must get ready to be shipped to the front. He must defend our ideological principles. The banker is too old to be of service; the salesmen I was talking about are too clever; so the genius has to serve, though God knows, since we have so few of them, you would think we might be able to spare one now and then.

I hope that Walt Disney is exempted, because he's the man, though I doubt that he realizes it, to illustrate what I have to say. In fact, he's been doing it all along, unconsciously. He's the master of the nightmare. He's the Gustave Doré of the world of Henry Ford & Co., Inc. The Mannerheim Line is just a scratch on the surface. True, the temperature was abnormal — about forty degrees below zero on the average. (Amazing how men can be trained to kill in all kinds of weather. Almost as intelligent as horses.) But as I was saying, Disney has all kinds of temperature — a temperature to suit every fresh horror. He doesn't have to think: the newspapers are always on tap. Of course they're not real men and women. Oh no! They're more real than real men and women: they're dream creatures. They tell us what we look like beneath the covering of flesh. A fascinating world, what? Really, when you think about it, even more fascinating than Dali's cream puffs. Dali thinks too much. Besides, he has only two hands. Disney has a million. And besides hands he has voices — the voice of the hyena, the voice of the donkey, the voice of the dinosaur. The Soviet film, for example, is intimidating enough, but slow, ponderous, cumbersome, unwieldy. It takes time in real life to demolish all those concrete pill-boxes, cut all that barbed wire, kill all those soldiers, burn all those villages. Slow work. Disney works fast — like greased lightning. That's how we'll all operate soon. What we dream we become. We'll get the knack of it soon. We'll learn how to annihilate the whole planet in the wink of an eye — just wait and see.

The capital of the new planet — the one, I mean, which will kill itself off — of course Detroit. I realized that the moment I arrived. At first I thought I'd go and see Henry Ford, give him my congratulations. But then I thought — what's the use? He wouldn't know what I was talking about. Neither would Mr. Cameron most likely. That lovely Ford evening hour! Every time I hear it announced I think of Céline—Ferdinand, as he so affectionately calls himself. Yes, I think of Céline standing outside the factory gates (pp. 222–225, I think it is: *Journey to the End of the Night*). Will he get the job? Sure he will. He gets it. He goes through the baptism—the baptism of stultification through noise. He sings a wonderful song there for a few pages about the machine, the blessings that it showers upon mankind. Then he meets Molly. Molly is just a whore. You'll find another Molly in *Ulysses,* but Molly the whore of Detroit is much better. Molly has a soul. Molly is the milk of human kindness. Céline pays a tribute to her at the end of the chapter. It's remarkable because all the other characters are paid off in one way or another. Molly is whitewashed. Molly, believe it or not, looms up bigger and holier than Mr. Ford's huge enterprise. Yes, that's the beautiful and surprising thing about Céline's chapter on Detroit — that he makes the body

of a whore triumph over the soul of the machine. You wouldn't
suspect that there was such a thing as a soul if you went to Detroit.
Everything is too new, too slick, too bright, too ruthless. Souls don't
grow in factories. Souls are killed in factories — even the niggardly
ones. Detroit can do in a week for the white man what the South
couldn't do in a hundred years to the Negro. That's why I like the
Ford evening hour — it's so soothing, so inspiring.

Of course Detroit isn't the worst place—not by a long shot. That's
what I said about Pittsburgh. That's what I'll say about other places
too. None of them is the worst. There is no worst or worstest. The
worst is in process of becoming. It's inside us now, only we haven't
brought it forth. Disney dreams about it — and he gets paid for it,
that's the curious thing. People bring their children to look and scream
with laughter. (Ten years later it happens now and then that they
fail to recognize the little monster who so joyfully clapped his hands
and screamed with delight. It's always hard to believe that a Jack-
the-Ripper could have sprung out of your own loins.) However. . . .
It's cold in Detroit. A gale is blowing. Happily I am not one of those
without work, without food, without shelter. I am stopping at the
gay Detroiter, the Mecca of the futilitarian salesmen. There is a
swanky haberdashery shop in the lobby. Salesmen love silk shirts.
Sometimes they buy cute little panties too — for the ministering angels
in the aeroplanes. They buy any and everything — just to keep money
in circulation. The men of Detroit who are left out in the cold freeze
to death in woolen underwear. The temperature in winter is distinctly sub-tropical. The buildings are straight and cruel. The wind
is like a double-bladed knife. If you're lucky you can go inside where
it's warm and see the Mannerheim Line. A cheering spectacle. See
how ideological principles can triumph in spite of sub-normal tempera-
tures. See men in white cloaks crawling through the snow on their
bellies; they have scissors in their hands, big ones, and when they
reach the barbed wire they cut, cut, cut. Now and then they get shot
doing it — but then they become heroes — and besides there are always
others to take their places, all armed with scissors. Very edifying, very
instructive. Heartening, I should say. Outside, on the streets of Detroit,
the wind is howling and people are running for shelter. But it's
warm and cosy in the cinema. After the spectacle a nice warm cup
of chocolate in the lobby of the hotel. Men talking buttons and chewing gum there. Not the same men as in the aeroplane—different ones.
Always find them where it's warm and comfortable. Always buying
and selling. And of course a pocketful of cigars. Things are picking up

in Detroit. Defense orders, you know. The taxi driver told me he expetced to get his job back soon. In the factory, I mean. What would happen if the war suddenly stopped I can't imagine. There would be a lot of broken hearts. Maybe another crisis. People wouldn't know what to do for themselves if peace were suddenly declared. Everybody would be laid off. The bread lines would start up. Strange, how we can manage to feed the world and not learn how to feed ourselves.

I remember when the wireless came how everybody thought—how wonderful! now we will be in communication with the whole world! And television — how marvelous! now we shall be able to see what's going on in China, in Africa, in the remotest parts of the world! I used to think that perhaps one day I'd own a little apparatus which by turning a dial would enable me to see Chinamen walking through the streets of Peking or Shanghai or savages in the heart of Africa performing their rites of initiation. What do we actually see and hear to-day? What the censors permit us to see and hear, nothing more. India is just as remote as it ever was — in fact, I think it is even more so now than it was fifty years ago. In China a great war is going on — a revolution fraught with far greater significance for the human race than this little affair in Europe. Do you see anything of it in the news reels? Even the newspapers have very little to say about it. Five million Chinese can die of flood, famine or pestilence or be driven from their homes by the invader, and the news (a headliner for one day usually) leaves us unruffled. In Paris I saw one news reel of the bombing of Shanghai and that was all. It was too horrible — the French couldn't stomach it. To this day we haven't been shown the real pictures of the first World War. You have to have influence to get a glimpse of those fairly recent horrors. . . . There are the "educational" pictures, to be sure. Have you seen them? Nice, dull, soporific, hygienic, statistical poems fully castrated and sprinkled with lysol. The sort of thing the Baptist or Methodist Church could endorse.

The news reels deal largely with diplomatic funerals, christenings of battleships, fires and explosions, aeroplane wrecks, athletic contests, beauty parades, fashions, cosmetics and political speeches. Educational pictures deal largely with machines, fabrics, commodities and crime. If there's a war on we get a glimpse of foreign scenery. We get about as much information about the other peoples of this globe, through the movies and the radio, as the Martians get about us. And this abysmal separation is reflected in the American physiognomy. In the towns and cities you find the typical American everywhere. His expression is mild, bland, pseudo-serious and definitely fatuous. He is usually neatly dressed in a cheap ready-made suit, his shoes shined, a fountain pen and pencil in his breast pocket, a brief case under his arm — and of course he wears glasses, the model changing with the changing styles. He looks as though he were turned out by a university with the aid of a chain store cloak and suit house. One looks like the other, just as the automobiles, the radios and the telephones do. This is the type between 25 and 40. After that age we get another type — the middle-aged man who is already fitted with a set of false teeth, who puffs and pants, who insists on wearing a belt though he should be wearing a truss. He is a man who eats and drinks too much, smokes too much, sits too much, talks too much and is always on the edge of a break-down. Often he dies of heart failure in the next few years. In a city like Cleveland this type comes to apotheosis. So do the buildings, the restaurants, the parks, the war memorials. The most typical American city I have struck thus far. Thriving, prosperous, active, clean, spacious, sanitary, vitalized by a liberal infusion of foreign blood and by the ozone from the lake, it stands out in my mind as the composite of many American cities. Possessing all the virtues, all the prerequisites for life, growth, blossoming, it remains nevertheless a thoroughly dead place — a deadly, dull, dead place. (In Cleveland to see "The Doctor's Dilemma" is an exciting event.) I would rather die in Richmond somehow, though God knows Richmond has little enough to offer. But in Richmond, or in any Southern city for that matter, you do see types now and then which depart from the norm. The South is full of eccentric characters; it still fosters individuality. And the most individualistic are of course from the land, from the out of the way places. When you go through a sparsely settled state like South Carolina you do meet men, interesting men — jovial, cantankerous, disputative, pleasure-loving, independent-thinking creatures who disagree with everything, on principle, but who make life charming and gracious. There can hardly be any greater contrast between two regions in these United States, in my mind, than between a state like Ohio and a state like South Carolina. Nor can there be a greater contrast in these States than between two cities like Cleveland and Charleston, for example. In the latter place you actually have to pin a man to the mat before you can talk business to him. And if he happens to be a good business man, this chap from Charleston, the chances are that he is also a fanatic about something unheard of. His face registers changes of expression, his eyes light up, his hair stands on end, his voice swells with passion, his cravet slips out of place, his suspenders are apt to come undone, he spits and curses, he coos and prances, he pirouettes now and then. And there's one thing he never dangles in front of your nose — his time-piece. He has time, oodles of time. And he accomplishes everything he chooses to accomplish in due time, with the result that the air is not filled with dust and machine oil and cash register clickings. The great time-wasters, I find, are in the North, among the busy-bodies. Their whole life, one might say, is just so much time wasted. The fat, puffy, wattle-faced man of forty-five who has turned asexual is the greatest monument to futility that America has created. He's a nymphomaniac of energy accomplishing nothing. He's an hallucination of the Paleolithic man. He's a statistical bundle of fat and jangled nerves for the insurance man to convert into a frightening thesis. He sows the land with prosperous, restless, empty-headed, idle-handed widows who gang together in ghoulish sororities where politics and diabetes go hand in hand.

About Detroit, before I forget it — yes, it was here that Swami Vivekananda kicked over the traces. Some of you who read this may be old enough to remember the stir he created when he spoke before the Parliament of Religions in Chicago back in the early Nineties. The story of the pilgrimage of this man who electrified the American people reads like a legend. At first unrecognized, rejected, reduced to starvation and forced to beg in the streets, he was finally hailed as the greatest spiritual leader of our time. Offers of all kinds were showered upon him; the rich took him in and tried to make a monkey of him. In Detroit, after six weeks of it, he rebelled. All contracts were cancelled and from that time on he went alone from town to town at the invitation of such or such a society. Here are the words of Romain Rolland:

"His first feeling of attraction and admiration for the formidable power of the young republic had faded. Vivekananda almost at once fell foul of the brutality, the inhumanity, the littleness of spirit, the narrow fanaticism, the monumental ignorance, the crushing incomprehension, so frank and sure of itself with regard to all who thought, who believed, who regarded life differently from the paragon nation of the human race . . . And so he had no patience. He hid nothing. He stigmatised the vices and crimes of the Western civilisation with its characteristics of violence, pillage and destruction. Once when he was to speak at Boston on a beautiful religious subject particularly dear to him (Ramakrishna), he felt such repulsion at the sight of his audience, the artificial and cruel crowd of men of affairs and of the world, that he refused to yield them the key of his sanctuary, and brusquely changing the subject, he inveighed furiously against a civilisation represented by such foxes and wolves. The scandal was terrific. Hundreds noisily left the hall and the Press was furious. He was especially bitter against false Christianity and religious hypocrisy: 'With all your brag and boasting, where has your Christianity succeeded without the sword? Yours is a religion preached in the name of luxury. It is all hypocrisy that I have heard in this country. All this prosperity, all this from Christ! Those who call upon Christ care nothing but to amass riches! Christ would not find a stone on which to lay his head among you . . . You are not Christians. Return to Christ!' "

Rolland goes on to contrast this reaction with that inspired by England. "He came as an enemy and he was conquered." Vivekananda himself admitted that his ideas about the English had been revolutionized. "No one," he said, "ever landed on English soil with more hatred in his heart for a race than I did for the English . . . There is none among you . . . who loves the English people more than I do now."

A familiar theme—one hears it over and over again. I think of so many eminent men who visited these shores only to return to their native land saddened, disgusted and disillusioned. There is one thing America has to give, and that they are all in agreement about: MONEY. And as I write this there comes to my mind the case of an obscure individual whom I knew in Paris, a painter of Russian birth who during the twenty years that he lived in Paris knew scarcely a day when he was not hungry. He was quite a figure in Montparnasse — every one wondered how he managed to survive so long without money. Finally he met an American who made it possible for him to visit this country which he had always longed to see and which he hoped to make his adopted land. He stayed a year, travelling about, making portraits, received hospitably by rich and poor. For the first time in his whole life he knew what it was to have money in his pocket, to sleep in a clean, comfortable bed, to be warm, to be well nourished — and what is more important, to have his talent recognized. One day, after he had been back a few weeks I ran into him at a bar. I was extremely curious to hear what he might have to say about America. I had heard of his success and I wondered why he had returned.

He began to talk about the cities he had visited, the people he had met, the houses he had put up at, the meals he had been fed, the museums he had visited, the money he had made. "At first it was wonderful," he said. "I thought I was in Paradise. But after six months of it I began to be bored. It was like living with children — but *vicious* children. What good does it do to have money in your pocket if you can't enjoy yourself? What good is fame if nobody understands what you're doing? You know what my life is like here. I'm a man without a country. If there's a war I'll either be put in a concentration camp or asked to fight for the French. I could have escaped that in America. I could have become a citizen and made a good living. But I'd rather take my chances here. Even if there's only a few year left those few years are worth more here than a lifetime in America. There's no real life for an artist in America — only a living death. By the way, have you got a few francs to lend me? I'm broke again. But I'm happy. I've got my old studio back again — I appreciate that lousy place now. Maybe it was good for me to go to America — if only to make me realize how wonderful is this life which I once thought unbearable."

How many letters I received while in Paris from Americans who had returned home — all singing the same song. "If I could only be back there again. I would give my right arm to be able to return. I didn't realize what I was giving up." Et cetera, et cetera. I never received one letter from a repatriated American saying that he was happy to be home again. When this war is over there will be an exodus to Europe such as this country has never seen. We try to pretend now, because France has collapsed, that she was degenerate. There are artists and art critics in this country who, taking advantage of the situation, endeavor with utter shamelessness to convince the American public that we have nothing to learn from Europe, that Europe, France more particularly, is dead. What an abominable lie! France prostrate and defeated is more alive than we have ever been. Art does not die because of a military defeat, or an economic collapse, or a political débâcle. Moribund France produced more art than young and vigorous America, than fanatical Germany or proselytizing Russia. Art is not born of a dead people.

There are evidences of a very great art in Europe as long ago as twenty-five thousand years, and in Egypt as far back as sixty thousand years. Money had nothing to do with the production of these treasures. Money will have nothing to do with the art of the future. Money will pass away. Even now we are able to realize the futility of money. Had we not become the arsenal of the world, and thus staved off the gigantic collapse of our economic system, we might have witnessed the spectacle of the richest nation on earth starving to death in the midst of the accumulated gold of the entire world. The war is only an interruption of the inevitable disaster which impends. We have a few years ahead of us and then the whole structure will come toppling down and engulf us. Putting a few millions back to work making engines of destruction is no solution of the problem. When the destruction brought about by war is complete another sort of destruction will set in. And it will be far more drastic, far more terrible than the destruction which we are now witnessing. The whole planet will be in the throes of revolution. And the fires will rage until the very foundations of this present world crumble. Then we shall see who has life, the life more abundant. Then we shall see whether the ability to make money and the ability to survive are one and the same. Then we shall see the meaning of true wealth.

I had to cover a tremendous stretch of country before I got the inspiration to begin this book. When I think of what I would have seen in Europe, Asia, or Africa, in the space of ten thousand miles, I feel as though I had been cheated. Sometimes I think that the best books on America are the imaginary ones written by those who have never seen the country. Before I get through with my journey I intend to describe some American scenes as I pictured them in my mind's eye when in Paris. Mobile is one of them.

Meanwhile I have good news for you — I'm going to take you to Chicago, to the Mecca Apartments on the South Side. It's a Sunday morning and my cicerone has borrowed a car to take me around. We stop at a flea market on the way. My friend explains to me that he was raised here in the ghetto; he tries to find the spot where his home used to be. It's a vacant lot now. There are acres and acres of vacant lots here on the South Side. It looks like Belgium did after the World War. Worse, if anything. Reminds me of a diseased jawbone, some of it smashed and pulverized, some of it charred and ulcerated. The flea market is more reminiscent of Cracow than of Clignancourt, but the effect is the same. We are at the back door of civilization, amidst the dregs and débris of the disinherited. Thousands, hundreds of thousands, maybe millions of Americans, are still poor enough to rummage through this offal in search of some sorely needed object. Nothing is too dilapidated or rust-bitten or disease-laden to discourage the hungry buyer. You would think the five-and-ten cent store could satisfy the humblest wants, but the five-and-ten cent store is really expensive in the long run, as one soon learns. The congestion is terrific — we have to elbow our way through the throng. It's like the banks of the Ganges except that there is no odor of sanctity about. As we push our way through the crowd my feet are arrested by a strange sight. There in the middle of the street, dressed in full regalia, is an American Indian. He's selling a snake oil. Instantly the thought of the other miserable derelicts stewing around in this filth and vermin is gone. *"A World I Never Made,"* wrote James Farrell. Well, there stands the real author of the book — an outcast, a freak, a hawker of snake oil. On that same spot the buffaloes once roamed; now it is covered with broken pots and pans, with wornout watches, with dismantled chandeliers, with busted shoes which even an Igorote would spurn. Of course if you walk on a few blocks you can see the other side of the picture — the grand façade of Michigan Avenue where it seems as if the whole world were composed of millionaires. At night you can see the great monument to chewing gum lit up by flood-lights and marvel that such a monstrosity of architecture should be singled out for special attention. If you wander down the steps leading to the rear of the building and squint your eyes and sharpen your imagination a bit you can even imagine yourself back in Paris, on the Rue Broca. No Bubu here, of course, but perhaps you will run into one of Al Capone's ex-comrades. It must be pleasant to be stuck up behind the glitter of the bright lights.

We dig further into the South Side, getting out now and then to stetch our legs. Interesting evolution going on here. Rows of old mansions flanked by vacant lots. A dingy hotel sticking up like a Mayan ruin in the midst of yellow fangs and chalk teeth. Once respectable dwelling places given up now to the dark-skinned people we "liberated." No heat, no gas, no plumbing, no water, no nothing — sometimes not even a window-pane. Who owns these houses? Better not inquire too closely. What do they do with them when the darkies move out? Tear them down, of course. Federal housing projects. Model tenement houses. . . . I think of old Genoa, one of the last ports I stopped at on my way back to America. Very old, this section. Nothing much to brag about in the way of conveniences. But what a difference between the slums of Genoa and the slums of Chicago! Even the Armenian section of Athens is preferable to this. For twenty years the Armenian refugees of Athens have lived like goats in the little quarter which they made their own. There were no old mansions to take over — not even an abandoned factory. There was just a plot of land on which they erected their homes out of whatever came to hand. Men like Henry Ford and Rockefeller contributed unwittingly to the creation of this paradise which was entirely built of remnants and discarded objects. I think of this Armenian quarter because as we were walking through the slums of Chicago my friend called my attention to a flower-pot on the window-sill of a wretched hovel. "You see," he said, "even the poorest among them have their flowers." But in Athens I saw dovecotes, solariums, verandas floating without support, rabbits sunning themselves on the roofs, goats kneeling before ikons, turkeys tied to the door-knobs. Everybody had flowers — not just flower-pots. A door might be made of Ford fenders and look inviting. A chair might be made of gasoline tins and be pleasant to sit on. There were bookshops where you could read about Buffalo Bill or Jules Verne or Hermes Trismegistus. There was a spirit here which a thousand years of misery had not squelched. Chicago's South Side, on the other hand, is like a vast, unorganized lunatic asylum. Nothing can flourish here but vice and disease. I wonder what the great Emancipator would say if he could see the glorious freedom in which the black man moves now. We made them free, yes — free as rats in a dark cellar.

Well, here we are — the Mecca Apartments! A great quadrangular cluster of buildings, once in good taste, I suppose — architecturally. After the whites moved out the colored people took over. Before it reached its present condition it went through a sort of Indian Summer. Every other apartment was a dive. The place glowed with prostitution. It must have been a Mecca indeed for the lonely darky in search of work.

It's a queer building now. The locks are dismantled, the doors unhinged, the globes busted. You enter what seems like the corridor of some dismal Catholic institution, or a deaf and dumb asylum, or a Bronx sanatorium for the discreet practice of abortion. You come to a turn and you find yourself in a court surrounded by several tiers of balconies. In the center of the court is an abandoned fountain covered with a huge wire mesh like the oldfashioned cheese covers. You can imagine what a charming spot this was in the days when the ladies of easy virtue held sway here. You can imagine the peals of laughter which once flooded the court. Now there is a strained silence, except for the sound of roller skates, a dry cough, an oath in the dark. A man and woman are leaning over the balcony rail above us. They look down at us without expression. Just looking. *Dreaming?* Hardly. Their bodies are too worn, their souls too stunted, to permit indulgence in that cheapest of all luxuries. They stand there like animals in the field. The man spits. It makes a queer, dull smack as it hits the pavement. Maybe that's his way of signing the Declaration of Independence. Maybe he didn't know he spat. Maybe it was his ghost that spat. I look at the fountain again. It's been dry a long time. And maybe it's covered like a piece of old cheese so that people won't spit in it and bring it back to life. It would be a terrible thing for Chicago if this black fountain of life should suddenly erupt! My friend assures me there's no danger of that. I don't feel so sure about it. Maybe he's right. Maybe the Negro will always be our friend, no matter what we do to him. I remember a conversation with a colored maid in the home of one of my friends. She said, "I do think we have more love for you than you have for us." "You don't hate us ever?" I asked. "Lord no!" she answered, "we just feel sorry for you. You has all the power and the wealth but you ain't happy."

As we were walking back to the car we heard a great voice shouting as if from the roof-tops. We walked another block and still the voice resounded as mighty as before. We were puzzled. We turned round and retraced our steps. The voice grew stronger and stronger. It was the voice of a preacher and he was shouting with the lungs of a bull: "Jesus is the light of the world!" And then other voices joined in. "*Jesus! Jesus! The light of the world!*" We looked about in perplexity. There was nothing in sight but a Jewish synagogue. And from it, from the very walls, it seemed, came this stentorian voice bellowing about the light of the world. Finally we observed some Negroes entering the tabernacle and when we lifted our eyes we saw the amplifiers attached like gargoyles to the cornice of the building. For three blocks, clear as a bell, the voice followed us. It was like a maniac rising up out of No Man's Land and shouting *Peace!* As we stepped into the car I saw a beautiful colored woman hanging out of a window in what looked like a deserted house. What a vista her eyes took in from the fifth floor of that blackened morgue! Even up there she could hear the preacher talking about the light of the world. It was Sunday and she had nothing to do. Downstairs a ragged urchin was putting a number on the door in green chalk — so that the postman would deliver the letters to the right address, no doubt. A few blocks yonder lay the slaughterhouse and on a bright day, if the wind were propitious, one could get a whiff from where she was of the blood of the lamb, of thousands of lambs, millions of lambs, in fact. "There were nothing but cribs around here years ago," my friend was saying. Cribs, cribs. I wasn't paying attention. What's he talking about, I thought to myself. I was thinking of the Lamb of God lying in the manger at the Bethlehem Steel Plant. "There, you see?" he said, nudging me and turning his eyes upward towards the Negress on the fifth floor. She was beckoning to us. She had found God, no doubt, up there in

Nigger Heaven. If she was thinking of something else I couldn't tell it. She looked positively ecstatic. No heat, no gas, no water; the windows shattered, the mice making merry, the garbage lying in the gutter. She beckoned to us as though to say: "Come I am the light of the world! I pay no rent, I do no work, I drink nothing but blood."

We got into the car, rode a few blocks and got out to visit another shell crater. The street was deserted except for some chickens grubbing for food between the slats of a crumbling piazza. More vacant lots, more gutted houses; fire escapes clinging to the walls with their iron teeth, like drunken acrobats. A Sunday atmosphere here. Everything serene and peaceful. Like Louvain or Rheims between bombardments. Like Phoebus, Virginia, dreaming of bringing her steeds to water, or like modern Eleusis smothered by a wet sock. Then suddenly I saw it chalked up on the side of a house in letters ten feet high:

GOOD NEWS! GOD IS LOVE!

When I saw these words I got down on my knees in the open sewer which had been conveniently placed there for the purpose and I offered up a short prayer, a silent one, which must have registered as far as Mound City, Illinois, where the colored muskrats have built their igloos. It was time for a good stiff drink of cod liver oil but as the varnish factories were all closed we had to repair to the abattoir and quaff a bucket of blood. Never has blood tasted so wonderful! it was like taking Vitamines A, B, C, D, E in quick succession and then chewing a stick of cold dynamite. Good news! Aye, wonderful news — for Chicago. I ordered the chauffeur to take us immediately to Mundelein so that I could bless the cardinal and all the real estate operations, but we only got as far as the Bahai Temple. A workman who was shoveling sand opened the door of the temple and showed us around. He kept telling us that we all worshipped the same God, that all religions were alike in essence. In the little pamphlet which he handed us to read I learned that the Forerunner of the Faith, the Founder of the Faith, and the authorized Interpreter and Exemplar of Baha'u'llah's teaching all suffered persecution and martyrdom for daring to make God's love all-inclusive. It's a queer world, even in this enlightened period of civilization. The Bahai temple has been twenty years building and is not finished yet. The architect was Mr. Bourgeois, believe it or not. The interior of the temple, in its unfinished state, makes you think of a stage setting for *Joan of Arc*. The circular meeting place on the ground floor resembles the hollow of a shell and inspires peace and meditation as few places of worship do.

The movement has already spread over most of the globe, thanks to its persecutors and detractors. There is no color line, as in Christian churches, and one can believe as he pleases. It is for this reason that the Bahai movement is destined to outlast all the other religious organizations on this continent. The Christian Church in all its freakish ramifications and efflorescences is as dead as a doornail; it will pass away utterly when the political and social systems in which it is now embedded collapse. The new religion will be based on deeds, not beliefs. "Religion is not for empty bellies," said Ramakrishna. Religion is always revolutionary, far more revolutionary than bread-and-butter philosophies, The priest is always in league with the devil, just as the political leader always leads to death. People are trying to get together, it seems to me. Their representatives, in every walk of life, keep them apart by breeding hatred and fear. The exceptions are so rare that when they occur the impulse is to set them apart, make supermen of them, or gods, anything but men and women like ourselves. And in removing them thus to the ethereal realms the revolution of love which they came to preach is nipped in the bud. But the good news is always there, just around the corner, chalked up on the wall of a deserted house: GOD IS LOVE! I am sure that when the citizens of Chicago read these lines they will get up en masse and make a pilgrimage to that house. It is easy to find because it stands in the middle of a vacant lot on the South Side. You climb down a manhole in La Salle Street and let yourself drift with the sewer water. You can't miss it because it's written in white chalk in letters ten feet high. All you need to do when you find it is to shake yourself like a sewer-rat and dust yourself off. God will do the rest. . . .

even nice girls

Gael Greene

The name of the game is Cool.

And she *can* be cool, the American coed. Cool in the hipster sense. She can be calmly, casually, matter-of-factly, coolly erotic.

The rules of the game are: there are no rules. But there is a firm understanding: ostentatious display of virginity is strictly uncool. Among the coolest, the diaphragm is a status symbol; as a cool Cornell sophomore remarked with almost angry impatience — "Well really, what does morality have to do with it?"

The voice of the cool coed is speaking out at colleges and universities across the country, sounding the slogans, the boasts, and the doubts of a new sex freedom. Although definitely a minority voice, the cool coed, as champion of the new sex ethic, makes a loud, impressive, and persuasive noise. The more conservative college girl echoes the cool coed's slogans — often in the same hip language — although she would not dream of emulating her sexual behavior.

It is startling to hear the idiom of the junky or the argument of the existentialist coming from a primly dressed Wisconsin University farm girl or in the soft drawl of a Mississippi deb at the University of Maryland. Even if she has yet to pick up the idiom — even if she is too naive to recognize the genesis of the argument, the college girl reflects fragments of the new ethic in what she says about sex.

The fact is morality has a great deal to do with sex on the American campus, but the word "morality" is avoided. Hours are consumed in sober, painfully candid, and sometimes desperate search for answers, *the* answer, for values, for a reasonable code of behavior — over tap-water tea and pretzels in dormitory ironing rooms or a sorority house lounge. But girls do not like to call it a moral dilemma because morality is an absolute, and absolutes are constantly under fire as part of the education process.

Most college girls would consider it sophomoric to judge in terms of Good and Evil what goes on in the cemetery across from the University of Michigan's Stockwell Hall or on a sticky leather sofa in the blackness of a Dartmouth fraternity's TV room.

Sex to these girls is healthy or unhealthy. It is wise or foolish. It is glorious or wasted. It is repressed, childish, neurotic, or mature, meaningful, wholesome. It is "whatever I can get away with and still be a 'nice girl,'" a Swarthmore junior said. "It is whatever I do as long as no one is hurt and I can live with it," a Mt. Holyoke senior said. "It is nobody's business but mine," volunteered a slim 17-year-old Queens College freshman who recently "celebrated my first anniversary of freedom from virginity" on a ski weekend at Stowe "with my deliverer, of course." It is something each girl must decide for herself," suggested a tall, suntanned Stanford University education major who is, she confesses with an apologetic shrug, a virgin but does not feel compromised if she spends weekends with her steady, skiing at Aspen, where "we sleep together, shower together, admire each other, and play wild, mad games."

Virgin and nonvirgin, sexually emancipated and romantically, stubbornly, or fearfully chaste, with few exceptions college girls agree: Sexual behavior is something you have to decide for yourself. Rarely do they condemn another for behavior they might regard as personally unwise; although in certain sexually sophisticated circles a virgin might find herself an object of derision. Discretion is essential to survival on some campuses; candor to the point of sexual boasting is a must on others.

Petting is increasingly widespread, increasingly intimate, involving, according to Temple University sociologist Robert Bell, far more incidence of oral-genital stimulation than most behaviorists would concede. "The meaning of the word virginity has been grossly perverted," a Pembroke junior observed, and her comment was echoed by at least a dozen coeds.

There are no comprehensive, recent statistics on campus premarital intercourse, but recognized authorities in the field—Oregon State University's Lester A. Kirkendal for one — are convinced that it is increasing. Engagement, not marriage, is regarded as license to enjoy complete sexual intimacy by most college girls, and some stretch that license to being pinned, lavaliered, going steady, or — simply — in love. Though college girls invoke the name of love as though it were a magic wand with the power to transform brass into wedding-ring gold, love is but one of the many forces that ultimately pushes — or leads — a girl to the prenuptial bed. They talk about themselves as if they were idealists and romantics with iron wills. But their actions often are those of moths or wind-up dolls.

It is not the drastic revolution wrought by two world wars — female suffrage, the automobile, Freud, and the shedding of Victorian repressions — that are reflected so vividly in the sexual climate of the sixties. It is far subtler, a nuance of evolution in just seven years since I was last on the campus of the University of Michigan.

"Playing house" or "going all the way" (two euphemisms current where girls can't quite get themselves to call it an affair) is no longer universally regarded as cheap, desperate, promiscuous, loose, or "strictly for girls who can't get a man any other way."

Girls who signed out for home Saturday night and went to motels with young men did not advertise it then. And I was rather shocked to learn that some of the most sheltered and coddled offspring of proper bourgeois Baltimore made little or no pretense about where they were going when they left their University of Maryland sorority house with toothbrush and a change of underwear in a shoebox to return the following morning at 11:30 A.M. — motel checkout time.[1] But even the motel-goers maintain an apple-cheeked innocence. "We don't have affairs," a pretty junior corrected me when I used the term. "An affair is something for Liz and Richard Burton. We have relations," she exclaimed. But spending the night in a motel with a young man does not mean "relations" can be taken for granted. "You never know what goes on behind locked doors, do you?" a second junior suggested.

This, then, is the new style in sex ethics. Mama, the Church, Baltimore (and Springfield and Three Rivers), and the Dean of Women may pledge allegiance to the traditional standards of chastity and worship at the altar of purity in soul and reputation, but the accepted, vigorously voiced public moral codes are practically meaningless to young women of today. This does not mean, however, that they are unaware or able to ignore their existence.

"Most of us start out with the basic freshman orientation," a shiny-faced, delicate-featured Radcliffe junior began. "I mean we all get sort of the same 'nice girls don't' routine at home. Well, I for one really believed it. There just wasn't any doubt in my mind that I would be a virgin when I got married. But then I came up here and there they were — all those nice girls, much nicer than I if you talk about family and background — and they were doing it. I felt betrayed. Maybe all I had holding my determination together was just that one idea: 'nice girls don't.' My virginity lasted exactly four months. Not that I gave in without an utterly unsophisticated struggle. But frankly, my heart probably wasn't in protecting it any longer. The truth is, nice girls do."

"Nice girls don't" — "your reputation will be ruined" — "no man will ever marry you" — "pregnancy is unavoidable." These are the threats girls hear from those who urge them to "stay out of trouble." When they discover how little wallop these traditional threats seem to pack, some girls react as though they have indeed been betrayed. Their intelligence has been insulted. In fury at being so unfairly misled, they may seek revenge — a very complicated revenge — in bed. Or they may simply be left with no particular justification for refraining from

1. Restrictions on overnight absences designed to halt the motel traffic were announced by Maryland's Dean of Women, Helen E. Clark, October 31, 1963.

the siren call to sensuous ecstasy or instant intimacy or the bed of ·a particular young man.

"I used to think it would show on your face," said a Marygrove sophomore, "or you could always tell a girl who went to bed with a boy by her mascara or a skintight sweater. That's ridiculous," she said with a giggle, tugging at her own outsize Shetland. And it is *not* the girl in the skintight sweater. It's the president of the snootiest sorority on campus and the frumpy Phi Beta Kappa with the contact lenses. It's the marriage-minded mama's girl and the marriage-panicked maiden who plays little Miss Chastity with dates who might be marital potentials and then sneaks quietly off to a young teaching fellow's apartment Sunday afternoon and begs him to relieve her of her maidenhood.

Hearing what these girls have to say, sitting in on their spirited and challenging after-hours bull sessions, eavesdropping on an after-the-big-weekend-date train and at countless plastic-and-vinyl-and-incandescent-bright student unions, I was struck both by what has not changed at all and how much has happened in the past decade to provide an atmosphere in which sexual freedom — and sexual panic — can flourish.

"Sex," suggests critic and English professor David Boroff, "is the politics of the sixties — the last arena of adventure in the quasi-welfare state in which we now live." Sex, says David Riesman "provides a kind of defense against the threat of total apathy. . . . [The other-directed person] looks to it for reassurance that he is alive." Riesman obviously knows his confused and threatened other-directed American college girl. But then the other-directed college girl often knows her Riesman. His analysis may become her rationalization. "I suppose I slip into bed too easily," said a UCLA coed. "And often with the wrong guy and for the wrong reasons. But most of the time I'm nothing. A cipher. A vegetable. In bed, at least, I'm alive." Is she that perceptive? you wonder. Or is such neat analysis designed to distract you and the girl herself from deep motivations? What came first: Riesman, the bed, or the zero of her ego?

The college girl, it is true, had Riesman a decade ago, and we had witnessed, as Boroff describes it, the sexualization of our culture in our heroes, the ingenuous virility of the late Clark Gable giving way to the inarticulate Brando "whose arrogant sexuality clearly announces his intentions."[2]

2. "Sex: The Quiet Revolution," by David Boroff. *Esquire Magazine,* July, 1962.

But we had not yet witnessed Hollywood's curiously belated coming of age. Three-times married Doris Day was still a virgin. Movie stars married their lovers or at least made a pretense of wholesomely continent courtship if they knew what was good for their box office. A newly grown-up child star did not celebrate the shedding of her husband by coolly and openly voyaging around the world with Warren Beatty. An Elsa Martinelli would not have welcomed an inquiring journalist from *Esquire* into her Manhattan hotel suite to meet her suite-mate lover and hear all about "Accommodation—Italian Style."[3] Elizabeth Taylor Hilton Wilding was still paying lip service to her fan magazine image and it would be two husbands and one Richard Burton later before Max Lerner would be inspired to comment on ". . . the dawning recognition that even a movie goddess has the right to her frailties and pleasures and joys, and that the kind of morality she practices has little to do with the kind of job she does as an actress."[4] "What are you trying to do now?" an interviewer for *Look* magazine asked Miss Taylor and she answered: "I try not to live a lie." It is an answer with a persuasive appeal for the college girl. Idealistic and essentially conservative, the college girl might be appalled by the imperiousness and self-centeredness of the *Cleopatra* affair, but her sympathies are likely to be stirred by that cry against the life of hypocrisy. And she cannot help but notice that, so far at least, as Lerner points out, Elizabeth Taylor seems to be getting away with it.

Sex in the past decade has become more explicit, rawer, as well as more public. We gulp our sex straight. Language that would once have prompted a lady to burst into tears or leave the room now punctuates cocktail-party chatter. Eavesdrop on an after-hours gossip session in a college dorm with your eyes closed and pick up all the old four-letter Anglo-Saxons plus a few you might not yet have heard. You

3. "Accommodation—Italian Style," by Gay Talese. *Esquire Magazine,* February, 1963. Talese opens with a quote from Elsa:

> " 'Willy and I started living together in Tanganyika,' she said.
> " 'No,' Willy corrected. 'St. Tropez.'
> " 'Oh yes,' she said, after a pause, wondering how she could have forgotten. 'St. Tropez.'
> "Elsa Martinelli was sitting next to her lover, Willy Rizzo, the photographer, on a white damask sofa in an elegant hotel overlooking Central Park. It was like so many other hotels that they had chosen since their love began in the spring of 1960; it was a big, expensive, No-Questions-Asked hotel, and its room clerks were among the most sophisticated men in the world. . . ."

4. "Gilded Rebel," by Max Lerner. *The New York Post,* April 20, 1963.

might think you had walked into an army barracks, were it not for the sweet soprano trills and the soft scent of Blue Grass. "There are a certain number of short Anglo-Saxon words for bodily functions that were regarded as a secret language for men," critic Malcolm Cowley testified in a requiem for gentler days at the Post Office Department hearings on *Lady Chatterley's Lover*. ". . . No woman was supposed to know them unless she was an utterly degraded woman . . . [but] there is no more secret language for males. That has been abolished." "Of all the roles imaginable for the Supreme Court of the United States," writes *The New York Times* high-court reporter, Anthony Lewis, "liberating this country from puritanism might seem the least likely. . . . The United States has moved from one of the most timid countries in dealing with sex in the arts to what many believe is now by far the most liberated in the Western world. The nine no-longer-so-old men are responsible."[5]

It has been quite a leap from the morality and romanticism of Hemingway, whose illicit lovers have to be punished by ("It's just a dirty trick") death in the rain, to the matter-of-fact sex of fiction today. A big fat romantic Hemingway-type death would seem almost merciful to contemporary literature's unpunished illicit lovers forced to sprawl about brooding while passion dies of sheer boredom.

Can it be less than a decade since *Marjorie Morningstar* (now regarded by most college girls as "a kind of humorless *Much Ado About Nothing* in modern dress," suggests writer Gloria Steinem)[6] was taken seriously enough to precipitate outbreaks of sexual panic? "I suspect Herman Wouk would be somewhat upset if he realized how many nice middle-class Jewish girls lost their virginity because of him," a self-described "ex-nice" Hunter College graduate told me. "Silly as it sounds, I know for sure at least three girls who gave up the good fight just to prove they weren't Marjories."

There are, of course, legions of diehard Marjories on the campus today, but many of them seem pressured and torn by the challenge of the campus counterpart to Marjorie's younger sister, Merrit, well-stacked heroine of Glendon Swarthout's *Where the Boys Are,* a saga of the adolescent lemmings who descend on Fort Lauderdale for Spring Vacation suntans and sex. "In my opinion," says Merrit, "it's

5. "Sex . . . And The Supreme Court," by Anthony Lewis. *Esquire Magazine,* June, 1963.
6. "The Moral Disarmament of Betty Coed," by Gloria Steinem. *Esquire Magazine,* September, 1962.

ridiculous and picky of society to turn it [virginity] into an *institution*. The whole deal is simply not that *monumental*. And I am not merely a poor loser either. . . . What with pimples and puberty boys have enough to endure without being terrorized about the sanctity of every so-called vestal in his neighborhood nor do I think a girl's misplacing it somewhere as catastrophic as The Decline and Fall of the Roman Empire."

Where do wholesome Middle-Western teenagers like Merrit pick up this brash confidence? From each other, of course. From the "strong youth 'subculture,'" which is confident, vocal, and self-conscious,"[7] spawned by the increasing complexities of contemporary life and alienation within the family. Adolescents don't really speak to adults, don't actually expect to be understood, may even disdain adult approval of their heroes. Adolescence is not envious of adult standing. Adolescence is seen as a golden time of sanity before the inevitable acceptance of adult world hypocrisy. The move is too fast for Holden Caulfield and his admirers.

Life has indeed been sharply accelerated sexually.[8] The drama of gender begins early.[9] Never did it begin earlier than for the child now or soon to be a college girl of the sixties, born in the decade when Middle-Class Mamas, terrorized into raising baby by the book, moved from the rigidity of the Toilet-Training Thirties to the permissiveness, even anarchy, of the forties and fifties. The college girl of today

7. "The Role of the Counselor in Sex Behavior and Standards," by Kate Hevner Mueller. *Journal of the National Association of Women Deans and Counselors,* January, 1963.
8. It has speeded up biologically too. Dr. Thomas E. Cone Jr. of the U.S. Naval Hospital in Bethesda, Md., reported to the recent International Congress on Pediatrics that in 1900, American girls first menstruated at the average age of 14. The average has dropped to 13 — a statistic duly noted by one sanitary-napkin firm that recently featured a pigtailed child in their magazine ads. She might have been 13 — she might have been 10.
9. Sex-directed education, often neglecting allover female potential to concentrate on educating girls for their sexual function — marriage and motherhood — takes over where popularity-panicked parents leave off. Betty Friedan, author of *The Feminine Mystique,* describes a lesson plan for a junior high life adjustment course: "Entitled *The Slick Chick,* it gives functional 'do's and don't's for dating' to girls of 11, 12, 13 — a kind of early or forced recognition of their sexual function. . . . Though many have nothing yet to fill a brassiere, they are told archly not to wear a sweater without one, and to be sure to wear slips so boys can't see through their skirts. It is hardly surprising that by the sophomore year, many bright girls are more than conscious of their sexual function. . . . One cannot help wondering (especially when some of these girls get pregnant as high school sophomores and marry at 15 or 16) if they have not been educated for their sexual function too soon. . . .'"

probably played post office at mixed parties by the age of nine, began dating for the afternoon movies at ten, has her hair done once a week at a neighborhood beauty parlor by twelve, has gone steady at least once by thirteen, suffered from a broken heart or a slight fissure by 13¼.

With a buying power that packs an impressive wallop, the teen-ager is the pet of manufacturers, who woo her with sex and encourage her to spend $25 million a year on deodorants, $20 million on lipstick, $9 million on home permanents. In her 30AA bra and Jackie Kennedy hairdo, she is a living, fire-breathing *femme fatale* at 14. There is no time to be a child. She is quickly an adolescent and a teenager, a strange interim plateau that is fraught with paradox and goes on forever. "In the first decade of life the boy and girl learn that love is good and sex is evil," as Morton Hunt notes in *The Natural History of Love;* "in the second decade that love is still better, while sex has been slightly upgraded to the status of a forbidden fruit; and in the third decade that love is better than ever, while sex has suddenly become normal and healthful and is, in fact, a major means of ex-pressing one's higher sentiments."[10]

While young people cope with this unsatisfactory and bewildering inheritance, time presses from another direction. War. Not a new specter, war has been haunting college students since 1914. Peace marches and bomb-banning demonstrations are not new. But only within the last decade has the total annihilation of the Earth become another dimension of everyday existence. "Today every inhabitant of this planet must contemplate the day when this planet may no longer be habitable," the late President Kennedy said; and in psychiatric sessions as well as school essays, young people reveal how vividly they have indeed contemplated the threat. "They are not primarily afraid of hardships. Rather it is the thought that there may not be continuity and sense in the life that lies ahead."[11] They react "live now." They react "how dare you tell me what to do — you who made the world what it is." They react "I won't think about it." "I woke up one night and I thought, 'I am going to die a virgin,' " a Stanford coed recalled. "I decided it was time to do something about it." "During the Cuban crisis my best friend got on the phone with the boy she'd been dating," a Berkeley junior said. "She told him, 'Listen, I'm ready to get laid.' "

10. N.Y.: Alfred A. Knopf, Inc., 1959.
11. "Children and the Threat of Nuclear War," by Sibylle Escalona. A Child Study Association Publication with the National Institute of Mental Health.

"We were sitting around," a Barnard senior said, "and we were telling each other how if this is really the end of the world coming, what would we do. It was the morning when no one knew what Russia would do about the Cuban blockade. We decided we'd run to the nearest frat house and grab the first available man." "We had just seen 'On the Beach' again," a Hollins senior said, "and I was thinking 'If I'm not married by the time I'm 21, I *will* have an affair.' " "I don't expect to live out the second half of my life," a City College of New York sophomore said. And a pretty, sensitive, not too happily promiscuous Barnard senior, commenting on a plea for chastity by her college's former president, Millicent McIntosh, remarked: "I agree with Mrs. McIntosh that sexual freedom is not easy to handle. She says, 'Wait.' But she's a Quaker, you know, and an optimist. Maybe I could go along with her if I had faith in the sanity of the world. But I don't."

Sex on the campus reflects all the factors contributing to teenage marriage — the search for emotional security, the need for a deep emotional attachment, fear, alienation, ego deficiencies, hedonism, the big sell on togetherness, constant sexual stimulation, love as a panacea, the idea of love as instant medium for gender identification and re-lease from the tensions of home — where parents seem to alternate between overprotectiveness, apology, and unjustified demands. A girl tends to seek a sympathetic, understanding stand-in parent. Her steady becomes, as William Graham Cole suggests, "parent, comfort, con-fessor and arbiter" of sexual codes.[12] The monogamy of most col-legiate lovers is positively tame. Except in the South, stag lines have just about disappeared. Couples become each other's property, sticking together through bliss and boredom in an imitation of married life that often leads to married life[13] (witness the blossoming of campus housing for newlyweds), both with and without benefit of shotgun.

It was one thing to give women the right to vote. It is quite another to make such a noisy fuss about her right to an orgasm. It is a fuss that dates back to the twenties but has taken its time to filter through to the most conservative quarters of the middle class. Colleges had a less complicated task keeping nubile young women out of the pre-nuptial bed in the days when sex was an unpleasant duty, possibly

12. "Early Marriage," by William Graham Cole. *The Nation Magazine,* February 8, 1958.
13. Population Reference Bureau (1961) statistics show that 12 percent or 162,000 college women were married; 77,000 high school girls had husbands.

vile and disgusting, endured for the sake of a husband's animal de-
sires. But the day the word started getting around that sex was the
great ecstasy of woman's existence linked to the edict that it must be
foresworn until marriage, the task became Herculean. "Have you
noticed?" asked a recent graduate of Smith, "how even the sex manu-
als reflect the change. Not so long ago the best seller was *Love
without Fear.* Today it's *Sex without Guilt.* And even the 'guilt' tends
to sound a little old-fashioned."

Is it any wonder that educators look back to the mid-1950's
nostalgically as "the good old days of sexual innocence?" The Kinsey
works themselves took a toll of this innocence. "In the years that
have elapsed since their publication," medical sociologist Dr. Celia S.
Deschin of the Adelphi Graduate School of Social Work, writes,
"Kinsey's findings have become a new kind of social norm. . . . I find
those favoring higher moral standards are often reluctant to express
their opinions too openly — so widespread is the notion that to be
normal is to have a lot of sexual involvements." "Gradually . . . one
after another of the 'old-fashioned' standards have been questioned
and put aside. . . ." Barnard President Millicent McIntosh lamented
in a recent plea for chastity.[14] And it was an ultimatum on the subject, from Vassar's Sarah Gibson Blanding, that became the campus
cause célèbre in spring of 1962. Her highly publicized pronouncement that premarital sex relations constitute "offensive and vulgar
behavior" and her suggestion that Vassarites who disagreed should
resign aroused a storm of outrage on campuses across the nation, not
the mildest of which echoed through the vestal halls of Vassar. "If
Vassar is to become the Poughkeepsie Victorian Seminary for Young
Virgins, then the change of policy had better be made explicit in
admissions catalogues," a cynical Vassarite was quoted. Some equally
cynical Yale lads predicted "a mass exodus from Poughkeepsie of indignant Vassar women wearing their diaphragms as badges of courage." Such an exodus failed to materialize. A survey by the *Vassar
Miscellany News* indicated only two students planned to resign. None
has to date.[15]

14. "Out of a Morals Revolution: A Moral Revolution," by Millicent
    McIntosh. *Glamour Magazine,* January, 1963.
15. The Vassar Questionnaire was answered by 1,040 students and the results
    were printed in the April 11, 1962, issue of the *Vassar Miscellany News:*
    Question 1. Do you agree with the position taken by Miss Blanding in
    her speech Wednesday night?
    52 percent — Yes   40 percent — No   Rest — Undecided
    Question 2. Do you believe that social morals are a personal matter that

How shall the colleges be involved in the debate over sex ethics and sex behavior? "How much authority must still be invoked in order to keep human error at a safe minimum for inexperienced youth? At what age in any one individual's development do we withdraw authority and fear, and allow rational and social sanctions to take over?" Educators were asked these questions and collegiate sex made predictable headlines when the Association of Women Deans and Counselors devoted its entire January, 1963, issue to "Student Sex Standards and Behavior." The gist of its several articles, by some of the most respected authorities in the field: student sex behavior and sex ethics have become national problems, "unacknowledged, unsavory and unsolved"; youth, alienated from adult contact and influence, makes its own sexual decisions; the power of such traditional fear-evoking threats as pregnancy, venereal disease, and community disapproval is decreasing; neither parents nor teachers have been facing the problem with honesty, courage, or adequate insight.

But the point that didn't make headlines was a suggestion many student counselors and advisers dare not utter aloud: that sex on the campus is more an adult problem than it is a youth problem; that, as Lester Kirkendall has stated over and over again in his 30 years of working with youth, young people are not sex obsessed. "They are more moral, more straightforward, more honest than most adults when it comes to thinking about and searching for meaningful answers to the sexual dilemma." Adults, Kirkendall writes, are crippled by fear . . . fear "which pervades our whole society, makes both teachers and administrators evasive and dishonest when issues arise involving sex."

When Vassar's Miss Blanding spoke of the indecency of premarital sex, editors and headline writers spread the word about the "ban against free love" and sober articles appeared applauding the stand

---

should be of concern to the college only when they bring the name of Vassar into public disrepute?

81 percent — Yes   15 percent — No   Rest — Undecided

Question 3. Do you think the purpose of Miss Blanding's speech was to determine your personal moral standards and the moral standards of every Vassar student?

32 percent — Yes   65 percent — No   Rest — Undecided

Question 4. Do you think that the speech reflected a change in the administration's attitude toward its students' moral standards?

29 percent — Yes   62 percent — No   Rest — Undecided

Question 5. Do you take the suggestion of withdrawal for the reasons suggested in the speech seriously?

28 percent — Yes   65 percent — No   Rest — Undecided

against promiscuity. But premarital intercourse is neither free love nor promiscuity.

Cool is rarely as cool as it looks. Young people today are so very vulnerable and alone they could scarcely bear exposure to the scorns of contemporary existence without borrowing the pose of blasé disdain from the Beats. The first beatitude of the cool is simply: no sweat. An Eastern women's college dean, obviously taken in by the pose, is quoted as saying: "It isn't that they're preoccupied with sex. It's that they accept it so easily and then turn to you and say, 'And now what?'" Most of the college girls I interviewed *are* preoccupied with sex. They do care. They do not accept it so easily, they confess privately, as they pretend publicly. They do not all have the courage of their free-love convictions. Even those who embrace the "sweet" life often discover they have more courage than conviction.

The college girl *has* sexual problems: misunderstanding and abuse of sex freedom, guilt and self-recrimination, the burden of constantly reevaluating her own inner convictions to form and reform the sexual code she must author herself, and, I suspect, far more incidence of pregnancy than has yet been documented.

But it is a mistake to lump all premarital sexual acts into such categories as "scandalous," "unsavory" and "disaster." Dr. Walter Stokes, the psychiatrist, told the 34 educators who recently assembled behind closed doors at a Columbia Teachers Conference on sex behavior: "Anything that promotes successful interpersonal relations is moral." Stated more cautiously, this has been Kirkendall's thesis. "Sex that builds and does not hurt is good," an earnest Antioch junior put it. "There is good love and bad love and just because you happen to be married is no guarantee of either," a Wisconsin University sophomore suggested.

Men and women at all levels of society are questioning sexual codes; values are changing. College students are not a separate population; they are a vocal, intelligent, and intellectually curious segment of our society. They have every right to question too.

The dilemma "created by an uneasy equilibrium between two contradictory values," as sociologist Winston Ehrmann has written,[16] has created the unique patterns of American courtship and dating. The conflict between sex as sin, and sex as the ultimate expression of romantic love has led youth, on its own, to "invent" new social de-

16. "The Variety and Meaning of Premarital Heterosexual Experience for the College Student," by Winston W. Ehrmann. *Journal of the National Association of Women Deans and Counselors,* January, 1963.

vices — dating, petting, going steady, and intercourse under an elaborate code of what is considered proper.

How these "inventions" work and how they fail is the subject of this book. Some readers will be shocked, alarmed, and offended by what these college girls had to say and how they said it; but with wisdom, charity, patience, and the courage to rise above one's own personal anxieties, they may grasp an essential message: that the love-making of young people is, as Ehrmann notes, not merely exploitive, animal, selfish, or "a single set of mechanical acts in which young people engage solely to have 'fun.'" It is also affection, chivalry, romantic, idealistic, fulfilling, and "a way of reaching identity and growing up." Educators can have little hope of ever influencing the values on which youth base their codes of sexual behavior without at least this much faith.

notes of a native son

James Baldwin

On the 29th of July, in 1943, my father died. On the same day, a few hours later, his last child was born. Over a month before this, while all our energies were concentrated in waiting for these events, there had been, in Detroit, one of the bloodiest race riots of the century. A few hours after my father's funeral, while he lay in state in the undertaker's chapel, a race riot broke out in Harlem. On the morning of the 3rd of August, we drove my father to the graveyard through a wilderness of smashed plate glass.

The day of my father's funeral had also been my nineteenth birthday. As we drove him to the graveyard, the spoils of injustice, anarchy, discontent, and hatred were all around us. It seemed to me that God himself had devised, to mark my father's end, the most sustained and brutally dissonant of codas. And it seemed to me, too, that the violence which rose all about us as my father left the world had been devised as a corrective for the pride of his eldest son. I had declined to

From *Notes of a Native Son* by James Baldwin. Reprinted by permission of the Beacon Press, copyright 1955 by James Baldwin.

believe in that apocalypse which had been central to my father's vision; very well, life seemed to be saying, here is something that will certainly pass for an apocalypse until the real thing comes along. I had inclined to be contemptuous of my father for the conditions of his life, for the conditions of our lives. When his life had ended I began to wonder about that life and also, in a new way, to be apprehensive about my own.

I had not known my father very well. We had got on badly, partly because we shared, in our different fashions, the vice of stubborn pride. When he was dead I realized that I had hardly ever spoken to him. When he had been dead a long time I began to wish I had. It seems to be typical of life in America where opportunities, real and fancied, are thicker than anywhere else on the globe, that the second generation has no time to talk to the first. No one, including my father, seems to have known exactly how old he was, but his mother had been born during slavery. He was of the first generation of free men. He, along with thousands of other Negroes, came North after 1919 and I was part of that generation which had never seen the landscape of what Negroes sometimes call the Old Country.

He had been born in New Orleans and had been a quite young man there during the time that Louis Armstrong, a boy, was running errands for the dives and honky-tonks of what was always presented to me as one of the most wicked of cities — to this day, whenever I think of New Orleans, I also helplessly think of Sodom and Gomorrah. My father never mentioned Louis Armstrong, except to forbid us to play his records; but there was a picture of him on our wall for a long time. One of my father's strong-willed female relatives had placed it there and forbade my father to take it down. He never did, but he eventually maneuvered her out of the house and when, some years later, she was in trouble and near death, he refused to do anything to help her.

He was, I think, very handsome. I gather this from photographs and from my own memories of him, dressed in his Sunday best and on his way to preach a sermon somewhere, when I was little. Handsome, proud, and ingrown, "like a toe-nail," somebody said. But he looked to me, as I grew older, like pictures I had seen of African tribal chieftains: he really should have been naked, with war-paint on and barbaric mementos, standing among spears. He could be chilling in the pulpit and indescribably cruel in his personal life and he was certainly the most bitter man I have ever met; yet it must be said that there was something else in him, buried in him, which lent him his tremendous power and, even, a rather crushing charm. It had something to do with his blackness, I think — he was very black — with his blackness and his beauty, and with the fact that he knew that he was black but did not know that he was beautiful. He claimed to be proud of his blackness but it had also been the cause of much humiliation and it had fixed bleak boundaries to his life. He was not a young man when we were growing up and he had already suffered many kinds of ruin; in his outrageously demanding and protective way he loved his children, who were black like him and menaced, like him; and all these things sometimes showed in his face when he tried, never to my knowledge with any success, to establish contact with any of us. When he took one of his children on his knee to play, the child always became fretful and began to cry; when he tried to help one of us with our homework the absolutely unabating tension which emanated from him caused our minds and our tongues to become paralyzed, so that he, scarcely knowing why flew into a rage and the child, not knowing why, was punished. If it ever entered his head to bring a surprise home for his children, it was, almost unfailingly, the wrong surprise and even the big watermelons he often brought home on his back in the summertime led to the most appalling scenes. I do not remember in all those years, that one of his children was ever glad to see him come home. From what I was able to gather of his early life, it seemed that this inability to establish contact with other people had always marked him and had been one of the things which had driven him out of New Orleans. There was something in him therefore, groping and tentative, which was never expressed and which was buried with him. One saw it most clearly when he was facing new people and hoping to impress them. But he never did, not for long. We went from church to smaller and more improbable church, he found himself in less and less demand as a minister, and by the time he died none of his friends had come to see him for a long time. He had lived and died in an intolerable bitterness of spirit and it frightened me, as we drove him to the graveyard through those unquiet, ruined streets, to see how powerful and overflowing this bitterness could be and to realize that this bitterness now was mine.

When he died I had been away from home for a little over a year. In that year I had had time to become aware of the meaning of all my father's bitter warnings, had discovered the secret of his proudly pursed lips and rigid carriage: I had discovered the weight of white people in the world. I saw that this had been for my ancestors and now would be for me an awful thing to live with and that the bitterness which had helped to kill my father could also kill me.

He had been ill a long time — in the mind, as we now realized, reliving instances of his fantastic intransigence in the new light of his affliction and endeavoring to feel a sorrow for him which never, quite, came true. We had not known that he was being eaten up by paranoia, and the discovery that his cruelty, to our bodies and our minds, had been one of the symptoms of his illness was not, then, enough to enable us to forgive him. The younger children felt, quite simply, relief that he would not be coming home anymore. My mother's observation that it was he, after all, who had kept them alive all these years meant nothing because the problems of keeping children alive are not real for children. The older children felt, with my father gone, that they could invite their friends to the house without fear that their friends would be insulted or, as had sometimes happened with me, being told that their friends were in league with the devil and intended to rob our family of everything we owned. (I didn't fail to wonder, and it made me hate him, what on earth we owned that anybody else would want.)

His illness was beyond all hope of healing before anyone realized that he was ill. He had always been so strange and had lived, like a prophet, in such unimaginably close communion with the Lord that his long silences which were punctuated by moans and hallelujahs and snatches of old songs while he sat at the living-room window never seemed odd to us. It was not until he refused to eat because, he said, his family was trying to poison him that my mother was forced to accept as a fact what had, until then, been only an unwilling suspicion. When he was committed, it was discovered that he had tuberculosis and, as it turned out, the disease of his mind allowed the disease of his body to destroy him. For the doctors could not force him to eat, either, and, though he was fed intravenously, it was clear from the beginning that there was no hope for him.

In my mind's eye I could see him, sitting at the window, locked up in his terrors; hating and fearing every living soul including his children who had betrayed him, too, by reaching towards the world which had despised him. There were nine of us. I began to wonder what it could have felt like for such a man to have had nine children whom he could barely feed. He used to make little jokes about our poverty, which never, of course, seemed very funny to us; they could not have seemed very funny to him, either, or else our all too feeble response to them would never have caused such rages. He spent great energy and achieved, to our chagrin, no small amount of success in keeping us away from the people who surrounded us, people who had all-night rent parties to which we listened when we should have been sleeping, people who cursed and drank and flashed razor blades on Lenox Avenue. He could not understand why, if they had so much energy to spare, they could not use it to make their lives better. He treated almost everybody on our block with a most uncharitable asperity and neither they, nor of course, their children were slow to reciprocate.

The only white people who came to our house were welfare workers and bill collectors. It was almost always my mother who dealt with them, for my father's temper, which was at the mercy of his pride, was never to be trusted. It was clear that he felt their very presence in his home to be a violation: this was conveyed by his carriage almost ludicrously stiff, and by his voice, harsh and vindictively polite. When I was around nine or ten I wrote a play which was directed by a young, white schoolteacher, a woman, who then took an interest in me, and gave me books to read and, in order to corroborate my theatrical bent, decided to take me to see what she somewhat tactlessly referred to as "real" plays. Theatergoing was forbidden in our house, but, with the really cruel intuitiveness of a child, I suspected that the color of this woman's skin would carry the day for me. When, at school, she suggested taking me to the theater, I did not, as I might have done if she had been a Negro, find a way of discouraging her, but agreed that she should pick me up at my house one evening. I then, very cleverly, left all the rest to my mother, who suggested to my father, as I knew she would, that it would not be very nice to let such a kind woman make the trip for nothing. Also, since it was a schoolteacher, I imagine that my mother countered the idea of sin with the idea of "education," which word, even with my father, carried a kind of bitter weight.

Before the teacher came my father took me aside to ask *why* she was coming, what *interest* she could possibly have in our house, in a boy like me. I said I didn't know but I, too, suggested that it had something to do with education. And I understood that my father was waiting for me to say something — I didn't quite know what; perhaps that I wanted his protection against this teacher and her "education." I said none of these things and the teacher came and we went out. It was clear, during the brief interview in our living room, that my father was agreeing very much against his will and that he would have refused permission if he had dared. The fact that he did not dare caused me to despise him: I had no way of knowing that he was facing in that living room a wholly unprecedented and frightening situation.

Later, when my father had been laid off from his job, this woman became very important to us. She was really a very sweet and generous woman and went to a great deal of trouble to be of help to us, particularly during one awful winter. My mother called her by the highest name she knew: she said she was a "christian." My father could scarcely disagree but during the four or five years of our relatively close association he never trusted her and was always trying to surprise in her open, Midwestern face the genuine, cunningly hidden, and hideous motivation. In later years, particularly when it began to be clear that this "education" of mine was going to lead me to perdition, he became more explicit and warned me that my white friends in high school were not really my friends and that I would see, when I was older, how white people would do anything to keep a Negro down. Some of them could be nice, he admitted, but none of them were to be trusted and most of them were not even nice. The best thing was to have as little to do with them as possible. I did not feel this way and I was certain, in my innocence, that I never would.

But the year which preceded my father's death had made a great change in my life. I had been living in New Jersey, working in defense plants, working and living among southerners, white and black. I knew about the south, of course, and about how southerners treated Negroes and how they expected them to behave, but it had never entered my mind that anyone would look at me and expect *me* to behave that way. I learned in New Jersey that to be a Negro meant, precisely, that one was never looked at but was simply at the mercy of the reflexes the color of one's skin caused in other people. I acted in New Jersey as I had always acted, that is as though I thought a great deal of myself — I had to *act* that way — with results that were, simply, unbelievable. I had scarcely arrived before I had earned the enmity, which was extraordinarily ingenious, of all my superiors and nearly all my co-workers. In the beginning, to make matters worse, I simply did not know what was happening. I did not know what I had done, and I shortly began to wonder what *anyone* could possibly do, to bring about such unanimous, active, and unbearably vocal hostility. I knew about jim-crow but I had never experienced it. I went to the same self-service restaurant three times and stood with all the Princeton boys before the counter, waiting for a hamburger and coffee; it was always an extraordinarily long time before anything was set before me; but it was not until the fourth visit that I learned that, in fact, nothing had ever been set before me: I had simply picked something up. Negroes were not served there, I was told, and they had been waiting for me to realize that I was always the only Negro present. Once I was told this, I determined to go there all the time. But now they were ready for me and, though some dreadful scenes were subsequently enacted in that restaurant, I never ate there again.

It was the same story all over New Jersey, in bars, bowling alleys, diners, places to live. I was always being forced to leave, silently, or with mutual imprecations. I very shortly became notorious and children giggled behind me when I passed and their elders whispered or shouted — they really believed that I was mad. And it did begin to work on my mind, of course; I began to be afraid to go anywhere and to compensate for this I went places to which I really should not have gone and where, God knows, I had no desire to be. My reputation in town naturally enhanced my reputation at work and my working day became one long series of acrobatics designed to keep me out of trouble. I cannot say that these acrobatics succeeded. It began to seem that the machinery of the organization I worked for was turning over, day and night, with but one aim: to eject me. I was fired once, and contrived, with the aid of a friend from New York, to get back on the payroll; was fired again, and bounced back again. It took a while to fire me for the third time, but the third time took. There were no loopholes anywhere. There was not even any way of getting back inside the gates.

That year in New Jersey lives in my mind as though it were the year during which, having an unsuspected predilection for it, I first contracted some dread, chronic disease, the unfailing symptom of which is a kind of blind fever, a pounding in the skull and fire in the bowels. Once this disease is contracted, one can never be really care-free again, for the fever, without an instant's warning, can recur at any moment. It can wreck more important things than race relations. There is not a Negro alive who does not have this rage in his blood — one has the choice, merely, of living with it consciously or sur-rendering to it. As for me, this fever has recurred in me, and does, and will until the day I die.

My last night in New Jersey, a white friend from New York took me to the nearest big town, Trenton, to go to the movies and have a few drinks. As it turned out, he also saved me from, at the very least, a violent whipping. Almost every detail of that night stands out very clearly in my memory. I even remember the name of the movie we saw because its title impressed me as being so patly ironical. It was a movie about the German occupation of France, starring Maureen O'Hara and Charles Laughton and called *This Land Is Mine*. I remember the name of the diner we walked into when the movie ended: it was the "American Diner." When we walked in the counterman asked what we wanted and I remember answering with the casual sharpness which had become my habit: "We want a hamburger and a cup of coffee, what do you think we want?" I do not know why, after a year of such rebuffs, I so completely failed to anticipate his answer, which was, of course, "We don't serve Negroes here." This reply failed to discompose me, at least for the moment. I made some sardonic comment about the name of the diner and we walked out into the streets.

This was the time of what was called the "brown-out," when the lights in all American cities were very dim. When we re-entered the streets something happened to me which had the force of an optical illusion, or a nightmare. The streets were very crowded and I was facing north. People were moving in every direction but it seemed to me, in that instant, that all of the people I could see, and many more than that, were moving toward me, against me, and that everyone was white. I remember how their faces gleamed. And I felt, like a physical sensation, a *click* at the nape of my neck as though some interior string connecting my head to my body had been cut. I began to walk. I heard my friend call after me, but I ignored him. Heaven only knows what was going on in his mind, but he had the good sense not to touch me — I don't know what would have happened if he had — and to keep me in sight. I don't know what was going on in my mind, either; I certainly had no conscious plan. I wanted to do something to crush these white faces, which were crushing me. I walked for perhaps a block or two until I came to an enormous, glittering, and fashionable restaurant in which I knew not even the intercession of the Virgin would cause me to be served. I pushed through the doors and took the first vacant seat I saw, at a table for two, and waited.

I do not know how long I waited and I rather wonder, until today, what I could possibly have looked like. Whatever I looked like, I frightened the waitress who shortly appeared, and the moment she appeared all of my fury flowed towards her. I hated her for her white face, and for her great, astounded, frightened eyes. I felt that if

she found a black man so frightening I would make her fright worth-
while.

She did not ask me what I wanted, but repeated, as though she had
learned it somewhere, "We don't serve Negroes here." She did not
say it with the blunt, derisive hostility to which I had grown so accustomed, but, rather, with a note of apology in her voice, and fear. This
made me colder and more murderous than ever. I felt I had to do
something with my hands. I wanted her to come close enough for me
to get her neck between my hands.

So I pretended not to have understood her, hoping to draw her
closer. And she did step a very short step closer, with her pencil
poised incongruously over her pad, and repeated the formula: ". . .
don't serve Negroes here."

Somehow, with the repetition of that phrase, which was already
ringing in my head like a thousand bells of a nightmare, I realized
that she would never come any closer and that I would have to strike
from a distance. There was nothing on the table but an ordinary
watermug half full of water, and I picked this up and hurled it with
all my strength at her. She ducked and it missed her and shattered
against the mirror behind the bar. And, with that sound, my frozen
blood abruptly thawed, I returned from wherever I had been, I *saw,*
for the first time, the restaurant, the people with their mouths open,
already, as it seemed to me, rising as one man, and I realized what I
had done, and where I was, and I was frightened. I rose and began
running for the door. A round, potbellied man grabbed me by the
nape of the neck just as I reached the doors and began to beat me
about the face. I kicked him and got loose and ran into the streets.
My friend whispered, "*Run!*" and I ran.

My friend stayed outside the restaurant long enough to misdirect
my pursuers and the police, who arrived, he told me, at once. I do
not know what I said to him when he came to my room that night.
I could not have said much. I felt, in the oddest, most awful way,
that I had somehow betrayed him. I lived it over and over and over
again, the way one relives an automobile accident after it has happened and one finds oneself alone and safe. I could not get over two
facts, both equally difficult for the imagination to grasp, and one was
that I could have been murdered. But the other was that I had been
ready to commit murder. I saw nothing very clearly but I did see
this: that my life, my *real* life, was in danger, and not from anything
other people might do but from the hatred I carried in my own heart.

2

I had returned home around the second week in June — in great haste because it seemed that my father's death and my mother's confinement were both but a matter of hours. In the case of my mother, it soon became clear that she had simply made a miscalculation. This had always been her tendency and I don't believe that a single one of us arrived in the world, or has since arrived anywhere else, on time. But none of us dawdled so intolerably about the business of being born as did my baby sister. We sometimes amused ourselves, during those endless, stifling weeks, by picturing the baby sitting within in the safe, warm dark, bitterly regretting the necessity of becoming a part of our chaos and stubbornly putting it off as long as possible. I understood her perfectly and congratulated her on showing such good sense so soon. Death, however, sat as purposefully at my father's bedside as life stirred within my mother's womb and it was harder to understand why he so lingered in that long shadow. It seemed that he had bent, and for a long time, too, all of his energies towards dying. Now death was ready for him but my father held back.

All of Harlem, indeed, seemed to be infected by waiting. I had never before known it to be so violently still. Racial tensions throughout this country were exacerbated during the early years of the war, partly because the labor market brought together hundreds of thousands of ill-prepared people and partly because Negro soldiers, regardless of where they were born, received their military training in the south. What happened in defense plants and army camps had repercussions, naturally, in every Negro ghetto. The situation in Harlem had grown bad enough for clergymen, policemen, educators, politicians, and social workers to assert in one breath that there was no "crime wave" and to offer, in the very next breath, suggestions as to how to combat it. These suggestions always seemed to involve playgrounds, despite the fact that racial skirmishes were occurring in the playgrounds, too. Playground or not, crime wave or not, the Harlem police force had been augmented in March, and the unrest grew — perhaps, in fact, partly as a result of the ghetto's hatred of policemen. Perhaps the most revealing news item, out of the steady parade of reports of muggings, stabbings, shootings, assaults, gang wars, and accusations of police brutailty, is the item concerning six Negro girls who set upon a white girl in the subway because, as they all too accurately put it, she was stepping on their toes. Indeed she was, all over the nation.

I had never before been so aware of policemen, on foot, on horseback, on corners, everywhere, always two by two. Nor had I ever been so aware of small knots of people. They were on stoops and on corners and in doorways, and what was striking about them, I think, was that they did not seem to be talking. Never, when I passed these groups, did the usual sound of a curse or a laugh ring out and neither did there seem to be any hum of gossip. There was certainly, on the other hand, occurring between them communication extraordinarily intense. Another thing that was striking was the unexpected diversity of the people who made up these groups. Usually, for example, one would see a group of sharpies standing on the street corner, jiving the passing chicks; or a group of older men, usually, for some reason, in the vicinity of a barber shop, discussing baseball scores, or the numbers, or making rather chilling observations about women they had known. Women, in a general way, tended to be seen less often together — unless they were church women, or very young girls, or prostitutes met together for an unprofessional instant. But that summer I saw the strangest combinations: large, respectable, churchly matrons standing on the stoops or the corners with their hair tied up, together with a girl in sleazy satin whose face bore the marks of gin and the razor, or heavyset, abrupt, no-nonsense older men, in company with the most disreputable and fanatical "race" men, or these same "race" men with the sharpies, or these sharpies with the churchly women. Seventh Day Adventists and Methodists and Spiritualists seemed to be hobnobbing with Holyrollers and they were all, alike, entangled with the most flagrant disbelievers; something heavy in their stance seemed to indicate that they had all, incredibly, seen a common vision, and on each face there seemed to be the same strange, bitter shadow.

The churchly women and the matter-of-fact, no-nonsense men had children in the Army. The sleazy girls they talked to had lovers there, the sharpies and the "race" men had friends and brothers there. It would have demanded an unquestioning patriotism, happily as uncommon in this country as it is undesirable, for these people not to have been disturbed by the bitter letters they received, by the newspaper stories they read, not to have been enraged by the posters, then to be found all over New York, which described the Japanese as "yellow-bellied Japs." It was only the "race" men, to be sure, who spoke ceaselessly of being revenged — how this vengeance was to be

exacted was not clear — for the indignities and dangers suffered by
Negro boys in uniform; but everybody felt a directionless, hopeless
bitterness, as well as that panic which can scarcely be suppressed when
one knows that a human being one loves is beyond one's reach, and
in danger. This helplessness and this gnawing uneasiness does something, at length, to even the toughest mind. Perhaps the best way to
sum all this up is to say that the people I knew felt, mainly, a peculiar
kind of relief when they knew that their boys were being shipped out
of the south, to do battle overseas. It was, perhaps, like feeling that
the most dangerous part of a dangerous journey had been passed and
that now, even if death should come, it would come with honor and
without the complicity of their countrymen. Such a death would be,
in short, a fact with which one could hope to live.

It was on the 28th of July, which I believe was a Wednesday, that
I visited my father for the first time during his illness and for the
last time in his life. The moment I saw him I knew why I had put
off this visit so long. I had told my mother that I did not want to see
him because I hated him. But this was not true. It was only that I
had hated him and I wanted to hold on to this hatred. I did not want
to look on him as a ruin: it was not a ruin I had hated. I imagine
that one of the reasons people cling to their hates so stubbornly is
because they sense, once hate is gone, that they will be forced to deal
with pain.

We traveled out to him, his older sister and myself, to what seemed
to be the very end of a very Long Island. It was hot and dusty and
we wrangled, my aunt and I, all the way out, over the fact that I had
recently begun to smoke and, as she said, to give myself airs. But I
knew that she wrangled with me because she could not bear to face
the fact of her brother's dying. Neither could I endure the reality of
her despair, her unstated bafflement as to what had happened to her
brother's life, and her own. So we wrangled and I smoked and from
time to time she fell into a heavy reverie. Covertly, I watched her
face, which was the face of an old woman; it had fallen in, the eyes
were sunken and lightless; soon she would be dying, too.

In my childhood — it had not been so long ago — I had thought her
beautiful. She had been quick-witted and quick-moving and very
generous with all the children and each of her visits had been an
event. At one time one of my brothers and myself had thought of
running away to live with her. Now she could no longer produce out
of her handbag some unexpected and yet familiar delight. She made
me feel pity and revulsion and fear. It was awful to realize that she

no longer caused me to feel affection. The closer we came to the hospital the more querulous she became and at the same time, naturally, grew more dependent on me. Between pity and guilt and fear I began to feel that there was another me trapped in my skull like a jack-in-the-box who might escape my control at any moment and fill the air with screaming.

She began to cry the moment we entered the room and she saw him lying there, all shriveled and still, like a little black monkey. The great, gleaming apparatus which fed him and would have compelled him to be still even if he had been able to move brought to mind, not beneficence, but torture; the tubes entering his arm made me think of pictures I had seen when a child, of Gulliver, tied down by the pygmies on that island. My aunt wept and wept, there was a whistling sound in my father's throat; nothing was said; he could not speak. I wanted to take his hand, to say something. But I do not know what I could have said, even if he could have heard me. He was not really in that room with us, he had at last really embarked on his journey; and though my aunt told me that he said he was going to meet Jesus, I did not hear anything except that whistling in his throat. The doctor came back and we left, into that unbearable train again, and home. In the morning came the telegram saying that he was dead. Then the house was suddenly full of relatives, friends, hysteria, and confusion and I quickly left my mother and the children to the care of those impressive women who, in Negro communities at least, automatically appear at times of bereavement armed with lotions, proverbs, and patience, and an ability to cook. I went downtown. By the time I returned, later the same day, my mother had been carried to the hospital and the baby had been born.

3

For my father's funeral I had nothing black to wear and this posed a nagging problem all day long. It was one of those problems, simple, or impossible of solution, to which the mind insanely clings in order to avoid the mind's real trouble. I spent most of that day at the downtown apartment of a girl I knew, celebrating my birthday with whiskey and wondering what to wear that night. When planning a birthday celebration one naturally does not expect that it will be up against competition from a funeral and this girl had anticipated taking me out that night, for a big dinner and a night club afterwards. Sometimes during the course of that long day we decided that we would go out anyway, when my father's funeral service was over. I imagine *I* decided it, since, as the funeral hour approached, it became clearer and clearer to me that I would not know what to do with myself when it was over. The girl, stifling her very lively concern as to the possible effects of the whiskey on one of my father's chief mourners, concentrated on being conciliatory and practically helpful. She found a black shirt for me somewhere and ironed it and, dressed in the darkest pants and jacket I owned, and slightly drunk, I made my way to my father's funeral.

The chapel was full, but not packed, and very quiet. There were, mainly, my father's relatives, and his children, and here and there I saw faces I had not seen since childhood, the faces of my father's one-time friends. They were very dark and solemn now, seeming somehow to suggest that they had known all along that something like this would happen. Chief among the mourners was my aunt, who had quarreled with my father all his life; by which I do not mean to suggest that her mourning was insincere or that she had not loved him. I suppose that she was one of the few people in the world who had, and their incessant quarreling proved precisely the strength of the tie that bound them. The only other person in the world, as far as I knew, whose relationship to my father rivaled my aunt's in depth was my mother, who was not there.

It seemed to me, of course, that it was a very long funeral. But it was, if anything, a rather shorter funeral than most, nor, since there were no overwhelming, uncontrollable expressions of grief, could it be called — if I dare use the word — successful. The minister who preached my father's funeral sermon was one of the few my father had still been seeing as he neared his end. He presented to us in his sermon a man whom none of us had ever seen — a man thoughtful, patient, and forbearing, a Christian inspiration to all who knew him, and a model for his children. And no doubt the children, in their disturbed and guilty state, were almost ready to believe this; he had been remote enough to be anything and, anyway, the shock of the incontrovertible, that it was really our father lying up there in that casket, prepared the mind for anything. His sister moaned and this grief-stricken moaning was taken as corroboration. The other faces held a dark, non-committal thoughtfulness. This was not the man they had known, but they had scarcely expected to be confronted with *him;* this was, in a sense deeper than questions of fact, the man they had not known, and the man they had not known may have been the real one. The real man, whoever he had been, had suffered and now he was dead: this was all that was sure and all that mattered now. Every man in the chapel hoped that when his hour came he, too, would be eulogized, which is to say forgiven, and that all of his lapses, greeds, errors, and strayings from the truth would be invested with coherence and looked upon with charity. This was perhaps the last thing human beings could give each other and it was what they demanded, after all, of the Lord. Only the Lord saw the midnight tears, only He was present when one of His children, moaning and wringing hands, paced up and down the room. When one slapped one's child in anger the recoil in the heart reverberated through heaven and became part of the pain of the universe. And when the children were hungry and sullen and distrustful and one watched them, daily, growing wilder, and further away, and running headlong into danger, it was the Lord who knew what the charged heart endured as the strap was laid to the backside; the Lord alone who knew what one *would* have said if one had had, like the Lord, the gift of the living word. It was the Lord who knew of the impossibility every parent in that room faced: how to prepare the child for the day when the child would be despised and how to *create* in the child — by what means? — a stronger antidote to this poison than one had found for oneself. The avenues, side streets, bars, billiard halls, hospitals, police stations, and even the playgrounds of Harlem — not to mention the houses of correction, the jails, and the morgue — testified to the potency of the poison while remaining silent as to the efficacy of whatever antidote, irresistibly raising the question of whether or not such an antidote existed; raising, which was worse, the question of whether or not an antidote was desirable; perhaps poison should be fought with poison. With these several schisms in the mind and with more terrors in the heart than could be named, it was better not to judge the man who had gone down under an impossible burden. It was better to remember: *Thou knowest this man's fall; but thou knowest not his wrassling.*

While the preacher talked and I watched the children — years of changing their diapers, scrubbing them, slapping them, taking them to school, and scolding them had had the perhaps inevitable result of making me love them, though I am not sure I knew this then — my mind was busily breaking out with a rash of disconnected impressions. Snatches of popular songs, indecent jokes, bits of books I had read, movie sequences, face, voices, political issues — I thought I was going mad; all these impressions suspended, as it were, in the solution of the faint nausea produced in me by the heat and liquor. For a moment

I had the impression that my alcoholic breath, inefficiently disguised with chewing gum, filled the entire chapel. Then someone began singing one of my father's favorite songs and, abruptly, I was with him, sitting on his knee, in the hot, enormous, crowded church which was the first church we attended. It was the Abyssinia Baptist Church on 138th Street. We had not gone there long. With this image, a host of others came. I had forgotten, in the rage of my growing up, how proud my father had been of me when I was little. Apparently, I had had a voice and my father had liked to show me off before the members of the church. I had forgotten what he had looked like when he was pleased but now I remembered that he had always been grinning with pleasure when my solos ended. I even remembered certain expressions on his face when he teased my mother — had he loved her? I would never know. And when had it all begun to change? For now it seemed that he had not always been cruel. I remembered being taken for a haircut and scraping my knee on the footrest of the barber's chair and I remembered my father's face as he soothed my crying and applied the stinging iodine. Then I remembered our fights, fights which had been of the worst possible kind because my technique had been silence.

I remembered the one time in all our life together when we had really spoken to each other.

It was on a Sunday and it must have been shortly before I left home. We were walking, just the two of us, in our usual silence, to or from church. I was in high school and had been doing a lot of writing and I was, at about this time, the editor of the high school magazine. But I had also been a Young Minister and had been preaching from the pulpit. Lately, I had been taking fewer engagements and preached as rarely as possible. It was said in the church, quite truthfully, that I was "cooling off."

My father asked me abruptly, "You'd rather write than preach, wouldn't you?"

I was astonished at his question — because it was a real question. I answered, "Yes."

That was all we said. It was awful to remember that that was all we had *ever* said.

The casket now was opened and the mourners were being led up the aisle to look for the last time on the deceased. The assumption was that the family was too overcome with grief to be allowed to make this journey alone and I watched while my aunt was led to the casket and, muffled in black, and shaking, led back to her seat. I disapproved of forcing the children to look on their dead father, considering that the shock of his death, or, more truthfully, the shock of death as a reality, was already a little more than a child could bear, but my judgment in this matter had been overruled and there they were, bewildered and frightened and very small, being led, one by one, to the casket. But there is also something very gallant about children at such moments. It has something to do with their silence and gravity and with the fact that one cannot help them. Their legs, somehow, seem *exposed,* so that it is at once incredible and terribly clear that their legs are all they have to hold them up.

I had not wanted to go to the casket myself and I certainly had not wished to be led there, but there was no way of avoiding either of these forms. One of the deacons led me up and I looked on my father's face. I cannot say that it looked like him at all. His blackness had been equivocated by powder and there was no suggestion in that casket of what his power had or could have been. He was simply an old man dead, and it was hard to believe that he had ever given anyone either joy or pain. Yet, his life filled that room. Further up the avenue his wife was holding his newborn child. Life and death so close together, and love and hatred, and right and wrong, said something to me which I did not want to hear concerning man, concerning the life of man.

After the funeral, while I was downtown desperately celebrating my birthday, a Negro soldier, in the lobby of the Hotel Braddock, got into a fight with a white policeman over a Negro girl. Negro girls, white policemen, in or out of uniform, and Negro males — in or out of uniform — were part of the furniture of the lobby of the Hotel Braddock and this was certainly not the first time such an incident had occurred. It was destined, however, to receive unprecedented publicity, for the fight between the policeman and the soldier ended with the shooting of the soldier. Rumor, flowing immediately to the streets outside, stated that the soldier had been shot in the back, an instantaneous and revealing invention, and that the soldier had died protecting a Negro woman. The facts were somewhat different — for example, the soldier had not been shot in the back, and was not dead, and the girl seems to have been as dubious a symbol of womanhood as her white counterpart in Georgia usually is, but no one was interested in the facts. They preferred the invention because this invention expressed and corroborated their hates and fears so perfectly. It is just as well to remember that people are always doing this. Perhaps many of those legends, including Christianity, to which the world clings began their conquest of the world with just some such concerted surrender to distortion. The effect, in Harlem, of this particular legend was like the effect of a lit match in a tin of gasoline. The mob gathered before the doors of the Hotel Braddock simply began to swell and to spread in every direction, and Harlem exploded.

The mob did not cross the ghetto lines. It would have been easy, for example, to have gone over Morningside Park on the west side or to have crossed the Grand Central railroad tracks at 125th Street on the east side, to wreak havoc in white neighborhoods. The mob seems to have been mainly interested in something more potent and real than the white face, that is, in white power, and the principal damage done during the riot of the summer of 1943 was to white business establishments in Harlem. It might have been a far bloodier story, of course, if, at the hour the riot began, these establishments had still been open. From the Hotel Braddock the mob fanned out, east and west along 125th Street, and for the entire length of Lenox, Seventh, and Eighth avenues. Along each of these avenues, and along each major side street — 116th, 125th, 135th, and so on — bars, stores, pawnshops, restaurants, even little luncheonettes had been smashed open and entered and looted — looted, it might be added, with more haste than efficiency. The shelves really looked as though a bomb had struck them. Cans of beans and soup and dog food, along with toilet paper, corn flakes, sardines, and milk tumbled every which way, and abandoned cash registers and cases of beer leaned crazily out of the splintered windows and were strewn along the avenues. Sheets, blankets, and clothing of every description formed a kind of path, as though people had dropped them while running. I truly had not realized that Harlem *had* so many stores until I saw them all smashed open; the first time the word *wealth* ever entered my mind in relation to Harlem was when I saw it scattered in the streets. But one's first, incongruous impression of plenty was countered immediately by an impression of waste. None of this was doing anybody any good. It would have been better to have left the plate glass as it had been and the goods lying in the stores.

It would have been better, but it would also have been intolerable, for Harlem had needed something to smash. To smash something is the ghetto's chronic need. Most of the time it is the members of the ghetto who smash each other, and themselves. But as long as the ghetto walls are standing there will always come a moment when these outlets do not work. That summer, for example, it was not enough to get into a fight on Lenox Avenue, or curse out one's cronies in the barber shops. If ever, indeed, the violence which fills Harlem's churches, pool halls, and bars erupts outward in a more direct fashion, Harlem and its citizens are likely to vanish in an apocalyptic flood. That this is not likely to happen is due to a great many reasons, most hidden and powerful among them the Negro's real relation to the white American. This relation prohibits, simply, anything as uncomplicated and satisfactory as pure hatred. In order really to hate white people, one has to blot so much out of the mind — and the heart — that this hatred itself becomes an exhausting and self-destructive pose. But this does not mean, on the other hand, that love comes easily: the white world is too powerful, too complacent, too ready with gratuitous humiliation, and, above all, too ignorant and too innocent for that. One is absolutely forced to make perpetual qualifications and one's own reactions are always canceling each other out. It is this, really, which has driven so many people mad, both white and black. One is always in the position of having to decide between amputation and gangrene. Amputation is swift but time may prove that the amputation was not necessary — or one may delay the amputation too long. Gangrene is slow, but it is impossible to be sure that one is reading one's symptoms right. The idea of going through life as a cripple is more than one can bear, and equally unbearable is the risk of swelling up slowly, in agony, with poison. And the trouble, finally, is that the risks are real even if the choices do not exist.

"But as for me and my house," my father had said, "we will serve the Lord." I wondered, as we drove him to his resting place, what this line had meant for him. I had heard him preach it many times. I had preached it once myself, proudly giving it an interpretation different from my father's. Now the whole thing came back to me, as though my father and I were on our way to Sunday school and I were memorizing the golden text: *And if it seem evil unto you to serve the Lord, choose you this day whom you will serve; whether the gods which your fathers served that were on the other side of the flood, or the gods of the Amorites, in which land ye dwell: but as for me and my house, we will serve the Lord.* I suspected in these familiar lines a meaning which had never been there for me before. All of my father's texts and songs, which I had decided were meaningless, were arranged before me at his death like empty bottles, waiting to hold the meaning which life would give them for me. This was his legacy: nothing is ever escaped. That bleakly memorable morning I hated the unbelievable streets and the Negroes and whites who had, equally, made them that way. But I knew that it was folly, as my father would have said, this bitterness was folly. It was necessary to hold on to the things that mattered. The dead man mattered, the new life mattered; blackness and whiteness did not matter; to believe that they did was to acquiesce in one's own destruction. Hatred, which could destroy so much, never failed to destroy the man who hated and this was an immutable law.

It began to seem that one would have to hold in the mind forever two ideas which seemed to be in opposition. The first idea was acceptance, the acceptance, totally without rancor, of life as it is, and men as they are: in the light of this idea, it goes without saying that injustice is a commonplace. But this did not mean that one could be complacent, for the second idea was of equal power: that one must never, in one's own life, accept these injustices as commonplace but must fight them with all one's strength. This fight begins, however, in the heart and it now had been laid to my charge to keep my own heart free of hatred and despair. This intimation made my heart heavy and, now that my father was irrecoverable, I wished that he had been beside me so that I could have searched his face for the answers which only the future would give me now.

government by publicity

William J. Lederer

Outside the closed door a guard stopped unauthorized persons from entering. Inside, a Congressional investigating committee impatiently waited to go into action. Puffing pipes and cigarettes, the Congressmen were reading a piece of paper marked CONFIDENTIAL. In the center of the group stood a public-relations expert; he was talking slowly, carefully explaining the confidential paper. It was an instruction sheet telling how to get maximum headlines and publicity from the approaching Congressional investigation.

The expert made clear to committeemen how to terminate each day's session so that it would have the greatest news value, how to squeeze the most newspaper space for a press release, how to handle witnesses so that they don't dissipate the publicity angle the committee might be trying to exploit for that day.*

The desire of this committee for publicity is common among governmental circles. Almost every official, from the president down, has been guilty of manipulating and managing the news in the predatory struggle for headlines. Washington officials have plenty of free assistance in their "government by publicity." *There are twice as many governmental public-relations men in Washington as there are journalists.*

In the effort to influence our votes and our opinions, Congressmen — along with most other public servants — often forget that one of their primary functions is to inform the country about the conditions and problems of the nation; and to describe important issues so that we can understand them. It was because of this requirement that the post of "public information officer" (or public affairs officer or press attachés) was established.

However, in practice, public information officers (who speak for the various governmental departments) have become prostituted. They have ceased serving you and me. Instead they have developed into press-agents. Almost all of their energies and talents are spent keeping themselves and their bosses in power, obtaining appropriations, or making the bureau "look good," frequently at the expense of other bureaus. In short, much of our government's energy is squandered in obaining a pre-determined public opinion. Officials try by selective information releases to have us accept what they believe is proper; as if fearing the decisions we might make on our own if we had all of the truth.

Senators and Congressmen (who are so inclined) seem to publicize themselves with more vigor and skill than other public servants. Perhaps it is because the floors of the Senate and of the House provide a better national spotlight.

Although he is dead now — and almost forgotten — Senator Joseph McCarthy was a master at manipulating public opinion to gain his own end — which was personal power. He effectively used headlines to frighten people, to strangle the usefulness of officials, and to eliminate anyone who impeded his obsessions.

McCarthy succeeded because he discovered and made full use of a tradition of American journalism — that most newspapermen report

* The points listed on the confidential instructions are given in Douglass Cater's book, *The Fourth Branch of Government.*

the news "straight." This means that if a prominent person says something sensational — even if untrue — the press normally will report the statement exactly as spoken. The substance of the speech will not be challenged; and no discussion of its veracity (or lack of veracity) is given to the reader. The press simply acts as a mirror. Therefore the irrational blatherings of a fool get as much publicity as the studied wisdom of a patriotic genius, if the fool is "news" at the time of his blather. The more violent and impossible the speech, usually the larger the headline and the more space it gets on page one.

When a Congressional investigator or a public official as prominent as McCarthy explodes verbally in public, the press merely describes what has happened. Background material or significance of what has been said is not included. *It is up to the reader* (who cannot ask questions or challenge alleged facts) *to differentiate between truth and falsehood.* The gentlemen of the press maintain this is the citizen's responsibility; even though, generally, you and I are not equipped to carry such a complex burden alone. Apparently they forget that we are depending upon them to supply us with *full* information on events.

When McCarthy, from the floor of the Senate, said he had in his hand a list of 205 card-carrying State Department Communists — we were offered no reason to doubt that he really had such a list. It said so in the papers. If our journalists had asked McCarthy for a look at the names and he had refused, we assumed that the press would expose the faker in headlines.

No such thing happened. McCarthy dramatically said he had the 205 Communists' names written on a piece of paper (which he did not); and the press gave us his speech "straight" — thus compounding the deception.

McCarthy knew this would happen; and it was this well-placed confidence which permitted him to shoot his mouth off for several years — always getting publicity from his accusations and ravings. His speeches were news; and the press built McCarthyism into prominence.

It did more than influence us. When one side of an issue is plastered all over the papers day after day, a dangerous phenomenon can take place: The continuous publishing of a viewpoint unconsciously persuades the government that the viewpoint is true; and that it represents a mandate from the people.

What screams from TV, radio, and press is interpreted as public opinion. Which, of course, it is not.

This, then, in addition to personal aggrandizement, often is the aim of Congressional investigations — the circus-type ones which take place on stage before television, radio, and press. We have permitted them to take place even though the sole legitimate objective of investigation is to get information for effective legislation. Douglass Cater, Washington newsman, in his excellent book, *The Fourth Branch of Government,* brilliantly shows how many Congressional investigations simply are a technique for making and controlling news. Investigations, then, often are entertainment spectaculars created to attract public attention. They are a means of molding national opinion or creating fame for the investigators.

Cater wrote, "The most notable committee investigations are seldom point of fact 'investigations.' They are planned deliberately to move from a preconceived idea to a predetermined conclusion. The skill and resourcefulness of the chairman and sizable staff are pitted against any effort to alter its destined course. Whatever investigating is done takes place well in advance of the public hearing. The hearing is the final act in the drama. Its intent, by the staging of an arresting spectacle, is to attract public attention, to alarm or to allay, to enlighten, or yes, sometimes to obscure."

Cater tells how in some of the sensational investigations the information uncovered by the committee was of no legislative importance, ". . . the chairmen sought to dispense with the formality of a report altogether, each making vague assertions that the public had 'the facts' and could form its own judgments." And further, "reporters who have sat through countless hours of these investigations can vouchsafe how difficult it is for a witness to overcome the enormous publicity advantage of a biased committee."

Of course there are some committees, such as the House Committee on Government Activities, whose hearings are modest, dignified, and scholarly. In its quiet way, this committee has discovered information of enormous importance to America — material which influences United States foreign policy and legislation. Yet — despite the fact that this committee's reports are written in clear, readable English and are unclassified, they hardly get a line in the press; and the public is unaware of the Committee's accomplishments.

Is our ignorance the fault of the press for not bringing the committee to our notice in headlines? Is it the fault of the Congressmen for being dignified, fair, and scholarly — instead of putting on a flamboyant show? Or is it possible that we only show interest in political vaudeville acts?

Although the Congress probably is particularly effective in "prospering by publicity," almost every other governmental activity, likewise, tries to brain-wash America into accepting their points of view.

During my last few trips to Washington I met many public-information officers, some of them old friends. I asked each the same question, "What project are you working on now?" Their replies, boiled down, are significant:

The Air Force: "Missiles belong to the Air Force. We've got to get the Polaris away from the Navy."

The Navy: "Something has to be done to stop the Air Force from deceiving the public on their Minute Man program."

State Department: "We are laying low until we see what happens when Kennedy gets in."

The Army: "The Air Force has all the money and the Army is suffering. We want some of the big dough which the fly-boys are hogging, and often wasting."

The missions which our governmental public relations are trying to accomplish may be ethical and legitimate; and they may not. But they are using psychological tricks to capture you and me into a preconceived opinion. The image they are trying to impress on us is created with slanted press releases, cleverly timed speeches, spectacular exhibits, the "leaking" of favorable bits of news to journalists, and having magazines and television publish praising pieces (laudatory articles or pieces which damage their opponents). This is not-too-honest propaganda. We are being treated as bored customers who are shopping for a deodorant or a new car, not as citizens whose independent opinions mold the destiny of our democracy.

We have almost no assurance whether public information coming from Washington is true or not. Some civil servants dish it out for a dozen different reasons, few of them being to inform the country. Occasionally an official — and John Foster Dulles did this frequently — will irresponsibly use the press (and the public) as a means of testing a proposed policy: Dulles would call a private meeting of favored journalists. Everything he told them was "not for attribution." This means his name could not be used. The resulting newspaper articles would start, "High officials in Washington claim that . . ."

On one occasion Dulles gave out a "not for attribution" story hinting that the United States might defend Quemoy and Matsu. After it was published and the public's reaction was noted, the White House released a story denying that any such action was being considered for Quemoy and Matsu at this time. Although his name was not on it,

Dulles authorized the second piece as well as the first. By this process of news chicanery he had found out what he wanted to know about the public's reaction. But he also confused the nation.

In *The Reporter* Magazine, Arthur M. Schlesinger, Jr., wrote: "Washington newspapermen today hardly know whether to believe the Secretary of State, because they do not know if he is speaking to them as reporters or seeking to use them as instruments of psychological warfare. . . . What is the responsibility of a newspaperman when he discovers that some rumored development of policy is really only a psychological warfare trick? Should he print the truth at the risk of wrecking the plans of the Secretary of State? Or should he suppress the truth, betray himself, and deceive the American people?"

A similar device used by Washington for influencing us is the clandestine "leak" to a reporter. Hardly a day goes by that we don't read a news story which contains the phrase, "According to well-informed sources . . ."

This means that someone has given out news which he couldn't do officially and honestly. Perhaps it is against the administration's policy; perhaps it is classified; or perhaps it is such a blatant distortion that the official is ashamed to be associated with it.

Of course it is possible the story is only an exciting rumor which a reporter picked up in a saloon, and didn't have the time or energy to track down and verify.

The hazy and vague explanation of "according to well-informed sources" is like writing the public an anonymous letter.

The government has been shameless in its efforts to attract our attention to a particular point of view, and in this manner mold public opinion. We often are enmeshed into preconceived opinions by the very people we elect and support — the civil servants who are supposed to be doing what *we* want.

The Air Force told its public-relations officers, according to Cater, that "flooding the public with facts is very helpful. But facts, facts and more facts are quite useless unless they implant logical conclusions. Facts must be convincing, demonstrated, living salesmen of practical benefits. These are the only kind of facts that mold opinion and channel the vibrant attentions of public thinking; always deciding issues in the end, altering military policy as surely as defeat in war — they make public opinion the most powerful tool of all, more powerful than war itself."

The Air Force has always worked hard to practice what it preaches; and by skillful publicity has been amazingly successful in favorably influencing legislation. During the first year of the Korean Conflict, the Air Force was probably the least effective of the four military services. But it managed to get the most effective publicity in the press.*

Then, too, there was so much one-sided publicity and news-muddying (control of our public opinion) during the Middle East Crisis in 1958 that our country enjoyed almost no discussion of national policies — either by Congress or by the public. This was the purpose of the administration. Those who spoke in opposition were scolded — by no less than the Speaker of the House and by President Eisenhower himself; and along with the scolding came the implication that anyone who asked questions or dissented came perilously close to being a traitor.

What is the result of all this? You and I are prisoners of our own government's self-generated publicity. Half the time we don't know what is really going on, and to find out we must apply the torch.

* An eight-month Summary of Military Public Relations at Nieman Foundation 1950–51.

section **2**

alienation,

fear,

and

anxiety

fiction

still life

Bernard Malamud

1

Months after vainly seeking a studio on the vie Margutta, del Babuino, della Croce, and elsewhere in that neighborhood, Arthur Fidelman settled for part of a crowded, windowy, attic-like atelier on a cobble-stone street in the Trastevere, strung high with sheets and underwear. He had, a week before, in "personal notices" in the American language newspaper in Rome, read: "Studio to share, cheap, many advantages, etc., A. Oliovino," and after much serious anguish (the curt advertisement having recalled dreams he had dreamed were dead), many indecisions, enunciations and renunciations, Fidelman had, one very cold late-December morning, hurried to the address given, a worn four-story building with a yellowish façade stained brown along the edges. On the top floor, in a thickly cluttered artist's studio smelling aromatically of turpentine and oil paints, the inspiring sight of an easel lit in unwavering light from the three large windows setting the former art student on fire once more to paint, he had dealt not with a pittore, as expected, but with a pittrice, Annamaria Oliovino.

The pittrice, a thin, almost gaunt, high-voiced, restless type, with short black uncombed hair, violet mouth, distracted eyes and tense neck, a woman with narrow buttocks and piercing breasts was in her way attractive if not in truth beautiful. She had on a thick black woolen sweater, eroded black velveteen culottes, black socks, and leather sandals spotted with drops of paint. Fidelman and she eyed each other stealthily and he realized at once she was, as a woman, indifferent to him or his type, who or which made no difference. But after ten minutes, despite the turmoil she exuded even as she dispassionately answered his hesitant questions, the art student, ever a sucker for strange beauty and all sorts of experiences, felt himself involved with and falling for her. Not my deep dish, he warned himself, aware of all the dangers to him and his renewed desire to create art; yet he was already half in love with her. It can't be, he thought in desperation; but it could. It had happened to him before. In her presence he tightly shut both eyes and wholeheartedly wished against what might be. Really he trembled, and though he labored to extricate his fate from hers, he was already a plucked bird, greased, and ready for frying. Fidelman protested within — cried out severely against the weak self, called himself ferocious names but could do not much, a victim of his familiar response, a too passionate fondness for strangers. So Annamaria, who had advertised a twenty thousand lire monthly rental, in the end doubled the sum, and Fidelman paid through both nostrils, cash for first and last months (should he attempt to fly by night) plus a deposit of ten thousand for possible damages. An hour later he moved in with his imitation leather suitcase. This happened in the dead of winter. Below the cold sunlit windows stood two frozen umbrella pines and beyond, in the near distance, sparkled the icy Tiber.

The studio was well heated, Annamaria had insisted, but the cold leaked in through the wide windows. It was more a blast; the art student shivered but was kept warm by his hidden love for the pittrice. It took him most of a day to clear himself a space to work, about a third of the studio was as much as he could manage. He stacked her canvases five deep against her portion of the walls, curious to examine them but Annamaria watched his every move (he noticed several self-portraits) although she was at the same time painting a monumental natura morta of a loaf of bread with two garlic bulbs ("Pane ed Aglii"). He moved stacks of *Oggi*, piles of postcards and yellowed letters, and a bundle of calendars going back to many years ago; also a Perugina candy box full of broken pieces of Etruscan pottery, one of small sea shells, and a third of medallions of various saints and of the Virgin, which she warned him to handle with care. He had uncovered a sagging cot by a dripping stone sink in his corner of the studio and there he slept. She furnished an old chafing dish and a broken table, and he bought a few household things he needed. Annamaria rented the art student an easel for a thousand lire a month. Her quarters were private, a room at the other end of the studio whose door she kept locked, handing him the key when he had to use the toilet. The wall was thin and the instrument noisy. He could hear the whistle and rush of her water, and though he tried to be quiet, because of the plumbing the bowl was always brimful and the pour of his stream embarrassed him. At night, if there was need, although he was tempted to use the sink, he fished out the yellowed, sedimented pot under his bed; once or twice, as he was using it in the thick of night, he had the impression she was awake and listening.

They painted in their overcoats, Annamaria wearing a black babushka, Fidelman a green wool hat pulled down over his frozen ears. She kept a pan of hot coals at her feet and every so often lifted a sandaled foot to toast it. The marble floor of the studio was sheer thick ice; Fidelman wore two pairs of tennis socks his sister Bessie had recently sent him from the States. Annamaria, a leftie, painted with a smeared leather glove on her hand, and theoretically his easel had been arranged so that he couldn't see what she was doing but he often sneaked looks at her work. The pittrice, to his surprise, painted with flicks of her fingers and wrists, peering at her performance with almost shut eyes. He noticed she alternated still lifes with huge lyric abstractions—massive whorls of red and gold exploding in all directions, these built on, entwined with, and ultimately concealing a small black religious cross, her first two brush strokes on every abstract canvas. Once when Fidelman gathered the nerve to ask her why the cross, she answered it was the symbol that gave the painting its meaning.

He was eager to know more but she was impatient. "Eh," she shrugged, "who can explain art."

Though her response to his various attempts to become better acquainted were as a rule curt, and her voluntary attention to him, shorter still — she was able, apparently, to pretend he wasn't there — Fidelman's feeling for Annamaria grew, and he was as unhappy in love as he had ever been.

But he was patient, a persistent virtue, served her often in various capacities, for instance carrying down four flights of stairs her two bags of garbage shortly after supper — the portinaia was crippled and the portiere never around — sweeping the studio clean each morning, even running to retrieve a brush or paint tube when she happened to drop one — offering any service any time, you name it. She accepted these small favors without giving them notice.

One morning after reading a many-paged letter she had just got in the mail, Annamaria was sad, sullen, unable to work; she paced around restlessly, it troubled him. But after feverishly painting a widening purple spiral that continued off the canvas, she regained a measure of repose. This heightened her beauty, lent it somehow a youthful quality it didn't ordinarily have—he guessed her to be no older than twenty-seven or -eight; so Fidelman, inspired by the change in her, hoping it might foretoken better luck for him, approached Annamaria, removed his hat and suggested since she went out infrequently why not lunch for a change at the trattoria at the corner, Guido's, where workmen assembled and the veal and white wine were delicious? She, to his surprise, after darting an uneasy glance out of the window at the tops of the motionless umbrella pines, abruptly assented. They ate well and conversed like human beings, although she mostly limited herself to answering his modest questions. She informed Fidelman she had come from Naples to Rome two years ago, although it seemed much longer, and he told her he was from the United States. Being so physically close to her, able to inhale the odor of her body—like salted flowers—and intimately eating together, excited Fidelman, and he sat very still, not to rock the boat and spill a drop of what was so precious to him. Annamaria ate hungrily, her eyes usually lowered. Once she looked at him with a shade of a smile and he felt beatitude; the art student contemplated many such meals though he could ill afford them, every cent he spent, saved and sent by Bessie.

After zuppa inglese and a peeled apple she patted her lips with a napkin, and still in good humor, suggested they take the bus to the Piazza del Popolo and visit some painter friends of hers.

"I'll introduce you to Alberto Moravia."

"With pleasure," Fidelman said, bowing.

But when they stepped into the street and were walking to the bus stop near the river a cold wind blew up and Annamaria turned pale.

"Something wrong?" Fidelman inquired.

"The East Wind," she answered testily.

"What wind?"

"The Evil Eye," she said with irritation. "Malocchio."

He had heard something of the sort. They returned quickly to the studio, their heads lowered against the noisy wind, the pittrice from time to time furtively crossing herself. A black-habited old nun passed them at the trattoria corner, from whom Annamaria turned in torment, muttering, "Jettatura! Porca miseria!" When they were upstairs in the studio she insisted Fidelman touch his testicles three times to undo or dispel who knows what witchcraft, and he modestly obliged. Her request had inflamed him although he cautioned himself to remember it was in purpose and essence, theological.

Later she received a visitor, a man who came to see her on Monday and Friday afternoons after his work in a government bureau. Her visitors, always men, whispered with her a minute, then left restlessly; most of them, excepting also Giancarlo Balducci, a crosseyed illustrator — Fidelman never saw again. But the one who came oftenest stayed longest, a solemn gray-haired gent, Augusto Ottogalli, with watery blue eyes and missing side teeth, old enough to be her father for sure. He wore a slanted black fedora, and a shabby gray overcoat too large for him, greeted Fidelman vacantly and made him inordinately jealous. When Augusto arrived in the afternoon the pittrice usually dropped anything she was doing and they retired to her room, at once locked and bolted. The art student wandered alone in the studio for dreadful hours. When Augusto ultimately emerged, looking disheveled, and if successful, defeated, Fidelman turned his back on him and the old man hastily let himself out of the door. After his visits, and only his, Annamaria did not appear in the studio for the rest of the day. Once when Fidelman knocked on her door to invite her out to supper, she told him to use the pot because she had a headache and was sound asleep. On another occasion when Augusto was locked long in her room with her, after a tormenting two hours Fidelman tip-toed over and put his jealous ear to the door. All he could hear was the buzz and sigh of their whispering. Peeking through the keyhole he saw them both in their overcoats, sitting on her bed, Augusto tightly clasping her hands, whispering passionately, his nose empurpled with emotion, Annamaria's white face averted. When the art student checked an hour afterward, they were still at it, the old man imploring, the pittrice weeping. The next time, Augusto came with a priest, a portly, heavy-breathing man with a doubtful face. But as soon as they appeared in the studio Annamaria, enraged to fury, despite the impassioned entreatments of Augusto, began to throw at them anything of hers or Fidelman's she could lay hands on.

"Bloodsuckers!" she shouted, "scorpions! parasites!" until they had hastily retreated. Yet when Augusto, worn and harried, returned alone, without complaint she retired to her room with him.

2

Fidelman's work, despite the effort and despair he gave it, was going poorly. Every time he looked at unpainted canvas he saw harlequins, whores, tragic kings, fragmented musicians, the sick and the dread. Still, tradition was tradition and what if he should want to make more? Since he had always loved art history he considered embarking on a "Mother and Child," but was afraid her image would come out too much Bessie — after all, fifteen years between them. Or maybe a moving "Pietà," the dead son's body held like a broken wave in mama's frail arms? A curse on art history — he fought the fully prefigured picture though some of his former best paintings had jumped in every detail to the mind. Yet if so, where's true engagement? Sometimes I'd like to forget every picture I've seen, Fidelman thought. Almost in panic he sketched in charcoal a coattailed "Figure of a Jew Fleeing" and quickly hid it away. After that, ideas, prefigured or not, were scarce. "Astonish me," he muttered to himself, wondering whether to return to surrealism. He also considered a series of "Relations to Place and Space," constructions in squares and circles, the pleasures of tri-dimensional geometry of linear abstraction, only he had little heart for it. The furthest abstraction, Fidelman thought, is the blank canvas. A moment later he asked himself, if painting shows who you are, why should not painting?

After the incident with the priest Annamaria was despondent for a week, stayed in her room sometimes bitterly crying, Fidelman often standing helplessly by her door. However this was a prelude to a burst of creativity by the pittrice. Works by the dozens leaped from her brush and stylus. She continued her lyric abstractions based on the theme of a hidden cross and spent hours with a long black candle, burning holes in heavy white paper ("Buchi Spontanei"). Having mixed coffee grounds, sparkling bits of crushed mirror and ground-up sea shells, she blew the dust on mucilaged paper ("Velo nella Nebbia"). She composed collages of rags and toilet tissue. After a dozen linear studies ("Linee Discendenti"), she experimented with gold leaf sprayed with umber, the whole while wet combed in long undulations with a fine comb. She framed this in a black frame and hung it on end like a diamond ("Luce di Candela"). Annamaria worked intently, her brow furrowed, violet mouth tightly pursed, eyes lit, nostrils palpitating in creative excitement. And when she had temporarily run out of new ideas she did a mythological bull in red clay ("La Donna Toro"), afterwards returning to nature morte with bunches of bananas; then self-portraits.

The pittrice occasionally took time out to see what Fidelman was up to, although not much, and then editing his efforts. She changed lines and altered figures, or swabbed paint over whole compositions that didn't appeal to her. There was not much that did, but Fidelman was grateful for any attention she gave his work, and even kept at it to incite her criticism. He could feel his heart beat in his teeth whenever she stood close to him modifying his work, he deeply breathing her intimate smell of sweating flowers. She used perfume only when Augusto came and it disappointed Fidelman that the old man should evoke the use of bottled fragrance; yet he was cheered that her natural odor which he, so to say, got for free, was so much more exciting than the stuff she doused herself with for her decrepit Romeo. He had noticed she had a bit of soft belly but he loved the pliant roundness and often daydreamed of it. Thinking it might please her, for he pleased her rarely (he reveried how it would be once she understood the true depth of his love for her), the art student experimented with some of the things Annamaria had done — the spontaneous holes, for instance, several studies of "Lines Ascending," and two lyrical abstract expressionistic pieces based on, interwoven with, and ultimately concealing a Star of David, although for these attempts he soon discovered he had earned, instead of her good will, an increased measure of scorn.

However, Annamaria continued to eat lunch with him at Guido's, and more often than not, supper, although she said practically nothing during meals and afterwards let her eye roam over the faces of the men at the other tables. But there were times after they had eaten when she would agree to go for a short walk with Fidelman, if there was no serious wind; and once in a while they entered a movie in the Trastevere, for she hated to cross any of the bridges of the Tiber, and then only in a bus, sitting stiffly, staring ahead. As they were once riding, Fidelman seized the opportunity to hold her tense fist in his, but as soon as they were across the river she tore it out of his grasp. He was by now giving her presents — tubes of paints, the best brushes, a few yards of Belgian linen, which she accepted without comment; she also borrowed small sums from him, nothing startling

— a hundred lire today, five hundred tomorrow. And she announced one morning that he would thereafter, since he used so much of both, have to pay additional for water and electricity — he already paid extra for the heatless heat. Fidelman, though continually worried about money, assented. He would have given his last lira to lie on her soft belly, but she offered niente, not so much as a caress; until one day, he was permitted to look on as she sketched herself nude in his presence. Since it was bitter cold the pittrice did this in two stages. First she removed her sweater and brassiere, and viewing herself in a long, faded mirror, quickly sketched the upper half of her body before it turned blue. He was dizzily enamored of her form and flesh. Hastily fastening the brassiere and pulling on her sweater, Annamaria stepped out of her sandals and peeled off her culottes, and white panties torn at the crotch, then drew the rest of herself down to her toes. The art student begged permission to sketch along with her but the pittrice denied it, so he had, as best one can, to commit to memory her lovely treasures — the hard, piercing breasts, narrow shapely buttocks, vine-hidden labia, the font and sweet beginning of time. After she had drawn herself and dressed, and when Augusto appeared and they had retired behind her bolted door, Fidelman sat motionless on his high stool before the glittering blue-skied windows, slowly turning to ice to faint strains of Bach.

3

The art student increased his services to Annamaria, her increase was scorn, or so it seemed. This severely bruised his spirit. What have I done to deserve such treatment? That I pay my plenty of rent on time? That I buy her all sorts of presents, not to mention two full meals a day? That I live in flaming hot and freezing cold? That I passionately adore each sweet-and-sour bit of her? He figured it bored her to see so much of him. For a week Fidelman disappeared during the day, sat in cold libraries or stood around in frosty museums. He tried painting after midnight and into the early morning hours but the pittrice found out and unscrewed the bulbs before she went to bed. "Don't waste my electricity, this isn't America." He screwed in a dim blue bulb and worked silently from one a.m. to five. At dawn he discovered he had painted a blue picture. Fidelman wandered in the streets of the city. At night he slept in the studio and could hear her sleeping in her room. She slept restlessly, dreamed badly, and often moaned. He dreamed he had three eyes.

For two weeks he spoke to no one but a dumpy four-and-a-half foot female on the third floor, and to her usually to say no. Fidelman, having often heard the music of Bach drifting up from below, had tried to picture the lady piano player, imagining a quiet blonde with a slender body, a woman of grace and beauty. It had turned out to be Clelia Montemaggio, a middle-aged old maid music teacher, who sat at an old upright piano, her apartment door open to let out the cooking smells, particularly fried fish on Friday. Once when coming up from bringing down the garbage, Fidelman had paused to listen to part of a partita at her door and she had lassoed him in for an espresso and pastry. He ate and listened to Bach, her plump bottom moving spryly on the bench as she played not badly. "Lo spirito," she called to him raptly over her shoulder, "l'architettura!" Fidelman nodded. Thereafter whenever she spied him in the hall she attempted to entice him with cream-filled pastries and J.S.B., whom she played apparently exclusively.

"Come een," she called in English, "I weel play for you. We weel talk. There is no use for too much solitude." But the art student, burdened by his, spurned hers.

Unable to work, he wandered in the streets in a desolate mood, his spirit dusty in a city of fountains and leaky water taps. Water, water everywhere, spouting, flowing, dripping, whispering secrets, love love love, but not for him. If Rome's so sexy, where's mine? Fidelman's Romeless Rome. It belonged least to those who yearned most for it. With slow steps he climbed the Pincio, if possible to raise his spirits gazing down at the rooftops of the city, spires, cupolas, towers, monuments, compounded history and past time. It was in sight, possessible, all but its elusive spirit; after so long he was still straniero. He was then struck by a thought: if you could paint this sight, give it its quality in yours, the spirit belonged to you. History become esthetic! Fidelman's scalp thickened. A wild rush of things he might paint swept sweetly through him: saints in good and bad health, whole or maimed, in gold and red; nude gray rabbis at Auschwitz, black or white Negroes — what not when *any* color dripped from your brush? And if these, so also ANNAMARIA ES PULCHRA. He all but cheered. What more intimate possession of a woman! He would paint her, whether she permitted or not, posed or not — she was his to paint, he could with eyes shut. Maybe something will come after all of my love for her. His spirits elevated, Fidelman ran most of the way home.

It took him eight days, a labor of love. He tried her as nude and although able to imagine every inch of her, could not commit it to canvas. Then he suffered until it occurred to him to paint her as "Virgin with Child." The idea astonished and elated him. Fidelman went feverishly to work and caught an immediate likeness in paint. Annamaria, saintly beautiful, held in her arms the infant resembling his little nephew Georgie. The pittrice, aware, of course, of his continuous activity, cast curious glances his way, but Fidelman, painting in the corner by the stone sink, kept the easel turned away from her. She pretended unconcern. Done for the day he covered the painting and carefully guarded it. The art student was painting Annamaria in a passion of tenderness for the infant at her breast, her face responsive to its innocence. When, on the ninth day, in trepidation Fidelman revealed his work, the pittrice's eyes clouded and her underlip curled. He was about to grab the canvas and smash it up all over the place when her expression fell apart. The art student postponed all movement but visible trembling. She seemed at first appalled, a darkness descended on her, she was undone. She wailed wordlessly, then sobbed, "You have seen my soul." They embraced tempestuously, her breasts stabbing him, Annamaria bawling on his shoulder. Fidelman kissed her wet face and salted lips, she murmuring as he fooled with the hook of her brassiere under her sweater, "Aspetta, aspetta, caro, Augusto viene." He was mad with expectation and suspense.

Augusto, who usually arrived punctually at four, did not appear that Friday afternoon. Uneasy as the hour approached, Annamaria seemed relieved as the streets grew dark. She had worked badly after viewing Fidelman's painting, sighed frequently, gazed at him with sweet-sad smiles. At six she gave in to his urging and they retired to her room, his unframed "Virgin with Child" already hanging above her bed, replacing a gaunt self-portrait. He was curiously disappointed in the picture — surfacy thin — and made a mental note to borrow it back in the morning to work on it more. But the conception, at least, deserved the reward. Annamaria cooked supper. She cut his meat for him and fed him forkfuls. She peeled Fidelman's orange and stirred sugar in his coffee. Afterwards, at his nod, she locked and bolted the studio and bedroom doors and they undressed and slipped under her blankets. How good to be for a change on this side of the locked door, Fidelman thought, relaxing marvelously. Annamaria, however, seemed tensely alert to the noises of the old building, including a parrot screeching, some shouting kids running up the stairs, a soprano singing "Ritorna, vincitor!" But she calmed down and then hotly embraced Fidelman. In the middle of a passionate kiss the doorbell rang.

Annamaria stiffened in his arms. "Diavolo! Augusto!"

"He'll go away," Fidelman advised. "Both doors locked."

But she was at once out of bed, drawing on her culottes. "Get dressed," she said.

He hopped up and hastily got into his pants.

Annamaria unlocked and unbolted the inner door and then the outer one. It was the postman waiting to collect ten lire for an overweight letter from Naples.

After she had read the long letter and wiped away a tear they undressed and got back into bed.

"Who is he to you?" Fidelman asked.

"Who?"

"Augusto."

"An old friend. Like a father. We went through much together."

"Were you lovers?"

"Look, if you want me, take me. If you want to ask questions, go back to school."

He determined to mind his business.

"Warm me," she said, "I'm freezing."

Fidelman stroked her slowly. After ten minutes she said, " 'Gioco di mano, gioco di villano.' Use your imagination."

He used his imagination and she responded with excitement. "Dolce tesoro," she whispered, flicking the tip of her tongue into his ear, then with little bites biting his ear lobe.

The door bell rang loudly.

"For Christ's sake, don't answer," Fidelman groaned. He tried to hold her down but she was already up, hunting her robe.

"Put on your pants," she hissed.

He had thoughts of waiting for her in bed but it ended with his dressing fully. She sent him to the door. It was the crippled portinaia, the art student having neglected to take down the garbage.

Annamaria furiously got the two bags and handed them to her.

In bed she was so cold her teeth chattered.

Tense with desire Fidelman warmed her.

"Angelo mio," she murmured. "Amore, possess me."

He was about to when she rose in a hurry. "The cursed door again!"

Fidelman gnashed his teeth. "I heard nothing."

In her torn yellow silk robe she hurried to the front door, opened and shut it, quickly locked and bolted it, did the same in her room and slid into bed.

"You were right, it was nobody."

She embraced him, her hairy armpits perfumed. He responded with postponed passion.

"Enough of antipasto," Annamaria said. She reached for his member.

Overwrought, Fidelman though fighting himself not to, spent himself in her hand. Although he mightily willed resurrection, his wilted flower bit the dust.

She furiously shoved him out of bed, into the studio, flinging his clothes after him.

"Pig, beast, onanist!"

4

At least she lets me love her. Daily Fidelman shopped, cooked, and cleaned for her. Every morning he took her shopping sack off the hook, went to the street market and returned with the bag stuffed full of greens, pasta, eggs, meat, cheese, wine, bread. Annamaria insisted on three hearty meals a day although she had once told him she no longer enjoyed eating. Twice he had seen her throw up her supper. What she enjoyed he didn't know except it wasn't Fidelman. After he had served her at her table he was allowed to eat alone in the studio. At two every afternoon she took her siesta, and though it was forbidden to make noise, he was allowed to wash the dishes, dust and clean her room, swab the toilet bowl. She called, Fatso, and in he trotted to get her anything she had run out of — drawing pencils, sanitary belt, safety pins. After she waked from her nap, rain or shine, snow or hail, he was now compelled to leave the studio so she could work in peace and quiet. He wandered, in the tramontana, from one cold two-bit movie to another. At seven he was back to prepare her supper, and twice a week Augusto's, who sported a new black hat and spiffy overcoat, and pitied the art student with both wet blue eyes but wouldn't look at him. After supper, another load of dishes, the garbage downstairs, and when Fidelman returned, with or without Augusto Annamaria was already closeted behind her bolted door. He checked through the keyhole on Mondays and Fridays but she and the old gent were always fully clothed. Fidelman had more than once complained to her that his punishment exceeded his crime, but the pittrice said he was a type she would never have any use for. In fact he did not exist for her. Not existing how could he paint, although he told himself he must? He couldn't. He aimlessly froze wherever he went, a mean cold that seared his lungs, although under his overcoat he wore a new thick sweater Bessie had knitted for him, and two woolen scarves around his neck. Since the night Annamaria had kicked him out of bed he had not been warm; yet he often dreamed of ultimate victory. Once when he was on his lonely way out of the house — a night she was giving a party for some painter friends, Fidelman, a drooping butt in the corner of his mouth, carrying the garbage bags, met Clelia Montemaggio coming up the stairs.

"You look like a frozen board," she said. "Come in and enjoy the warmth and a little Bach."

Unable to unfreeze enough to say no, he continued down with the garbage.

"Every man gets the woman he deserves," she called after him.

"Who got," Fidelman muttered. "Who gets."

He considered jumping into the Tiber but it was full of ice that winter.

One night at the end of February, Annamaria, to Fidelman's astonishment — deeply affected him — said he might go with her to a party at Giancarlo Balducci's studio on the Via dell'Oca; she needed somebody to accompany her in the bus across the bridge and Augusto was flat on his back with the Asian flu. The party was lively — painters, sculptors, some writers, two diplomats, a prince and a visiting Hindu sociologist, their ladies and three hotsy-totsy, scantily dressed, unattached girls. One of them, a shapely beauty with orange hair, bright eyes, and warm ways became interested in Fidelman, except that he was dazed by Annamaria, seeing her in a dress for the first time, a ravishing, rich, ruby-colored affair. The crosseyed host had provided simply a huge cut glass bowl of spiced mulled wine, and the guests dipped ceramic glasses into it, and guzzled away. Everyone but the art student seemed to be enjoying himself. One or two of the men disappeared into other rooms with female friends or acquaintances and Annamaria, in a gay mood, did a fast shimmy to rhythmic handclapping. She was drinking steadily and when she wanted her glass filled, politely called him "Arturo." He began to have mild thoughts of possibly possessing her.

The party bloomed, at least forty, and turned wildish. Practical jokes were played. Fidelman realized his left shoe had been smeared with mustard. Balducci's black cat mewed at a fat lady's behind, a slice of sausage pinned to her dress. Before midnight there were two fist fights, Fidelman enjoying both but not getting involved, though once he was socked on the neck by a sculptor who had aimed at a painter. The girl with the orange hair, still interested in the art stu-

dent, invited him to join her in Balducci's bedroom, but he continued
to be devoted to Annamaria, his eyes tied to her every move. He was
jealous of the illustrator, who whenever near her, nipped her bottom.

One of the sculptors, Orazio Pinello, a slender man with a darkish
face, heavy black brows, and bleached blond hair, approached Fidelman. "Haven't we met before, caro?"

"Maybe," the art student said, perspiring lightly. "I'm Arthur
Fidelman, an American painter."

"You don't say? Action painter?"

"Always active."

"I refer of course to Abstract Expressionism."

"Of course. Well, sort of. On and off."

"Haven't I seen some of your work around? Galleria Schneider?
Some symmetric, hard-edge, biomorphic forms? Not bad as I remember."

Fidelman thanked him, in full blush.

"Who are you here with?" Orazio Pinello asked.

"Annamaria Oliovino."

"Her?" said the sculptor. "But she's a fake."

"Is she?" Fidelman said with a sigh.

"Have you looked at her work?"

"With one eye. Her art is bad but I find her irresistible."

"Peccato." The sculptor shrugged and drifted away.

A minute later there was another fist fight, during which the bright-
eyed orange head conked Fidelman with a Chinese vase. He went
out cold and when he came to, Annamaria and Balducci were un-
dressing him in the illustrator's bedroom. Fidelman experienced an
almost overwhelming pleasure, then Balducci explained that the art
student had been chosen to pose in the nude for drawings both he and
the pittrice would do of him. He explained there had been a discussion
as to which of them did male nudes best and they had decided to
settle it in a short contest. Two easels had been wheeled to the center
of the studio; a half hour was allotted to the contestants, and the
guests would judge who had done the better job. Though he at first
objected because it was a cold night, Fidelman nevertheless felt
warmish from wine so he agreed to pose; besides he was proud of his
muscles and maybe if she sketched him nude it might arouse her
interest for a tussle later. And if he wasn't painting he was at least
being painted.

So the pittrice and Giancarlo Balducci, in paint-smeared smocks,
worked for thirty minutes by the clock, the whole party silently look-

ing on, with the exception of the orange-haired tart, who sat in the corner eating a prosciutto sandwich. Annamaria, her brow furrowed, lips pursed, drew intensely with crayon; Balducci worked calmly in colored chalk. The guests were absorbed, although after ten minutes the Hindu went home. A journalist locked himself in the painter's bedroom with orange head and would not admit his wife who pounded on the door. Fidelman, standing barefoot on a bathmat, was eager to see what Annamaria was accomplishing but had to be patient. When the half hour was up he was permitted to look. Balducci had drawn a flock of green and black abstract testiculate circles. Fidelman shuddered. But Annamaria's drawing was representational, not Fidelman although of course inspired by him: A gigantic funereal phallus that resembled a broken-backed snake. The blond sculptor inspected it with half-closed eyes, then yawned and left. By now the party was over, the guests departed, lights out except for a few dripping white candles. Balducci was collecting his ceramic glasses and emptying ash trays, and Annamaria had thrown up. The art student afterwards heard her begging the illustrator to sleep with her but Balducci complained of fatigue.

"I will if he won't," Fidelman offered.

Annamaria, enraged, spat on her picture of his unhappy phallus. "Don't dare come near me," she cried. "Malocchio! Jettatura!"

5

The next morning he awoke sneezing, a nasty cold. How can I go on? Annamaria, showing no signs of pity or remorse, continued shrilly to berate him. "You've brought me nothing but bad luck since you came here. I'm letting you stay because you pay well but I warn you to keep out of my sight."

"But how — " he asked hoarsely.

"That doesn't concern me."

" — how will I paint?"

"Who cares? Paint at night."

"Without light—"

"Paint in the dark. I'll buy you a can of black paint."

"How can you be so cruel to a man who loves —"

"I'll scream," she said.

He left in anguish. Later while she was at her siesta he came back, got some of his things and tried to paint in the hall. No dice. Fidelman wandered in the rain. He sat for hours on the Spanish Steps.

Then he returned to the house and went slowly up the stairs. The door was locked. "Annamaria," he hoarsely called. Nobody answered. In the street he stood at the river wall, watching the dome of St. Peter's in the distance. Maybe a potion, Fidelman thought, or an amulet? He doubted either would work. How do you go about hanging yourself? In the late afternoon he went back to the house — would say he was sick, needed rest, possibly a doctor. He felt feverish. She could hardly refuse.

But she did, although explaining she felt bad herself. He held onto the bannister as he went down the stairs. Clelia Montemaggio's door was open. Fidelman paused, then continued down but she had seen him. "Come een, come een."

He went reluctantly in. She fed him camomile tea and panettone. He ate in a wolfish hurry as she seated herself at the piano.

"No Bach, please, my head aches from various troubles."

"Where's your dignity?" she asked.

"Try Chopin, that's lighter."

"Respect yourself, please."

Fidelman removed his hat as she began to play a Bach prelude, her bottom rhythmic on the bench. Though his cold oppressed him and he could hardly breathe, tonight the spirit, the architecture, moved him. He felt his face to see if he were crying but only his nose was wet. On the top of the piano Clelia had placed a bowl of white carnations in full bloom. Each white petal seemed a white flower. If I could paint those gorgeous flowers, Fidelman thought. If I could paint something. By Jesus, if I could paint myself, that'd show them! Astonished by the thought he ran out of the house.

The art student hastened to a costume shop and settled on a cassock and fuzzy black soupbowl biretta, envisaging another Rembrandt: "Portrait of the Artist as Priest." He hurried with his bulky package back to the house. Annamaria was handing the garbage to the portinaia as Fidelman thrust his way into the studio. He quickly changed into the priest's vestments. The pittrice came in wildly to tell him where he got off, but when she saw Fidelman already painting himself as priest, with a moan she rushed into her room. He worked with smoking intensity and in no time created an amazing likeness. Annamaria, after stealthily re-entering the studio, with heaving bosom and agitated eyes closely followed his progress. At last, with a cry she threw herself at his feet.

"Forgive me, Father, for I have sinned — "

Dripping brush in hand, he stared down at her. "Please, I — "

"Oh, Father, if you knew how I have sinned. I've been a whore — "

After a moment's thought, Fidelman said, "If so, I absolve you."

"Not without penance. First listen to the rest. I've had no luck with men. They're all bastards. Or else I jinx them. If you want the truth I am an Evil Eye myself. Anybody who loves me is cursed."

He listened, fascinated.

"Augusto is really my uncle. After many others he became my lover. At least he's gentle. My father found out and swore he'd kill us both. When I got pregnant I was scared to death. A sin can go too far. Augusto told me to have the baby and leave it at an orphanage, but the night it was born I was confused and threw it into the Tiber. I was afraid it was an idiot."

She was sobbing. He drew back.

"Wait," she wept. "The next time in bed Augusto was impotent. Since then he's been imploring me to confess so he can get back his powers. But everytime I step into the confessional my tongue turns to bone. The priest can't tear a word out of me. That's how it's been all my life, don't ask me why because I don't know."

She grabbed his knees, "Help me, Father, for Christ's sake."

Fidelman, after a short tormented time, said in a quavering voice, "I forgive you, my child."

"The penance," she wailed, "first the penance."

After reflecting, he replied, "Say one hundred times each, Our Father and Hail Mary."

"More," Annamaria wept. "More, more. Much more."

Gripping his knees so hard they shook she burrowed her head into his black-buttoned lap. He felt the surprised beginnings of an erection.

"In that case," Fidelman said, shuddering a little, "better undress."

"Only," Annamaria said, "if you keep your vestments on."

"Not the cassock, too clumsy."

"At least the biretta."

He agreed to that.

Annamaria undressed in a swoop. Her body was extraordinarily lovely, the flesh glowing. In her bed they tightly embraced. She clasped his buttocks, he cupped hers. Pumping slowly he nailed her to her cross.

the jelly-bean

F. Scott Fitzgerald

1

Jim Powell was a Jelly-bean. Much as I desire to make him an appealing character, I feel that it would be unscrupulous to deceive you on that point. He was a bred-in-the-bone, dyed-in-the-wool, ninety-nine three-quarters per cent Jelly-bean and he grew lazily all during Jelly-bean season, which is every season, down in the land of the Jelly-beans well below the Mason-Dixon line.

Now if you call a Memphis man a Jelly-bean he will quite possibly pull a long sinewy rope from his hip pocket and hang you to a convenient telegraph-pole. If you call a New Orleans man a Jelly-bean he will probably grin and ask you who is taking your girl to the Mardi Gras ball. The particular Jelly-bean patch which produced the protagonist of this history lies somewhere between the two — a little city of forty thousand that has dozed sleepily for forty thousand years in southern Georgia, occasionally stirring in its slumbers and muttering something about a war that took place sometime, somewhere, and that everyone else has forgotten long ago.

Jim was a Jelly-bean. I write that again because it has such a pleasant sound — rather like the beginning of a fairy story — as if Jim were nice. It somehow gives me a picture of him with a round, appetizing face and all sorts of leaves and vegetables growing out of his cap. But Jim was long and thin and bent at the waist from stooping over pool-tables, and he was what might have been known in the indiscriminating North as a corner loafer. "Jelly-bean" is the name throughout the undissolved Confederacy for one who spends his life conjugating the verb to idle in the first person singular — I am idling, I have idled, I will idle.

Jim was born in a white house on a green corner. It had four weather-beaten pillars in front and a great amount of lattice-work in the rear that made a cheerful criss-cross background for a flowery sun-drenched lawn. Originally the dwellers in the white house had owned the ground next door and next door to that and next door to that, but this had been so long ago that even Jim's father scarcely remembered it. He had, in fact, thought it a matter of so little moment that when he was dying from a pistol wound got in a brawl he neglected even to tell little Jim, who was five years old and miserably frightened. The white house became a boarding-house run by a tight-lipped lady from Macon, whom Jim called Aunt Mamie and detested with all his soul.

He became fifteen, went to high school, wore his hair in black snarls, and was afraid of girls. He hated his home where four women and one old man prolonged an interminable chatter from summer to summer about what lots the Powell place had originally included and what sort of flowers would be out next. Sometimes the parents of little girls in town, remembering Jim's mother and fancying a re-semblance in the dark eyes and hair, invited him to parties, but parties made him shy and he much preferred sitting on a disconnected axle in Tilly's Garage, rolling the bones or exploring his mouth endlessly with a long straw. For pocket money, he picked up odd jobs, and it was due to this that he stopped going to parties. At his third party little Marjorie Haight had whispered indiscreetly and within hearing distance that he was a boy who brought the groceries sometimes. So instead of the two-step and polka, Jim had learned to throw any number he desired on the dice and had listened to spicy tales of all the shootings that had occurred in the surrounding country during the past fifty years.

He became eighteen. The war broke out and he enlisted as a gob and polished brass in the Charleston Navy-yard for a year. Then, by way of variety, he went North and polished brass in the Brooklyn Navy-yard for a year.

When the war was over he came home. He was twenty-one, his trousers were too short and too tight. His buttoned shoes were long and narrow. His tie was an alarming conspiracy of purple and pink marvellously scrolled, and over it were two blue eyes faded like a piece of very good old cloth long exposed to the sun.

In the twilight of one April evening when a soft gray had drifted down along the cottonfields and over the sultry town, he was a vague figure leaning against a board fence, whistling and gazing at the moon's rim above the lights of Jackson Street. His mind was working persistently on a problem that had held his attention for an hour. The Jelly-bean had been invited to a party.

Back in the days when all the boys had detested all the girls, Clark Darrow and Jim had sat side by side in school. But, while Jim's social aspirations had died in the oily air of the garage, Clark had alternately fallen in and out of love, gone to college, taken to drink, given it up, and, in short, become one of the best beaux of the town. Nevertheless Clark and Jim had retained a friendship that, though casual, was perfectly definite. That afternoon Clark's ancient Ford had slowed up beside Jim, who was on the sidewalk and, out of a clear sky, Clark had invited him to a party at the country club. The impulse that made him do this was no stranger than the impulse which made Jim accept. The latter was probably an unconscious ennui, a half-frightened sense of adventure. And now Jim was soberly thinking it over.

He began to sing, drumming his long foot idly on a stone block in the sidewalk till it wobbled up and down in time to the low throaty tune:

> *"One mile from Home in Jelly-bean town,*
> *Lives Jeanne, the Jelly-bean Queen.*
> *She loves her dice and treats 'em nice;*
> *No dice would treat her mean."*

He broke off and agitated the sidewalk to a bumpy gallop.

"Daggone!" he muttered, half aloud.

They would all be there — the old crowd, the crowd to which, by right of the white house, sold long since, and the portrait of the officer in gray over the mantel, Jim should have belonged. But that crowd had grown up together into a tight little set as gradually as the girls' dresses had lengthened inch by inch, as definitely as the boys' trousers had dropped suddenly to their ankles. And to that society of first names and dead puppy-loves Jim was an outsider — a running mate of poor whites. Most of the men knew him, condescendingly; he tipped his hat to three or four girls. That was all.

When the dusk had thickened into a blue setting for the moon, he walked through the hot, pleasantly pungent town to Jackson Street. The stores were closing and the last shoppers were drifting homeward, as if borne on the dreamy revolution of a slow merry-go-round. A street-fair farther down made a brilliant alley of vari-colored booths and contributed a blend of music to the night—an oriental dance on a calliope, a melancholy bugle in front of a freak show, a cheerful rendition of "Back Home in Tennessee" on a hand-organ.

The Jelly-bean stopped in a store and bought a collar. Then he sauntered along toward Soda Sam's, where he found the usual three or four cars of a summer evening parked in front and the little darkies running back and forth with sundaes and lemonades.

"Hello, Jim."

It was a voice at his elbow — Joe Ewing sitting in an automobile with Marylyn Wade. Nancy Lamar and a strange man were in the back seat.

The Jelly-bean tipped his hat quickly.

"Hi, Ben — " then, after an almost imperceptible pause — "How y' all?"

Passing, he ambled on toward the garage where he had a room upstairs. His "How y' all" had been said to Nancy Lamar, to whom he had not spoken in fifteen years.

Nancy had a mouth like a remembered kiss and shadowy eyes and blue-black hair inherited from her mother who had been born in Budapest. Jim passed her often in the street, walking small-boy fashion with her hands in her pockets and he knew that with her inseparable Sally Carrol Hopper she had left a trail of broken hearts from Atlanta to New Orleans.

For a few fleeting moments Jim wished he could dance. Then he laughed and as he reached his door began to sing softly to himself:

> *"Her Jelly Roll can twist your soul,*
> *Her eyes are big and brown,*
> *She's the Queen of the Queens of the Jelly-beans —*
> *My Jeanne of Jelly-bean Town."*

2

At nine-thirty Jim and Clark met in front of Soda Sam's and started for the Country Club in Clark's Ford.

"Jim," asked Clark casually, as they rattled through the jasmine-scented night, "how do you keep alive?"

The Jelly-bean paused, considered.

"Well," he said finally, "I got a room over Tilly's garage. I help him some with the cars in the afternoon an' he gives it to me free. Sometimes I drive one of his taxies and pick up a little thataway. I get fed up doin' that regular though."

"That all?"

"Well, when there's a lot of work I help him by the day — Saturdays usually — and then there's one main source of revenue I don't generally mention. Maybe you don't recollect I'm about the champion crap-shooter of this town. They make me shoot from a cup now because once I get the feel of a pair of dice they just roll for me."

Clark grinned appreciatively.

"I never could learn to set 'em so's they'd do what I wanted. Wish you'd shoot with Nancy Lamar some day and take all her money away from her. She will roll 'em with the boys and she loses more than her daddy can afford to give her. I happen to know she sold a good ring last month to pay a debt."

The Jelly-bean was non-committal.

"The white house on Elm Street still belong to you?"

Jim shook his head.

"Sold. Got a pretty good price, seein' it wasn't in a good part of town no more. Lawyer told me to put it into Liberty bonds. But Aunt Mamie got so she didn't have no sense, so it takes all the interest to keep her up at Great Farms Sanitarium."

"Hm."

"I got an old uncle up-state an' I reckon I kin go up there if ever I get sure enough pore. Nice farm, but not enough niggers around to work it. He's asked me to come up and help him, but I don't guess I'd take much to it. Too doggone lonesome —— "He broke off suddenly. "Clark, I want to tell you I'm much obliged to you for askin' me out, but I'd be a lot happier if you'd just stop the car right here an' let me walk back into town."

"Shucks!" Clark grunted." Do you good to step out. You don't have to dance — just get out there on the floor and shake."

"Hold on," exclaimed Jim uneasily, "Don't you go leadin' me up to any girls and leavin' me there so I'll have to dance with 'em."

Clark laughed.

" 'Cause," continued Jim desperately, "without you swear you won't do that I'm agoin' to get out right here an' my good legs goin' carry me back to Jackson Street."

They agreed after some argument that Jim, unmolested by females, was to view the spectacle from a secluded settee in the corner where Clark would join him whenever he wasn't dancing.

So ten o'clock found the Jelly-bean with his legs crossed and his arms conservatively folded, trying to look casually at home and politely uninterested in the dancers. At heart he was torn between overwhelming self-consciousness and an intense curiosity as to all that went on around him. He saw the girls emerge one by one from the dressing-room, stretching and pluming themselves like bright birds, smiling over their powdered shoulders at the chaperones, casting a quick glance around to take in the room and, simultaneously, the room's reaction to their entrance — and then, again like birds, alighting and nestling in the sober arms of their waiting escorts. Sally Carrol

Hopper, blonde and lazy-eyed, appeared clad in her favorite pink and blinking like an awakened rose. Marjorie Haight, Marylyn Wade, Harriet Cary, all the girls he had seen loitering down Jackson Street by noon, now, curled and brilliantined and delicately tinted for the overhead lights, were miraculously strange Dresden figures of pink and blue and red and gold, fresh from the shop and not yet fully dried.

He had been there half an hour, totally uncheered by Clark's jovial visits which were each one accompanied by a "Hello, old boy, how you making out?" and a slap at his knee. A dozen males had spoken to him or stopped for a moment beside him, but he knew that they were each one surprised at finding him there and fancied that one or two were even slightly resentful. But at half past ten his embarrassment suddenly left him and a pull of breathless interest took him completely out of himself — Nancy Lamar had come out of the dressing-room.

She was dressed in yellow organdie, a costume of a hundred cool corners, with three tiers of ruffles and a big bow in back until she shed black and yellow around her in a sort of phosphorescent lustre. The Jelly-bean's eyes opened wide and a lump arose in his throat. For a minute she stood beside the door until her partner hurried up. Jim recognized him as the stranger who had been with her in Joe Ewing's car that afternoon. He saw her set her arms akimbo and say something in a low voice, and laugh. The man laughed too and Jim experienced the quick pang of a weird new kind of pain. Some ray had passed between the pair, a shaft of beauty from that sun that had warmed him a moment since. The Jelly-bean felt suddenly like a weed in a shadow.

A minute later Clark approached him, bright-eyed and glowing.

"Hi, old man," he cried with some lack of originality. "How you making out?"

Jim replied that he was making out as well as could be expected.

"You come along with me," commanded Clark. "I've got something that'll put an edge on the evening."

Jim followed him awkwardly across the floor and up the stairs to the locker-room where Clark produced a flask of nameless yellow liquid.

"Good old corn."

Ginger ale arrived on a tray. Such potent nectar as "good old corn" needed some disguise beyond seltzer.

"Say, boy," exclaimed Clark breathlessly, "doesn't Nancy Lamar look beautiful?"

Jim nodded.

"Mighty beautiful," he agreed.

"She's all dolled up to a fare-you-well to-night," continued Clark. "Notice that fellow she's with?"

"Big fella? White pants?"

"Yeah. Well, that's Ogden Merritt from Savannah. Old man Merritt makes the Merritt safety razors. This fella's crazy about her. Been chasing after her all year.

"She's a wild baby," continued Clark, "but I like her. So does everybody. But she sure does do crazy stunts. She usually gets out alive, but she's got scars all over her reputation from one thing or another she's done."

"That so?" Jim passed over his glass. "That's good corn."

"Not so bad. Oh, she's a wild one. Shoots craps, say, boy! And she do like her high-balls. Promised I'd give her one later on."

"She in love with this — Merritt?"

"Damned if I know. Seems like all the best girls around here marry fellas and go off somewhere."

He poured himself one more drink and carefully corked the bottle.

"Listen, Jim, I got to go dance and I'd be much obliged if you just stick this corn right on your hip as long as you're not dancing. If a man notices I've had a drink he'll come up and ask me and before I know it it's all gone and somebody else is having my good time."

So Nancy Lamar was going to marry. This toast of a town was to become the private property of an individual in white trousers — and all because white trousers' father had made a better razor than his neighbor. As they descended the stairs Jim found the idea inexplicably depressing. For the first time in his life he felt a vague and romantic yearning. A picture of her began to form in his imagination — Nancy walking boylike and debonnaire along the street, taking an orange as tithe from a worshipful fruit-dealer, charging a dope on a mythical account at Soda Sam's, assembling a convoy of beaux and then driving off in triumphal state for an afternoon of splashing and singing.

The Jelly-bean walked out on the porch to a deserted corner, dark between the moon on the lawn and the single lighted door of the ballroom. There he found a chair and, lighting a cigarette, drifted into the thoughtless reverie that was his usual mood. Yet now it was a reverie made sensuous by the night and by the hot smell of damp powder puffs, tucked in the fronts of low dresses and distilling a thousand rich scents to float out through the open door. The music itself, blurred by a loud trombone, became hot and shadowy, a languorous overtone to the scraping of many shoes and slippers.

Suddenly the square of yellow light that fell through the door was obscurred by a dark figure. A girl had come out of the dressing-room and was standing on the porch not more than ten feet away. Jim heard a low-breathed "doggone" and then she turned and saw him. It was Nancy Lamar.

Jim rose to his feet.

"Howdy?"

"Hello — " She paused, hesitated and then approached. "Oh, it's — Jim Powell."

He bowed slightly, tried to think of a casual remark.

"Do you suppose," she began quickly, "I mean — do you know anything about gum?"

"What?"

"I've got gum on my shoe. Some utter ass left his or her gum on the floor and of course I stepped in it."

Jim blushed, inappropriately.

"Do you know how to get it off?" she demanded petulantly. "I've tried a knife. I've tried every damn thing in the dressing-room. I've tried soap and water — and even perfume and I've ruined my powder-puff trying to make it stick to that."

Jim considered the question in some agitation.

"Why — I think maybe gasoline —— "

The words had scarcely left his lips when she grasped his hand and pulled him at a run off the low veranda, over a flower bed and at a gallop toward a group of cars parked in the moonlight by the first hole of the golf course.

"Turn on the gasolene," she commanded breathlessly.

"What?"

"For the gum of course. I've got to get it off. I can't dance with gum on."

Obediently Jim turned to the cars and began inspecting them with a view to obtaining the desired solvent. Had she demanded a cylinder he would have done his best to wrench one out.

"Here," he said after a moment's search. "Here's one that's easy. Got a handkerchief?"

"It's up-stairs wet. I used it for the soap and water."

Jim laboriously explored his pockets.

"Don't believe I got one either."

"Doggone it! Well, we can turn it on and let it run on the ground."

He turned the spout; a dripping began.

"More!"

He turned it on fuller. The dripping became a flow and formed an oily pool that glistened brightly, reflecting a dozen tremulous moons on its quivering bosom.

"Ah," she sighed contentedly, "let it all out. The only thing to do is to wade in it."

In desperation he turned on the tap full and the pool suddenly widened sending tiny rivers and trickles in all directions.

"That's fine. That's something like."

Raising her skirts she stepped gracefully in.

"I know this'll take it off," she murmured.

Jim smiled.

"There's lots more cars."

She stepped daintily out of the gasolene and began scraping her slippers, side and bottom, on the running-board of the automobile. The Jelly-bean contained himself no longer. He bent double with explosive laughter and after a second she joined in.

"You're here with Clark Darrow, aren't you?" she asked as they walked back toward the veranda.

"Yes."

"You know where he is now?"

"Out dancin', I reckon."

"The deuce. He promised me a highball."

"Well," said Jim, "I guess that'll be all right. I got his bottle right here in my pocket."

She smiled at him radiantly.

"I guess maybe you'll need ginger ale though," he added.

"Not me. Just the bottle."

"Sure enough?"

She laughed scornfully.

"Try me. I can drink anything any man can. Let's sit down."

She perched herself on the side of a table and he dropped into one of the wicker chairs beside her. Taking out the cork she held the flask to her lips and took a long drink. He watched her fascinated.

"Like it?"

She shook her head breathlessly.

"No, but I like the way it makes me feel. I think most people are that way."

Jim agreed.

"My daddy liked it too well. It got him."

"American men," said Nancy gravely, "don't know how to drink."

"What?" Jim was startled.

"In fact," she went on carelessly, "they don't know how to do anything very well. The one thing I regret in my life is that I wasn't born in England."

"In England?"

"Yes. It's the one regret of my life that I wasn't."

"Do you like it over there."

"Yes. Immensely. I've never been there in person, but I've met a lot of Englishmen who were over here in the army, Oxford and Cambridge men — you know, that's like Sewanee and University of Georgia are here—and of course I've read a lot of English novels."

Jim was interested, amazed.

"D' you ever hear of Lady Diana Manners?" she asked earnestly. No, Jim had not.

"Well, she's what I'd like to be. Dark, you know, like me, and wild as sin. She's the girl who rode her horse up the steps of some cathedral or church or something and all the novelists made their heroines do it afterwards."

Jim nodded politely. He was out of his depths.

"Pass the bottle," suggested Nancy. "I'm going to take another little one. A little drink wouldn't hurt a baby.

"You see," she continued, again breathless after a draught. "People over there have style. Nobody has style here. I mean the boys here aren't really worth dressing up for or doing sensational things for. Don't you know?"

"I suppose so — I mean I suppose not," murmured Jim.

"And I'd like to do 'em an' all. I'm really the only girl in town that has style."

She stretched out her arms and yawned pleasantly.

"Pretty evening."

"Sure is," agreed Jim.

"Like to have boat," she suggested dreamily. "Like to sail out on a silver lake, say the Thames, for instance. Have champagne and caviare sandwiches along. Have about eight people. And one of the men would jump overboard to amuse the party and get drowned like a man did with Lady Diana Manners once."

"Did he do it to please her?"

"Didn't mean drown himself to please her. He just meant to jump overboard and make everybody laugh."

"I reckin they just died laughin' when he drowned."

"Oh, I suppose they laughed a little," she admitted. "I imagine she did, anyway. She's pretty hard, I guess — like I am."

"You hard?"

"Like nails." She yawned again and added, "Give me a little more from that bottle."

Jim hesitated but she held out her hand defiantly.

"Don't treat me like a girl," she warned him. "I'm not like any girl *you* ever saw." She considered. "Still, perhaps you're right. You got — you got old head on young shoulders."

She jumped to her feet and moved toward the door. The Jelly-bean rose also.

"Good-bye," she said politely, "good-bye. Thanks, Jelly-bean."

Then she stepped inside and left him wide-eyed upon the porch.

3

At twelve o'clock a procession of cloaks issued single file from the women's dressing-room and, each one paring with a coated beau like dancers meeting in a cotillion figure, drifted through the door with sleepy happy laughter — through the door into the dark where autos backed and snorted and parties called to one another and gathered around the water-cooler.

Jim, sitting in his corner, rose to look for Clark. They had met at eleven; then Clark had gone in to dance. So, seeking him, Jim wandered into the soft-drink stand that had once been a bar. The room was deserted except for a sleepy Negro dozing behind the counter and two boys lazily fingering a pair of dice at one of the tables. Jim was about to leave when he saw Clark coming in. At the same moment Clark looked up.

"Hi, Jim!" he commanded. "C'mon over and help us with this bottle. I guess there's not much left, but there's one all around."

Nancy, the man from Savannah, Marylyn Wade, and Joe Ewing were lolling and laughing in the doorway. Nancy caught Jim's eye and winked at him humorously.

They drifted over to a table and arranging themselves around it waited for the waiter to bring ginger ale. Jim, faintly ill at ease, turned his eyes on Nancy, who had drifted into a nickel crap game with the two boys at the next table.

"Bring them over here," suggested Clark.

Joe looked around.

"We don't want to draw a crowd. It's against club rules."

"Nobody's around," insisted Clark, "except Mr. Taylor. He's walking up and down like a wild-man trying to find out who let all the gasolene out of his car."

There was a general laugh.

"I bet a million Nancy got something on her shoe again. You can't park when she's around."

"O Nancy, Mr. Taylor's looking for you!"

Nancy's cheeks were glowing with excitement over the game. "I haven't seen his silly little flivver in two weeks."

Jim felt a sudden silence. He turned and saw an individual of uncertain age standing in the doorway.

Clark's voice punctuated the embarrassment.

"Won't you join us, Mr. Taylor?"

"Thanks."

Mr. Taylor spread his unwelcome presence over a chair. "Have to, I guess. I'm waiting till they dig me up some gasolene. Somebody got funny with my car."

His eyes narrowed and he looked quickly from one to the other. Jim wondered what he had heard from the doorway — tried to remember what had been said.

"I'm right to-night," Nancy sang out, "and my four bits is in the ring."

"Faded!" snapped Taylor suddenly.

"Why, Mr. Taylor, I didn't know you shot craps!" Nancy was overjoyed to find that he had seated himself and instantly covered her bet. They had openly disliked each other since the night she had definitely discouraged a series of rather pointed advances.

"All right, babies, do it for your mamma. Just one little seven." Nancy was *cooing* to the dice. She rattled them with a brave underhand flourish, and rolled them out on the table.

"Ah-h! I suspected it. And now again with the dollar up."

Five passes to her credit found Taylor a bad loser. She was making it personal, and after each success Jim watched triumph flutter across her face. She was doubling with each throw — such luck could scarcely last.

"Better go easy," he cautioned her timidly.

"Ah, but watch this one," she whispered. It was eight on the dice and she called her number.

"Little Ada, this time we're going South."

Ada from Decatur rolled over the table. Nancy was flushed and half-hysterical, but her luck was holding. She drove the pot up and up, refusing to drag. Taylor was drumming with his fingers on the table, but he was in to stay.

Then Nancy tried for a ten and lost the dice. Taylor seized them avidly. He shot in silence, and in the hush of excitement the clatter of one pass after another on the table was the only sound.

Now Nancy had the dice again, but her luck had broken. An hour passed. Back and forth it went. Taylor had been at it again — and again and again. They were even at last — Nancy lost her ultimate five dollars.

"Will you take my check," she said quickly, "for fifty, and we'll shoot it all?" Her voice was a little unsteady and her hand shook as she reached to the money.

Clark exchanged an uncertain but alarmed glance with Joe Ewing. Taylor shot again. He had Nancy's check.

"How 'bout another?" she said wildly. "Jes' any bank'll do — money everywhere as a matter of fact."

Jim understood — the "good old corn" he had given her — the "good old corn" she had taken since. He wished he dared interfere — a girl of that age and position would hardly have two bank accounts. When the clock struck two he contained himself no longer.

"May I — can't you let me roll 'em for you?" he suggested, his low, lazy voice a little strained.

Suddenly sleepy and listless, Nancy flung the dice down before him.

"All right — old boy? As Lady Diana Manners says, 'Shoot 'em, Jelly-bean' — My luck's gone."

"Mr. Taylor," said Jim, carelessly, "we'll shoot for one of those there checks against the cash."

Half an hour later Nancy swayed forward and clapped him on the back.

"Stole my luck, you did." She was nodding her head sagely.

Jim swept up the last check and putting it with the others tore them into confetti and scattered them on the floor. Someone started singing, and Nancy kicking her chair backward rose to her feet.

"Ladies and gentlemen," she announced. "Ladies — that's you Marylyn. I want to tell the world that Mr. Jim Powell, who is a well-known Jelly-bean of this city, is an exception to a great rule — 'lucky in dice — unlucky in love.' He's lucky in dice, and as matter fact I — I *love* him. Ladies and gentlemen, Nancy Lamar, famous darkhaired beauty often featured in the *Herald* as one th' most popular members of younger set as other girls are often featured in this particular case. Wish to announce — wish to announce, anyway, Gentlemen —— " She tipped suddenly. Clark caught her and restored her balance.

"My error," she laughed, "she stoops to — stoops to — anyways —— We'll drink to Jelly-bean . . . Mr. Jim Powell, King of the Jelly-beans."

And a few minutes later as Jim waited hat in hand for Clark in the darkness of that same corner of the porch where she had come searching for gasolene, she appeared suddenly beside him.

"Jelly-bean," she said, "are you here, Jelly-bean? I think — " and her slightest unsteadiness seemed part of an enchanted dream — "I think you deserve one of my sweetest kisses for that, Jelly-bean."

For an instant her arms were around his neck — her lips were pressed to his.

"I'm a wild part of the world, Jelly-bean, but you did me a good turn."

Then she was gone, down the porch, over the cricket-loud lawn. Jim saw Merritt come out the front door and say something to her angrily — saw her laugh and, turning away, walk with averted eyes to his car. Marylyn and Joe followed, singing a drowsy song about a Jazz baby.

Clark came out and joined Jim on the steps. "All pretty lit, I guess," he yawned. "Merritt's in a mean mood. He's certainly off Nancy."

Over east along the golf course a faint rug of gray spread itself across the feet of the night. The party in the car began to chant a chorus as the engine warmed up.

"Good-night everybody," called Clark.

"Good-night, Clark."

"Good-night."

There was a pause, and then a soft happy voice added,

"Good-night, Jelly-bean."

The car drove off to a burst of singing. A rooster on a farm across the way took up a solitary mournful crow, and behind them a last Negro waiter turned out the porch light. Jim and Clark strolled over toward the Ford, their shoes crunching raucously on the gravel drive.

"Oh boy!" sighed Clark softly, "how you can set those dice!"

It was still too dark for him to see the flush on Jim's thin cheeks — or to know that it was a flush of unfamiliar shame.

4

Over Tilly's garage a bleak room echoed all day to the rumble and snorting down-stairs and the singing of the Negro washers as they turned the hose on the cars outside. It was a cheerless square of a room, punctuated with a bed and a battered table on which lay half a dozen books — Joe Miller's "Slow Train thru Arkansas," "Lucille," in an old edition very much annotated in an old-fashioned hand; "The Eyes of the World," by Harold Bell Wright, and an ancient prayer-book of the Church of England with the name Alice Powell and the date 1831 written on the fly-leaf.

The East, gray when the Jelly-bean entered the garage, became a rich and vivid blue as he turned on his solitary electric light. He snapped it out again, and going to the window rested his elbows on the sill and stared into the deepening morning. With the awakening of his emotions, his first perception was a sense of futility, a dull ache at the utter grayness of his life. A wall had sprung up suddenly around him hedging him in, a wall as definite and tangible as the white wall of his bare room. And with his perception of this wall all that had been the romance of his existence, the casualness, the light-hearted improvidence, the miraculous open-handedness of life faded out. The Jelly-bean strolling up Jackson Street humming a lazy song, known at every shop and street stand, cropful of easy greeting and local wit, sad sometimes for only the sake of sadness and the flight of time — that Jelly-bean was suddenly vanished. The very name was a reproach, a triviality. With a flood of insight he knew that Merritt must despise him, that even Nancy's kiss in the dawn would have awakened not jealousy but only a contempt for Nancy's so lowering herself. And on his part the Jelly-bean had used for her a dingy subterfuge learned from the garage. He had been her moral laundry, the stains were his.

As the gray became blue, brightened and filled the room, he crossed to his bed and threw himself down on it, gripping the edges fiercely.

"I love her," he cried aloud, "God!"

As he said this something gave way within him like a lump melting in his throat. The air cleared and became radiant with dawn, and turning over on his face he began to sob dully into the pillow.

In the sunshine of three o'clock Clark Darrow chugging painfully along Jackson Street was hailed by the Jelly-bean, who stood on the curb with his fingers in his vest pockets.

"Hi!" called Clark, bringing his Ford to an astonishing stop along-side. "Just get up?"

The Jelly-bean shook his head.

"Never did go to bed. Felt sorta restless, so I took a long walk this morning out in the country. Just got into town this minute."

"Should think you *would* feel restless. I been feeling thataway all day —— "

"I'm thinkin' of leavin' town," continued the Jelly-bean, absorbed by his own thoughts. "Been thinkin' of goin' up on the farm, and takin' a little that work off Uncle Dun. Reckin I been bummin' too long."

Clark was silent and the Jelly-bean continued:

"I reckin maybe after Aunt Mamie dies I could sink that money of mine in the farm and make somethin' out of it. All my people originally came from that part up there. Had a big place."

Clark looked at him curiously .

"That's funny," he said. "This — this sort of affected me the same way."

The Jelly-bean hesitated.

"I don't know," he began slowly, "somethin' about — about that girl last night talkin' about a lady named Diana Manners — an Eng-lish lady, sorta got me thinkin'!" He drew himself up and looked oddly at Clark, "I had a family once," he said defiantly.

Clark nodded.

"I know."

"And I'm the last of 'em," continued the Jelly-bean, his voice rising slightly, "and I ain't worth shucks. Name they call me by means jelly — weak and wobbly like. People who weren't nothin' when my folks was a lot turn up their noses when they pass me on the street."

Again Clark was silent.

"So I'm through. I'm goin' to-day. And when I come back to this town it's going to be like a gentleman."

Clark took out his handkerchief and wiped his damp brow.

"Reckon you're not the only one it shook up," he admitted gloomily. "All this thing of girls going round like they do is going to stop right quick. Too bad, too, but everybody'll have to see it thataway."

"Do you mean," demanded Jim in surprise, "that all that's leaked out?"

"Leaked out? How on earth could they keep it secret. It'll be an-nounced in the papers to-night. Doctor Lamar's got to save his name somehow."

Jim put his hands on the sides of the car and tightened his long fingers on the metal.

"Do you mean Taylor investigated those checks?"

It was Clark's turn to be surprised.

"Haven't you heard what happened?"

Jim's startled eyes were answer enough.

"Why," announced Clark dramatically, "those four got another bottle of corn, got tight and decided to shock the town — so Nancy and that fella Merritt were married in Rockville at seven o'clock this morning."

A tiny indentation appeared in the metal under the Jelly-bean's fingers.

"Married?"

"Sure enough. Nancy sobered up and rushed back into town, crying and frightened to death — claimed it'd all been a mistake. First Doctor Lamar went wild and was going to kill Merritt, but finally they got it patched up some way, and Nancy and Merritt went to Savannah on the two-thirty train."

Jim closed his eyes and with an effort overcame a sudden sickness.

"It's too bad," said Clark philosophically. "I don't mean the wedding — reckon that's all right, though I don't guess Nancy cared a darn about him. But it's a crime for a nice girl like that to hurt her family that way."

The Jelly-bean let go the car and turned away. Again something was going on inside him, some inexplicable but almost chemical change.

"Where you going?" asked Clark.

The Jelly-bean turned and looked dully back over his shoulder.

"Got to go," he muttered. "Been up too long; feelin' right sick."

"Oh."

The street was hot at three and hotter still at four, the April dust seeming to enmesh the sun and give it forth again as a world-old joke forever played on an eternity of afternoons. But at half past four a first layer of quiet fell and the shades lengthened under the awnings and heavy foliaged trees. In this heat nothing mattered. All life was weather, a waiting through the hot where events had no significance for the cool that was soft and caressing like a woman's hand on a tired forehead. Down in Georgia there is a feeling — perhaps inarticulate — that this is the greatest wisdom of the South — so after a while the Jelly-bean turned into a pool-hall on Jackson Street where he was sure to find a congenial crowd who would make all the old jokes — the ones he knew.

the best of everything

Richard Yates

Nobody expected Grace to do any work the Friday before her wedding. In fact nobody would let her, whether she wanted to or not.

A gardenia corsage lay in a cellophane box beside her typewriter— from Mr. Atwood, her boss—and tucked inside the envelope that came with it was a ten-dollar gift certificate from Bloomingdale's. Mr. Atwood had treated her with a special shy courtliness ever since the time she necked with him at the office Christmas party, and now when she went in to thank him he was all hunched over, rattling desk drawers, blushing and grinning and barely meeting her eyes.

"Aw, now, don't mention it, Grace," he said. "Pleasure's all mine. Here, you need a pin to put that gadget on with?"

"There's a pin that came with it," she said, holding up the corsage. "See? A nice white one."

Beaming, he watched her pin the flowers high on the lapel of her suit. Then he cleared his throat importantly and pulled out the writing panel of his desk, ready to give the morning's dictation. But it turned out there were only two short letters, and it wasn't until an hour later, when she caught him handing over a pile of Dictaphone cylinders to Central Typing, that she realized he had done her a favor.

"That's very sweet of you, Mr. Atwood," she said, "but I do think you ought to give me all your work today, just like any oth — "

"Aw, now, Grace," he said. "You only get married once."

The girls all made a fuss over her too, crowding around her desk and giggling, asking again and again to see Ralph's photograph ("Oh, he's *cute!*"), while the office manager looked on nervously, reluctant to be a spoilsport but anxious to point out that it was, after all, a working day.

Then at lunch there was the traditional little party at Schrafft's — nine women and girls, giddy on their unfamiliar cocktails, letting their chicken à la king grow cold while they pummeled her with old times and good wishes. There were more flowers and another gift — a silver candy dish for which all the girls had whisperingly chipped in.

Grace said "Thank you" and "I certainly do appreciate it" and "I don't know what to say" until her head rang with the words and the corners of her mouth ached from smiling, and she thought the afternoon would never end.

Ralph called up about four o'clock, exuberant. "How ya doin', honey?" he asked, and before she could answer he said, "Listen. Guess what I got?"

"I don't know. A present or something? What?" She tried to sound excited, but it wasn't easy.

"A bonus. Fifty dollars." She could almost see the flattening of his lips as he said "fifty dollars" with the particular earnestness he reserved for pronouncing sums of money.

"Why, that's lovely, Ralph," she said, and if there was any tiredness in her voice he didn't notice it.

"Lovely, huh?" he said with a laugh, mocking the girlishness of the word. "*Ya like* that, huh Gracie? No, but I mean I was really surprised, ya know it? The boss siz, 'Here, Ralph,' and he hands me this envelope. He don't even crack a smile or nothin', and I'm wonderin', what's the deal here? I'm getting fired here, or what? He siz, 'G-ahead, Ralph, open it.' So I open it, and then I look at the boss and he's grinning a mile wide." He chuckled and sighed. "Well, so listen, honey. What time ya want me to come over tonight?"

"Oh, I don't know. Soon as you can, I guess."

"Well listen, I gotta go over to Eddie's house and pick up that bag he's gonna loan me, so I might as well do that, go on home and eat, and then come over to your place around eight-thirty, nine o'clock. Okay?"

"All right," she said. "I'll see you then, darling." She had been calling him "darling" for only a short time — since it had become irrevocably clear that she was, after all, going to marry him — and the word still had an alien sound. As she straightened the stacks of stationery in her desk (because there was nothing else to do), a familiar little panic gripped her; she couldn't marry him — she hardly even *knew* him. Sometimes it occurred to her differently, that she couldn't marry him because she knew him too well, and either way it left her badly shaken, vulnerable to all the things that Martha, her roommate, had said from the very beginning.

"Isn't he funny?" Martha had said after their first date. "He says 'terlet.' I didn't know people really said 'terlet.'" And Grace had giggled, ready enough to agree that it was funny. That was a time when she had been ready to agree with Martha on practically anything — when it often seemed, in fact, that finding a girl like Martha from an ad in the *Times* was just about the luckiest thing that had ever happened to her.

But Ralph had persisted all through the summer, and by fall she had begun standing up for him. "What don't you *like* about him, Martha? He's perfectly nice."

"Oh, everybody's perfectly nice, Grace," Martha would say in her college voice, making perfectly nice a faintly absurd thing to be, and then she'd look up crossly from the careful painting of her fingernails. "It's just that he's such a little — a little *white worm*. Can't you see that?"

"Well, I certainly don't see what his *complexion* has to do with — "

"Oh God, *you* know what I mean. Can't you see what I *mean?* Oh, and all those friends of his, his Eddie and his Marty and his George with their mean, ratty little clerks' lives and their mean, ratty little. . . . It's just that they're all *alike,* those people. All they ever say is 'Hey, wha' happen t'ya Giants?' and 'Hey, wha' happen t'ya Yankees?' and they all live way out in Sunnyside or Woodhaven or some awful place, and their mothers have those damn little china elephants on the mantelpiece." And Martha would frown over her nail polish again, making it clear that the subject was closed.

All that fall and winter she was confused. For a while she tried going out only with Martha's kind of men — the kind that used words like "amusing" all the time and wore small-shouldered flannel suits like a uniform; and for a while she tried going out with no men at all. She even tried that crazy business with Mr. Atwood at the office Christmas party. And all the time Ralph kept calling up, hanging around, waiting for her to make up her mind. Once she took him home to meet her parents in Pennsylvania (where she never would have dreamed of taking Martha), but it wasn't until Easter time that she finally gave in.

They had gone to a dance somewhere in Queens, one of the big American Legion dances that Ralph's crowd was always going to, and when the band played "Easter Parade" he held her very close, hardly moving, and sang to her in a faint, whispering tenor. It was the kind of thing she'd never have expected Ralph to do — a sweet, gentle thing — and it probably wasn't just then that she decided to marry him, but it always seemed so afterwards. It always seemed she had decided that minute, swaying to the music with his husky voice in her hair:

> *"I'll be all in clover*
> *And when they look you over*
> *I'll be the proudest fella*
> *In the Easter Parade...."*

That night she had told Martha, and she could still see the look on Martha's face. "Oh, Grace, you're not — surely you're not *serious.* I mean, I thought he was more or less of a *joke* — you can't really mean you want to — "

"Shut up! You just shut up, Martha!" And she'd cried all night. Even now she hated Martha for it; even as she stared blindly at a row of filing cabinets along the office wall, half sick with fear that Martha was right.

The noise of giggles swept over her, and she saw with a start that two of the girls — Irene and Rose — were grinning over their type-writers and pointing at her. "*We* saw ya!" Irene sang. "*We* saw ya! Mooning again, huh Grace?" Then Rose did a burlesque of mooning, heaving her meager breasts and batting her eyes, and they both collapsed in laughter.

With an effort of will Grace resumed the guileless, open smile of a bride. The thing to do was concentrate on plans.

Tomorrow morning, "bright and early," as her mother would say, she would meet Ralph at Penn Station for the trip home. They'd arrive about one, and her parents would meet the train. "Good t'see ya, Ralph!" her father would say, and her mother would probably kiss him. A warm, homely love filled her: *they* wouldn't call him a white worm; *they* didn't have any ideas about Princeton men and "interesting" men and all the other kinds of men Martha was so stuck-up about. Then her father would probably take Ralph out for a beer and show him the paper mill where he worked (and at least Ralph wouldn't be snobby about a person working in a paper mill, either), and then Ralph's family and friends would come down from New York in the evening.

She'd have time for a long talk with her mother that night, and the next morning, "bright and early" (her eyes stung at the thought of her mother's plain, happy face), they would start getting dressed for the wedding. Then the church and the ceremony, and then the reception (Would her father get drunk? Would Muriel Ketchel sulk about not being a bridesmaid?), and finally the train to Atlantic City, and the hotel. But from the hotel on she couldn't plan any more. A door would lock behind her and there would be a wild, fantastic silence, and nobody in all the world but Ralph to lead the way.

"Well, Grace," Mr. Atwood was saying, "I want to wish you every happiness." He was standing at her desk with his hat and coat on, and all around her were the chattering and scraping-back of chairs that meant it was five o'clock.

"Thank you, Mr. Atwood." She got to her feet, suddenly surrounded by all the girls in a bedlam of farewell.

"All the luck in the world, Grace."

"Drop us a card, huh Grace? From Atlantic City?"

"So long, Grace."

"G'night, Grace, and listen: the best of everything."

Finally she was free of them all, out of the elevator, out of the building, hurrying through the crowds to the subway.

When she got home Martha was standing in the door of the kitchenette, looking very svelte in a crisp new dress.

"Hi, Grace. I bet they ate you alive today, didn't they?"

"Oh no," Grace said. "Everybody was — real nice." She sat down, exhausted, and dropped the flowers and the wrapped candy dish on a table. Then she noticed that the whole apartment was swept and dusted, and the dinner was cooking in the kitchenette. "Gee, everything looks wonderful," she said. "What'd you do all this for?"

"Oh, well, I got home early anyway," Martha said. Then she smiled, and it was one of the few times Grace had ever seen her look shy. "I just thought it might be nice to have the place looking decent for a change, when Ralph comes over."

"Well," Grace said, "it certainly was nice of you."

The way Martha looked now was even more surprising: she looked awkward. She was turning a greasy spatula in her fingers, holding it delicately away from her dress and examining it, as if she had something difficult to say. "Look, Grace," she began. "You do understand why I can't come to the wedding, don't you?"

"Oh, sure," Grace said, although in fact she didn't, exactly. It was something about having to go up to Harvard to see her brother before he went into the Army, but it had sounded like a lie from the beginning.

"It's just that I'd hate you to think I — well, anyway, I'm glad if you do understand. And the other thing I wanted to say is more important."

"What?"

"Well, just that I'm sorry for all the awful things I used to say about Ralph. I never had a right to talk to you that way. He's a very sweet boy and I — well, I'm sorry, that's all."

It wasn't easy for Grace to hide a rush of gratitude and relief when she said, "Why, that's all right, Martha, I — "

"The chops are on fire!" Martha bolted for the kitchenette, "It's all right," she called back. "They're edible." And when she came out to serve dinner all her old composure was restored. "I'll have to eat and run," she said as they sat down. "My train leaves in forty minutes."

"I thought it was *tomorrow* you were going."

"Well, it was, actually," Martha said, "but I decided to go tonight. Because you see, Grace, another thing — if you can stand one more apology — another thing I'm sorry for is that I've hardly ever given you and Ralph a chance to be alone here. So tonight I'm going to clear out." She hesitated. "It'll be a sort of wedding gift from me, okay?" And then she smiled, not shyly this time but in a way that was more in character — the eyes subtly averted after a flicker of special meaning. It was a smile that Grace — through stages of suspicion, bewilderment, awe, and practiced imitation — had long ago come to associate with the word "sophisticated."

"Well, that's very sweet of you," Grace said, but she didn't really get the point just then. It wasn't until long after the meal was over and the dishes washed, until Martha had left for her train in a whirl of cosmetics and luggage and quick goodbyes, that she began to understand.

She took a deep, voluptuous bath and spent a long time drying herself, posing in the mirror, filled with a strange, slow excitement. In her bedroom, from the rustling tissues of an expensive white box, she drew the prizes of her trousseau — a sheer nightgown of white nylon and a matching negligee — put them on, and went to the mirror again. She had never worn anything like this before, or felt like this, and the thought of letting Ralph see her like this sent her into the kitchenette for a glass of the special dry sherry Martha kept for cocktail parties. Then she turned out all the lights but one and, carrying her glass, went to the sofa and arranged herself there to wait for him. After a while she got up and brought the sherry bottle over to the coffee table, where she set it on a tray with another glass.

When Ralph left the office he felt vaguely let down. Somehow, he'd expected more of the Friday before his wedding. The bonus check had been all right (though secretly he'd been counting on twice that amount), and the boys had bought him a drink at lunch and kidded around in the appropriate way ("Ah, don't feel too bad, Ralph — worse things could happen"), but still there ought to have been a real party. Not just the boys in the office, but Eddie, and *all* his friends. Instead there would only be meeting Eddie at the White Rose like every other night of the year, and riding home to borrow Eddie's suitcase and to eat, and then having to ride all the way back to Manhattan just to see Gracie for an hour or two. Eddie wasn't in the bar when he arrived, which sharpened the edge of his loneliness. Morosely he drank a beer, waiting.

Eddie was his best friend, and an ideal best man because he'd been in on the courtship of Gracie from the start. It was in this very bar, in fact, that Ralph had told him about their first date last summer: "Ooh, Eddie — what a paira *knockers!*"

And Eddie had grinned. "Yeah? So what's the roommate like?"

"Ah, you don't want the roommate, Eddie. The roommate's a dog. A snob, too, I think. No, but this *other* one, this little *Gracie* — boy, I mean, she is *stacked.*"

Half the fun of every date — even more than half — had been telling Eddie about it afterwards, exaggerating a little here and there, asking Eddie's advice on tactics. But after today, like so many other pleasures, it would all be left behind. Gracie had promised him at least one night off a week to spend with the boys, after they were married, but even so it would never be the same. Girls never understood a thing like friendship.

There was a ball game on the bar's television screen and he watched it idly, his throat swelling in a sentimental pain of loss. Nearly all his life had been devoted to the friendship of boys and men, to trying to be a good guy, and now the best of it was over.

Finally Eddie's stiff finger jabbed the seat of his pants in greeting. "Whaddya say, sport?"

Ralph narrowed his eyes to indolent contempt and slowly turned around. "Wha' happen ta you, wise guy? Get lost?"

"Whaddya — in a hurry a somethin'?" Eddie barely moved his lips when he spoke. "Can't wait two minutes?" He slouched on a stool and slid a quarter at the bartender. "Draw one, there, Jack."

They drank in silence for a while, staring at the television. "Got a little bonus today," Ralph said. "Fifty dollars."

"Yeah?" Eddie said. "Good."

A batter struck out; the inning was over and the commercial came on. "So?" Eddie said, rocking the beer around in his glass. "Still gonna get married?"

"Why not?" Ralph said with a shrug. "Listen, finish that, willya? I wanna get a move on."

"Wait awhile, wait awhile. What's ya hurry?"

"C'mon, willya?" Ralph stepped impatiently away from the bar. "I wanna go pick up ya bag."

"Ah, bag schmagg."

Ralph moved up close again and glowered at him. "Look, wise guy. Nobody's gonna *make ya* loan me the goddamn bag, ya know. I don't wanna break ya *heart* or nothin' — "

"Arright, arright, arright. You'll getcha bag. Don't worry so much." He finished the beer and wiped his mouth. "Let's go."

Having to borrow a bag for his wedding trip was a sore point with Ralph; he'd much rather have bought one of his own. There was a fine one displayed in the window of a luggage shop they passed every night on their way to the subway — a big, tawny Gladstone with a zippered compartment on the side, at thirty-nine ninety-five — and Ralph had had his eye on it ever since Easter time. "Think I'll buy that," he told Eddie, in the same offhand way that a day or so before he had announced his engagement ("Think I'll marry the girl"). Eddie's response to both remarks had been the same: "Whaddya — crazy?" Both times Ralph had said, "Why not?" and in defense of the bag he had added, "Gonna get married, I'll *need* somethin' like that." From then on it was as if the bag, almost as much as Gracie herself, had become a symbol of the new and richer life he sought. But after the ring and the new clothes and all the other expenses, he'd found at last that he couldn't afford it; he had settled for the loan of Eddie's, which was similar but cheaper and worn, and without the zippered compartment.

Now as they passed the luggage shop he stopped, caught in the grip of a reckless idea. "Hey wait awhile, Eddie. Know what I think I'll do with that fifty-dollar bonus? I think I'll buy that bag right now." He felt breathless.

"Whaddya — crazy? Forty bucks for a bag you'll use maybe one time a year? Ya crazy, Ralph? C'mon."

"Ah — I dunno. Ya think so?"

"Listen, you better *keep* ya money, boy. You're gonna *need* it."

"Ah — yeah," Ralph said at last. "I guess ya right." And he fell in step with Eddie again, heading for the subway. This was the way things usually turned out in his life; he could never own a bag like that until he made a better salary, and he accepted it — just as he'd accepted without question, after the first thin sigh, the knowledge that he'd never possess his bride until after the wedding.

The subway swallowed them, rattled and banged them along in a rocking, mindless trance for half an hour, and disgorged them at last into the cool early evening of Queens.

Removing their coats and loosening their ties, they let the breeze dry their sweated shirts as they walked. "So what's the deal?" Eddie asked. "What time we supposed to show up in this Pennsylvania burg tomorra?"

"Ah, suit yourself," Ralph said. "Any time in the evening's okay."

"So whadda we do then? What the hell can ya *do* in a hillbilly town like that, anyway?"

"Ah, I dunno," Ralph said defensively. "Sit around and talk, I guess; drink beer with Gracie's old man or somethin'; I dunno."

"Jesus," Eddie said. "Some weekend. Big, big deal."

Ralph stopped on the sidewalk, suddenly enraged, his damp coat wadded in his fist. "Look, you bastid. Nobody's gonna *make* ya come, ya know — you or Marty or George or any a the rest of 'em. Get that straight. You're not doin' *me* no favors, unnastand?"

"Whatsa matta?" Eddie inquired. "Whatsa matta? Can'tcha take a joke?"

"Joke," Ralph said. "You're fulla jokes." And plodding sullenly in Eddie's wake, he felt close to tears.

They turned off into the block where they both lived, a double row of neat, identical houses bordering the street where they'd fought and loafed and played stickball all their lives. Eddie pushed open the front door of his house and ushered Ralph into the vestibule, with its homely smell of cauliflower and overshoes. "G'wan in," he said, jerking a thumb at the closed livingroom door, and he hung back to let Ralph go first.

Ralph opened the door and took three steps inside before it hit him like a sock on the jaw. The room, dead silent, was packed deep with grinning, red-faced men — Marty, George, the boys from the block, the boys from the office — everybody, all his friends, all on their feet and poised motionless in a solid mass. Skinny Maguire was crouched at the upright piano, his spread fingers high over the keys, and when he struck the first rollicking chords they all roared into song, beating time with their fists, their enormous grins distorting the words:

"Fa he's a jally guh fella
Fa he's a jally guh fella
Fa he's a jally guh fell-ah
That nobody can deny!"

Weakly Ralph retreated a step on the carpet and stood there wide-eyed, swallowing, holding his coat. *"That nobody can deny!"* they sang, *"That nobody can deny!"* And as they swung into the second chorus Eddie's father appeared through the dining-room curtains, bald and beaming, in full song, with a great glass pitcher of beer in either hand. At last Skinny hammered out the final line:

"That — no — bod — dee — can — dee — nye!"

And they all surged forward cheering, grabbing Ralph's hand, pounding his arms and his back while he stood trembling, his own voice lost under the noise. "Gee, fellas — thanks. I — don't know what to — thanks, fellas. . . ."

Then the crowd cleaved in half, and Eddie made his way slowly down the middle. His eyes gleamed in a smile of love, and from his bashful hand hung the suitcase — not his own, but a new one: the big, tawny Gladstone with the zippered compartment on the side.

"Speech!" they were yelling. *"Speech! Speech!"*

But Ralph couldn't speak and couldn't smile. He could hardly even see.

At ten o'clock Grace began walking around the apartment and biting her lip. What if he wasn't coming? But of course he was coming. She sat down again and carefully smoothed the billows of nylon around her thighs, forcing herself to be calm. The whole thing would be ruined if she was nervous.

The noise of the doorbell was like an electric shock. She was half-way to the door before she stopped, breathing hard, and composed herself again. Then she pressed the buzzer and opened the door a crack to watch for him on the stairs.

When she saw he was carrying a suitcase, and saw the pale serious-ness of his face as he mounted the stairs, she thought at first that he knew; he had come prepared to lock the door and take her in his arms. "Hello, darling," she said softly, and opened the door wider.

"Hi, baby." He brushed past her and walked inside. "Guess I'm late, huh? You in bed?"

"No." She closed the door and leaned against it with both hands holding the doorknob at the small of her back, the way heroines close doors in the movies. "I was just — waiting for you."

He wasn't looking at her. He went to the sofa and sat down, holding the suitcase on his lap and running his fingers over its surface. "Gracie," he said, barely above a whisper. "Look at this."

She looked at it, and then into his tragic eyes.

"Remember," he said, "I told you about that bag I wanted to buy? Forty dollars?" He stopped and looked around. "Hey, where's Martha? She in bed?"

"She's gone, darling," Grace said, moving slowly toward the sofa. "She's gone for the whole weekend." She sat down beside him, leaned close, and gave him Martha's special smile.

"Oh yeah?" he said. "Well anyway, listen. I said I was gonna borrow Eddie's bag instead, remember?"

"Yes."

"Well, so tonight at the White Rose I siz, 'C'mon, Eddie, let's go home pick up ya bag.' He siz, 'Ah, bag schmagg.' I siz, 'Whatsa matta?' but he don't say nothin', see? So we go home to his place and the living-room door's shut, see?"

She squirmed closer and put her head on his chest. Automatically he raised an arm and dropped it around her shoulders, still talking. "He siz, 'G'ahead, Ralph, open the door.' I siz, 'Whatsa deal?' He siz 'Never mind, Ralph, open the door.' So I open the door, and oh Jesus." His fingers gripped her shoulder with such intensity that she looked up at him in alarm.

"They was all there, Gracie," he said. "All the fellas. Playin' the piana, singin', cheerin' — " His voice wavered and his eyelids fluttered shut, their lashes wet. "A big surprise party," he said, trying to smile. "Fa me. Can ya beat that, Gracie? And then — and then Eddie comes out and — Eddie comes out and hands me this. The very same bag I been lookin' at all this time. He bought it with his own money and he didn't say nothin', just to give me a surprise. 'Here, Ralph,' he siz. 'Just to let ya know you're the greatest guy in the world.'" His fingers tightened again, trembling. "I cried, Gracie," he whispered. "I couldn't help it. I don't think the fellas saw it or anything, but I was cryin'." He turned his face away and worked his lips in a tremendous effort to hold back the tears.

"Would you like a drink, darling?" she asked tenderly.

"Nah, that's all right, Gracie. I'm all right." Gently he set the suitcase on the carpet. "Only, gimme a cigarette, huh?"

She got one from the coffee table, put it in his lips and lit it. "Let me get you a drink," she said.

He frowned through the smoke. "Whaddya got, that sherry wine?

Nah, I don't like that stuff. Anyway, I'm fulla beer." He leaned back and closed his eyes. "And then Eddie's mother feeds us this terrific meal," he went on, and his voice was almost normal now. "We had *steaks;* we had French-fried *potatas"* — his head rolled on the sofa-back with each item of the menu — "lettuce-and-tomata *salad, pickles, bread, butter* — everything. The works."

"Well," she said. "Wasn't that nice."

"And afterwards we had ice cream and coffee," he said, "and all the beer we could drink. I mean, it was a real spread."

Grace ran her hands over her lap, partly to smooth the nylon and partly to dry the moisture on her palms. "Well, that certainly was nice of them," she said. They sat there silent for what seemed a long time.

"I can only stay a minute, Gracie," Ralph said at last. "I promised 'em I'd be back."

Her heart thumped under the nylon. "Ralph, do you — do you like this?"

"What, honey?"

"My negligee. You weren't supposed to see it until — after the wedding, but I thought I'd — "

"Nice," he said, feeling the flimsy material between thumb and index finger, like a merchant. "Very nice. Wudga pay fa this, honey?"

"Oh — I don't know. But do you like it?"

He kissed her and began, at last, to stroke her with his hands. "Nice," he kept saying. "Nice. Hey, I like this." His hand hesitated at the low neckline, slipped inside and held her breast.

"I do love you, Ralph," she whispered. "You know that, don't you?"

His fingers pinched her nipple, once, and slid quickly out again. The policy of restraint, the habit of months was too strong to break. "Sure," he said. "And I love you, baby. Now you be a good girl and get ya beauty sleep, and I'll see ya in the morning. Okay?"

"Oh, Ralph. Don't go. Stay."

"Ah, I promised the fellas, Gracie." He stood up and straightened his clothes. "They're waitin' fa me, out home."

She blazed to her feet, but the cry that was meant for a woman's appeal came out, through her tightening lips, as the whine of a wife: "Can't they wait?"

"Whaddya — *crazy?"* He backed away, eyes round with righteousness. She would *have* to understand. If this was the way she acted before the wedding, how the hell was it going to be afterwards?

"Have a *heart,* willya? Keep the fellas waitin' *tonight?* After all they done fa *me?*"

After a second or two, during which her face became less pretty than he had ever seen it before, she was able to smile. "Of course not, darling. You're right."

He came forward again and gently brushed the tip of her chin with his fist, smiling, a husband reassured. " 'At's more like it," he said. "So I'll see ya, Penn Station, nine o'clock tomorra. Right, Gracie? Only, before I go — " he winked and slapped his belly. "I'm fulla beer. Mind if I use ya terlet?"

When he came out of the bathroom she was waiting to say goodnight, standing with her arms folded across her chest, as if for warmth. Lovingly he hefted the new suitcase and joined her at the door. "Okay, then, baby," he said, and kissed her. "Nine o'clock. Don't forget, now."

She smiled tiredly and opened the door for him. "Don't worry, Ralph," she said. "I'll be there."

larchmoor is not the world

R. V. Cassill

In the winter the glassed arcade between Thornton and Gillespie Halls was filled with potted flowers so it smelled and looked like a greenhouse. Last night's storm, blowing in across the athletic fields of the Northwest campus, had left a shape of frozen snow like a white boomerang in the corner of each pane behind the rows of geraniums and ferns.

The first time Dr. Cameron walked through the arcade on this particular day, he stopped to point with his pipestem at the ranked greenery so slightly and perilously separated from the outside cold. "There," he rumbled to Mr. Wilks of History, "is your symbol for this young women's seminary. There is your Larchmoor girl cut off by a pane of glass from the blast of your elements. A visible defiance of the nature of things, made possible by a corrupt technology."

By permission of the author.

Mr. Wilks grimaced and chuckled, weighed this illustration of their common attitude toward the college in which they taught, finally amended, "The glass is wrong. Glass they could see through. See the world in which they don't live, even though. . . ." His thought trailed off in a giggle. At Larchmoor, Mr. Wilks seemed to spend most of his energy looking behind him to see if he had been overheard.

"True," Dr. Cameron said. As they loitered through the arcade the music and the rumble of the student lounge rose to them from the floor below. It rose, mixed inextricably with the smell of baked goods from the dining hall and the moist smell of steam from laboring radiators. Now and then a cry, barbaric, probably happy but otherwise meaningless, punctuated the noise. "The analogy breaks down, true. Listen to them down there. One gets to be like an animal trainer. Sensitive to their noises. If I had no calendar I could tell by their tone that Christmas vacation started this afternoon."

"Then there's an identifying noise that distinguishes Christmas vacation from the beginning of — say — spring vacation?"

"Hmm. Yes, that's right. In seven years my ear has become acutely attuned to it. You'll pick it up eventually. Unhappily, in learning their mass sound you'll become unable to distinguish one of them from the others. Compensation at work. They will seem to you one single enormous female juvenile named Shirley or whatever the name would happen to be of the child movie star ascendant in the year of their birth." Dr. Cameron's baby-pink face grew almost radiant. "Tomorrow," he said, "the sons of bitches will all be gone home and we'll have three weeks of peace. Shantih."

The second time he went through the arcade that day he met Sandra White, dressed for her journey with high heels now and a fur coat, looking like the ads in the fashion magazines with the good sharp empty Nordic shape of her head an appurtenance to the excellent clothes — looking five years older than she had looked that morning in his American Literature class. Her manner, too, had been changed with her clothes, so that she spoke to him as a young matron patronizing an old and crotchety, really lovable duck who had "made his lah-eef out of literature."

"Dr. Cameron. Thank *you* for the list of books," she said. "I don't think I'll give any presents this Christmas except books and I. . . ." Yet because this was so obviously a statement coined to please him, both became momentarily embarrassed. It was the girl who first recovered and went on, "I think I'll get Daddy the Dos Passos' *USA.*"

"Hmmm." He chewed his pipestem and stared at the glass roof of the arcade, then smiled.

"Well," she said in defense, "Daddy is really searching . . . for . . . *that* kind of Americanism. He's not just a businessman. He's really — "

"Yes," he said. "I understand you to say you wanted this list of books for yourself, not just for presents."

"Oh. I'm going to ask for the Yeats for myself," she said. Her tone, demanding that this would please him, produced from the efficient catalog of his memory the image of her eyes becoming feminine-dramatic in that class hour a week before when he had quoted, "An aged man is but a paltry thing . . . unless soul clap its hands and sing and louder sing for every tatter in its mortal dress." Well, the quotation had been an indulgence for him and not intended for the class at all. It had been a parade before their innocent minds of a conscious expression of his own dilemma. He had spoken the lines to his class with the motives that lead a man to confess to his dog the sentiments for which he has no human confidant. But this little female, Sandra, whatever those words may have meant to her, had caught something of their importance to him and trapped him now into paying for the indulgence with a compliment to her taste.

"Fine," he said, "that's fine."

With a still doubtful look she said, "Merry Christmas," and let him go on to his office.

Here was the sanctuary which he had been seven years in building. A desk barred off one corner of the room. When students came in he sat behind it like a magistrate at the bar. Three walls, excepting door and window spaces, were lined to the ceiling with books. "I bought them," he once told Wilks, "but only for insulation and display. It's fatuous to assume that anybody can own books. I think that President Herman is pleased to find them there when he brings down parents and the prospective customers to exhibit me as a mechanism of the English department."

His swivel chair took most of the space behind the desk. It made of the corner an efficient nest, for he could swing to any of the cabinets and drawers in which he filed themes. Also within reach were the two material items he needed for his intellectual life. One was a bolt tied on a length of wrapping cord that he sometimes swung as a pendulum. The other was a motto that he had lettered painstakingly on colored paper. Originally it had come from an examination paper handed in to him during his first year at Larchmoor. "Shelley's main purpose was to write a lot of poems," it said. "This it came easy for him to do."

Sometimes, when he was alone, he would place the inscription before him on his desk and sit laughing crazily at it until all the stains of teaching at Larchmoor were washed away. Then purified, without moving except to throw his shoulders back, he would watch that fraction of the campus where the pendulum of seasons appeared before his window.

This afternoon, the sunlight was a strange and clamorous orange that moved on the black tree trunks and the snow. Here nature dramatized the quality of a Beckmann painting — black cedars over water, it might have been, or such a landscape as the horns in Sibelius presented with not so much art as longing, such a landscape as might contain a golden mute princess called out by Death, that central myth that all the Romantics had exploited.

The embroidered, death-bidden, golden will-o'-the-wisp (and Sandra White now drifted on his mind's screen in a role that would have surprised her. Not as an intellect that shared his understanding of poetry but, wrapped in a rich cocoon of fur, wool, and silk that protected her delicacies from the blowing cold, as the image itself which the poets had conceived and desired — the figure on the Grecian urn, the witchlady on the mead, or that which Malraux's Dutchman saw on the Shanghai sidewalks, proud and strutting beyond the reach of the proletariat's desire) which like Shelley's Beatrice must be the fairest, youngest, purest of flesh to satisfy the snowy mouth of the Death the Romantics had imagined.

The peacefulness of snow is pure commercial folklore, he speculated, and in art the cold North always somehow emerges as the symbol of hungry frenzy — like the gelid and perfect tyranny which Plato described as the worst disaster of all that society can manage. The disorder of cold which had wrought the counter disorder of Northern art — the wind-whipped fires in the snowfield — with its load of desire protesting too much.

If Dr. Cameron had moved closer to his window, he would necessarily have seen more than this private landscape of a few trees, snow, and sun in which his mind pursued the lost girl. He would have seen more than twenty Larchmoor girls standing in the slush in front of the Kampus Kabin while they waited for taxis. They bounced, giggled, sang ("a woman, a woman, a woman without a man, teedlededum, bumph"), chewed gum, shifted packages or suitcases from hand to hand, stamped their fur-topped boots in the muck of the road. He knew they were there, not five degrees outside the arc of vision which the window gave him. "But I have the right not to look."

With the arrival of each Christmas vacation since he had come to Larchmoor, he had discovered himself confronted with a particular crisis of fatigue and depression. The beginning of yet another school year and the first exacting months hollowed him emotionally, and the pleasures of intellect had lost their recreational power. While the girls went off to whatever indulgences the society provided for its most expensive and pampered stock, he went to his bachelor rooms to read and smoke incessantly, and considered how he might get a job elsewhere until always, with the passing of the actual and figurative solstice, the change of renewal occurred. What was compounded of hatred and contempt for Larchmoor led him first to review the other places he had taught — the two big universities where the younger assistants whinnied like mares around the head of the department, and the religious college where he had been forbidden to smoke on campus and required to attend chapel daily — then led through a couple of drinking bouts with some one of his friends, like Mr. Wilks. There had always been younger men like Mr. Wilks coming and going as Larchmoor instructors. Just out of graduate school, they regarded Larchmoor as a stepping stone to bigger schools, but while they stayed — one or two each year succeeding those who had gone — they formed a fit audience though few for such occasions as the Christmas drunks. Those times gave him the chance to elaborate with perverse brilliance on the attractions Larchmoor had for him.

They would be sitting in the easy chairs of his rooms with a litter of crackers and cheese on a card table between them, the black windows frosting over, and in the late hours the monologue would pause only when one or another went unsteadily to the bathroom. "Do you remember reading about that Jap general on Iwo Jima . . . said, 'I will die here' . . . the component of all the forces of his life . . . so that even the melodrama was right for the bandy-legged little bastard. Fitting. The answer is a kind of balance — not balance — but that second in the pendulum's swing when all the forces are composed so there must be an instant of harmony that the eye isn't quick enough to catch when one reasons that there must be no motion. Still . . . The effort of the mind to perpetuate that second by selection out of all the comic and vicious flux in us and around us is the same as the slave's impulse to throw off his ropes. . . . Larchmoor locks up kids that should be out and doing things. Their bad luck is good for me. There are different ages, and for me freedom doesn't exist in the world. It's an asylum growth. . . . I've got my office for asylum like a rat's nest in the corner of a busy house. I don't huddle there

because I'm interested in the house. Nobody but a damn fool would be
concerned with Larchmoor as Larchmoor. . . . It gives me a stable
place to sit and watch the 'pismires' " — here he smiled — " 'and the
stars.' And don't you know, Wilks, that a man has to actually utter
his ideas? Your gloomy newspapers tell you that. It's such an un-
deniable premise of the search for freedom. Here I can say whatever
I please to my classes. Elsewhere, in these days, I might be quickly
apprehended as a Communist or an atheist, but when I say something
to my girls they put it in their notebooks and there's an end to it.
Oh, I have my disguises here. On another level I can talk to the
vermin Herman" — Larchmoor's president — "the same way. As far
as that goes. When he asked me what I thought of the new dormitory
with the air-conditioned bedsprings, I made some trivial remark about
painting 'our outward walls so costly gay.' And he thought it was my
stamp of approval, yes he did. . . . And then we mustn't fool ourselves.
Where else could I go? I'm not a scholar in the sense that I've ever
felt a mission to get my name in *PMLA,* or write a book on Chaucer's
cook's marmal. I'm a reader, that's all I amount to. 'Whatever games
are played with us, we must play no games with ourselves, but deal
in our privacy with the last honesty and truth.' Larchmoor not only
lets but forces me to be honest with myself. The games it plays with
me are not much bother. To them I'm just an old gaffer that talks
like Bartlett's quotations. I have a place here. They pay me as a fix-
ture. . . . The girls are pretty. Like old David's, my bones need the
warmth provided by a moderate proximity of young female flesh. My
disguises . . . I look too old to notice them. I am too old to letch for
any of them, but by God they're pleasant furniture. . . . At Larchmoor
I come close to balancing. If it were any better I'd get involved with
it. No doubt I've searched subconsciously for Larchmoor all my life.
I'm preoccupied with how I die. Like the Jap general. That isn't
morbid at my age. More natural. I want to die in this moral Iwo
Jima . . . and be buried under the hockey field."

He had put on his overcoat to go home when he passed through
the glassed arcade for the third time that day. This time a clatter of
heels on the tile floor rang behind him. There was a hand on his arm
and Shirley Bridges' face suddenly thrust so close to his own that he
jumped back. At first, the circles of white around her eyes and the
chalky stripes on either side of her mouth struck him as an antic
fashion culled from the pages of *Vogue* and destined to become a part
of the fluctuating uniform of Larchmoor. But even as he began to

smile, her hand clawed down his sleeve until she had hold of his bare
wrist and he understood that her face was marked with some girlish
emotion. Her hand on his wrist was wet and cold. He felt pain in the
back of his skull and then a release of anger. "What's the trouble,
Miss Bridges?" He lifted her fingers one at a time from their hysterical
grasp. "Are you ill?"

To his exasperation she said, "No. My grade. You — "

"I understand," he said. He cleared his throat the better to snarl.
"In spite of your studious industry, I, I, I have so seriously misprized
you that I reported you to the Dean, who maliciously put you on
academic probation. Now you're going to be forbidden the delights of
the jukebox and the downtown dance hall for the rest of the semester."
The tonic of anger had blurred away any distinctions he might have
tried to make between her and The Larchmoor Girl in a more tem-
perate season. "Every coercion will be applied to force you to the unreasonable humiliation of reading your books. I am committed to the
belief that you will live through it. Now, if you will excuse me, may
I bid you a Merry Chirstmas?"

"Please," she said. In the blue expanse of her eyes the pupil diminished nastily like an insect pulling its wings to its body.

He felt the burning of his face. She'd better not put her hands on
me again, he thought. "Don't take all this so intensely. There really
isn't any reason you can't make up your work. Weren't you the one
last fall who was, well — so sublimely confident of her ability? You
sometimes make interesting comments in class. I think you just need
to decide to do some work."

"No," she said. "Talk to me." Her mouth hung loose like a bright
ribbon, and her tongue arched against her lower teeth.

"You're *not* well."

She nodded. "Talk to me in your office. Please."

One hall on their way led past the president's office and reception
rooms. She would not go this way. Without quite knowing why, he
let her guide him down a roundabout stairway.

While he lit his pipe and rocked squeaking in his swivel chair, he
looked at the girl's hands. The lacquered nails were broader than they
were long and the fingers were tapered like a child's from the palm.
How do they manage to look like *women?* he asked himself. What
corruption and tampering with mortality in the flesh is it that lets
them or makes them look generally the same from fifteen to thirty-five,
brushed and painted and girdled to a formula that here across his desk

was breaking down into its sodden components? He noted that two beads of spittle had stuck in the corners of Shirley's mouth.

What would be the effect, he wondered, if he should announce at once that he had reconsidered her case and had already decided to give her an A for the semester?

"You restore my faith," he said. "In seven years of teaching here I have never seen a Larchmoor girl who spent the day before a vacation even thinking about the college, let alone the grades she might get in one class in Biblical Literature."

"They're going to kick me out," she said.

"Oh nonsense. No final grades go in for six weeks yet."

"They are," she insisted. "They sent for Daddy. He's in President Herman's office now. I know they sent for him to take me out of school."

"Because of your grades? Not because of your grades, surely."

"Oh. I thought if I could get my grades straightened out that would help."

"You mean you've got in some kind of trouble. If your grades were good you might get by with it?"

The note of sarcasm was heavy enough to warn her of a trap. She said, "No. I don't think there would be any trouble if my grades were all right. I could work everything else out, I know."

"If you're in difficulty you ought to have gone to your housemother, not to me."

"Honest, it's the grades and my classes and things."

Dr. Cameron shook his head. His white mustache dipped at the ends as he made a face. "I'm guilty of many things, but I have never given any grades I didn't think were deserved; so there isn't much use to talk about that. Nevertheless I might tell you something that will reassure you. Among other things Larchmoor is a commercial institution. I have even heard President Herman speak of it as a business. You pay a considerable tuition here which would have to be refunded if you were dropped before the end of the semester. I have no doubt that the administration will find some way to avoid that unpleasant necessity." This will end the interview, he thought. She can understand that better than anything. Coin is the sea that bore them hither and will bear them hence. It is the direct communication, the basis of knowledge on which whatever they might get from the library or classroom would only be fluff. "Does that explain exactly why they aren't going to kick you out?"

"It isn't that way, is it?"

He grinned like a devil. "Undoubtedly." Less because she demanded it than because of the habit of explanation he went on, "There's much more to it than that. I have simply given you a short cut to understanding why you won't be expelled. From your side of the fence everything seems to be an absolute. Every rule, every pronouncement, perhaps. I'm old enough to know there are no absolutes. Everyone here who has anything to do with your case lives in a tangle of confusions and opinions not so different from your own. Out of these will come some compromise that won't be too hard on you. That's the truth. That's the way the world goes. Compromise, compromise. President Herman's decrees and judgments may seem absolute and final to a freshman. They're not, really. He's not God Almighty."

"They're all God Almighty," the girl said. "My father is God Almighty too." He was not sure whether she meant this as a joke or as an attempt at philosophy, but whichever it was it seemed to amuse her. "That's why it's so goofy. They say I destroyed their faith. Didn't you hear about that, Dr. Cameron? It happened in your Biblical Lit class so I guess you knew about it. It's so funny because I think there is God Almighty. Lots of them. You're another one, because remember at the first of the year you told us to use our minds and question things, and then I was the only one that argued, and you're going to give me an F."

"You haven't handed in any work," he said irrelevantly. He turned the swivel chair sharply sideways so the old bearings screamed. So the other little ones had sat in class all semester being careful to hear nothing, read nothing before their open eyes except what confirmed those memories of Sunday school they liked to call "their faith." All right. He had known that and had remarked on it caustically. But here was the other twist — that they were leagued, each little monster with her shining braids, to smell out differences within the herd which had not been apparent to him. He labored his memory for images of the class from which this one girl would appear standing like a martyr among the Philistian mob. She said that she had "argued." He could remember nothing of the sort. Each day she had seemed as impersonal as a ninepin in a row of her classmates. Her eyes had been as blue as theirs, her hair more blond than some; the courtesy of her bored attention had been the same, though she had not taken notes so assiduously as a few. Somehow, on a level of intuition that he could only guess at, they had found the intolerable difference in her. He remembered the wetness of her hand on his wrist and wondered if it had been fear they smelled.

"I thought you got along all right with the girls," he said.

"I will try. I will get along if they'll let me stay. I think I was just beginning to make some friends." She drew in her upper arms against her breasts and shivered.

"That sort of thing has to happen. I don't suppose it's possible to *make* friends."

The idea, with her own interpretation, had not helped. "I know I could," she said.

"Don't you have any — well, people, girls you run around with here?"

"Oh yes. My roommate. And there's lots of others. I know how to make them like me if I could stay."

If there had been someone impartial with them — Mr. Wilks perhaps — to whom he could have rationalized the abyss he glimpsed, letting orderly words mount like a steel bridge over it, he might still have kept himself from involvement. "One must not seek the contagion of the herd," he would have said. "God knows what conformities they may exact from her once she has kissed the rod. Whatever it may cost to maintain even the fear, if it's only the fear that distinguishes one . . ." If he could have found the words on which he depended.

" 'Larchmoor, calm and serene on thy hill,' " he muttered. "Now Miss Bridges, Shirley, maybe we ought to look at this another way. Suppose they . . . suppose you leave Larchmoor now. There are bigger schools you might go to where you'd have a better chance to be yourself."

"Bigger?" she said. "Oh no."

"You mustn't forget that there is time for anything you want to do."

"Not if I go home," she said.

"But you're wrong. There will be fifty years ahead of you," he said, realizing that she could not believe this. "Larchmoor is not the world. Every possibility is open at your age."

"Would you go to the president and tell him I'm a good student? Could you give me any kind of a good grade if I'd work all through vacation?" She rose and came around the desk and stood just in front of him, just beyond arm's length from him. She stood very straight facing him and neither swaying nor looking at him.

"Please," he said. "Sit down. I'm afraid I don't understand at all. I can't understand why it's so important for you to stay here. You have so many years ahead of you. There is plenty of time. Go home for a while."

She sighed like a child, heavily. "I guess I ought to tell you why they sent for Daddy. It was because when the railroad agents came out to sell tickets home I was the only girl in school who wasn't going. I would have stayed here if they would have let me. Then I got scared and rented a hotel room downtown."

He was afraid to ask any further questions. Once again his necessary refuge was not in forty years of the poor scholar's study but only in the pipe which he could chew and smoke and scrape ostentatiously, as he did now. His eyebrows arched as though to admonish her to say no more.

"I can't go home. I'm afraid of Daddy. That was the reason."

"Now, now. You could surely explain to him. . . . Grades aren't that important."

"He fought me last summer with his fists. I'm not quite as strong as he is. He knocked me down and was choking me when Mother came and made him stop." The words were rushing from her throat like a foul torrent heaved up by the convulsions of her body as she writhed from side to side. "Don't know what he'll do to me now. Now. Now."

The revelation of pain, however confused, was not to be doubted.

(So Shelley's Beatrice would have said, "Reach me that handkerchief — my brain is hurt.")

Then as though she was rid of it, she quieted. "I hit him first and cut his face with my ring." She held up her right hand, showing the ring, and for the first time that afternoon laughed shortly.

Resentment mixed with his bewilderment and horror. All around about them, he thought, on the walls and towers of Larchmoor, on the stubblefields and highways for unimaginable miles lies the snow. It's as if she's trying to drag me with her into elements that neither of us, teacher or student, should ever have to face. She's trying to elect me not just her father, but as she said, God Almighty.

"Why?" he asked. His voice seemed to boom.

"I don't know why he did it," she said with crazy slyness, her face weird.

(*Oh, icehearted counselor . . .*
If I could find a word that might make known
The crime of my destroyer. . . .)

"Are you sure you're well? Have you told anybody else about this?"

She shook her head. "They sent me downtown to see the psychiatrist when they found out I wasn't going home. I told him. He said he'd help me. I think he's the one that told them to send for Daddy to come and get me. I'm in trouble, so they're afraid I'll dirty up their college. But I would be good and everybody would get to like me if I could stay."

The president's secretary knocked on his door and put her head in. "Oh, good," she said, seeing them both, and then bobbing her head as though to confirm a suspicion that they were both quite real. "Can I speak to you privately, Dr. Cameron?" She pulled the door tight behind him and whispered, "Wheeeew, what a relief. The whole campus has been upside down looking for Shirley Bridges. Her father wants her upstairs. We couldn't find her in her room and they thought she might have done away with herself."

"Who thought that?" he demanded angrily.

"I don't know. We were all worried."

"But why should anyone think such a thing?"

"We've been having a lot of trouble with her. Her father says she gets in trouble wherever she goes. He just can't seem to do anything with her. He's going to take her home. I guess it's a good thing he came when he did. We had to send her to the psychiatrist last week."

"Oh, that's nonsense. Anyone can go to a psychiatrist."

"Well," she said. "Well, don't pick on me. Will you send her right up to the president's office?"

Instead he went himself. The noise in the halls was faint and infrequent now. Buses and taxis had carried most of the students to the depot. He passed one of the maids locking her mops into a closet and slowed his angry, absorbed march to say Merry Christmas to her.

A little man whose mouth protruded as though he were deciding whether or not to whistle sat in the president's reception room. He looked as sleek and innocent as a little dachshund perched on the edge of an overstuffed lounge. Dr. Cameron nodded stiffly to him. So this is the fistfighter, he thought. The champ.

"Go right in," the secretary said.

The hand in which President Herman held his glasses dangled over a chairback. He gestured with the glasses to indicate that Dr. Cameron should sit down.

"I'm glad you've come, Arthur," he said. "I understand from Miss Lee that Shirley Bridges has been in your office all afternoon. We've been very much concerned with Shirley today."

"As well we might be."

"Yes. Oh, yes."

"She's in a very tight spot. You might call it a kind of snare that tightens the more she struggles."

"She's not well. Upset mentally. There are always the few who can't adjust to Larchmoor. Her father is very much concerned with her, poor fellow." He sighed. His eyes rolled up under their thick lids.

"The girl has a rather different interpretation of him."

"You mean about her father's beating her? That's an unsavory story for her to tell, isn't it?" He looked challengingly across his desk like a lawyer requiring a yes-or-no answer. He's no fool, Cameron thought. This is going to be difficult. The president continued, "Shirley is quite an actress. Her talent should find its outlet on the stage. She's told that story to several people around here. Did she just tell you today? She seems to have fled to you as a last resort. If I'm not mistaken, she told the same story to the housemother before she'd been here two weeks. With different embellishments, I suppose. She'd broken this or that rule and seemed to think the story would be a kind of excuse. Don't you think a less unpleasant story might have served her better?"

"And what if it is true?"

"Do you believe it?"

"Suppose I did not. Why did Miss Lee say to me 'they thought she might have done away with herself'? Whether you believe the story or not, you seem to recognize a terrible situation there."

"I'm sure that I have no idea what Miss Lee may have meant." There was a clock on President Herman's desk with ornate bronze scrolls representing the tails of mermaids. With a lead pencil's point he traced out first one then the other of these scrolls. "I have, just as an assumption, gone so far as to assume that Shirley's story with all its — its morbid implications — might have some foundation. I have a psychiatrist's report in which such possibilities are examined. Inconclusively, anyway. I don't put much stock in psychiatry. It's best not to. But if they had any basis, I would say they were the best of reasons why Shirley — and her father — ought to scamper away from Larchmoor, wouldn't you, Arthur?"

"I would not. She needs something to hang on to. Let her stay, Dr. Herman."

"Mr. Bridges has decided, I think, that he'll take her home. That was all settled before you came up, Arthur."

"Are you going to let him? Whatever else is true, that girl's afraid of him."

"Is she? Maybe she's been up to something that ought to make her afraid of him." He sighed deeply for Larchmoor's sake. "That kind

of thing has happened here before. Another good reason she shouldn't
be here. Arthur, do you imagine that I am going to tell a parent —
a *parent* — that Larchmoor forbids him to take his daughter home?"
He chuckled at the impossibility.

> (*"Think of the offender's gold, his dreaded hate,
> And the strange horror of the accuser's tale
> Baffling belief and overpowering speech."*)

"Larchmoor isn't a hospital, Arthur. If Shirley is having mental
troubles and her father isn't, ah, just the one to see that she's taken
care of properly, some of the family will surely handle it."

"They will? How do we know? 'O that the vain remorse which
must chastise crimes done had but as loud a voice to warn —' "

President Herman tapped his pencil impatiently on the desk top.
"That's all very well," he said.

"It means, in the language of the Rotary Club, 'Don't expect
George to do it.' "

"You think I might understand the language of the Rotary Club?"

"In the situation that's what it means. It's from a play. The *Cenci*.
By Shelley. He was an English poet." He had seen the warning glitter
in President Herman's eyes but he could not stop his sarcasm.

Yet President Herman maintained the reserve which had helped
him greatly in administering a school so old and prosperous as Larchmoor for so many years.

"Arthur, do you realize the scandal we narrowly missed? Seems
she had rented a hotel room downtown and told her roommate she
was going to stay there and 'get soused.' Can you imagine?"

"So her roomrate told you that? My God, my God. Doesn't Larchmoor ever produce anything but little stoolies? I don't understand
that girl, but I believe she needs help. And as soon as there is some
suspicion that she might, every student and old maid housemother
and the administration itself set on her. Did you ever see a flock of
chickens go after one with a broken leg?"

Now President Herman's face had grown faintly red. "I must say,
Arthur, that I'm considerably interested in hearing your opinion of
Larchmoor. You've always seemed rather reticent and noncommittal.
All these years. I'm glad to know what you think of us."

The two old men glared at each other. "I apologize," Dr. Cameron
said. "That was an unfortunate outburst. Let me begin again and
appeal to you in the name of the Christian principles which guide
Larchmoor."

"I resent your sneering when you say 'Christian principles.'"

Both of them stood up. "If I sneered," said Dr. Cameron, "the intonation was superfluous. I told that girl . . ." Compromise, compromise were the words he had in mind. He could see no reason now for saying them.

Blinded by his feeling — the whole compounded hate for Larchmoor, which must gloss over everything — he stumbled against a little mahogany coffee table as he turned to leave. This little and inconsequential piece of reality that had tripped him up was, finally, his undoing. President Herman might have forgiven him or forgotten the hot things he had said. But when he felt the table strike his shins, he stood for just one second watching it, then he kicked it with all his might. It flew against the wall, its glass top tinkling, and lay on its side.

He threw his hands above his head in a terrible gesture. "You dull, criminal, unperceiving bastards," he shouted and rushed from the room.

If Mr. Bridges had still been outside in the waiting room, he would have struck the man, and seen how good he was with his fists at anything besides beating up his daughter. The little dachshund man had gone. No one was there but Miss Lee, the secretary. She was watching him with terror, and it did him good to see her cringe.

Without beginning to think what he would say to Shirley, only aware that it was now he who must and would protect her, he went to his office with all the speed his old legs could manage.

She was not there. He hunted, ridiculously, in the offices next his own and in the nearby classrooms, almost dark now. He had a tremendous fear for the girl. His head began to ache as he trotted from room to room.

There is a long hall in the buildings at Larchmoor, beneath the glassed arcade and extending through the principal structures as an evidence that Larchmoor girls not only don't have to go out in the weather as they pass from bedroom to dining room to classroom, but that they need not even veer from a luxuriously straight path. After the classrooms, Dr. Cameron went to the end of this hall. There, far off, down a long perspective of windows and doors, he saw Shirley and her father. They were talking, and as he watched, the dachshund man took her coat from the rack outside the student lounge and held it for her while she put her arms into it and flipped her hair up over the collar. They went out the front door together.

He got his coat and overshoes. He took from his desk the gloves which he had been almost ready to put on two hours ago. He walked down the hall toward the door from which Shirley and her father had left, but slowly, reluctantly. Was it all a lie that she had told him? If he were going to come back at the end of vacation, would he have heard that one of the busy-bodies on the Larchmoor payroll had unearthed the plot? "She just tried to fix it so she could stay in the hotel with her boy friend. Got caught at it." No, no, it couldn't be just that. Whatever it was, though, however muddled and sordid, the walls of Larchmoor — that were bigger, much bigger than Larchmoor; as big as money and complacency — were going to enclose it gently in indestructible steam heat. He was the only one who had been pro-jected, tossed, into the cold, where an old scholar had to worry about rent.

The lights along Larchmoor's main walk had a festive air. Each one had been wreathed in red and green for holiday. At the bases of the lampposts and in the trees overhead, driven back only a little, lurked the blue shadows of the absolute snow. It was not Shirley who had lured him out of his warm corner into this, not any real Shirley that he had been protecting or that had determined he would die in the real cold, he thought, defending himself against self-ridicule, self-obloquy. The realer Beatrice, the gold-embroidered princess, the beau-tiful lady without mercy and without hope had brought him out of the door.

drama

cat on a hot tin roof

Tennessee Williams

CHARACTERS

MARGARET

BRICK

MAE, sometimes called Sister Woman

BIG MAMA

DIXIE, a little girl

BIG DADDY

REVEREND TOOKER

GOOPER, sometimes called Brother Man

DOCTOR BAUGH, pronounced "Baw"

LACEY, a Negro servant

SOOKEY, another

Another little girl and two small boys

(The playing script of Act III also includes TRIXIE, another little girl, also DAISY, BRIGHTIE and SMALL, servants.)

Notes for the designer

The set is the bed-sitting-room of a plantation home in the Mississippi Delta. It is along an upstairs gallery which probably runs around the entire house; it has two pairs of very wide doors opening

onto the gallery; showing white balustrades against a fair summer
sky that fades into dusk and night during the course of the play,
which occupies precisely the time of its performance, excepting, of
course, the fifteen minutes of intermission.

Perhaps the style of the room is not what you would expect in the
home of the Delta's biggest cotton-planter. It is Victorian with a
touch of the Far East. It hasn't changed much since it was occupied
by the original owners of the place, Jack Straw and Peter Ochello, a
pair of old bachelors who shared this room all their lives together.
In other words, the room must evoke some ghosts; it is gently and
poetically haunted by a relationship that must have involved a
tenderness which was uncommon. This may be irrelevant or un-
necessary, but I once saw a reproduction of a faded photograph of the
verandah of Robert Louis Stevenson's home on that Samoan Island
where he spent his last years, and there was a quality of tender light
on weathered wood, such as porch furniture made of bamboo and
wicker, exposed to tropical suns and tropical rains, which came to
mind when I thought about the set for this play, bringing also to
mind the grace and comfort of light, the reassurance it gives, on a
late and fair afternoon in summer, the way that no matter what, even
dread of death, is gently touched and soothed by it. For the set is the
background for a play that deals with human extremities of emotion,
and it needs that softness behind it.

The bathroom door, showing only pale-blue tile and silver towel
racks, is in one side wall; the hall door in the opposite wall. Two
articles of furniture need mention: a big double bed which staging
should make a functional part of the set as often as suitable, the
surface of which should be slightly raked to make figures on it seen
more easily; and against the wall space between the two huge double
doors upstage: a monumental monstrosity peculiar to our times, a
huge console combination of radio-phonograph (Hi-Fi with three
speakers) TV set *and* liquor cabinet, bearing and containing many
glasses and bottles, all in one piece, which is a composition of
muted silver tones, and the opalescent tones of reflecting glass,
a chromatic link, this thing, between the sepia (towny gold) tones
of the interior and the cool (white and blue) tones of the gallery and
sky. This piece of furniture (?!), this monument is a very complete
and compact little shrine to virtually all the comforts and illusions
behind which we hide from such things as the characters in the play
are faced with. . . . The set should be far less realistic than I have so
far implied in this description of it. I think the walls below the
ceiling should dissolve mysteriously into air; the set should be roofed
by the sky; stars and moon suggested by traces of milky pallor, as
if they were observed through a telescope lens out of focus.

Anything else I can think of? Oh, yes, fanlights (transoms shaped like an open glass fan) above all the doors in the set, with panes of blue and amber, and above all, the designer should take as many pains to give the actors room to move about freely (to show their restlessness, their passion for breaking out) as if it were a set for a ballet.

An evening in summer. The action is continuous, with two inter-missions.

ACT ONE: *At the rise of the curtain someone is taking a shower in the bathroom, the door of which is half open. A pretty young woman, with anxious lines in her face, enters the bedroom and crosses to the bathroom door.*

MARGARET (*shouting above roar of water*): One of those no-neck monsters hit me with a hot buttered biscuit so I have t' change!
(MARGARET'S *voice is both rapid and drawling. In her long speeches she has the vocal tricks of a priest delivering a liturgical chant, the lines are almost sung, always continuing a little beyond her breath so she has to gasp for another. Sometimes she inter-sperses the lines with a little wordless singing, such as "Da-da-daaaa!"*
Water turns off and BRICK *calls out to her, but is still unseen. A tone of politely feigned interest, masking indifference, or worse, is characteristic of his speech with* MARGARET.)
BRICK: Wha'd you say, Maggie? Water was on s' loud I couldn't hearya. . . .
MARGARET: Well, I! — just remarked that! — one of th' no-neck mon-sters messed up m' lovely lace dress so I got t' — cha-a-ange. . . .
(*She opens and kicks shut drawers of the dresser.*)
BRICK: Why d'ya call Gooper's kiddies no-neck monsters?
MARGARET: Because they've got no necks! Isn't that a good enough reason?
BRICK: Don't they have any necks?
MARGARET: None visible. Their fat little heads are set on their fat little bodies without a bit of connection.
BRICK: That's too bad.
MARGARET: Yes, it's too bad because you can't wring their necks if they've got no necks to wring! Isn't that right honey? (*She steps out of her dress, stands in a slip of ivory satin and lace.*) Yep, they're no-neck monsters, all no-neck people are monsters . . .
(CHILDREN *shriek downstairs.*)

Hear them? Hear them screaming? I don't know where their voice-boxes are located since they don't have necks. I tell you I got so nervous at that table tonight I thought I would throw back my head and utter a scream you could hear across the Arkansas border an' parts of Louisiana an' Tennessee. I said to your charming sister-in-law, Mae, honey, couldn't you feed those precious little things at a separate table with an oilcloth cover? They make such a mess an' the lace cloth looks *so* pretty! She made enormous eyes at me and said, "Ohhh, noooooo! On Big Daddy's birthday? Why, he would never forgive me!" Well, I want you to know, Big Daddy hadn't been at the table two minutes with those five no-neck monsters slobbering and drooling over their food before he threw down his fork an' shouted, "Fo' God's sake, Gooper, why don't you put them pigs at a trough in th' kitchen?" — Well, I swear, I simply could have di-ieed!

Think of it, Brick, they've got five of them and number six is coming. They've brought the whole bunch down here like animals to display at a county fair. Why, they have those children doin' tricks all the time! "Junior, show Big Daddy how you do this, show Big Daddy how you do that, say your little piece fo' Big Daddy, Sister. Show your dimples, Sugar. Brother, show Big Daddy how you stand on your head!" — It goes on all the time, along with constant little remarks and innuendos about the fact that you and I have not produced any children, are totally childless and therefore totally useless! — Of course it's comical but it's also disgusting since it's so obvious what they're up to!

BRICK (*without interest*): What are they up to, Maggie?

MARGARET: Why, you know what they're up to!

BRICK (*appearing*): No, I don't know what they're up to.

(*He stands there in the bathroom doorway drying his hair with a towel and hanging onto the towel rack because one ankle is broken, plastered and bound. He is still slim and firm as a boy. His liquor hasn't started tearing him down outside. He has the additional charm of that cool air of detachment that people have who have given up the struggle. But now and then, when disturbed, something flashes behind it, like lightning in a fair sky, which shows that at some deeper level he is far from peaceful. Perhaps in a stronger light he would show some signs of deliquescence, but the fading, still warm, light from the gallery treats him gently.*)

MARGARET: I'll tell you what they're up to, boy of mine! — They're up to cutting you out of your father's estate, and — (*She freezes momentarily before her next remark. Her voice drops as if it were somehow a personally embarrassing admission.*) — Now we know that Big Daddy's dyin' of — *cancer*. . . . (*There are voices on the lawn below: long-drawn calls across distance. Margaret raises her lovely bare arms and powders her armpits with a light sigh. She adjusts the angle of a magnifying mirror to straighten an eyelash, then rises fretfully saying:*) There's so much light in the room it —

BRICK (*softly but sharply*): Do we?

MARGARET: Do we what?

BRICK: Know Big Daddy's dyin' of cancer?

MARGARET: Got the report today.

BRICK: Oh . . .

MARGARET (*letting down bamboo blinds which cast long, gold-fretted shadows over the room*): Yep, got th' report just now . . . it didn't surprise me, Baby. . . . (*Her voice has range, and music; sometimes it drops low as a boy's and you have a sudden image of her playing boys' games as a child.*) I recognized the symptoms soon's we got here last spring and I'm willin' to bet you that Brother Man and his wife were pretty sure of it, too. That more than likely explains why their usual summer migration to the coolness of the Great Smokies was passed up this summer in favor of — hustlin' down here ev'ry whipstitch with their whole screamin' tribe! And why so many allusions have been made to Rainbow Hill lately. You know what Rainbow Hill is? Place that's famous for treatin' alcoholics an' dope fiends in the movies!

BRICK: I'm not in the movies.

MARGARET: No, and you don't take dope. Otherwise you're a perfect candidate for Rainbow Hill, Baby, and that's where they aim to ship you — over my dead body! Yep, over my dead body they'll ship you there, but nothing would please them better. Then Brother Man could get a-hold of the purse strings and dole out remittances to us, maybe get power-of-attorney and sign checks for us and cut off our credit wherever, whenever he wanted! Son-of-a-bitch! — How'd you like that, Baby? — Well, you've been doin' just about ev'rything in your power to bring it about, you've just been doin' ev'rything you can think of to aid and abet them in this scheme of theirs! Quittin' work, devoting yourself to the occupation of drinkin'! — Breakin' your ankle last night on the high school athletic field: doin' what? Jumpin' hurdles? At two or three in the morning? Just fantastic! Got in the paper. *Clarksdale Register* carried a nice little item about it, human interest story about a well-known former athlete stagin' a one-man track meet on the Glorious Hill High School athletic field last night, but was slightly out of condition and didn't clear the first hurdle! Brother Man Gooper claims he exercised his influence t' keep it from goin' out over AP or UP or every goddam "P." But, Brick. You still have one big advantage!

(*During the above swift flood of words,* BRICK *has reclined with contrapuntal leisure on the snowy surface of the bed and has rolled over carefully on his side or belly.*)

BRICK (*wryly*): Did you *say* something, Maggie?

MARGARET: Big Daddy dotes on you, honey. And he can't stand Brother Man and Brother Man's wife, that monster of fertility, Mae; she's downright odious to him! Know how I know? By little expressions that flicker over his face when that woman is holding fo'th on one of her choice topics such as — how she refused twilight sleep! — when the twins were delivered! Because she feels motherhood's an experience that a woman ought to experience fully! — in order to fully appreciate the wonder and beauty of it! HAH! (*This loud "HAH!" is accompanied by a violent action such as slamming a drawer shut.*) — and how she made Brother Man come in an' stand beside her in the delivery room so he would not miss out on the "wonder and beauty" of it either! — producin' those no-neck monsters. . . . (*A speech of this kind would be antipathetic from almost anybody but* MARGARET; *she makes it oddly funny, because her eyes constantly twinkle and her voice shakes with laughter which is basically indulgent.*) — Big Daddy shares my attitude toward those two! As for me, well — I give him a laugh now and then and he tolerates me. In fact! — I sometimes suspect that Big Daddy harbors a little unconscious "lech" fo' me. . . .

BRICK: What makes you think that Big Daddy has a lech for you, Maggie?

MARGARET: Way he always drops his eyes down my body when I'm talkin' to him, drops his eyes to my boobs an' licks his old chops! Ha ha!

BRICK: That kind of talk is disgusting.

MARGARET: Did anyone ever tell you that you're an ass-aching Puritan, Brick?

I think it's mighty fine that that ole fellow, on the doorstep of death, still takes in my shape with what I think is deserved appreciation!

And you wanta know something else? Big Daddy didn't know how many little Maes and Goopers had been produced! "How many kids have you got?" he asked at the table, just like Brother Man and his wife were new acquaintances to him! Big Mama said he was jokin', but that ole boy wasn't jokin', Lord, no!

And when they infawmed him that they had five already and were turning out number six! — the news seemed to come as a sort of unpleasant surprise . . .

> (CHILDREN *yell below.*)

Scream, monsters!

> (*Turns to* BRICK *with a sudden, gay, charming smile which fades as she notices that he is not looking at her but into fading gold space with a troubled expression.*
>
> (*It is constant rejection that makes her humor "bitchy."*)

Yes, you should of been at that supper-table, Baby.

> (*Whenever she calls him "baby" the word is a soft caress.*)

Y'know, Big Daddy, bless his ole sweet soul, he's the dearest ole thing in the world, but he does hunch over his food as if he preferred not to notice anything else. Well, Mae an' Gooper were side by side at the table, direckly across from Big Daddy, watchin' his face like hawks while they jawed an' jabbered about the cuteness an' brilliance of th' no-neck monsters!

> (*She giggles with a hand fluttering at her throat and her breast and her long throat arched.*
>
> (*She comes downstage and recreates the scene with voice and gesture.*)

And the no-neck monsters were ranged around the table, some in high chairs and some on th' *Books of Knowledge,* all in fancy little paper taps in honor of Big Daddy's birthday, and all through dinner, well, I want you to know that Brother Man an' his partner never once, for one moment, stopped exchanging pokes an' pinches an' kicks an' signs an' signals! — Why, they were like a couple of cardsharps fleecing a sucker. — Even Big Mama, bless her ole sweet soul, she isn't th' quickest an' brightest thing in the world, she finally noticed, at last, an' said to Gooper, "Gooper, what are you an' Mae makin' all these signs at each other about?" — I swear t' goodness, I nearly choked on my chicken!

> (MARGARET, *back at the dressing-table, still doesn't see* BRICK. *He is watching her with a look that is not quite definable. — Amused? shocked? contemptuous? — part of those and part of something else.*)

Y'know — your brother Gooper still cherishes the illusion he took
a giant step up on the social ladder when he married Miss Mae
Flynn of the Memphis Flynns.

(MARGARET *moves about the room as she talks, stops before the
mirror, moves on.*)

But I have a piece of Spanish news for Gooper. The Flynns never
had a thing in this world but money and they lost that, they were
nothing at all but fairly successful climbers. Of course, Mae Flynn
came out in Memphis eight years before I made my debut in Nash-
ville, but I had friends at Ward-Belmont who came from Memphis
and they used to come to see me and I used to go to see them for
Christmas and spring vacations, and so I know who rates an' who
doesn't rate in Memphis society. Why, y'know ole Papa Flynn, he
barely escaped doing time in the Federal pen for shady manipula-
tions on th' stock market when his chain stores crashed, and as for
Mae having been a cotton carnival queen, as they remind us so
often, lest we forget, well, that's one honor that I don't envy her
for! — Sit on a brass throne on a tacky float an' ride down Main
Street, smilin', bowin', and blowin' kisses to all the trash on the
street —

(*She picks out a pair of jeweled sandals and rushes to the dress-
ing-table.*)

Why, year before last, when Susan McPheeters was singled out fo'
that honor, y'know what happened to her? Y'know what happened
to poor little Susie McPheeters?

BRICK (*absently*): No. What happened to little Susie McPheeters?

MARGARET: Somebody spit tobacco juice in her face.

BRICK (*dreamily*): Somebody spit tobacco juice in her face?

MARGARET: That's right, some old drunk leaned out of a window in
the Hotel Gayoso and yelled, "Hey, Queen, hey, hey, there,
Queenie!" Poor Susie looked up and flashed him a radiant smile
and he shot out a squirt of tobacco juice right in poor Susie's face.

BRICK: Well, what d'you know about that.

MARGARET (*gaily*): What do I know about it? I was there, I saw it!

BRICK (*absently*): Must have been kind of funny.

MARGARET: Susie didn't think so. Had hysterics. Screamed like a
banshee. They had to stop th' parade an' remove her from her
throne an' go on with —

(*She catches sight of him in the mirror, gasps slightly, wheels
about to face him. Count ten.*)

— Why are you looking at me like that?

BRICK (*whistling softly, now*): Like what, Maggie?

MARGARET (*intensely, fearfully*): The way y' were lookin' at me just now, befo' I caught your eye in the mirror and you started t' whistle! I don't know how t' describe it but it froze my blood! — I've caught you lookin' at me like that so often lately. What are you thinkin' of when you look at me like that?

BRICK: I wasn't conscious of lookin' at you, Maggie.

MARGARET: Well, I was conscious of it! What were you thinkin'?

BRICK: I don't remember thinking of anything, Maggie.

MARGARET: Don't you think I know that — ? Don't you — ? — Think I know that — ?

BRICK (*coolly*): Know what, Maggie?

MARGARET (*struggling for expression*): That I've gone through this — hideous! — transformation, become — hard! Frantic!

(*Then she adds, almost tenderly:*)

— cruel!!

That's what you've been observing in me lately. How could y' help but observe it? That's all right. I'm not — thin-skinned any more, can't afford t' be thin-skinned any more.

(*She is now recovering her power.*)

— But Brick? Brick?

BRICK: Did you say something?

MARGARET: I was goin' t' say something: that I get — lonely. Very!

BRICK: Ev'rybody gets that . . .

MARGARET: Living with someone you love can be lonelier — than living entirely alone! — if the one that y' love doesn't love you. . . .

(*There is a pause.* BRICK *hobbles downstage and asks, without looking at her:*)

BRICK: Would you like to live alone, Maggie?

(*Another pause: then — after she has caught a quick, hurt breath:*)

MARGARET: No! — God! — I wouldn't!

(*Another gasping breath. She forcibly controls what must have been an impulse to cry out. We see her deliberately, very forcibly, going all the way back to the world in which you can talk about ordinary matters.*)

Did you have a nice shower?

BRICK: Uh-huh.

MARGARET: Was the water cool?

BRICK: No.

MARGARET: But it made y' feel fresh, huh?

BRICK: Fresher. . . .

MARGARET: I know something would make y' feel much fresher!

BRICK: What?

MARGARET: An alcohol rub. Or cologne, a rub with cologne!

BRICK: That's good after a workout but I haven't been workin' out, Maggie.

MARGARET: You've kept in good shape, though.

BRICK (*Indifferently*): You think so, Maggie?

MARGARET: I always thought drinkin' men lost their looks, but I was plainly mistaken.

BRICK (*wryly*): Why, thanks, Maggie.

MARGARET: You're the only drinkin' man I know that it never seems t' put fat on.

BRICK: I'm gettin' softer, Maggie.

MARGARET: Well, sooner or later it's bound to soften you up. It was just beginning to soften up Skipper when —

(*She stops short.*)

I'm sorry. I never could keep my fingers off a sore — I wish you *would* lose your looks. If you did it would make the martyrdom of Saint Maggie a little more bearable. But no such goddam luck. I actually believe you've gotten better looking since you've gone on the bottle. Yeah, a person who didn't know you would think you'd never had a tense nerve in your body or a strained muscle.

(*There are sounds of croquet on the lawn below: the click of mallets, light voices, near and distant.*)

Of course, you always had that detached quality as if you were playing a game without much concern over whether you won or lost, and now that you've lost the game, not lost but just quit playing, you have that rare sort of charm that usually only happens in very old or hopelessly sick people, the charm of the defeated. — You look so cool, so cool, so enviably cool.

(*Music is heard.*)

They're playing croquet. The moon has appeared and it's white, just beginning to turn a little bit yellow. . . .

You were a wonderful lover. . . .

Such a wonderful person to go to bed with, and I think mostly because you were really indifferent to it. Isn't that right? Never had any anxiety about it, did it naturally, easily, slowly, with absolute confidence and perfect calm, more like opening a door for a lady or seating her at a table than giving expression to any longing for her. Your indifference made you wonderful at lovemaking — strange? — but true. . . .

You know, if I thought you would never, never, never make love to me again — I would go downstairs to the kitchen and pick out the longest and sharpest knife I could find and stick it straight into my heart, I swear that I would!

But one thing I don't have is the charm of the defeated, my hat is still in the ring, and I am determined to win!

(*There is the sound of croquet mallets hitting croquet balls.*)

— What is the victory of a cat on a hot tin roof? — I wish I knew. . . .

Just staying on it, I guess, as long as she can. . . .

(*More croquet sounds.*)

Later tonight I'm going to tell you I love you an' maybe by that time you'll be drunk enough to believe me. Yes, they're playing croquet. . . .

Big Daddy is dying of cancer. . . .

What were you thinking of when I caught you looking at me like that? Were you thinking of Skipper?

(BRICK *takes up his crutch, rises.*)

Oh, excuse me, forgive me, but laws of silence don't work! No, laws of silence don't work. . . .

(BRICK *crosses to the bar, takes a quick drink, and rubs his head with a towel.*)

Laws of silence don't work. . . .

When something is festering in your memory or your imagination, laws of silence don't work, it's just like shutting a door and locking it on a house on fire in hope of forgetting that the house is burning. But not facing a fire doesn't put it out. Silence about a thing just magnifies it. It grows and festers in silence, becomes malignant. . . .

Get dressed, Brick.

(*He drops his crutch.*)

BRICK: I've dropped my crutch.

(*He has stopped rubbing his hair dry but still stands hanging onto the towel rack in a white towel-cloth robe.*)

MARGARET: Lean on me.

BRICK: No, just give me my crutch.

MARGARET: Lean on my shoulder.

BRICK: I don't want to lean on your shoulder, I want my crutch!

(*This is spoken like sudden lightning.*) Are you going to give me my crutch or do I have to get down on my knees on the floor and —

MARGARET: Here, here, take it, take it!

(*She has thrust the crutch at him.*)

BRICK (*hobbling out*): Thanks . . .

MARGARET: We mustn't scream at each other, the walls in this house have ears. . . . (*He hobbles directly to liquor cabinet to get a new drink.*) — but that's the first time I've heard you raise your voice in a long time, Brick. A crack in the wall? — Of composure?

— I think that's a good sign. . . .

A sign of nerves in a player on the defensive!

(BRICK *turns and smiles at her coolly over his fresh drink.*)

BRICK: It just hasn't happened yet, Maggie.

MARGARET: What?

BRICK: The click I get in my head when I've had enough of this stuff to make me peaceful. . . .

Will you do me a favor?

MARGARET: Maybe I will. What favor?

BRICK: Just, just keep your voice down!

MARGARET (*in a hoarse whisper*): I'll do you that favor, I'll speak in a whisper, if not shut up completely, if you will do me a favor and make that drink your last one till after the party.

BRICK: What party?

MARGARET: Big Daddy's birthday party.

BRICK: Is this Big Daddy's birthday?

MARGARET: You know this is Big Daddy's birthday!

BRICK: No, I don't, I forgot it.

MARGARET: Well, I remembered it for you. . . .

(*They are both speaking as breathlessly as a pair of kids after a fight, drawing deep exhausted breaths and looking at each other with faraway eyes, shaking and panting together as if they had broken apart from a violent struggle.*)

BRICK: Good for you, Maggie.

MARGARET: You just have to scribble a few lines on this card.

BRICK: You scribble something, Maggie.

MARGARET: It's got to be your handwriting; it's your present, I've given him my present; it's got to be your handwriting!

(*The tension between them is building again, the voices becoming shrill once more.*)

BRICK: I didn't get him a present.

MARGARET: I got one for you.

BRICK: All right. You write the card, then.

MARGARET: And have him know you didn't remember his birthday?

BRICK: I didn't remember his birthday.

MARGARET: You don't have to prove you didn't!

BRICK: I don't want to fool him about it.

MARGARET: Just write "Love, Brick!" for God's —

BRICK: No.

MARGARET: You've got to!

BRICK: I don't have to do anything I don't want to do. You keep forgetting the conditions on which I agreed to stay on living with you.

MARGARET *(out before she knows it)*: I'm not living with you. We occupy the same cage.

BRICK: You've got to remember the conditions agreed on.

MARGARET: They're impossible conditions!

BRICK: Then why don't you — ?

MARGARET: HUSH! Who is out there? Is somebody at the door?

(*There are footsteps in hall.*)

MAE *(outside)*: May I enter a moment?

MARGARET: Oh, you! Sure. Come in, Mae.

(MAE *enters bearing aloft the bow of a young lady's archery set.*)

MAE: Brick, is this thing yours?

MARGARET: Why, Sister Woman — that's my Diana Trophy. Won it at the intercollegiate archery contest on the Ole Miss campus.

MAE: It's a mighty dangerous thing to leave exposed round a house full of nawmal rid-blooded children attracted t'weapons.

MARGARET: "Nawmal rid-blooded children attracted t'weapons" ought t'be taught to keep their hands off things that don't belong to them.

MAE: Maggie, honey, if you had children of your own you'd know how funny that is. Will you please lock this up and put the key out of reach?

MARGARET: Sister Woman, nobody is plotting the destruction of your kiddies. — Brick and I still have our special archers' license. We're goin' deer-huntin' on Moon Lake as soon as the season starts. I love to run with dogs through chilly woods, run, run, leap over obstructions —

(*She goes into the closet carrying the bow.*)

MAE: How's the injured ankle, Brick?

BRICK: Doesn't hurt. Just itches.

MAE: Oh, my! Brick — Brick, you should've been downstairs after supper! Kiddies put on a show. Polly played the piano, Buster an' Sonny drums, an' then they turned out the lights an' Dixie an'

Trixie puhfawmed a toe dance in fairy costume with spahkluhs! Big Daddy just beamed! He just beamed!

MARGARET (*from the closet with a sharp laugh*): Oh, I bet. It breaks my heart that we missed it! (*She reenters.*) But Mae? Why did y'give dawgs' names to all your kiddies?

MAE: Dogs' names?

(*Margaret has made this observation as she goes to raise the bamboo blinds, since the sunset glare has diminished. In crossing she winks at* BRICK.)

MARGARET (*sweetly*): Dixie, Trixie, Buster, Sonny, Polly! — Sounds like four dogs and a parrot . . . animal act in a circus!

MAE: Maggie? (MARGARET *turns with a smile.*) Why are you so catty?

MARGARET: Cause I'm a cat! But why can't you take a joke, Sister Woman?

MAE: Nothin' pleases me more than a joke that's funny. You know the real names of our kiddies. Buster's real name is Robert. Sonny's real name is Saunders. Trixie's real name is Marlene and Dixie's — (*Someone downstairs calls for her. "Hey, Mae!" — She rushes to door, saying:*)

Intermission is over!

MARGARET (*as* MAE *closes door*): I wonder what Dixie's real name is?

BRICK: Maggie, being catty doesn't help things any . . .

MARGARET: I know! *WHY!* — Am I so catty? — Cause I'm consumed with envy an' eaten up with longing? — Brick, I've laid out your beautiful Shantung silk suit from Rome and one of your monogrammed silk shirts. I'll put your cuff-links in it, those lovely star sapphires I get you to wear so rarely. . . .

BRICK: I can't get trousers on over this plaster cast.

MARGARET: Yes, you can, I'll help you.

BRICK: I'm not going to get dressed, Maggie.

MARGARET: Will you just put on a pair of white silk pajamas?

BRICK: Yes, I'll do that, Maggie.

MARGARET: Thank you, thank you so much!

BRICK: Don't mention it.

MARGARET: Oh, Brick! How long does it have t' go on? This punishment? Haven't I done time enough, haven't I served my term, can't I apply for a — pardon?

BRICK: Maggie, you're spoiling my liquor. Lately your voice always sounds like you'd been running upstairs to warn somebody that the house was on fire!

MARGARET: Well, no wonder, no wonder. Y'know what I feel like, Brick?

   (*Children's and grownups' voices are blended, below, in a loud but uncertain rendition of "My Wild Irish Rose."*)

   I feel all the time like a cat on a hot tin roof!

BRICK: Then jump off the roof, jump off it, cats can jump off roofs and land on their four feet uninjured!

MARGARET: Oh, yes!

BRICK: Do it! — fo' God's sake, do it . . .

MARGARET: Do what?

BRICK: Take a lover!

MARGARET: I can't see a man but you! Even with my eyes closed I just see you! Why don't you get ugly, Brick, why don't you please get fat or ugly or something so I could stand it? (*She rushes to hall door, opens it, listens.*) The concert is still going on! Bravo, no-necks, bravo! (*She slams and locks door fiercely.*)

BRICK: What did you lock the door for?

MARGARET: To give us a little privacy for a while.

BRICK: You know better, Maggie.

MARGARET: No, I don't know better. . . .

   (*She rushes to gallery doors, draws the rose-silk drapes across them.*)

BRICK: Don't make a fool of yourself.

MARGARET: I don't mind makin' a fool of myself over you!

BRICK: I mind, Maggie. I feel embarrassed for you.

MARGARET: Feel embarrassed! But don't continue my torture. I can't live on and on under these circumstances.

BRICK: You agreed to —

MARGARET: I know but —

BRICK: — accept that condition!

MARGARET: I can't! Can't! Can't!

   (*She seizes his shoulder.*)

BRICK: Let go!

   (*He breaks away from her and seizes the small boudoir chair and raises it like a lion-tamer facing a big circus cat. Count five. She stares at him with her fist pressed to her mouth, then bursts into shrill, almost hysterical laughter. He remains grave for moment, then grins and puts the chair down.* BIG MAMA *calls through closed door.*)

BIG MAMA: Son? Son? Son?

BRICK: What is it, Big Mama?

BIG MAMA(*outside*): Oh, son! We got the most wonderful news about Big Daddy. I just had t' run up an' tell you right this — (*She rattles the knob.*) — What's this door doin', locked, faw? You all think there's robbers in the house?

MARGARET: Big Mama, Brick is dressin', he's not dressed yet.

BIG MAMA: That's all right, it won't be the first time I've seen Brick not dressed. Come on, open the door!

(MARGARET, *with a grimace, goes to unlock and open the hall door, as Brick hobbles rapidly to the bathroom and kicks the door shut.* BIG MAMA *has disappeared from the hall.*)

MARGARET: Big Mama?

(BIG MAMA *appears through the opposite gallery doors behind* MARGARET, *huffing and puffing like an old bulldog. She is a short, stout woman; her sixty years and 170 pounds have left her somewhat breathless most of the time; she's always tensed like a boxer, or rather, a Japanese wrestler. Her "family" was maybe a little superior to* BIG DADDY'*s, but not much. She wears a black or silver lace dress and at least half a million in flashy gems. She is very sincere.*)

BIG MAMA (*loudly, startling* MARGARET): Here — I come through Gooper's and Mae's gallery door. Where's Brick? *Brick* — Hurry on out of there, son, I just have a second and want to give you the news about Big Daddy. — I hate locked doors in a house. . . .

MARGARET (*with affected lightness*): I've noticed you do, Big Mama, but people have got to have *some* moments of privacy, don't they?

BIG MAMA: No, ma'am, not in *my* house. (*Without pause*) Whacha took off you' dress faw? I thought that little lace dress was so sweet on yuh, honey.

MARGARET: I thought it looked sweet on me, too, but one of m' cute little table-partners used it for a napkin so — !

BIG MAMA (*picking up stockings on floor*): What?

MARGARET: You know, Big Mama, Mae and Gooper's so touchy about those children — thanks, Big Mama . . . (BIG MAMA *has thrust the picked-up stockings in* MARGARET'*s hand with a grunt.*) — that you just don't dare to suggest there's any room for improvement in their —

BIG MAMA: Brick, hurry out! — Shoot, Maggie, you just don't like children.

MARGARET: I do SO like children! Adore them! — well brought up!

BIG MAMA (*gentle — loving*): Well, why don't you have some and bring them up well, then, instead of all the time pickin' on Gooper's an' Mae's?

GOOPER (*shouting up the stairs*): Hey, hey, Big Mama, Betsy an' Hugh got to go, waitin' t' tell yuh g'by!

BIG MAMA: Tell 'em to hold their hawses, I'll be right down in a jiffy! (*She turns to the bathroom door and calls out.*) Son? Can you hear me in there? (*There is a muffled answer.*) We just got the full report from the laboratory at the Ochsner Clinic, completely negative, son, ev'rything negative, right on down the line! Nothin' a-tall's wrong with him but some little functional thing called a spastic colon. Can you hear me, son?

MARGARET: He can hear you, Big Mama.

BIG MAMA: Then why don't he say something? God Almighty, a piece of news like that should make him shout. It made *me* shout, I can tell you. I shouted and sobbed and fell right down on my knees — Look! (*She pulls up her skirt.*) See the bruises where I hit my kneecaps? Took both doctors to haul me back on my feet! (*She laughs — she always laughs like hell at herself.*) Big Daddy was furious with me! But ain't that wonderful news? (*Facing bathroom again, she continues:*) After all the anxiety we been through to git a report like that on Big Daddy's birthday? Big Daddy tried to hide how much of a load that news took off his mind, but didn't fool *me.* He was mighty close to crying about it *himself!* (*Goodbyes are shouted downstairs, and she rushes to door.*) Hold those people down there, don't let them go! — Now, git dressed, we're all comin' up to this room fo' Big Daddy's birthday party because of your ankle. — How's his ankle, Maggie?

MARGARET: Well, he broke it, Big Mama.

BIG MAMA: I know he broke it. (*A phone is ringing in hall. A Negro voice answers "Mistuh Polly's res'dence."*) I mean does it hurt him much still.

MARGARET: I'm afraid I can't give you that information, Big Mama. You'll have to ask Brick if it hurts much still or not.

SOOKEY (*in the hall*): It's Memphis, Miss Polly, it's Miss Sally in Memphis.

BIG MAMA: Awright, Sookey. (BIG MAMA *rushes into the hall and is heard shouting on the phone:*) Hello, Miss Sally. How are you, Miss Sally? — Yes, well, I was just gonna call you about it. Shoot! — (*She raises her voice to a bellow.*) Miss Sally? Don't ever call me from the Gayoso Lobby, too much talk goes on in that hotel lobby, no wonder you can't hear me! Now listen, Miss

Sally. They's nothin' serious wrong with Big Daddy. We got the
report just now, they's nothin' wrong but a thing called a — spastic!
Spastic! — colon . . . (*She appears at the hall door and calls to*
MARGARET.) — Maggie, come out here and talk to that fool on the
phone. I'm shouted breathless!

MARGARET (*goes out and is heard sweetly at phone*): Miss Sally?
This is Brick's wife, Maggie. So nice to hear your voice. Can you
hear *mine? * Well, *good!* — Big Mama just wanted you to know that
they've got the report from the Ochsner Clinic and what Big Daddy
has is a spastic colon. Yes. Spastic colon, Miss Sally. That's right,
spastic colon. G'bye, Miss Sally, hope I'll see you real soon!
(*Hangs up a little before Miss Sally was probably ready to terminate
the talk. She returns through the hall door.*) She heard me perfectly.
I've discovered with deaf people the thing to do is not shout at
them but just enunciate clearly. My rich old Aunt Cornelia was
deaf as the dead but I could make her hear me just by sayin' each
word slowly, distinctly, close to her ear. I read her the *Commercial
Appeal* ev'ry night, read her the classified ads in it, even, she never
missed a word of it. But was she a mean ole thing! Know what I
got when she died? Her unexpired subscription to five magazines
and the Book-of-the-Month Club and a library full of ev'ry dull
book ever written! All else went to her hellcat of a sister . . .
meaner than she was, even!

> (BIG MAMA *has been straightening things up in the room during
> this speech.*)

BIG MAMA (*closing closet door on discarded clothes*): Miss Sally
sure is a case! Big Daddy says she's always got her hand out fo'
something. He's not mistaken. That poor ole thing always has her
hand out fo' somethin'. I don't think Big Daddy gives her as much
as he should. (*Somebody shouts for her downstairs and she shouts:*)
I'm comin'! (*She starts out. At the hall door, turns and jerks a
forefinger, first toward the bathroom door, then toward the liquor
cabinet, meaning "Has Brick been drinking?"* MARGARET *pretends
not to understand, cocks her head and raises her brows as if the
pantomimic performance was completely mystifying to her.* BIG
MAMA *rushes back to* MARGARET) Stop playin' so dumb! — I
mean has he been drinkin' that stuff much yet?

MARGARET (*with a little laugh*): Oh I think he had a highball after
supper.

BIG MAMA: Don't laugh about it! — Some single men stop drinkin'

when they get married and others start! Brick never touched liquor
before he — !

MARGARET (*crying out*): THAT'S NOT FAIR!

BIG MAMA: Fair or not fair I want to ask you a question, one question: D'you make Brick happy in bed?

MARGARET: Why don't you ask if he makes *me* happy in bed?

BIG MAMA: Because I know that —

MARGARET: It works both ways!

BIG MAMA: Something's not right! You're childless and my son
drinks! (*Someone has called her downstairs and she has rushed to
the door on the line above. She turns at the door and points at the
bed.*) — When a marriage goes on the rocks, the rocks are there,
right there!

MARGARET: That's — (BIG MAMA *has swept out of the room and
slammed the door.*) — not — fair . . . (MARGARET *is alone, completely alone, and she feels it. She draws in, hunches her shoulders,
raises her arms with fists clenched, shuts her eyes tight as a child
about to be stabbed with a vaccination needle. When she opens her
eyes again, what she sees is the long oval mirror and she rushes
straight to it, stares into it with a grimace and says: "Who are
you?" — Then she crouches a little and answers herself in a different
voice which is high, thin, mocking: "I am Maggie the Cat!" —
Straightens quickly as bathroom door opens a little and* BRICK *calls
out to her.*)

BRICK: Has Big Mama gone?

MARGARET: She's gone. (*He opens the bathroom door and hobbles
out, with his liquor glass now empty, straight to the liquor cabinet.
He is whistling softly.* MARGARET's *head pivots on her long, slender
throat to watch him. She raises a hand uncertainly to the base of her
throat, as if it was difficult for her to swallow, before she speaks*)
You know, our sex life didn't just peter out in the usual way, it was
cut off short, long before the natural time for it to, and it's going
to revive again, just as sudden as that. I'm confident of it. That's
what I'm keeping myself attractive for. For the time when you'll
see me again like other men see me. Yes, like other men see me.
They still see me, Brick, and they like what they see. Uh-huh. Some
of them would give their — Look, Brick! (*She stands before the
long oval mirror, touches her breast and then her hips with her
two hands.*) How high my body stays on me! — Nothing has fallen
on me — not a fraction. . . . (*Her voice is soft and trembling: a
pleading child's. At this moment as he turns to glance at her — a*

look which is like a player passing a ball to another player, third down and goal to go — she has to capture the audience in a grip so tight that she can hold it till the first intermission without any lapse of attention.) Other men still want me. My face looks strained, sometimes, but I've kept my figure as well as you've kept yours, and men admire it. I still turn heads on the street. Why, last week in Memphis everywhere that I went men's eyes burned holes in my clothes, at the country club and in restaurants and department stores, there wasn't a man I met or walked by that didn't just eat me up with his eyes and turn around when I passed him and look back at me. Why, at Alice's party for her New York cousins, the best lookin' man in the crowd — followed me upstairs and tried to force his way in the powder room with me, followed me to the door and tried to force his way in!

BRICK: Why didn't you let him, Maggie?

MARGARET: Because I'm not that common, for one thing. Not that I wasn't almost tempted to. You like to know who it was? It was Sonny Boy Maxwell, that's who!

BRICK: Oh, yeah, Sonny Boy Maxwell, he was a good end-runner but had a little injury to his back and had to quit.

MARGARET: He has no injury now and has no wife and still has a lech for me.

BRICK: I see no reason to lock him out of a powder room in that case.

MARGARET: And have someone catch me at it? I'm not that stupid. Oh, I might sometime cheat on you with someone, since you're so insultingly eager to have me do it! — But if I do, you can be damned sure it will be in a place and a time where no one but me and the man could possibly know. Because I'm not going to give you any excuse to divorce me for being unfaithful or anything else. . . .

BRICK: Maggie, I wouldn't divorce you for being unfaithful or anything else. Don't you know that? Hell. I'd be relieved to know that you found yourself a lover.

MARGARET: Well, I'm taking no chances. No, I'd rather stay on this hot tin roof.

BRICK: A hot tin roof's 'n uncomfo'table place t' stay on. . . . (*He starts to whistle softly.*)

MARGARET (*through his whistle*):Yeah, but I can stay on it just as long as I have to.

BRICK: You could leave me, Maggie. (*He resumes whistle. She wheels about to glare at him.*)

MARGARET: Don't want to and will not! Besides if I did, you don't have a cent to pay for it but what you get from Big Daddy and he's dying of cancer!

> (*For the first time a realization of* BIG DADDY's *doom seems to penetrate to* BRICK's *consciousness, visibly, and he looks at* MARGARET.)

BRICK: Big Mama just said he wasn't, that the report was okay.

MARGARET: That's what she thinks because she got the same story that they gave Big Daddy. And was just as taken in by it as he was, poor ole things. . . . But tonight they're going to tell her the truth about it. When Big Daddy goes to bed, they're going to tell her that he is dying of cancer. (*She slams the dresser drawer.*) — It's malignant and it's terminal.

BRICK: Does Big Daddy know it?

MARGARET: Hell, do they *ever* know it? Nobody says, "You're dying." You have to fool them. They have to fool themselves.

BRICK: Why?

MARGARET: Why? Because human beings dream of life everlasting, that's the reason! But most of them want it on earth and not in heaven. (*He gives a short, hard laugh at her touch of humor.*) Well. . . . (*She touches up her mascara.*) That's how it is, anyhow. . . . (*She looks about.*) Where did I put down my cigarette? Don't want to burn up the home-place, at least not with Mae and Gooper and their five monsters in it! (*She has found it and sucks at it greedily. Blows out smoke and continues.*) So this is Big Daddy's last birthday. And Mae and Gooper, they know it, oh, *they* know it, all right. They got the first information from the Ochsner Clinic. That's why they rushed down here with their no-neck monsters. Because. Do you know something? Big Daddy's made no will? Big Daddy's never made out any will in his life, and so this campaign's afoot to impress him, forcibly as possible, with the fact that you drink and I've borne no children!

> (*He continues to stare at her a moment, then mutters something sharp but not audible and hobbles rather rapidly out onto the long gallery in the fading, much faded, gold light.*)

MARGARET (*continuing her liturgical chant*): Y'know, I'm fond of Big Daddy, I am genuinely fond of that old man, I really am, you know. . . .

BRICK (*faintly, vaguely*): Yes, I know you are. . . .

MARGARET: I've always sort of admired him in spite of his coarseness, his four-letter words and so forth. Because Big Daddy *is* what he *is,* and he makes no bones about it. He hasn't turned gentleman farmer, he's still a Mississippi red neck, as much of a red neck as he must have been when he was just overseer here on the old Jack Straw and Peter Ochello place. But he got hold of it an' built it into th' biggest an' finest plantation in the Delta. — I've always liked Big Daddy. . . . (*She crosses to the proscenium.*) Well, this is Big Daddy's last birthday. I'm sorry about it. But I'm facing the facts. It takes money to take care of a drinker and that's the office that I've been elected to lately.

BRICK: You don't have to take care of me.

MARGARET: Yes, I do. Two people in the same boat have got to take care of each other. At least you want money to buy more Echo Spring when this supply is exhausted, or will you be satisfied with a ten-cent beer? Mae an' Gooper are plannin' to freeze us out of Big Daddy's estate because you drink and I'm childless. But we can defeat that plan. We're going to defeat that plan! Brick, y'know, I've been so God damn disgustingly poor all my life! — That's the truth, Brick!

BRICK: I'm not sayin' it isn't.

MARGARET: Always had to suck up to people I couldn't stand because they had money and I was poor as Job's turkey. You don't know what that's like. Well, I'll tell you, it's like you would feel a thousand miles away from Echo Spring! — And had to get back to it on that broken ankle . . . without a crutch! That's how it feels to be as poor as Job's turkey and have to suck up to relatives that you hated because they had money and all you had was a bunch of hand-me-down clothes and a few old moldy three per cent government bonds. My daddy loved his liquor, he fell in love with his liquor the way you've fallen in love with Echo Spring! — And my poor Mama, having to maintain some semblance of social position, to keep appearances up, on an income of one hundred and fifty dollars a month on those old government bonds! When I came out, the year that I made my debut, I had just two evening dresses! One Mother made me from a pattern in *Vogue,* the other a hand-me-down from a snotty rich cousin I hated! — The dress that I married you in was my grandmother's weddin' gown. . . . So that's why I'm like a cat on a hot tin roof!

(BRICK *is still on the gallery. Someone below calls up to him*

in a warm Negro voice, "Hiya, Mistuh Brick, how yuh feelin?"
BRICK *raises his liquor glass as if that answered the question.*)

MARGARET: You can be young without money but you can't be old without it. You've got to be old *with* money because to be old without it is just too awful, you've got to be one or the other, either *young* or *with money,* you can't be old and *without* it. — That's the truth, Brick. . . .

(BRICK *whistles softly, vaguely.*)

Well, now I'm dressed, I'm all dressed, there's nothing else for me to do. (*Forlornly, almost fearfully.*) I'm dressed, all dressed, nothing else for me to do. . . . (*She moves about restlessly, aimlessly, and speaks, as if to herself.*) I know when I made my mistake. — What am I — ?Oh! — my bracelets. . . . (*She starts working a collection of bracelets over her hands onto her wrists, about six on each, as she talks.*) I've thought a whole lot about it and now I know when I made my mistake. Yes, I made my mistake when I told you the truth about that thing with Skipper. Never should have confessed it, a fatal error, tellin' you about that thing with Skipper.

BRICK: Maggie, shut up about Skipper. I mean it, Maggie; you got to shut up about Skipper.

MARGARET: You ought to understand that Skipper and I —

BRICK: You don't think I'm serious, Maggie? You're fooled by the fact that I am saying this quiet? Look, Maggie. What you're doing is a dangerous thing to do. You're — you're — you're — foolin' with something that — nobody ought to fool with.

MARGARET: This time I'm going to finish what I have to say to you. Skipper and I made love, if love you could call it, because it made both of us feel a little bit closer to you. You see, you son of a bitch, you asked too much of people, of me, of him, of all the unlucky poor damned sons of bitches that happen to love you, and there was a whole pack of them, yes, there was a pack of them besides me and Skipper, you asked too goddam much of people that loved you, you — superior creature! — you godlike being! — And so we made love to each other to dream it was you, both of us! Yes, yes, yes! Truth, truth! What's so awful about it? I like it, I think the truth is — yeah! I shouldn't have told you. . . .

BRICK (*holding his head unnaturally still and uptilted a bit*): It was Skipper that told me about it. Not you, Maggie.

MARGARET: I told you!

BRICK: After he told me!

MARGARET: What does it matter who — ?

(BRICK *turns suddenly out upon the gallery and calls:*)

BRICK: Little girl! Hey, little girl!

LITTLE GIRL (*at a distance*): What, Uncle Brick?

BRICK: Tell the folks to come up! — Bring everybody upstairs!

MARGARET: I can't stop myself! I'd go on telling you this in front of them all, if I had to!

BRICK: Little girl! Go on, go on, will you? Do what I told you, call them!

MARGARET: Because it's got to be told and you, you! — you never let me! (*She sobs, then controls herself, and continues almost calmly.*) It was one of those beautiful, ideal things they tell about in the Greek legends, it couldn't be anything else, you being you, and that's what made it so sad, that's what made it so awful, because it was love that never could be carried through to anything satisfying or even talked about plainly. Brick, I tell you, you got to believe me, Brick, I *do* understand all about it! I — I think it was — noble! Can't you tell I'm sincere when I say I respect it? My only point, the only point that I'm making, is life has got to be allowed to continue even after the dream of life is — all — over. . . .

(BRICK *is without his crutch. Leaning on furniture, he crosses to pick it up as she continues as if possessed by a will outside herself:*)

Why I remember when we double-dated at college, Gladys Fitzgerald and I and you and Skipper, it was more like a date between you and Skipper. Gladys and I were just sort of tagging along as if it was necessary to chaperone you! — to make a good public impression —

BRICK (*turns to face her, half lifting his crutch*): Maggie, you want me to hit you with this crutch? Don't you know I could kill you with this crutch?

MARGARET: Good Lord, man, d' you think I'd care if you did?

BRICK: One man has one great good true thing in his life. One great good thing which is true! — I had friendship with Skipper. — You are naming it dirty!

MARGARET: I'm not naming it dirty! I am naming it clean.

BRICK: Not love with you, Maggie, but friendship with Skipper was that one great true thing, and you are naming it dirty!

MARGARET: Then you haven't been listenin', not understood what I'm saying! I'm naming it so damn clean that it killed poor Skipper! — You two had something that had to be kept on ice, yes, incorruptible, yes! — and death was the only icebox where you could keep it. . . .

BRICK: I married you, Maggie. Why would I marry you, Maggie, if I was — ?

MARGARET: Brick, don't brain me yet, let me finish! — I know, believe me I know, that it was only Skipper that harbored even any unconscious desire for anything not perfectly pure between you two! — Now let me skip a little. You married me early that summer we graduated out of Ole Miss, and we were happy, weren't we, we were blissful, yes, hit heaven together ev'ry time that we loved! But that fall you an' Skipper turned down wonderful offers of jobs in order to keep on bein' football heroes — pro-football heroes. You organized the Dixie Stars that fall, so you could keep on bein' teammates forever! But somethin' was not right with it! — *Me included!* — between you. Skipper began hittin' the bottle . . . you got a spinal injury — couldn't play the Thanksgivin' game in Chicago, watched it on TV from a traction bed in Toledo. I joined Skipper. The Dixie Stars lost because poor Skipper was drunk. We drank together that night all night in the bar of the Blackstone and when cold day was comin' up over the Lake an' we were comin' out drunk to take a dizzy look at it, I said, "SKIPPER! STOP LOVIN' MY HUSBAND OR TELL HIM HE'S GOT TO LET YOU ADMIT IT TO HIM!" — one way or another!

HE SLAPPED ME HARD ON THE MOUTH! — then turned and ran without stopping once, I am sure, all the way back into his room at the Blackstone. . . .

— When I came to his room that night, with a little scratch like a shy little mouse at his door, he made that pitiful, ineffectual little attempt to prove that what I had said wasn't true. . . .

(BRICK *strikes at her with crutch, a blow that shatters the gemlike lamp on the table.*)

— In this way, I destroyed him, by telling him truth that he and his world which he was born and raised in, yours and his world, had told him could not be told?

— From then on Skipper was nothing at all but a receptacle for liquor and drugs. . . .

— Who shot cock-robin? I with my — (*She throws back her head with tight shut eyes.*) — merciful arrow! (BRICK *strikes at her; misses.*)

Missed me! — Sorry, — I'm not tryin' to whitewash my behavior, Christ, no! Brick, I'm not good. I don't know why people have to pretend to be good, nobody's good. The rich or the well-to-do can afford to respect moral patterns, conventional moral patterns, but I could never afford to, yeah, but — I'm honest! Give me credit for just that, will you *please?* — Born poor, raised poor, except to die poor unless I manage to get us something out of what Big Daddy leaves when he dies of cancer! But Brick?! — Skipper is dead! I'm alive! Maggie the cat is —

(BRICK *hops awkwardly forward and strikes at her again with his crutch.*)

— alive! I am alive, alive! I am . . .

(*He hurls the crutch at her, across the bed she took refuge behind, and pitches forward on the floor as she completes her speech.*)

— alive!

(*A little girl,* DIXIE, *bursts into the room, wearing an Indian war bonnet and firing a cap pistol at* MARGARET *and shouting:* "Bang, bang, bang!"

(*Laughter downstairs floats through the open hall door.* MARGARET *had crouched gasping to bed at child's entrance. She now rises and says with cool fury:*)

Little girl, your mother or someone should teach you — (*Gasping*) — to knock at a door before you come into a room. Otherwise people might think that you — lack — good breeding. . . .

DIXIE: Yanh, yanh, yanh, what is Uncle Brick doin' on th' floor?

BRICK: I tried to kill your Aunt Maggie, but I failed — and I fell. Little girl, give me my crutch so I can get up off th' floor.

MARGARET: Yes, give your uncle his crutch, he's a cripple, honey, he broke his ankle last night jumping hurdles on the high school athletic field!

DIXIE: What were you jumping hurdles for, Uncle Brick?

BRICK: Because I used to jump them, and people like to do what they used to do, even after they've stopped being able to do it. . . .

MARGARET: That's right, that's your answer, now go away, little girl.

(DIXIE *fires cap pistol at* MARGARET *three times.*)

Stop, you stop that, monster! You little no-neck monster!

(*She seizes the cap pistol and hurls it through gallery doors.*)

DIXIE (*with a precocious instinct for the cruelest thing*): You're jealous! — You're just jealous because you can't have babies!

(*She sticks out her tongue at* MARGARET *as she sashays past her with her stomach stuck out, to the gallery.* MARGARET *slams the gallery doors and leans panting against them. There is a pause.*

BRICK *has replaced his spilt drink and sits, faraway, on the great four-poster bed.*)

MARGARET: You see? — they gloat over us being childless, even in front of their five little no-neck monsters!

(*Pause. Voices approach on the stairs.*)

Brick? — I've been to a doctor in Memphis, a — a gynecologist. . . . I've been completely examined, and there is no reason why we can't have a child whenever we want one. And this is my time by the calendar to conceive. Are you listening to me? Are you? Are you LISTENING TO ME!

BRICK: Yes. I hear you, Maggie. (*His attention returns to her inflamed face.*) — But how in hell on earth do you imagine — that you're going to have a child by a man that can't stand you?

MARGARET: That's a problem that I will have to work out. (*She wheels about to face the hall door.*) Here they come!

(*The lights dim.*)

(Curtain)

ACT TWO: *There is no lapse of time. Margaret and Brick are in the same positions they held at the end of Act I.*

MARGARET (*at door*): Here they come!

(BIG DADDY *appears first, a tall man with a fierce, anxious look, moving carefully not to betray his weakness even, or especially, to himself.*)

BIG DADDY: Well, Brick.

BRICK: Hello, Big Daddy. — Congratulations!

BIG DADDY: — Crap. . . .

(*Some of the people are approaching through the hall, others along the gallery: voices from both directions.* GOOPER *and* REVEREND TOOKER *become visible outside gallery doors, and their voices come in clearly.*

(*They pause outside as* GOOPER *lights a cigar.*)

REVEREND TOOKER (*vivaciously*): Oh, but St. Paul's in Grenada has three memorial windows, and the latest one is a Tiffany stained-glass window that cost twenty-five hundred dollars, a picture of Christ the Good Shepherd with a Lamb in His arms.

GOOPER: Who give that window, Preach?

REVEREND TOOKER: Clyde Fletcher's widow. Also presented St. Paul's with a baptismal font.

GOOPER: Y'know what somebody ought t' give your church is a *coolin'* system, Preach.

REVEREND TOOKER: Yes, siree, Bob! And y'know what Gus Hamma's family gave in his memory to the church at Two Rivers? A complete new stone parish-house with a basketball court in the basement and a —

BIG DADDY (*uttering a loud barking laugh which is far from truly mirthful*): Hey, Preach! What's all this talk about memorials, Preach? Y' think somebody's about t' kick off around here? 'S that it?

(*Startled by this interjection,* REVEREND TOOKER *decides to laugh at the question almost as loud as he can.*)

(*How he would answer the question we'll never know, as he's spared that embarrassment by the voice of* GOOPER'*s wife,* MAE, *rising high and clear as she appears with* "DOC" BAUGH, *the family doctor, through the hall door.*)

MAE (*almost religiously*): — Let's see now, they've had their *tyyyy*-phoïd shots, and their tetanus shots, their diphtheria shots and their hepatitis shots and their polio shots, they got those shots every month from May through September, and — Gooper? Hey! Gooper! — What all have the kiddies been shot faw?

MARGARET (*overlapping a bit*): Turn on the Hi-Fi, Brick! Let's have some music t' start off th' party with!

(*The talk becomes so general that the room sounds like a great aviary of chattering birds. Only Brick remains unengaged, leaning upon the liquor cabinet with his faraway smile, an ice cube in a paper napkin with which he now and then rubs his forehead. He doesn't respond to Margaret's command. She bounds forward and stoops over the instrument panel of the console.*)

GOOPER: We gave 'em that thing for a third anniversary present, got three speakers in it.

(*The room is suddenly blasted by the climax of a Wagnerian opera or a Beethoven symphony.*)

BIG DADDY: Turn that dam thing off!

(*Almost instant silence, almost instantly broken by the shouting charge of Big Mama, entering through hall door like a charging rhino.*)

BIG MAMA: Wha's my Brick, wha's mah precious baby!!

BIG DADDY: Sorry! Turn it back on!

(*Everyone laughs very loud. Big Daddy is famous for his jokes at Big Mama's expense, and nobody laughs louder at these jokes than Big Mama herself, though sometimes they're pretty cruel and Big Mama has to pick up or fuss with something to cover the hurt that the loud laugh doesn't quite cover.*

(On this occasion, a happy occasion because the dread in her heart has also been lifted by the false report on Big Daddy's condition, she giggles, grotesquely, coyly, in Big Daddy's direction and bears down upon Brick, all very quick and alive.)

BIG MAMA: Here he is, here's my precious baby! What's that you've got in your hand? You put that liquor down, son, your hand was made fo' holdin' somethin' better than that!

GOOPER: Look at Brick put it down!

(BRICK has obeyed BIG MAMA by draining the glass and handing it to her. Again everyone laughs, some high, some low.)

BIG MAMA: Oh, you bad boy, you, you're my bad little boy. Give Big Mama a kiss, you bad boy, you! — Look at him shy away, will you? Brick never liked bein' kissed or made a fuss over, I guess because he's always had too much of it!

Son, you turn that thing off!

(BRICK has switched on the TV set.)

I can't stand TV, radio was bad enough but TV has gone it one better, I mean — *(Plops wheezing in chair)* — one worse, ha ha! Now what'm I sittin' down here faw? I want t' sit next to my sweetheart on the sofa, hold hands with him and love him up a little!

(BIG MAMA has on a black and white figured chiffon. The large irregular patterns, like the markings of some massive animal, the luster of her great diamonds and many pearls, the brilliants set in the silver frames of her glasses, her riotous voice, booming laugh, have dominated the room since she entered. BIG DADDY has been regarding her with a steady grimace of chronic annoyance.)

BIG MAMA *(still louder)*: Preacher, Preacher, hey Preach! Give me you' hand an' help me up from this chair!

REVEREND TOOKER: None of your tricks, Big Mama!

BIG MAMA: What tricks? You give me you' hand so I can get up an' —

(REVEREND TOOKER extends her his hand. She grabs it and pulls him into her lap with a shrill laugh that spans an octave in two notes.)

Ever seen a preacher in a fat lady's lap? Hey, hey, folks!
Ever seen a preacher in a fat lady's lap?

(BIG MAMA *is notorious throughout the Delta for this sort of inelegant horseplay.* MARGARET *looks on with indulgent humor, sipping Dubonnet "on the rocks" and watching* BRICK, *but* MAE *and* GOOPER *exchange signs of humorless anxiety over these antics, the sort of behavior which* MAE *thinks may account for their failure to quite get in with the smartest young married set in Memphis, despite all. One of the* NEGROES, LACY *or* SOOKEY, *peeks in, cackling. They are waiting for a sign to bring in the cake and champagne. But* BIG DADDY's *not amused. He doesn't understand why, in spite of the infinite mental relief he's received from the doctor's report, he still has these same old fox teeth in his guts. "This spastic thing sure is something," he says to himself, but aloud he roars at* BIG MAMA:)

BIG DADDY: *BIG MAMA, WILL YOU QUIT HORSIN'?* — You're too old an' too fat fo' that sort of crazy kid stuff an' besides a woman with your blood-pressure — she had two hundred last spring! — is riskin' a stroke when you mess around like that. . . .

BIG MAMA: Here comes Big Daddy's birthday!

(NEGROES *in white jackets enter with an enormous birthday cake ablaze with candles and carrying buckets of champagne with satin ribbons about the bottle necks.*

(MAE *and* GOOPER *strike up song, and everybody, including the* NEGROES *and* CHILDREN, *joins in. Only* BRICK *remains aloof.*)

EVERYONE: Happy birthday to you.

Happy birthday to you.

Happy birthday, Big Daddy —

(*Some sing: "Dear, Big Daddy!"*)

Happy birthday to you.

(*Some sing: "How old are you?"*)

(MAE *has come down center and is organizing her children like a chorus. She gives them a barely audible: "One, two, three!" and they are off in the new tune.*)

CHILDREN: Skinamarinka — dinka — dink

Skinamarinka — do

We love you.

Skinamarinka — dinka — dink

Skinamarinka — do

(*All together, they turn to* BIG DADDY.)

Big Daddy, you!

(*They turn back front, like a musical comedy chorus.*)

We love you in the morning;

We love you in the night.
We love you when we're with you,
And we love you out of sight.
Skinamarinka — dinka — dink
Skinamarinka — do.
(MAE *turns to* BIG MAMA.)
Big Mamma, too!
(BIG MAMA *bursts into tears. The* NEGROES *leave.*)

BIG DADDY: Now Ida, what the hell is the matter with you?

MAE: She's just so happy.

BIG MAMA: I'm just so happy, Big Daddy, I have to cry or something. (*Sudden and loud in the hush:*) Brick, do you know the wonderful news that Doc Baugh got from the clinic about Big Daddy? Big Daddy's one hundred per cent!

MARGARET: Isn't that wonderful?

BIG MAMA: He's just one hundred per cent. Passed the examination with flying colors. Now that we know there's nothing wrong with Big Daddy but a spastic colon, I can tell you something. I was worried sick, half out of my mind, for fear that Big Daddy might have a thing like —

MARGARET (*cuts through this speech, jumping up and exclaiming shrilly*): Brick, honey, aren't you going to give Big Daddy his birthday present?
(*Passing by him, she snatches his liquor glass from him.*
(*She picks up a fancily wrapped package.*)
Here, it is, Big Daddy, this is from Brick!

BIG MAMA: This is the biggest birthday Big Daddy's ever had, a hundred presents and bushels of telegrams from —

MAE (*at same time*): What is it, Brick?

GOOPER: I bet 500 to 50 that Brick don't know what it is.

BIG MAMA: The fun of presents is not knowing what they are till you open the package. Open your present, Big Daddy.

BIG DADDY: Open it you'self. I want to ask Brick somethin! Come here, Brick.

MARGARET: Big Daddy's callin' you, Brick. (*She is opening the package.*)

BRICK: Tell Big Daddy I'm crippled.

BIG DADDY: I see you're crippled. I want to know how you got crippled.

MARGARET (*making diversionary tactics*): Oh, look, oh, look, why, it's a cashmere robe! (*She holds the robe up for all to see.*)

MAE: You sound surprised, Maggie.

MARGARET: I never saw one before.

MAE: That's funny. — Hah!

MARGARET (*turning on her fiercely, with a brilliant smile*): Why is it funny? All my family ever had was family — and luxuries such as cashmere robes still surprise me!

BIG DADDY (*ominously*): Quiet!

MAE (*heedless in her fury*): I don't see how you could be so surprised when you bought it yourself at Loewenstein's in Memphis last Saturday. You know how I know?

BIG DADDY: I said, Quiet!

MAE: — I know because the salesgirl that sold it to you waited on me and said, Oh, Mrs. Pollitt, your sister-in-law just bought a cashmere robe for your husband's father!

MARGARET: Sister Woman! Your talents are wasted as a housewife and mother, you really ought to be with the FBI or —

BIG DADDY: QUIET!

(REVEREND TOOKER's *reflexes are slower than the others'. He finishes a sentence after the bellow.*)

REVEREND TOOKER (*to Doc Baugh*): — the Stork and the Reaper are running neck and neck! (*He starts to laugh gaily when he notices the silence and* BIG DADDY's *glare. His laugh dies falsely.*)

BIG DADDY: Preacher, I hope I'm not butting in on more talk about memorial stained-glass windows, am I, Preacher?

(REVEREND TOOKER *laughs feebly, then coughs dryly in the embarrassed silence.*)

Preacher?

BIG MAMA: Now, Big Daddy, don't you pick on Preacher!

BIG DADDY (*raising his voice*): You ever hear that expression all hawk and no spit? You bring that expression to mind with that little dry cough of yours, all hawk an' no spit. . . .

(*The pause is broken only by a short startled laugh from Margaret, the only one there who is conscious of and amused by the grotesque.*)

MAE (*raising her arms and jangling her bracelets*): I wonder if the mosquitoes are active tonight?

BIG DADDY: What's that, little Mama? Did you make some remark?

MAE: Yes, I said I wondered if the mosquitoes would eat us alive if we went out on the gallery for a while.

BIG DADDY: Well, if they do, I'll have your bones pulverized for fertilizer!

BIG MAMA (*quickly*): Last week we had an airplane spraying the place and I think it done some good, at least I haven't had a —

BIG DADDY (*cutting her speech*): Brick, they tell me, if what they tell me is true, that you done some jumping last night on the high school athletic field?

BIG MAMA: Brick, Big Daddy is talking to you, son.

BRICK (*smiling vaguely over his drink*): What was that, Big Daddy?

BIG DADDY: They said you done some jumping on the high school track field last night.

BRICK: That's what they told me, too.

BIG DADDY: Was it jumping or humping that you were doing out there? What were you doing out there at three A.M., layin' a woman on that cinder track?

BIG MAMA: Big Daddy, you are off the sick-list, now, and I'm not going to excuse you for talkin' so —

BIG DADDY: Quiet!

BIG MAMA: — nasty in front of Preacher and —

BIG DADDY: *QUIET!* — I ast you, Brick, if you was cuttin' you'self a piece o' poon-tang last night on that cinder track? I thought maybe you were chasin' poon-tang on that track an' tripped over something in the heat of the chase — 'sthat it?

(GOOPER *laughs, loud and false, others nervously following suit.* BIG MAMA *stamps her foot, and purses her lips, crossing to* MAE *and whispering something to her as* BRICK *meets his father's hard, intent, grinning stare with a slow, vague smile that he offers all situations from behind the screen of his liquor.*)

BRICK: No, sir, I don't think so. . . .

MAE (*at the same time, sweetly*): Reverend Tooker, let's you and I take a stroll on the widow's walk.

(SHE *and the* PREACHER *go out on the gallery as* BIG DADDY *says:*)

BIG DADDY: Then what the hell were you doing out there at three o'clock in the morning?

BRICK: Jumping the hurdles, Big Daddy, runnin' and jumpin' the hurdles, but those high hurdles have gotten too high for me, now.

BIG DADDY: Cause you was drunk?

BRICK (*his vague smile fading a little*): Sober I wouldn't have tried to jump the low ones. . . .

BIG MAMA (*quickly*): Big Daddy, blow out the candles on your birthday cake!

MARGARET (*at the same time*): I want to propose a toast to Big

Daddy Pollitt on his sixty-fifth birthday, the biggest cotton-planter in —

BIG DADDY (*bellowing with fury and disgust*): I told you to stop it, now stop it, quit this — !

BIG MAMA (*coming in front of Big Daddy with the cake*): Big Daddy, I will not allow you to talk that way, not even on your birthday, I —

BIG DADDY: I'll talk like I want to on my birthday, Ida, or any other goddam day of the year and anybody here that don't like it knows what they can do!

BIG MAMA: You don't mean that!

BIG DADDY: What makes you think I don't mean it?

> (*Meanwhile various discreet signals have been exchanged and* GOOPER *has also gone out on the gallery.*)

BIG MAMA: I just know you don't mean it.

BIG DADDY: You don't know a goddam thing and you never did!

BIG MAMA: Big Daddy, you don't mean that.

BIG DADDY: Oh, yes, I do, oh, yes, I do, I mean it! I put up with a whole lot of crap around here because I thought I was dying. And you thought I was dying and you started taking over, well, you can stop taking over now, Ida, because I'm not gonna die, you can just stop now this business of taking over because you're not taking over because I'm not dying, I went through the laboratory and the goddam exploratory operation and there's nothing wrong with me but a spastic colon. And I'm not dying of cancer which you thought I was dying of. Ain't that so? Didn't you think that I was dying of cancer, Ida?

> (*Almost everybody is out on the gallery but the two old people glaring at each other across the blazing cake.*
>
> (BIG MAMA's *chest heaves and she presses a fat fist to her mouth.*
>
> (BIG DADDY *continues, hoarsely:*)

Ain't that so, Ida? Didn't you have an idea I was dying of cancer and now you could take control of this place and everything on it? I got that impression, I seemed to get that impression. Your loud voice everywhere, your fat old body butting in here and there!

BIG MAMA: Hush! The Preacher!

BIG DADDY: Rut the goddam preacher!

> (BIG MAMA *gasps loudly and sits down on the sofa which is almost too small for her.*)

Did you hear what I said? I said rut the goddam preacher!

(*Somebody closes the gallery doors from outside just as there is a burst of fireworks and excited cries from the children.*)

BIG MAMA: I never seen you act like this before and I can't think what's got in you!

BIG DADDY: I went through all that laboratory and operation and all just so I would know if you or me was boss here! Well, now it turns out that I am and you ain't — and that's my birthday present — and my cake and champagne! — because for three years now you been gradually taking over. Bossing. Talking. Sashaying your fat old body around the place I made! I made this place! I was overseer on it! I was the overseer on the old Straw and Ochello plantation. I quit school at ten! I quit school at ten years old and went to work like a nigger in the fields. And I rose to be overseer of the Straw and Ochello plantation. And old Straw died and I was Ochello's partner and the place got bigger and bigger and bigger and bigger and bigger! I did all that myself with no goddam help from you, and now you think you're just about to take over. Well, I am just about to tell you that you are not just about to take over, you are not just about to take over a God damn thing. Is that clear to you, Ida? Is that very plain to you, now? Is that understood completely? I been through the laboratory from A to Z. I've had the goddam exploratory operation, and nothing is wrong with me but a spastic colon — made spastic, I guess, by disgust! By all the goddam lies and liars that I have had to put up with, and all the goddam hypocrisy that I lived with all these forty years that we been livin' together! Hey! Ida!! Blow out the candles on the birthday cake! Purse up your lips and draw a deep breath and blow out the goddam candles on the cake!

BIG MAMA: Oh, Big Daddy, oh, oh, oh, Big Daddy!

BIG DADDY: What's the matter with you?

BIG MAMA: In all these years you never believed that I loved you??

BIG DADDY: Huh?

BIG MAMA: And I did, I did so much, I did love you! — I even loved your hate and your hardness, Big Daddy! (*She sobs and rushes awkwardly out onto the gallery.*)

BIG DADDY (*to himself*): Wouldn't it be funny if that was true. . . .

(*A pause is followed by a burst of light in the sky from the fireworks.*)

BRICK! HEY, BRICK!

(*He stands over his blazing birthday cake.*

(*After some moments,* BRICK *hobbles in on his crutch, holding his glass.*

(MARGARET *follows him with a bright, anxious smile.*)
I didn't call you, Maggie. I called Brick.

MARGARET: I'm just delivering him to you.

(*She kisses* BRICK *on the mouth which he immediately wipes with the back of his hand. She flies girlishly back out.* BRICK *and his father are alone.*)

BIG DADDY: Why did you do that?

BRICK: Do what, Big Daddy?

BIG DADDY: Wipe her kiss off your mouth like she'd spit on you.

BRICK: I don't know. I wasn't conscious of it.

BIG DADDY: That woman of yours has a better shape on her than Gooper's but somehow or other they got the same look about them.

BRICK: What sort of look is that, Big Daddy?

BIG DADDY: I don't know how to describe it but it's the same look.

BRICK: They don't look peaceful, do they?

BIG DADDY: No, they sure in hell don't.

BRICK: They look nervous as cats?

BIG DADDY: That's right, they look nervous as cats.

BRICK: Nervous as a couple of cats on a hot tin roof?

BIG DADDY: That's right, boy, they look like a couple of cats on a hot tin roof. It's funny that you and Gooper being so different would pick out the same type of woman.

BRICK: Both of us married into society, Big Daddy.

BIG DADDY: Crap . . . I wonder what gives them both that look?

BRICK: Well. They're sittin' in the middle of a big piece of land, Big Daddy, twenty-eight thousand acres is a pretty big piece of land and so they're squaring off on it, each determined to knock off a bigger piece of it than the other whenever you let it go.

BIG DADDY: I got a surprise for those women. I'm not gonna let it go for a long time yet if that's what they're waiting for.

BRICK: That's right, Big Daddy. You just sit tight and let them scratch each other's eyes out. . . .

BIG DADDY: You bet your life I'm going to sit tight on it and let those sons of bitches scratch their eyes out, ha ha ha. . . .
But Gooper's wife's a good breeder, you got to admit she's fertile. Hell, at supper tonight she had them all at the table and they had to put a couple of extra leafs in the table to make room for them, she's got five head of them, now, and another one's comin'.

BRICK: Yep, number six is comin'. . . .

BIG DADDY: Brick, you know, I swear to God, I don't know the way it happens?

BRICK: The way what happens, Big Daddy?

BIG DADDY: You git you a piece of land, by hook or crook, an' things start growin' on it, things accumulate on it, and the first thing you know it's completely out of hand, completely out of hand!

BRICK: Well, they say nature hates a vacuum, Big Daddy.

BIG DADDY: That's what they say, but sometimes I think that a vacuum is a hell of a lot better than some of the stuff that nature replaces it with.

Is someone out there by that door?

BRICK: Yep.

BIG DADDY: Who? (*He has lowered his voice.*)

BRICK: Someone int'rested in what we say to each other.

BIG DADDY: Gooper? —— *GOOPER!*

(*After a discreet pause,* MAE *appears in the gallery door.*)

MAE: Did you call Gooper, Big Daddy?

BIG DADDY: Aw, it was you.

MAE: Do you want Gooper, Big Daddy?

BIG DADDY: No, and I don't want you. I want some privacy here, while I'm having a confidential talk with my son Brick. Now it's too hot in here to close them doors, but if I have to close those rutten doors in order to have a private talk with my son Brick, just let me know and I'll close 'em. Because I hate eavesdroppers, I don't like any kind of sneakin' an' spyin'.

MAE: Why, Big Daddy —

BIG DADDY: You stood on the wrong side of the moon, it threw your shadow!

MAE: I was just —

BIG DADDY: You was just nothing but spyin' an' you know it!

MAE (*begins to sniff and sob*): Oh, Big Daddy, you're so unkind for some reason to those that really love you!

BIG DADDY: Shut up, shut up, shut up! I'm going to move you and Gooper out of that room next to this! It's none of your goddam business what goes on in here at night between Brick an' Maggie. You listen at night like a couple of rutten peek-hole spies and go and give a report on what yu hear to Big Mama an' she comes to me and says they say such and such and so and so about what they heard goin' on between Brick an' Maggie, and Jesus, it makes me

sick. I'm goin' to move you an' Gooper out of that room, I can't
stand sneakin' an' spyin', it makes me sick. . . .

(MAE *throws back her head and rolls her eyes heavenward and
extends her arms as if invoking God's pity for this unjust martyrdom; then she presses a handkerchief to her nose and flies from
the room with a loud swish of skirts.*)

BRICK (*now at the liquor cabinet*): They listen, do they?

BIG DADDY: Yeah. They listen and give reports to Big Mama on what
goes on in here between you and Maggie. They say that — (*He
stops as if embarrassed.*) — You won't sleep with her, that you
sleep on the sofa. Is that true or not true? If you don't like Maggie,
get rid of Maggie! — What are you doin' there now?

BRICK: Fresh'nin' up my drink.

BIG DADDY: Son, you know you got a real liquor problem?

BRICK: Yes, sir, yes, I know.

BIG DADDY: Is that why you quit sports-announcing, because of this
liquor problem?

BRICK: Yes, sir, yes, sir, I guess so. (*He smiles vaguely and amiably
at his father across his replenished drink.*)

BIG DADDY: Son, don't guess about it, it's too important.

BRICK (*vaguely*): Yes, sir.

BIG DADDY: And listen to me, don't look at the damn chandelier. . . .
(*Pause.* BIG DADDY'S *voice is husky.*) — Somethin' else we picked
up at th' big fire sale in Europe. (*Another pause.*) Life is important. There's nothing else to hold onto. A man that drinks is throwing his life away. Don't do it, hold onto your life. There's nothing
else to hold onto. . . .
Sit down over here so we don't have to raise our voices, the walls
have ears in this place.

BRICK (*hobbling over to sit on the sofa beside him*): All right, Big
Daddy.

BIG DADDY: Quit! — how'd that come about? Some disappointment?

BRICK: I don't know. Do you?

BIG DADDY: I'm askin' you, God damn it! How in hell would I know
if you don't?

BRICK: I just got out there and found that I had a mouth full of
cotton. I was always two or three beats behind what was goin' on
on the field and so I —

BIG DADDY: Quit!

BRICK (*amiably*): Yes, quit.

BIG DADDY: Son?

BRICK: Huh?

BIG DADDY (*inhales loudly and deeply from his cigar; then bends suddenly a little forward, exhaling loudly and raising a hand to his forehead*): — Whew! — ha ha! — I took in too much smoke, it made me a little light-headed. . . .

(*The mantel clock chimes.*)

Why is it so damn hard for people to talk?

BRICK: Yeah. . . . (*The clock goes on sweetly chiming till it has completed the stroke of ten.*) — Nice peaceful-soundin' clock, I like to hear it all night. . . .

(*He slides low and comfortable on the sofa;* BIG DADDY *sits up straight and rigid with some unspoken anxiety. All his gestures are tense and jerky as he talks. He wheezes and pants and sniffs through his nervous speech, glancing quickly, shyly, from time to time, at his son.*)

BIG DADDY: We got that clock the summer we wint to Europe, me an' Big Mama on that damn Cook's Tour, never had such an awful time in my life, I'm tellin' you, son, those gooks over there, they gouge your eyeballs out in their grand hotels. And Big Mama bought more stuff than you could haul in a couple of boxcars, that's no crap. Everywhere she wint on this whirlwind tour, she bought, bought, bought. Why, half that stuff she bought is still crated up in the cellar, under water last spring! (*He laughs.*) That Europe is nothin' on earth but a great big auction, that's all it is, that bunch of old worn-out places, it's just a big firesale, the whole rutten thing, an' Big Mama wint wild in it, why, you couldn't hold that woman with a mule's harness! Bought, bought, bought! — lucky I'm a rich man, yes siree, Bob, an' half that stuff is mildewin' in th' basement. It's lucky I'm a rich man, it sure is lucky, well, I'm a rich man, Brick, yep, I'm a mighty rich man. (*His eyes light up for a moment.*) Y'know how much I'm worth? Guess, Brick! Guess how much I'm worth!

(BRICK *smiles vaguely over his drink.*)

Close on ten million in cash an' blue chip stocks, outside, mind you, of twenty-eight thousand acres of the richest land this side of the valley Nile!

(*A puff and crackle and the night sky blooms with an eerie greenish glow.* CHILDREN *shriek on the gallery.*)

But a man can't buy his life with it, he can't buy back his life with it when his life has been spent, that's one thing not offered in the Europe fire-sale or in the American markets or any markets on earth, a man can't buy his life with it, he can't buy back his life when his life is finished. . . .

That's a sobering thought, a very sobering thought, and that's a thought that I was turning over in my head, over and over and over — until today. . . .

I'm wiser and sadder, Brick, for this experience which I just gone through. They's one thing else that I remember in Europe.

BRICK: What is that, Big Daddy?

BIG DADDY: The hills around Barcelona in the country of Spain and the children running over those bare hills in their bare skins beggin' like starvin' dogs with howls and screeches, and how fat the priests are on the streets of Barcelona, so many of them and so fat and so pleasant, ha ha! — Y'know I could feed that country? I got money enough to feed that goddam country, but the human animal is a selfish beast and I don't reckon the money I passed out there to those howling children in the hills around Barcelona would more than upholster one of the chairs in this room, I mean pay to put a new cover on this chair!

Hell, I threw them money like you'd scatter feed corn for chickens, I threw money at them just to get rid of them long enough to climb back into th' car and — drive away. . . .

And then in Morocco, them Arabs, why, prostitution begins at four or five, that's no exaggeration, why, I remember one day in Marrakech, that old walled Arab city, I set on a broken-down wall to have a cigar, it was fearful hot there and this Arab woman stood in the road and looked at me till I was embarrassed, she stood stock still in the dusty hot road and looked at me till I was embarrassed. But listen to this. She had a naked child with her, a little naked girl with her, barely able to toddle, and after a while she set this child on the ground and give her a push and whispered something to her. This child came toward me, barely able t' walk, come toddling up to me and —

Jesus, it makes you sick t' remember a thing like this!

It stuck out its hand and tried to unbutton my trousers!

That child was not yet five! Can you believe me? Or do you think that I am making this up? I wint back to the hotel and said to Big Mama, Git packed! We're clearing out of this country. . . .

BRICK: Big Daddy, you're on a talkin' jag tonight.

BIG DADDY (*ignoring this remark*): Yes, sir, that's how it is, the human animal is a beast that dies but the fact that he's dying don't give him pity for others, no, sir, it —

— Did you say something?

BRICK: Yes.

BIG DADDY: What?

BRICK: Hand me over that crutch so I can get up.

BIG DADDY: Where you goin'?

BRICK: I'm takin' a little short trip to Echo Spring.

BIG DADDY: To where?

BRICK: Liquor cabinet. . . .

BIG DADDY: Yes, sir, boy — (*He hands* BRICK *the crutch.*) — the human animal is a beast that dies and if he's got money he buys and buys and buys and I think the reason he buys everything he can buy is that in the back of his mind he has the crazy hope that one of his purchases will be life everlasting! — Which it never can be. . . . The human animal is a beast that —

BRICK (*at the liquor cabinet*): Big Daddy, you sure are shootin' th' breeze here tonight.

(*There is a pause and voices are heard outside.*)

BIG DADDY: I been quiet here lately, spoke not a word, just sat and stared into space. I had something heavy weighing on my mind but tonight that load was took off me. That's why I'm talking. — The sky looks diff'rent to me. . . .

BRICK: You know what I like to hear most?

BIG DADDY: What?

BRICK: Solid quiet. Perfect unbroken quiet.

BIG DADDY: Why?

BRICK: Because it's more peaceful.

BIG DADDY: Man, you'll hear a lot of that in the grave. (*He chuckles agreeably.*)

BRICK: Are you through talkin' to me?

BIG DADDY: Why are you so anxious to shut me up?

BRICK: Well, sir, ever so often you say to me, Brick, I want to have a talk with you, but when we talk, it never materializes. Nothing is said. You sit in a chair and gas about this and that and I look like I listen. I try to look like I listen, but I don't listen, not much. Communication is — awful hard between people an' — somehow between you and me, it just don't —

BIG DADDY: Have you ever been scared? I mean have you ever felt downright terror of something? (*He gets up.*) Just one moment. I'm going to close these doors. . . . (*He closes doors on gallery as if he were going to tell an important secret.*)

BRICK: What?

BIG DADDY: Brick?

BRICK: Huh?

BIG DADDY: Son, I thought I had it!

BRICK: Had what? Had what, Big Daddy?

BIG DADDY: Cancer!

BRICK: Oh . . .

BIG DADDY: I thought the old man made out of bones had laid his cold and heavy hand on my shoulder!

BRICK: Well, Big Daddy, you kept a tight mouth about it.

BIG DADDY: A pig squeals. A man keeps a tight mouth about it, in spite of a man not having a pig's advantage.

BRICK: What advantage is that?

BIG DADDY: Ignorance — of mortality — is a comfort. A man don't have that comfort, he's the only living thing that conceives of death, that knows what it is. The others go without knowing which is the way that anything living should go, go without knowing, without any knowledge of it, and yet a pig squeals, but a man sometimes, he can keep a tight mouth about it. Sometimes he — (*There is a deep, smoldering ferocity in the old man.*) — can keep a tight mouth about it. I wonder if —

BRICK: What, Big Daddy?

BIG DADDY: A whiskey highball would injure this spastic condition?

BRICK: No, sir, it might do it good.

BIG DADDY (*grins suddenly, wolfishly*): Jesus, I can't tell you! The sky is open! Christ, it's open again! It's open, boy, it's open!
(BRICK *looks down at his drink.*)

BRICK: You feel better, Big Daddy?

BIG DADDY: Better? Hell! I can breathe! — All of my life I been like a doubled up fist. . . . (*He pours a drink.*) — Poundin', smashin', drivin'! — now I'm going to loosen these doubled up hands and touch things easy with them. . . . (*He spreads his hands as if caressing the air.*) You know what I'm contemplating?

BRICK (*vaguely*): No, sir. What are you contemplating?

BIG DADDY: Ha ha! — Pleasure! — pleasure with women!
(BRICK'S *smile fades a little but lingers.*)
Brick, this stuff burns me! —
— Yes, boy. I'll tell you something that you might not guess. I still have desire for women and this is my sixty-fifth birthday.

BRICK: I think that's mighty remarkable, Big Daddy.

BIG DADDY: Remarkable?

BRICK: Admirable, Big Daddy.

BIG DADDY: You're damn right it is, remarkable and admirable both. I realize now that I never had me enough. I let many chances slip by because of scruples about it, scruples, convention — crap. . . . All that stuff is bull, bull, bull! — It took the shadow of death to make me see it. Now that shadow's lifted, I'm going to cut loose and have, what is it they call it, have me a — ball!

BRICK: A ball, huh?

BIG DADDY: That's right, a ball, a ball! Hell! — I slept with Big Mama till, let's see, five years ago, till I was sixty and she was fifty-eight, and never even liked her, never did!

> (*The phone has been ringing down the hall.* BIG MAMA *enters, exclaiming:*)

BIG MAMA: Don't you men hear that phone ring? I heard it way out on the gall'ry.

BIG DADDY: There's five rooms off this front gall'ry that you could go through. Why do you go through this one?

> (BIG MAMA *makes a playful face as she bustles out the hall door.*) Hunh! — Why, when Big Mama goes out of a room, I can't remember what that woman looks like, but when Big Mama comes back into the room, boy, then I see what she looks like, and I wish I didn't! (*Bends over laughing at this joke till it hurts his guts and he straightens with a grimace. The laugh subsides to a chuckle as he puts the liquor glass a little distrustfully down on the table.*)

> (BRICK *has risen and hobbled to the gallery doors.*)

Hey! Where you goin'?

BRICK: Out for a breather.

BIG DADDY: Not yet you ain't. Stay here till this talk is finished, young fellow.

BRICK: I thought it was finished, Big Daddy.

BIG DADDY: It ain't even begun.

BRICK: My mistake. Excuse me. I just wanted to feel that river breeze.

BIG DADDY: Turn on the ceiling fan and set back down in that chair.

> (BIG MAMA'S *voice rises, carrying down the hall.*)

BIG MAMA: Miss Sally, you're a case! You're a caution, Miss Sally. Why didn't you give me a chance to explain it to you?

BIG DADDY: Jesus, she's talking to my old maid sister again.

BIG MAMA: Well, goodbye, now, Miss Sally. You come down real soon, Big Daddy's dying to see you! Yaisss, goodbye, Miss Sally. . . .

> (*She hangs up and bellows with mirth.* BIG DADDY *groans and covers his ears as she approaches.*)

> (*Bursting in:*)

Big Daddy, that was Miss Sally callin' from Memphis again! You know what she done, Big Daddy? She called her doctor in Memphis to git him to tell her what that spastic thing is! Ha-*HAAAA!* — And called back to tell me how relieved she was that — Hey! Let me in!

(BIG DADDY *has been holding the door half closed aaginst her.*)

BIG DADDY: Naw I ain't. I told you not to come and go through this room. You just back out and go through those five other rooms.

BIG MAMA: Big Daddy? Big Daddy? Oh, big Daddy! — You didn't mean those things you said to me, did you?

(*He shu:s door firmly against her but she still calls.*)

Sweetheart? Sweetheart? Big Daddy? You didn't mean those awful things you said to me? — I know you didn't. I know you didn't mean those things in your heart. . . .

(*The childlike voice fades with a sob and her heavy footsteps retreat down the hall.* BRICK *has risen once more on his crutches and starts for the gallery again.*)

BIG DADDY: All I ask of that woman is that she leave me alone. But she can't admit to herself that she makes me sick. That comes of having slept with her too many years. Should of quit much sooner but that old woman she never got enough of it — and I was good in bed . . . I never should of wasted so much of it on her. . . . They say you got just so many and each one is numbered. Well, I got a few left in me, a few, and I'm going to pick me a good one to spend 'em on! I'm going to pick me a choice one. I don't care how much she costs, I'll smother her in minks! Ha ha! I'll strip her naked and smother her in minks and choke her with diamonds! Ha ha! I'll strip her naked and choke her with diamonds and smother her with minks and hump her from hell to breakfast. Ha aha ha ha ha!

MAE (*gaily at door*): Who's that laughin' in there?

GOOPER: Is Big Daddy laughin' in there?

BIG DADDY: Crap! — them two — drips. . . . (*He goes over and touches* BRICK's *shoulder.*) Yes, son. Brick boy. — I'm happy! I'm happy, son, I'm happy! (*He chokes a little and bites his under lip, pressing his head quickly, shyly against his son's head and then, coughing with embarrassment, goes uncertainly back to the table where he set down the glass. He drinks and makes a grimace as it burns his guts. Brick sighs and rises with effort.*) What makes you so restless? Have you got ants in your britches?

BRICK: Yes, sir . . .

BIG DADDY: Why?

BRICK: — Something — hasn't — happened. . . .

BIG DADDY: Yeah? What is that!

BRICK (*sadly*): — the click. . . .

BIG DADDY: Did you say click?

BRICK: Yes, click.

BIG DADDY: What click?

BRICK: A click that I get in my head that makes me peaceful.

BIG DADDY: I sure in hell don't know what you're talking about, but it disturbs me.

BRICK: It's just a mechanical thing.

BIG DADDY: What is a mechanical thing?

BRICK: This click that I get in my head that makes me peaceful. I got to drink till I get it. It's just a mechanical thing, something like a — like a — like a —

BIG DADDY: Like a —

BRICK: Switch clicking off in my head, turning the hot light off and the cool night on and — (*He looks up, smiling sadly.*) — all of a sudden there's — peace!

BIG DADDY (*whistles long and soft with astonishment; he goes back to Brick and clasps his son's two shoulders*): Jesus! I didn't know it had gotten that bad with you. Why, boy, you're — alcoholic!

BRICK: That's the truth, Big Daddy. I'm alcoholic.

BIG DADDY: This shows how I — let things go!

BRICK: I have to hear that little click in my head that makes me peaceful. Usually I hear it sooner than this, sometimes as early as — noon, but —

— Today it's — dilatory. . . .

— I just haven't got the right level of alcohol in my bloodstream yet!

> (*This last statement is made with energy as he freshens his drink.*)

BIG DADDY: Uh — huh. Expecting death made me blind. I didn't have no idea that a son of mine was turning into a drunkard under my nose.

BRICK (*gently*): Well, now you do, Big Daddy, the news has penetrated.

BIG DADDY: UH-huh, yes, now I do, the news has — penetrated. . . .

BRICK: And so if you'll excuse me —

BIG DADDY: No, I won't excuse you.

BRICK: — I'd better sit by myself till I hear that click in my head, it's just a mechanical thing but it don't happen except when I'm alone or talking to no one. . . .

BIG DADDY: You got a long, long time to sit still, boy, and talk to no one, but now you're talkin' to me. At last I'm talking to you. And you set there and listen until I tell you the conversation is over!

BRICK: But this talk is like all the others we've ever had together in our lives! It's nowhere, nowhere! — it's — it's *painful*, Big Daddy. . . .

BIG DADDY: All right, then let it be painful, but don't you move from that chair! — I'm going to remove that crutch. . . . (*He seizes the crutch and tosses it across room.*)

BRICK: I can hop on one foot, and if I fall, I can crawl!

BIG DADDY: If you ain't careful you're gonna crawl off this plantation and then, by Jesus, you'll have to hustle your drinks along Skid Row!

BRICK: That'll come, Big Daddy.

BIG DADDY: Naw, it won't. You're my son and I'm going to straighten you out; now that I'm straightened out, I'm going to straighten out you!

BRICK: Yeah?

BIG DADDY: Today the report come in from Ochsner Clinic. Y'know what they told me? (*His face glows with triumph.*) The only thing that they could detect with all the instruments of science in that great hospital is a little spastic condition of the colon! And nerves torn to pieces by all that worry about it.

(*A little girl bursts into room with a sparkler clutched in each fist, hops and shrieks like a monkey gone mad and rushes back out again as* BIG DADDY *strikes at her.*)

(*Silence. The two men stare at each other. A woman laughs gaily outside.*)

I want you to know I breathed a sigh of relief almost as powerful as the Vicksburg tornado!

BRICK: You weren't ready to go?

BIG DADDY: GO WHERE? — crap. . . .

— When you are gone from here, boy, you are long gone and no where! The human machine is not no different from the animal machine or the fish machine or the bird machine or the reptile machine or the insect machine! It's just a whole God damn lot more complicated and consequently more trouble to keep together. Yep. I thought I had it. The earth shook under my foot, the sky come down like the black lid of a kettle and I couldn't breathe! —

Today!! — that lid was lifted, I drew my first free breath in — how many years? — *God!* — three. . . .

(There is laughter outside, running footsteps, the soft, plushy sound and light of exploding rockets.

*(*BRICK *stares at him soberly for a long moment; then makes a sort of startled sound in his nostrils and springs up on one foot and hops across the room to grab his crutch, swinging on the furniture for support. He gets the crutch and flees as if in horror for the gallery. His father seizes him by the sleeve of his white silk pajamas.)*

Stay here, you son of a bitch! — till I say go!

BRICK: I can't.

BIG DADDY: You sure in hell will, God damn it.

BRICK: No, I can't. We talk, you talk, in — circles! We get nowhere, nowhere! It's always the same, you say you want to talk to me and don't have a ruttin' thing to say to me!

BIG DADDY: Nothin' to say when I'm tellin' you I'm going to live when I thought I was dying?!

BRICK: Oh — that! — Is that what you have to say to me?

BIG DADDY: Why, you son of a bitch! Ain't that, ain't that — important?!

BRICK: Well, you said that, that's said, and now I —

BIG DADDY: Now you set back down.

BRICK: You're all balled up, you —

BIG DADDY: I ain't balled up!

BRICK: You are, you're all balled up!

BIG DADDY: Don't tell me what I am, you drunken whelp! I'm going to tear this coat sleeve off if you don't set down!

BRICK: Big Daddy —

BIG DADDY: Do what I tell you! I'm the boss here, now! I want you to know I'm back in the driver's seat now!

*(*BIG MAMA *rushes in, clutching her great heaving bosom.)*

What in hell do you want in here, Big Mama?

BIG MAMA: Oh, Big Daddy! Why are you shouting like that? I just cain't stainnnnnnnnd — it. . . .

BIG DADDY *(raising the back of his hand above his head)*: GIT! — outa here.

(She rushes back out, sobbing.)

BRICK *(softly, sadly)*: Christ. . . .

BIG DADDY *(fiercely)*: Yeah! Christ! — is right . . . (BRICK *breaks loose and hobbles toward the gallery.* BIG DADDY *jerks his crutch from under* BRICK *so he steps with the injured ankle. He utters a hissing cry of anguish, clutches a chair and pulls it over on top of him on the floor.*) Son of a — tub of — hog fat. . . .

BRICK: Big Daddy! Give me my crutch. (BIG DADDY *throws the crutch out of reach.*) Give me that crutch, Big Daddy.

BIG DADDY: Why do you drink?

BRICK: Don't know, give me my crutch!

BIG DADDY: You better think why you drink or give up drinking!

BRICK: Will you please give me my crutch so I can get up off this floor?

BIG DADDY: First you answer my question. Why do you drink? Why are you throwing your life away, boy, like somethin' disgusting you picked up on the street?

BRICK (*getting onto his knees*): Big Daddy, I'm in pain, I stepped on that foot.

BIG DADDY: Good! I'm glad you're not too numb with the liquor in you to feel some pain!

BRICK: You — spilled my — drink . . .

BIG DADDY: I'll make a bargain with you. You tell me why you drink and I'll hand you one. I'll pour you the liquor myself and hand it to you.

BRICK: Why do I drink?

BIG DADDY: Yeah! Why?

BRICK: Give me a drink and I'll tell you.

BIG DADDY: Tell me first!

BRICK: I'll tell you in one word.

BIG DADDY: What word?

BRICK: DISGUST! (*The clock chimes softly, sweetly. Big Daddy gives it a short, outraged glance.*) Now how about that drink?

BIG DADDY: What are you disgusted with? You got to tell me that, first. Otherwise being disgusted don't make no sense!

BRICK: Give me my crutch.

BIG DADDY: You heard me, you got to tell me what I asked you first.

BRICK: I told you, I said to kill my disgust!

BIG DADDY: DISGUST WITH WHAT!

BRICK: You strike a hard bargain.

BIG DADDY: What are you disgusted with? — an' I'll pass you the liquor.

BRICK: I can hop on one foot, and if I fall, I can crawl.

BIG DADDY: You want liquor that bad?

BRICK (*dragging himself up, clinging to bedstead*): Yeah, I want it that bad.

BIG DADDY: If I give you a drink, will you tell me what it is you're disgusted with, Brick?

BRICK: Yes, sir, I will try to. (*The old man pours him a drink and solemnly passes it to him. There is silence as* BRICK *drinks.*) Have you ever heard the word "mendacity"?

BIG DADDY: Sure. Mendacity is one of them five dollar words that cheap politicians throw back and forth at each other.

BRICK: You know what it means?

BIG DADDY: Don't it mean lying and liars?

BRICK: Yes, sir, lying and liars.

BIG DADDY: Has someone been lying to you?

CHILDREN (*chanting in chorus offstage*): We want Big Dad-dee! We want Big Dad-dee!

(GOOPER *appears in the gallery door.*)

GOOPER: Big Daddy, the kiddies are shouting for you out there.

BIG DADDY (*fiercely*): Keep out, Gooper!

GOOPER: 'Scuse me!

(BIG DADDY *slams the doors after* GOOPER.)

BIG DADDY: Who's been lying to you, has Margaret been lying to you, has your wife been lying to you about something, Brick?

BRICK: Not her. That wouldn't matter.

BIG DADDY: Then who's been lying to you, and what about?

BRICK: No one single person and no one lie. . . .

BIG DADDY: Then what, what then, for Christ's sake?

BRICK: — The whole, the whole — thing. . . .

BIG DADDY: Why are you rubbing your head? You got a headache?

BRICK: No, I'm tryin' to —

BIG DADDY: — Concentrate, but you can't because your brain's all soaked with liquor, is that the trouble? Wet brain! (*He snatches the glass from* BRICK's *hand.*) What do you know about this mendacity thing? Hell! I could write a book on it! Don't you know that? I could write a book on it and still not cover the subject? Well, I could, I could write a goddam book on it and still not cover the subject anywhere near enough! — Think of all the lies I got to put up with! — Pretenses! Ain't that mendacity? Having to pretend stuff you don't think or feel or have any idea of? Having for instance to act like I care for Big Mama! — I haven't been able to stand the sight, sound, or smell of that woman for forty years now! — even when I laid her! — regular as a piston. . . .

Pretend to love that son of a bitch of a Gooper and his wife Mae
and those five same screechers out there like parrots in a jungle?
Jesus! Can't stand to look at 'em! Church! — it bores the Bejesus
out of me, but I go! — I go an' sit there and listen to the fool
preacher! Clubs! — Elks! Masons! Rotary! — crap! (*A spasm of
pain makes him clutch his belly. He sinks into a chair and his
voice is softer and hoarser.*) You I do like for some reason, did
always have some kind of real feeling for — affection — respect —
yes, always. . . . You and being a success as a planter is all I ever
had any devotion to in my whole life! — and that's the truth. . . .
I don't know why, but it is! I've lived with mendacity! — Why
can't you live with it? Hell you *got* to live with it, there's nothing
else to *live* with except mendacity, is there?

BRICK: Yes, sir. Yes, sir there is something else that you can live with!

BIG DADDY: What?

BRICK (*lifting his glass*): This! — Liquor. . . .

BIG DADDY: That's not living, that's dodging away from life.

BRICK: I want to dodge away from it.

BIG DADDY: Then why don't you kill yourself, man?

BRICK: I like to drink. . . .

BIG DADDY: Oh, God, I can't talk to you. . . .

BRICK: I'm sorry, Big Daddy.

BIG DADDY: Not as sorry as I am. I'm tell you something. A little
while back when I thought my number was up — (*This speech
should have torrential pace and fury.*) — before I found out it was
just this — spastic — colon, I thought about you. Should I or should
I not, if the jig was up, give you this place when I go — since I
hate Gooper an' Mae an' know that they hate me, and since all five
same monkeys are little Maes an' Goopers. — And I thought, No!
— Then I thought, Yes! — I couldn't make up my mind. I hate
Gooper and his five same monkeys and that bitch Mae! Why should
I turn over twenty-eight thousand acres of the richest land this side
of the valley Nile to not my kind? — But why in hell, on the other
hand, Brick — should I subsidize a goddam fool on the bottle? —
Liked or not liked, well, maybe even — loved! — Why should I
do that? — Subsidize worthless behavior? Rot? Corruption?

BRICK (*smiling*): I understand.

BIG DADDY: Well, if you do, you're smarter than I am, God damn it,
because I don't understand. And this I will tell you frankly. I didn't
make up my mind at all on that question and still to this day I
ain't made out no will! — Well, now I don't *have* to. The pressure

is gone. I can just wait and see if you pull yourself together or if you don't.

BRICK: That's right, Big Daddy.

BIG DADDY: You sound like you thought I was kidding.

BRICK (*rising*): No, sir, I know you're not kidding.

BIG DADDY: But you don't care — ?

BRICK (*hobbling toward the gallery door*): No, sir, I don't care. . . . Now how about taking a look at your birthday fireworks and getting some of that cool breeze off the river? (*He stands in the gallery doorway as the night sky turns pink and green and gold with successive flashes of light.*)

BIG DADDY: *WAIT!* — Brick. . . . (*His voice drops. Suddenly there is something shy, almost tender, in his restraining gesture.*) Don't let's — leave it like this, like them other talks we've had, we've always — talked around things, we've — just talked around things for some rutten reason. I don't know what, it's always like something was left not spoken, something avoided because neither of us was honest enough with the — other. . . .

BRICK: I never lied to you, Big Daddy.

BIG DADDY: Did I ever to you?

BRICK: No, sir. . . .

BIG DADDY: Then there is at least two people that never lied to each other.

BRICK: But we've never talked to each other.

BIG DADDY: We can now.

BRICK: Big Daddy, there don't seem to be anything much to say.

BIG DADDY: You say that you drink to kill your disgust with lying.

BRICK: You said to give you a reason.

BIG DADDY: Is liquor the only thing that'll kill this disgust?

BRICK: Now. Yes.

BIG DADDY: But not once, huh?

BRICK: Not when I was still younger an' believing. A drinking man's someone who wants to forget he isn't still young an' believing.

BIG DADDY: Believing what?

BRICK: Believing. . . .

BIG DADDY: Believing what?

BRICK (*stubbornly evasive*): Believing. . . .

BIG DADDY: I don't know what the hell you mean by believing and I don't think you know what you mean by believing, but if you still got sports in your blood, go back to sports announcing and —

BRICK: Sit in a glass box watching games I can't play? Describing

what I can't do while players do it? Sweating out their disgust and
confusion in contests I'm not fit for? Drinkin' a coke, half bourbon,
so I can stand it? That's no goddam good any more, no help —
time just outran me, Big Daddy — got there first. . . .

BIG DADDY: I think you're passing the buck.

BRICK: You know many drinkin' men?

BIG DADDY (*with a slight, charming smile*): I have known a fair
number of that species.

BRICK: Could any of them tell you why he drank?

BIG DADDY: Yep, you're passin' the buck to things like time and disgust with "mendacity" and — crap! — if you got to use that kind
of language about a thing, it's ninety-proof bull, and I'm not buying
any.

BRICK: I had to give you a reason to get a drink!

BIG DADDY: You started drinkin' when your friend Skipper died.

(*Silence for five beats. Then* BRICK *makes a startled movement,
reaching for his crutch.*)

BRICK: What are you suggesting?

BIG DADDY: I'm suggesting nothing. (*The shuffle and clop of* BRICK's
rapid hobble away from his father's steady, grave attention.) — But
Gooper an' Mae suggested that there was something not right
exactly in your —

BRICK (*stopping short downstage as if backed to a wall*): "Not
right"?

BIG DADDY: Not, well, exactly normal in your friendship with —

BRICK: They suggested that, too? I thought that was Maggie's suggestion. (BRICK's *detachment is at last broken through. His heart
is accelerated; his forehead sweat-beaded; his breath becomes more
rapid and his voice hoarse. The thing they're discussing, timidly
and painfully on the side of* BIG DADDY, *fiercely, violently on*
BRICK's *side, is the inadmissible thing that Skipper died to disavow
between them. The fact that if it existed it had to be disavowed to
"keep face" in the world they lived in, may be at the heart of the
"mendacity" that* BRICK *drinks to kill his disgust with. It may be
the root of his collapse. Or maybe it is only a single manifestation
of it, not even the most important. The bird that I hope to catch in
the net of this play is not the solution of one man's psychological
problem. I'm trying to catch the true quality of experience in a
group of people, that cloudy, flickering, evanescent — fiercely
charged! — interplay of live human beings in the thundercloud of
a common crisis. Some mystery should be left in the revelation of*

character in a play, just as a great deal of mystery is always left in the revelation of character in life, even in one's own character to himself. This does not absolve the playwright of his duty to observe and probe as clearly and deeply as he legitimately *can: but it should steer him away from "pat" conclusions, facile definitions which make a play just a play, not a snare for the truth of human experience.*)

(*The following scene should be played with great concentration, with most of the power leashed but palpable in what is left unspoken.*) Who else's suggestion is it, is it yours? How many others thought that Skipper and I were —

BIG DADDY (*gently*): Now, hold on, hold on a minute, son. — I knocked around in my time.

BRICK: What's that got to do with —

BIG DADDY: I said 'Hold on!' — I bummed, I bummed this country till I was —

BRICK: Whose suggestion, who else's suggestion is it?

BIG DADDY: Slept in hobo jungles and railroad Y's and flophouses in all cities before I —

BRICK: Oh, you think so, too, you call me your son and a queer. Oh! Maybe that's why you put Maggie and me in this room that was Jack Straw's and Peter Ochello's, in which that pair of old sisters slept in a double bed where both of 'em died!

BIG DADDY: Now just don't go throwing rocks at — (*Suddenly* REVEREND TOOKER *appears in the gallery doors, his head slightly, playfully, fatuously cocked, with a practised clergyman's smile, sincere as a bird-call blown on a hunter's whistle, the living embodiment of the pious, conventional lie.* BIG DADDY *gasps a little at this perfectly timed, but incongruous, apparition.*) — What're you lookin' for, Preacher?

REVEREND TOOKER: The gentleman's lavatory, ha ha! — heh, heh . . .

BIG DADDY (*with strained courtesy*): — Go back out and walk down to the other end of the gallery, Reverend Tooker, and use the bathroom connected with my bedroom, and if you can't find it, ask them where it is!

REVEREND TOOKER: Ah, thanks. (*He goes out with a deprecatory chuckle.*)

BIG DADDY: It's hard to talk in this place . . .

BRICK: Son of a — !

BIG DADDY (*leaving a lot unspoken*): — I seen all things and understood a lot of them, till 1910. Christ, the year that — I had worn my shoes through, hocked my — I hopped off a yellow dog freight car half a mile down the road, slept in a wagon of cotton outside the gin — Jack Straw an' Peter Ochello took me in. Hired me to manage this place which grew into this one. — When Jack Straw died — why, old Peter Ochello quit eatin' like a dog does when its master's dead, and died, too!

BRICK: Christ!

BIG DADDY: I'm just saying I understand such —

BRICK (*violently*): Skipper is dead. I have not quit eating!

BIG DADDY: No, but you started drinking.

(BRICK *wheels on his crutch and hurls his glass across the room shouting.*)

BRICK: YOU THINK SO, TOO?

BIG DADDY: Shhh! (*Footsteps run on the gallery. There are women's calls.* BIG DADDY *goes toward the door.*) Go way! — Just broke a glass. . . .

(BRICK *is transformed, as if a quiet mountain blew suddenly up in volcanic flame.*)

BRICK: You think so, too? You think so, too? You think me an' Skipper did, did, did! — sodomy! — together?

BIG DADDY: Hold — !

BRICK: That what you —

BIG DADDY: — *ON* — a minute!

BRICK: You think we did dirty things between us, Skipper an' —

BIG DADDY: Why are you shouting like that? Why are you —

BRICK: — Me, is that what you think of Skipper, is that —

BIG DADDY: — so excited? I don't think nothing. I don't know nothing. I'm simply telling you what —

BRICK: You think that Skipper and me were a pair of dirty old men?

BIG DADDY: Now that's —

BRICK: Straw? Ochello? A couple of —

BIG DADDY: Now just —

BRICK: — ducking sissies? Queers? Is that what you —

BIG DADDY: Shhh.

BRICK: — think?

(*He loses his balance and pitches to his knees without noticing the pain. He grabs the bed and drags himself up.*)

BIG DADDY: Jesus — Whew. . . . Grab my hand!

BRICK: Naw, I don't want your hand. . . .

BIG DADDY: Well, I want yours. Git up! (*He draws him up, keeps*

an arm about him with concern and affection.) You broken out in
a sweat! You're panting like you'd run a race with —

BRICK (*freeing himself from his father's hold*): Big Daddy, you
shock me, Big Daddy, you, you — shock me! Talkin' so — (*He
turns away from his father.*) — casually! — about a — thing like
that . . . — Don't you know how people *feel* about things like that?
How, how disgusted they are by things like that? Why, at Ole
Miss when it was discovered a pledge to our fraternity, Skipper's and
mine, did a, attempted to do a, unnatural thing with — We not
only dropped him like a hot rock! — We told him to git off the
campus, and he did, he got! — All the way to —

(*He halts, breathless.*)

BIG DADDY: — Where?

BRICK: — North Africa, last I heard!

BIG DADDY: Well, I have come back from further away than that. I
have just now returned from the other side of the moon, death's
country, son, and I'm not easy to shock by anything here. (*He
comes downstage and faces out.*) Always, anyhow, lived with too
much space around me to be infected by ideas of other people. One
thing you can grow on a big place more important than cotton! —
is *tolerance!* — I grown it.

(*He returns toward* BRICK.)

BRICK: Why can't exceptional friendship, real, real, deep, deep
friendship! between two men be respected as something clean
and decent without being thought of as —

BIG DADDY: It can, it is, for God's sake.

BRICK: — Fairies. . . .

(*In his utterance of this word, we gauge the wide and profound
reach of the conventional mores he got from the world that
crowned him with early laurel.*)

BIG DADDY: I told Mae an' Gooper —

BRICK: Frig Mae and Gooper, frig all dirty lies and liars! — Skipper
and me had a clean, true thing between us! — had a clean friendship, practically all our lives, till Maggie got the idea you're talking about. Normal? No! — It was too rare to be normal, any true
thing between two people is too rare to be normal. Oh, once in a
while he put his hand on my shoulder or I'd put mine on his, oh,
maybe even, when we were touring the country in pro-football an'
shared hotel-rooms we'd reach across the space between the two
beds and shake hands to say goodnight, yeah, one or two times we —

BIG DADDY: Brick, nobody thinks that that's not normal!

BRICK: Well, they're mistaken, it was! It was a pure an' true thing an' that's not normal.

(*They both stare straight at each other for a long moment. The tension breaks and both turn away as if tired.*)

BIG DADDY: Yeah, it's — hard t' — talk. . . .

BRICK: All right, then, let's — let it go. . . .

BIG DADDY: Why did Skipper crack up? Why have you?

(BRICK *looks back at his father again. He has already decided, without knowing that he has made this decision, that he is going to tell his father that he is dying of cancer. Only this could even the score between them: one inadmissible thing in return for another.*)

BRICK (*ominously*): All right. You're asking for it, Big Daddy. We're finally going to have that real true talk you wanted. It's too late to stop it, now, we got to carry it through and cover every subject. (*He hobbles back to the liquor cabinet.*) Uh-huh. (*He opens the ice bucket and picks up the silver tongs with slow admiration of their frosty brightness.*) Maggie declares that Skipper and I went into pro-football after we left "Ole Miss" because we were scared to grow up . . . (*He moves downstage with the shuffle and clop of a cripple on a crutch. As* MARGARET *did when her speech became "recitative," he looks out into the house, commanding its attention by his direct, concentrated gaze — a broken, "tragically elegant" figure telling simply as much as he knows of "the Truth":*) — Wanted to — keep on tossing — those long, long! — high, high! — passes that — couldn't be intercepted except by time, the aerial attack that made us famous! And so we did, we did, we kept it up for one season, that aerial attack, we held it high! — Yeah, but — that summer, Maggie, she laid the law down to me, said, Now or never, and so I married Maggie. . . .

BIG DADDY: How was Maggie in bed?

BRICK (*wryly*): Great! the greatest! (BIG DADDY *nods as if he thought so.*) She went on the road that fall with the Dixie Stars. Oh, she made a great show of being the world's best sport. She wore a — wore a — tall bearskin cap! A shako, they call it, a dyed moleskin coat, a moleskin coat dyed red! — Cut up crazy; Rented hotel ballrooms for victory celebrations, wouldn't cancel them when it — turned out — defeat. . . . MAGGIE THE CAT! Ha ha! (BIG DADDY *nods.*) — But Skipper, he had some fever which came back on him which doctors couldn't explain and I got that injury —

turned out to be just a shadow on the X-ray plate — and a touch of bursitis. . . . I lay in a hospital bed, watched our games on TV, saw Maggie on the bench next to Skipper when he was hauled out of a game for stumbles, fumbles! — Burned me up the way she hung on his arm! — Y'know, I think that Maggie had always felt sort of left out because she and me never got any closer together than two people just get in bed, which is not much closer than two cats on a — fence humping. . . . So! She took this time to work on poor dumb Skipper. He was a less than average student at Ole Miss, you know that, don't you?! — Poured in his mind the dirty, false idea that what we were, him and me, was a frustrated case of that ole pair of sisters that lived in this room, Jack Straw and Peter Ochello! — He, poor Skipper, went to bed with Maggie to prove it wasn't true, and when it didn't work out, he thought it *was* true! — Skipper broke in two like a rotten stick — nobody ever turned so fast to a lush — or died of it so quick. . . . — Now are you satisfied?

(BIG DADDY *has listened to this story, dividing the grain from the chaff. Now he looks at his son.*)

BIG DADDY: Are you satisfied?

BRICK: With what?

BIG DADDY: That half-ass story!

BRICK: What's half-ass about it?

BIG DADDY: Something's left out of that story. What did you leave out?

(*The phone has started ringing in the hall. As if it reminded him of something,* BRICK *glances suddenly toward the sound and says:*)

BRICK: Yes! — I left out a long-distance call which I had from Skipper, in which he made a drunken confession to me and on which I hung up! — last time we spoke to each other in our lives. . . .

(*Muted ring stops as someone answers phone in a soft, indistinct voice in hall.*)

BIG DADDY: You hung up?

BRICK: Hung up. Jesus! Well —

BIG DADDY: Anyhow now! — we have tracked down the lie with which you're disgusted and which you are drinking to kill your disgust with, Brick. You been passing the buck. This disgust with mendacity is disgust with yourself. You! — dug the grave of your friend and kicked him in it! — before you'd face truth with him!

BRICK: His truth, not mine!

BIG DADDY: His truth, okay! But you wouldn't face it with him!

BRICK: Who can face truth? Can you?

BIG DADDY: Now don't start passin' the rotten buck again, boy!

BRICK: How about these birthday congratulations, these many, many happy returns of the day, when ev'rybody but you knows there won't be any! (*Whosoever has answered the hall phone lets out a high, shrill laugh; the voice becomes audible saying: "no, no, you got it all wrong! Upside down! Are you crazy?"*) (BRICK *suddenly catches his breath as he realized that he has made a shocking disclosure. He hobbles a few paces, then freezes, and without looking at his father's shocked face, says:*) Let's, let's — go out, now, and —

(BIG DADDY *moves suddenly forward and grabs hold of the boy's crutch like it was a weapon for which they were fighting for possession.*)

BIG DADDY: Oh, no, no! No one's going out. What did you start to say?

BRICK: I don't remember.

BIG DADDY: "Many happy returns when they know there won't be any"?

BRICK: Aw, hell, Big Daddy, forget it. Come on out on the gallery and look at the fireworks they're shooting off for your birthday. . . .

BIG DADDY: First you finish that remark you were makin' before you cut off. "Many happy returns when they know there won't be any"? — Ain't that what you just said?

BRICK: Look, now. I can get around without that crutch if I have to but it would be a lot easier on the furniture an' glassware if I didn't have to go swinging along like Tarzan of th' —

BIG DADDY: FINISH! WHAT YOU WAS SAYIN'!

(*An eerie green glow shows in sky behind him.*)

BRICK (*sucking the ice in his glass, speech, becoming thick*): Leave th' place to Gooper and Mae an' their five little same little monkeys. All I want is —

BIG DADDY: "LEAVE TH' PLACE," did you say?

BRICK (*vaguely*): All twenty-eight thousand acres of the richest land this side of the valley Nile.

BIG DADDY: Who said I was "leaving the place" to Gooper or anybody? This is my sixty-fifth birthday! I got fifteen years or twenty years left in me! I'll outlive *you!* I'll bury you an' have to pay for your coffin!

BRICK: Sure. Many happy returns. Now let's go watch the fireworks, come on, let's —

BIG DADDY: Lying, have they been lying? About the report from th' — clinic? Did they, did they — find something? — *Cancer.* Maybe?

BRIDK: Mendacity is a system that we live in. Liquor is one way out an' death's the other. . . .

(*He takes the crutch from* BIG DADDY'S *loose grip and swings out on the gallery leaving the doors open. A song, "Pick a Bale of Cotton," is heard.*)

MAE (*appearing in door*): Oh, Big Daddy the field-hands are singin' fo' you!

BIG DADDY (*shouting hoarsely*): BRICK! BRICK!

MAE: He's outside drinkin', Big Daddy.

BIG DADDY: BRICK!

(MAE *retreats, awed by the passion of his voice.* CHILDREN *call* BRICK *in tones mocking* BIG DADDY. *His face crumbles like broken yellow plaster about to fall into dust. There is a glow in the sky.* BRICK *swings back through the doors, slowly, gravely, quite soberly.*)

BRICK: I'm sorry Big Daddy. My head don't work any more and it's hard for me to understand how anybody could care if he lived or was dying or cared about anything but whether or not there was liquor left in the bottle and so I said what I said without thinking. In some ways I'm no better than the others, in some ways worse because I'm less alive. Maybe it's being alive that makes them lie, and being almost *not* alive makes one sort of accidentally truthful — I don't know but — anyway — we've been friends . . . — And being friends is telling each other the truth. . . . (*There is a pause.*) You told *me!* I told *you!*

(*A* CHILD *rushes into the room and grabs a fistful of fire-crackers and runs out again.*)

CHILD (*screaming*): Bang, bang, bang, bang, bang, bang, bang, bang!

BIG DADDY (*slowly and passionately*): CHRIST — DAMN — ALL — LYING SONS OF — BITCHES! (*He straightens at last and crosses to the inside door. At the door he turns and looks back as if he had some desperate question he couldn't put into words. Then he nods reflectively and says in a hoarse voice:*)Yes, all liars, all liars, all lying dying liars! (*This is said slowly, slowly, with a fierce revulsion. He goes on out.*) — Lying! Dying! Liars!

(*His voice dies out. There is the sound of a child being slapped.*)

It rushes, hideously bawling, through room and out the hall door. BRICK *remains motionless as the lights dim out and the curtain falls.*)

Curtain

ACT THREE: *There is no lapse of time.*
MAE *enters with* REVEREND TOOKER.

MAE: Where is Big Daddy! Big Daddy?

BIG MAMA (*entering*): Too much smell of burnt fireworks makes me feel a little bit sick at my stomach. — Where is Big Daddy?

MAE: That's what I want to know, where has Big Daddy gone?

BIG MAMA: He must have turned in, I reckon he went to baid. . . .
(GOOPER *enters.*)

GOOPER: Where is Big Daddy?

MAE: We don't know where he is!

BIG MAMA: I reckon he's gone to baid.

GOOPER: Well, then, now we can talk.

BIG MAMA: What is this talk, what talk?
(MARGARET *appears on gallery, talking to* DR. BAUGH.)

MARGARET (*musically*): My family freed their slaves ten years before abolition, my great-great-grandfather gave his slaves their freedom five years before the war between the States started!

MAE: Oh, for God's sake! Maggie's climbed back up in her family tree!

MARGARET (*sweetly*): What, Mae? — Oh, where's Big Daddy?!
(*The pace must be very quick. Great Southern animation.*)

BIG MAMA (*addressing them all*): I think Big Daddy was just worn out. He loves his family, he loves to have them around him, but it's a strain on his nerves. He wasn't himself tonight, Big Daddy wasn't himself, I could tell he was all worked up.

REVEREND TOOKER: I think he's remarkable.

BIG MAMA: Yaisss! Just remarkable. Did you all notice the food he ate at that table? Did you all notice the supper he put away? Why, he ate like a hawss!

GOOPER: I hope he doesn't regret it.

BIG MAMA: Why, that man — ate a huge piece of cawn-bread with molasses on it! Helped himself twice to hoppin' john.

MARGARET: Big Daddy loves hoppin' john. — We had a real country dinner.

BIG MAMA (*overlapping Margaret*): Yais, he simply adores it! An' candied yams? That man put away enough food at that table to stuff a nigger *field*-hand!

GOOPER (*with grim relish*): I hope he don't have to pay for it later on. . . .

BIG MAMA (*fiercely*): What's that, Gooper?

MAE: Gooper says he hopes Big Daddy doesn't suffer tonight.

BIG MAMA: Oh, shoot, Gooper says, Gooper says! Why should Big Daddy suffer from satisfying a normal appetite? There's nothin' wrong with that man but nerves, he's sound as a dollar! And now he knows he is an' that's why he ate such a supper. He had a big load off his mind, knowin' he wasn't doomed t' — what he thought he was doomed to. . . .

MARGARET (*sadly and sweetly*): Bless his old sweet soul. . . .

BIG MAMA (*vaguely*): Yais, bless his heart, wher's Brick?

MAE: Outside.

GOOPER: — Drinkin' . . .

BIG MAMA: I know he's drinkin'. You all don't have to keep tellin' *me* Brick is drinkin'. Cain't I see he's drinkin' without you continually tellin' me that boy's drinkin'?

MARGARET: Good for you, Big Mama! (*She applauds.*)

BIG MAMA: Other people *drink* and *have* drunk an' will *drink,* as long as they make that stuff an' put it in bottles.

MARGARET: That's the truth. I never trusted a man that didn't drink.

MAE: Gooper never drinks. Don't you trust Gooper?

MARGARET: Why, Gooper don't you drink? If I'd known you didn't drink, I wouldn't of made that remark —

BIG MAMA: Brick?

MARGARET: — at least not in your presence. (*She laughs sweetly.*)

BIG MAMA: Brick!

MARGARET: He's still on the gall'ry. I'll go bring him in so we can talk.

BIG MAMA (*worriedly*): I don't know what this mysterious family conference is about. (*Awkward silence.* BIG MAMA *looks from face to face, then belches slightly and mutters, "Excuse me. . . ." She opens an ornamental fan suspended about her throat, a black lace fan to go with her black lace gown, and fans her wilting corsage, sniffing nervously and looking from face to face in the uncomfortable silence as* MARGARET *calls "Brick?" and* BRICK *sings to the moon on the gallery.*) I don't know what's wrong here, you all have such long faces! Open that door on the hall and let some air circulate through here, will you please, Gooper?

MAE: I think we'd better leave that door closed, Big Mama, till after the talk.

BIG MAMA: Reveren' Tooker, will *you* please open that door?!

REVEREND TOOKER: I sure will, Big Mama.

MAE: I just didn't think we ought t' take any chance of Big Daddy hearin' a word of this discussion.

BIG MAMA: I swan! Nothing's going to be said in Big Daddy's house that he cain't hear if he wants to!

GOOPER: Well, Big Mama, it's —

   (MAE *gives him a quick, hard poke to shut him up. He glares at her fiercely as she circles before him like a burlesque ballerina, raising her skinny bare arms over her head, jangling her bracelets, exclaiming:*)

MAE: A breeze! A breeze!

REVEREND TOOKER: I think this house is the coolest house in the Delta. — Did you all know that Halsey Banks' widow put air-conditioning units in the church and rectory at Friar's Point in memory of Halsey?

   (*General conversation has resumed; everybody is chatting so that the stage sounds like a big bird-cage.*)

GOOPER: Too bad nobody cools your church off for you. I bet you sweat in that pulpit these hot Sundays, Reverend Tooker.

REVEREND TOOKER: Yes, my vestments are drenched.

MAE (*at the same time to Dr. Baugh*): You reckon those vitamin B_{12} injections are what they're cracked up t' be, Doc Baugh?

DOCTOR BAUGH: Well, if you want to be stuck with something I guess they're as good to be stuck with as anything else.

BIG MAMA (*at gallery door*): Maggie, Maggie, aren't you comin' with Brick?

MAE (*suddenly and loudly, creating a silence*): I have a strange feeling, I have a peculiar feeling!

BIG MAMA (*turning from gallery*): What feeling?

MAE: That Brick said somethin' he shouldn't of said t' Big Daddy.

BIG MAMA: Now what on earth could Brick of said t' Big Daddy that he shouldn't say?

GOOPER: Big Mama, there's somethin' —

MAE: NOW, WAIT!

   (*She rushes up to Big Mama and gives her a quick hug and kiss.*

BIG MAMA *pushes her impatiently off as the* REVEREND TOOKER'*s voice rises serenely in a little pocket of silence:*)

REVEREND TOOKER: Yes, last Sunday the gold in my chasuble faded into th' purple. . . .

GOOPER: Reveren', you must of been preachin' hell's fire last Sunday!
(*He guffaws at this witticism but the* REVEREND *is not sincerely amused. At the same time* BIG MAMA *has crossed over to* DR. BAUGH *and is saying to him:*)

BIG MAMA (*her breathless voice rising high-pitched above the others*): In my day they had what they call the Keeley cure for heavy drinkers. But now I understand they just take some kind of tablets, they call them "Annie Bust" tablets. But *Brick* don't need to take *nothin'*.

(BRICK *appears in gallery doors with Margaret behind him.*)

BIG MAMA (*unaware of his presence behind her*): That boy is just broken up over Skipper's death. You know how poor Skipper died. They gave him a big, big dose of that sodium amytal stuff at his home and then they called the ambulance and give him another big, big dose of it at the hospital and that and all of the alcohol in his system fo' months an' months an' months just proved too much for his heart. . . . I'm scared of needles! I'm more scared of a needle than the knife. . . . I think more people have been needled out of this world than — (*She stops short and wheels about.*) *OH!* — here's Brick! My precious baby —

(*She turns upon Brick with short, fat arms extended, at the same time uttering a loud, short sob, which is both comic and touching. (Brick smiles and bows slightly, making a burlesque gesture of gallantry for Maggie to pass before him into the room. Then he hobbles on his crutch directly to the liquor cabinet and there is absolute silence, with everybody looking at Brick as everybody has always looked at Brick when he spoke or moved or appeared. One by one he drops ice cubes in his glass, then suddenly, but not quickly, looks back over his shoulder with a wry, charming smile, and says:*)

BRICK: I'm sorry! Anyone else?

BIG MAMA (*sadly*): No, son. I wish you wouldn't!

BRICK: I wish I didn't have to, Big Mama, but I'm still waiting for that click in my head which makes it all smooth out!

BIG MAMA: Aw, Brick, you — BREAK MY HEART!

MARGARET (*at the same time*): Brick, go sit with Big Mama!

BIG MAMA: I just cain't staiiiiiiiiii-nnnnnd — it. . . . (*She sobs.*)

MAE: Now that we're all assembled —

GOOPER: We kin talk. . . .

BIG MAMA: Breaks my heart. . . .

MARGARET: Sit with Big Mama, Brick, and hold her hand.

> (BIG MAMA *sniffs very loudly three times, almost like three drum beats in the pocket of silence.*)

BRICK: You do that, Maggie. I'm a restless cripple. I got to stay on my crutch.

> (BRICK *hobbles to the gallery door; leans there as if waiting.* (MAE *sits beside* BIG MAMA, *while* GOOPER *moves in front and sits on the end of the couch, facing her.* REVEREND TOOKER *moves nervously into the space between them; on the other side,* DR. BAUGH *stands looking at nothing in particular and lights a cigar.* MARGARET *turns away.*)

BIG MAMA: Why're you all surroundin' me — like this? Why're you all starin' at me like this an' makin' signs at each other?

> (REVEREND TOOKER *steps back startled.*)

MAE: Calm yourself, Big Mama.

BIG MAMA: Calm you'self, you'self, Sister Woman. How could I calm myself with everyone starin' at me as if big drops of blood had broken out on m'face? What's this all about, Annh! What?

> (GOOPER *coughs and takes a center position.*)

GOOPER: Now, Doc Baugh.

MAE: Doc Baugh?

BRICK (*suddenly*): SHHH! — (*Then he grins and chuckles and shakes his head regretfully.*) — Naw! — that wasn't th' click.

GOOPER: Brick, shut up or stay out there on the gallery with your liquor! We got to talk about a serious matter. Big Mama wants to know the complete truth about the report we got today from the Ochsner Clinic.

MAE (*eagerly*): — on Big Daddy's condition!

GOOPER: Yais, on Big Daddy's condition, we got to face it.

DOCTOR BAUGH: Well. . . .

BIG MAMA (*terrified, rising*): Is there? Something? Something that I? Don't — Know?

> (*In these few words, this startled, very soft, question, Big Mama reviews the history of her forty-five years with Big Daddy, her great, almost embarrassingly true-hearted and simple-minded devotion to Big Daddy, who must have had something Brick has, who made himself loved so much by the "simple expedient" of*)

not loving enough to disturb his charming detachment, also once coupled, like Brick's, with virile beauty.

(BIG MAMA *has a dignity at this moment: she almost stops being fat.*)

DOCTOR BAUGH (*after a pause, uncomfortably*): Yes? — Well —

BIG MAMA: *I!!!* — want to — knowwwwwww. . . . (*Immediately she thrusts her fist to her mouth as if to deny that statement.*

(*Then, for some curious reason, she snatches the withered corsage from her breast and hurls it on the floor and steps on it with her short, fat feet.*) — Somebody must be lyin'! — I want to know!

MAE: Sit down, Big Mama, sit down on this sofa.

MARGARET (*quickly*): Brick, go sit with Big Mama.

BIG MAMA: What is it, what is it?

DOCTOR BAUGH: I never have seen a more thorough examination than Big Daddy Pollitt was given in all my experience with the Ochsner Clinic.

GOOPER: It's one of the best in the country.

MAE: It's THE best in the country — bar none!

(*For some reason she gives* GOOPER *a violent poke as she goes past him. He slaps at her hand without removing his eyes from his mother's face.*)

DOCTOR BAUGH: Of course they were ninety-nine and nine-tenths percent sure before they even started.

BIG MAMA: Sure of what, sure of what, sure of — what? — what!

(*She catches her breath in a startled sob.* MAE *kisses her quickly. She thrusts* MAE *fiercely away from her, staring at the doctor.*)

MAE: Mommy, be a brave girl!

BRICK (*in the doorway, softly*):
    "By the light, by the light,
    Of the sil-ve-ry mo-ooo-n . . ."

GOOPER: Shut up! — Brick.

BRICK: — Sorry. . . .

(*He wanders out on the gallery.*)

DOCTOR BAUGH: But now, you see, Big Mama, they cut a piece off this growth, a specimen of the tissue and —

BIG MAMA: Growth? You told Big Daddy —

DOCTOR BAUGH: Now wait.

BIG MAMA (*fiercely*): You told me and Big Daddy there wasn't a thing wrong with him but —

MAE: Big Mama, they always —

GOOPER: Let Doc Baugh talk, will yuh?

BIG MAMA: — little spastic condition of — (*Her breath gives out in a sob.*)

DOCTOR BAUGH: Yes, that's what we told Big Daddy. But we had this bit of tissue run through the laboratory and I'm sorry to say the test was positive on it. It's — well — malignant. . . .
(*Pause.*)

BIG MAMA: — Cancer?! Cancer?!
(DR. BAUGH *nods gravely.*)
(BIG MAMA *gives a long gasping cry.*)

MAE and GOOPER: Now, now, now, Big Mama, you had to know. . . .

BIG MAMA: Why didn't they cut it out of him? Hanh? Hanh?

DOCTOR BAUGH: Involved too much, Big Mama, too many organs affected.

MAE: Big Mama, the liver's affected and so's the kidneys, both! It's gone way past what they call a —

GOOPER: A surgical risk.

MAE: — Uh-huh. . . .
(BIG MAMA *draws a breath like a dying gasp.*)

REVEREND TOOKER: Tch, tch, tch, tch, tch!

DOCTOR BAUGH: Yes, it's gone past the knife.

MAE: That's why he's turned yellow, Mommy!

BIG MAMA: Git away from me, git away from me, Mae! (*She rises abruptly.*) I want Brick! Where's Brick? Where is my only son?

MAE: Mama! Did she say "only son"?

GOOPER: What does that make me?

MAE: A sober responsible man with five precious children! — Six!

BIG MAMA: I want Brick to tell me! Brick! Brick!

MARGARET (*rising from her reflections in a corner*): Brick was so upset he went back out.

BIG MAMA: Brick!

MARGARET: Mama, let me tell you!

BIG MAMA: No, no, leave me alone, you're not my blood!

GOOPER: Mama, I'm your son! Listen to me!

MAE: Gooper's your son, he's your first-born!

BIG MAMA: Gooper never liked Daddy.

MAE (*as if terribly shocked*): That's not TRUE!
(*There is a pause. The minister coughs and rises.*)

REVEREND TOOKER (*to* MAE): I think I'd better slip away at this point.

MAE (*sweetly and sadly*): Yes, Doctor Tooker, you go.

REVEREND TOOKER (*discreetly*): Goodnight, goodnight, everybody, and God bless you all . . . on this place. . . .

(*He slips out.*)

DOCTOR BAUGH: That man is a good man but lacking in tact. Talking about people giving memorial windows — if he mentioned one memorial window, he must have spoke of a dozen, and saying how awful it was when somebody died intestate, the legal wrangles, and so forth.

(MAE *coughs, and points at* BIG MAMA.)

DOCTOR BAUGH: Well, Big Mama. . . .

(*He sighs.*)

BIG MAMA: It's all a mistake, I know it's just a bad dream.

DOCTOR BAUGH: We're gonna keep Big Daddy as comfortable as we can.

BIG MAMA: Yes, it's just a bad dream, that's all it is, it's just an awful dream.

GOOPER: In my opinion Big Daddy is having some pain but won't admit that he has it.

BIG MAMA: Just a dream, a bad dream.

DOCTOR BAUGH: That's what lots of them do, they think if they don't admit they're having the pain they can sort of escape the fact of it.

GOOPER (*with relish*): Yes, they get sly about it, they get real sly about it.

MAE: Gooper and I think —

GOOPER: Shut up, Mae! — Big Daddy ought to be started on morphine.

BIG MAMA: Nobody's going to give Big Daddy morphine.

DOCTOR BAUGH: Now, Big Mama, when that pain strikes it's going to strike mighty hard and Big Daddy's going to need the needle to bear it.

BIG MAMA: I tell you, nobody's going to give him morphine.

MAE: Big Mama, you don't want to see Big Daddy suffer, you know you —

(GOOPER *standing beside her gives her a savage poke.*)

DOCTOR BAUGH (*placing a package on the table*): I'm leaving this stuff here, so if there's a sudden attack you all won't have to send out for it.

MAE: I know how to give a hypo.

GOOPER: Mae took a course in nursing during the war.

MARGARET: Somehow I don't think Big Daddy would want Mae to give him a hypo.

MAE: You think he'd want *you* to do it?
  (DR. BAUGH *rises.*)

GOOPER: Doctor Baugh is goin'.

DOCTOR BAUGH: Yes, I got to be goin'. Well, keep your chin up, Big Mama.

GOOPER (*with jocularity*): She's gonna keep both chins up, aren't you Big Mama? (BIG MAMA *sobs.*) Now stop that, Big Mama.

MAE: Sit down with me, Big Mama.

GOOPER (*at door with* DR. BAUGH): Well, Doc, we sure do appreciate all you done. I'm telling you, we're surely obligated to you for —
  (DR. BAUGH *has gone out without a glance at him.*)

GOOPER: — I guess that doctor has got a lot on his mind but it wouldn't hurt him to act a little more human. . . . (BIG MAMA *sobs.*) Now be a brave girl, Mommy.

BIG MAMA: It's not true, I know that it's just not true!

GOOPER: Mama, those tests are infallible!

BIG MAMA: Why are you so determined to see your father daid?

MAE: Big Mama!

MARGARET (*gently*): I know what Big Mama means.

MAE (*fircely*): Oh, do you?

MARGARET (*quietly and very sadly*): Yes, I think I do.

MAE: For a newcomer in the family you sure do show a lot of understanding.

MARGARET: Understanding is needed on this place.

MAE: I guess you must have needed a lot of it in your family, Maggie, with your father's liquor problem and now you've got Brick with his!

MARGARET: Brick does not have a liquor problem at all. Brick is devoted to Big Daddy. This thing is a terrible strain on him.

BIG MAMA: Brick is Big Daddy's boy, but he drinks too much and it worries me and Big Daddy, and, Margaret, you've got to cooperate with us, you've got to cooperate with Big Daddy and me in getting Brick straightened out. Because it will break Big Daddy's heart if Brick don't pull himself together and take hold of things.

MAE. Take hold of what things, Big Mama?

BIG MAMA: The place.
  (*There is a quick violent look between* MAE *and* GOOPER.)

GOOPER: Big Mama, you've had a shock.

MAE: Yais, we've all had a shock, but. . . .

GOOPER: Let's be realistic —

MAE: — Big Daddy would never, would *never,* be foolish enough to —

GOOPER: — put this place in irresponsible hands!

BIG MAMA: Big Daddy ain't going to leave the place in anybody's hands; Big Daddy is *not* going to die. I want you to get that in your heads, all of you!

MAE: Mommy, Mommy, Big Mama, we're just as hopeful an' optimistic as you are about Big Daddy's prospects, we have faith in *prayer* — but nevertheless there are certain matters that have to be discussed an' dealt with, because otherwise —

GOOPER: Eventualities have to be considered and now's the time. . . . Mae, will you please get my briefcase out of our room?

MAE: Yes, honey.

(*She rises and goes out through the hall door.*)

GOOPER (*standing over* BIG MAMA): Now Big Mom. What you said just now was not at all true and you know it. I've always loved Big Daddy in my own quiet way. I never made a show of it, and I know that Big Daddy has always been fond of me in a quiet way, too, and he never made a show of it neither.

(MAE *returns with* GOOPER's *briefcase.*)

MAE: Here's your briefcase, Gooper, honey.

GOOPER (*handing the briefcase back to her*): Thank you. . . . Of cou'se my relationship with Big Daddy is different from Brick's.

MAE: You're eight years older'n Brick an' always had t'carry a bigger load of th' responsibilities than Brick ever had t'carry. He never carried a thing in his life but a football or a highball.

GOOPER: Mae, will y' let me talk, please?

MAE: Yes, honey.

GOOPER: Now, a twenty-eight thousand acre plantation's a mighty big thing t'run.

MAE: Almost singlehanded.

(MARGARET *has gone out onto the gallery, and can be heard calling softly to* BRICK.)

BIG MAMA: You never had to run this place! What are you talking about? As if Big Daddy was dead and in his grave, you had to run it? Why, you just helped him out with a few business details and had your law practice at the same time in Memphis!

MAE: Oh, Mommy, Mommy, Big Mommy! Let's be fair! Why, Gooper has given himself body and soul to keeping this place up for the past five years since Big Daddy's health started failing. Gooper won't say it, Gooper never thought of it as a duty, he just did it. And what did Brick do? Brick kept living in his past glory at college! Still a football player at twenty-seven!

MARGARET (*returning alone*): Who are you talking about, now? Brick? A football player? He isn't a football player and you know it. Brick is a sports announcer on TV and one of the best-known ones in the country!

MAE: I'm talking about what he was.

MARGARET: Well, I wish you would just stop talking about my husband.

GOOPER: I've got a right to discuss my brother with other members of MY OWN family which don't include *you*. Why don't you go out there and drink with Brick?

MARGARET: I've never seen such malice toward a brother.

GOOPER: How about his for me? Why, he can't stand to be in the same room with me!

MARGARET: This is a deliberate campaign of vilification for the most disgusting and sordid reason on earth, and I know what it is! It's avarice, avarice, greed, greed!

BIG MAMA: Oh, I'll scream! I will scream in a moment unless this stops!

(GOOPER *has stalked up to* MARGARET *with clenched fists at his sides as if he would strike her.* MAE *distorts her face again into a hideous grimace behind* MARGARET'*s back.*)

MARGARET: We only remain on the place because of Big Mama and Big Daddy. If it is true what they say about Big Daddy we are going to leave here just as soon as it's over. Not a moment later.

BIG MAMA (*sobs*): Margaret. Child. Come here. Sit next to Big Mama.

MARGARET: Precious Mommy. I'm sorry, I'm sorry, I — !

(*She bends her long graceful neck to press her forehead to* BIG MAMA'*s bulging shoulder under its black chiffon.*)

GOOPER: How beautiful, how touching, this display of devotion!

MAE: Do you know why she's childless? She's childless because that big beautiful athlete husband of hers won't go to bed with her!

GOOPER: You jest won't let me do this in a nice way, will yah? Aw right — Mae and I have five kids with another one coming! I don't give a goddam if Big Daddy likes me or don't like me or did or never did or will or will never! I'm just appealing to a sense of common decency and fair play. I'll tell you the truth. I've resented Big Daddy's partiality to Brick ever since Brick was born, and the way I've been treated like I was just barely good enough to spit on and sometimes not even good enough for that. Big Daddy is dying of cancer, and it's spread all through him and it's attacked all his vital organs including the kidneys and right now he is sinking into uremia, and you all know what uremia is, it's poisoning of the whole system due to the failure of the body to eliminate its poisons.

MARGARET (*to herself, downstage, hissingly*): Poisons, poisons! Venomous thoughts and words! In hearts and minds! — That's poisons!

GOOPER (*overlapping her*): I am asking for a square deal, and I expect to get one. But if I don't get one, if there's any peculiar shenanigans going on around here behind my back, or before me, well, I'm not a corporation lawyer for nothing, I know how to protect my own interests. — Oh! A late arrival!

(BRICK *enters from the gallery with a tranquil, blurred smile, carrying an empty glass with him.*)

MAE: Behold the conquering hero comes!

GOOPER: The fabulous Brick Pollitt! Remember him? — Who could forget him!

MAE: He looks like he's been injured in a game!

GOOPER: Yep, I'm afraid you'll have to warm the bench at the Sugar Bowl this year, Brick! (MAE *laughs shrilly.*) Or was it the Rose Bowl that he made that famous run in?

MAE: The punch bowl honey. It was in the punch bowl, the cut-glass punch bowl!

GOOPER: Oh, that's right, I'm getting the bowls mixed up!

MARGARET: Why don't you stop venting your malice and envy on a sick boy?

BIG MAMA: Now you two hush, I mean it, hush, all of you, hush!

GOOPER: All right, Big Mama. A family crisis brings out the best and the worst in every member of it.

MAE: That's the truth.

MARGARET: Amen!

BIG MAMA: I said, hush! I won't tolerate any more catty talk in my house.

(MAE *gives Gooper a sign indicating briefcase.* BRICK's *smile has grown both brighter and vaguer. As he prepares a drink, he sings softly:*)

BRICK:
>   Show me the way to go home,
>   I'm tired and I wanta go to bed,
>   I had a little drink about an hour ago —

GOOPER (*at the same time*): Big Mama, you know it's necessary for me t'go back to Memphis in th' mornin' t'represent the Parker estate in a lawsuit.

>   (MAE *sits on the bed and arranges papers she has taken from the briefcase.*)

BRICK (*continuing the song*):
>   Wherever I may roam,
>   On land or sea or foam.

BIG MAMA: Is it, Gooper?

MAE: Yaiss.

GOOPER: That's why I'm forced to — to bring up a problem that —

MAE: Somethin' that's too important t' be put off!

GOOPER: If Brick was sober, he ought to be in on this.

MARGARET: Brick is present, we're here.

GOOPER: Well, good. I will now give you this outline my partner, Tom Bullitt, an me have drawn up — a sort of dummy — trustee-ship.

MARGARET: Oh, that's it! You'll be in charge an' dole out remittances, will you?

GOOPER: This we did as soon as we got the report on Big Daddy from th' Ochsner Laboratories. We did this thing, I mean we drew up this dummy outline with the advice and assistance of the Chairman of the Boa'd of Directors of th' Southern Plantahs Bank and Trust Company in Memphis, C. C. Bellowes, a man who handles estates for all th' prominent fam'lies in West Tennessee and th' Delta.

BIG MAMA: Gooper?

GOOPER (*crouching in front of* BIG MAMA): Now this is not — not final, or anything like it. This is just a preliminary outline. But it does provide a basis — a design — a — possible, feasible — plan!

MARGARET: Yes, I'll bet.

MAE: It's a plan to protect the biggest estate in the Delta from ir-responsibility an' —

BIG MAMA: Now you listen to me, all of you, you listen here! They's not goin' to be any more catty talk in my house! And Gooper, you put that away before I grab it out of your hand and tear it right up! I don't know what the hell's in it, and I don't want to know what the hell's in it. I'm talkin' in Big Daddy's language now; I'm his wife, not his widow, I'm still his wife! And I'm talkin' to you in his language an —

GOOPER: Big Mama, what I have here is —

MAE: Gooper explained that it's just a plan. . . .

BIG MAMA: I don't care what you got there. Just put it back where it came from, an' don't let me see it again, not even the outside of the envelope of it! Is that understood? Basis! Plan! Preliminary! Design! I say — what is it Big Daddy always says when he's disgusted?

BRICK (*from the bar*): Big Daddy says "crap" when he's disgusted.

BIG MAMA (*rising*): That's right — CRAP! I say CRAP too, like Big Daddy!

MAE: Coarse language doesn't seem called for in this —

GOOPER: Somethin' in me is deeply outraged by hearin' you talk like this.

BIG MAMA: Nobody's goin' to take nothin'! — till Big Daddy lets go if it, and maybe, just possibly, not — not even then! No, not even then!

BRICK:

> You can always hear me singin' this song,
> Show me the way to go home.

BIG MAMA: Tonight Brick looks like he used to look when he was a little boy, just like he did when he played wild games and used to come home all sweaty and pink-cheeked and sleepy, with his — red curls shining. . . .

> (*She comes over to him and runs her fat shaky hand through his hair. He draws aside as he does from all physical contact and continues the song in a whisper, opening the ice bucket and dropping in the ice cubes one by one as if he were mixing some important chemical formula.*)

BIG MAMA (*continuing*): Time goes by so fast. Nothin' can outrun it. Death commences too early — almost before you're half-acquainted with life — you meet with the other. . . . Oh, you know we just got to love each other an' stay together, all of us, just as close as we can, especially now that such a *black* thing has come and moved into this place without invitation.

> (*Awkwardly embracing* BRICK, *she presses her head to his shoulder,* GOOPER *has been returning papers to* MAE *who has restored them to briefcase with an air of severely tried patience.*)

GOOPER: Big Mama? Big Mama?

> (*He stands behind her, tense with sibling envy.*)

BIG MAMA (*oblivious of* GOOPER): Brick, you hear me, don't you?

MARGARET: Brick hears you, Big Mama, he understands what you're saying.

BIG MAMA: Oh, Brick, son of Big Daddy! Big Daddy does so love you! Y'know what would be his fondest dream come true? If before he passed on, if Big Daddy has to pass on, you gave him a child of yours, a grandson as much like his son as his son is like Big Daddy!

MAE (*zipping briefcase shut: an incongruous sound*): Such a pity that Maggie an' Brick can't oblige!

MARGARET (*suddenly and quietly but forcefully*): Everybody listen. (*She crosses to the center of the room, holding her hands rigidly together.*)

MAE: Listen to what, Maggie?

MARGARET: I have an announcement to make.

GOOPER: A sports announcement. Maggie?

MARGARET: Brick and I are going to — have a child! (BIG MAMA *catches her breath in a loud gasp. Pause.* BIG MAMA *rises.*)

BIG MAMA: Maggie! Brick! This is too good to believe!

MAE: That's right, too good to believe.

BIG MAMA: Oh, my, my! This is Big Daddy's dream, his dream come true! I'm going to tell him right now before he —

MARGARET: We'll tell him in the morning. Don't disturb him now.

BIG MAMA: I want to tell him before he goes to sleep, I'm going to tell him his dream's come true this minute! And Brick! A child will make you pull yourself together and quit this drinking! (*She seizes the glass from his hand.*) The responsibilities of a father will — (*Her face contorts and she makes an excited gesture; bursting into sobs she rushes out, crying.*) I'm going to tell Big Daddy right this minute!

(*Her voice fades out down the hall.* BRICK *shrugs slightly and drops an ice cube into another glass.* MARGARET *crosses quickly to his side, saying something under her breath, and she pours the liquor for him, staring up almost fiercely into his face.*)

BRICK (*coolly*): Thank you, Maggie, that's a nice big shot. (MAE *has joined* GOOPER *and she gives him a fierce poke, making a low hissing sound and a grimace of fury.*)

GOOPER (*pushing her aside*): Brick could you possibly spare me one small shot of that liquor?

BRICK: Why, help yourself, Gooper boy.

GOOPER: I will.

MAE (*shrilly*): Of course we know that this is —

GOOPER: Be still Mae!

MAE: I won't be still I know she's made this up!

GOOPER: God damn it, I said to shut up!

MARGARET: Gracious! I didn't know that my little announcement was going to provoke such a storm!

MAE: That woman isn't pregnant!

GOOPER: Who said she was?

MAE: She did.

GOOPER: The doctor didn't. Doc Baugh didn't.

MARGARET: I haven't gone to Doc Baugh.

GOOPER: Then who'd you go to, Maggie?

MARGARET: One of the best gynecologists in the South.

GOOPER: Uh huh, uh huh! — I see. . . . (*He takes out pencil and notebook.*) — May we have his name, please?

MARGARET: No, you may not, Mister Prosecuting Attorney!

MAE: He doesn't have any name, he doesn't exist!

MARGARET: Oh, he exists all right, and so does my child, Brick's baby!

MAE: You can't conceive a child by a man that won't sleep with you unless you think you're —

(BRICK *has turned on the phonograph. A scat son cuts* MAE's *speech.*)

GOOPER: Turn that off!

MAE: We know it's a lie because we hear you in here; he won't sleep with you, we hear you! So don't imagine you're going to put a trick over on us, to fool a dying man with a —

(*A long drawn cry of agony and rage fills the house.* MARGARET *turns phonograph down to a whisper. The cry is repeated.*)

MAE (*awed*): Did you hear that, Gooper, did you hear that?

GOOPER: Sounds like the pain has struck.

MAE: Go see, Gooper!

GOOPER: Come along and leave these love birds together in their nest!

(*He goes out first.* MAE *follows but turns at the door, contorting her face and hissing at* MARGARET.)

MAE: Liar!

(*She slams the door.* MARGARET *exhales with relief and moves a little unsteadily to catch hold of* BRICK's *arm.*

MARGARET: Thank you for — keeping still . . .

BRICK: O.K. Maggie.

MARGARET: It was gallant of you to save my face!

BRICK: — It hasn't happened yet.

MARGARET: What?

BRICK: The click. . . .

MARGARET: — the click in your head that makes you peaceful, honey?

BRICK: Uh-huh. It hasn't happened. . . . I've got to make it happen before I can sleep. . . .

MARGARET: — I — know what you — mean. . . .

BRICK: Give me that pillow in the big chair, Maggie.

MARGARET: I'll put it on the bed for you.

BRICK: No, put it on the sofa, where I sleep.

MARGARET: Not tonight, Brick.

BRICK: I want it on the sofa. That's where I sleep. (*He has hobbled to the liquor cabinet. He now pours down three shots in quick succession and stands waiting, silent. All at once he turns with a smile and says:*) There!

MARGARET: What?

BRICK: The click. . . .

> (*His gratitude seems almost infinite as he hobbles out on the gallery with a drink. We hear his crutch as he swings out of sight. Then, at some distance, he begins singing to himself a peaceful song.* MARGARET *holds the big pillow forlornly as if it were her only companion, for a few moments, then throws it on the bed. She rushes to the liquor cabinet, gathers all the bottles in her arms, turns about undecidedly, then runs out of the room with them, leaving the door ajar on the dim yellow hall.* BRICK *is heard hobbling back along the gallery, singing his peaceful song. He comes back in, sees the pillow on the bed, laughs lightly, sadly, picks it up. He has it under his arm as* MARGARET *returns to the room.* MARGARET *softly shuts the door and leans against it, smiling softly at* BRICK.)

MARGARET: Brick, I used to think that you were stronger than me and I didn't want to be overpowered by you. But now, since you've taken to liquor — you know what? — I guess it's bad, but now I'm stronger than you and I can love you more truly!

Don't move that pillow. I'll move it right back if you do! — Brick? (*She turns out all the lamps but a single rose-silk-shaded one by the bed.*) I really have been to a doctor and I know what to do and — Brick? — this is my time by the calendar to conceive!

BRICK: Yes, I understand, Maggie. But how are you going to conceive a child by a man in love with his liquor?

MARGARET: By locking his liquor up and making him satisfy my desire before I unlock it!

BRICK: Is that what you've done, Maggie?

MARGARET: Look and see. That cabinet's mighty empty compared to before!

BRICK: Well, I'll be a son of a —

(*He reaches for his crutch but she beats him to it and rushes out on the gallery, hurls the crutch over the rail and comes back in, panting. There are running footsteps. Big Mama bursts into the room, her face all awry, gasping stammering.*)

BIG MAMA: Oh, my God, oh, my God, oh, my God, where is it?

MARGARET: Is this what you want, Big Mama?

(MARGARET *hands her the package left by the doctor.*)

BIG MAMA: I can't bear it, oh, God! Oh, Brick! Brick, baby! (*She rushes at him. He averts his face from her sobbing kisses.* MARGARET *watches with a tight smile.*) My son, Big Daddy's boy! Little Father!

(*The groaning cry is heard again. She runs out, sobbing.*)

MARGARET: And so tonight we're going to make the lie true, and when that's done, I'll bring the liquor back here and we'll get drunk together, here, tonight, in this place that death has come into. . . . — What do you say?

BRICK: I don't say anything. I guess there's nothing to say.

MARGARET: Oh, you weak people, you weak, beautiful people! — who give up. — What you want is someone to — (*She turns out the rose-silk lamp.*) — take hold of you. — Gently, gently, with love! And — (*The curtain begins to fall slowly.*) I do love you, Brick, I do!

BRICK (*smiling with charming sadness*): Wouldn't it be funny if that was true?

The curtain comes down

note of explanation

Some day when time permits I would like to write a piece about the influence, its dangers and its values, of a powerful and highly imaginative director upon the development of a play, before and during production. It does have dangers, but it has them only if the playwright is excessively malleable or submissive, or the director is excessively insistent on ideas or interpretations of his own. Elia Kazan and I have enjoyed the advantages and avoided the dangers of this highly explosive relationship because of the deepest mutual respect for each other's creative functions we have worked together three times with a phenomenal absence of friction between us and each occasion has increased the trust.

If you don't want a director's influence on your play, there are two ways to avoid it, and neither is good. One way is to arrive at an absolutely final draft of your play before you let your director see it, then hand it to him saying, Here it is, take it or leave it! The other way is to select a director who is content to put your play on the stage precisely as you conceived it with no ideas of his own. I said neither is a good way, and I meant it. No living playwright, that I can think of, hasn't something valuable to learn about his own work from a director so keenly perceptive as Elia Kazan. It so happened that in the case of *Streecar*, Kazan was given a script that was completely finished. In the case of *Cat*, he was shown the first typed version of the play, and he was excited by it, but he had definite reservations about it which were concentrated in the third act. The gist of his reservations can be listed as three points: one, he felt that Big Daddy was too valid and important a character to disappear from the play except as an offstage cry after the second act curtain; two, he felt that the character of Brick should undergo some apparent mutation as a result of the virtual vivisection that he undergoes in his interview with his father in Act Two. Three, he felt that the character of Margaret, while he understood that I sympathized with her myself, should be, if possible, more clearly sympathetic to an audience.

It was only the third of three suggestions that I embraced wholeheartedly from the outset, because it so happened that Maggie the Cat had become steadily more charming to me as I worked on her characterization. I didn't want Big Daddy to reappear in Act Three and I felt that the moral paralysis of Brick was a root thing in his tragedy, and to show a dramatic progression would obscure the meaning of that tragedy in him and because I don't believe that a conversation, however revelatory, ever effects so immediate a change in the heart or even conduct of a person in Brick's state of spiritual disrepair.

However, I wanted Kazan to direct the play, and though these suggestions were not made in the form of an ultimatum, I was fearful that I would lose his interest if I didn't re-examine the script from his point of view. I did. And you will find included in this published script the new third act that resulted from his creative influence on the play. The reception of the playing-script has more than justified, in my opinion, the adjustments made to that influence.

A failure reaches fewer people, and touches fewer, than does a play that succeeds.

It may be that *Cat* number one would have done just as well, or nearly, as *Cat* number two; it's an interesting question. At any rate, with the publication of both third acts in this volume, the reader can, if he wishes, make up his own mind about it.

Tennessee Williams

ACT THREE
AS PLAYED IN NEW YORK PRODUCTION

BIG DADDY *is seen leaving as at the end of Act* II.

BIG DADDY (*shouts, as he goes out DR on gallery*): ALL — LYIN' — DYIN' — LIARS! LIARS! LIARS!

(*After* BIG DADDY *has gone,* MARGARET *enters from DR on gallery, into room through DS door. She X to* BRICK *at LC.*)

MARGARET: Brick, what in the name of God was goin' on in this room?

(DIXIE *and* TRIXIE *rush through the room from the hall, L to gallery R, brandishing cap pistols, which they fire repeatedly, as they shout: "Bang! Bang! Bang!"* MAE *appears from DR gallery entrance, and turns the children back UL, along gallery. At the same moment,* GOOPER, REVEREND TOOKER *and* DR. BAUGH *enter from L in the hall.*)

MAE: Dixie! You quit that! Gooper, will y'please git these kiddies t'baid? Right now?

(GOOPER *and* REVEREND TOOKER X *along upper gallery.* DR. BAUGH *holds, UC, near hall door.* REVEREND TOOKER X *to* MAE *near section of gallery just outside doors, R.*)

GOOPER (*urging the children along*): Mae — you seen Big Mama?

MAE: Not yet.

(DIXIE *and* TRIXIE *vanish through hall, L.*)

REVEREND TOOKER (*to* MAE): Those kiddies are so full of vitality. I think I'll have to be startin' back to town.

(MARGARET *turns to watch and listen.*)

MAE: Not yet, Preacher. You know we regard you as a member of this fam'ly, one of our closest an' dearest, so you just got t'be with us when Doc Baugh gives Big Mama th' actual truth about th' report from th' clinic. (*Calls through door:*) Has Big Daddy gone to bed, Brick?

(GOOPER *has gone out DR at the beginning of the exchange between* MAE *and* REVEREND TOOKER.)

MARGARET (*replying to* MAE): Yes, he's gone to bed. (*To* BRICK:) Why'd Big Daddy shout "liars"?

GOOPER (*off DR*): Mae!

(MAE *exits DR.* REVEREND TOOKER *drifts along upper gallery.*)

BRICK: I didn't lie to Big Daddy. I've lied to nobody, nobody but myself, just lied to myself. The time has come to put me in Rainbow Hill, put me in Rainbow Hill, Maggie, I ought to go there.

MARGARET: Over my dead body! (BRICK *starts R. She holds him.*) Where do you think you're goin'?

(MAE *enters from DR on gallery,* X *to* REVEREND TOOKER, *who comes to meet her.*)

BRICK (X *below to* C): Out for some air, I want air —

GOOPER (*entering from DR to* MAE, *on gallery*): Now, where is that old lady?

MAE: Cantcha find her, Gooper?

(REVEREND TOOKER *goes out DR.*)

GOOPER (X *to* DOC *above hall door*): She's avoidin' this talk.

MAE: I think she senses somethin'.

GOOPER (*calls off* L): Sookey! Go find Big Mama an' tell her Doc Baugh an' the Preacher've got to go soon.

MAE: Don't let Big Daddy hear yuh!

(*Brings* DR. BAUGH *to R on gallery.*)

REVEREND TOOKER (*off DR, calls*): Big Mama.

SOOKEY and DAISY (*running from L to R on lawn, calling*): Miss Ida! Miss Ida!

(*They go out UR.*)

GOOPER (*calling off upper gallery*): Lacey, you look downstairs for Big Mama!

MARGARET: Brick, they're going to tell Big Mama the truth now, an' she needs you!

(REVEREND TOOKER *appears in lawn area, UR,* X C.)

DOCTOR BAUGH (*to* MAE, *on R gallery*): This is going to be painful.

MAE: Painful things can't always be avoided.

DOCTOR BAUGH: That's what I've noticed about 'em, Sister Woman.

REVEREND TOOKER (*on lawn, points off R*): I see Big Mama!

(*Hurries off L and reappears shortly in hall.*)

GOOPER (*hurrying into hall*): She's gone round the gall'ry to Big Daddy's room. Hey, Mama! (*Off:*) Hey, Big Mama! Come here!

MAE (*calls*): Hush, Gooper! Don't holler, go to her!

(GOOPER *and* REVEREND TOOKER *now appear together in hall.*
BIG MAMA *runs in from DR, carrying a glass of milk. She X past*
DR. BAUGH *to* MAE, *on R gallery.* DR. BAUGH *turns away.*)

BIG MAMA: Here I am! What d'you all want with me?

GOOPER (*steps toward* BIG MAMA): Big Mama, I told you we got to
have this talk.

BIG MAMA: What talk you talkin' about? I saw the light go on in
Big Daddy's bedroom an' took him his glass of milk, an' he just
shut the shutters right in my face. (*Steps into room through R
door.*) When old couples have been together as long as me an'
Big Daddy, they, get irritable with each other just from too much
— devotion! Isn't that so?

(*X below wicker seat to RC area.*)

MARGARET (*X to* BIG MAMA, *embracing her*): Yes, of course it's so.
(BRICK *starts out UC through hall, but sees* GOOPER *and* REVER-
END TOOKER *entering, so he hobbles through C out DS door
and onto gallery.*)

BIG MAMA: I think Big Daddy was just worn out. He loves his fam'ly.
He loves to have 'em around him, but it's a strain on his nerves.
He wasn't himself tonight, Brick — (*XC toward* BRICK. BRICK
passes her on his way out, DS.) Big Daddy wasn't himself, I could
tell he was all worked up.

REVEREND TOOKER (*USC*): I think he's remarkable.

BIG MAMA: Yaiss! Just remarkable. (*Faces US, turns, X to bar, puts
down glass of milk.*) Did you notice all the food he ate at that
table? (*XR a bit.*) Why he ate like a hawss!

GOOPER (*USC*): I hope he don't regret it.

BIG MAMA (*turns US toward* GOOPER): What! Why that man ate
a huge piece of cawn bread with molasses on it! Helped himself
twice to hoppin' john!

MARGARET (*X to* BIG MAMA): Big Daddy loves hoppin' john. We
had a real country dinner.

BIG MAMA: Yais, he simply adores it! An' candied yams. Son — (*X
to DS door, looking out at* BRICK. MARGARET *X above* BIG
MAMA *to her L.*) That man put away enough food at that table
to stuff a fieldhand.

GOOPER: I hope he don't have to pay for it later on.

BIG MAMA (*turns US*): What's that, Gooper?

MAE: Gooper says he hopes Big Daddy doesn't suffer tonight.

BIG MAMA (*turns to* MARGARET, *DC*): Oh, shoot, Gooper says,
Gooper says! Why should Big Daddy suffer for satisfyin' a nawmal

appetite? There's nothin' wrong with that man but nerves; he's sound as a dollar! An' now he knows he is, an' that's why he ate such a supper. He had a big load off his mind, knowin' he wasn't doomed to — what — he thought he was — doomed t' —

(*She wavers.* MARGARET *puts her arms around* BIG MAMA.)

GOOPER (*urging* MAE *forward*): MAE!

(MAE *runs forward below wicker seat. She stands below* BIG MAMA, MARGARET *above* BIG MAMA. *They help her to the wicker seat.* BIG MAMA *sits.* MARGARET *sits above her.* MAE *stands behind her.*)

GARET *sits above her.* MAE *stands behind her.*)

MARGARET: Bless his ole sweet soul.

BIG MAMA: Yes — bless his heart.

BRICK (*DS on gallery, looking out front*): Hello, moon, I envy you, you cool son of a bitch.

BIG MAMA: I want Brick!

MARGARET: He just stepped out for some fresh air.

BIG MAMA: Honey! I want Brick!

MAE: Bring li'l Brother in here so we kin talk.

(MARGARET *rises, X through DS door to* BRICK *on gallery.*)

BRICK (*to the moon*): I envy you — you cool son of a bitch.

MARGARET: Brick, what're you doin' out here on the gall'ry, baby?

BRICK: Admirin' an' complimentin' th' man in the moon.

(MAE *X to* DR. BAUGH *on R gallery.* REVEREND TOOKER *and* GOOPER *move R UC, looking at* BIG MAMA.)

MARGARET (*to* BRICK): Come in, Baby. They're gettin' ready to tell Big Mama the truth.

BRICK: I can't witness that thing in there.

MAE: Doc Baugh, d'you think those vitamin B_{12} injections are all they're cracked up t'be?

(*Enters room to upper side, behind wicker seat.*)

DOCTOR BAUGH (*X to below wicker seat*): Well, I guess they're as good t'be stuck with as anything else.

(*Looks at watch; X through to LC.*)

MARGARET (*to* BRICK): Big Mama needs you!

BRICK: I can't witness that thing in there!

BIG MAMA: What's wrong here? You all have such long faces, you sit here waitin' for somethin' like a bomb — to go off.

GOOPER: We're waitin' for Brick an' Maggie to come in for this talk.

MARGARET (*X above* BRICK, *to his R*): Brother Man an' Mae have

got a trick up their sleeves, an' if you don't go in there t'help Big
Mama, y'know what I'm goin' to do — ?

BIG MAMA: Talk. Whispers! Whispers! (*Looks out DR.*) Brick! . . .

MARGARET (*answering* BIG MAMA'S *call*): Comin', Big Mama! (*To*
BRICK.) I'm going' to take every dam' bottle on this place an' pitch
it off th' levee into th' river!

BIG MAMA: Never had this sort of atmosphere here before.

MAE (*sits above* BIG MAMA *on wicker seat*): Before what, Big
Mama?

BIG MAMA: This occasion. What's Brick an' Maggie doin' out there
now?

GOOPER (*X DC, looks out*): They seem to be havin' some little
altercation.

(BRICK *X toward DS step.* MAGGIE *moves R above him to portal
DR.* REVEREND TOOKER *joins* DR. BAUGH, *LC.*)

BIG MAMA (*taking a pill from pill box on chain at her wrist*): Give
me a little somethin' to wash this tablet down with. Smell of burnt
fireworks always makes me sick.

(MAE *X to bar to pour glass of water.* DR. BAUGH *joins her.*
GOOPER *X to* REVEREND TOOKER, *LC.*)

BRICK (*to* MAGGIE): You're a live cat, aren't you?

MARGARET: You're dam' right I am!

BIG MAMA: Gooper, will y'please open that hall door — an' let some
air circulate in this stiflin' room?

(GOOPER *starts US, but is restrained by* MAE *who X through C
with glass of water.* GOOPER *turns to men DLC.*)

MAE (*X to* BIG MAMA *with water, sits above her*): Big Mama, I
think we ought to keep that door closed till after we talk.

BIG MAMA: I swan!

(*Drinks water. Washes down pill.*)

MAE: I just don't think we ought to take any chance of Big Daddy
hearin' a word of this discussion.

BIG MAMA (*hands glass to* MAE): What discussion of what? Maggie!
Brick! Nothin' is goin' to be said in th' house of Big Daddy Pollitt
that he can't hear if he wants to!

(MAE *rises, X to bar, puts down glass, joins* GOOPER *and the two
men, LC.*)

BRICK: How long are you goin' to stand behind me, Maggie?

MARGARET: Forever, if necessary.

(BRICK *X US to R gallery door.*)

BIG MAMA: Brick!

(MAE *rises, looks out DS, sits.*)

GOOPER: That boy's gone t'pieces — he's just gone t'pieces.

DOCTOR BAUGH: Y'know, in my day they used to have somethin' they called the Keeley cure for drinkers.

BIG MAMA: Shoot!

DOCTOR BAUGH: But nowadays, I understand they take some kind of tablets that kill their taste for the stuff.

GOOPER (*turns to* DR. BAUGH): Call 'em anti-bust tablets.

BIG MAMA: Brick don't need to take nothin'. That boy is just broken up over Skipper's death. You know how poor Skipper died. They gave him a big, big dose of that sodium amytal stuff at his home an' then they called the ambulance an' give him another big, big dose of it at th' hospital an' that an' all the alcohol in his system fo' months an' months just proved too much for his heart an' his heart quit beatin'. I'm scared of needles! I'm more scared of a needle than th' knife —

(BRICK *has entered the room to behind the wicker seat. He rests his hand on* BIG MAMA'S *head.* GOOPER *has moved a bit URC, facing* BIG MAMA.)

BIG MAMA: Oh! Here's Brick! My precious baby!

(DR. BAUGH X *to bar, puts down drink.* BRICK X *below* BIG MAMA *through C to bar.*)

BRICK: Take it, Gooper!

MAE (*rising*): What?

BRICK: Gooper knows what. Take it, Gooper!

(MAE *turns to* GOOPER *URC.* DR. BAUGH X *to* REVEREND TOOKER. MARGARET, *who has followed* BRICK *US on R gallery before he entered the room, now enters room, to behind wicker seat.*)

BIG MAMA (*to* BRICK): You just break my heart.

BRICK (*at bar*): Sorry — anyone else?

MARGARET: Brick, sit with Big Mama an' hold her hand while we talk.

BRICK: You do that, Maggie. I'm a restless cripple. I got to stay on my crutch.

(MAE *sits above* BIG MAMA. GOOPER *moves in front, below, and sits on couch, facing* BIG MAMA. REVEREND TOOKER *closes in to RC.* DR. BAUGH X *DC, faces upstage, smoking cigar.* MARGARET *turns away to R doors.*)

BIG MAMA: Why're you all surroundin' me? — like this? Why're you all starin' at me like this an' makin' signs at each other? (BRICK

hobbles out hall door and X along R gallery.) I don't need nobody
to hold my hand. Are you all crazy? Since when did Big Daddy or
me need anybody — ?

(REVEREND TOOKER *moves behind wicker seat.*)

MAE: Calm yourself, Big Mama.

BIG MAMA: Calm you'self you'self, Sister Woman! How could I
calm myself with everyone starin' at me as if big drops of blood
had broken out on m'face? What's this all about, Annh! What?

GOOPER: Doc Baugh — (MAE *rises.*) Sit down, Mae — (MAE *sits.*)
— Big Mama wants to know the complete truth about th' report
we got today from the Ochsner Clinic!

(DR. BAUGH *buttons his coat, faces group at RC.*)

BIG MAMA: Is there somethin' — somethin' that I don't know?

DOCTOR BAUGH: Yes — well . . .

BIG MAMA (*rises*): I — want to — knowwwww! (X *to* DR. BAUGH.)
Somebody must be lyin'! I want to know!

(MAE, GOOPER, REVEREND TOOKER *surround* BIG MAMA.)

MAE: Sit down, Big Mama, sit down on this sofa!

(BRICK *has passed* MARGARET *Xing DR on gallery.*)

MARGARET: Brick! Brick!

BIG MAMA: What is it, what is it?

(BIG MAMA *drives* DR. BAUGH *a bit DLC. Others follow, surrounding* BIG MAMA.)

DOCTOR BAUGH: I never have seen a more thorough examination
than Big Daddy was given in all my experience at the Ochsner
Clinic.

GOOPER: It's one of th' best in th' country.

MAE: It's the best in th' country — bar none!

DOCTOR BAUGH: Of course they were ninety-nine and nine-tenths
per cent certain before they even started.

BIG MAMA: Sure of what, sure of what, sure of what — what!?

MAE: Now, Mommy, be a brave girl!

BRICK (*on DR gallery, covers his ears, sings*): "By the light, by the
light, of the silvery moon!"

GOOPER (*breaks DR. Calls out to* BRICK): Shut up, Brick!

(*Returns to group LC.*)

BRICK: Sorry . . .

(*Continues singing.*)

DOCTOR BAUGH: But now, you see, Big Mama, they cut a piece off
this growth, a specimen of the tissue, an' —

BIG MAMA: Growth? You told Big Daddy —

DOCTOR BAUGH: Now, wait —

BIG MAMA: You told me an' Big Daddy there wasn't a thing wrong with him but —

MAE: Big Mama, they always —

GOOPER: Let Doc Baugh talk, will yuh?

BIG MAMA: — little spastic conditions of —

REVEREND TOOKER (*throughout all this*): Shh! Shh! Shh!

    (BIG MAMA *breaks UC, they all follow.*)

DOCTOR BAUGH: Yes, that's what we told Big Daddy. But we had this bit of tissue run through the laboratory an' I'm sorry t'say the test was positive on it. It's malignant.

    (*Pause.*)

BIG MAMA: Cancer! Cancer!

MAE: Now now, Mommy —

GOOPER (*at the same time*): You had to know, Big Mama.

BIG MAMA: Why didn't they cut it out of him? Hanh? Hannh?

DOCTOR BAUGH: Involved too much, Big Mama, too many organs affected.

MAE: Big Mama, the liver's affected, an' so's the kidneys, both. It's gone way past what they call a —

GOOPER: — a surgical risk.

    (BIG MAMA *gasps.*)

REVEREND TOOKER: Tch, tch, tch.

DOCTOR BAUGH: Yes, it's gone past the knife.

MAE: That's why he's turned yellow!

    (BRICK *stops singing, turns away UR on gallery.*)

BIG MAMA (*pushes MAE DS*): Git away from me, git away from me, Mae! (*X DSR.*) I want Brick! Where's Brick! Where's my only son?

MAE (*a step after* BIG MAMA): Mama! Did she say "only" son?

GOOPER (*following* BIG MAMA): What does that make me?

MAE (*above* GOOPER): A sober responsible man with five precious children — six!

BIG MAMA: I want Brick! Brick! Brick!

MARGARET (*a step to* BIG MAMA *above couch*): Mama, let me tell you.

BIG MAMA (*pushing her aside*): No, no, leave me alone, you're not my blood!

    (*She rushes onto the DS gallery.*)

GOOPER (*X to* BIG MAMA *on gallery*): Mama! I'm your son! Listen to me!

MAE: Gooper's your son, Mama, he's your first-born!

BIG MAMA: Gooper never liked Daddy!

MAE: That's not true!

REVEREND TOOKER (*UC*): I think I'd better slip away at this point. Goodnight, goodnight everybody, and God bless you all — on this place.

(*Goes out through hall.*)

DOCTOR BAUGH (*X DR to above DS door*): Well, Big Mama —

BIG MAMA (*leaning against* GOOPER, *on lower gallery*): It's all a mistake, I know it's just a bad dream.

DOCTOR BAUGH: We're gonna keep Big Daddy as comfortable as we can.

BIG MAMA: Yes, it's just a bad dream, that's all it is, it's just an awful dream.

GOOPER: In my opinion Big Daddy is havin' some pain but won't admit that he has it.

BIG MAMA: Just a dream, a bad dream.

DOCTOR BAUGH: That's what lots of 'em do, they think if they don't admit they're havin' the pain they can sort of escape th' fact of it.

(BRICK *X US on R gallery.* MARGARET *watches him from R door.*)

GOOPER: Yes, they get sly about it, get real sly about it.

MAE (*X to R of* DR. BAUGH): Gooper an' I think —

GOOPER: Shut up, Mae! — Big Mama, I really do think Big Daddy should be started on morphine.

BIG MAMA (*pulling away from* GOOPER): Nobody's goin' to give Big Daddy morphine!

DOCTOR BAUGH: Now, Big Mama, when that pain strikes it's goin' to strike mighty hard an' Big Daddy's goin' t'need the needle to bear it.

BIG MAMA (*X to* DR. BAUGH): I tell you, nobody's goin' to give him morphine!

MAE: Big Mama, you don't want to see Big Daddy suffer, y'know y' —

DOCTOR BAUGH (*X to bar*): Well, I'm leavin' this stuff here (*Puts packet of morphine, etc., on bar.*) so if there's a sudden attack you won't have to send out for it.

(BIG MAMA *hurries to L side bar.*)

MAE (*X C, below* DR. BAUGH): I know how to give a hypo.

BIG MAMA: Nobody's goin' to give Big Daddy morphine!

GOOPER (*X C*): Mae took a course in nursin' durin' th' war.

MARGARET: Somehow I don't think Big Daddy would want Mae t'give him a hypo.

MAE (*to* MARGARET): You think he'd want you to do it?

DOCTOR BAUGH: Well —

GOOPER: Well, Doc Baugh is goin' —

DOCTOR BAUGH: Yes, I got to be goin'. Well, keep your chin up, Big Mama.

> (*X to hall.*)

GOOPER (*as he and* MAE *follow* DR. BAUGH *into the hall*): She's goin' to keep her ole chin up, aren't you, Big Mama? (*They go out L.*) Well, Doc, we sure do appreciate all you've done. I'm telling you, we're obligated —

BIG MAMA: Margaret!

> (*X RC.*)

MARGARET (*meeting* BIG MAMA *in front of wicker seat*): I'm right here, Big Mama.

BIG MAMA: Margaret, you've got to cooperate with me an' Big Daddy to straighten Brick out now —

GOOPER (*off L, returning with* MAE): I guess that Doctor has got a lot on his mind, but it wouldn't hurt him to act a little more human —

BIG MAMA: — because it'll break Big Daddy's heart if Brick don't pull himself together an' take hold of things here.

> (BRICK *X DSR on gallery.*)

MAE (*UC, overhearing*): Take hold of what things, Big Mama?

BIG MAMA (*sits in wicker chair,* MARGARET *standing behind chair*): The place.

GOOPER (*UC*): Big Mama, you've had a shock.

MAE (*X with* GOOPER *to* BIG MAMA): Yais, we've all had a shock, but —

GOOPER: Let's be realistic —

MAE: Big Daddy would not, would never, be foolish enough to —

GOOPER: — put this place in irresponsible hands!

BIG MAMA: Big Daddy ain't goin' t'put th' place in anybody's hands, Big Daddy is not goin' t'die! I want you to git that into your haids, all of you!

> (MAE *sits above* BIG MAMA, MARGARET *turns R to door,* GOOPER *X LC a bit.*)

MAE: Mommy, Mommy, Big Mama, we're just as hopeful an' optimistic as you are about Big Daddy's prospects, we have faith in prayer — but nevertheless there are certain matters that have to be discussed an' dealt with, because otherwise —

GOOPER: Mae, will y'please get my briefcase out of our room?

MAE: Yes, honey.

(*Rises, goes out through hall L.*)

MARGARET (*X to* BRICK *on DS gallery*): Hear them in there?

(*X back to R gallery door.*)

GOOPER (*stands above* BIG MAMA. *Leaning over her*): Big Mama, what you said just now was not at all true, an' you know it. I've always loved Big Daddy in my own quiet way. I never made a show of it. I know that Big Daddy has always been fond of me in a quiet way, too.

(MARGARET *drifts UR on gallery.* MAE *returns, X to* GOOPER'S *L with briefcase.*)

MAE: Here's your briefcase, Gooper, honey.

(*Hands it to him.*)

GOOPER (*hands briefcase back to* MAE): Thank you. Of cou'se, my relationship with Big Daddy is different from Brick's.

MAE: You're eight years older'n Brick an' always had t'carry a bigger load of th' responsibilities than Brick ever had t'carry; he never carried a thing in his life but a football or a highball.

GOOPER: Mae, will y'let me talk, please?

MAE: Yes, honey.

GOOPER: Now, a twenty-eight thousand acre plantation's a mighty big thing t'run.

MAE: Almost single-handed!

BIG MAMA: You never had t'run this place, Brother Man, what're you talkin' about, as if Big Daddy was dead an' in his grave, you had to run it? Why, you just had t'help him out with a few business details an' had your law practice at the same time in Memphis.

MAE: Oh, Mommy, Mommy, Mommy! Let's be fair! Why, Gooper has given himself body an' soul t'keepin' this place up fo' the past five years since Big Daddy's health started failin'. Gooper won't say it, Gooper never thought of it as a duty, he just did it. An' what did Brick do? Brick kep' livin' in his past glory at college!

(GOOPER *places a restraining hand on* MAE'S *leg;* MARGARET *drifts DS in gallery.*)

GOOPER: Still a football player at twenty-seven!

MARGARET (*bursts into UR door*): Who are you talkin' about now? Brick? A football player? He isn't a football player an' you know it! Brick is a sports announcer on TV an' one of the best-known ones in the country!

MAE (*breaks UC*): I'm talkin' about what he was!

MARGARET (*X to above lower gallery door*): Well, I wish you would stop talkin' about my husband!

GOOPER (*X to above* MARGARET): Listen, Margaret, I've got a right to discuss my own brother with other members of my own fam'ly, which don't include you! (*Pokes finger at her; she slaps his finger away.*) Now, why don't you go on out there an' drink with Brick?

MARGARET: I've never seen such malice toward a brother.

GOOPER: How about his for me? Why he can't stand to be in the same room with me!

BRICK (*on lower gallery*): That's the truth!

MARGARET: This is a deliberate campaign of vilification for the most disgusting and sordid reason on earth, and I know what it is! It's avarice, avarice, greed, greed!

BIG MAMA: Oh, I'll scream, I will scream in a moment unless this stops! Margaret, child, come here, sit next to Big Mama.

MARGARET (*X to* BIG MAMA, *sits above her*): Precious Mommy.
      (GOOPER *X to bar.*)

MAE: How beautiful, how touchin' this display of devotion! Do you know why she's childless? She's childless because that big, beautiful athlete husband of hers won't go to bed with her, that's why!
      (*X to L of bed, looks at* GOOPER.)

GOOPER: You jest won't let me do this the nice way, will yuh? Aw right — (*X to above wicker seat.*) I don't give a goddam if Big Daddy likes me or don't like me or did or never did or will or will never! I'm just appealin' to a sense of common decency an' fair play! I'm tellin' you th' truth — (*X DS through lower door to* BRICK *on DR gallery.*) I've resented Big Daddy's partiality to Brick ever since th' goddam day you were born, son, an' th' way I've been treated, like I was just barely good enough to spit on, an' sometimes not even good enough for that. (*X back through room to above wicker seat.*) Big Daddy is dyin' of cancer an' it's spread all through him an' it's attacked all his vital organs includin' the kidneys an' right now he is sinkin' into uremia, an' you all know what uremia is, it's poisonin' of the whole system due to th' failure of th' body to eliminate its poisons.

MARGARET: Poisons, poisons, venomous thoughts and words! In hearts and minds! That's poisons!

GOOPER: I'm askin' for a square deal an' by God I expect to get one. But if I don't get one, if there's any peculiar shenanigans goin' on around here behind my back, well I'm not a corporation lawyer for nothin'! (*X DS toward lower gallery door, on apex.*) I know how to protect my own interests.

(*Rumble of distant thunder.*)

BRICK (*entering the room through DS door*): Storm comin' up.

GOOPER: Oh, a late arrival!

MAE (*X through C to below bar, LCO*): Behold, the conquerin' hero comes!

GOOPER (*X through C to bar, following* BRICK, *imitating his limp*): The fabulous Brick Pollitt! Remember him? Who could forget him?

MAE: He looks like he's been injured in a game!

GOOPER: Yep, I'm afraid you'll have to warm th' bench at the Sugar Bowl this year, Brick! Or was it the Rose Bowl that he made his famous run in.

(*Another rumble of thunder, sound of wind rising.*)

MAE (*X to L of* BRICK, *who has reached the bar*): The punch bowl, honey, it was the punch bowl, the cut-glass punch bowl!

GOOPER: That's right! I'm always gettin' the boy's bowls mixed up!

(*Pats* BRICK *on the butt.*)

MARGARET (*rushes at* GOOPER, *striking him*): Stop that! You stop that!

(*Thunder.* MAE X *toward* MARGARET *from L of* GOOPER, *flails at* MARGARET; GOOPER *keeps the women apart.* LACEY *runs through the US lawn area in a raincoat.*)

DAISY and SOOKEY (*off UL*): Storm! Storm comin'! Storm! Storm!

LACEY (*running out UR*): Brightie, close them shutters!

GOOPER (*X onto R gallery, calls after* LACEY): Lacey, put the top up on my Cadillac, will yuh?

LACEY (*off R*): Yes, suh, Mistah Pollit!

GOOPER (*X to above* BIG MAMA): Big Mama, you know it's goin' to be necessary for me t'go back to Memphis in th' mornin' t'represent the Parker estate in a lawsuit.

(MAE *sits on L side bed, arranges papers she removes from briefcase.*)

BIG MAMA: Is it, Gooper?

MAE: Yaiss.

GOOPER: That's why I'm forced to — to bring up a problem that —

MAE: Somethin' that's too important t' be put off!

GOOPER: If Brick was sober, he ought to be in on this. I think he ought to be present when I present this plan.

MARGARET (*UC*): Brick is present, we're present!

GOOPER: Well, good. I will now give you this outline my partner, Tom Bullit, an' me have drawn up — a sort of dummy — trustee-ship!

MARGARET: Oh, that's it! You'll be in charge an' dole out remittances, will you?

GOOPER: This we did as soon as we got the report on Big Daddy from th' Ochsner Laboratories. We did this thing, I mean we drew up this dummy outline with the advice and assistance of the Chairman of the Boa'd of Directors of th' Southern Plantuhs Bank and Trust Company in Memphis, C. C. Bellowes, a man who handles estates for th' prominent fam'lies in West Tennessee and th' Delta!

BIG MAMA: Gooper?

GOOPER (*X behind seat to below* BIG MAMA): Now this is not — not final, or anything like it, this is just a preliminary outline. But it does provide a — basis — a design — a — possible, feasible — plan!

(*He waves papers* MAE *has thrust into his hand, US.*)

MARGARET (*X DL*): Yes, I'll bet it's a plan!

(*Thunder rolls. Interior lighting dims.*)

MAE: It's a plan to protect the biggest estate in the Delta from ir-responsibility an' —

BIG MAMA: Now you listen to me, all of you, you listen here! They's not goin' to be no more catty talk in my house! And Gooper, you put that away before I grab it out of your hand and tear it right up! I don't know what the hell's in it, and I don't want to know what the hell's in it. I'm talkin' in Big Daddy's language now, I'm his wife, not his widow, I'm still his wife! And I'm talkin' to you in his language an' —

GOOPER: Big Mama, what I have here is —

MAE: Gooper explained that it's just a plan . . .

BIG MAMA: I don't care what you got there, just put it back where it come from an' don't let me see it again, not even the outside of the envelope of it! Is that understood? Basis! Plan! Preliminary! De-sign! — I say — what is it that Big Daddy always says when he's disgusted?

(*Storm clouds race across sky.*)

BRICK (*from bar*): Big Daddy says "crap" when he is disgusted.

BIG MAMA (*rising*): That's right — Crapppp! I say crap too, like Big Daddy!

(*Thunder rolls.*)

MAE: Coarse language don't seem called for in this —

GOOPER: Somethin' in me is deeply outraged by this.

BIG MAMA: Nobody's goin' to do nothin'! till Big Daddy lets go of it, and maybe just possibly not — not even then! No, not even then!

(*Thunder clap. Glass crash, off L. Off UR, children commence crying. Many storm sounds, L and R: barnyard animals in terror, papers crackling, shutters rattling. SOOKEY and DAISY hurry from L to R in lawn area. Inexplicably, DAISY hits together two leather pillows. They cry, "Storm! Storm!" SOOKEY waves a piece of wrapping paper to cover lawn furniture. MAE exits to hall and upper gallery. Strange man runs across lawn, R to L. Thunder rolls repeatedly.*)

MAE: Sookey, hurry up an' git that po'ch fu'niture covahed; want th' paint to come off?

(*Starts DR on gallery. GOOPER runs through hall to R gallery.*)

GOOPER (*yells to LACY, who appears from R*): Lacey, put mah car away!

LACEY: Cain't, Mistah Pollit, you got the keys!

(*Exit US.*)

GOOPER: Naw, you got 'em, man. (*Exit DR. Reappears UR, calls to MAE:*) Where th' keys to th' car, honey?

(*Runs C.*)

MAE (*DR on gallery*): You got 'em in your pocket!

(*Exit DR. GOOPER exits UR. Dog howls. DAISY and SOOKEY sing off UR to comfort children. MAE is heard placating the children. Storm fades away. During the storm, MARGARET X and sits on couch, DR. BIG MAMA X DC.*)

BIG MAMA: BRICK! Come here, Brick, I need you.

(*Thunder distantly. Children whimper, off L MAE consoles them. BRICK X to R of BIG MAMA.*)

BIG MAMA: Tonight Brick looks like he used to look when he was a little boy just like he did when he played wild games in the orchard back of the house and used to come home when I hollered myself hoarse for him! all — sweaty — and pink-cheeked — an' sleepy with his curls shinin' — (*Thunder distantly. Children whimper, off L. MAE consoles them. Dog howls, off.*) Time goes by so fast. Nothin' can outrun it. Death commences too early — almost before you're half-acquainted with life — you meet with the other. Oh, you know we just got to love each other, an' stay together all of us just as close as we can, specially now that such a *black* thing has come and moved into this place without invitation. (*Dog howls, off.*) Oh, Brick, son of Big Daddy, Big Daddy does so love you. Y'know what would be his fondest dream come true? If before he passed on, if Big Daddy has to pass on . . . (*Dog howls, off.*) You give him a child of yours, a grandson as much like his son as his son is like Big Daddy. . . .

MARGARET: I know that's Big Daddy's dream.

BIG MAMA: That's his dream.

BIG DADDY (*off DR on gallery*): Looks like the wind was takin' liberties with this place.

(LACEY *appears UL, X to UC in lawn area;* BRIGHTIE *and* SMALL *appear UR on lawn.* BIG DADDY *X onto the UR gallery.*)

LACY: Evenin', Mr. Pollitt.

BRIGHTIE and SMALL: Evenin', Cap'n. Hello, Cap'n.

MARGARET (*X to R door*): Big Daddy's on the gall'ry.

BIG DADDY: Strawm cross th' river, Lacey?

LACEY: Gone to Arkansas, Cap'n.

(BIG MAMA *has turned toward the hall door at the sound of* BIG DADDY's *voice on the gallery. Now she X's DSR and out the DS door onto the gallery.*)

BIG MAMA: I can't stay here. He'll see somethin' in my eyes.

BIG DADDY (*on upper gallery, to the boys*): Stawm done any damage around here?

BRIGHTIE: Took the po'ch off ole Aunt Crawley's house.

BIG DADDY: Ole Aunt Crawley should of been settin' on it. It's time fo' th' wind to blow that ole girl away! (FIELD-HANDS *laugh, exit, UR.* BIG DADDY *enters room, UC, hall door.*) Can I come in?

(*Puts his cigar in ash tray on bar.* MAE *and* GOOPER *hurry along the upper gallery and stand behind* BIG DADDY *in hall door.*)

MARGARET: Did the storm wake you up, Big Daddy?

BIG DADDY: Which stawm are you talkin' about — th' one outside or th' hullaballoo in here?

(GOOPER *squeezes past* BIG DADDY.)

GOOPER (*X toward bed, where legal papers are strewn*): 'Scuse me, sir . . .

(MAE *tries to squeeze past* BIG DADDY *to join* GOOPER, *but* BIG DADDY *puts his arm firmly around her.*)

BIG DADDY: I heard some mighty loud talk. Sounded like somethin' important was bein' discussed. What was the powwow about?

MAE (*flustered*): Why — nothin', Big Daddy . . .

BIG DADDY (*X DLC, taking* MAE *with him*): What is that pregnant-lookin' envelope you're puttin' back in your briefcase, Gooper?

GOOPER (*at foot of bed, caught, as he stuffs papers into envelope*): That? Nothin', suh — nothin' much of anythin' at all . . .

BIG DADDY: Nothin'? It looks like a whole lot of nothing! (*Turns US to group:*) You all know th' story about th' young married couple —

GOOPER: Yes, sir!

BIG DADDY: Hello, Brick —

BRICK: Hello, Big Daddy.

> (*The group is arranged in a semi-circle above* BIG DADDY, MAR-
> GARET *at the extreme R, then* MAE *and* GOOPER, *then* BIG
> MAMA, *with* BRICK *at L.*)

BIG DADDY: Young married couple took Junior out to th' zoo one Sunday, inspected all of God's creatures in their cages, with satisfaction.

GOOPER: Satisfaction.

BIG DADDY (*X USC, face front*): This afternoon was a warm afternoon in spring an' that ole elephant had somethin' else on his mind which was bigger'n peanuts. You know this story, Brick?

> (GOOPER *nods.*)

BRICK: No, sir, I don't know it.

BIG DADDY: Y'see, in th' cage adjoinin' they was a young female elephant in heat!

BIG MAMA (*at* BIG DADDY's *shoulder*): Oh, Big Daddy!

BIG DADDY: What's the matter, preacher's gone, ain't he? All right. That female elephant in the next cage was permeatin' the atmosphere about her with a powerful and excitin' odor of female fertility! Huh! Ain't that a nice way to put it, Brick?

BRICK: Yes, sir, nothin' wrong with it.

BIG DADDY: Brick says the's nothin' wrong with it!

BIG MAMA: Oh, Big Daddy!

BIG DADDY (*X DSC*): So this ole bull elephant still had a couple of fornications left in him. He reared back his trunk an' got a whiff of that elephant lady next door! — began to paw at the dirt in his cage an' butt his head against the separatin' partition and, first thing y'know, there was a conspicuous change in his profile — very conspicuous! Ain't I tellin' this story in decent language, Brick?

BRICK: Yes, sir, too ruttin' decent!

BIG DADDY: So, the little boy pointed at it and said, "What's that?" His Mam said, "Oh, that's — nothin'!" — His Papa said, "She's spoiled!"

> (FIELD-HANDS *sing off R, featuring* SOOKEY: *"I Just Can't Stay Here by Myself," through following scene.* BIG DADDY X *to* BRICK *at L.*)

BIG DADDY: You didn't laugh at that story, Brick.

> (BIG MAMA X *DRC crying.* MAGRARET *goes to her.* MAE *and* GOOPER *hold URC.*)

BRICK: No, sir, I didn't laugh at that story.

> (*On the lower gallery,* BIG MAMA *sobs.* BIG DADDY *looks toward her.*)

BIG DADDY: What's wrong with that long, thin woman over there, loaded with diamonds? Hey, what's-your-name, what's the matter with you?

MARGARET (X *toward* BIG DADDY): She had a slight dizzy spell, Big Daddy.

BIG DADDY (*ULC*): You better watch that, BIG MAMA. A stroke is a bad way to go.

MARGARET (X *to* BIG DADDY *at C*): Oh, Brick, Big Daddy has on your birthday present to him, Brick, he has on your cashmere robe, the softest material I have ever felt.

BIG DADDY: Yeah, this is my soft birthday, Maggie. . . . Not my gold or my silver birthday, but my soft birthday, everything's got to be soft for Big Daddy on this soft birthday.

> (MAGGIE *kneels before* BIG DADDY *C. As* GOOPER *and* MAE *speak,* BIG MAMA X *USRC in front of them, hushing them with a gesture.*)

GOOPER: Maggie, I hate to make such a crude observation, but there is somethin' a little indecent about your —

MAE: Like a slow-motion football tackle —

MARGARET: Big Daddy's got on his Chinese slippers that I gave him, Brick. Big Daddy, I haven't given you my big present yet, but now I will, now's the time for me to present it to you! I have an announcement to make!

MAE: What? What kind of announcement?

GOOPER: A sports announcement, Maggie?

MARGARET: Announcement of life beginning! A child is coming, sired by Brick, and out of Maggie the Cat! I have Brick's child in my body, an' that's my birthday present to Big Daddy on this birthday!

(BIG DADDY *looks at* BRICK *who* X *behind* BIG DADDY *to DS portal, L.*)

BIG DADDY: Get up, girl, get up off your knees, girl. (BIG DADDY *helps* MARGARET *rise. He* X *above her, to her R, bites off the end of a fresh cigar, taken from his bathrobe pocket, as he studies* MARGARET.) Uh-huh, this girl has life in her body, that's no lie!

BIG MAMA: BIG DADDY'S DREAM COME TRUE!

BRICK: *JESUS!*

BIG DADDY (X R *below wicker seat*): Gooper, I want my lawyer in the mornin'.

BRICK: Where are you goin', Big Daddy?

BIG DADDY: Son, I'm goin' up on the roof to the belvedere on th' roof to look over my kingdom before I give up my kingdom — twenty-eight thousand acres of th' richest land this side of the Valley Nile!

(*Exit through R doors, and DR on gallery.*)

BIG MAMA (*following*): Sweetheart, sweetheart, sweetheart — can I come with you?

(*Exits DR.* MARGARET *is DSC in mirror area.*)

GOOPER (X *to bar*): Brick, could you possibly spare me one small shot of that liquor?

BRICK (*DLC*): Why, help yourself, Gooper boy.

GOOPER: I will.

MAE (X *forward*): Of course we know that this is a lie!

GOOPER (*drinks*): Be still, Mae!

MAE (X *to* GOOPER *at bar*): I won't be still! I know she's made this up!

GOOPER: God damn it, I said to shut up!

MAE: That woman isn't pregnant!

GOOPER: Who said she was?

MAE: She did.

GOOPER: The doctor didn't. Doc Baugh didn't.

MARGARET (X R *to above couch*): I haven't gone to Doc Baugh.

GOOPER (X *through to L of* MARGARET): Then who'd you go to, Maggie?

(*Offstage song finishes.*)

MARGARET: One of the best gynecologists in the South.

GOOPER: Uh-huh, I see — (*Foot on end of couch, trapping* MAR-GARET.) May we have his name please?

MARGARET: No, you may not, Mister — Prosecutin' Attorney!

MAE (*X to R of* MARGARET, *above*): He doesn't have any name, he doesn't exist!

MARGARET: He does so exist, and so does my baby, Brick's baby!

MAE: You can't conceive a child by a man that won't sleep with you unless you think you're — (*Forces* MARGARET *onto couch, turns away C.*) BRICK *starts C for* MAE.) He drinks all the time to be able to tolerate you! Sleeps on the sofa to keep out of contact with you!

GOOPER (*X above* MARGARET, *who lies face down on couch*): Don't try to kid us, Margaret —

MAE (*X to bed, L side, rumpling pillows*): How can you conceive a child by a man that won't sleep with you? How can you conceive? How can you? How can you!

GOOPER (*sharply*): *MAE!*

BRICK (*X below* MAE *to her R, takes hold of her*): Mae, Sister Woman, how d'you know that I don't sleep with Maggie?

MAE: We occupy the next room an' th' wall between isn't sound-proof.

BRICK: Oh . . .

MAE: We hear the nightly pleadin' and the nightly refusal. So don't imagine you're goin' t'put a trick over on us, to fool a dyin' man with — a —

BRICK: Mae, Sister Woman, not everybody makes much noise about love. Oh, I know some people are huffers an' puffers, but others are silent lovers.

GOOPER (*behind seat, R*): This talk is pointless, completely.

BRICK: How d'y'know that we're not silent lovers? Even if y'got a peep-hole drilled in the wall, how can y'tell if sometime when Gooper's got business in Memphis an' you're playin' scrabble at the country club with other ex-queens of cotton, Maggie and I don't come to some temporary agreement? How do you know that — ? (*He X above wicker seat to above R and couch.*)

MAE: Brick, I never thought that you would stoop to her level, I just never dreamed that you would stoop to her level.

GOOPER: I don't think Brick will stoop to her level.

BRICK (*sits R of* MARGARET *on couch*): What is your level? Tell me your level so I can sink or rise to it. (*Rises.*) You heard what Big Daddy said. This girl has life in her body.

MAE: That is a lie!

BRICK: No, truth is something desperate; an' she's got it. Believe me, it's somethin' desperate, an' she's got it. (*X below seat to below bar.*) An' now if you will stop actin' as if Brick Pollitt was dead an' buried, invisible, not heard, an go on back to your peep-hole in the wall — I'm drunk, and sleepy — not as alive as Maggie, but still alive. . . .

   (*Pours drink, drinks.*)

GOOPER (*picks up briefcase from R foot of bed*): Come on, Mae. We'll leave these love birds together in their nest.

MAE: Yeah, nest of lice! Liars!

GOOPER: Mae — Mae, you jes' go on back to our room —

MAE: Liars!

   (*Exits through hall.*)

GOOPER (*DR above* MARGARET): We're jest goin' to wait an' see. Time will tell. (*X to R of bar.*) Yes, sir, little brother, we're just goin' to wait an' see!

   (*Exit, hall. The clock strikes twelve.* MAGGIE *and* BRICK *exchange a look. He drinks deeply, puts his glass on the bar. Gradually, his expression changes. He utters a sharp exhalation. The exhalation is echoed by the singers, off* UR, *who commence vocalizing with* "Gimme a Cool Drink of Water Fo' I Die," *and continue till end of act.*)

MARGARET (*as she hears* BRICK's *exhalation*): The click? (BRICK *looks toward the singers, happily, almost gratefully. He* XR *to bed, picks up his pillow, and starts toward head of couch,* DR, *Xing above wicker seat.* MARGARET *seizes the pillow from his grasp, rises, stands facing* C, *holding the pillow close.* BRICK *watches her with growing admiration. She moves quickly* USC, *throwing pillow onto bed. She X to bar.* BRICK *counters below wicker seat, watching her.* MARGARET *grabs all the bottles from the bar. She goes into hall, pitches the bottles, one after the other, off the platform into the* UL *lawn area. Bottles break, off* L. MARGARET *re-enters the room, stands* UC, *facing* BRICK.) Echo Spring has gone dry, and no one but me could drive you to town for more.

BRICK: Lacey will get me —

MARGARET: Lacey's been told not to!

BRICK: I could drive —

MARGARET: And you lost your driver's license! I'd phone ahead and have you stopped on the highway before you got halfway to Ruby Lightfoot's gin mill. I told a lie to Big Daddy, but we can make that lie come true. And then I'll bring you liquor, and we'll get

drunk together, here, tonight, in this place that death has come into!
What do you say? What do you say, Baby?

BRICK (*X to L side bed*): I admire you, Maggie.

(BRICK *sits on edge of bed. He looks up at the overhead light,
then at* MARGARET. *She reaches for the light, turns it out; then
she kneels quickly beside* BRICK *at foot of bed.*)

MARGARET: Oh, you weak, beautiful people who give up with such
grace. What you need is someone to take hold of you — gently,
with love, and hand your life back to you, like something gold
you let go of — and I can! I'm determined to do it — and nothing's
more determined than a cat on a tin roof — is there? Is there, Baby?

(*She touches his cheek, gently.*)

Curtain

poetry

an old man replaced

Russell Edson

An old woman put a stone on her husband's chair at dinner. When the old man came in he said, a stone is on my chair.

The old woman said, the stone and I are having dinner.

No no, said the old man, the stone may have some tea in the kitchen with the maid, but the old man must sit on his chair; even if he only pretends to eat, still he must sit there; he might slip his plate under the table to the stone, but still he must sit in his chair.

No no, said the old woman, the stone has been invited to be the new old man; but it still wishes to be a stone, too, so you can't even be a stone. Perhaps if you laid on the floor you could be a rug, or, if you went outside you could be someone passing the house.

Russell Edson, *The Very Thing That Happens.* Copyright © 1960, 1964 by Russell Edson. Reprinted by permission of the publisher, New Directions Publishing Corporation.

No no, said the old man, a stone is to be defeated if I am again to be an old man, and sit in the old man's chair.

No no, said the old woman, you will give the stone indigestion, and I hate dyspepsia in a stone.

The old man said, why is it that you love a stone and not the old man?

The old woman said, it is not so much that I love a stone, as that I don't love you.

The old man said, ah, that puts a new light on it, and I begin to understand the symbolism: the stone has not replaced me, it's simply that I haven't replaced myself over the years.

The old woman said, I don't know what you mean, but if you're looking for a handout, go to the kitchen and ask the maid; but do please leave the stone and me in peace.

So the old man went out into the garden.

Perhaps in time she will forget me, and begin to see me as a stone, he said, and take me back into the dining room. I know many hours must pass. . . Rains and seasons. . .

man and wife

Robert Lowell

Tamed by *Miltown,* we lie on Mother's bed;
the rising sun in war paint dyes us red;
in broad daylight her gilded bed-posts shine,
abandoned, almost Dionysian.
At last the trees are green on Marlborough Street,
blossoms on our magnolia ignite
the morning with their murderous five days' white.
All night I've held your hand,
as if you had
a fourth time faced the kingdom of the mad —
its hackneyed speech, its homicidal eye —
and dragged me home alive. . . . Oh my *Petite,*
clearest of all God's creatures, still all air and nerve:
you were in your twenties, and I,
once hand on glass
and heart in mouth,
outdrank the Rahvs in the heat
of Greenwich Village, fainting at your feet —
too boiled and shy
and poker-faced to make a pass,
while the shrill verve
of your invective scorched the traditional South.
Now, twelve years later, you turn your back.
Sleepless, your hold
your pillow to your hollows like a child;
your old-fashioned tirade —
loving, rapid, merciless —
breaks like the Atlantic Ocean on my head.

360 STOP *here*

the advantages of learning

Kenneth Rexroth

dramatic monologue

Lonely, beatnik-type intellectual.

I am a man with no ambitions
And few friends, wholly incapable
of making a living, growing no
Younger, fugitive from some just doom.
Lonely, ill clothed, what does it matter?
At midnight I make myself a jug
Of hot white wine and cardamon seeds.
In a torn grey robe and old beret,
I sit in the cold writing poems.
Drawing nudes on the crooked margins,
Copulating with sixteen year old
Nymphomaniacs of my imagination.

From Kenneth Rexroth. *Natural Numbers.* Copyright 1940 by Kenneth Rexroth. Reprinted by permission of New Directions Publishing Corporation.

Child gaining independence from his parents. will hurt just as ~~some~~ the jumped on his father's head.

step on his head

James Laughlin

"Let's step on daddy's head" shout
the children, my dear children, as
we walk in the country on a sunny

summer day my shadow bobs dark on
the road, as we walk and they jump
on its head and my love of them

fills me all full of soft feelings
Now I duck with my head so they'll
miss when they jump & they screech

From James Laughlin, *The Wild Anemone and Other Poems.* All rights reserved. Reprinted by permission of New Directions Publishing Corp.

with delight and I moan "Oh you're
hurting you're hurting me, Stop!" and
they jump all the harder and love

fills the whole road. But I see it run
on through the years and I know
how some day they must jump when

it won't be this shadow but really
my head (as I stepped on my own
father's head) it will hurt really

hurt, and I wonder if then I will
have love enough. Will I have love
enough when it's not just a game?

man without sense of direction

John Crowe Ransom

Tell this to ladies: how a hero man
Assail a thick and scandalous giant
Who casts true shadow in the sun,
And die, but play no truant.

large force to overcome
doesn't ignore his duty.

This is more horrible: that the darling egg
Of the chosen people hatch a creature
Of noblest mind and powerful leg
Who cannot fathom nor perform his nature.

The larks' tongues are never stilled
Where the pale spread straw of sunlight lies
Then what invidious gods have willed
Him to be seized so otherwise?

Birds of the field and beasts of the stable
Are swollen with rapture and make uncouth
Demonstration of joy, which is a babble
Offending the ear of the fervorless youth.

Love — is it the cause? the proud shamed spirit?
Love has slain some whom it possessed,
But his was requited beyond his merit
And won him in bridal the loveliest.

Yet scarcely he issues from the warm chamber,
Flushed with her passion, when cold as dead
Once more he walks where waves past number
Of sorrow buffet his curse-hung head.

Whether by street, or in field full of honey,
Attended by clouds of the creatures of air
Or shouldering the city's companioning many,
His doom is on him; and how can he care

For the shapes that would fiddle upon his senses,
Wings and faces and mists that move,
Words, sunlight, the blue air which rinses
The pure pale head which he must love?

And he writhes like an antique man of bronze
That is beaten by furies visible,
Yet he is punished not knowing his sins
And for his innocence walks in hell.

He flails his arms, he moves his lips:
"Rage have I none, cause, time, nor country —
Yet I have traveled land and ships
And knelt my seasons in the chantry."

So he stands muttering; and rushes
Back to the tender thing in his charge
With clamoring tongue and taste of ashes
And a small passion to feign large.

But let his cold lips be her omen,
She shall not kiss that harried one
To peace, as men are served by women
Who comfort them in darkness and in sun.

grandfather in the old men's home

W. S. Merwin

Gentle at last, and as clean as ever,
He did not even need drink any more,
And his good sons unbent and brought him
Tobacco to chew, both times when they came
To be satisfied he was well cared for.
And he smiled all the time to remember
Grandmother, his wife, wearing the true faith
Like an iron nightgown, yet brought to birth
Seven times and raising the family
Through her needle's eye while he got away
Down the green river, finding directions
For boats. And himself coming home sometimes
Well-heeled but blind drunk, to hide all the bread
And shoot holes in the bucket while he made
His daughters pump. Still smiled as kindly in
His sleep beside the other clean old men
To see Grandmother, every night the same,
Huge in her age, with her thumbed-down mouth, come
Hating the river, filling with her stare
His gliding dream, while he turned to water,
While the children they both had begotten,
With old faces now, but themselves shrunken
To child-size again, stood ranged at her side,
Beating their little Bibles till he died.

in the smoking car

Richard Wilbur

The eyelids meet. He'll catch a little nap.
The grizzled, crew-cut head drops to his chest.
It shakes above the briefcase on his lap.
Close voices breathe, 'Poor sweet, he did his best.'

'Poor sweet, poor sweet,' the bird-hushed glades repeat,
Through which in quiet pomp his litter goes,
Carried by native girls with naked feet.
A sighing stream concurs in his repose.

Could he but think, he might recall to mind
The righteous mutiny or sudden gale
That beached him here; the dear ones left behind . . .
So near the ending, he forgets the tale.

Were he to lift his eyelids now, he might
Behold his maiden porters, brown and bare.
But even here he has no appetite.
It is enough to know that they are there.

Enough that now a honeyed music swells,
The gentle, mossed declivities begin,
And the whole air is full of flower-smells.
Failure, the longed-for valley, takes him in.

richard cory

Edwin Arlington Robinson

[handwritten: iambic pentameter]

Whenever Richard Cory went down town,   A
We people on the pavement looked at him: B
He was a gentleman from sole to crown,   A
Clean favored, and imperially slim.   B   *[handwritten: quatrain]*

And he was always quietly arrayed,
And he was always human when he talked;
But still he fluttered pulses when he said,
"Good-morning," and he glittered when he walked.

And he was rich — yes, richer than a king —
And admirably schooled in every grace:
In fine, we thought that he was everything
To make us wish that we were in his place.

So on we worked, and waited for the light,
And went without the meat, and cursed the bread;
And Richard Cory, one calm summer night,
Went home and put a bullet through his head.

counting the mad

Donald Justice

This one was put in a jacket,
This one was sent home,
This one was given bread and meat

But would eat none,
And this one cried No No No No
All day long.

This one looked at the window
As though it were a wall,
This one saw things that were not there,
This one things that were,
And this one cried No No No No
All day long.

This one thought himself a bird,
This one a dog,
⌈And this one thought himself a man,⌉
|An ordinary man,|
|And cried and cried No No No No|
⌊All day long.⌋

nobody loses all the time

E. E. Cummings

nobody loses all the time

i had an uncle named
Sol who was a born failure and
nearly everybody said he should have gone
into vaudeville perhaps because my Uncle Sol could
sing McCann He Was a Diver on Xmas Eve like Hell Itself which
may or may not account for the fact that my Uncle

Sol indulged in that possibility most inexcusable
of all to use a highfalootin phrase
luxuries that is or to
wit farming and be
it needlessly
added

my Uncle Sol's farm
failed because the chickens
ate the vegetables so
my Uncle Sol had a
chicken farm till the
skunks ate the chickens when

my Uncle Sol
had a skunk farm but
the skunks caught cold and
died and so
my Uncle Sol imitated the
skunks in a subtle manner

or by drowning himself in the watertank
but somebody who'd given my Uncle Sol a Victor
Victrola and records while he lived presented to
him upon the auspicious occasion of his decease a
scrumptious not to mention splendiferous funeral with
tall boys in black gloves and flowers and everything and

i remember we all cried like the Missouri
when my Uncle Sol's coffin lurched because
somebody pressed a button
(and down went
my Uncle
Sol

and started a worm farm)

Muzak — a mechanization or corruption of music.

nonfiction

las vegas (what?) las vagas (can't hear you! too noisy) las vagas!!!!

Tom Wolfe

Hernia, hernia, hernia, hernia, hernia, hernia, hernia, hernia, hernia, hernia, hernia, hernia, hernia, HERNia; hernia, HERNia, hernia, hernia, hernia, hernia, HERNia, HERNia, HERNia, hernia, hernia, hernia, hernia, hernia, hernia, hernia, eight is the point, the point is eight; hernia hernia, HERNia; hernia hernia, hernia, hernia, all right, hernia, hernia, hernia, hernia, hard eight, hernia, hernia, hernia, HERNia, hernia, hernia, hernia, HERNia, hernia, hernia, hernia, HERNia, hernia, hernia, hernia, hernia

"What is all this *hernia hernia* stuff?"

This was Raymond talking to the wavy-haired fellow with the stick, the dealer, at the craps table about 3:45 Sunday morning. The

Reprinted from *The Kandy Kolored Tangerine Flake Streamline Baby* by Tom Wolfe, by permission of Farrar, Straus & Giroux, Inc. Copyright © 1963 by Thomas K. Wolfe, Jr.

First published in Esquire Magazine.

stickman had no idea what this big wiseacre was talking about, but he resented the tone. He gave Raymond that patient arch of the eyebrows known as a Red Hook brushoff, which is supposed to convey some such thought as, I am a very tough but cool guy, as you can tell by the way I carry my eyeballs low in the pouches, and if this wasn't such a high-class joint we would take wiseacres like you out back and beat you into jellied madrilene.

At this point, however, Raymond was immune to subtle looks.

The stickman tried to get the game going again, but every time he would start up his singsong, by easing the words out through the nose, which seems to be the style among craps dealers in Las Vagas — "All right, a new shooter . . . eight is the point, the point is eight" and so on — Raymond would start droning along with him in exactly the same tone of voice, "Hernia, hernia, hernia; hernia, HERNia, HERNia, hernia; hernia, hernia, hernia."

Everybody at the craps table was staring in consternation to think that anybody would try to needle a tough, hip, elite *soldat* like a Las Vegas craps dealer. The gold-lamé odalisques of Los Angeles were staring. The Western sports, fifty-eight-year-old men who wear Texas string ties, were staring. The old babes at the slot machines, holding Dixie Cups full of nickles, were staring at the craps tables, but cranking away the whole time.

Raymond, who is thirty-four years old and works as an engineer in Phoenix, is big but not terrifying. He has the sort of thatchwork hair that grows so low all along the forehead there is no logical place to part it, but he tries anyway. He has a huge, prognathous jaw, but it is as smooth, soft and round as a melon, so that Raymond's total effect is that of an Episcopal divinity student.

The guards were wonderful. They were dressed in cowboy uniforms like Bruce Cabot in *Sundown* and they wore sheriff's stars.

"Mister, is there something we can do for you?"

"The expression is 'Sir,'" said Raymond. "You said 'Mister.' The expression is 'Sir.' How's your old Cosa Nostra?"

Amazingly, the casino guards were easing Raymond out peaceably, without putting a hand on him. I had never seen the fellow before, but possibly because I had been following his progress for the last five minutes, he turned to me and said, "Hey, do you have a car? This wild stuff is starting again."

The gist of it was that he had left his car somewhere and he wanted to ride up the Strip to the Stardust, one of the big hotel-casinos. I am describing this big goof Raymond not because he is a typical Las

Vegas tourist, although he has some typical symptoms, but because he is a good example of the marvelous impact Las Vegas has on the senses. Raymond's senses were at a high pitch of excitation, the only trouble being that he was going off his nut. He had been up since Thursday afternoon, and it was now about 3:45 A.M. Sunday. He had an envelope full of pep pills — amphetamine — in his left coat pocket and an envelope full of Equanils — meprobamate — in his right pocket, or were the Equanils in the left and the pep pills in the right? He could tell by looking, but he wasn't going to look anymore. He didn't care to see how many were left.

He had been rolling up and down the incredible electric-sign gauntlet of Las Vegas' Strip, U.S. Route 91, where the neon and the par lamps — bubbling, spiraling, rocketing, and exploding in sunbursts ten stories high out in the middle of the desert — celebrate one-story casinos. He had been gambling and drinking and eating now and again at the buffet tables the casinos keep heaped with food day and night, but mostly hopping himself up with good old amphetamine, cooling himself down with meprobamate, then hooking down more alcohol, until now, after sixty hours, he was slipping into the symptoms of toxic schizophrenia.

He was also enjoying what the prophets of hallucinogen call "consciousness expansion." The man was psychedelic. He was beginning to isolate the components of Las Vegas' unique bombardment of the senses. He was quite right about this *hernia hernia* stuff. Every casino in Las Vegas is, among the other things, a room full of craps tables with dealers who keep up a running singsong that sounds as though they are saying "hernia, hernia, hernia, hernia, hernia" and so on. There they are day and night, easing a running commentary through their nostrils. What they have to say contains next to no useful instruction. Its underlying message is, We are the initiates, riding the crest of chance. That the accumulated sound comes out "hernia" is merely an unfortunate phonetic coincidence. Actually, it is part of something rare and rather grand: a combination of baroque stimuli that brings to mind the bronze gongs, no larger than a blue plate, that Louis XIV, his ruff collars larded with the lint of the foul Old City of Byzantium, personally hunted out in the bazaars of Asia Minor to provide exotic acoustics for his new palace outside Paris.

The sounds of the craps dealer will be in, let's say, the middle register. In the lower register will be the sound of the old babes at the slot machines. Men play the slots too, of course, but one of the indelible images of Las Vegas is that of the old babes at the row upon

row of slot machines. There they are at six o'clock Sunday morning
no less than at three o'clock Tuesday afternoon. Some of them pack
their old hummocky shanks into Capri pants, but many of them just
put on the old print dress, the same one day after day, and the old
hob-heeled shoes, looking like they might be going out to buy eggs
in Tupelo, Mississippi. They have a Dixie Cup full of nickles or dimes
in the left hand and an Iron Boy work glove on the right hand to keep
the callouses from getting sore. Every time they pull the handle, the
machines makes a sound much like the sound a cash register makes
before the bell rings, then the slot pictures start clattering up from left
to right, the oranges, lemons, plums, cherries, bells, bars, buckaroos —
the figure of a cowboy riding a bucking bronco. The whole sound
keeps churning up over and over again in eccentric series all over the
place, like one of those random-sound radio symphonies by John
Cage. You can hear it at any hour of the day or night all over Las
Vegas. You can walk down Fremont Street at dawn and hear it without even walking in a door, that and the spins of the wheels of fortune,
a boring and not very popular sort of simplified roulette, as the tabs
flap to a stop. As an overtone, or at times simply as a loud sound,
comes the babble of the casino crowds, with an occasional shriek from
the craps tables, or, anywhere from 4 P.M. to 6 A.M., the sound of brass
instruments or electrified string instruments from the cocktail-lounge
shows.

The crowd and band sounds are not very extraordinary, of course.
But Las Vegas' Muzak is. Muzak pervades Las Vegas from the time
you walk into the airport upon landing to the last time you leave
the casinos. It is piped out to the swimming pool. It is in the drug-
stores. It is as if there were a communal fear that someone, somewhere in Las Vegas, was going to be left with a totally vacant minute
on his hands.

Las Vegas has succeeded in wiring an entire city with this electronic
stimulation, day and night, out in the middle of the desert. In the
automobile I rented, the radio could not be turned off, no matter which
dial you went after. I drove for days in a happy burble of Action
Checkpoint News, "Monkey No. 9," "Donna, Donna, the Prima
Donna," and picking-and-singing jingles for the Frontier Bank and
the Fremont Hotel.

One can see the magnitude of the achievement. Las Vegas takes
what in other American towns is but a quixotic inflamation of the
senses for some poor salary mule in the brief interval between the

flagstone rambler and the automatic elevator downtown and magnifies it, foliates it, embellishes it into an institution.

For example, Las Vegas is the only town in the world whose sky-line is made up neither of buildings, like New York, nor of trees, like Wilbraham, Massachusetts, but signs. One can look at Las Vegas from a mile away on Route 91 and see no buildings, no trees, only signs. But such signs! They tower. They revolve, they oscillate, they soar in shapes before which the existing vocabulary of art history is helpless. I can only attempt to supply names — Boomerang Modern, Palette Curvilinear, Flash Gordon Ming-Alert Spiral, McDonald's Ham-burger Parabola, Mint Casino Elliptical, Miami Beach Kidney. Las Vegas' sign makers work so far out beyond the frontiers of conven-tional studio art that they have no names themselves for the forms they create. Vaughan Cannon, one of those tall, blond Westerners, the builders of places like Las Vegas and Los Angeles, whose eyes seem to have been bleached by the sun, is in the back shop of the Young Electric Sign Company out on East Charleston Boulevard with Herman Boernge, one of his designers, looking at the model they have pre-pared for the Lucky Strike Casino sign, and Cannon points to where the sign's two great curving faces meet to form a narrow vertical face and says:

"Well, here we are again — what do we call that?"

"I don't know," says Boernge. "It's sort of a nose effect. Call it a nose."

Okay, a nose, but it rises sixteen stories high about a two-story building. In Las Vegas no farseeing entrepreneur buys a sign to fit a building he owns. He rebuilds the building to support the biggest sign he can get up the money for and, if necessary, changes the name. The Lucky Strike Casino today is the Lucky Casino, which fits better when recorded in sixteen stories of flaming peach and incandescent yellow in the middle of the Mojave Desert. In the Young Electric Sign Co. era signs have become the architecture of Las Vegas, and the most whimsical, Yale-seminar-frenzied devices of the two late geniuses of Baroque Modern, Frank Lloyd Wright and Eero Saarinen, seem rather stuffy business, like a jest at a faculty meeting, compared to it. Men like Boernge, Kermit Wayne, Ben Mitchem and Jack Larsen, formerly an artist for Walt Disney, are the designer-sculptor geniuses of Las Vegas, but their motifs have been carried faithfully throughout the town by lesser men, for gasoline stations, motels, funeral parlors, churches, public buildings, flophouses and sauna baths.

Then there is a stimulus that is both visual and sexual — the Las

Vegas buttocks décolletage. This is a form of sexually provocative dress seen more and more in the United States, but avoided like Broadway message-embroidered ("Kiss Me, I'm Cold") underwear in the fashion pages, so that the euphemisms have not been established and I have no choice but clinical terms. To achieve buttocks décolletage a woman wears bikini-style shorts that cut across the round fatty masses of the buttocks rather than cupping them from below, so that the outer-lower edges of these fatty masses, or "cheeks," are exposed. I am in the cocktail lounge of the Hacienda Hotel, talking to managing director Dick Taylor about the great success his place has had in attracting family and tour groups, and all around me the waitresses are bobbing on their high heels, bare legs and décolletage-bare backsides, set off by pelvis-length lingerie of an uncertain denomination. I stare, but I am new here. At the White Cross Rexall drugstore on the Strip a pregnant brunette walks in off the street wearing black shorts with buttocks décolletage aft and illusion-of-cloth nylon lingerie hanging fore, and not even the old mom's-pie pensioners up near the door are staring. They just crank away at the slot machines. On the streets of Las Vegas, not only the show girls, of which the town has about two hundred fifty, bona fide, in residence, but girls of every sort, including, especially, Las Vegas' little high-school buds, who adorn what locals seeking roots in the sand call "our city of churches and schools," have taken up the chic of wearing buttocks décolletage step-ins under flesh-tight slacks, with the outline of the undergarment showing through fashionably. Others go them one better. They achieve the effect of having been dipped once, briefly, in Helenca stretch nylon. More and more they look like those wonderful old girls out of Flash Gordon who were wrapped just once over in Baghdad pantaloons of clear polyethylene with only Flash Gordon between them and the insane red-eyed assaults of the minions of Ming. It is as if all the hip young suburban gals of America named Lana, Deborah and Sandra, who gather wherever the arc lights shine and the studs steady their coiffures in the plate-glass reflection, have convened in Las Vegas with their bouffant hair above and anatomically stretch-pant-swathed little bottoms below, here on the new American frontier. But exactly!

None of it would have been possible, however, without one of those historic combinations of nature and art that creates an epoch. In this case, the Mojave Desert plus the father of Las Vagas, the late Benjamin "Bugsy" Siegel.

Bugsy was an inspired man. Back in 1944 the city fathers of Las Vegas, their Protestant rectitude alloyed only by the giddy prospect of gambling revenues, were considering the sort of ordinance that would have preserved the town with a kind of Colonial Williamsburg dinkiness in the motif of the Wild West. All new buildings would have to have at least the façade of the sort of place where piano players used to wear garters on their sleeves in Virginia City around 1880. In Las Vegas in 1944, it should be noted, there was nothing more stimulating in the entire town than a Fremont Street bar where the composer of "Deep in the Heart of Texas" held forth and the regulars downed fifteen-cent beer.

Bugsy pulled into Las Vegas in 1945 with several million dollars that, after his assassination, was traced back in the general direction of gangster-financiers. Siegel put up a hotel-casino such as Las Vegas had never seen and called it the Flamingo — all Miami Modern, and the hell with piano players with garters and whatever that was all about. Everybody drove out Route 91 just to gape. Such shapes! Boomerang Modern supports, Palette Curvilinear bars, Hot Shoppe Cantilever roofs and a scalloped swimming pool. Such colors! All the new electrochemical pastels of the Florida littoral: tangerine, broiling magenta, livid pink, incarnadine, fuchsia demure, Congo ruby, methyl green, viridine, aquamarine, phenosafranine, incandescent orange, scarlet-fever purple, cyanic blue, tessellated bronze, hospital-fruit-basket orange. And such signs! Two cylinders rose at either end of the Flamingo — eight stories high and covered from top to bottom with neon rings in the shape of bubbles that fizzed all eight stories up into the desert sky all night long like an illuminated whisky-soda tumbler filled to the brim with pink champagne.

The business history of the Flamingo, on the other hand, was not such a smashing success. For one thing, the gambling operation was losing money at a rate that rather gloriously refuted all the recorded odds of the gaming science. Siegel's backers apparently suspected that he was playing both ends against the middle in collusion with professional gamblers who hung out at the Flamingo as though they had liens on it. What with one thing and another, someone decided by the night of June 20, 1947, that Benny Siegel, lord of the Flamingo, had had it. He was shot to death in Los Angeles.

Yet Siegel's aesthetic, psychological and cultural insights, like Cézanne's, Freud's and Max Weber's, could not die. The Siegel vision and the Siegel aesthetic were already sweeping Las Vegas like gold fever. And there were builders of the West equal to the opportunity.

All over Las Vegas the incredible electric pastels were repeated. Overnight the Baroque Modern forms made Las Vegas one of the few architecturally unified cities of the world — the style was late American Rich — and without the bother and bad humor of a City Council ordinance. No enterprise was too small, too pedestrian or too solemn for The Look. The Supersonic Carwash, the Mercury Jetaway, Gas Vegas Village and Terrible Herbst gasoline stations, the Par-a-Dice Motel, the Palm Mortuary, the Orbit Inn, the Desert Moon, the Blue Onion Drive-in — on it went, like Wildwood, New Jersey, entering Heaven.

The atmosphere of the six-mile-long Strip of hotel-casinos grips even those segments of the population who rarely go near it. Barely twenty-five-hundred feet off the Strip, over by the Convention Center, stands Landmark Towers, a shaft thirty stories high, full of apartments, supporting a huge circular structure shaped like a space observation platform, which was to have contained the restaurant and casino. Somewhere along the way Landmark Towers went bankrupt, probably at that point in the last of the many crises when the construction workers *still* insisted on spending half the day flat on their bellies with their heads, tongues and eyeballs hanging over the edge of the tower, looking down into the swimming pool of the Playboy Apartments below, which has a "nudes only" section for show girls whose work calls for a tan all over.

Elsewhere, Las Vegas' beautiful little high-school buds in their buttocks-décolletage stretch pants are back on the foam-rubber upholstery of luxury broughams peeling off the entire chick ensemble long enough to establish the highest venereal-disease rate among high-school students anywhere north of the yaws-rotting shanty jungles of the Eighth Parallel. The Negroes who have done much of the construction work in Las Vegas' sixteen-year boom are off in their ghetto on the west side of town, and some of them are smoking marijuana, eating peyote buttons and taking horse (heroin), which they get from Tijuana, I mean it's simple, baby, right through the mails, and old Raymond, the Phoenix engineer, does not have the high life to himself.

I am on the third floor of the Clark County Courthouse talking to Sheriff Captain Ray Gubser, another of these strong, pale-eyed Western-builder types, who is obligingly explaining to me law enforcement on the Strip, where the problem is not so much the drunks, crooks or roughhousers, but these nuts on pills who don't want to ever go to

bed, and they have hallucinations and try to bring down the casinos
like Samson. The county has two padded cells for them. They cool
down after three or four days and they turn out to be somebody's
earnest breadwinner back in Denver or Minneapolis, loaded with the
right credentials and pouring soul and apologiae all over the county
cops before finally pulling out of never-never land for good by plane.
Captain Gubser is telling me about life and eccentric times in Las
Vegas, but I am distracted. The captain's office has windows out on
the corridor. Coming down the corridor is a covey of girls, skipping
and screaming, giggling along, their heads exploding in platinum-
and-neon-yellow bouffants or beehives or raspberry-silk scarves, their
eyes appliquéd in black like mail-order decals, their breasts aimed up
under their jerseys at the angle of anti-aircraft automatic weapons,
and, as they swing around the corner toward the elevator, their glutei
maximi are bobbing up and down with their pumps in the inevitable
buttocks décolletage pressed out against black, beige and incarnadine
stretch pants. This is part of the latest shipment of show girls to Las
Vegas, seventy in all, for the "Lido de Paris" revue at the Stardust, to
be entitled *Bravo!,* replacing the old show, entitled *Voilà.* The girls
are in the county courthouse getting their working papers, and fifteen
days from now these little glutei maximi and ack-ack breasts with
stars pasted on the tips will be swinging out over the slack jaws and
cocked-up noses of patrons sitting at stageside at the Stardust. I am
still listening to Gubser, but somehow it is a courthouse where mere
words are beaten back like old atonal Arturo Toscanini trying to sing
along with the NBC Symphony. There he would be, flapping his
little toy arms like Tony Galento shadowboxing with fate, bawling
away in the face of union musicians who drowned him without a
bubble. I sat in on three trials in the courthouse, and it was wonderful,
because the courtrooms are all blond-wood modern and look like
sets for TV panel discussions on marriage and the teenager. What the
judge has to say is no less formal and no more fatuous than what
judges say everywhere, but inside of forty seconds it is all meaningless because the atmosphere is precisely like a news broadcast over
Las Vegas' finest radio station, KORK. The newscast, as it is called,
begins with a series of electronic wheeps out on that far edge of sound
where only quadrupeds can hear. A voice then announces that this is
Action Checkpoint News. "The news — all the news — flows first
through Action Checkpoint! — then reaches You! at the speed of
Sound!" More electronic wheeps, beeps and lulus, and then an item:
"Cuban Premier Fidel Castro nearly drowned yesterday." Urp!

Wheep! Lulu! No news a KORK announcer has ever brought to
Las Vegas at the speed of sound, or could possibly bring, short of
word of the annihilation of Los Angeles, could conceivably compete
within the brain with the giddiness of this electronic jollification.

The wheeps, beeps, freeps, electronic lulus, Boomerang Modern
and Flash Gordon sunbursts soar on through the night over the
billowing hernia-hernia sounds and the old babes at the slots — until
it is 7:30 A.M. and I am watching five men at a green-topped card
table playing poker. They are sliding their Bee-brand cards into their
hands and squinting at the pips with a set to the lips like Conrad
Veidt in a tunic collar studying a code message from S.S. headquarters.
Big Sid Wyman, the old Big-Time gambler from St. Louis, is there,
with his eyes looking like two poached eggs engraved with a road map
of West Virginia after all night at the poker table. Sixty-year-old
Chicago Tommy Hargan is there with his topknot of white hair pulled
back over his little pink skull and a mountain of chips in front of his
old caved-in sternum. Sixty-two-year-old Dallas Maxie Welch is there,
fat and phlegmatic as an Indian Ocean potentate. Two Los Angeles
biggies are there exhaling smoke from candela-green cigars into the
gloom. It looks like the perfect vignette of every Big Time back
room, "athletic club," snooker house and floating poker game in the
history of the guys-and-dolls lumpen-bourgeoisie. But what is all this?
Off to the side, at a rostrum, sits a flawless little creature with bouffant
hair and Stridex-pure skin who looks like she is polished each morning
with a rotary buffer. Before her on the rostrum is a globe of coffee
on a hot coil. Her sole job is to keep the poker players warmed up
with coffee. Meanwhile, numberless uniformed lackeys are cocked
and aimed about the edges to bring the five Big Timers whatever else
they might desire, cigarettes, drinks, napkins, eyeglass-cleaning tissues, plug-in telephones. All around the poker table, at a respectful
distance of ten feet, is a fence with the most delicate golden pickets.
Upon it, even at this narcoleptic hour, lean men and women in their
best clothes watching the combat of the titans. The scene is the
charmed circle of the casino of the Dunes Hotel. As everyone there
knows, or believes, these fabulous men are playing for table stakes
of fifteen or twenty thousand dollars. One hundred dollars rides on a
chip. Mandibles gape at the progress of the battle. And now Sid
Wyman, who is also a vice-president of the Dunes, is at a small
escritoire just inside the golden fence signing a stack of vouchers for
such sums as $4500, all printed in the heavy Mondrianesque digits of a
Burroughs business check-making machine. It is as if America's guys-

and-dolls gamblers have somehow been tapped upon the shoulder, knighted, initiated into a new aristocracy.

Las Vegas has become, just as Bugsy Siegel dreamed, the American Monte Carlo — without any of the inevitable upper-class baggage of the Riviera casinos. At Monte Carlo there is still the plush mustiness of the 19th century noble lions — of Baron Bleichroden, a big winner at roulette who always said, "My dear friends, it is so easy on Black." Of Lord Jersey, who won seventeen maximum bets in a row — on black, as a matter of fact — nodded to the croupier, and said, "Much obliged, old sport, old sport," took his winnings to England, retired to the country and never gambled again in his life. Or of the old Duc de Dinc who said he could win only in the high-toned Club Privé, and who won very heavily one night, saw two Englishmen gaping at his good fortune, threw them every mille-franc note he had in his hands and said, "Here. Englishmen without money are altogether odious." Thousands of Europeans from the lower orders now have the money to go to the Riviera, but they remain under the century-old status pall of the aristocracy. At Monte Carlo there are still Wrong Forks, Deficient Accents, Poor Tailoring, Gauche Displays, Nouveau Richness, Cultural Aridity — concepts unknown in Las Vegas. For the grand debut of Monte Carlo as a resort in 1879 the architect Charles Garnier designed an opera house for the Place du Casino, and Sarah Bernhardt read a symbolic poem. For the debut of Las Vegas as a resort in 1946 Bugsy Seigel hired Abbot and Costello, and there, in a way, you have it all.

I am in the office of Major A. Riddle — Major is his name — the president of the Dunes Hotel. He combs his hair straight back and wears a heavy gold band on his little finger with a diamond sunk into it. As everywhere else in Las Vegas, someone has turned on the air conditioning to the point where it will be remembered, all right, as Las Vegas-style air conditioning. Riddle has an appointment to see a doctor at 4:30 about a crimp in his neck. His secretary, Maude Mc-Bride, has her head down and is rubbing the back of her neck. Lee Fisher, the P.R. man, and I are turning ours from time to time to keep the pivots from freezing up. Riddle is telling me about "the French war" and moving his neck gingerly. The Stardust bought and imported a version of the Lido de Paris spectacular, and the sight of all those sequined giblets pooning around on flamingo legs inflamed the tourists. The Tropicana fought back with the Folies Bergère, the New Frontier installed "Paree Ooh La La," the Hacienda reached for the puppets "Les Poupées de Paris," and the Silver Slipper called in Lili St. Cyr, the stripper, which was going French after a fashion. So the Dunes has bought up the third and last of the great Paris girlie shows, the Casino de Paris. Lee Fisher says, "And we're going to do things they *can't* top. In this town you're got to move ahead in quantum jumps."

Quantum? But exactly! The beauty of the Dunes' Casino de Paris show is that it will be beyond art, beyond dance, beyond spectacle, even beyond the titillations of the winking crotch. The Casino de Paris will be a behemoth piece of American calculus, like Project Mercury.

"This show alone will cost us two and a half million a year to operate and one and a half million to produce," Major A. Riddle is saying. "The costumes alone will be fantastic. There'll be more than five hundred costumes and — well, they'll be fantastic.

"And this machine — by the time we get through expanding the stage, this machine will cost us $250,000."

"Machine?"

"Yes. Sean Kenny is doing the staging. The whole set moves electronically right in front of your eyes. He used to work with this fellow Lloyd Wright."

"Frank Lloyd Wright?"

"Yes. Kenny did the staging for *Blitz*. Did you see it? Fantastic. Well, it's all done electronically. They built this machine for us in Glasgow, Scotland, and it's being shipped here right now. It moves all over the place and creates smoke and special effects. We'll have everything. You can stage a bombardment with it. You'll think the whole theatre is blowing up.

"You'll have to program it. They had to use the same mechanism that's in the Skybolt Missile to build it. It's called a 'Celson' or something like that. That's how complicated this thing is. They have to have the same thing as the Skybolt Missile."

As Riddle speaks, one gets a wonderful picture of sex riding the crest of the future. Whole tableaux of bare-bottomed Cosmonaughties will be hurtling around the Casino de Paris Room of the Dunes Hotel at fantastic speed in elliptical orbits, a flash of the sequined giblets here, a blur of the black-rimmed decal eyes there, a wink of the crotch here and there, until, with one vast Project Climax for our times, Sean Kenny, who used to work with this fellow Frank Lloyd Wright, presses the red button and the whole yahooing harem, shrieking ooh-la-la amid the din, exits in a mushroom cloud.

The allure is most irresistible not to the young but the old. No one in Las Vegas will admit it — it is not the modern, glamorous notion — but Las Vegas is a resort for old people. In those last years before the tissue deteriorates and the wires of the cerebral cortex hang in the skull like a clump of dried seaweed, they are seeking liberation.

At eight o'clock Sunday morning it is another almost boringly sunny day in the desert, and Clara and Abby, both about sixty, and their husbands, Earl, sixty-three, and Ernest, sixty-four, come squinting out of the Mint Casino onto Fremont Street.

"I don't know what's wrong with me," Abby says. "Those last three drinks, I couldn't even feel them. It was just like drinking fizz. You know what I mean?"

"Hey," says Ernest, "how about that place back 'ere? We ain't been back 'ere. Come on."

The others are standing there on the corner, squinting and looking doubtful. Abby and Clara both entered old babehood. They have that fleshy, humped-over shape across the bask of the shoulders. Their torsos are hunched up into fat little loaves supported by bony, atrophied leg stems sticking up into their hummocky hips. Their hair has been fried and dyed into improbable designs.

"You know what I mean? After a while it just gives me gas," says Abby. "I don't even feel it."

"Did you see me over there?" says Earl. "I was just going along, nice and easy, not too much, just riding along real nice. You know? And then, boy, I don't know what happened to me. First thing I know I'm laying down fifty dollars. . . ."

Abby lets out a great belch. Clara giggles.

"Gives me gas," Abby says mechanically.

"Hey, how about that place back 'ere?" says Ernest.

". . . Just nice and easy as you please. . . ."

". . . get me all fizzed up. . . ."

"Aw, come on. . . ."

And there at eight o'clock Sunday morning stand four old parties from Albuquerque, New Mexico, up all night, squinting at the sun, belching from a surfeit of tall drinks at eight o'clock Sunday morning, and — marvelous! — there is no one around to snigger at what an old babe with decaying haunches looks like in Capri pants with her heels jacked up on decorated wedgies.

"Where do we *come* from?" Clara said to me, speaking for the first time since I approached them on Fremont Street. "He wants to know where we come from. I think it's past your bedtime, sweets."

"Climb the stairs and go to bed," said Abby.

Laughter all around.

"Climb the stairs" was Abby's finest line. At present there are almost no stairs to climb in Las Vegas. Avalon homes are soon to go up, advertising "Two-Story Homes!" as though this were an incredibly lavish and exotic concept. As I talked to Clara, Abby, Earl and Ernest, it came out that "climb the stairs" was a phrase they brought along to Albuquerque with them from Marshalltown, Iowa, those many years ago, along with a lot of other baggage, such as the entire cupboard of Protestant taboos against drinking, lusting, gambling, staying out late, getting up late, loafing, idling, lollygagging around the streets and wearing Capri pants — all designed to deny a person short-term pleasures so he will center his energies on bigger, long-term goals.

"We was in 'ere" — the Mint — "a couple of hours ago, and that old boy was playing the guitar, you know, 'Walk right in, set right down,' and I kept hearing an old song I haven't heard for twenty years. It has this little boy and his folks keep telling him it's late and he has to go to bed. He keeps saying, 'Don't make me go to bed and I'll be good.' Am I *good*, Earl? Am I *good?*"

The liberated cortex in all its glory is none other than the old babes at the slot machines. Some of them are tourists whose husbands said, *Here is fifty bucks, go play the slot machines,* while they themselves went off to more complex pleasures. But most of these old babes are part of the permanent landscape of Las Vegas. In they go to the Golden Nugget or the Mint, with their Social Security check or their pension check from the Ohio telephone company, cash it at the casino cashier's, pull out the Dixie Cup and the Iron Boy work glove, disappear down a row of slots and get on with it. I remember particularly talking to another Abby — a widow, sixty-two years old, built short and up from the bottom like a fire hydrant. After living alone for twelve years in Canton, Ohio, she had moved out to Las Vegas to live with her daughter and her husband, who worked for the Army.

"They were wonderful about it," she said. "Perfect hypocrites. She kept saying, you know, 'Mother, we'd be delighted to have you, only we don't think you'll *like* it. It's practically a fron*tier* town,' she says. 'It's so *gar*ish,' she says. So I said, I told her, 'Well, if you'd rather I didn't come. . . .' 'Oh, no!' she says. I wish I could have heard what her husband was saying. He calls me 'Mother.' '*Mother,*' he says. Well, once I was here, they figured, well, I *might* make a good baby-sitter and dishwasher and duster and mopper. The children are nasty little things. So one day I was in town for something or other and I just played a slot machine. It's fun — I can't describe it to you. I suppose I lose. I lose a little. And *they* have fits about it. 'For God's sake, Grandmother,' and so forth. They always say '*Grand*mother' when I am supposed to 'act my age' or crawl through a crack in the floor. Well, I'll tell you, the slot machines are a *whole lot* better than sitting in that little house all day. They kind of get you; I can't explain it."

The childlike megalomania of gambling is, of course, from the same cloth as the megalomania of the town. And, as the children of the liberated cortex, the old guys and babes are running up and down the Strip around the clock like everybody else. It is not by chance that much of the entertainment in Las Vegas, especially the second-stringers who perform in the cocktail lounges, will recall for an aging man what was glamorous twenty-five years ago when he had neither the money nor the freedom of spirit to indulge himself in it. In the big theatre-dining room at the Desert Inn, The Painted Desert Room, Eddie Fisher's act is on and he is saying cozily to a florid guy at a table right next to the stage, "Manny, you know you shouldn'a sat this close — you know you're in for it now, Manny, baby," while Manny beams with fright. But in the cocktail lounge, where the idea is chiefly just to keep the razzle-dazzle going, there is Hugh Farr, one of the stars of another era in the West, composer of two of the five Western songs the Library of Congress has taped for posterity, "Cool Water" and "Tumbling Tumbleweed," when he played the violin for the Sons of the Pioneers. And now around the eyes he looks like an aging Chinese savant, but he is wearing a white tuxedo and powder-blue leather boots and playing his sad old Western violin with an electric cord plugged in it for a group called The Country Gentlemen. And there is Ben Blue, looking like a waxwork exhibit of vaudeville, doffing his straw skimmer to reveal the sculptural qualities of his skull. And down at the Flamingo cocktail lounge — Ella Fitzgerald is in the main room — there is Harry James, looking old and pudgy in one of those toy Italian-style show-biz suits. And the Ink Spots are at the New Frontier and Louis Prima is at the Sahara, and the old parties are seeing it all, roaring through the dawn into the next day, until the sun seems like a par lamp fading in and out. The casinos, the bars, the liquor stores are open every minute of every day, like a sempiternal wading pool for the childhood ego. ". . . Don't make me go to bed. . . ."

Finally the casualties start piling up. I am in the manager's office of a hotel on the Strip. A man and his wife, each about sixty, are in there, raging. Someone got into their room and stole seventy dollars from her purse, and they want the hotel to make it up to them. The man pops up and down from a chair and ricochets back and forth across the room, flailing his great pig's-knuckle elbows about.

"What kind of security you call that? Walk right in the god-dern room and just help themselves. And where do you think I found your security man? Back around the corner reading a god-dern detective magazine!"

He had scored a point there, but he was wearing a striped polo shirt with a hip Hollywood solid-color collar, and she had on Capri pants, and hooked across their wrinkly old faces they both had rimless, wraparound French sunglasses of the sort young-punk heroes in *nouvelle vague* movies wear, and it was impossible to give any earnest contemplation to a word they said. They seemed to have the great shiny popeyes of a praying mantis.

"Listen, Mister," she is saying, "I don't care about the seventy bucks. I'd lose seventy bucks at your craps table and I wouldn't think nothing of it. I'd play seventy bucks just like that, and it wouldn't mean nothing. I wouldn't regret it. But when they can just walk in — and you don't give a damn — for Christ's sake!"

They are both zeroing in on the manager with their great insect corneas. The manager is a cool number in a white-on-white shirt and silver tie.

"This happened three days ago. Why didn't you tell us about it then?"

"Well, I was gonna be a nice guy about it. Seventy dollars," he said, as if it would be difficult for the brain to grasp a sum much smaller. "But then I found your man back there reading a god-dern detective magazine. *True Detectives* it was. Had a picture on the front of some floozie with one leg up on a chair and her garter showing. Looked like a god-derned athlete's-foot ad. Boy, I went into a slow burn. But when I am burned up, I am *burned up!* You get me, Mister? There he was, reading the god-derned *True Detectives*."

"Any decent hotel would have insurance," she says.

The manager says, "I don't know a hotel in the world that offers insurance against theft."

"Hold on, Mister," he says, "are you calling my wife a liar? You just get smart, and I'm gonna pop you one! I'll pop you one right now if you call my wife a liar."

At this point the manager lowers his head to one side and looks up at the old guy from under his eyebrows with a version of the Red Hook brush-off, and the old guy begins to cool off.

But others are beyond cooling off. Hornette Reilly, a buttery hipped whore from New York City, is lying in bed with a bald-headed guy from some place who has skin like oatmeal. He is asleep or passed out or something. Hornette is relating all this to the doctor over the Princess telephone by the bed.

"Look," she says, "I'm breaking up. I can't tell you how much I've drunk. About a bottle of brandy since four o'clock, I'm not kidding. I'm in bed with a guy. Right this minute. I'm talking on the telephone to you and this slob is lying here like an animal. He's all fat and his skin looks like oatmeal — what's happening to me? I'm going to take some more pills. I'm not kidding, I'm breaking up. I'm going to kill myself. You've got to put me in Rose de Lima. I'm breaking up, and I don't even know what's happening to me."

"So naturally you want to go to Rose de Lima."

"Well, yeah."

"You can come by the office, but I'm not sending you to Rose de Lima."

"Doctor, I'm not kidding."

"I don't doubt that you're sick, old girl, but I'm not sending you to Rose de Lima to sober up."

The girls do not want to go to the County Hospital. They want to go to Rose de Lima, where the psychiatric cases receive milieu therapy. The patients dress in street clothes, socialize and play games with the staff, eat well and relax in the sun, all paid for by the State. One of the folk heroines of the Las Vegas floozies, apparently, is the call girl who last year was spending Monday through Friday at Rose de Lima and "turning out," as they call it, Saturdays and Sundays on the Strip, to the tune of $200 to $300 a weekend. She looks upon herself not as a whore, or even a call girl, but as a lady of assignation. When some guy comes to the Strip and unveils the little art-nouveau curves in his psyche and calls for two girls to perform arts upon one another, this one consents to be the passive member of the team only. A Rose de Lima girl, she draws the line.

At the County Hospital the psychiatric ward is latched, bolted, wired up and jammed with patients who are edging along the walls in the inner hall, the only place they have to take a walk other than the courtyard.

A big brunette with the remnants of a beehive hairdo and decal eyes and an obvious pregnancy is the liveliest of the lot. She is making eyes at everyone who walks in. She also nods gaily toward vacant place places along the wall.

"Mrs. ——— is refusing medication," a nurse tells one of the psychiatrists. "She won't even open her mouth."

Presently the woman, in a white hospital tunic, is led up the hall. She looks about fifty, but she has extraordinary lines on her face.

"Welcome home," says Dr. ———.

"This is not my home," she says.

"Well, as I told you before, it has to be for the time being."

"Listen, you didn't analyze me."

"Oh, yes. Two psychiatrists examined you — all over again."

"You mean that time in jail."

"Exactly."

"You can't tell anything from that. I was excited. I had been out on the Strip, and then all that stupid — "

Three-fourths of the 640 patients who clustered into the ward last year were casualties of the Strip or the Strip milieu of Las Vegas, the psychiatrist tells me. He is a bright and energetic man in a shawl-collared black silk suit with brass buttons.

"I'm not even her doctor," he says. "I don't know her case. There's nothing I can do for her."

Here, securely out of sight in this little warren, are all those who have taken the loop-the-loop and could not stand the centripety. Some, like Raymond, who has been rocketing for days on pills and liquor, who has gone without sleep to the point of anoxia, might pull out of the toxic reaction in two or three days, or eight or ten. Others have conflicts to add to the chemical wackiness. A man who has thrown all his cash to the flabby homunculus who sits at every craps table stuffing the take down an almost hidden chute so it won't pile up in front of the customers' eyes; a man who has sold the family car for next to nothing at a car lot advertising "Cash for your car — *right now*" and then thrown that to the homunculus, too, but also still has the family waiting guiltlessly, guilelessly back home; well, he has troubles.

". . . After I came here and began doing personal studies," the doctor is saying, "I recognized extreme aggressiveness continually. It's not merely what Las Vegas can do to a person, it's the type of person it attracts. Gambling is a very aggressive pastime, and Las Vegas attracts aggressive people. They have an amazing capacity to louse up a normal situation."

The girl, probably a looker in more favorable moments, is pressed face into the wall, cutting glances at the doctor. The nurse tells her something and she puts her face in her hands, convulsing but not making a sound. She retreats to her room, and then the sounds come shrieking out. The doctor rushes back. Other patients are sticking their heads out of their rooms along the hall.

"The young girl?" a quiet guy says to a nurse. "The young girl," he says to somebody in the room.

But the big brunette just keeps rolling her decal eyes.

Out in the courtyard — all bare sand — the light is a kind of light-bulb twilight. An old babe is rocking herself back and forth on a straight chair and putting one hand out in front from time to time and pulling it in toward her bosom.

It seems clear enough to me. "A slot machine?" I say to the nurse, but she says there is no telling.

". . . and yet the same aggressive types are necessary to build a frontier town, and Las Vegas is a frontier town, certainly by any psychological standard," Dr. —— is saying. "They'll undertake anything and they'll accomplish it. The building here has been incredible. They don't seem to care what they're up against, so they do it."

I go out to the parking lot in back of the County Hospital and it doesn't take a second; as soon as I turn on the motor I'm swinging again with Action Checkpoint News, "Monkey No. 9," "Donna, Donna, the Prima Donna," and friendly picking and swinging for the Fremont Hotel and Frontier Federal. Me and my big white car are sailing down the Strip and the Boomerang Modern, Palette Curvi-linear, Flash Gordon Ming-Alert Spiral, McDonald's Hamburger Para-bola, Mint Casino Elliptical and Miami Beach Kidney sunbursts are exploding in the Young Electric Sign Company's Grand Gallery for all the sun kings. At the airport there was that bad interval between the rental-car stall and the terminal entrance, but once through the automatic door the Muzak came bubbling up with "Song of India." On the upper level around the ramps the slots were cranking away. They are placed like "traps," a word Las Vegas picked up from golf. And an old guy is walking up the ramp, just off the plane from Denver, with a huge plastic bag of clothes slung over the left shoulder and a two-suiter suitcase in his right hand. He has to put the suitcase down on the floor and jostle the plastic bag all up around his neck to keep it from falling, but he manages to dig into his pocket for a couple of coins and get going on the slot machines. All seems right, but walking out to my plane I sense that something is missing. Then

I recall sitting in the cocktail lounge of the Dunes at 3 P.M. with Jack Heskett, district manager of the Federal Sign and Signal Corporation, and Marty Steinman, the sales manager, and Ted Blaney, a designer. They are telling me about the sign they are building for the Dunes to put up at the airport. It will be five thousand square feet of free-standing sign, done in flaming-lake red on burning-desert gold. The d — the D — alone in the word Dunes, written in Cyrillic modern, will be practically two stories high. An inset plexiglas display, the largest revolving, trivision plexiglas sign in the world, will turn and show first the Dunes, with its twenty-two-story addition, then the seahorse swimming pool, then the new golf course. The scimitar curves of the sign will soar to a huge roaring diamond at the very top. "You'll be able to see it from an airplane fifteen miles away," says Jack Heskett. "Fifty miles," says Lee Fisher. And it will be sixty-five feet up in the air — because the thing was, somebody was out at the airport and they noticed there was only one display to be topped. That was that shaft about sixty feet high with the lit-up globe and the beacon lights, which is to say, the control tower. Hell, you can only see that forty miles away. But exactly!

the silence of oswald

John Clellon Holmes

allusion - past hist. or myth. event.

The author most assumes readers know about it.

"Wasn't there anyone to give you the lecture on Cuba? Don't you sense the enormity of your mistake — you invade a country without understanding its music."

Norman Mailer in an Open Letter to JFK

In a special sense that had little to do with his politics, John Kennedy was *our* president, the first president with whom people of my age could feel a personal identification. Whether we agreed with him or not, we assumed that we could address him as Mailer does above, without being scoffed at for suggesting that intelligence about a country's soul was as essential to foreign policy as intelligence about its Coastal Defenses. Kennedy brought a style, eloquence, taste, courage and relish-for-the-game (perhaps the best qualities of youth) back into public life again, and I think we all became a little more interested in politics during his Administration than we had been in ten years.

If we were sometimes suspicious of his motives, critical of his accomplishments, and wary of his charm, it was not because he resembled his predecessors, but precisely because he was so different from them that we judged him by different standards — standards based on reality rather than realpolitik, the standards by which we judged each other. For a brief time, America was a more exciting place to live in day-to-day. The rhetorical grunts that usually characterize our political hog-wallow were temporarily out of fashion, and a certain sharp-eyed wit and grace (as distant from the locker-room wowser and the Fred Waring fox-trot as Abilene is from Boston) were definitely in. For once, we had a Chief Executive and his Lady who could be viewed as sexual objects with no feeling of disrespect, and if we cavilled at the fact that Nelson Algren and Norman Mailer remained uninvited to the White House, it was not because good writers never appeared there. The persistent feeling that this man might decisively affect the quality of American public-life for decades to come must have plagued even the most cynical of us. And then, with the suddenness of a rifle-shot, it was over.

Probably the most universal reaction to the assassination was the shocking realization that some promise, some hope, some still-unplumbed *chance* for a shift in mood had been inexplicably lost. At least, the words that kept running through *my* head during those awful days after Dallas had nothing to do with political parties or programs: "Now it's back to America-as-usual," I thought. And yet something huge and terrible and *new* seemed to be shuddering in the air, as if a phantom-Caliban had broken out of the cellars in the national psyche, and struck down our Ariel for no other reason than a desire to wreck the play. The age-old American belief in the perfectability of men *through* politics, and the bitter, violent hatred (equally age-old) which this belief can rouse in the murky corners of the soul, had collided, and the best we had to offer to this moment in history had been savagely cut down by — what? A madman? A disgruntled ideologist? A pawn in some sinister plot?

Whether out of frustrated vengeance or honest bewilderment, we turned to the figure of Lee Harvey Oswald, as you sometimes turn ahead to the last chapter of a murder-mystery, acknowledging the fact that the more cruel and gratuitous the crime, the greater is the need to understand it if one is to accept a loss as stunning as Kennedy's was to us, and still keep one's perspective. But instead of a clear motive, an articulate gesture, and a coherent human being, we found only a further riddle, a more impenetrable silence, a man of paper. Oswald looked out at us from our TV sets — querulous, ungiving, and mockingly enigmatic. We saw his death flood, with the anguish of surprise, across his face, and we saw his secrets and his reasons perish with him. I think that the suspicion that we might never know the whole truth, and that it was somehow crucial that we do if that Caliban-side of American life was ever to be disarmed (and *some* good come out of it), drove not a few of us a little off center for a time.

In any case, the necessity to understand Lee Harvey Oswald became a governmental, as well as a personal, fixation in the months that followed, resulting in the publication of the Warren Report a year later, in which most of the important *factual* questions about Oswald seemed to be answered, except in the minds of chronic skeptics and conspiracy-hunters. For despite the fact that the case against Oswald appeared to be damning as early as January 1964, the rumors, theories, and dark allegations mounted steadily nevertheless, and the Report did little to bring these speculations to an end.

Indeed, they have continued unabated to this day. The competence of the Commission itself has been seriously questioned. Doubts as to the thoroughness and neutrality of its investigation have been raised, and it now seems likely that the Commission's work was hurried, haphazard in certain respects, and ultimately unsuccessful in accounting for gaps in the evidence and discrepancies in the testimony, to explain which fantastic theories have been propounded (like the so-called Second Oswald Theory, which literally creates "two" questions for every one it answers). None of these speculations, however intriguing they may be, have come up with a single scrap of positive evidence that alters the strong feeling one has after reading the Report: That despite all the gaps and all the discrepancies, in all probability it was Lee Harvey Oswald who killed John Kennedy, aided and abetted in the act by an incredible run of luck but by no one else, and that, so far at least, there is small reason to assume that the assassination did not occur more or less as the Warren Report describes it. The single most interesting question — the question of *Why?* — has not been answered by any of these post-Report theories because, quite simply, they never raise it.

Why have so many people lavished so much torturous logic on the mostly-inconsequential holes in the case against Oswald? Why have these skeptics continued to erect ever more elaborate explanations, all of which are based on nothing more damning than the conflict of recollection and the difficulty of making an airtight reconstruction of an event after the fact, that are typical of any murder case where there is neither an eye-witness nor a confession? And finally, why do most of us feel that somehow something *is* missing, even in the Report, that would make the assassination of this popular and gifted young president comprehensible?

The reasons may be more simple than the sort of subjective politicking and simplistic psychologizing to which we are all prone in moments of crisis. For an almost-unbroken chain of facts *is* incomprehensible unless the man they indict is comprehensible too, and without an over-riding motive all evidence remains circumstantial. The Warren Report notwithstanding, we are forced to conclude that few of the facts therein do much to answer the blunt questions: Given Oswald, why Kennedy? What was the reason for this seemingly-absurd act?   ← MAIN   POINT

Probably no one will ever be able to answer these questions for certain, and yet if we accept the broad conclusions of the Report, that Oswald was guilty and he acted alone (and I *still* see no way to avoid doing so), we are compelled to look more deeply into the life and character of Lee Harvey Oswald in the hope of discovering the psychic drives that produced his crime. Certainly I cannot have been alone in plodding through every one of the Warren Report's 800-odd pages for the sole purpose of understanding Oswald, and thus ridding myself of what had become something of an obsession. For the feeling persisted in me that somehow Oswald embodied, albeit to an extreme, a condition of Being that is growing more and more prevalent in our time.

Two kinds of motivation were ascribed to Oswald — politics and/or madness — and yet the persistent doubts, echoed in the Report itself, indicated how unsatisfactory these explanations were, to reasonable and unreasonable men alike. On the one hand, the political overtones of the assassination (a left-winger killing a liberal President) are so confused and contradictory that they supply no really conclusive reason for the crime; and on the other, Oswald under arrest never ex-

*modern philosophy there & only
exist now. We only we're dying
know. here is the thing we do.*

hibited (as did Jack Ruby) the self-aggrandizement, disassociation and rapid alternation of mood that characterize a seriously demented man. He was a psychopath all right — that was clear — but what kind of psychopath? What aggravated his condition beyond bearing? And, above all, what was the specific need in this peculiar man that demanded this particular expression?

A "deep" reading of the Report gave me, at least, a hint of an answer to these questions, for such a reading gradually makes clear that Oswald's action may have been nothing less than his decisive move *beyond* politics, and *out* of mere neurosis, into that frightening existential realm from which people sometimes violently gesture back at the reality they feel has excluded them. (Camus' novel, *The Stranger,* which is an account of an utterly gratuitous murder, is a chilling examination of just such a feeling of exclusion.) That people *do* act for reasons of this sort is evidenced every day in newspaper stories of cases of "meaningless" violence on the part of alienated, socially disoriented individuals; and perhaps it is because the victim, in this case, was a President, and the assassin a political dissenter, that we have failed to glimpse what has been under our noses all along.

alienation

Consider Oswald's human situation. His life was as unremittingly bleak, loveless and thwarting as any described in a Dostoievskyan novel. Growing up in a society that provided an unskilled but reasonably intelligent man almost nothing meaningful on which to expend his idealism, his personal environment continually sabotaged his efforts to discover his own value as a human being. The sobering fact is that there are possibly millions of people in the U.S. who are indistinguishable from Oswald, except for the crime he committed. Rootless, traditionless, fatherless, unloved by his "self-involved" mother, emotionally displaced by their peripatetic life together, moving restlessly from flat to flat, city to city, always crushingly alone, his hours occupied by TV and chance books, friendless and rejected, and so withdrawing more and more from any renewing contact with others, Oswald was that typical figure of the modern world: the anonymous, urban mass man, who most always has the same blank, half-scornful, sullen expression on his face. Oswald's photos, as an example, are all alarmingly alike, and he always looks the same: cautious, irritable, hungry, *masked.* To him, the world was as impersonal as the camera, and he turned the same face to both.

He appears to have embraced Marxism because, in the U.S. of the 1950s, it was the most unpopular, rebellious, and socially outrageous creed he could espouse. The society which gave him no place, and did not deign to notice him *even* as a dissident, had to be spurned in its turn: "I reject the world that has rejected me," as Jean Genet has put it. Nevertheless, Oswald exhibited the neurotic's standard ambivalence toward authority: To escape from one (his mother), he embraced another (the Marines); to defy the U.S., he defended the U.S.S.R. But he was happy nowhere; the psychic heat in him intensified, demanding ceaseless changes of mind to accommodate it, and his few short years were marked by a bewildering number of conflicting political and emotional attitudes. There are those hundreds of dreary "official" letters to the Soviet authorities, the State Department, the Navy Department, the FBI and almost everyone else, the sole reason for which was to define and get on the record his chameleonlike changes of status. Like many of us in this bureaucratized world, he searched for himself in his dossier.

Everything disappointed him; nothing gave him a feeling of his own distinct being; he tried over and over again to find a situation in which he could experience himself as alive, productive, a person of consequence; and one of the most interesting clues to his personality lies in the odd fact of his always writing about his actions (in his Historic Diary) in the present tense. The entry recording his suicide attempt in Russia is a telling example (the spelling and punctuation are Oswald's): "I am shocked!! My dreams! . . . I have waited for 2 year to be accepted. My fondes dreams are shattered because of a petty offial . . . I decide to end it. Soak rist in cold water to numb the pain, Than slash my leftwrist. Than plaug wrist into bathtum of hot water . . . Somewhere, a violin plays, as I wacth my life whirl away. I think to myself 'How easy to Die' and 'A Sweet Death, (to violins).' "

This is an astonishing image of a man observing himself as if he were not himself, at once self-dramatic and objective, pathetic and theatrical, but, above all, *cold.* The very precision of his account of the preparations, the alert recording of his sensory perceptions, and particularly the ironic comment to the end, form a picture of a man cruelly isolated in himself, to whom lonely communion with his own thoughts and the sort of false, reportorial objectivity that results are the normal way he experiences his consciousness. Such a man often becomes a melancholic, or an artist, or a killer.

Oswald's inherent dissent soon overran his political convictions. Pinning his hopes on Russia, he was relieved for a time; losing those hopes in disappointment, he returned to the U.S., only to feel the pressure of exclusion rising in him once again. He vacillated between

Cuba and Russia; he made abortive attempts to find a place for himself in various radical movements. Everywhere he was blocked, rejected, ignored. His inability to arrange an escape to Havana seems
to have left him, at the last, utterly bereft, utterly placeless, finally
outside the conflicting political solutions to his discontent. It thrust
him back upon himself, reduced him to having to live with the facts
of his social impotence and his personal inadequacy, without even the
illusion that he was enduring this pain in the name of something
outside himself. As a result, the hammer on the rifle of his already
alienated nature was cocked.   Metaphor

His wife never appears to have understood the sort of man he was.
She comes through the Report as shallow, adaptable, materialistic and
self-centered; a simple, affectionate creature, rather like *The Stranger's*
mistress, with little or no understanding of the existential attraction
of underground politics to the young, disaffected American, or even of
the "complex fate" of Oswald's relentlessly dispiriting life. She chides
him for his failures, she complains about his ideas; she is easily accepted into the Dallas Russian colony, while he is not; in *his* country,
she finds what he has never found — friends. Oswald's male pride is
constantly abused by their acquaintances, by his job losses, by their
poverty, his family, and ultimately by Marina herself in the most un-
forgivable way: She ridicules his sexual performance. He beats her
up; he is puritanical in specifically sexual ways (he flies into a fury
because the zipper on her skirt is not properly fastened in front of
others); he doesn't want her to smoke, or drink, or use cosmetics. He
discovers her letter to a former beau in Russia, lamenting that she
hadn't married *him.* The pattern of exclusion and failure becomes
more and more personal and interiorized; it reaches that pitch of
psychological pressure where a man acts decisively to overcome everything, or goes under and loses his image of himself. And no matter
how extravagant or idiotic that image may be, a man must have a
self-image or go mad.

Viewed in this light, Oswald's crime may have been a last desperate attempt to become part of reality again, to force his way back
into the reality that had ignored him, so that he could experience
himself as *acting,* as living, as committed. "Men also secrete the in-
human," Camus has written. "Sometimes, in [our] moments of lucidity, the mechanical aspect of their gestures and their senseless pantomime make everything about them seem stupid." And when we are
possessed by such a feeling, we have lost that sense of immediate

contact with the world that is the strongest check on the violent whims that sometimes stir in all of us.

For there comes a moment when we realize that we can break through the invisible and intangible wall that separates us from the person standing right next to us; when we realize that we have been drifting along, as if under water, in the terror and *silence* of isolation; when we see things with the "hopeless lucidity" that Sartre has described somewhere, and realize that only an unwarranted act, an abrupt breaking through the wall, will restore us to reality, and obliterate that silence that imprisons us; when we realize that *they* are not mechanical dolls, automatons moving through a dream from which only *we* are excluded, but human — because they will bleed, hurt, die and (perhaps most important of all) turn toward us at the last their shocked faces, across which no hint of our existence has ever glimmered before, startled now by the abrupt recognition of our presence among them. When Marina joined *them,* when she crossed over to the other side of the wall, refusing even to talk to Oswald that last night, refusing even to consider moving into Dallas with him, she (in one sense) put the cartridge in the chamber of his life, and President Kennedy was doomed.   *metaphor*

Still, it is possible that Oswald was not absolutely committed to his act. He may have taken the rifle to work that day merely to experience the strange and lonesome thrill of being able to hold someone's life in his hands for a single giddy moment. After all, this is why people peer through binoculars in big cities — to initiate an intimacy that is not threatening because it is an illusion. This is why people expose themselves on subway platforms, without actually planning to assault the observer, and, in some cases, hoping not even to be noticed by him. This is why people carry weapons they could never bring themselves to use. It is the urge of the outsider, the isolated, to feign a breakthrough into the unknown possibilities of ongoing reality, and it is at least conceivable that Oswald intended to do nothing but *view* Kennedy through the telescopic sight of his rifle, and feel for a moment the omnipotence and self-importance that his whole life (and now his wife as well) had denied him.

Once having reached this point, however, circumstances would have pushed him over. For circumstances, the accidents of as-yet-unrealized time, often create the pressure of the finger on the trigger, and psychologists believe that people always act by some logic of self-interest as their peril. What might have happened, for instance, if the Negro youth who had eaten his lunch at Oswald's window a scant half hour before had remained there instead of going down to a lower floor to watch the motorcade with his friends? What would have happened had someone asked Oswald to watch the motorcade with *him?* No one can say, and yet one is left with the uneasy feeling that an act of friendship, a recognition, a movement toward human contact, at a hundred different junctures during Oswald's life might have radically altered the course he traveled. So why not at this most crucial of junctures? If, for instance, Marina had discussed their situation with him that last night, and perhaps allowed that discussion to lead to some sort of minimal reconciliation in their bed, would Oswald have needed this ultimate, severing act to relieve himself of the unendurable *silence* that enclosed him? No one can ever say.

Certainly, his psychopathy was real, constantly expanding and dangerous. He had tried to kill General Walker some months earlier, after planning the attempt for many weeks, only to miss a far easier shot than the apparently impulsive one that hit the President — a clear indication to me that the first was only another muddled political gesture, whereas the second was something deeper and more mysterious. By November 1963, his need had grown to proportions that no single annealing act on the part of any one person, much less the environment, could have dissipated. And yet there are probably thousands of people who are daily caught in psychic binds not unlike his — so many cocked rifles walking anonymously through the streets — and little or nothing in our society, or in our mostly naïve conceptions of our responsibility to each other's lonely struggle to keep from drowning in it, offers any sure way by which these cocked rifles can be disarmed. At least not until they have gone off, and it is too late.

Oswald's relation to reality is succinctly described by the "we" in Camus' "A man is talking on the telephone. We cannot hear him behind the glass partition, but we can see his senseless mimicry. We wonder why he is alive?" It was this glass partition that separated Oswald from the rest of us, and made him feel that he was only a "thing" in our eyes, a piece of meaningless, uncared-for flotsam. But a man cannot exist this way, at least not a man who is the intelligent, articulate and impatient neurotic that Oswald seems to have been. Such a man often feels that only two alternatives are open to him: to rashly insist on being his idealized image of himself, or to slavishly become the nonentity the world tells him over and over again that he is.

The fact remains that in the urbanized and impersonal America of his day, Oswald's resources were never used, his affections were never aroused, his concern for the future was never harnessed, and yet, on the evidence, he seems to have been reasonably brave, potentially decisive, mostly hard-working and certainly untiring in his efforts to break out of the dead end of his existence. At least all these qualities were present in him, in embryo, and only soured and became destructive when he could find no place to utilize them creatively.

One indication of the blistered wasteland of his human and social hopes lies in this passage, which he wrote after his disappointment with Russia: "I wonder what would happen if somebody was to stand up and say he was utterly opposed not only to the governments, but to the people, to the entire land and complete foundations of his socially." We need no longer wonder, for he has given us one answer to the question, and perhaps it was this very "wondering" of his that led him (still uncommitted to the act itself) to that window. In any case, his words stand as a twisted rebuke to a society that can seem to recognize only its madmen or its heroes, but steadfastly ignores the countless millions of anonymous people yearning to feel some responsibility, some faith, some ultimate *stake* in the world around them.

In a larger sense, the two polar aspects of the contemporary American character collided that day in Dallas — a consideration which, in going beyond politics, goes far to explain why it *had* to be Kennedy. For John Kennedy was everything that Lee Oswald was not. He existed directly in the vivid center of reality, he was potent in every way, his life and personality were one continuous action and interaction; he was neither dualistic, separated nor helpless; he had never been prevented from experiencing himself as alive and consequential. Oswald struck back at everything he was *not,* but in a sense he was performing a Kennedylike act (as far as he could imagine one), and was attempting to *become* the sort of man he killed by the very *act* of killing. And so all that was most starved, thwarted and hopeless in our national life took its pathetic and sullen revenge on all that was most vital, potent and attractive.

The horror of Oswald's loneliness, the extremity of his hunger, the appalling facelessness and spirit-withering *silence* of his whole life exploded in a bitter and anguished threat: Either he would be admitted onto life's stage or he would pull that stage down in total ruin; he would be recognized as having that sense of uniqueness that a human being *has* to have if he is to outwit the despair that leads to madness, or he would turn his very powerlessness into a source of power. Those who are imprisoned in the silence of reality always use a gun (or, if they are more fortunate, a pen) to speak for them, and perhaps the prince and the pauper in the human spirit are doomed to meet face to face, no matter what. But certainly the job of a sane and mature society is to see that this meeting does not take place through the sights of a high-powered rifle.

In one sense, we are poorer for the loss of them *both*. Though we lost Oswald years before we lost Kennedy, how many losses of *any* human potential can our besieged society afford? The fact is that a man will affirm his humanity at all costs, even if it means denying the humanity of others, and the whole ghastly nightmare of modern history has been endured for nothing if we have not understood that paradox at last. Oswald's blind insistence that he *was* a man, no matter what the sum of his life might indicate, had to be made in terms that the world could comprehend and, denied every other exit from that smothering silence, he resorted to the only language that our time seems to offer to the voiceless: He took a gun and aimed it at the center of the life from which he felt orphaned, and so broke into the stream of reality at last, by arresting it.

For a moment, he must have felt the exhilaration, the keenness to sensory stimuli and the virile power of choice that characterized a man functioning at the top of himself as a human being. Certainly his sinister calm before the Dallas police, his refusal to be trapped by their web of logic and his perfectly blank-faced denials of any complicity in the assassination suggest a man whose darker conflicts are at least temporarily at rest, a man at ominous peace with his divided life.

But if all this is true, it is too harsh a comment on our world, and its attritions, to be merely a psychological footnote to a political tragedy. Instead, it should remind us that history is, at the last, only the exterior appearance of far more important inner events — such as those that Lee Harvey Oswald suffered until he could suffer no more, and so struck back out of his wound.

intellectual foolery:

john barth's huge allegorical novel

Hayden Carruth

John Barth's new novel is a huge allegory so brilliantly conceived that one feels it simply must succeed. And it very nearly does; many readers will get from it, or at least from parts of it, that intense, quickening delight which comes only from good satire. In the school of Philosophical Bawdry, so prominent in our fiction during the past decade, *Giles Goat-Boy* is probably the best American example so far.

And yet the fact also is, unhappily, that long before the end, which comes on the 744th page, most readers will be sick of it.

Like all good allegorists, Mr. Barth begins with a conceit simple enough to permit almost endless elaboration. It is this: the World is a University. But of course this equivalence must never be stated outright; Mr. Barth knows that the rules of allegory forbid it. Instead, he merely thrusts us right away into a University so vast that from the start we make the equivalence ourselves. We recognize that this campus is all the earth, our whole world, and from our recognition springs our knowledge of all the other equivalences as well.

We know instantly, for example, Who is meant by the Founder. We know who were the Grand Tutors of the Old and New Syllabi, including the last and foremost, Enos Enoch. We see that in this University to pass is salvation, to fail is damnation, and hence the Finals, Graduation, and Commencement take on their "real" meaning. We know — too well — the Dean o' Flunks. And we know also the whole history of this University down to its present schismatic division between the East Campus and the West. Indeed, there is nothing in the entire history of mankind, from Stoicism to Existentialism, from the misty Orient to the pragmatic Occident, that cannot be translated into the terms of Mr. Barth's novelized history of studentdom.

Into this University a boy is born. For somewhat complex reasons, however, he is not raised as a human child but as a goat, and does not discover his own humanity until he is fourteen years old. Predictably, the discovery throws him into a considerable flap, from which he emerges at last with a resolve not merely to investigate his own extraordinary and new-found qualities as a man, but to make

With permission of Chicago Daily News.

himself into something more than a man; a hero, a messiah; in short, a new Grand Tutor who will save the University from its present schism and bring peace to all the campus. The book, therefore, is a long, bawdy account of his adventures as he tries, in spite of his goatish background, which he never succeeds in putting entirely behind him, to carry out his high purpose.

Many criticisms will be brought against it. Literal-minded Christians, and some not so literal-minded, will have no choice but to call the book an immense blasphemy. Others will wonder if the Goat-Boy's claim to Grand Tutorship is justifiable, or if the wisdom he professes to attain at the end is a genuine wisdom. But these are matters for the individual reader to decide.

A commoner criticism, probably, will concern the structure of the book, the detailed elaboration of the campus-world allegory. Without doubt it is carried beyond the point of surfeit. Many passages in which famous events or points of view from the world are satirically recast in the language of the campus extend too far; the satirical point is lost. Mr. Barth has been indulging himself, playing with his own cleverness, when he should have been attending to the proper business of constructing an allegory. But in the end this too becomes a subjective criticism, since the point of surfeit will depend upon the individual reader's tolerance for Mr. Barth's kind of intellectual foolery.

A more objective criticism concerns his style, especially since Mr. Barth has said that for him style is the substance of art. In his work language is — or is intended to be — more than an instrument of satire, it is an element of satire. Thus his style uses, and at the same time pokes fun at, many other styles: political bombast, technical jargon, business and advertising argot, the rhetoric of academia, and especially scripture and liturgy; it is full of leering pedantries and archaisms. Its satiric force is sustained in the best passages by a tense, self-conscious irony that keeps the reader elevated, so to speak, above a direct involvement in the flow of language, aware of the intended tongue-in-cheek effect. It is a kind of purposeful stylistic insincerity. But in too many passages this verbal tension slackens, Mr. Barth cannot keep it up, and the reader is permitted to drift into the immediate flow of word and phrase. The effect is lost; the satire turns into the thing satirized.

The best example occurs in the middle of the book where, for purposes of the narrative, we are presented with a modern verse translation of a classical Greek drama. For two pages the translation is a fine satire; it gives us the errors of our translators in exaggerated particularity: false rhymes, jingly meters, misplaced pedantries, inappropriate colloquialisms, etc. But the translation goes on for thirty pages or more. And very soon the reader finds himself no longer laughing at a satire but, instead, groaning over one more extremely bad modern version of the Oedipus legend.

Could the necessary tension of verbal satire be sustained in any case for 744 pages? It would be a remarkable feat. One is reminded of other writers who have used ironic archaism successfully but within a smaller compass: on the serious side, the marvelous polemics of Edward Dalhberg; in a comic spirit, the disquisitions of S. J. Perelman. Indeed, to one reader Mr. Barth's style seems farther from its putative sources — the Scriptures; Mallory and Florio and Burton — than it is from a much more recent classic called *Dawn Ginsbergh's Revenge.* Mr. Barth might have fared better if he had confined himself, not to the narrow scope of that little masterpiece, for obviously he had a broader end in view, but at least to something more like it.

# of death and unreason

Theodore H. White

It was hot; the sun was blinding; there would be a moment of cool shade ahead under the overpass they were approaching.

But the trip, until this moment, had been splendid. For the President was beginning, with this journey, the campaign of 1964 — testing the politics of his leadership, and hearing the people clap in the streets.

He had just turned easily, but with grace and precision as was his style, to wave at the Texans who cheered him — when the sound rapped above the noise.

It was a blunt crack, like the sound of a motorcycle backfiring (which is what his wife thought it was), followed in about five

From *The Making of the President 1964* by Theodore H. White. Used by permission.

seconds by two more; then, suddenly, the sniper's bullets had found their mark and John Fitzgerald Kennedy lay fallen, his head in his wife's lap.

There is an amateur's film, 400 feet long, twenty-two seconds in all, which catches alive the moment of death. The film is soundless but in color. Three motorcycle outriders come weaving around the bend, leading the black Presidential limousine; a gay patch of background frolics behind them — mint-green grasses, yellow-green foliage. The President turns in the back seat, all the way around to his right, and flings out his hand in greeting. Then the hand bends quickly up as if to touch his throat, as if something hurts. His wife, at this moment, is also leaning forward, turning to the right. Slowly he leans back to her, as if to rest his head on her shoulder. She quickly puts her arm around him, and leans even farther forward to look at him. Then, brutally, unbelievably, the head of the President is jolted by some invisible and terrible second impact. It is flung up, jerked up. An amber splash flicks in a fractional second from his head into the air. One notices the red roses spill from her lap as the President's body topples from sight.

That is all. But one who has seen the filmed action knows that though, technically, his pulse beat for another twenty minutes and some flow of blood went on, President Kennedy had ceased to be from the moment the second bullet entered his skull. He had died quickly, painlessly, perhaps even without consciousness of his own end. The faint recall of the President's wife a few days later may be the most accurate recapture of his sense of the moment — she remembered that, as he turned between shots, an expression of puzzlement, almost quizzical, crossed his face.

miss lonelyhearts of miss lonelyhearts

Nathanael West

Dear Miss Lonelyhearts of Miss Lonelyhearts —
  I am twenty-six years old and in the newspaper game. Life for
me is a desert empty of comfort. I cannot find pleasure in food, drink,
or women — nor do the arts give me joy any longer. The Leopard of
Discontent walks the streets of my city; the Lion of Discouragement
crouches outside the walls of my citadel. All is desolation and a
vexation of the spirit. I feel like hell. How can I believe, how can
I have faith in this day and age? Is it true that the greatest scientists
believe again in you?
  I read your column and like it very much. There you once wrote:
'When the salt has lost its savour, who shall savour it again?' Is the
answer: 'None but the Saviour?'
  Thanking you very much for a quick reply, I remain yours truly,
                                                    A regular Subscriber

section 3 affirmative
re-orientation

DifferENT
Style!
   Faulkner uses
long, complicated
sentences.

1) Character of the Father
2) What Happened?

point of view - 3rd person (impersonal)

3rd Person
1) Omniscence (meaning God) (tells what people are
   thinking, doing ect.)

* 2) limited omniscence - see into one person's
       mind

* this story is 3rd person limited omniscence

Conflict: Man versus himself (boy)

boy is the most important in the story. (He has the conflict)

attempts to concentrate on food instead of the trial.

fiction

meaning "in the family", "flood" "feathers".

barn burning

one, long sentence (hungry, little, illiterate)

William Faulkner

The store in which the Justice of the Peace's court was sitting smelled of cheese. The boy, crouched on his nail keg at the back of the crowded room, knew he smelled cheese, and more; from where he sat he could see the naked shelves close-packed with the solid, squat, dynamic shapes of tin cans whose labels his stomach read, not from the lettering which meant nothing to his mind but from the scarlet devils and the silver curve of fish — this, the cheese which he knew he smelled and the hermetic meat which his intestines believed he smelled coming in intermittent gusts momentary and brief between the other constant one, the smell and sense just a little of fear because mostly of despair and grief, the old fierce pull of blood. He could not see the table where the Justice sat and before which his father and his father's enemy (*our enemy* he thought in that despair; *ourn! mine and hisn both! He's my father!*) stood, but he could hear them, the two of them that is, because his father had said no word yet:

"But what proof have you, Mr. Harris?"

Boy is
70 years
old.
May 1896

"I told you. The hog got into my corn. I caught it up and sent it
back to him. He had no fence that would hold it. I told him so, warned
him. The next time I put the hog in my pen. When he came to get it
I gave him enough wire to patch up his pen. The next time I put the
hog up and kept it. I rode down to his house and saw the wire I gave
him still rolled on to the spool in his yard. I told him he could have
the hog when he paid me a dollar pound fee. That evening a nigger
came with the dollar and got the hog. He was a strange nigger. He
said, 'He say to tell you wood and hay kin burn.' I said, 'What?' 'That
whut he say to tell you,' the nigger said. 'Wood and hay kin burn.'
That night my barn burned. I got the stock out but I lost the barn."

"Where is the nigger? Have you got him?"

"He was a strange nigger, I tell you. I don't know what became of
him."

"But that's not proof. Don't you see that's not proof?"

"Get that boy up here. He knows." For a moment the boy thought
too that the man meant his older brother until Harris said, "Not him.
The little one. The boy," and, crouching, small for his age, small and
wiry like his father, in patched and faded jeans even too small for him,
with straight, uncombed, brown hair and eyes gray and wild as storm
scud, he saw the men between himself and the table part and become
a lane of grim faces, at the end of which he saw the Justice, a shabby,
collarless, graying man in spectacles, beckoning him. He felt no
floor under his bare feet; he seemed to walk beneath the palpable
weight of the grim turning faces. His father, stiff in his black Sunday
coat donned not for the trial but for the moving, did not even look at
him. *He aims for me to lie,* he thought, again with that frantic grief
and despair. *And I will have to do hit.*

"What's your name, boy?" the Justice said.

"Colonel Sartoris Snopes," the boy whispered.

"Hey?" the justice said. "Talk louder. Colonel Sartoris? I reckon
anybody named for Colonel Sartoris in this country can't help but
tell the truth, can they? The boy said nothing. *Enemy! Enemy!* he
thought; for a moment he could not even see, could not see that the
Justice's face was kindly nor discern that his voice was troubled when
he spoke to the man named Harris: "Do you want me to question this
boy?" But he could hear, and during those subsequent long seconds
while there was absolutely no sound in the crowded little room save
that of quiet and intent breathing it was as if he had swung outward
at the end of a grape vine, over a ravine, and at the top of the swing

had been caught in a prolonged instant of mesmerized gravity, weight-less in time.

"No!" Harris said violently, explosively. "Damnation! Send him out of here!" Now time, the fluid world, rushed beneath him again, through the smell of cheese and sealed meat, the fear and despair and the old grief of blood:

"This case is closed. I can't find against you, Snopes, but I can give you advice. Leave this country and don't come back to it."

His father spoke for the first time, his voice cold and harsh, level, without emphasis: "I aim to. I don't figure to stay in a country among people who . . ." he said something unprintable and vile, addressed to no one.

"That'll do," the Justice said. "Take your wagon and get out of this country before dark. Case dismissed."

His father turned, and he followed the stiff black coat, the wiry figure walking a little stiffly from where a Confederate provost's man's musket ball had taken him in the heel on a stolen horse thirty years ago, followed the two backs now, since his older brother had appeared from somewhere in the crowd, no taller than the father but thicker, chewing tobacco steadily, between the two lines of grim-faced men and out of the store and across the worn gallery and down the sagging steps and among the dogs and half-grown boys in the mild May dust, where as he passed a voice hissed:

"Barn burner!"

Again he could not see, whirling; there was a face in a red haze, moonlike, bigger than the full moon, the owner of it half again his size, he leaping in the red haze toward the face, feeling no blow, feel-ing no shock when his head struck the earth, scrabbling up and leap-ing again, feeling no blow this time either and tasting no blood, scrabbling up to see the other boy in full flight and himself already leap-ing into pursuit as his father's hand jerked him back, the harsh, cold voice speaking above him: "Go get in the wagon."

It stood in a grove of locusts and mullberries across the road. His two hulking sisters in their Sunday dresses and his mother and her sister in calico and sunbonnets were already in it, sitting on and among the sorry residue of the dozen and more movings which even the boy could remember — the battered stove, the broken beds and chairs, the clock inlaid with mother-of-pearl, which would not run, stopped at some fourteen minutes past two o'clock of a dead and forgotten day and time, which had been his mother's dowry. She was crying, though when she saw him she drew her sleeve across her face and began to descend from the wagon. "Get back," the father said.

"He's hurt. I got to get some water and wash his . . ."

"Get back in the wagon," his father said. He got in too, over the tail-gate. His father mounted to the seat where the older brother already sat and struck the gaunt mules two savage blows with the peeled willow, but without heat. It was not even sadistic; it was exactly that same quality which in later years would cause his descendants to over-run the engine before putting a motor car into motion, striking and reining back in the same movement. The wagon went on, the store with its quiet crowd of grimly watching men dropped behind; a curve in the road hid it. *Forever* he thought. *Maybe he's done satisfied now, now that he has* . . . stopping himself, not to say it aloud even to himself. His mother's hand touched his shoulder.

"Does hit hurt?" she said.

"Naw," he said. "Hit don't hurt. Lemme be."

"Can't you wipe some of the blood off before hit dries?"

"I'll wash to-night," he said. "Lemme be, I tell you."

The wagon went on. He did not know where they were going. None of them ever did or ever asked, because it was always somewhere, always a house of sorts waiting for them a day or two days or even three days away. Likely his father had already arranged to make a crop on another farm before he . . . Again he had to stop himself. He (the father) always did. There was something about his wolflike independence and even courage when the advantage was at least neutral which impressed strangers, as if they got from his latent ravening ferocity not so much a sense of dependability as a feeling that his ferocious conviction in the rightness of his own actions would be of advantage to all whose interest lay with his.

That night they camped, in a grove of oaks and beeches where a spring ran. The nights were still cool and they had a fire against it, of a rail lifted from a nearby fence and cut into lengths — a small fire, neat, niggard almost, a shrewd fire; such fires were his father's habit and custom always, even in freezing weather. Older, the boy might have remarked this and wondered why not a big one; why should not a man who had not only seen the waste and extravagance of war, but who had in his blood an inherent voracious prodigality with material not his own, have burned everything in sight? Then he might have gone a step farther and thought that that was the reason: that niggard blaze was the living fruit of nights passed during those four years in the woods hiding from all men, blue or gray, with his strings

wasteful

of horses (captured horses, he called them). And older still, he might have divined the true reason: that the element of fire spoke to some deep mainspring of his father's being, as the element of steel or of powder spoke to other men, as the one weapon for the preservation of integrity, else breath were not worth the breathing, and hence to be regarded with respect and used with discretion.

But he did not think this now and he had seen those same niggard blazes all his life. He merely ate his supper beside it and was already half asleep over his iron plate when his father called him, and once more he followed the stiff back, the stiff and ruthless limp, up the slope and on to the starlit road where, turning, he could see his father against the stars but without face or depth — a shape black, flat, and bloodless as though cut from tin in the iron folds of the frockcoat which had not been made for him, the voice harsh like tin and without heat like tin:

"You were fixing to tell them. You would have told him." He didn't answer. His father struck him with the flat of his hand on the side of the head, hard but without heat, exactly as he had struck the two mules at the store, exactly as he would strike either of them with any stick in order to kill a horse fly, his voice still without heat or anger: "You're getting to be a man. You got to learn. You got to learn to stick to your own blood or you ain't going to have any blood to stick to you. Do you think either of them, any man there this morning, would? Don't you know all they wanted was a chance to get at me because they knew I had them beat? Eh?" Later, twenty years later, he was to tell himself, "If I had said they wanted only truth, justice, he would have hit me again." But now he said nothing. He was not crying. He just stood there. "Answer me," his father said.

"Yes," he whispered. His father turned.

"Get on to bed. We'll be there to-morrow."

To-morrow they were there. In the early afternoon the wagon stopped before a paintless two-room house identical almost with the dozen others it had stopped before even in the boy's ten years, and again, as on the other dozen occasions, his mother and aunt got down and began to unload the wagon, although his two sisters and his father and brother had not moved.

"Likely hit ain't fitten for hawgs," one of the sisters said.

"Nevertheless, fit it will and you'll hog it and like it," his father said. "Get out of them chairs and help your Ma unload."

The two sisters got down, big, bovine, in a flutter of cheap ribbons; one of them drew from the jumbled wagon bed a battered lantern, the

other a worn broom. His father handed the reins to the older son and
began to climb stiffly over the wheel. "When they get unloaded, take
the team to the barn and feed them." Then he said, and at first the
boy thought he was still speaking to his brother: "Come with me."

"Me?" he said.

"Yes," his father said. "You."

"Abner," his mother said. His father paused and looked back —
the harsh level stare beneath the shaggy, graying, irascible brows.

"I reckon I'll have a word with the man that aims to begin tomorrow owning me body and soul for the next eight months."

They went back up the road. A week ago — or before last night,
that is — he would have asked where they were going, but not now.
His father had struck him before last night but never before had he
paused afterward to explain why; it was as if the blow and the following calm, outrageous voice still rang, repercussed, divulging nothing
to him save the terrible handicap of being young, the light weight of
his few years, just heavy enough to prevent his soaring free of the
world as it seemed to be ordered but not heavy enough to keep him
footed solid in it, to resist it and try to change the course of its events.

Presently he could see the grove of oaks and cedars and the other
flowering trees and shrubs where the house would be, though not the
house yet. They walked beside a fence massed with honeysuckle and
Cherokee roses and came to a gate swinging open between two brick
pillars, and now, beyond a sweep of drive, he saw the house for the
first time and at that instant he forgot his father and the terror and
despair both, and even when he remembered his father again (who
had not stopped) the terror and despair did not return. Because, for
all the twelve movings, they had sojourned until now in a poor
country, a land of small farms and fields and houses, and he had never
seen a house like this before. *Hit's big as a courthouse* he thought
quietly, with a surge of peace and joy whose reason he could not
have thought into words, being too young for that: *They are safe from
him. People whose lives are a part of this peace and dignity are beyond his touch, he no more to them than a buzzing wasp: capable of
stinging for a little moment but that's all; the spell of this peace and
dignity rendering even the barns and stable and cribs which belong to
it impervious to the puny flames he might contrive* . . . this, the peace
and joy, ebbing for an instant as he looked again at the stiff black
back, the stiff and implacable limp of the figure which was not
dwarfed by the house, for the reason that it had never looked big
anywhere and which now, against the serene columned backdrop, had

more than ever that impervious quality of something cut ruthlessly from tin, depthless, as though, sidewise to the sun, it would cast no shadow. Watching him, the boy remarked the absolutely undeviating course which his father held and saw the stiff foot come squarely down in a pile of fresh droppings where a horse had stood in the drive and which his father could have avoided by a simple change of stride. But it ebbed only for a moment, though he could not have thought this into words either, walking on in the spell of the house, which he could even want but without envy, without sorrow, certainly never with that ravening and jealous rage which unknown to him walked in the ironlike black coat before him: *Maybe he will feel it too. Maybe it will even change him now from what maybe he couldn't help but be.*

They crossed the portico. Now he could hear his father's stiff foot as it came down on the boards with clocklike finality, a sound out of all proportion to the displacement of the body it bore and which was not dwarfed either by the white door before it, as though it had attained to a sort of vicious and ravening minimum not to be dwarfed by anything — the flat, wide, black hat, the formal coat of broadcloth which had once been black but which had now that friction-glazed greenish cast of the bodies of old house flies, the lifted sleeve which was too large, the lifted hand like a curled claw. The door opened so promptly that the boy knew the Negro must have been watching them all the time, an old man with neat grizzled hair, in a linen jacket, who stood barring the door with his body, saying, "Wipe yo foots, white man, fo you come in here. Major ain't home nohow."

"Get out of my way, nigger," his father said, without heat too, flinging the door back and the Negro also and entering, his hat still on his head. And now the boy saw the prints of the stiff foot on the doorjamb and saw them appear on the pale rug behind the machine-like deliberation of the foot which seemed to bear (or transmit) twice the weight which the body compassed. The Negro was shouting "Miss Lula! Miss Lula!" somewhere behind them, then the boy, deluged as though by a warm wave by a suave turn of carpeted stair and a pendant glitter of chandeliers and a mute gleam of gold frames, heard the swift feet and saw her too, a lady — perhaps he had never seen her like before either — in a gray, smooth gown with lace at the throat and an apron tied at the waist and the sleeves turned back, wiping cake or biscuit dough from her hands with a towel as she came up the hall, looking not at his father at all but at the tracks on the blond rug with an expression of incredulous amazement.

"I tried," the Negro cried. "I tole him to . . ."

"Will you please go away?" she said in a shaking voice. "Major de Spain is not at home. Will you please go away?"

His father had not spoken again. He did not speak again. He did not even look at her. He just stood stiff in the center of the rug, in his hat, the shaggy iron-gray brows twitching slightly above the pebble-colored eyes as he appeared to examine the house with brief delibera-tion. Then with the same deliberation he turned; the boy watched him pivot on the good leg and saw the stiff foot drag round the arc of the turning, leaving a final long and fading smear. His father never looked at it, he never once looked down at the rug. The Negro held the door. It closed behind them, upon the hysteric and indistinguishable woman-wail. His father stopped at the top of the steps and scraped his boot clean on the edge of it. At the gate he stopped again. He stood for a moment, planted stiffly on the stiff foot, looking back at the house. "Pretty and white, ain't it?" he said. "That's sweat. Nigger sweat. Maybe it ain't white enough yet to suit him. Maybe he wants to mix some white sweat with it."

Two hours later the boy was chopping wood behind the house within which his mother and aunt and the two sisters (the mother and aunt, not the two girls, he knew that; even at this distance and muffled by walls the flat loud voices of the two girls emanated an incorrigible idle inertia) were setting up the stove to prepare a meal, when he heard the hooves and saw the linen-clad man on a fine sorrel mare, whom he recognized even before he saw the rolled rug in front of the Negro youth following on a fat bay carriage horse — a suffused, angry face vanishing, still at full gallop, beyond the corner of the house where his father and brother were sitting in the two tilted chairs; and a moment later, almost before he could have put the axe down, he heard the hooves again and watched the sorrel mare go back out of the yard, already galloping again. Then his father began to shout one of the sisters' names, who presently emerged backward from the kitchen door dragging the rolled rug along the ground by one end while the other sister walked behind it.

"If you ain't going to tote, go on and set up the wash pot," the first said.

"You, Sarty!" the second shouted. "Set up the wash pot!" His father appeared at the door, framed against that shabbiness, as he had been against that other bland perfection, impervious to either, the mother's anxious face at his shoulder.

"Go on," the father said. "Pick it up." The two sisters stooped, broad, lethargic; stooping, they presented an incredible expanse of pale cloth and a flutter of tawdry ribbons.

"If I thought enough of a rug to have to git hit all the way from France I wouldn't keep hit where folks coming in would have to tromp on hit," the first said. They raised the rug.

"Abner," the mother said. "Let me do it."

"You go back and git dinner," his father said. "I'll tend to this."

From the woodpile through the rest of the afternoon the boy watched them, the rug spread flat in the dust beside the bubbling wash-pot, the two sisters stooping over it with that profound and lethargic reluctance, while the father stood over them in turn, implacable and grim, driving them though never raising his voice again. He could smell the harsh homemade lye they were using; he saw his mother come to the door once and look toward them with an expression not anxious now but very like despair; he saw his father turn, and he fell to with the axe and saw from the corner of his eye his father raise from the ground a flattish fragment of field stone and examine it and return to the pot, and this time his mother actually spoke: "Abner. Abner. Please don't. Please, Abner."

Then he was done too. It was dusk; the whippoorwills had already begun. He could smell coffee from the room where they would presently eat the cold food remaining from the mid-afternoon meal, though when he entered the house he realized they were having coffee again probably because there was a fire on the hearth, before which the rug now lay spread over the backs of the two chairs. The tracks of his father's foot were gone. Where they had been were now long, water-cloudy scorifications resembling the sporadic course of a lilliputian mowing machine.

It still hung there while they ate the cold food and then went to bed, scattered without order or claim up and down the two rooms, his mother in one bed, where his father would later lie, the older brother in the other, himself, the aunt, and the two sisters on pallets on the floor. But his father was not in bed yet. The last thing the boy remembered was the depthless, harsh silhouette of the hat and coat bending over the rug and it seemed to him that he had not even closed his eyes when the silhouette was standing over him, the fire almost dead behind it, the stiff foot prodding him awake. "Catch up the mule," his father said.

When he returned with the mule his father was standing in the black door, the rolled rug over his shoulder. "Ain't you going to ride?" he said.

italics (handwritten)

"No. Give me your foot."

He bent his knee into his father's hand, the wiry, surprising power flowed smoothly, rising, he rising with it, on to the mule's bare back (they had owned a saddle once; the boy could remember it though not when or where) and with the same effortlessness his father swung the rug up in front of him. Now in the starlight they retraced the afternoon's path, up the dusty road rife with honeysuckle, through the gate and up the black tunnel of the drive to the lightless house, where he sat on the mule and felt the rough warp of the rug drag across his thighs and vanish.

"Don't you want me to help?" he whispered. His father did not answer and now he heard again that stiff foot striking the hollow portico with that wooden and clocklike deliberation, that outrageous overstatement of the weight it carried. The rug, hunched, not flung (the boy could tell that even in the darkness) from his father's shoulder struck the angle of wall and floor with a sound unbelievably loud, thunderous, then the foot again, unhurried and enormous; a light came on in the house and the boy sat, tense, breathing steadily and quietly and just a little fast, though the foot itself did not increase its beat at all, descending the steps now; now the boy could see him.

"Don't you want to ride now?" he whispered. "We kin both ride now," the light within the house altering now, flaring up and sinking. *He's coming down the stairs now,* he thought. He had already ridden the mule up beside the horse block; presently his father was up behind him and he doubled the reins over and slashed the mule across the neck, but before the animal could begin to trot the hard, thin arm came round him, the hard, knotted hand jerking the mule back to a walk.

refuse to ride (handwritten, left margin)

In the first red rays of the sun they were in the lot, putting plow gear on the mules. This time the sorrel mare was in the lot before he heard it at all, the rider collarless and even bareheaded, trembling, speaking in a shaking voice as the woman in the house had done, his father merely looking up once before stooping again to the hame he was buckling, so that the man on the mare spoke to his stooping back:

"You must realize you have ruined that rug. Wasn't there anybody here, any of your women . . ." he ceased, shaking, the boy watching him, the older brother leaning now in the stable door, chewing, blinking slowly and steadily at nothing apparently. "It cost a hundred dollars. But you never had a hundred dollars. You never will. So I'm going to charge you twenty bushels of corn against your crop. I'll add

coat — a black
up everytime a father comes
— important something
his mother did the work.

it in your contract and when you come to the commissary you can sign it. That won't keep Mrs. de Spain quiet but maybe it will teach you to wipe your feet off before you enter her house again."

Then he was gone. The boy looked at his father, who still had not spoken or even looked up again, who was now adjusting the logger-head in the hame.

"Pap," he said. His father looked at him — the inscrutable face, the shaggy brows beneath which the gray eyes glinted coldly. Suddenly the boy went toward him, fast, stopping as suddenly. "You done the best you could!" he cried. "If he wanted hit done different why didn't he wait and tell you how? He won't git no twenty bushels! He won't git none! We'll gether hit and hide hit! I kin watch . . ."

"Did you put the cutter back in that straight stock like I told you?"

"No, sir," he said.

"Then go do it."

That was Wednesday. During the rest of the week he worked steadily, at what was within his scope and some which was beyond it, with an industry that did not need to be driven nor even com-manded twice; he had this from his mother, with the difference that some at least of what he did he liked to do, such as splitting wood with the half-size axe which his mother and aunt had earned, or saved money somehow, to present him with at Christmas. In company with the two older women (and on one afternoon, even one of the sisters), he built pens for the shoat and cow which were a part of his father's contract with the landlord, and one afternoon, his father being absent, gone somewhere on one of the mules, he went to the field.

They were running a middle buster now, his brother holding the plow straight while he handled the reins, and walking beside the straining mule, the rich black soil shearing cool and damp against his bare ankles, he thought *Maybe this is the end of it. Maybe even that twenty bushels that seems hard to have to pay for just a rug will be a cheap price for him to stop forever and always from being what he used to be;* thinking, dreaming now, so that his brother had to speak sharply to him to mind the mule: *Maybe he even won't collect the twenty bushels. Maybe it will all add up and balance and vanish — corn, rug, fire; the terror and grief, the being pulled two ways like between two teams of horses — gone, done with for ever and ever.*

Then it was Saturday; he looked up from beneath the mule he was harnessing and saw his father in the black coat and hat. "Not that," his father said. "The wagon gear." And then, two hours later, sitting in the wagon bed behind his father and brother on the seat, the wagon

bravery

accomplished a final curve, and he saw the weathered paintless store with its tattered tobacco and patent-medicine posters and the tethered wagons and saddle animals below the gallery. He mounted the gnawed steps behind his father and brother, and there again was the lane of quiet, watching faces for the three of them to walk through. He saw the man in spectacles sitting at the plank table and he did not need to be told this was a Justice of the Peace; he sent one glare of fierce, exultant, partisan defiance at the man in collar and cravat now, whom he had seen but twice before in his life, and that on a galloping horse, who now wore on his face an expression not of rage but of amazed unbelief which the boy could not have known was at the incredible circumstance of being sued by one of his own tenants, and came and stood against his father and cried at the Justice: "He ain't done it! He ain't burnt . . ."

"Go back to the wagon," his father said.

"Burnt?" the Justice said. "Do I understand this rug was burned too?"

"Does anybody here claim it was?" his father said. "Go back to the wagon." But he did not, he merely retreated to the rear of the room, crowded as that other had been, but not to sit down this time, instead, to stand pressing among the motionless bodies, listening to the voices:

"And you claim twenty bushels of corn is too high for the damage you did to the rug?"

"He brought the rug to me and said he wanted the tracks washed out of it. I washed the tracks out and took the rug back to him."

"But you didn't carry the rug back to him in the same condition it was in before you made the tracks on it."

His father did not answer, and now for perhaps half a minute there was no sound at all save that of breathing, the faint, steady suspiration of complete and intent listening.

"You decline to answer that, Mr. Snopes?" Again his father did not answer. "I'm going to find against you, Mr. Snopes. I'm going to find that you were responsible for the injury to Major de Spain's rug and hold you liable for it. But twenty bushels of corn seems a little high for a man in your circumstances to have to pay. Major de Spain claims it cost a hundred dollars. October corn will be worth about fifty cents. I figure that if Major de Spain can stand a ninety-five dollar loss on something he paid cash for, you can stand a five-dollar loss you haven't earned yet. I hold you in damages to Major de Spain to the amount of ten bushels of corn over and above your contract with him, to be paid to him out of your crop at gathering time. Court adjourned."

It had taken no time hardly, the morning was but half begun. He thought they would return home and perhaps back to the field, since they were late, far behind all other farmers. But instead his father passed on behind the wagon, merely indicating with his hand for the older brother to follow with it, and crossed the road toward the black-smith shop opposite, pressing on after his father, overtaking him, speaking, whispering up at the harsh, calm face beneath the weathered hat: "He won't git no ten bushels neither. He won't git one. We'll . . ." until his father glanced for an instant down at him, the face absolutely calm, the grizzled eyebrows tangled above the cold eyes, the voice almost pleasant, almost gentle:

"You think so? Well, we'll wait till October anyway."

The matter of the wagon — the setting of a spoke or two and the tightening of the tires — did not take long either, the business of the tires accomplished by driving the wagon into the spring branch behind the shop and letting it stand there, the mules nuzzling into the water from time to time, and the boy on the seat with the idle reins, looking up the slope and through the sooty tunnel of the shed where the slow hammer rang and where his father sat on an upended cypress bolt, easily, either talking or listening, still sitting there when the boy brought the dripping wagon up out of the branch and halted it before the door.

"Take them on to the shade and hitch," his father said. He did so and returned. His father and the smith and a third man squatting on his heels inside the door were talking, about crops and animals; the boy, squatting too in the ammoniac dust and hoof-parings and scales of rust, heard his father tell a long and unhurried story out of the time before the birth of the older brother even when he had been a profes-sional horsetrader. And then his father came up beside him where he stood before a tattered last year's circus poster on the other side of the store, gazing rapt and quiet at the scarlet horses, the incredible poisings and convolutions of tulle and tights and the painted leers of come-dians, and said, "It's time to eat."

But not at home. Squatting beside his brother against the front wall, he watched his father emerge from the store and produce from a paper sack a segment of cheese and divide it carefully and deliberately into three with his pocket knife and produce crackers from the same sack. They all three squatted on the gallery and ate, slowly, without talking; then in the store again, they drank from a tin dipper tepid water smelling of the cedar bucket and of living beech trees. And still they did not go home. It was a horse lot this time, a tall rail fence upon and along which men stood and sat and out of which one by one horses were led, to be walked and trotted and then cantered back and forth along the road while the slow swapping and buying went on and the sun began to slant westward, they — the three of them — watching and listening, the older brother with his muddy eyes and his steady, inevitable tobacco, the father commenting now and then on certain of the animals, to no one in particular.

It was after sundown when they reached home. They ate supper by lamplight, then, sitting on the doorstep, the boy watched the night fully accomplish, listening to the whippoorwills and the frogs, when he heard his mother's voice: "Abner! No! No! Oh, God. Oh, God. Abner!" and he rose, whirled, and saw the altered light through the door where a candle stub now burned in a bottleneck on the table and his father, still in the hat and coat, at once formal and burlesque as though dressed carefully for some shabby and ceremonial violence, emptying the reservoir of the lamp back into the five-gallon kerosene can from which it had been filled, while the mother tugged at his arm until he shifted the lamp to the other hand and flung her back, not savagely or viciously, just hard, into the wall, her hands flung out against the wall for balance, her mouth open and in her face the same quality of hopeless despair as had been in her voice. Then his father saw him standing in the door.

"Go to the barn and get that can of oil we were oiling the wagon with," he said. The boy did not move. Then he could speak.

"What . . ." he cried. "What are you . . ."

"Go get that oil," his father said. "Go."

Then he was moving, running, outside the house, toward the stable: this the old habit, the old blood which he had not been permitted to choose for himself, which had been bequeathed him willy nilly and which had run for so long (and who knew where, battening on what of outrage and savagery and lust) before it came to him. *I could keep on,* he thought. *I could run on and on and never look back, never need to see his face again. Only I can't. I can't,* the rusted can in his hand now, the liquid sploshing in it as he ran back to the house and into it, into the sound of his mother's weeping in the next room, and handed the can to his father.

"Ain't you going to even send a nigger?" he cried. "At least you sent a nigger before!"

This time his father didn't strike him. The hand came even faster *stick to his own kind.*

than the blow had, the same hand which had set the can on the table with almost excruciating care flashing from the can toward him too quick for him to follow it, gripping him by the back of his shirt and on to tiptoe before he had seen it quit the can, the face stooping at him in breathless and frozen ferocity, the cold, dead voice speaking over him to the older brother who leaned against the table, chewing with that steady, curious, sidewise motion of cows.

"Empty the can into the big one and go on. I'll catch up with you."

"Better tie him up to the bedpost," the brother said.

"Do like I told you," the father said. Then the boy was moving, his bunched shirt and the hard, bony hand between his shoulder-blades, his toes just touching the floor, across the room and into the other one, past the sisters sitting with spread heavy thighs in the two chairs over the cold hearth, and to where his mother and aunt sat side by side on the bed, the aunt's arms about his mother's shoulders.

"Hold him," the father said. The aunt made a startled movement. "Not you," the father said. "Lennie. Take hold of him. I want to see you do it." His mother took him by the wrist. "You'll hold him better than that. If he gets loose don't you know what he is going to do? He will go up yonder." He jerked his head toward the road. "Maybe I'd better tie him."

"I'll hold him," his mother whispered.

"See you do then." Then his father was gone, the stiff foot heavy and measured upon the boards, ceasing at last.

Then he began to struggle. His mother caught him in both arms, he jerking and wrenching at them. He would be stronger in the end, he knew that. But he had no time to wait for it. "Lemme go!" he cried. "I don't want to have to hit you!"

"Let him go!" the aunt said. "If he don't go, before God, I am going up there myself!"

"Don't you see I can't?" his mother cried. "Sarty! Sarty! No! No! Help me, Lizzie!"

Then he was free. His aunt grasped at him but it was too late. He whirled, running, his mother stumbled forward onto her knees behind him, crying to the nearer sister: "Catch him, Net! Catch him!" But that was too late too, the sister (the sisters were twins, born at the same time, yet either of them now gave the impression of being, encompassing as much living meat and volume and weight as any other two of the family) not yet having begun to rise from the chair, her head, face, alone merely turned, presenting to him in the flying instant an astonishing expanse of young female features untroubled by any surprise even, wearing only an expression of bovine interest. Then he was out of the room, out of the house, in the mild dust of the starlit road and the heavy rifeness of honeysuckle, the pale ribbon unspooling with terrific slowness under his running feet, reaching the gate at last and turning in, running, his heart and lungs drumming, on up the drive toward the lighted house, the lighted door. He did not knock, he burst in, sobbing for breath, incapable for the moment of speech; he saw the astonished face of the Negro in the linen jacket without knowing when the Negro had appeared.

"De Spain!" he cried, panted. "Where's . . ." then he saw the white man too emerging from a white door down the hall. "Barn!" he cried. "Barn!"

"What?" the white man said. "Barn?"

"Yes!" the boy cried. "Barn!"

"Catch him!" the white man shouted.

But it was too late this time too. The Negro grasped his shirt, but the entire sleeve, rotten with washing, carried away, and he was out that door too and in the drive again, and had actually never ceased to run even while he was screaming into the white man's face.

Behind him the white man was shouting, "My horse! Fetch my horse!" and he thought for an instant of cutting across the park and climbing the fence into the road, but he did not know the park nor how high the vine-massed fence might be and he dared not risk it. So he ran on down the drive, blood and breath roaring; presently he was in the road again though he could not see it. He could not hear either: the galloping mare was almost upon him before he heard her, and even then he held his course, as if the very urgency of his wild grief and need must in a moment more find him wings, waiting until the ultimate instant to hurl himself aside and into the weed-choked road-side ditch as the horse thundered past and on, for an instant in furious silhouette against the stars, the tranquil early summer night sky which, even before the shape of the horse and rider vanished, stained abruptly and violently upward: a long, swirling roar incredible and soundless, blotting the stars, and he springing up and into the road again, run-ning again, knowing it was too late yet still running even after he heard the shot and, an instant later, two shots, pausing now without knowing he had ceased to run, crying "Pap! Pap!", running again before he knew he had begun to run, stumbling, tripping over some-thing and scrabbling up again without ceasing to run, looking back-ward over his shoulder at the glare as he got up, running on among the invisible trees, panting, sobbing, "Father! Father!"

At midnight he was sitting on the crest of a hill. He did not know it was midnight and he did not know how far he had come. But there was no glare behind him now and he sat now, his back toward what he had called home for four days anyhow, his face toward the dark woods which he would enter when breath was strong again, small, shaking steadily in the chill darkness, hugging himself into the remainder of his thin, rotten shirt, the grief and despair now no longer terror and fear but just grief and despair. *Father. My father,* he thought. "He was brave!" he cried suddenly, aloud but not loud, no more than a whisper: "He was! He was in the war! He was in Colonel Sartoris' cav'ry!" not knowing that his father had gone to that war a private in the fine old European sense, wearing no uniform, admitting the authority of and giving fidelity to no man or army or flag, going to war as Malbrouck himself did: for booty — it meant nothing and less than nothing to him if it were enemy booty or his own.

The slow constellations wheeled on. It would be dawn and then sun-up after a while and he would be hungry. But that would be tomorrow and now he was only cold, and walking would cure that. His breathing was easier now and he decided to get up and go on, and then he found that he had been asleep because he knew it was almost dawn, the night almost over. He could tell that from the whippoorwills. They were everywhere now among the dark trees below him, constant and inflectioned and ceaseless, so that, as the instant for giving over to the day birds drew nearer and nearer, there was no interval at all between them. He got up. He was a little stiff, but walking would cure that too as it would the cold, and soon there would be the sun. He went on down the hill, toward the dark woods within which the liquid silver voices of the birds called unceasing — the rapid and urgent beating of the urgent and quiring heart of the late spring night. He did not look back.

report on the barnhouse effect

Kurt Vonnegut, Jr.

Let me begin by saying that I don't know any more about where Professor Arthur Barnhouse is hiding than anyone else does. Save for one short, enigmatic message left in my mail box on Christmas Eve, I have not heard from him since his disappearance a year and a half ago.

What's more, readers of this article will be disappointed if they expect to learn how *they* can bring about the so-called "Barnhouse Effect." If I were able and willing to give away that secret, I would certainly be something more important than a psychology instructor.

I have been urged to write this report because I did research under the professor's direction and because I was the first to learn of his astonishing discovery. But while I was his student I was never entrusted with knowledge of how the mental forces could be released and directed. He was unwilling to trust anyone with that information.

I would like to point out that the term "Barnhouse Effect" is a creation of the popular press, and was never used by Professor Barnhouse. The name he chose for the phenomenon was "*dynamopsychism,*" or *force of the mind.*

I cannot believe that there is a civilized person yet to be convinced that such a force exists, what with its destructive effects on display in every national capital. I think humanity has always had an inkling that this sort of force does exist. It has been common knowledge that some people are luckier than others with inanimate objects like dice. What Professor Barnhouse did was to show that such "luck" was a measurable force, which in his case could be enormous.

By my calculations, the professor was about fifty-five times more powerful than a Nagasaki-type atomic bomb at the time he went into hiding. He was not bluffing when, on the eve of "Operation Brainstorm," he told General Honus Barker: "Sitting here at the dinner table, I'm pretty sure I can flatten anything on earth — from Joe Louis to the Great Wall of China."

There is an understandable tendency to look upon Professor Barnhouse as a supernatural visitation. The First Church of Barnhouse in Los Angeles has a congregation numbering in the thousands. He is

Reprinted with permission of the author.

godlike in neither appearance nor intellect. The man who disarms
the world is single, shorter than the average American male, stout,
and averse to exercise. His I.Q. is 143, which is good but certainly not
sensational. He is quite mortal, about to celebrate his fortieth birthday,
and in good health. If he is alone now, the isolation won't bother him
too much. He was quiet and shy when I knew him, and seemed to
find more companionship in books and music than in his associations
at the college.

Neither he nor his powers fall outside the sphere of Nature. His
dynamopsychic radiations are subject to many known physical laws
that apply in the field of radio. Hardly a person has not now heard
the snarl of "Barnhouse static" on his home receiver. Contrary to what
one might expect, the radiations are affected by sunspots and variations in the ionosphere.

However, his radiations differ from ordinary broadcast waves in
several important ways. Their total energy can be brought to bear on
any single point the professor chooses, and that energy is undiminished
by distance. As a weapon, then, dynamopsychism has an impressive advantage over bacteria and atomic bombs, beyond the fact that it costs
nothing to use: it enables the professor to single out critical individuals
and objects instead of slaughtering whole populations in the process of
maintaining international equilibrium.

As General Honus Barker told the House Military Affairs Committee: "Until someone finds Barnhouse, there is no defense against
the Barnhouse Effect." Efforts to "jam" or block the radiations have
failed. Premier Slezak could have saved himself the fantastic expense
of his "Barnhouseproof" shelter. Despite the shelter's twelve-foot-
thick lead armor, the premier has been floored twice while in it.

There is talk of screening the population for men potentially as
powerful dynamopsychically as the professor. Senator Warren Foust
demanded funds for this purpose last month, with the passionate
declaration: "He who rules the Barnhouse Effect rules the world!"
Commissar Kropotnik said much the same thing, so another costly
armaments race, with a new twist, has begun.

This race at least has its comical aspects. The world's best gamblers
are being coddled by governments like so many nuclear physicists.
There may be several hundred persons with dynamopsychic talent
on earth, myself included, but, without knowledge of the professor's
technique, they can never be anything but dice-table despots. With the
secret, it would probably take them ten years to become dangerous

weapons. It took the professor that long. He who rules the Barnhouse Effect is Barnhouse and will be for some time.

Popularly, the "Age of Barnhouse" is said to have begun a year and a half ago, on the day of Operation Brainstorm. That was when dynamopsychism became significant politically. Actually, the phenomenon was discovered in May, 1942, shortly after the professor turned down a direct commission in the Army and enlisted as an artillery private. Like X-rays and vulcanized rubber, dynamopsychism was discovered by accident.

From time to time Private Barnhouse was invited to take part in games of chance by his barrack mates. He knew nothing about the games, and usually begged off. But one evening, out of social grace, he agreed to shoot craps. It was a terrible or wonderful thing that he played, depending upon whether or not you like the world as it now is.

"Shoot sevens, Pop," someone said.

So "Pop" shot sevens — ten in a row to bankrupt the barracks. He retired to his bunk and, as a mathematical exercise, calculated the odds against his feat on the back of a laundry slip. His chances of doing it, he found, were one in almost ten million! Bewildered, he borrowed a pair of dice from the man in the bunk next to his. He tried to roll sevens again, but got only the usual assortment of numbers. He lay back for a moment, then resumed his toying with the dice. He rolled ten more sevens in a row.

He might have dismissed the phenomenon with a low whistle. But the professor instead mulled over the circumstances surrounding his two lucky streaks. There was one single factor in common: on both occasions, *the same thought train had flashed through his mind just before he threw the dice.* It was that thought train which aligned the professor's brain cells into what has since become the most powerful weapon on earth.

The soldier in the next bunk gave dynamopsychism its first token of respect. In an understatement certain to bring wry smiles to the faces of the world's dejected demagogues, the soldier said, "You're hotter'n a two-dollar pistol, Pop." Professor Barnhouse was all of that. The dice that did his bidding weighed but a few grams, so the forces involved were minute; but the unmistakable fact that there were such forces was earth-shaking.

Professional caution kept him from revealing his discovery immediately. He wanted more facts and a body of theory to go with them. Later, when the atomic bomb was dropped on Hiroshima, it was fear that made him hold his peace. At no time were his experiments, as Premier Slezak called them, "a bourgeois plot to shackle the true democracies of the world." The professor didn't know where they were leading.

In time, he came to recognize another startling feature of dynamopsychism: *its strength increased with use.* Within six months, he was able to govern dice thrown by men the length of a barracks distant. By the time of his discharge in 1945, he could knock bricks loose from chimneys three miles away.

Charges that Professor Barnhouse could have won the last war in a minute, but did not care to do so, are perfectly senseless. When the war ended, he had the range and power of a 37-millimeter cannon, perhaps — certainly no more. His dynamopsychic powers graduated from the small-arms class only after his discharge and return to Wyandotte College.

I enrolled in the Wyandotte Graduate School two years after the professor had rejoined the faculty. By chance, he was assigned as my thesis adviser. I was unhappy about the assignment, for the professor was, in the eyes of both colleagues and students, a somewhat ridiculous figure. He missed classes or had lapses of memory during lectures. When I arrived, in fact, his shortcomings had passed from the ridiculous to the intolerable.

"We're assigning you to Barnhouse as a sort of temporary thing," the dean of social studies told me. He looked apologetic and perplexed. "Brilliant man, Barnhouse, I guess. Difficult to know since his return, perhaps, but his work before the war brought a great deal of credit to our little school."

When I reported to the professor's laboratory for the first time, what I saw was more distressing than the gossip. Every surface in the room was covered with dust; books and apparatus had not been disturbed for months. The professor sat napping at his desk when I entered. The only signs of recent activity were three overflowing ash trays, a pair of scissors, and a morning paper with several items clipped from its front page.

As he raised his head to look at me, I saw that his eyes were clouded with fatigue. "Hi," he said, "just can't seem to get my sleeping done at night." He lighted a cigarette, his hands trembling slightly. "You the young man I'm supposed to help with a thesis?"

"Yes, sir," I said. In minutes he converted my misgivings to alarm.

"You an overseas veteran?" he asked.

"Yes, sir."

"Not much left over there, is there?" He frowned. "Enjoy the last war?"

"No, sir."

"Look like another war to you?"

"Kind of, sir."

"What can be done about it?"

I shrugged. "Looks pretty hopeless."

He peered at me intently. "Know anything about international law, the U.N., and all that?"

"Only what I pick up from the papers."

"Same here," he sighed. He showed me a fat scrapbook packed with newspaper clippings. "Never used to pay any attention to international politics. Now I study them the way I used to study rats in mazes. Everybody tells me the same thing — 'Looks hopeless.' "

"Nothing short of a miracle — " I began.

"Believe in magic?" he asked sharply. The professor fished two dice from his vest pocket. "I will try to roll twos," he said. He rolled twos three time in a row. "One chance in about 47,000 of that happening. There's a miracle for you." He beamed for an instant, then brought the interview to an end, remarking that he had a class which had begun ten minutes ago.

He was not quick to take me into his confidence, and he said no more about his trick with the dice. I assumed they were loaded, and forgot about them. He set me the task of watching male rats cross electrified metal strips to get to food or female rats — an experiment that had been done to everyone's satisfaction in the 1930s. As though the pointlessness of my work were not bad enough, the professor annoyed me further with irrelevant questions. His favorites were: "Think we should have dropped the atomic bomb on Hiroshima?" and "Think every new piece of scientific information is a good thing for humanity?"

However, I did not feel put upon for long. "Give those poor animals a holiday," he said one morning, after I had been with him only a month. "I wish you'd help me look into a more interesting problem — namely, my sanity."

I returned the rats to their cages.

"What you must do is simple," he said, speaking softly. "Watch the inkwell on my desk. If you see nothing happen to it, say so, and I'll go quietly — relieved, I might add — to the nearest sanitarium."

I nodded uncertainly.

He locked the laboratory door and drew the blinds, so that we were in twilight for a moment. "I'm odd, I know," he said. "It's fear of myself that's made me odd."

"I've found you somewhat eccentric, perhaps, but certainly not — "

"If nothing happens to that inkwell, 'crazy as a bedbug' is the only description of me that will do," he interrupted, turning on the overhead lights. His eyes narrowed. "To give you an idea of how crazy, I'll tell you what's been running through my mind when I should have been sleeping. I think maybe I can save the world. I think maybe I can make every nation a *have* nation, and do away with war for good. I think maybe I can clear roads through jungles, irrigate deserts, build dams overnight."

"Yes, sir."

"Watch the inkwell!"

Dutifully and fearfully I watched. A high-pitched humming seemed to come from the inkwell; then it began to vibrate alarmingly, and finally to bound about the top of the desk, making two noisy circuits. It stopped, hummed again, glowed red, then popped in splinters with a blue-green flash.

Perhaps my hair stood on end. The professor laughed gently. "Magnets?" I managed to say at last.

"Wish to Heaven it were magnets," he murmured. It was then that he told me of dynamopsychism. He knew only that there was such a force; he could not explain it. "It's me and me alone — and it's awful."

"I'd say it was amazing and wonderful!" I cried.

"If all I could do was make inkwells dance, I'd be tickled silly with the whole business." He shrugged disconsolately. "But I'm no toy, my boy. If you like, we can drive around the neighborhood, and I'll show you what I mean." He told me about pulverized boulders, shattered oaks and abandoned farm buildings demolished within a fifty-mile radius of the campus. "Did every bit of it sitting right here, just thinking — not even thinking hard."

He scratched his head nervously. "I have never dared to concentrate as hard as I can for fear of the damage I might do. I'm to the point where a mere whim is a blockbuster." There was a depressing pause. "Up until a few days ago, I've thought it best to keep my secret for fear of what use it might be put to," he continued. "Now I realize that I haven't any more right to it than a man has a right to own an atomic bomb."

He fumbled through a heap of papers. "This says about all that needs to be said, I think." He handed me a draft of a letter to the Secretary of State.

> *Dear Sir:*
>
> *I have discovered a new force which costs nothing to use, and which is probably more important than atomic energy. I should like to see it used most effectively in the cause of peace, and am, therefore, requesting your advice as to how this might best be done.*
>
>

Yours truly,

A. Barnhouse.

"I have no idea what will happen next," said the professor.

There followed three months of perpetual nightmare, wherein the nation's political and military great came at all hours to watch the professor's trick with fascination.

We were quatered in an old mansion near Charlottesville, Virginia, to which we had been whisked five days after the letter was mailed. Surrounded by barbed wire and twenty guards, we were labeled "Project Wishing Well," and were classified as Top Secret.

For companionship we had General Honus Barker and the State Department's William K. Cuthrell. For the professor's talk of peace-through-plenty they had indulgent smiles and much discourse on practical measures and realistic thinking. So treated, the professor, who had at first been almost meek, progressed in a matter of weeks toward stubbornness.

He had agreed to reveal the thought train by means of which he aligned his mind into a dynamopsychic transmitter. But, under Cuthrell's and Barker's nagging to do so, he began to hedge. At first he declared that the information could be passed on simply by word of mouth. Later he said that it would have to be written up in a long report. Finally, at dinner one night, just after General Barker had read the secret orders for Operation Brainstorm, the professor announced, "The report may take as long as five years to write." He looked fiercely at the general. "Maybe twenty."

The dismay occasioned by this flat announcement was offset somewhat by the exciting anticipation of Operation Brainstorm. The general was in a holiday mood. "The target ships are on their way to the Caroline Islands at this very moment," he declared ecstatically. "One hundred and twenty of them! At the same time, ten V-2s are being readied for firing in New Mexico, and fifty radio-controlled jet bombers are being equipped for a mock attack on the Aleutians. Just think of it!" Happily he reviewed his orders. "At exactly 1100 hours next Wednesday, I will give you the order to *concentrate;* and you, professor, will think as hard as you can about sinking the target ships, destroying the V-2s before they hit the ground, and knocking down the bombers before they reach the Aleutians! Think you can handle it?"

The professor turned gray and closed his eyes. "As I told you before, my friend, I don't know what I can do." He added bitterly, "As for this Operation Brainstorm, I was never consulted about it, and it strikes me as childish and insanely expensive."

General Barker bridled. "Sir," he said, "your field is psychology, and I wouldn't presume to give you advice in that field. Mine is national defense. I have had thirty years of experience and success, Professor, and I'll ask you not to criticize my judgment."

The professor appealed to Mr. Cuthrell. "Look," he pleaded, "isn't it war and military matters we're all trying to get rid of? Wouldn't it be a whole lot more significant and lots cheaper for me to try moving cloud masses into drought areas, and things like that? I admit I know next to nothing about international politics, but it seems reasonable to suppose that nobody would want to fight wars if there were enough of everything to go around. Mr. Cuthrell, I'd like to try running generators where there isn't any coal or water power, irrigating deserts, and so on. Why, you could figure out what each country needs to make the most of its resources, and I could give it to them without costing American taxpayers a penny."

"Eternal vigilance is the price of freedom," said the general heavily.

Mr. Cuthrell threw the general a look of mild distaste. "Unfortunately, the general is right in his own way," he said. "I wish to Heaven the world were ready for ideals like yours, but it simply isn't. We aren't surrounded by brothers, but by enemies. It isn't a lack of food or resources that has us on the brink of war — it's a struggle for power. Who's going to be in charge of the world, our kind of people or theirs?"

The professor nodded in reluctant agreement and arose from the table. "I beg your pardon, gentlemen. You are, after all, better qualified to judge what is best for the country. I'll do whatever you say." He turned to me. "Don't forget to wind the restricted clock and put the confidential cat out," he said gloomily, and ascended the stairs to his bedroom.

For reasons of national security, Operation Brainstorm was carried on without the knowledge of the American citizenry which was footing the bill. The observers, technicians and military men involved in the activity knew that a test was under way — a test of what, they had no idea. Only thirty-seven key men, myself included, knew what was afoot.

In Virignia, the day for Operation Brainstorm was unseasonably cool. Inside, a log fire crackled in the fireplace, and the flames were reflected in the polished metal cabinets that lined the living room. All that remained of the room's lovely old furniture was a Victorian love seat, set squarely in the center of the floor, facing three television receivers. One long bench had been brought in for the ten of us privileged to watch. The television screens showed, from left to right, the stretch of desert which was the rocket target, the guinea-pig fleet, and a section of the Aleutian sky through which the radio-controlled bomber formation would roar.

Ninety minutes before H hour the radios announced that the rockets were ready, that the observation ships had backed away to what was thought to be a safe distance, and that the bombers were on their way. The small Virginia audience lined up on the bench in order of rank, smoked a great deal, and said little. Professor Barnhouse was in his bedroom. General Barker bustled about the house like a woman preparing Thanksgiving dinner for twenty.

At ten minutes before H hour the general came in, shepherding the professor before him. The professor was comfortably attired in sneakers, gray flannels, a blue sweater and a white shirt open at the neck. The two of them sat side by side on the love seat. The general was rigid and perspiring; the professor was cheerful. He looked at each of the screens, lighted a cigarette and settled back, comfortable and cool.

"Bombers sighted!" cried the Aleutian observers.

"Rockets away!" barked the New Mexico radio operator.

All of us looked quickly at the big electric clock over the mantel, while the professor, a half-smile on his face, continued to watch the television sets. In hollow tones, the general counted away the seconds remaining. "Five . . . four . . . three . . . two . . . one . . . *Concentrate!*"

Professor Barnhouse closed his eyes, pursed his lips, and stroked his temples He held the position for a minute. The television images were scrambled, and the radio signals were drowned in the din of Barnhouse static. The professor sighed, opened his eyes and smiled confidently.

"Did you give it everything you had?" asked the general dubiously. "I was wide open," the professor replied.

The television images pulled themselves together, and mingled cries of amazement came over the radios tuned to the observers. The Aleutian sky was streaked with the smoke trails of bombers screaming down in flames. Simultaneously, there appeared high over the rocket target a cluster of white puffs, followed by faint thunder.

General Barker shook his head happily. "By George!" he crowed. "Well, sir, by George, by George, by George!"

"Look!" shouted the admiral seated next to me. "The fleet — it wasn't touched!"

"The guns seem to be drooping," said Mr. Cuthrell.

We left the bench and clustered about the television sets to examine the damage more closely. What Mr. Cuthrell had said was true. The ships' guns curved downward their muzzles resting on the steel decks. We in Virginia were making such a hullabaloo that it was impossible to hear the radio reports. We were so engrossed, in fact, that we didn't miss the professor until two short snarls of Barnhouse static shocked us into sudden silence. The radios went dead.

We looked around apprehensively. The professor was gone. A harassed guard threw open the front door from the outside to yell that the professor had escaped. He brandished his pistol in the direction of the gates, which hung open, limp and twisted. In the distance, a speeding government station wagon topped a ridge and dropped from sight into the valley beyond. The air was filled with choking smoke, for every vehicle on the grounds was ablaze. Pursuit was impossible.

"What in God's name got into him?" bellowed the general.

Mr. Cuthrell, who had rushed out onto the front porch, now slouched back into the room, reading a penciled note as he came. He thrust the note into my hands. "The good man left this billet-doux under the door knocker. Perhaps our young friend here will be kind enough to read it to you gentlemen, while I take a restful walk through the woods."

"*Gentlemen,*" I read aloud, "*As the first superweapon with a conscience, I am removing from your national defense stockpile. Setting a new precedent in the behavior of ordnance, I have humane reasons for going off. A. Barnhouse.*"

Since that day, of course, the professor has been systematically destroying the world's armaments, until there is now little with which to equip an army other than rocks and sharp sticks. His activities haven't exactly resulted in peace, but have, rather, precipitated a bloodless and entertaining sort of war that might be called the "War of the Tattletales." Every nation is flooded with enemy agents whose sole mission is to locate military equipment, which is promptly wrecked when it is brought to the professor's attention in the press.

Just as every day brings news of more armaments pulverized by dynamopsychism, so has it brought rumors of the professor's whereabouts. During the last week alone, three publications carried articles proving variously that he was hiding in an Inca ruin in the Andes, in the sewers of Paris, and in the unexplored lower chambers of Carlsbad Caverns. Knowing the man, I am inclined to regard such hiding places as unnecessarily romantic and uncomfortable. While there are numerous persons eager to kill him, there must be millions who would care for him and hide him. I like to think that he is in the home of such a person.

One thing is certain: at this writing, Professor Barnhouse is not dead. Barnhouse static jammed broadcasts not ten minutes ago. In the eighteen months since his disappearance, he has been reported dead some half-dozen times. Each report has stemmed from the death of an unidentified man resembling the professor, during a period free of the static. The first three reports were followed at once by renewed talk of rearmament and recourse to war. The saber rattlers have learned how imprudent premature celebrations of the professor's demise can be.

Many a stouthearted patriot has found himself prone in the tangled bunting and timbers of a smashed reviewing stand, seconds after having announced that the archtyranny of Barnhouse was at an end. But those who would make war if they could, in every country in the world, wait in sullen silence for what must come — the passing of Professor Barnhouse.

To ask how much longer the professor will live is to ask how much longer we must wait for the blessings of another world war. He is of short-lived stock: his mother lived to be fifty-three, his father to be forty-nine; and the life-spans of his grandparents on both sides were of the same order. He might be expected to live, then, for perhaps fifteen years more, if he can remain hidden from his enemies. When one considers the number and vigor of these enemies, however, fifteen years seems an extraordinary length of time, which might better be revised to fifteen days, hours or minutes.

The professor knows that he cannot live much longer. I say this because of the message left in my mailbox on Christmas Eve. Unsigned, typewritten on a soiled scrap of paper, the note consisted of ten sentences. The first nine of these, each a bewildering tangle of psychological jargon and references to obscure texts, made no sense to me at first reading. The tenth, unlike the rest, was simply constructed and contained no large words — but its irrational content made it the most puzzling and bizarre sentence of all. I nearly threw the note away, thinking it a colleague's warped notion of a pratcical joke. For some reason, though, I added it to the clutter on top of my desk, which included, among other mementos, the professor's dice.

It took me several weeks to realize that the message really meant something, that the first nine sentences, when unsnarled, could be taken as instructions. The tenth still told me nothing. It was only last night that I discovered how it fitted in with the rest. The sentence appeared in my thoughts last night, while I was toying absently with the professor's dice.

I promised to have this report on its way to the publishers today. In view of what has happened, I am obliged to break that promise, or release the report incomplete. The delay will not be a long one, for one of the few blessings accorded a bachelor like myself is the ability to move quickly from one abode to another, or from one way of life to another. What property I want to take with me can be packed in a few hours. Fortunately, I am not without substantial private means, which may take as long as a week to realize in liquid and anonymous form. When this is done, I shall mail the report.

I have just returned from a visit to my doctor, who tells me my health is excellent. I am young, and, with any luck at all, I shall live to a ripe old age indeed, for my family on both sides is noted for longevity.

Briefly, I propose to vanish.

Sooner or later, Professor Barnhouse must die. But long before then I shall be ready. So, to the saber rattlers of today — and even, I hope, of tomorrow — I say: Be advised. Barnhouse will die. But not the Barnhouse Effect.

Last night, I tried once more to follow the oblique instructions on the scrap of paper. I took the professor's dice, and then, with the last, nightmarish sentence flitting through my mind, I rolled fifty consecutive sevens.

Good-by.

breakfast

John Steinbeck

This thing fills me with pleasure. I don't know why, I can see it in the smallest detail. I find myself recalling it again and again, each time bringing more detail out of a sunken memory, remembering brings the curious warm pleasure.

It was very early in the morning. The eastern mountains were black-blue, but behind them the light stood up faintly colored at the mountain rims with a washed red, growing colder, greyer and darker as it went up and overhead until, at a place near the west, it merged with pure night.

And it was cold, not painfully so, but cold enough so that I rubbed my hands and shoved them deep into my pockets, and I hunched my shoulders up and scuffled my feet on the ground. Down in the valley where I was, the earth was that lavender grey of dawn. I walked along a country road and ahead of me I saw a tent that was only a little lighter grey than the ground. Beside the tent there was a flash of orange fire seeping out of the cracks of an old rusty iron stove. Grey smoke spurted up out of the stubby stovepipe, spurted up a long way before it spread out and dissipated.

I saw a young woman beside the stove, really a girl. She was dressed in a faded cotton skirt and waist. As I came close I saw that she carried a baby in a crooked arm and the baby was nursing, its head under her waist out of the cold. The mother moved about, poking the fire, shifting the rusty lids of the stove to make a greater draft, opening the oven door; and all the time the baby was nursing, but that didn't interfere with the mother's work, nor with the light quick gracefulness of her movements. There was something very precise and practiced in her movements. The orange fire flicked out of the cracks in the stove and threw dancing reflections on the tent.

I was close now and I could smell frying bacon and baking bread, the warmest, pleasantest odors I know. From the east the light grew swiftly. I came near to the stove and stretched my hands out to it and shivered all over when the warmth struck me. Then the tent flap jerked up and a young man came out and an older man followed him. They were dressed in new blue dungarees and in new dungaree coats with the brass buttons shining. They were sharp-faced men, and they looked much alike.

The younger had a dark stubble beard and the older had a grey stubble beard. Their heads and faces were wet, their hair dripped with water, and water stood out on their stiff beards and their cheeks shone with water. Together they stood looking quietly at the lightening east; they yawned together and looked at the light on the hill rims. They turned and saw me.

"Morning," said the older man. His face was neither friendly nor unfriendly.

"Morning, sir," I said.

"Morning," said the young man.

The water was slowly drying on their faces. They came to the stove and warmed their hands at it.

The girl kept to her work, her face averted and her eyes on what she was doing. Her hair was tied back out of her eyes with a string and it hung down her back and swayed as she worked. She set tin cups on a big packing box, set tin plates and knives and forks out too. Then she scooped fried bacon out of the deep grease and laid it on a big tin platter, and the bacon cricked and rustled as it grew crisp. She opened the rusty oven door and took out a square pan full of high big biscuits.

When the smell of that hot bread came out, both of the men inhaled deeply. The young man said softly, "Keerist!"

The elder man turned to me, "Had your breakfast?"

"No."

"Well, sit down with us, then."

That was the signal. We went to the packing case and squatted on the ground about it. The young man asked, "Picking cotton?"

"No."

"We had twelve days' work so far," the young man said.

The girl spoke from the stove. "They even got new clothes."

The two men looked down at their new dungarees and they both smiled a little.

The girl set out the platter of bacon, the brown high biscuits, a bowl of bacon gravy and a pot of coffee, and then she squatted down by the box too. The baby was still nursing, its head up under her waist out of the cold. I could hear the sucking noises it made.

We filled our plates, poured bacon gravy over our biscuits and sugared our coffee. The older man filled his mouth full and he chewed and chewed and swallowed. Then he said, "God Almighty, it's good," and he filled his mouth again.

The young man said, "We been eating good for twelve days."

We all ate quickly, frantically, and refilled our plates and ate quickly again until we were full and warm. The hot bitter coffee scalded our throats. We threw the last little bit with the grounds in it on the earth and refilled our cups.

There was color in the light now, a reddish gleam that made the air seem colder. The two men faced the east and their faces were lighted by the dawn, and I looked up for a moment and saw the image of the mountain and the light coming over it reflected in the older man's eyes.

Then the two men threw the grounds from their cups on the earth and they stood up together. "Got to get going," the older man said.

The younger turned to me. " 'Fyou want to pick cotton, we could maybe get you on."

"No. I got to go along. Thanks for breakfast."

The older man waved his hand in a negative. "O.K. Glad to have you." They walked away together. The air was blazing with light at the eastern skyline. And I walked away down the country road.

That's all. I know, of course, some of the reasons why it was pleasant. But there was some element of great beauty there that makes the rush of warmth when I think of it.

the berry patch

Wallace Stegner

That day the sun came down in a vertical fall of heat, but the wind came under it, flat out of the gap beyond Mansfield, and cooled a sweating forehead as fast as the sun could heat it. In the washed ruts of the trail there were no tracks.

"Lord," Perley Hill said. "It's a day for seeing things, right enough."

He jerked off his tie and unbuttoned his shirt, rolled up his sleeves

and set his right arm gingerly on the hot door, and as Alma steered
the Plymouth up the long slope of Stannard he looked back across
the valley to where the asbestos mine on Belvidere blew up its perpetual white plume, and on down south across the hills folding back
in layers of blue to Mansfield and Elmore and the sharkfin spine of
Camel's Hump. Just across the valley the lake was like a mirror
leaned on edge against the hills, with the white houses of the village
propped against its lower edge to keep it from sliding down into the
river valley.

"It's pretty on a clear day," Alma said, without looking.

Perley continued to look down. "Things show up," he said. "There's
Donald Swain's place."

" 'Twon't be his much longer," Alma said.

Perley glanced at her. She was watching the road with rigid concentration. "Having trouble?" he said.

"I thought I told you. He's in hospital in St. Johnsbury. Stomach
trouble or something. With Henry and George in the navy, Allen
can't run it alone. Donald's had him put it up for sale."

"I guess you did tell me," he said. "I forgot."

"Already sold half his cows," Alma said.

They passed an abandoned farm, with a long meadow that flowed
downhill between tight walls of spruce. "Looks like a feller could've
made that pay," Perley said. "How long's it been since Gardner left
here?"

"I remember coming up here to pick apples when I was about
fifteen," Alma said. "Must be ten-twelve years since anybody's worked
this place."

Perley drummed on the door, grinning a little to himself at the way
Alma never took her eyes off the road when she talked. She faced
it as if it were a touchy bull-critter. "Kind of proud of yourself since
you learned to drive, ain't you?" he said. "Be putting Sam Boyce out
of business, taxiing people around."

She took her foot off the accelerator. "Why, you can drive," she
said. "I didn't mean —— "

"Go ahead," Perley said. "Any OPA agents around, you can do the
explaining about the pleasure driving."

" 'Tisn't pleasure driving," Alma said. "Berrying's all right to do."

Perley watched the roadside, the chokecherry bushes getting heavy
with green clusters already, the daisies and paintbrush just going out,
but still lush in the shaded places, the fireweed and green goldenrod
flowing back into every little bay in the brush.

Just as Alma shifted and crawled out onto a level before an abandoned schoolhouse, a partridge swarmed out of a beech, and Perley bent to look upward. "See them two little ones hugging the branch?" he said. "They'd sit there and never move till you knocked them off with a stick."

Alma pulled off the road into the long grass. An old skid road wormed up the hill through heavy timber, and the air was rich with the faint, warm, moist smell of woods after rain. Perley stretched till his muscles cracked, yawned, stepped out to look across the broken stone wall that disappeared into deep brush.

"Makes a feller just want to lay down in the cool," he said. "If I lay down will you braid my hair full of daisies?"

The berry pails in her hands, Alma looked at him seriously. "Well, if you'd rather just lay down," she said. "We don't have to —— "

"I guess I can stay up a mite longer," Perley said.

"But if you'd rather," she said, and looked at him as if she didn't quite know what he'd like to do, but was willing to agree to anything he said. She'd been that way ever since he came home. If he yawned, she wondered if he didn't want to go to bed. If he sat down, she brought a pillow or a magazine as if he might be going to stay there all day.

He reached in and got the big granite kettle and set it over her head like a helmet, and then fended her off with one hand while he got the blanket, the lunch box, the Mason jar of water. "Think the army had wrapped me up in cellophane too pretty to touch," he said.

"Well," she said, "I just wanted to be sure." She looked at his face and added, "You big lummox."

He nested the pails, hooked his arm through the basket, slung the blanket across his shoulder, picked up the water jar. "If I just had me a wife would do for me," he said, "I'd lay down and get my strength back. With the wife I got, I s'pose I got to work."

"Here," Alma said mildly. "Give me some of them things. You'll get so toggled up I'll have to cut you out with the pliers."

All the way up the skid road under the deep shade their feet made trails in the wet grass. Perley jerked his head at them. "Nobody been in since yesterday anyway," he said.

"Wa'n't any tracks on the road."

"Thought somebody might've walked," Perley said. "Haven't, though."

"Be nice if we had the patch all to our lonesomes," she said.

They came out of the woods into a meadow. A house that had once stood at the edge was a ruined foundation overgrown with fireweed, and the hurricane of 1938 had scooped a path two hundred yards long and fifty wide out of the maples behind. Root tables lay up on edge, trunks were crisscrossed, flat, leaning, dead and half-dead. Perley went over and looked into the tangle. "Plenty raspberries," he said.

"I've got my face fixed for blueberries," Alma said. "We can get some of those too, though. They're about gone down below."

Perley was already inspecting the ruined cellar. "Ha!" he said. "Gooseberries, too. A mess of 'em."

"It's blueberries I'm interested in," she said.

"Well, I'll find you some blueberries then." He tightroped the foundation and jumped clear of the gooseberry bushes. Fifty feet down the meadow he went into a point with lifted foot, the pails dangling in one hand. "Hey!" he said. "Hey!"

When she got to his side he was standing among knee-high bushes, and all down the falling meadow, which opened on the west into a clear view of the valley, the village, the lake, the hills beyond hills and the final peaks, the dwarf bushes were so laden that the berries gleamed through the covering leaves like clusters of tiny flowers.

"Thunderation," Perley said. "I never saw a patch like that in fifteen years."

Before she could say anything he had stripped off the army shirt and the white undershirt and hung them on a bush, and was raking the berries into a pail with his spread fingers.

By the time two buckets were full the wind had shifted so that the trees cut it off, and it was hot in the meadow. They went back into the shade by the old foundation and ate lunch and drank from the spring. Then they lay down on the blanket and looked up at the sky. The wind came in whiffs along the edge of the blowdown, and the sweet smell of the raspberry patch drifted across them. Away down along the view that this house had had once, the lake looked more than ever like a mirror tipped against the hills. Below the village Donald Swain's white house and round red barn were strung on a white thread of road.

Perley rolled over on his side and looked at his wife. "I guess I never asked you," he said, "how you were getting along."

"I get along all right."

"You don't want me to sell any cows?"

"You know you wouldn't want to do that. You were just getting the herd built up."

"A herd's no good if you can't get help."

"People are good about helping," she said.

"What'll you do when there ain't any more people around? Seems like half the place has gone down country or into the army already."

"It's been going since the Civil War," Alma said, "and still there always seems to be somebody around to neighbor with."

He rolled onto his back again and plucked a spear of grass. "We should be haying," he said, "right now."

"Sunday," she said.

"Sunday or no Sunday. There's still those two top meadows. Those city kids you got can't get all that hay in."

"All they need is somebody to keep 'em from raring back in the breeching," Alma said. "I'll be behind with a pitchfork if I have to."

"I can see you."

She did not stir from her comfortable sprawl, but her voice went up crisply. "You thought we ought to sell when you got called up," she said. "Well, you've been gone going on a year, and hasn't anything gone wrong, has there? Got seven new calves, an't you? Milk checks have got bigger, an't they? Learned to drive the tractor and the car, didn't I? Got ten run of wood coming from DeSerres for the loan of the team, an't we, and saved the price of feed all that time last winter."

"Allen Swain can't make it go," Perley said.

"His farm don't lay as good as ours, and he's got a mortgage," she said. "Mortgage," the way she said it, sounded like an incurable disease. She half rose on her elbow to look at him. "And I an't Allen Swain, either."

"So you want to be a farmer."

"I am," she said.

Perley picked another stem of grass and grinned up into the tops of the maples. They had been growing densely before the hurricane, and the going down of trees on every side had left them standing tall and spindly. The wind went through their leaves high up, a good stiff wind that bent and threshed their tops, but only a creeping breath disturbed the grass below. It was like lying deep down in a soft, warm, sweet-smelling nest.

"Laying here, you wouldn't think anything could ever touch you," he said. "Wind could blow up there like all get-out, and you'd never feel it." Alma's hand fell across his chest, and he captured it. "Unless you stuck your head out," he said.

For a while he lay feeling the pulse in her wrist.

"Smell them raspberries?" he said once, and squirmed his shoulders more comfortable against the ground. "There ain't anything smells sweeter, even flowers." Alma said nothing.

"Funny about a berry patch," he said. "Nobody ever plowed it, or planted it, or cultivated it, or fertilized it, or limed it, but there it is. You couldn't grub it out if you tried. More you plow it up, the more berries there is next year. Burn it over, it's up again before anything else. Blow everything down, that's just what it likes."

He filled his lungs with the ripe berry odor and let the breath bubble out between his lips. "Don't seem as if you'd ever have to move," he said. "Just lay here and reach up and pick a mouthful and then lay some more and let the wind blow over way up there and you never even feel it."

"It's nice," Alma said. "I didn't hardly think the blueberries would be ripe yet, it's been so rainy."

"Makes you think the world's all right," Perley said, "the way they come along every year, rain or shine."

Alma stirred. "We'd better get busy," she said. "Some gooseberries, too, if you'd like some."

"Might use a pie," he said. He sat up and stretched for the pails. There were only the granite kettle and the two-quart milk pail left. "You lay still," he said. "I'll get some."

" 'Tisn't as if I needed a rest," she said. "Here I've been just having fun all day."

"Well, take the kettle then. It's easier to pick into." He picked up the milk pail.

"Perley," Alma said.

"Uh?"

"This is what you want to do, isn't it? I mean, you wouldn't rather go see somebody?"

He watched her steadily. "Why?"

"Well, it's only two more days. I just ——"

"I already saw everybody I want to see," he said. "I was saving the last couple days."

"Well, all right," she said, and went into the blowdown with the kettle.

He picked very fast, wanting to surprise her with how many he had, and when after a half-hour he worked back toward the side where she was picking he had the pail filled and overflowing, mounded an inch above the brim. He liked the smell of his hand when he scratched his nose free of a tickling cobweb. For a moment he stood, turning his face upward to watch the unfelt upper-air wind thresh through the tops of the maples, and then he came up softly behind Alma where she bent far in against a root table to reach a loaded vine. He bent in after her and kissed the back of her neck.

"How're you doing?" she said, and worked her way out. Her shirt was unbuttoned halfway down, her throat was brown even in the hollow above where her collarbones joined, and her eyes sought his with that anxiety to know that he was content, that he was doing what he wanted to do, which she had shown all the time of his furlough. "I got quite a mess," she said, and showed the berries in her pail. "How about you?"

"All I want," Perley said. He was watching the sun dapple the brown skin of her throat as the wind bent the thin tops of the maples. "I wouldn't want any more," he said.

drama

visit to a small planet

Gore Vidal

CHARACTERS

Kreton	*General Powers*
Roger Spelding	*Aide*
Ellen Spelding	*Paul Laurent*
Mrs. Spelding	*Second Visitor*
John Randolph	*President of Paraguay*

ACT ONE: *Stock Shot: The night sky, stars. Then slowly a luminous object arcs into view. As it is almost upon us, dissolve to the living room of the Spelding house in Maryland.*
Superimpose card: "THE TIME: THE DAY AFTER TOMORROW"

The room is comfortably balanced between the expensively decorated and the homely. Roger Spelding is concluding his TV broadcast. He is middle-aged, unctuous, resonant. His wife, bored and vague, knits passively while he talks at his desk. Two technicians are on hand, operating the equipment. His daughter, Ellen, a lively girl of twenty, fidgets as she listens.

SPELDING (*into microphone*): . . . and so, according to General Powers . . . who should know if anyone does . . . the flying object which has given rise to so much irresponsible conjecture is nothing more than a meteor passing through the earth's orbit. It is not, as many believe, a secret weapon of this country. Nor is it a space-ship as certain lunatic elements have suggested. General Powers has assured me that it is highly doubtful there is any form of life on other planets capable of building a space-ship. "If any traveling is to be done in space, we will do it first." And those are his exact words. . . . Which winds up another week of news. (*Crosses to pose with wife and daughter.*) This is Roger Spelding, saying good night to Mother and Father America, from my old homestead in Silver Glen, Maryland, close to the warm pulse-beat of the nation.

TECHNICIAN: Good show tonight, Mr. Spelding.

SPELDING: Thank you.

TECHNICIAN: Yes sir, you were right on time.

    (SPELDING *nods wearily, his mechanical smile and heartiness suddenly gone.*)

MRS. SPELDING: Very nice, dear. Very nice.

TECHNICIAN: See you next week, Mrs. Spelding.

SPELDING: Thank you, boys.

    (TECHNICIANS *go.*)

SPELDING: Did you like the broadcast, Ellen?

ELLEN: Of course I did, Daddy.

SPELDING: Then what did I say?

ELLEN: Oh, that's not fair.

SPELDING: It's not very flattering when one's own daughter won't listen to what one says while millions of people . . .

ELLEN: I always listen, Daddy, you know that.

MRS. SPELDING: We love your broadcasts, dear. I don't know what we'd do without them.

SPELDING: Starve.

ELLEN: I wonder what's keeping John?

SPELDING: Certainly not work.

ELLEN: Oh, Daddy, stop it! John works very hard and you know it.

MRS. SPELDING: Yes, he's a perfectly nice boy, Roger. I like him.

SPELDING: I know. I know: he has every virtue except the most important one: he has no get-up-and-go.

ELLEN (*precisely*): He doesn't want to get up and he doesn't want to go because he's already where he wants to be on his own farm which is exactly where I'm going to be when we're married.

SPELDING: More thankless than a serpent's tooth is an ungrateful child.

ELLEN: I don't think that's right. Isn't it "more deadly . . ."

SPELDING: Whatever the exact quotation is, I stand by the sentiment.

MRS. SPELDING: Please don't quarrel. It always gives me a headache.

SPELDING: I never quarrel. I merely reason, in my simple way, with Miss Know-it-all here.

ELLEN: Oh, Daddy! Next you'll tell me I should marry for money.

SPELDING: There is nothing wrong with marrying a wealthy man. The horror of it has always eluded me. However, my only wish is that you marry someone hard-working, ambitious, a man who'll make his mark in the world. Not a boy who plans to sit on a farm all his life, growing peanuts.

ELLEN: English walnuts.

SPELDING: Will you stop correcting me?

ELLEN: But, Daddy, John grows walnuts . . .

(JOHN *enters, breathlessly.*)

JOHN: Come out! Quickly. It's coming this way. It's going to land right here!

SPELDING: *What's* going to land?

JOHN: The space-ship. Look!

SPELDING: Apparently you didn't hear my broadcast. The flying object in question is a meteor not a space ship.

(JOHN *has gone out with* ELLEN. SPELDING *and* MRS. SPELDING *follow.*)

MRS. SPELDING: Oh, my! Look! Something *is* falling! Roger, you don't think it's going to hit the house, do you?

SPELDING: The odds against being hit by a falling object that size are, I should say, roughly, ten million to one.

JOHN: Ten million to one or not it's going to land right here and it's *not* falling.

SPELDING: I'm sure it's a meteor.

MRS. SPELDING: Shouldn't we go down to the cellar?

SPELDING: If it's not a meteor, it's an optical illusion . . . mass hysteria.

ELLEN: Daddy, it's a real space ship. I'm sure it is.

SPELDING: Or maybe a weather balloon. Yes, that's what it is. General Powers said only yesterday . . .

JOHN: It's landing!

SPELDING: I'm going to call the police . . . the army! (*Bolts inside.*)

ELLEN: Oh look how it shines!

JOHN: Here it comes!

MRS. SPELDING: Right in my rose garden!

ELLEN: Maybe it's a balloon.

JOHN: No, it's a space ship and right in your own backyard.

ELLEN: What makes it shine so?

JOHN: I don't know but I'm going to find out. (*Runs off toward the light.*)

ELLEN: Oh, darling, don't! John, please! John, John come back!
(SPELDING, *wide-eyed, returns.*)

MRS. SPELDING: Roger, it's landed right in my rose garden.

SPELDING: I got General Powers. He's coming over. He said they've been watching this thing. They . . . they don't know what it is.

ELLEN: You mean it's nothing of ours?

SPELDING: They believe it . . . (*Swallows hard.*) . . . it's from outer space.

ELLEN: And John's down there! Daddy, get a gun or something.

SPELDING: Perhaps we'd better leave the house until the army gets here.

ELLEN: We can't leave John.

SPELDING: I can. (*Peers nearsightedly.*) Why, it's not much larger than a car. I'm sure it's some kind of meteor.

ELLEN: Meteors are blazing hot.

SPELDING: This is a cold one . . .

ELLEN: It's opening . . . the whole side's opening! (*Shouts.*) John! Come back! Quick. . . .

MRS. SPELDING: Why, there's a man getting out of it! (*Sighs.*) I feel much better already. I'm sure if we ask him, he'll move that thing for us. Roger, you ask him.

SPELDING (*ominously*): If it's really a man?

ELLEN: John's shaking hands with him. (*Calls.*) John darling, come on up here . . .

MRS. SPELDING: And bring your friend . . .

SPELDING: There's something wrong with the way that creature looks . . . If it is a man and not a . . . not a monster.

MRS. SPELDING: He looks perfectly nice to me.

(JOHN *and the* VISITOR *appear. The* VISITOR *is in his forties, a mild, pleasant-looking man with side-whiskers and dressed in the fashion of 1860. He pauses when he sees the three people, in silence for a moment. They stare back at him, equally interested.*)

VISITOR: I seem to've made a mistake. I am sorry. I'd better go back and start over again.

SPELDING: My dear sir, you've only just arrived. Come in, come in. I don't need to tell you what a pleasure this is . . . Mister . . . Mister . . .

VISITOR: Kreton . . . This is the wrong costume, isn't it?

SPELDING: Wrong for what?

KRETON: For the country, and the time.

SPELDING: Well, it's a trifle old-fashioned.

MRS. SPELDING: But really awfully handsome.

KRETON: Thank you.

MRS. SPELDING (*to husband*): Ask him about moving that thing off my rose bed.

(SPELDING *leads them all into living room.*)

SPELDING: Come on in and sit down. You must be tired after your trip.

KRETON: Yes, I am a little. (*Looks around delightedly.*) Oh, it's better than I'd hoped!

SPELDING: Better? What's better?

KRETON: The house . . . that's what you call it? Or is this an apartment?

SPELDING: This is a house in the State of Maryland, U.S.A.

KRETON: In the late 20th century! To think this is really the 20th century. I must sit down a moment and collect myself. The *real* thing! (*He sits down.*)

ELLEN: You . . . you're not an American, are you?

KRETON: What a nice thought! No, I'm not.

JOHN: You sound more English.

KRETON: Do I? Is my accent very bad?

JOHN: No, it's quite good.

SPELDING: Where *are* you from, Mr. Kreton?

KRETON (*evasively*): Another place.

SPELDING: On this earth of course.

KRETON: No, not on this planet.

ELLEN: Are you from Mars?

KRETON: Oh dear no, not Mars. There's nobody on Mars . . . at least no one I know.

ELLEN: I'm sure you're teasing us and this is all some kind of publicity stunt.

KRETON: No, I really am from another place.

SPELDING: I don't suppose you'd consent to my interviewing you on television?

KRETON: I don't think your authorities will like that. They are terribly upset as it is.

SPELDING: How do you know?

KRETON: Well, I . . . pick up things. For instance, I know that in a few minutes a number of people from your Army will be here to question me and they . . . like you . . . are torn by doubt.

SPELDING: How extraordinary!

ELLEN: Why did you come here?

KRETON: Simply a visit to your small planet. I've been studying it for years. In fact, one might say, you people are my hobby. Especially, this period of your development.

JOHN: Are you the first person from your . . . your planet to travel in space like this?

KRETON: Oh my no! Everyone travels who wants to. It's just that no one wants to visit you. I can't think why. *I* always have. You'd be surprised what a thorough study I've made. (*Recites.*) The planet, Earth, is divided into five continents with a number of large islands. It is mostly water. There is one moon. Civilization is only just beginning. . . .

SPELDING: Just beginning! My dear sir, we have had. . . .

KRETON (*blandly*): You are only in the initial stages, the most fascinating stages as far as I'm concerned . . . I do hope I don't sound patronizing.

ELLEN: Well, we are very proud.

KRETON: I know and that's one of your most endearing, primitive traits. Oh, I can't believe I'm here at last!

(GENERAL POWERS, *a vigorous product of the National Guard, and his* AIDE *enter.*)

POWERS: All right folks. The place is surrounded by troops. Where is the monster?

KRETON: I, my dear General, am the monster.

POWERS: What are you dressed up for, a fancy-dress party?

KRETON: I'd hoped to be in the costume of the period. As you see I am about a hundred years too late.

POWERS: Roger, who is this joker?

SPELDING: This is Mr. Kreton . . . General Powers. Mr. Kreton arrived in that thing outside. He is from another planet.

POWERS: I don't believe it.

ELLEN: It's true. We saw him get out of the flying saucer.

POWERS (*to* AIDE): Captain, go down and look at that ship. But be careful. Don't touch anything. And don't let anybody else near it. (AIDE *goes.*) So you're from another planet.

KRETON: Yes. My, that's a very smart uniform but I prefer the ones made of metal, the ones you used to wear, you know: with the feathers on top.

POWERS: That was five hundred years ago . . . Are you sure you're not from the Earth?

KRETON: Yes.

POWERS: Well, I'm not. You've got some pretty tall explaining to do.

KRETON: Anything to oblige.

POWERS: All right, which planet?

KRETON: None that you have ever heard of.

POWERS: Where is it?

KRETON: You wouldn't know.

POWERS: This solar system?

KRETON: No.

POWERS: Another system?

KRETON: Yes.

POWERS: Look, Buster, I don't want to play games: I just want to know where you're from. The law requires it.

KRETON: It's possible that I could explain it to a mathematician but I'm afraid I couldn't explain it to you, not for another five hundred years and by then of course you'd be dead because you people do die, don't you?

POWERS: What?

KRETON: Poor fragile butterflies, such brief little moments in the sun. . . . You see *we* don't die.

POWERS: You'll die all right if it turns out you're a spy or a hostile alien.

KRETON: I'm sure you wouldn't be so cruel.

(AIDE *returns; he looks disturbed.*)

POWERS: What did you find?

AIDE: I'm not sure, General.

POWERS (*heavily*): Then do your best to describe what the object is like.

AIDE: Well, it's elliptical, with a fourteen foot diameter. And it's made of an unknown metal which shines and inside there isn't anything.

POWERS: Isn't anything?

AIDE: There's nothing inside the ship: No instruments, no food, nothing.

POWERS (*to* KRETON): What did you do with your instrument board?

KRETON: With my what? Oh, I don't have one.

POWERS: How does the thing travel?

KRETON: I don't know.

POWERS: You don't know. Now look, Mister, you're in pretty serious trouble. I suggest you do a bit of coöperating. You claim you travelled here from outer space in a machine with no instruments . . .

KRETON: Well, these cars are rather common in my world and I suppose, once upon a time, I must've known the theory on which they operate but I've long since forgotten. After all, General, we're not mechanics, you and I.

POWERS: Roger, do you mind if we use your study?

SPELDING: Not at all. Not at all, General.

POWERS: Mr. Kreton and I are going to have a chat. (*To* AIDE) Put in a call to the Chief of Staff.

AIDE: Yes, General.

(SPELDING *rises, leads* KRETON *and* POWERS *into next room, a handsomely furnished study, many books and a globe of the world.*)

SPELDING: This way, gentlemen. (KRETON *sits down comfortably beside the globe which he twirls thoughtfully. At the door,* SPELDING *speaks in a low voice to* POWERS.) I hope I'll be the one to get the story first, Tom.

POWERS: There isn't any story. Complete censorship. I'm sorry but this house is under martial law. I've a hunch we're in trouble. (*He shuts the door.* SPELDING *turns and rejoins his family.*)

ELLEN: I think he's wonderful, whoever he is.

MRS. SPELDING: I wonder how much damage he did to my rose garden . . .

JOHN: It's sure hard to believe he's really from outer space. No instruments, no nothing . . . boy, they must be advanced scientifically.

MRS. SPELDING: Is he spending the night, dear?

SPELDING: What?

MRS. SPELDING: Is he spending the night?

SPELDING: Oh yes, yes. I suppose he will be.

MRS. SPELDING: Then I'd better go make up the bedroom. He seems perfectly nice to me. I like his whiskers. They're so very . . . comforting. Like Grandfather Spelding's. (*She goes.*)

SPELDING (*bitterly*): I *know* this story will leak out before I can interview him. I just know it.

ELLEN: What does it mean, we're under martial law?

SPELDING: It means we have to do what General Powers tells us to do. (*He goes to the window as a soldier passes by.*) See?

JOHN: I wish I'd taken a closer look at that ship when I had the chance.

ELLEN: Perhaps he'll give us a ride in it.

JOHN: Traveling in space! Just like those stories. You know: intergalactic drive stuff.

SPELDING: *If* he's not an impostor.

ELLEN: I have a feeling he isn't.

JOHN: Well, I better call the family and tell them I'm all right.
   (*He crosses to telephone by the door which leads into hall.*)

AIDE: I'm sorry, sir, but you can't use the phone.

SPELDING: He certainly can. This is my house . . .

AIDE (*mechanically*): This house is a military reservation until the crisis is over: Order General Powers. I'm sorry.

JOHN: How am I to call home to say where I am?

AIDE: Only General Powers can help you. You're also forbidden to leave this house without permission.

SPELDING: You can't do this!

AIDE: I'm afraid, sir, we've done it.

ELLEN: Isn't it exciting!

   Cut to study.

POWERS: Are you deliberately trying to confuse me?

KRETON: Not deliberately, no.

POWERS: We have gone over and over this for two hours now and all that you've told me is that you're from another planet in another solar system . . .

KRETON: In another dimension. I think that's the word you use.

POWERS: In another dimension and you have come here as a tourist.

KRETON: Up to a point, yes. What did you expect?

POWERS: It is my job to guard the security of this country.

KRETON: I'm sure that must be very interesting work.

POWERS: For all I know, you are a spy, sent here by an alien race to study us, preparatory to invasion.

KRETON: Oh, none of my people would dream of invading you.

POWERS: How do I know that's true?

KRETON: You don't, so I suggest you believe me. I should also warn you: I can tell what's inside.

POWERS: What's inside?

KRETON: What's inside your mind.

POWERS: You're a mind reader?

KRETON: I don't really read it. I hear it.

POWERS: What am I thinking?

KRETON: That I am either a lunatic from the earth or a spy from another world.

POWERS: Correct. But then you could've guessed that. (*Frowns.*) What am I thinking now?

KRETON: You're making a picture. Three silver stars. You're pinning them on your shoulder, instead of the two stars you now wear.

POWERS (*startled*): That's right. I was thinking of my promotion.

KRETON: If there's anything I can do to hurry it along, just let me know.

POWERS: You can. Tell me why you're here.

KRETON: Well, we don't travel much, my people. We used to but since we see everything through special monitors and recreators, there is no particular need to travel. However, *I* am a hobbyist. I love to gad about.

POWERS (*taking notes*): Are you the first to visit us?

KRETON: Oh, no! We started visiting you long before there were people on the planet. However, we are seldom noticed on our trips. I'm sorry to say I slipped up, coming in the way I did . . . but then this visit was all rather impromptu. (*Laughs.*) I am a creature of impulse, I fear.

   (AIDE *looks in.*)

AIDE: Chief of Staff on the telephone, General.

POWERS (*picks up phone*): Hello, yes, sir. Powers speaking. I'm talking to him now. No, sir. No, sir. No, we can't determine what method of power was used. He won't talk. Yes, sir. I'll hold him here. I've put the house under martial law . . . belongs to a friend of mine, Roger Spelding, the TV commentator, Roger Spelding, the TV . . . What? Oh, no, I'm sure he won't say anything. Who . . . oh, yes, sir. Yes, I realize the importance of it. Yes, I will. Good-by. (*Hangs up.*) The President of the United States wants to know all about you.

KRETON: How nice of him! And I want to know all about him. But

I do wish you'd let me rest a bit first. Your language is still not familiar to me. I had to learn them all, quite exhausting.

POWERS: You speak all our languages?

KRETON: Yes, all of them. But then it's easier than you might think since I can see what's inside.

POWERS: Speaking of what's inside, we're going to take your ship apart.

KRETON: Oh, I wish you wouldn't.

POWERS: Security demands it.

KRETON: In that case my security demands you leave it alone.

POWERS: You plan to stop us?

KRETON: I already have . . . Listen.

(*Far-off shouting.* AIDE *rushes into the study.*)

AIDE: Something's happened to the ship, General. The door's shut and there's some kind of wall all around it, an invisible wall. We can't get near it.

KRETON (*to camera*): I hope there was no one inside.

POWERS (*to* KRETON): How did you do that?

KRETON: I couldn't begin to explain. Now if you don't mind, I think we should go in and see our hosts.

(*He rises, goes into living room.* POWERS *and* AIDE *look at each other.*)

POWERS: Don't let him out of your sight.

Cut to living room as POWERS *picks up phone.* KRETON *is with* JOHN *and* ELLEN.

KRETON: I don't mind curiosity but I really can't permit them to wreck my poor ship.

ELLEN: What do you plan to do, now you're here?

KRETON: Oh, keep busy. I have a project or two . . . (*Sighs.*) I can't believe you're real!

JOHN: Then we're all in the same boat.

KRETON: Boat? Oh, yes! Well, I should have come ages ago but I . . . I couldn't get away until yesterday.

JOHN: Yesterday? It only took you a day to get here?

KRETON: One of my days, not yours. But then you don't know about time yet.

JOHN: Oh, you mean relativity.

KRETON: No, it's much more involved than that. You won't know about time until . . . now let me see if I remember . . . No, I don't but it's about two thousand years.

JOHN: What do we do between now and then?

KRETON: You simply go on the way you are, living your exciting primitive lives . . . you have no idea how much fun you're having now.

ELLEN: I hope you'll stay with us while you're here.

KRETON: That's very nice of you. Perhaps I will. Though I'm sure you'll get tired of having a visitor under foot all the time.

ELLEN: Certainly not. And Daddy will be deliriously happy. He can interview you by the hour.

JOHN: What's it like in outer space?

KRETON: Dull.

ELLEN: I should think it would be divine!

(POWERS *enters.*)

KRETON: No, General, it won't work.

POWERS: What won't work?

KRETON: Trying to blow up my little force field. You'll just plough up Mrs. Spelding's garden.

(POWERS *snarls and goes into study.*)

ELLEN: Can you tell what we're all thinking?

KRETON: Yes. As a matter of fact, it makes me a bit giddy. Your minds are not at all like ours. You see we control our thoughts while you . . . well, it's extraordinary the things you think about!

ELLEN: Oh, how awful! You can tell everything we think?

KRETON: Everything! It's one of the reasons I'm here, to intoxicate myself with your primitive minds . . . with the wonderful rawness of your emotions! You have no idea how it excites me! You simply seethe with unlikely emotions.

ELLEN: I've never felt so sordid.

JOHN: From now on I'm going to think about agriculture.

SPELDING (*entering*): You would.

ELLEN: Daddy!

KRETON: No, no. You must go right on thinking about Ellen. Such wonderfully purple thoughts!

SPELDING: Now see here, Powers, you're carrying this martial law thing too far . . .

POWERS: Unfortunately, until I have received word from Washington as to the final disposition of this problem, you must obey my orders: no telephone calls, no communication with the outside.

SPELDING: This is unsupportable.

KRETON: Poor Mr. Spelding! If you like, I shall go. That would solve everything, wouldn't it?

POWERS: You're not going anywhere, Mr. Kreton, until I've had my instructions.

KRETON: I sincerely doubt if you could stop me. However, I put it up to Mr. Spelding. Shall I go?

SPELDING: Yes! (POWERS *gestures a warning.*) Do stay, I mean, we want you to get a good impression of us . . .

KRETON: And of course you still want to be the first journalist to interview me. Fair enough. All right, I'll stay on for a while.

POWERS: Thank you.

KRETON: Don't mention it.

SPELDING: General, may I ask our guest a few questions?

POWERS: Go right ahead, Roger. I hope you'll do better than I did.

SPELDING: Since you read our minds, you probably already know what our fears are.

KRETON: I do, yes.

SPELDING: We are afraid that you represent a hostile race.

KRETON: And I have assured General Powers that my people are not remotely hostile. Except for me, no one is interested in this planet's present stage.

SPELDING: Does this mean you might be interested in a later stage?

KRETON: I'm not permitted to discuss your future. Of course my friends think me perverse to be interested in a primitive society but there's no accounting for tastes, is there? You are my hobby. I love you. And that's all there is to it.

POWERS: So you're just here to look around . . . sort of going native.

KRETON: What a nice expression! That's it exactly. I am going native.

POWERS (*grimly*): Well, it is my view that you have been sent here by another civilization for the express purpose of reconnoitering prior to invasion.

KRETON: That would be your view! The wonderfully primitive assumption that all strangers are hostile. You're almost too good to be true, General.

POWERS: You deny your people intend to make trouble for us?

KRETON: I deny it.

POWERS: Then are they interested in establishing communication with us? trade? that kind of thing?

KRETON: We have always had communication with you. As for trade, well, we do not trade . . . that is something peculiar only to your social level. (*Quickly.*) Which I'm not criticizing! As you know, I approve of everything you do.

POWERS: I give up.

SPELDING: You have no interest then in . . . well, trying to dominate the earth.

KRETON: Oh, yes!

POWERS: I thought you just said your people weren't interested in us.

KRETON: They're not, but *I* am.

POWERS: You!

KRETON: Me . . . I mean I. You see I've come here to take charge.

POWERS: Of the United States?

KRETON: No, of the whole world. I'm sure you'll be much happier and it will be great fun for me. You'll get used to it in no time.

POWERS: This is ridiculous. How can one man take over the world?

KRETON (*gaily*): Wait and see!

POWERS (*to* AIDE): Grab him!

(POWERS *and* AIDE *rush* KRETON *but within a foot of him, they stop, stunned.*)

KRETON: You can't touch me. That's part of the game. (*He yawns.*) Now, if you don't mind, I shall go up to my room for a little lie-down.

SPELDING: I'll show you the way.

KRETON: That's all right. I know the way. (*Touches his brow.*) Such savage thoughts! My head is vibrating like a drum. I feel quite giddy, all of you thinking away. (*He starts to the door; he pauses beside* MRS. SPELDING.) No, it's not a dream, dear lady. I shall be here in the morning when you wake up. And now, good night, dear, wicked children. . . .

(*He goes as we fade out.*)

ACT TWO: *Fade in on* KRETON'S *bedroom next morning. He lies fully clothed on bed with cat on his lap.*

KRETON: Poor cat! Of course I sympathize with you. Dogs are distasteful. What? Oh, I can well believe they do: yes, yes, how disgusting. They don't ever groom their fur! But you do constantly, such a fine coat. No, no, I'm not just saying that. I really mean it: exquisite texture. Of course, I wouldn't say it was nicer than skin but even so. . . . What? Oh, no! They chase you! Dogs chase you for no reason at all except pure malice? You poor creature. Ah, but you do fight back! That's right! give it to them: slash, bite, scratch! Don't let them get away with a trick. . . . No! Do dogs

really do that? Well, I'm sure you don't. What . . . oh, well, yes
I completely agree about mice. They are delicious! (Ugh!) Pounce,
snap and there is a heavenly dinner. No, I don't know any mice
yet . . . they're not very amusing? But after all think how you
must terrify them because you are so bold, so cunning, so beautifully predatory! (*Knock at door.*) Come in.

ELLEN (*enters*): Good morning. I brought you your breakfast.

KRETON: How thoughtful! (*Examines bacon.*) Delicious, but I'm
afraid my stomach is not like yours, if you'll pardon me. I don't
eat. (*Removes pill from his pocket and swallows it.*) This is all
I need for the day. (*Indicates cat.*) Unlike this creature, who would
eat her own weight every hour, given a chance.

ELLEN: How do you know?

KRETON: We've had a talk.

ELLEN: You can speak to the cat?

KRETON: Not speak exactly but we communicate. I look inside and
the cat coöperates. Bright red thoughts, very exciting, though rather
on one level.

ELLEN: Does kitty like us?

KRETON: No. I wouldn't say she did. But then she has very few
thoughts not connected with food. Have you, my quadruped
criminal?

(*He strokes the cat, which jumps to the floor.*)

ELLEN: You know you've really upset everyone.

KRETON: I supposed that I would.

ELLEN: Can you really take over the world, just like that?

KRETON: Oh, yes.

ELLEN: What do you plan to do when you have taken over?

KRETON: Ah, that is my secret.

ELLEN: Well, I think you'll be a very nice President, if they let you
of course.

KRETON: What a sweet girl you are! Marry him right away.

ELLEN: Marry John?

KRETON: Yes. I see it in your head and in his. He wants you very
much.

ELLEN: Well, we plan to get married this summer, if father doesn't
fuss too much.

KRETON: Do it before then. I shall arrange it all if you like.

ELLEN: How?

KRETON: I can convince your father.

ELLEN: That sounds awfully ominous. I think you'd better leave poor Daddy alone.

KRETON: Whatever you say. (*Sighs.*) Oh, I love it so! When I woke up this morning I had to pinch myself to prove I was really here.

ELLEN: We were all doing a bit of pinching too. Ever since dawn we've had nothing but visitors and phone calls and troops outside in the garden. No one has the faintest idea what to do about you.

KRETON: Well, I don't think they'll be confused much longer.

ELLEN: How do you plan to conquer the world?

KRETON: I confess I'm not sure. I suppose I must make some demonstration of strength, some colorful trick that will frighten everyone . . . though I much prefer taking charge quietly. That's why I've sent for the President.

ELLEN: The President? Our President?

KRETON: Yes, he'll be along any minute now.

ELLEN: But the President just doesn't go around visiting people.

KRETON: He'll visit me. (*Chuckles.*) It may come as a surprise to him, but he'll be in this house in a very few minutes. I think we'd better go downstairs now. (*To cat.*) No, I will not give you a mouse. You must get your own. Be self-reliant. Beast!

(*Dissolve to the study.* POWERS *is reading book entitled: "The Atom and You". Muffled explosions off-stage.*)

AIDE (*entering*): Sir, nothing seems to be working. Do we have the General's permission to try a fission bomb on the force field?

POWERS: No . . . no. We'd better give it up.

AIDE: The men are beginning to talk.

POWERS (*thundering*): Well, keep them quiet (*Contritely.*) I'm sorry, Captain. I'm on edge. Fortunately, the whole business will soon be in the hands of the World Council.

AIDE: What will the World Council do?

POWERS: It will be interesting to observe them.

AIDE: You don't think this Kreton can really take over the world, do you?

POWERS: Of course not. Nobody can.

(*Dissolve to living room,* MRS. SPELDING *and* SPELDING *are talking.*)

MRS.SPELDING: You still haven't asked Mr. Kreton about moving that thing, have you?

SPELDING: There are too many important things to ask him.

MRS. SPELDING: I hate to be a nag but you know the trouble I have had getting anything to grow in that part of the garden . . .

JOHN (*enters*): Good morning.

MRS. SPELDING: Good morning, John.

JOHN: Any sign of your guest?

MRS. SPELDING: Ellen took his breakfast up to him a few minutes ago.

JOHN: They don't seem to be having much luck, do they? I sure hope you don't mind my staying here like this.

(SPELDING *glowers*.)

MRS. SPELDING: Why, we love having you! I just hope your family aren't too anxious.

JOHN: One of the G.I.'s finally called them, said I was staying here for the week-end.

SPELDING: The rest of our lives, if something isn't done soon.

JOHN: Just how long do you think that'll be, Dad?

SPELDING: Who knows?

(KRETON *and* ELLEN *enter*.)

KRETON: Ah, how wonderful to see you again! Let me catch my breath. . . . Oh, your minds! It's not easy for me; you know. So many crude thoughts blazing away! Yes, Mrs. Spelding, I will move the ship off your roses.

MRS. SPELDING: That's awfully sweet of you.

KRETON: Mr. Spelding, if any interviews are to be granted you will be the first, I promise you.

SPELDING: That's very considerate, I'm sure.

KRETON: So you can stop thinking those particular thoughts. And now where is the President?

SPELDING: The President?

KRETON: Yes, I sent for him. He should be here. (*He goes to the terrace window.*) Ah, that must be he. (*A swarthy man in uniform with a sash across his chest is standing, bewildered, on the terrace.* KRETON, *opens the glass doors.*) Come in, sir, come in. Your Excellency. Good of you to come on such short notice.

(*Man enters.*)

MAN (*in Spanish accent*): Where am I?

KRETON: You are the President, aren't you?

MAN: Of course I am the President. What am I doing here? I was dedicating a bridge and I find myself . . .

KRETON (*aware of his mistake*): Oh, dear! Where was the bridge?

MAN: Where do you think, you idiot, in Paraguay!

KRETON (*to others*): I seem to've made a mistake. Wrong President. (*Gestures and the man disappears.*) Seemed rather upset, didn't he?

JOHN: You can make people come and go just like that?

KRETON: Just like that.

(POWERS *looks into room from the study.*)

POWERS: Good morning, Mr. Kreton. Could I see you for a moment?

KRETON: By all means.

(*He crosses to the study.*)

SPELDING: I believe I am going mad.

(*Cut to study. The* AIDE *stands at attention while* POWERS *addresses* KRETON.)

POWERS: . . . and so we feel, the government of the United States feels that this problem is too big for any one country, therefore we are turning the whole affair over to Paul Laurent, the Secretary-General of the World Council.

KRETON: Very sensible. I should've thought of that myself.

POWERS: Mr. Laurent is on his way here now. And I may add, Mr. Kreton, you've made me look singularly ridiculous.

KRETON: I'm awfully sorry. (*Pause.*) No, you can't kill me.

POWERS: You were reading my mind again.

KRETON: I can't really help it, you know. And such black thoughts today, but intense, very intense.

POWERS: I regard you as a menace.

KRETON: I know you do and I think it's awfully unkind. I do mean well.

POWERS: Then go back where you came from and leave us alone.

KRETON: I'm afraid I can't do that just yet . . .

(*Phone rings, the* AIDE *answers it.*)

AIDE: He's outside? Sure, let him through. (*To* POWERS.) The Secretary-General of the World Council is here, sir.

POWERS (*to* KRETON): I hope you'll listen to him.

KRETON: Oh, I shall, of course. I love listening.

(*The door opens and* PAUL LAURENT, *middle-aged and serene, enters.* POWERS *and his* AIDE *stand to attention.* KRETON *goes forward to shake hands.*)

LAURENT: Mr. Kreton?

KRETON: At your service, Mr. Laurent.

LAURENT: I welcome you to this planet in the name of the World Council.

KRETON: Thank you sir, thank you.

LAURENT: Could you leave us alone for a moment. General?

POWERS: Yes, sir.

(POWERS *and* AIDE *go.* LAURENT *smiles at* KRETON.)

LAURENT: Shall we sit down?

KRETON: Yes. Yes I love sitting down. I'm afraid my manners are not quite suitable, yet.

(*They sit down.*)

LAURENT: Now, Mr. Kreton, in violation of all the rules of diplomacy, may I come to the point?

KRETON: You may.

LAURENT: Why are you here?

KRETON: Curiosity. Pleasure.

LAURENT: You are a tourist then in this time and place?

KRETON (*nods*): Yes. Very well put.

LAURENT: We have been informed that you have extraordinary powers.

KRETON: By your standards, yes, they must seem extraordinary.

LAURENT: We have also been informed that it is your intention to ... to take charge of this world.

KRETON: That is correct. . . . What a remarkable mind you have! I have difficulty looking inside it.

LAURENT (*laughs*): Practice. I've attended so many conferences. . . . May I say that your conquest of our world puts your status of tourist in a rather curious light?

KRETON: Oh, I said nothing about conquest.

LAURENT: Then how else do you intend to govern? The people won't allow you to direct their lives without a struggle.

KRETON: But I'm sure they will if I ask them to.

LAURENT: You believe you can do all this without, well, without violence?

KRETON: Of course I can. One or two demonstrations and I'm sure they'll do as I ask. (*Smiles*) Watch this.

(*Pause: Then shouting.* POWERS *bursts into room.*)

POWERS: Now what've you done?

KRETON: Look out the window, your Excellency. (LAURENT *goes to window. A rifle floats by, followed by an alarmed soldier.*) Nice, isn't it? I confess I worked out a number of rather melodramatic tricks last night. Incidentally, all the rifles of all the soldiers in the world are now floating in the air. (*Gestures*) Now they have them back.

POWERS (*to* LAURENT): You see, sir, I didn't exaggerate in my report.

LAURENT (*awed*): No, no, you certainly didn't.

KRETON: You were skeptical, were't you?

LAURENT: Naturally. But now I . . . now I think it's possible.

POWERS: That this . . . this gentleman is going to run everything?

LAURENT: Yes, yes I do. And it might be wonderful.

KRETON: You are more clever than the others. You begin to see that I mean only good.

LAURENT: Yes, only good. General, do you realize what this means? We can have one government . . .

KRETON: With innumerable bureaus, and intrigue. . . .

LAURENT (*excited*): And the world could be incredibly prosperous, especially if he'd help us with his superior knowledge.

KRETON (*delighted*): I will. I will. I'll teach you to look into one another's minds. You'll find it devastating but enlightening: all that self-interest, those lurid emotions . . .

LAURENT: No more countries. No more wars . . .

KRETON (*startled*): What? Oh, but I like a lot of countries. Besides, at this stage of your development you're supposed to have lots of countries and lots of wars . . . innumerable wars . . .

LAURENT: But you can help us change all that.

KRETON: Change all that! My dear, I am your friend.

LAURENT: What do you mean?

KRETON: Why, your deepest pleasure is violence. How can you deny that? It is the whole point to you, the whole point to my hobby . . . and you are my hobby, all mine.

LAURENT: But our lives are devoted to controlling violence, and not creating it.

KRETON: Now, don't take me for an utter fool. After all, I can see into your minds. My dear fellow, don't you know what you are?

LAURENT: What are we?

KRETON: You are savages. I have returned to the dark ages of an insignificant planet simply because I want the glorious excitement of being among you and revelling in your savagery! There is murder in all your hearts and I love it! It intoxicates me!

LAURENT (*slowly*): You hardly flatter us.

KRETON: I didn't mean to be rude but you did ask me why I am here and I've told you.

LAURENT: You have no wish then to . . . to help us poor savages.

KRETON: I couldn't even if I wanted to. You won't be civilized for at least two thousand years and you won't reach the level of my people for about a million years.

LAURENT (*sadly*): Then you have come here only to . . . to observe?

KRETON: No, more than that. I mean to regulate your past times. But don't worry: I won't upset things too much. I've decided I don't want to be known to the people. You will go right on with your countries, your squabbles, the way you always have, while I will secretly regulate things through you.

LAURENT: The World Council does not govern. We only advise.

KRETON: Well, I shall advise you and you will advise the governments and we shall have a lovely time.

LAURENT: I don't know what to say. You obviously have the power to do as you please.

KRETON: I'm glad you realize that. Poor Genearl Powers is now wondering if a hydrogen bomb might destroy me. It won't, General.

POWERS: Too bad.

KRETON: Now, your Excellency, I shall stay in this house until you have laid the groundwork for my first project.

LAURENT: And what is that to be?

KRETON: A War! I want one of your really splendid wars, with all the trimmings, all the noise and the fire . . .

LAURENT: A war! You're joking. Why at this moment we are working as hard as we know how not to have a war.

KRETON: But secretly you want one. After all, it's the one thing your little race does well. You'd hardly want me to deprive you of your simple pleasures, now would you?

LAURENT: I think you must be mad.

KRETON: Not mad, simply a philanthropist. Of course I myself shall get a great deal of pleasure out of a war (the vibrations must be incredible!) but I'm doing it mostly for you. So, if you don't mind, I want you to arrange a few incidents, so we can get one started spontaneously.

LAURENT: I refuse.

KRETON: In that event. I shall select someone else to head the World Council. Someone who will start a war. I suppose there exist a few people here who might like the idea.

LAURENT: How can you do such a horrible thing to us? Can't you see that we don't want to be savages?

KRETON: But you have no choice. Anyway, you're just pulling my leg! I'm sure you want a war as much as the rest of them do and that's what you're going to get: the biggest war you've ever had!

LAURENT (*stunned*): Heaven help us!

KRETON (*exuberant*): Heaven won't! Oh, what fun it will be! I can hardly wait!

(*He strikes the globe of the world a happy blow as we fade out.*)

ACT THREE: *Fade in on the study, two weeks later.* KRETON *is sitting at desk on which a map is spread out. He has a pair of dividers, some models of jet aircraft. Occasionally he pretends to dive bomb, imitating the sound of a bomb going off.* POWERS *enters.*

POWERS: You wanted me, sir?

KRETON: Yes, I wanted those figures on radioactive fall-out.

POWERS: They're being made up now. Anything else?

KRETON: Oh, my dear fellow, why do you dislike me so?

POWERS: I am your military aide, sir: I don't have to answer that question. It is outside the sphere of my duties.

KRETON: Aren't you at least happy about your promotion?

POWERS: Under the circumstances, no, sir.

KRETON: I find your attitude baffling.

POWERS: Is that all, sir?

KRETON: You have never said what you thought of my war plans. Not once have I got a single word of encouragement from you, a single compliment . . . only black thoughts.

POWERS: Since you read my mind, sir, you know what I think.

KRETON: True, but I can't help but feel that deep down inside of you there is just a twinge of professional jealousy. You don't like the idea of an outsider playing your game better than you do. Now confess!

POWERS: I am acting as your aide only under duress.

KRETON (*sadly*): Bitter, bitter . . . and to think I chose you especially as my aide. Think of all the other generals who would give anything to have your job.

POWERS: Fortunately, they know nothing about my job.

KRETON: Yes. I do think it wise not to advertise my presence, don't you?

POWERS: I can't see that it makes much difference, since you seem bent on destroying our world.

KRETON: I'm not going to destroy it. A few dozen cities, that's all, and not very nice cities either. Think of the fun you'll have building new ones when it's over.

POWERS: How many millions of people do you plan to kill?

KRETON: Well, quite a few, but they love this sort of thing. You can't convince me they don't. Oh, I know what Laurent says. But he's a misfit, out of step with his time. Fortunately, my new World Council is more reasonable.

POWERS: Paralyzed is the word, sir.

KRETON: You don't think they like me either?

POWERS: You *know* they hate you, sir.

KRETON: But love and hate are so confused in your savage minds and the vibrations of the one are so very like those of the other that I can't always distinguish. You see, we neither love nor hate in my world. We simply have hobbies. (*He strokes the globe of the world tenderly.*) But now to work. Tonight's the big night: first, the sneak attack, then: boom!

(*He claps his hands gleefully.*)

(*Dissolve to the living room, to* JOHN *and* ELLEN.)

ELLEN: I've never felt so helpless in my life.

JOHN: Here we all stand around doing nothing while he plans to blow up the world.

ELLEN: Suppose we went to the newspapers.

JOHN: He controls the press. When Laurent resigned they didn't even print his speech.

(*A gloomy pause.*)

ELLEN: What are you thinking about, John?

JOHN: Walnuts.

(*They embrace.*)

JOHN: No, I guess there's nothing.

ELLEN (*vehemently*): Oh! I could kill him!

(KRETON *and* POWERS *enter.*)

KRETON: Very good, Ellen, *very* good! I've never felt you so violent.

ELLEN: You heard what I said to John?

KRETON: Not in words, but you were absolutely bathed in malevolence.

POWERS: I'll get the papers you wanted, sir.

(POWERS *exits.*)

KRETON: I don't think he likes me very much but your father does. Only this morning he offered to handle my public relations and I said I'd let him. Wasn't that nice of him?

JOHN: I think I'll go get some fresh air.

(*He goes out through the terrace door.*)

KRETON: Oh, dear! (*Sighs.*) Only your father is really entering the spirit of the game. He's a much better sport than you, my dear.

ELLEN (*exploding*): Sport! That's it! You think we're sport. You think we're animals to be played with: well, we're not. We're people and we don't want to be destroyed.

KRETON (*patiently*): But *I* am not destroying you. You will be destroying one another of your own free will, as you have always done. I am simply a . . . a kibitzer.

ELLEN: No, you are a vampire!

KRETON: A vampire? You mean I drink blood? Ugh!

ELLEN: No, you drink emotions, our emotions. You'll sacrifice us all for the sake of your . . . your vibrations!

KRETON: Touché. Yet what harm am I really doing? It's true I'll enjoy the war more than anybody; but it will be your destructiveness after all, not mine.

ELLEN: You could stop it.

KRETON: So could you.

ELLEN: I?

KRETON: Your race. They could stop altogether but they won't. And I can hardly intervene in their natural development. The most I can do is help out in small, practical ways.

ELLEN: We are not what you think. We're not so . . . so primitive.

KRETON: My dear girl, just take this one household: your mother dislikes your father but she is too tired to do anything about it so she knits and she gardens and she tries not to think about him. Your father, on the other hand, is bored with all of you. Don't look shocked: he doesn't like you any more than you like him . . .

ELLEN: Don't say that!

KRETON: I am only telling you the truth. Your father wants you to marry someone important; therefore he objects to John while you, my girl . . .

ELLEN (*with a fierce cry,* ELLEN *grabs vase to throw*): You devil! (*Vase breaks in her hand.*)

KRETON: You see? That proves my point perfectly. (*Gently.*) Poor savage, I cannot help what you are. (*Briskly.*) Anyway. you will soon be distracted from your personal problems. Tonight is the night. If you're a good girl, I'll let you watch the bombing.

(*Dissolve to study: Eleven forty-five.* POWERS *and the* AIDE *gloomily await the war.*)

AIDE: General, isn't there anything we can do?

POWERS: It's out of our hands.

    (KRETON, *dressed as a Hussar with shako, enters.*)

KRETON: Everything on schedule?

POWERS: Yes, sir. Planes left for their targets at twenty-two hundred.

KRETON: Good . . . good. I myself, shall take off shortly after midnight to observe the attack first-hand.

POWERS: Yes, sir.

    (KRETON *goes into the living room where the family is gloomily assembled.*)

KRETON (*enters from study*): And now the magic hour approaches! I hope you're all as thrilled as I am.

SPELDING: You still won't tell us who's attacking whom?

KRETON: You'll know in exactly . . . fourteen minutes.

ELLEN (*bitterly*): Are we going to be killed too?

KRETON: Certainly not! You're quite safe, at least in the early stages of the war.

ELLEN: Thank you.

MRS. SPELDING: I suppose this will mean rationing again.

SPELDING: Will . . . will we see anything from here?

KRETON: No, but there should be a good picture on the monitor in the study. Powers is tuning in right now.

JOHN (*at window*): Hey look, up there! Coming this way!

    (ELLEN *joins him.*)

ELLEN: What is it?

JOHN: Why . . . it's another one! And it's going to land.

KRETON (*surprised*): I'm sure you're mistaken. No one would dream of coming here.

    (*He has gone to the window, too.*)

ELLEN: It's landing!

SPELDING: Is it a friend of yours, Mr. Kreton?

KRETON (*slowly*): No, no, not a friend . . .

    (KRETON *retreats to the study; he inadvertently drops a lace handkerchief beside the sofa.*)

JOHN: Here he comes.

ELLEN (*suddenly bitter*): Now we have two of them.

MRS. SPELDING: My poor roses.

    (*The new* VISITOR *enters in a gleam of light from his ship. He is wearing a most futuristic costume. Without a word, he walks past the awed family into the study.* KRETON *is cowering behind the globe.* POWERS *and the* AIDE *stare, bewildered, as the*

VISITOR *gestures sternly and* KRETON *reluctantly removes shako and sword. They communicate by odd sounds.*)

VISITOR (*to* POWERS): Please leave us alone.

(*Cut to living room as* POWERS *and the* AIDE *enter from the study.*)

POWERS (*to* ELLEN): Who on earth was that?

ELLEN: It's another one, another visitor.

POWERS: Now we're done for.

ELLEN: I'm going in there.

MRS. SPELDING: Ellen, don't you dare!

ELLEN: I'm going to talk to them.

(*Starts to door.*)

JOHN: I'm coming, too.

ELLEN (*grimly*): No, alone. I know what I want to say.

(*Cut to interior of the study, to* KRETON *and the other* VISITOR *as* ELLEN *enters.*)

ELLEN: I want you both to listen to me . . .

VISITOR: You don't need to speak. I know what you will say.

ELLEN: That you have no right here? That you mustn't . . .

VISITOR: I agree. Kreton has no right here. He is well aware that it is forbidden to interfere with the past.

ELLEN: The past?

VISITOR (*nods*): You are the past, the dark ages: we are from the future. In fact, we are your descendants on another planet. We visit you from time to time but we never interfere because it would change us if we did. Fortunately, I have arrived in time.

ELLEN: There won't be a war?

VISITOR: There will be no war. And there will be no memory of any of this. When we leave here you will forget Kreton and me. Time will turn back to the moment before his arrival.

ELLEN: Why did you want to hurt us?

KRETON (*heart-broken*): Oh, but I didn't! I only wanted to have . . . well, to have a little fun, to indulge my hobby . . . against the rules of course.

VISITOR (*to* ELLEN): Kreton is a rarity among us, Mentally and morally he is retarded. He is a child and he regards your period as his toy.

KRETON: A child, now really!

VISITOR: He escaped from his nursery and came back in time to you . . .

KRETON: And everything went wrong, everything! I wanted to visit 1860 . . . that's my real period but then something happened to the car and I ended up here, not that I don't find you nearly as interesting but . . .

VISITOR: We must go, Kreton.

KRETON (*to* ELLEN): You did like me just a bit, didn't you?

ELLEN: Yes, yes I did, until you let your hobby get out of hand. (*To* VISITOR.) What is the future like?

VISITOR: Very serene, very different . . .

KRETON: Don't believe him: it is dull, dull, dull beyond belief! One simply floats through eternity: no wars, no excitement . . .

VISITOR: It is forbidden to discuss these matters.

KRETON: I can't see what difference it makes since she's going to forget all about us anyway.

ELLEN: Oh, how I'd love to see the future . . .

VISITOR: It is against . . .

KRETON: Against the rules: how tiresome, you are (*To* ELLEN.) But, alas, you can never pay us a call because you aren't born yet! I mean where we are you are not. Oh, Ellen, dear, think kindly of me, until you forget.

ELLEN: I will.

VISITOR: Come. Time has begun to turn back. Time is bending.

(*He starts to door.* KRETON *turns conspiratorially to* ELLEN.)

KRETON: Don't be sad, my girl. I shall be back one bright day, but a bright day in 1860. I dote on the Civil War, so exciting . . .

VISITOR: Kreton!

KRETON: Only next time I think it'll be more fun if the South wins! (*He hurries after the* VISITOR.)

(*Cut to clock as the hands spin backwards. Dissolve to the living room, exactly the same as the first scene:* SPELDING, MRS. SPELD-ING, ELLEN.)

SPELDING: There is nothing wrong with marrying a wealthy man. The horror of it has always eluded me. However, my only wish is that you marry someone hard-working, ambitious, a man who'll make his mark in the world. Not a boy who is content to sit on a farm all his life, growing peanuts . . .

ELLEN: English walnuts! And he won't just sit there.

SPELDING: Will you stop contradicting me?

ELLEN: But, Daddy, John grows walnuts . . .

     (JOHN *enters.*)

JOHN: Hello, everybody.

MRS. SPELDING: Good evening, John.

ELLEN: What kept you, darling? You missed Daddy's broadcast.

JOHN: I saw it before I left home. Wonderful broadcast, sir.

SPELDING: Thank you, John.

     (JOHN *crosses to window.*)

JOHN: That meteor you were talking about, well, for a while it looked almost like a space ship or something. You can just barely see it now.

     (ELLEN *joins him at window. They watch, arms about one another.*)

SPELDING: Space ship! Nonsense! Remarkable what some people will believe, want to believe. Besides, as I said in the broadcast: if there's any traveling to be done in space we'll do it first.

He notices KRETON'S *handkerchief on sofa and picks it up. They all look at it, puzzled, as we cut to stock shot of the starry night against which two space ships vanish in the distance, one serene in its course, the other erratic, as we fade out.*

the wrecker

Saul Bellow

CAST
   A HUSBAND
   A WIFE
   A MOTHER-IN-LAW
   A CITY EMPLOYEE

SCENE: The living-room of a railroad flat on the East Side. Chesterfield suite, ribbon plants, rubber plants, all the cherished objects of the woman's temple, the man's asylum. At curtain wife and mother-in-law are discovered packing fragile articles into a barrel, wrapping them in paper.
   Suddenly, a huge crash backstage.

MOTHER-IN-LAW (*gives a shriek, suppresses it, asks angrily*) How can you stand it!

WIFE (*looks concerned; she leans forward slightly against the barrel, not daring to look in the direction of the noise*) I've been standing it since yesterday. I'll probably get used to it. They say you get used to any kind of noise.

MOTHER-IN-LAW: You should never have let him start.

WIFE: I held him back till yesterday, when the people downstairs moved. They were the last.

MOTHER-IN-LAW: The place is spooky. An empty building, and you on the third floor. They all left their trash on the stairs. It shows how inconsiderate people are. As long as there's a single tenant in the house they shouldn't have cluttered the staircase. I could hardly pass by.

WIFE (*sorrowfully patient with her mother*): I'm sorry mother, but it's the last time you'll be visiting me here anyway.

MOTHER-IN-LAW (*another rumbling noise offstage rear: she turns towards it*): I suppose he fought with all the neighbors enough.

You shouldn't be sorry to leave this . . . this dump. It ought to have been condemned years ago.

WIFE: Oh, I'm not exactly sorry. After fifteen years in the same place, though, you stop criticizing it. You never think whether it's a bad place or a good one.

MOTHER-IN-LAW: Nonsense. You ought to be happy to move into an elevator building. And get rid of the old dumbwaiter. And have white woodwork. And a toilet where you don't have to pull the chain. Things a person needs for her self-respect.

WIFE: It was good enough when I was a bride. (*Teary, thinking deep into the past.*) I was proud of it. And Albert used to be so kind about it. He helped me paper the walls. . . .

MOTHER-IN-LAW: Sarah, he's a neurotic.

WIFE: Oh, mother! You don't have to sound like a doctor.

    (*Terrible crash offstage*)

MOTHER-IN-LAW: Would any person in his right mind be doing that? Have you moved out the breakables?

WIFE: I took a lot of things over to the new apartment yesterday.

MOTHER-IN-LAW: I suppose you're trying to save money by doing the moving yourself. I'm positively disgusted. Why, on the bonus the City is offering you could have it all done for you while you went to Atlantic City or even Virginia Beach and took a rest. You'd come back to a clean house. He turns down the bonus the City's giving for moving a few days before the lease is up so they can start their work. He keeps you here, and you let him. Oh, it's maddening. A husband like that is maddening. I predict that on this very spot, in this very space, when the school is built they'll be teaching about men like him in the abnormal psychology course! Why, think what you could do with a thousand dollars. You could get a new coat.

WIFE: We could pay our debts.

MOTHER-IN-LAW: And last year he let his insurance policy lapse because of a hundred-dollar premium. He's of unsound mind. Don't try to tell me he's not.

WIFE (*mildly*): He doesn't believe in life insurance.

MOTHER-IN-LAW: I don't know where he gets his thoughts.

    (HUSBAND *enters pulling a mirror on casters, an oval mirror. He is wearing dusty overalls, a painter's cap and carries a hammer on his hip, a hatchet on the other side. He holds a short crowbar.*)

HUSBAND: I thought I'd better get this out of the way.

MOTHER-IN-LAW (*sarcastic*): Why not smash it. Break all the furniture too, while you're at it. It would be good for your temperament.

HUSBAND (*turning*): Oh, it's you. For once I'm glad to see you. Last night I dreamed you were here — like the bird at the battle. Welcome to the last of my house! (*He is very enthusiastic.*) (*To* WIFE.) Baby, I knocked out the pantry wall, and do you know what? now you can go from the kitchen to the dining-room without turning corners. It was thrilling to knock a hole in that wall. Oh! Wow, what excitement!

MOTHER-IN-LAW: Pretty expensive amusement.

HUSBAND: What do you mean, amusement!

MOTHER-IN-LAW: A thousand dollar amusement. Do you give any thought to what you could do with that money? Have you taken even five minutes off to sit down quietly in a corner and concentrate on what you could do? Your thoughts are always on the move, like the bottom of the sea.

HUSBAND: I have thought. With a thousand dollars I could pay off a lot of people who have never done anything except make me unhappy, and strengthen their hand so they make me and others like me still more unhappy. Installments! For a lot of stuff I never really needed!

MOTHER-IN-LAW: Like meat.

HUSBAND: Food I pay for. Those are debts of honor. But the other stuff. Huh!

MOTHER-IN-LAW: Like insurance.

HUSBAND: If I have to die, what will happen? The less secure Sarah is the more she'll feel my death. You want to be able to mourn for me, don't you, darling?

WIFE: Of course.

HUSBAND: There. And if I leave her too comfortable she won't feel my death acutely enough. Why should things be better when I die? The city is full of unhappy old women whose husbands left them well-off. It is like revenge from the grave. There lies the husband in the earth. With probably a telephone beside him . . . they say there is one beside Mary Baker Eddy. A monument to his wife's security. And now she goes shopping — she doesn't need anything. She goes to Schrafft's. She pesters the elevator starter to find her an Irish Sweepstakes ticket. She buys magazines and doesn't know what to do with herself.

MOTHER-IN-LAW (*snaps her fingers*): That! for you and your philosophy. A man who has no respect for a thousand dollars isn't intelligent. You're a scared to do better in life.

HUSBAND: I'm getting a thousand dollars' worth out of it. More. (*Shakes his crowbar like a spear.*) Oh, what am I wasting words on you for! Today I'm a man of deeds, like a hero out of Homer, like a man who does something for civilization.

WIFE: This is what he keeps saying.

HUSBAND: Where there's no demolition there's no advancement. The old must go down. You only see what is built. You forget what had to be taken away, and yet it is the same process. Man does not wait for time to do his work for him. He makes an end; he begins again.

(*Pounds the floor with the butt of his crowbar. A picture falls from the wall.*)

WIFE: Look what you've done!

MOTHER-IN-LAW: If you have to tear down walls, why don't you go downstairs and do it. They've moved out and nobody'll care. Then you'd have the bonus and your fun.

HUSBAND: It shows how little you understand. The neighbor's walls do not interest me. It was right here that everything happened to me. Here I was out of work, and looked at the walls. And here I was sick, and looked at the walls. And here I was blue, and here I cursed the world. And here maybe I learned my own limitations — oh, yes, that realization that I wasn't all I thought I was. It all took place within these walls. It went into them. And you ask me what I've got against them? *Plenty!* I *know* them. Oh, I've made a long study of them. There's a long history between us. And now that they have to come down why shouldn't I put my hand to the work? Who has a better right — a more sacred right? Why should I leave it to anyone? I will do it. Myself, I'll tear holes out. I'll see the East River through the dining-room. I'll have the satisfaction myself, and get my revenge for all those terrible times. What good will the walls downstairs do me? I want to take it out on my own walls. I know every lump, every blister, every face in the cracks of the ceiling. Now I'm going to see what this place is made of, what the walls are like inside. I'm going to tear out the laths and get behind all the swellings — like the brows, eyes, landscapes and so on. I'll find all the rats' nests and see if there are any treasures or bones. You can never tell what you'll find in an old building.

WIFE (*to* MOTHER): You see how overexcited he is?

MOTHER-IN-LAW: I see he's passing up an opportunity to make your life easier because he wants to play like a boy. Treasures! People ought to be forced to be their age. What if he put on a sailor suit and told you he was going to sail his little boat in Central Park pond? What a sex the males are! It's a miracle how anything ever works out.

HUSBAND: I am excited! I feel like Samson in the Temple of Gaza! (*So poses in the doorway.*) Take cover, ye Philistines, your oppression is ended. My strength has come back to me. Though you took my hair and put out my eyes and bound me in your mill your walls are doomed! Doomed!

MOTHER-IN-LAW (*a little frightened*): He's off his rock.

HUSBAND (*rousing himself*): I am not. (*Points at her with the crowbar; says seriously.*) Beware of diagnosing those near to you. You should never do that. Not even when it's true. At your age you should know better. What you think is lunacy is just happiness. You aren't used to it, probably haven't seen it in a long time. You've forgotten what it looks like.

WIFE: You are happy?

HUSBAND: Tremendously. Can't you see how happy I am? I'm a new man. And that's why I snap my fingers at the thousand dollar bonus. If I were as usual I'd need that thousand to help me bear it.

WIFE: Is it as bad as that to be as usual?

(*She is wounded.*)

HUSBAND: My dear, don't you take the blame for that. A daily life is a strange thing, and what are a husband and wife to do? They must live it together. Nobody is to blame. But these last two days I have carried a marvelous feeling in my heart. Like a poet. I have welcomed each night's sleep and blessed every morning's rising. I have been like a young boy reading a wonderful book who must put it down at night and says to himself, "Just close your eyes a while and when you open them again it will be morning and you can go on with it." And in the morning, which comes soon, it's very sweet; his book is still wonderful; it doesn't disappoint him. This is how my days have been since I started wrecking this apartment.

WIFE (*pathetic*): I didn't know you hated it so.

MOTHER-IN-LAW: All I can say is that I hope it will pass over before it gets to the Bellevue stage.

(*A ring at the door.* WIFE *answers and admits the* CITY EM-PLOYEE. *He has a portfolio under his arm — cardboard — and his double-breasted suit is chalkstriped. An eater of clams and drinker of beer. Seeing ladies he takes the toothpick from his mouth and with same hand removes his hat.*)

CITY EMPLOYEE: It gets kind of peculiar in a building when everybody leaves it.

WIFE: Oh, it's the man from the City.

MOTHER-IN-LAW (*best manners*): How do you do.

WIFE: It is spooky, isn't it. Yesterday as I was cooking supper it was the first time I could remember that there was no radio program downstairs at Pellegrini's, and nobody playing the piano. It was just like the last days of some poor old widow.

CITY EMPLOYEE: I come to open this bonus situation again. You understand, there's people waiting to start operations, the wrecking crew, the excavators, contractors. It's not exactly playing the game when everybody else has taken the bonus and moved out.

HUSBAND: My lease runs for three weeks yet.

CITY EMPLOYEE: You could be evicted with eminent domain.

HUSBAND: It still would take weeks. Try it.

CITY EMPLOYEE: It's no good trying to hold the City up for more dough, if that's your idea.

HUSBAND: So, you think I have an idea to get dough out of you?

MOTHER-IN-LAW: I wish I thought he was that smart.

CITY EMPLOYEE: Well, you don't want to put the City on the spot like this.

HUSBAND: What do I care about the City? It never did me a favor in all my life.

CITY EMPLOYEE: What are you talkin'. There's invisible benefits all over. The sidewalks, the sewers, the water, the bridges, the garbage, the police. . . .

HUSBAND: The police are no invisible benefit.

(*Swings his crowbar over his shoulder, turns about limberly and marches away.* CITY EMPLOYEE *stands amazed. A great crash is heard. Staggering.*)

CITY EMPLOYEE: What's that — what's he doin'?

MOTHER-IN-LAW: Can't you guess?

WIFE: Mother!

MOTHER-IN-LAW: Do you think you can keep it a secret? He's wrecking the house.

WIFE: Mother, that's downright disloyal.

CITY EMPLOYEE: Is he nuts or something? (*Slams hat against thigh.*) Who said he could? This is bought by the City. He's on m'nicipal

property. Why, it ain't legal anyhow. (*Another crash.* CITY EM-
PLOYEE *shouts down corridor.*) Hey!

(*No answer.* CITY EMPLOYEE *exits, rear.*)

MOTHER-IN-LAW: Now maybe we'll get somewhere with that stubborn man.

WIFE: Now he's in trouble.

MOTHER-IN-LAW: He deserves it.

WIFE: No he doesn't. You don't understand him.

MOTHER-IN-LAW: If I had to live with him fifteen years to understand him it wouldn't be worth it.

(CITY EMPLOYEE *re-enters covered with white dust, quivering with anger. He shouts down corridor, rear.*)

CITY EMPLOYEE: Who the hell do you think you are! (*Another crash.*) Who gave you the right? (*Sound of chopping.*) Lady, your husband better not carry this any further. I'm tellin' you for your own good. He's poundin' chunks out of the walls with a sledge hammer. This just is not allowed, and that's all.

WIFE: Why not? It's his right. Isn't a man's home his castle?

CITY EMPLOYEE (*startled, wiping his face*): He can have it for his castle, but not for his loony bin. Besides, it ain't his. The City bought it and they can get him for damaging municipal property.

WIFE: They've got their nerve. We paid enough rent before the City even heard of it.

MOTHER-IN-LAW: The way you stand up for him!

WIFE: Of course I do. Ain't I the man's wife? I know what he's been through if you don't, and if he wants his revenge on the place it's his by right.

CITY EMPLOYEE (*feels his ear*): Do I understand, lady, that he's passin' up the bonus just to do the wreckin' job on this place himself? (*Hears the* HUSBAND *hammering within. His face passes through wonder, outrage, envy and finally stops at an expression of law violated.*) It's not only crazy but illegal. It's real bad. For this he can go to jail. (*Draws forth notebook, looks about, makes notes.*) He don't even have a permit.

MOTHER-IN-LAW: I knew all along it was something fundamental.

WIFE: I don't understand why.

CITY EMPLOYEE: Lady, for one thing wrecking is a licensed occupation. You can't just go wreck. You have to know how. You must realize it's a profession like any other and you have to qualify for it. How does he know what to do about electricity, gas, water? Can he take out the bathtub or the toilet, any fixtures? He'd be shocked, suffocated or drowned. And what about the street? You have to protect your pedestrians. Where's your scaffold? Where's your dumping? He can get the book thrown at him.

(*Thunderous crash.* HUSBAND *enters carrying framed wedding picture.*)

HUSBAND: I think this wedding picture got jarred, dear. No real harm. Better put it away.

WIFE (*catches breath*): You're starting on the bedroom!

(*She takes picture from him, holds it tightly.*)

HUSBAND: I thought I might do a little work in there later today.

WIFE: The bedroom.

CITY EMPLOYEE: Listen bud, you're heading into all kinds of trouble.

WIFE (*from a different viewpoint*): Yes, Albert, you are.

HUSBAND: The City wants to have this place torn down, doesn't it? It wants a school built here, doesn't it? Suppose I volunteered my help in tearing down my own apartment? They'd never accept it. I'd have to see people and fill forms and answer questions and in the end I wouldn't get in on it. So I'm independently contributing my labor. What's wrong with that?

(*Hooks crowbar into mantelpiece and wrenches off top. Bric-a-brac goes flying.*)

WIFE (*wildly*): Oh, my things! The sea-shells! The little jug from Vermont! The little cups!

(*Goes on hands and knees.* MOTHER-IN-LAW, *muttering, helps.*)

HUSBAND: Oh, it's nothing, Sarah. I'll get you new knick-knacks. These are about worn out. Look at that grand cockroach. If it isn't the oldest resident in person! He's not even disturbed. What presence. This is what you call aristocracy. Fifteen years we've been his vassals. He's never done a lick of work, I'll bet. Why should he?

MOTHER-IN-LAW (*to* CITY EMPLOYEE): You see what's happening? But it's probably just temporary. You ought to give him till tomorrow to decide. He'll most likely come back to his senses.

CITY EMPLOYEE: He's off his control, all right, I can see that.

HUSBAND: See what a difference the point of view makes. I never was better. I am a magician. This joint is enchanted, you see. I'm getting rid of a lot of past life, dangerous to the soul. The past, you understand, is very dangerous if you don't deal with it. If I had a warehouse I could put this harmful past life into, or if I could take it to sea in a scow and dump it, let the seagulls have it, I'd be satisfied. You can't drag your heavy, heavy history around with you.

Suppose the humming bird had to keep remembering that in the ancient past it was a snake?

CITY EMPLOYEE (*touching his forehead*): Oh, man!

(*He goes out.*)

MOTHER-IN-LAW: I'd better talk to him. Maybe I can make him hold off a while. You'd better reason with *him* meanwhile and please God his mentality will return.

(*Exit.*)

WIFE (*broken cup in hand*): Albert. . . .

HUSBAND: Yes, darling?

WIFE: Isn't there anything — anything here you don't hold a grudge against?

HUSBAND (*speculative*): I suppose there is.

WIFE: You suffered in every room?

HUSBAND: Well, you carry it around from room to room, you see.

WIFE: The bedroom, too.

HUSBAND (*uneasy*): No more than the others, probably.

WIFE: Isn't there anything you'd like to save instead of wreck? You might remember something that made your life worth-while.

HUSBAND: Of course. You want to be fair about it.

WIFE (*with light irony*): The kitchen, perhaps, in memory of good meals. (*He shrugs. Wife changes tone.*) Albert, I have tried to make you a home. We've had many bad times, that's true. But didn't I comfort you? That time you came in and said your paycheck was stolen?

HUSBAND (*feebly*): It was, too.

WIFE: The time you were knocked down by the cab on Lexington Avenue and I brought you home from the hospital in a taxi, and when you woke up at night I'd go and make tea for you and stay awake with you. And what about the time the furniture company wanted to repossess the living-room suite . . . ?

HUSBAND: Yes, I remember.

WIFE: And what about the time we came back from Jones Beach that afternoon, and. . . .

HUSBAND: Sure, sure, that was great. That was a wonderful afternoon, wasn't it.

WIFE: What about all those good things?

HUSBAND: We haven't forgotten. Did I say we should? But let's not get sentimental, old girl. Because when you come right down to it, you can't check off every grievance against a happy time. You can't have happy times if you have to swallow all the grievances. Any-

482   **drama** | affirmative re-orientation

how, this is too much like bookkeeping. Why do you have to pretend to me that you're not sore at this joint, too? It never bored
you? Didn't it ever make you want to yell? Didn't you ever feel
here that you were in a cage? Didn't these walls ever look at you
with yellow foreheads and their lousy, dull eyes? Don't kid me.

WIFE (*hesitant*): Sometimes, of course.

HUSBAND (*hands her a hatchet*): What are you waiting for, then?
Be honest. Pitch in.

WIFE (*decisively rejects hatchet*): No, I'm not going to. I papered
and painted these walls myself, and washed the floors and the
woodwork.

HUSBAND: And swore at the landlord.

WIFE: Never mind the landlord. We lived here.

HUSBAND: We suffered here.

WIFE: That would have happened to you anywhere.

HUSBAND: Sometimes you ought to give in to your violent feelings,
Sarah. It's great to be angry. Anger is beautiful. It gives you a sense
of honor. It brings back your self-respect.

WIFE: All right, then. I am angry.

HUSBAND: About what?

WIFE: It's the bedroom I'm angry about. You haven't been happy,
and this is your way of saying it.

HUSBAND (*without enough emphasis*): Yes, I have been. Well, look
here, Sarah old girl. Let's not act in bad faith. I mean — you know.
If it isn't always what it should be, at least you don't have to think
you're protecting the home by pretending. Most likely it all clears
up in the end. . . .

WIFE: You don't love me.

HUSBAND (*indignant*): Of course I love you. Do you think I'm
wrecking this joint for myself? Every other hole I pound in the wall
is for you. I say, "This is for Sarah. This is where she bowed her
head. This is where she heard bad news. This is where she scalded
her foot. Where we argued. . . ."

WIFE: But the bedroom, Albert, the bedroom.

HUSBAND: Well, come and help me bust up the dining-room and we
can discuss the bedroom later. It's only another room.

WIFE: It isn't. And if you touch it. . . .

HUSBAND: Threats?

WIFE: You can't expect me to be overjoyed.

HUSBAND: And you can't expect me to be superhuman like you. If
you can forgive everything, that's your good luck. But if I did it I'd

be acting in bad faith. Things always should be nice, that's for sure. But tell me, why is it so glorious to tear this house down? Why is it ecstasy to see the ceilings fall, and chopping I feel like dancing, and the smell of dust makes my heart float with joy, like the smell of flowers, and I never feel tired?

WIFE: Have I tried to stop you? Did I insist about the thousand dollars? Did I complain at having to pack all the things myself?

HUSBAND: All that is true. Still, you should be glad I have found something that cries aloud to be done, an object. . . .

WIFE: Yes, I should be delighted that you don't knock me down; I should be pleased you don't batter me on the head with your axe, like the pantry shelves.

HUSBAND: Sweetheart, please understand. An object. . . .

WIFE: . . . is a substitute for me. Because I've had you in a trap. Was this your home or was it the Bastille? Did it mean nothing to you? Did you have to lie down each night worried that animals might bite you in your sleep, or people run in to attack you? You have no gratitude in your make-up. I often go back to where I used to live when I was a girl. The lot is vacant and nobody I know is there. I ask myself, "Where is everything that meant so much to me?" I'd bring it back if I could. Next year there'll be a school here, and children sitting where we used to. . . .

HUSBAND: They'll be studying history.

WIFE: And where will we be?

HUSBAND: In the new apartment.

WIFE: No, I'm speaking of the lives we used to lead here. Where will they be?

HUSBAND: And where will the lives the children will lead here be later on? You say this was the Bastille for me. Don't you mean that you want it to be a museum?

WIFE: Albert, I don't think I've made you a bad wife.

HUSBAND: Of course not.

WIFE: I've given in to your impulses and you always had my first consideration. I've never stood in your way. You want to wreck the house? Go ahead, wreck it!

HUSBAND: Angel!

WIFE: Only, if you wreck the bedroom, you'll be moving into the new apartment by yourself.

HUSBAND: You don't mean it!

WIFE: I'll leave you. It was you who told me anger was wonderful.

HUSBAND: You wouldn't do that.

WIFE: I will. And what else can I do? You force me into it.

HUSBAND: I am convinced now. Only the most ordinary men should become husbands. Whatever they may dream of, when you come right down to it women want their husbands to be ordinary and to make no trouble. Husbands are not heroes: heroes are not husbands. That's all there is to it.

WIFE: Do you call what you're doing heroism? (*She laughs.*)

HUSBAND: Amuse yourself if you like. It shows you never applied your mind to this subject. Does it say anywhere that Achilles ever built anything? Or Ulysses? They tore down Troy and killed everyone in it. Who were the heroes of the war? The fellows who dropped bombs on cities. A hero destroys the links with the past when they bother him. He frees himself from what other men have done before him.

WIFE (*indignant*): Other men before him? Are you trying to say. . . . What other men have ever been in that bedroom? Accusing me!

HUSBAND: No, no, no. Why do you have to be so damned literal? Besides . . . you don't have to protest so much. You'll make me think I'm missing up on something. Is it some other bedroom I should be thinking of tearing down? Is that it?

WIFE (*startled at first, then reproachful*): How can such things ever enter your mind? Oh, Albert!

HUSBAND: I always mean well, but my mind betrays me. Ah, Sarah, come along. (*Active again.*) Try it. When you've tried it you'll understand what I've been driving at. You have to prime yourself sometimes. Take one sock at a wall. Just one. See how different you'll feel. (*Hands her his hatchet.*) You don't realize what you'll get out of it.

WIFE: No. I've already told you what I'd do.

HUSBAND: Come, free yourself, Sarah.

WIFE: No, that's not what I call freeing myself. It's ingratitude.

HUSBAND: You're not big, but you sure are obstinate. And also because it was *your* house it was wonderful. That's how vain you are.

WIFE: Now I will leave. It's a lucky thing I thought of opening a bank account of my own.

HUSBAND: You're far too rigid — far, far. You have to learn to be more flexible. It's a practical matter. For the sake of your health.

WIFE (*sighs and shakes her head*): How many ideas you have. Do you want me to believe that what you're doing you're doing for your health's sake?

HUSBAND: Of course it's for my health. (*To audience.*) I'm dead serious. (*To* WIFE.) Now why else do you think I'm being so truthful? It's risky. If I say too much you'll get sore. But if I don't do it I feel sick. (*Puts back of hands to eyes and brings hands away with a whisking motion.*) Let's wipe out some of the falsehood. Let's admit what our souls tell us is true and stop denying it for the sake of keeping the peace or preserving the marriage and the home. Yes, just because of health. So the old bedroom will be destroyed, but maybe then the new one will be fit for princes and queens. Maybe it will make the roses bloom from the plaster and daisies from the rug.

WIFE (*half swayed*): Oh, Albert, do you really think so?

HUSBAND: Yes, yes. So come. We'll take some of the doors off the hinges and set them up. Have you noticed how pretty it is when the wreckers are working, with blue doors and pink doors standing outside? And you know how the plaster was always falling into the bath-tub, well now we can fill the tub with plaster. Rip up the old linoleum. Tear up the floors. Go through the place like a hurricane. Come on.

WIFE (*steels herself*): No.

HUSBAND (*turning*): You won't?

WIFE: I told you what I'd do.

HUSBAND: It's the bedroom?

WIFE: Yes, I'll leave.

HUSBAND (*furious*): All right, go then. Go. Damn! Take your shells and your damn precious female breakables, your Vermont jugs and your slave-chains of china, and get out of here. I'll wreck the joint myself. I'll demolish it; I'll raze it; I'll tear it to pieces; I'll level it down to the ground.

> (*Smites ceiling with crowbar. Chandelier falls and hits him on the head. He drops to floor.*)

WIFE (*rushing to him*): Oh, he's fractured his skull. Albert, Baby. Oh, sweetheart, what have you done? Mother! Mama! Oh, help. (*Kisses him, rubs his hands, examines his head, listens to his heart.*) It must be a concussion. I'll never forgive myself if it is. If he had to do it, at least I could have stuck by him and made him do it in a safer way. Oh, my little sweetheart. Little bright-thoughts. (*As he revives.*) My spunky one. You stood right up to me. Oh, honey, you were so right. Let's never quarrel. How does it feel?

> (*He groans, holds his head, starts to sit up.*)

HUSBAND: If it was any heavier it would have killed me. I bit my tongue.

WIFE: Albert, darling; Albert, look at me! (*She takes the hatchet and starts delicately to chip at the walls.*) Albert, you see, I've got the idea. It's just as you said. It really is glorious. (*Finds bulb and throws it down. Is slightly shocked by noise and own daring.*) Oh, Albert, how slow I am to learn anything. If I didn't have you to show me the way I'd be just a timid, conservative, pokey little creature worrying like a mole. Imagine how it would be to live a whole life without doing anything big.

    (*Chips away at the fireplace.*)

HUSBAND: Just about knocked my brains out. What are you doing?

    (*Watches.*)

WIFE: Doing? Why, what you tried to convince me to do, for my own good. And I couldn't agree with you more.

HUSBAND (*doesn't look happy about it*): Wait a minute.

WIFE (*still chipping*): Why, what's the matter? Is it the noise?

HUSBAND: Now hold on a minute.

WIFE: But you've convinced me. . . .

HUSBAND: Yes, but I'm not so sure . . . On you it doesn't look so good.

WIFE: Why not, I'd like to know. Now you want to stop me? Just as I've discovered what you meant? I know you didn't expect me to, but I have found out and you (*Shakes her head.*) don't want me to?

HUSBAND (*rising, uncomfortable*): It's not that exactly.

WIFE: How's your head?

HUSBAND: All right, I guess.

WIFE: You don't feel dizzy?

HUSBAND: Not very. It's a miracle.

WIFE (*hands him crowbar*): Then you can go back to work.

    (*Kisses him.*)

HUSBAND: I do think I need a little rest first.

WIFE: But not for long. I suddenly feel such strength in me. As soon as I picked up the hatchet it just poured into my hands. An hour ago they felt so feeble I couldn't have peeled a potato. Rest, dear, and then we can start on the bedroom together.

HUSBAND: The bedroom?

WIFE: Of course, the bedroom.

HUSBAND (*thinking*): You. . . .

WIFE: Of course. I. Now that I understand what you meant.

HUSBAND: Well, Sarah, (*Haltingly.*) is it really — I mean from your standpoint — such a good idea?

WIFE: You don't want to wreck it? I do, now. When I think of some of the things that happened, all of a sudden I want to express what I never dared. . . .

HUSBAND (*reprovingly*): Sarah!

WIFE: Well, I want to admit what's true, too. You have nothing against that, have you? There are a few places on the ceiling that just burn me up when I think of them. I've only now become conscious of it all.

HUSBAND: Sarah, don't you feel . . . ? Are you sure?

WIFE: Why, darling, you surprise me. Have you changed your mind about the bedroom? Why, silly, didn't you tell me a daily life was a strange thing, and what were husband and wife to do about it . . . they have to live it together?

HUSBAND: Yes, yes, of course. But. . . .

WIFE: And don't you want to wreck the house?

HUSBAND: Yes, but all at once you want to start with the bedroom. Tell me something. . . .

WIFE: What is there to tell? Do I have to draw pictures?

HUSBAND: Please, Sarah.

WIFE (*once more offers him the crowbar*): Are you with me or not? Are you going to back down or will you come alone?

HUSBAND: All right.

(*He is very reluctant.*)

WIFE: Better fetch a stepladder. I'm mad to get at that ceiling. (*Grips hatchet, and laughs exultantly.*) Something has just entered my mind.

HUSBAND: What?

WIFE: That maybe the best way to preserve the marriage is to destroy the home.

(*Embraces him.*)

HUSBAND (*mildly*): It may well be.

(*Curtain. After which, a thunderous crash*)

Final - Tuesday · 1230 - 230

Spondee - 2 accent syllables in a row
    baseball dat·dat

all poems

dactilic - accent on 1st syllable
    dat·da - dat·da - dat da

iambic - accent on 2nd syllable
    da dat - da·dat da·dat

poetry

birches

Robert Frost

[handwritten: iambic pentameter]

[handwritten: fact] When I see birches bend to left and right
Across the lines of straighter darker trees,
[handwritten: fic] I like to think some boy's been swinging them.
But swinging doesn't bend them down to stay.
[handwritten: fact] Ice-storms do that. Often you must have seen them
Loaded with ice a sunny winter morning
After a rain. They click upon themselves
As the breeze rises, and turn many-colored *[handwritten: description & imagination]*
As the stir cracks and crazes their enamel.
Soon the sun's warmth makes them shed crystal shells
[handwritten: fic] Shattering and avalanching on the snow-crust —
Such heaps of broken glass to sweep away *[handwritten: metaphor → extended.]*
You'd think the inner dome of heaven had fallen.
They are dragged to the withered bracken by the load,
And they seem not to break; though once they are bowed

So low for long, they never right themselves:
You may see their trunks arching in the woods
Years afterwards, trailing their leaves on the ground
Like girls on hands and knees that throw their hair
Before them over their heads to dry in the sun.
But I was going to say when Truth broke in
With all her matter-of-fact about the ice-storm
I should prefer to have some boy bend them
As he went out and in to fetch the cows —
Some boy too far from town to learn baseball,
Whose only play was that he found himself,
Summer or winter, and could play alone.
One by one he subdued his father's trees
By riding them down over and over again
Until he took the stiffness out of them,
And not one but hung limp, not one was left
For him to conquer. He learned all there was
To learn about not launching out too soon
And so not carrying the tree away
Clear to the ground. He always kept his poise
To the top branches, climbing carefully
With the same pains you use to fill a cup
Up to the brim, and even above the brim.
Then he flung outward, feet first, with a swish,
Kicking his way down through the air to the ground.
So was I once myself a swinger of birches.
And so I dream of going back to be.
It's when I'm weary of considerations,
And life is too much like a pathless wood
Where your face burns and tickles with the cobwebs
Broken across it, and one eye is weeping
From a twig's having lashed across it open.
I'd like to get away from earth awhile
And then come back to it and begin over.
May no fate willfully misunderstand me
And half grant what I wish and snatch me away
Not to return. Earth's the right place for love:
I don't know where it's likely to go better.
I'd like to go by climbing a birch tree,
And climb black branches up a snow-white trunk
Toward heaven, till the tree could bear no more,

But dipped its top and set me down again.
That would be good both going and coming back.
One could do worse than be a swinger of birches.

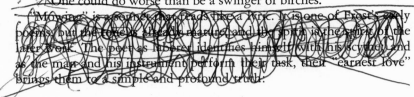

"Mowing" is a sonnet that reads like a lyric. It is one of Frost's early poems, but the tone is already mature and the spirit is the spirit of the later work. The poet as laborer identifies himself with his scythe, and as the man and his instrument perform their task, their "earnest love" brings them to a simple and profound truth:

The fact is the sweetest dream that labor knows.

"Birches" assured the reader that "Earth's the right place for love." "For love — and labor, too," adds the scythe, whispering to the ground.

sunday afternoon

Denise Levertov

After the First Communion
and the banquet of mangoes and
bridal cake, the young daughters
of the coffee merchant lay down
for a long siesta, and their white dresses
lay beside them in quietness
and the white veils floated
In their dreams as the flies buzzed.
But as the afternoon
burned to a close they rose
and ran about the neighbourhood
among the halfbuilt villas
alive, alive, kicking a basketball, wearing
other new dresses, of bloodred velvet.

river of my people

Pete Seeger

> There's a river of my people
> And its flow is swift and strong,
> Flowing to some mighty ocean
> Though its course is deep and long. } (2)
>
> Many rocks and reefs and mountains
> Seek to bar it from its way,
> But relentlessly this river
> Seeks its brothers at the sea. } (2)
>
> You will find me in the mainstream
> Steering surely through the foam,
> Far beyond its raging waters
> I can see our certain home. } (2)
>
> For I have met this river
> And I know its mighty force,
> And the courage that this gives me
> Will hold me to my course. } (2)
>
> O river of my people
> Together we must go,
> Hasten onward to that meeting
> Where my brothers wait I know. } (2)

our own odysseus

Frederic Will

i: calypso

Letters failing to leave that mark
Of decision which every woman requires,
I came to the city again,
Presuming the strongest parting was best,
And told her sister the plan to meet
In the public garden at eight.

A probe of sun that striped the delicious grass
Expired at the tip of my shoe, a robin
Hopped like a toy on exotic shrubs
And called the elaborate day to order,
And into it all she came
Like morning itself.

All was the same to the eye as before,
Intently and puzzled her smile
Put off an allowable kiss.
She sat on the narrow bench
And waited to hear me repeat
My lascivious slavery
Or some impossible hope of my own.
I fought with the need to please,
And touched her wrist through a red-silk sleeve.

"The wind has changed. Voices come
In the afternoon from every point of the compass.
Nothing is still inside, I move with my life."
She smiled, assuring her limpid eye
That only my style had changed. I gathered
A wedge of words:
                    "Living assembles
My strength, the staying is wrong at last.
Oceans remain to cross, my thought is still.

Reprinted with permission from the Southwest Review.

Your beauty will stay in the thought of your beauty,
Our love in the thought of our love."

                                        She turned,
Observing a wren in the grass, she turned
Before I could turn my shapeless talk
And even in that slight motion
I saw the change of a world
The loss of a world
And no word left for the finding.

ii: teiresias

My thought could not know him better
With the candles low and our chairs at the window
The city was still

Only a cab was heard from one to two
Lovers laughing in their own worlds
The sound of the turning world
It was warm in the room
He went on

"So it will be, choice upon choice gone,
All chance as lost as your ruined limbs.
So it will be in some room, your jaw sunk,
And your nails brittle, but you will leave much.
Stinking with time and place, your genitals
Empty, your fists soft, your eyes mere wells in your head,
So much will be left."

                        He turned to the window:
Then, drowning the kiting moon in his smoke, looked back.

"And all will be nothing, city on city sunk
In the eye's steep shaft,
Ticket by ticket the world crossed,
The last town as strange as the others,
Its name in a dubious alphabet
And your own name hard to remember.
All will be nothing, lost in the swamp
Of an old man's memory."

                                        Shadows had spread
In the room. I went to the window.
The city was still and crossed with channels of light,
A dog was barking, the stars were clear.
I touched the window, my hand as light as its light;
The pane was open, a breeze crossed the elm.
"So identity fails at last? My passport is lost
At the border, I leave my wallet in an inn?
I sit at a strange table, my friends forgotten,
The moon the only eye that remembers? Well
May it be so. I almost recall it now, that inn,
As though I had started there, and life
Was a going back. Someone is asking: "Your name
Old man? Your people? This is another country,
Your words are old." And this is the thought I await.
Only the world is left, the moon and sea are my speech,
I go out into the night. It is only the start.
I can remember nothing. Only the elements live.
I go to the shore where the moon has lighted
The sand. I start, and walk, and the world
Is new. Year after year I walk, shore
After shore, with the strength of rock. You smile?

He extinguished his cigarette. His fingers were thin
And nervous.

"So it will be in some room, your eyes mere wells
In your head and your jaws sunk.
But much must be left."

I saw him smile in the shadows.
His face was still.
His eyes were filmy and dead.

iii: penelope

Had I been longer away, a life, or briefer,
The time for ideas to change while habits stay:
Still, it was our house, our things in the house,
The lamp we bought in Berlin, the painting

My brother gave us in Paris. I stood in the hall,
You smiled, while all we could turn to advantage
Was weather.
               Her face was no longer mine,
Her voice was a stranger's. But the coffee was good:
I started the history then, from, well, birth
To death is not long — it took an hour to tell.
With all the details left out, that is.
From time to time she stopped me to ask of a friend
Or a certain city or word of another country:
Dusk was settling by six: I expected to stay, of course?

The dinner was quiet. She in her turn was quiet,
Saying as much and as little
As I had said. Her dress was an emerald woll,
She'd worn it once on the ship from Spain:
I had attempted to dance to hold her then.
She served the potatoes and spoke: of friends,
A summer abroad, the quiet shape of her days.
Her eye was her own, the screen of her soul,
And left me little for longing, except when her hand
Retrieved a rambunctious lock of hair, or her mouth
Laughed. Nothing but being together was quite the same.
Even the being together was different. I smoked
In the parlor later, a green cigar: she sneezed
And opened the window. She answered the phone
And spoke in a way I took for love
In words that I took for signs. It was hard.
At ten I started to go.
               Her face was no longer mine,
Her eye had history now, she stood like a woman
Given and worn with giving; her body had tired
Of its secrets. Her eye was no longer mine,
But something could smile between us. I took her hand,
Her hand remembered.
                  With nothing more certain than that
I left. She at the old door,
I at the old door leaving.

The stars were bright. There was no moon.

iv: odysseus

The train stopped often that night
In the towns with unknown names
And only a channel of bulbs
On a still main street.

An old man gaping like death, who'd slept
In the seat in front, got off.
I saw him limp with his bags as we left.
The train ground on, field after field lay slack
In the shapeless night.

The others who stayed were sleeping.
A negress and three black girls,
A nurse who slept outstretched in the dirty seat,
A porter who smoked and counted his stubs.
The floor was covered with crumbs
The windows with soot.

County by county the world went.
I blew my nose and used the latrine.
I stood in the observation car and reaped
The land with a glance.

And stopped at the least of the towns,
Taking my single bag.
There were none to see me go or arrive;
The town was still as a graveyard,
Only the cop was quick
Who drank his coffee at Burman's
And watched the desirable waitress.

Least of the towns, smallest,
Wood and stone on the ancient plain,
A store, a church, a courthouse square;
Only a stage-set, up for my random eye.
It was half-past four.
The sky was lighter. Orion was low.

By five I had crossed the town
To the first fields. The hills to the east were forming,
The dream of the sun was remembering the long sky.
I walked down the country road,
My back old, my eyes mere wells
In my skull, my hand the clutch of a bone
On my bag. Soon the town was too far to see.

The road was a dusty quai,
The fields a living ocean; wheat shoots
Tearing the humid ground, lines of green
Embroidered as far as the soil's cloth lay.
Nothing was silent: the sun-climb
Deafened from over the chunky hills,
The wheat split clod after noisy clod
And drank the elated dawn.

Nothing was still or held.
I sang with the others,
Caught the preposterous note of beginning
Till my back grew straight
And my eye whole,
And I enteerd the road's new country,
Younger than any child.

the picnic

John Logan

It is the picnic with Ruth in the spring.
Ruth was third on my list of seven girls
But the first two were gone (Betty) or else
Had someone (Ellen has accepted Doug).
Indian Gully the last day of school;

Girls make the lunches for the boys too.
I wrote a note to Ruth in algebra class
Day before the test. She smiled, and nodded.
We left the cars and walked through the young corn
The shoots green as paint and the leaves like tongues
Trembling. Beyond the fence where we stood
Some wild strawberry flowered by an elm tree
And Jack-in-the-pulpit was olive ripe.
A blackbird fled as I crossed, and showed
A spot of gold or red under its quick wing.
I held the wire for Ruth and watched the whip
Of her long, striped skirt as she followed.
Three freckles blossomed on her thin, white back
Underneath the loop where the blouse buttoned.
We went for our lunch away from the rest,
Stretched in the new grass, our heads close
Over unknown things wrapped up in wax papers.
Ruth tried for the same, I forget what it was,
And our hands were together. She laughed,
And a breeze caught the edge of her little
Collar and the edge of her brown, loose hair
That touched my cheek. I turned my face in-
to the gentle fall. I saw how sweet it smelled.
She didn't move her head or take her hand.
I felt a soft caving in my stomach
As at the top of the highest slide
When I had been a child, but was not afraid,
And did not know why my eyes moved with wet
As I brushed her cheek with my lips and brushed
Her lips with my own lips. She said to me
Jack, Jack, different than I had ever heard,
Because she wasn't calling me, I think,
Or telling me. She used my name to
Talk in another way I wanted to know.
She laughed again and then she took her hand;
I gave her what we both had touched — can't
Remember what it was, and we ate the lunch.
Afterward we walked in the small, cool creek
Our shoes off, her skirt hitched, and she smiling,
My pants rolled, and then we climbed up the high
Side of Indian Gully and looked

Where we had been, our hands together again.
It was then some bright thing came in my eyes,
Starting at the back of them and flowing
Suddenly through my head and down my arms
And stomach and my bare legs that seemed not
To stop in feet, not to feel the red earth
Of the Gully, as though we hung in a
Touch of birds. There was a word in my throat
With the feeling and I knew the first time
What it meant and I said, it's beautiful.
Yes, she said, and I felt the sound and word
In my hand join the sound and word in hers
As in one name said, or in one cupped hand.
We put back on our shoes and socks and we
Sat in the grass awhile, crosslegged, under
A blowing tree, not saying anything.
And Ruth played with shells she found in the creek,
As I watched. Her small wrist which was so sweet
To me turned by her breast and the shells dropped
Green, white, blue, easily into her lap,
Passing light through themselves. She gave the pale
Shells to me, and got up and touched her hips
With her light hands, and we walked down slowly
To play the school games with the others.

without invention

William Carlos Williams

Without invention nothing is well spaced,
unless the mind changes, unless
the stars are new measured, according
to their relative positions, the

From *Paterson, II* by William Carlos Williams. Copyright 1948 by William Carlos Williams, 1963 by Florence Williams. Reprinted by permission of the publisher, New Directions Publishing Corp.

line will not change, the necessity
will not matriculate: unless there is
a new mind there cannot be a new
line, the old will go on
repeating itself with recurring
deadliness: without invention
nothing lies under the witch-hazel
bush, the alder does not grow from among
the hummocks margining the all
but spent channel of the old swale,
the small foot-prints
of the mice under the overhanging
tufts of the bunch-grass will not
appear: without invention the line
will never again take on its ancient
divisions when the word, a supple word,
lived in it, crumbled now to chalk.

salutation

Ezra Pound

A generation of the thoroughly smug
    and thoroughly uncomfortable,
I have seen fishermen picnicking in the sun,
I have seen them with untidy families,
I have seen their smiles full of teeth
    and heard ungainly laughter.
And I am happier than you are,
And they were happier than I am;
And the fish swim in the lake
    and do not even own clothing.

a time to talk

Robert Frost

When a friend calls to me from the road
And slows his horse to a meaning walk,
I don't stand still and look around
On all the hills I haven't hoed,
And shout from where I am, "What is it?"
No, not as there is a time to talk.
I thrust my hoe in the mellow ground,
Blade-end up and five feet tall,
And plod: I go up to the stone wall
For a friendly visit.

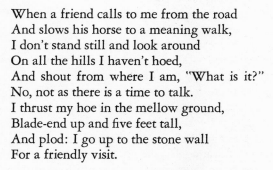

underwear

Lawrence Ferlinghetti

I didn't get much sleep last night
thinking about underwear
Have you ever stopped to consider
underwear in the abstract
When you really dig into it
some shocking problems are raised
Underwear is something
we all have to deal with
Everyone wears
some kind of underwear

Even Indians
wear underwear
Even Cubans
wear underwear
The Pope wears underwear I hope
Underwear is worn by Negroes
The Governor of Louisiana
wears underwear
I saw him on TV
He must have had tight underwear
He squirmed a lot
Underwear can really get you in a bind
Negroes often wear
white underwear
which may lead to trouble
You have seen the underwear ads
for men and women
so alike but so different
Women's underwear holds things up
Men's underwear holds things down
Underwear is one thing
men and women have in common
Underwear is all we have between us
You have seen the three-color pictures
with crotches encircled
to show the areas of extra strength
and three-way stretch
promising full freedom of action
Don't be deceived
It's all based on the two-party system
which doesn't allow much freedom of choice
the way things are set up
America in its Underwear
struggles thru the night
Underwear controls everything in the end
Take foundation garments for instance
They are really fascist forms
of underground government
making people believe
something but the truth
telling you what you can or can't do

Did you ever try to get around a girdle
Perhaps Non-Violent Action
is the only answer
Did Gandhi wear a girdle?
Did Lady Macbeth wear a girdle?
Was that why Macbeth murdered sleep?
And that spot she was always rubbing —
Was it really in her underwear?
Modern anglosaxon ladies
must have huge guilt complexes
always washing and washing and washing
Out damned spot — rub don't blot —
Underwear with spots very suspicious
Underwear with bulges very shocking
Underwear on clothesline a great flag of freedom
Someone has excaped his Underwear
May be naked somewhere
Help!
But don't worry
Everybody's still hung up in it
There won't be no real revolution
And poetry still the underwear of the soul
And underwear still covering
a multitude of faults
in the geological sense —
strange sedimentary stones, inscrutable cracks!
And that only the beginning
For does not the body stay alive
after death
and still need its underwear
or outgrow it
some organs said to reach full maturity
only after the head stops holding them back?
If I were you I'd keep aside
an oversize pair of winter underwear
Do not go naked into that good night
And in the meantime
keep calm and warm and dry
No use stirring ourselves up prematurely
'over Nothing'
Move forward with dignity

hand in vest
Don't get emotional
And death shall have no dominion
There's plenty of time my darling
Are we not still young and easy
Don't shout

jazz fantasia

Carl Sandburg

Drum on your drums, batter on your banjos, sob on the long and winding saxophones. Go to it, O jazzmen.

Sling your knuckles on the bottoms of the happy timpans, let your trombones ooze, and go hush-husha-hush with the slippery sand-paper.

Moan like an autumn wind high in the lonesome treetops, moan soft like you wanted somebody terrible, cry like a racing car slipping away from a motor-cycle cop, bang-bang! you jazzmen, bang alto-gether drums, traps, banjos, horns, tin cans — make two people fight on the top of a stairway and scratch each other's eyes in a clinch tumbling down the stairs.

Can the rough stuff . . . Now a Mississippi steamboat pushes up the night river with a hoo-hoo-hoo-oo . . . and the green lanterns calling to the high soft stars . . . a red moon rides on the humps of the low river hills . . . Go to it, O jazzmen.

nonfiction

my negro problem—*and ours*

Norman Podhoretz

> If we — and . . . I mean the relatively conscious whites
> and the relatively conscious blacks, who must, like
> lovers, insist on, or create, the consciousness of the
> others — do not falter in our duty now, we may be
> able, handful that we are, to end the racial nightmare,
> and achieve our country, and change the history of
> the world.
>
> — James Baldwin

Two ideas puzzled me deeply as a child growing up in Brooklyn
during the 1930's in what today would be called an integrated
neighborhood. One of them was that all Jews were rich; the other was
that all Negroes were persecuted. These ideas had appeared in print;
therefore they must be true. My own experience and the evidence of
my senses told they were not true, but that only confirmed what a day-
dreaming boy in the provinces — for the lower-class neighborhoods of
New York belong as surely to the provinces as any rural town in

Reprinted from *Doings and Undoings* by Norman Podhoretz, by permission of
Farrar, Straus & Giroux, Inc. Copyright © 1963 by Norman Podhoretz.

North Dakota — discovers very early: *his* experience is unreal and the evidence of his senses is not to be trusted. Yet even a boy with a head full of fantasies incongruously synthesized out of Hollywood movies and English novels cannot altogether deny the reality of his own experience — especially when there is so much deprivation in that experience. Nor can he altogether gainsay the evidence of his own senses — especially such evidence of the senses as comes from being repeatedly beaten up, robbed, and in general hated, terrorized, and humiliated.

And so for a long time I was puzzled to think that Jews were supposed to be rich when the only Jews I knew were poor, and that Negroes were supposed to be persecuted when it was the Negroes who were doing the only persecuting I knew about — and doing it, moreover, to *me.* During the early years of the war, when my older sister joined a left-wing youth organization, I remember my astonishment at hearing her passionately denounce my father for thinking that Jews were worse off than Negroes. To me, at the age of twelve, it seemed very clear that Negroes were better off than Jews — indeed, than *all* whites. A boy's world is contained within three or four square blocks, and in my world it was the whites, the Italians and Jews, who feared the Negroes, not the other way around. The Negroes were tougher than we were, more ruthless, and on the whole they were better athletes. What could it mean, then, to say that they were badly off and that we were more fortunate? Yet my sister's opinions, like print, were sacred, and when she told me about exploitation and economic forces I believed her. I believed her, but I was still afraid of Negroes. And I still hated them with all my heart.

It had not always been so — that much I can recall from early childhood. When did it start, this fear and this hatred? There was a kindergarten in the local public school, and given the character of the neighborhood, at least half of the children in my class must have been Negroes. Yet I have no memory of being aware of color differences at that age, and I know from observing my own children that they attribute no significance to such differences even when they begin noticing them. I think there was a day — first grade? second grade? — when my best friend Carl hit me on the way home from school and announced that he wouldn't play with me any more because I had killed Jesus. When I ran home to my mother crying for an explanation, she told me not to pay any attention to such foolishness, and then in Yiddish she cursed the *goyim* and the *schwartzes,* the *schwartzes* and the *goyim.* Carl, it turned out, was a *schwartze,* and so was added a third to the categories into which people were mysteriously divided.

Sometimes I wonder whether this is a true memory at all. It is blazingly vivid, but perhaps it never happened: can anyone really remember back to the age of six? There is no uncertainty in my mind, however, about the years that followed. Carl and I hardly ever spoke, though we met in school every day up through the eighth or ninth grade. There would be embarrassed moments of catching his eye or of his catching mine — for whatever it was that had attracted us to one another as very small children remained alive in spite of the fantastic barrier of hostility that had grown up between us, suddenly and out of nowhere. Nevertheless, friendship would have been impossible, and even if it had been possible, it would have been unthinkable. About that, there was nothing anyone could do by the time we were eight years old.

Item: The orphanage across the street is torn down, a city housing project begins to rise in its place, and on the marvelous vacant lot next to the old orphanage they are building a playground. Much excitement and anticipation as Opening Day draws near. Mayor La-Guardia himself comes to dedicate this great gesture of public benevolence. He speaks of neighborliness and borrowing cups of sugar, and of the playground he says that children of all races, colors, and creeds will learn to live together in harmony. A week later, some of us are swatting flies on the playground's inadequate little ball field. A gang of Negro kids, pretty much our own age, enter from the other side and order us out of the park. We refuse, proudly and indignantly, with superb masculine, fervor. There is a fight, they win, and we retreat, half whimpering, half with bravado. My first nauseating experience of cowardice. And my first appalled realization that there are people in the world who do not seem to be afraid of anything, who act as though they have nothing to lose. Therefore the playground becomes a battleground, sometimes quiet, sometimes the scene of athletic competition between Them and Us. But rocks are thrown as often as baseballs. Gradually we abandon the place and use the streets instead. The streets are safer, though we do not admit this to ourselves. We are not, after all, sissies — that most dreaded epithet of an American boyhood.

Item: I am standing alone in front of the building in which I live. It is late afternoon and getting dark. That day in school the teacher

had asked a surly Negro boy named Quentin a question he was unable to answer. As usual I had waved my arm eagerly ("Be a good
boy, get good marks, be smart, go to college, become a doctor") and,
the right answer bursting from my lips, I was held up lovingly by
the teacher as an example to the class. I had seen Quentin's face — a
very dark, very cruel, very Oriental-looking face — harden, and there
had been enough threat in his eyes to make me run all the way home
for fear that he might catch me outside.

Now, standing idly in front of my house, I see him approaching
from the project accompanied by his little brother who is carrying a
baseball bat and wearing a grin of malicious anticipation. As in a
nightmare, I am trapped. The surroundings are secure and familiar,
but terror is suddenly present and there is no one around to help. I am
locked to the spot. I will not cry out or run away like a sissy, and I
stand there, my heart wild, my throat clogged. He walks up, hurls the
familiar epithet ("Hey, mo'f —— r"), and to my surprise only pushes
me. It is a violent push, but not a punch. Maybe I can still back out
without entirely losing my dignity. Maybe I can still say, "Hey, c'mon
Quentin, whaddya wanna do *that* for? I dint do nothin' to you," and
walk away, not too rapidly. Instead, before I can stop myself, I push
him back — a token gesture — and I say, "Cut that out, I don't wanna
fight, I ain't got nothin' to fight about." As I turn to walk back into
the building, the corner of my eye catches the motion of the bat his
little brother has handed him. I try to duck, but the bat crashes
colored lights into my head.

The next thing I know, my mother and sister are standing over
me, both of them hysterical. My sister — she who was later to join
the "progressive" youth organization — is shouting for the police and
screaming imprecations at those dirty little black bastards. They take
me upstairs, the doctor comes, the police come. I tell them that the
boy who did it was a stranger, that he had been trying to get money
from me. They do not believe me, but I am too scared to give them
Quentin's name. When I return to school a few days later, Quentin
avoids my eyes. He knows that I have not squealed, and he is ashamed.
I try to feel proud, but in my heart I know that it was fear of what
his friends might do to me that had kept me silent, and not the code
of the street.

Item: There is an athletic meet in which the whole of our junior
high school is participating. I am in one of the seventh-grade rapid-
advance classes, and "segregation" has now set in with a vengeance.

In the last three or four years of the elementary school from which we have just graduated, each grade had been divided into three classes, according to "intelligence." (In the earlier grades the divisions had either been arbitrary or else unrecognized by us as having anything to do with brains.) These divisions by IQ, or however it was arranged, had resulted in a preponderance of Jews in the "1" classes and a corresponding preponderance of Negroes in the "3's," with the Italians split unevenly along the spectrum. At least a few Negroes had always made the "1's," just as there had always been a few Jewish kids among the "3's" and more among the "2's" (where Italians dominated). But the junior high's rapid-advance class of which I am now a member is overwhelmingly Jewish and entirely white — except for a shy lonely Negro girl with light skin and reddish hair.

The athletic meet takes place in a city-owned stadium far from the school. It is an important event to which a whole day is given over. The winners are to get those precious little medallions stamped with the New York City emblem that can be screwed into a belt and that prove the wearer to be a distinguished personage. I am a fast runner, and so I am assigned the position of anchor man on my class's team in the relay race. There are three other seventh-grade teams in the race, two of them all Negro, as ours is all white. One of the all-Negro teams is very tall — their anchor man waiting silently next to me on the line looks years older than I am, and I do not recognize him. He is the first to get the baton and crosses the finishing line in a walk. Our team comes in second, but a few minutes later we are declared the winners, for it has been discovered that the anchor man on the first-place team is not a member of the class. We are awarded the medallions, and the following day our home-room teacher makes a speech about how proud she is of us for being superior athletes as well as superior students. We want to believe that we deserve the praise, but we know that we could not have won even if the other class has not cheated.

That afternoon, walking home, I am waylaid and surrounded by five Negroes, among whom is the anchor man of the disqualified team. "Gimme my medal, mo'f —— r," he grunts. I do not have it with me and I tell him so. "Anyway, it ain't yours," I say foolishly. He calls me a liar on both counts and pushes me up against the wall on which we sometimes play handball. "Gimme my mo'f —— n' medal," he says again. I repeat that I have left it home. "Le's search the li'l mo'f —— r," one of them suggests, "he prolly got it *hid* in his mo'f —— n' *pants*." My panic is now unmanageable. (How many

times had I been surrounded like this and asked in soft tones, "Len'
me a nickel, boy." How many times had I been called a liar for
pleading poverty and pushed around, or searched, or beaten up, unless
there happened to be someone in the marauding gang like Carl who
liked me across that enormous divide of hatred and who would therefore say, "Aaah, c'mon, le's git someone else, *this* boy ain't got no
money on 'im.") I scream at them through tears of rage and self-
contempt, "Keep your f —— n' filthy lousy black hands offa me! I
swear I'll get the cops." This is all they need to hear, and the five of
them set upon me. They bang me around, mostly in the stomach and
on the arms and shoulders, and when several adults loitering near
the candy store down the block notice what is going on and begin to
shout, they run off and away.

I do not tell my parents about the incident. My team-mates, who
have also been waylaid, each by a gang led by his opposite number
from the disqualified team, have had their medallions taken from
them, and they never squeal either. For days, I walk home in terror,
expecting to be caught again, but nothing happens. The medallion is
put away in a drawer, never to be worn by anyone.

Obviously experiences like these have always been a common
feature of childhood life in working-class and immigrant neighborhoods, and Negros do not necessarily figure in them. Wherever, and
in whatever combination, they have lived together in the cities, kids
of different groups have been at war, beating up and being beaten up:
micks against kikes against wops against spiks against polacks. And
even relatively homogeneous areas have not been spared the warring
of the young: one black against another, one gang (called in my day, in
a pathetic effort at gentility, an "S.A.C.," or social-athletic club)
against another. But the Negro-white conflict had — and no doubt still
has — a special intensity and war conducted with a ferocity unmatched
by intramural white battling.

In my own neighborhood, a good deal of animosity existed between the Italian kids (most of whose parents were immigrants from
Sicily) and the Jewish kids (who came largely from East European
immigrant families). Yet everyone had friends, sometimes close
friends, in the other "camp," and we often visited one another's
strange-smelling houses, if not for meals, then for glasses of milk,
and occasionally for some special event like a wedding or a wake. If
it happened that we divided into warring factions and did battle, it
would invariably be half-hearted and soon patched up. Our parents,

to be sure, had nothing to do with one another and were mutually suspicious and hostile. But we, the kids, who all spoke Yiddish or Italian at home, were Americans, or New Yorkers, or Brooklyn boys: we shared a culture, the culture of the street, and at least for a while this culture proved to be more powerful than the opposing cultures of the home.

Why, *why* should it have been so different as between the Negroes and us? How was it borne in upon us so early, white and black alike, that we were enemies beyond any possibility of reconciliation? Why did we hate one another so?

I suppose if I tried, I could answer those questions more or less adequately from the perspective of what I have since learned. I could draw upon James Baldwin — what better witness is there? — to describe the sense of entrapment that poisons the soul of the Negro with hatred for the white man whom he knows to be his jailer. On the other side, if I wanted to understand how the white man comes to hate the Negro, I could call upon the psychologists who have spoken of the guilt that white Americans feel toward Negroes and that turns into hatred for lack of acknowledging itself as guilt. These are plausible answers and certainly there is truth in them. Yet when I think back upon my own experience of the Negro and his of me, I find myself troubled and puzzled, much as I was as a child when I heard that all Jews were rich and all Negroes persecuted. How could the Negroes in my neighborhood have regarded the whites across the street and around the corner as jailers? On the whole, the whites were not so poor as the Negroes, but they were quite poor enough, and the years were years of Depression. As for white hatred of the Negro, how could guilt have had anything to do with it? What share had these Italian and Jewish immigrants in the enslavement of the Negro? What share had they — downtrodden people themselves breaking their own necks to eke out a living — in the exploitation of the Negro?

No, I cannot believe that we hated each other back there in Brooklyn because they thought of us as jailers and we felt guilty toward them. But does it matter, given the fact that we all went through an unrepresentative confrontation? I think it matters profoundly, for if we managed the job of hating each other so well without benefit of the aids to hatred that are supposedly at the root of this madness everywhere else it must mean that the madness is not yet properly understood. I am far from pretending that I understand it, but I would insist that no view of the problem will begin to approach the truth unless it can account for a case like the one I have been trying to describe. Are the elements of any such view available to us?

At least two, I would say, are. One of them is a point we frequently come upon in the work of James Baldwin, and the other is a related point always stressed by psychologists who have studied the mechanisms of prejudice. Baldwin tells us that one of the reasons Negroes hate the white man is that the white man refuses to *look* at him: the Negro knows that in white eyes all Negroes are alike; they are faceless and therefore not altogether human. The psychologists, in their turn, tell us that the white man hates the Negro because he tends to project those wild impulses that he fears in himself onto an alien group which he then punishes with his contempt. What Baldwin does *not* tell us, however, is that the principle of facelessness is a two-way street and can operate in both directions with no difficulty at all. Thus, in my neighborhood in Brooklyn, *I* was as faceless to the Negroes as they were to me, and if they hated me because I never looked at them, I must also have hated them for never looking at *me*. To the Negroes, my white skin was enough to define me as the enemy, and in a war it is only the uniform that counts and not the person.

So with the mechanism of projection that the psychologists talk about: it too works in both directions at once. There is no question that the psychologists are right about what the Negro represents symbolically to the white man. For me as a child the life lived on the other side of the playground and down the block on Ralph Avenue seemed the very embodiment of the values of the street — free, independent, reckless, brave, masculine, erotic. I put the word "erotic" last, though it is usually stressed above all others, because in fact it came last, in consciousness as in importance. What mainly counted for me about Negro kids of my own age was that they were "bad boys." There were plenty of bad boys among the whites — this was, after all, a neighborhood with a long tradition of crime as a career open to aspiring talents — but the Negroes were *really* bad, bad in a way that beckoned to one, and made one feel inadequate. *We* all went home every day for a lunch of spinach-and-potatoes; *they* roamed around during lunch hour, munching on candy bars. In winter *we* had to wear itchy woolen hats and mittens and cumbersome galoshes; *they* were bare-headed and loose as they pleased. *We* rarely played hookey, or get into serious trouble in school, for all our street-corner bravado; *they* were defiant, forever staying out (to do what delicious things?), forever making disturbances in class and in the halls, forever being sent to the principal and returning uncowed. But most important of all, they were *tough;* beautifully, enviably tough, not giving a damn for anyone or anything. To hell with the teacher, the truant officer, the cop; to hell with the whole of the adult world that held *us* in its grip and that we never had the courage to rebel against except sporadically and in petty ways.

This is what I saw and envied and feared in the Negro: this is what finally made him faceless to me, though some of it, of course, was actually there. (The psychologists also tell us that the alien group which becomes the object of a projection will tend to respond by trying to live up to what is expected of them.) But what, on his side, did the Negro see in me that made me faceless to *him?* Did he envy me my lunches of spinach-and-potatoes and my itchy woolen caps and my prudent behavior in the face of authority, as I envied him his noon-time candy bars and his bare head in winter and his magnificent rebelliousness? Did those lunches and caps spell for him the prospect of powers and riches in the future? Did they mean that there were possibilities open to me that were denied to him? Very likely they did. But if so, one also supposes that he feared the impulses within himself toward submission to authority no less powerfully than I feared the impulses in myself toward defiance. If I represented the jailer to him, it was not because I was oppressing him or keeping him down: it was because I symbolized for him the dangerous and probably pointless temptation toward greater repression, just as he symbolized for me the equally perilous tug toward greater freedom. I personally was to be rewarded for this repression with a new and better life in the future, but how many of my friends paid an even higher price and were given only gall in return.

We have it on the authority of James Baldwin that all Negroes hate whites. I am trying to suggest that on their side all whites — all American whites, that is — are sick in their feelings about Negroes. There are Negroes, no doubt, who would say that Baldwin is wrong, but I suspect them of being less honest than he is, just as I suspect whites of self-deception who tell me they have no special feeling toward Negroes. Special feelings about color are a contagion to which white Americans seem susceptible even when there is nothing in their background to account for the susceptibility. Thus everywhere we look today in the North we find the curious phenomenon of white middle-class liberals with no previous personal experience of Negroes — people to whom Negroes have always been faceless in virtue rather than faceless in vice — discovering that their abstract commitment to the cause of Negro rights will not stand the test of a direct confrontation. We find such people fleeing in droves to the suburbs as the Negro population in the inner city grows; and when they stay in the city we find them sending their children to private school rather than to the "integrated" public school in the neighborhood. We find them resisting the demand that gerrymandered school districts be re-zoned for the purpose of overcoming de facto segregation; we find them judiciously considering whether the Negroes (for their own good, of course) are not perhaps pushing too hard; we find them clucking their tongues over Negro militancy; we find them speculating on the question of whether there may not, after all, be something in the theory that the races are biologically different; we find them saying that it will take a very long time for Negroes to achieve full equality, no matter what anyone does; we find them deploring the rise of black nationalism and expressing the solemn hope that the leaders of the Negro community will discover ways of containing the impatience and incipient violence within the Negro ghettos.*

But that is by no means the whole story; there is also the phenomenon of what Kenneth Rexroth once called "crow-jimism." There are the broken-down white boys like Vivaldo Moore in Baldwin's *Another Country* who go to Harlem in search of sex or simply to brush up against something that looks like primitive vitality, and who are so often punished by the Negroes they meet for crimes that they would have been the last ever to commit and of which they themselves have been as sorry victims as any of the Negroes who take it out on them. There are the writers and intellectuals and artists who romanticize Negroes and pander to them, assuming a guilt that is not properly theirs. And there are all the white liberals who permit Negroes to blackmail them into adopting a double standard of moral judgment, and who lend themselves — again assuming the responsibility for crimes they never committed — to cunning and contemptuous exploitation by Negroes they employ or try to befriend.

And what about me? What kind of feelings do I have about Negroes today? What happened to me, from Brooklyn, who grew up fearing and envying and hating Negroes? Now that Brooklyn is behind me, do I fear them and envy them and hate them still? The answer is yes, but not in the same proportions and certainly not in the same way. I now live on the upper west side of Manhattan, where there are many Negroes and many Puerto Ricans, and there are nights

---

* For an account of developments like these, see "The White Liberal's Retreat" by Murray Friedman in the January 1963 *Atlantic Monthly*.

when I experience the old apprehensiveness again, and there are streets that I avoid when I am walking in the dark, as there were streets that I avoided when I was a child. I find that I am not afraid of Puerto Ricans, but I cannot restrain my nervousness whenever I pass a group of Negroes standing in front of a bar or sauntering down the street. I know now, as I did not know when I was a child, that power is on my side, that the police are working for me and not for them. And knowing this I feel ashamed and guilty, like the good liberal I have grown up to be. Yet the twinges of fear and the resentment they bring and the self-contempt they arouse are not to be gainsaid.

But envy? Why envy? And hatred? Why hatred? Here again the intensities have lessened and everything has been complicated and qualified by the guilts and the resulting over-compensation that are the heritage of the enlightened middle-class world of which I am now a member. Yet just as in childhood I envied Negroes for what seemed to me their superior masculinity, so I envy them today for what seems to me their superior physical grace and beauty. I have come to value physical grace very highly, and I am now capable of aching with all my being when I watch a Negro couple on the dance floor, or a Negro playing baseball or basketball. They are on the kind of terms with their own bodies that I should like to be on with mine, and for that precious quality they seemed blessed to me.

The hatred I still feel for Negroes is the hardest of all the old feelings to face or admit, and it is the most hidden and the most over-larded by the conscious attitudes into which I have succeeded in willing myself. It no longer has, as for me it once did, any cause or justification (except, perhaps, that I am constantly being denied my right to an honest expression of the things I earned the right as a child to feel). How, then, do I know that this hatred has never entirely disappeared? I know it from the insane rage that can stir in me at the thought of Negro anti-Semitism; I know it from the disgusting prurience that can stir in me at the sight of a mixed couple; and I know it from the violence that can stir in me whenever I encounter that special brand of paranoid touchiness to which many Negroes are prone.

This, then, is where I am; it is not exactly where I think all other white liberals are, but it cannot be so very far away either. And it is because I am convinced that we white Americans are — for whatever reason, it no longer matters — so twisted and sick in our feelings about

Negroes that I despair of the present push toward integration. If the pace of progress were not a factor here, there would perhaps be no cause for despair: time and the law and even the international political situation are on the side of the Negroes, and ultimately, therefore, victory — of a sort, anyway — must come. But from everything we have learned from observers who ought to know, pace has become as important to the Negroes as substance. They want equality and they want it *now,* and the white world is yielding to their demand only as much and as fast as it is absolutely being compelled to do. The Negroes know this in the most concrete terms imaginable, and it is thus becoming increasingly difficult to buy them off with rhetoric and promises and pious assurances of support. And so within the Negro community we find more and more people declaring — as Harold R. Isaacs recently put it in an article in *Commentary* — that they want *out:* people who say that integration will never come, or that it will take a hundred or a thousand years to come, or that it will come at too high a price in suffering and struggle for the pallid and sodden life of the American middle class that at the very best it may bring.

The most numerous, influential, and dangerous movement that has grown out of Negro despair with the goal of integration is, of course, the Black Muslims. This movement, whatever else we may say about it, must be credited with one enduring achievement: it inspired James Baldwin to write an essay which deserves to be placed among the classics of our language. Everything Baldwin has ever been trying to tell us is distilled in *The Fire Next Time* into a statement of overwhelming persuasiveness and prophetic magnificence. Baldwin's message is and always has been simple. It is this: "Color is not a human or personal reality; it is a political reality." And Baldwin's demand is correspondingly simple: color must be forgotten, lest we all be smited with a vengeance "that does not really depend on, and cannot really be executed by, any person or organization, and that cannot be prevented by any police force or army: historical vengeance, a cosmic vengeance based on the law that we recognize when we say, 'Whatever goes up must come down.'" The Black Muslims Baldwin portrays as a sign and a warning to the intransigent white world. They come to proclaim how deep is the Negro's disaffection with the white world and all its works, and Baldwin implies that no American Negro can fail to respond somewhere in his being to their message: that the white man is the devil, that Allah has doomed him to destruction, and that the black man is about to inherit the earth. Baldwin of course knows that this nightmare inversion of the racism from which the black man has

suffered can neither win nor even point to the neighborhood in which
victory might be located. For in his view the neighborhood of victory
lies in exactly the opposite direction: the transcendence of color
through love.

Yet the tragic fact is that love is not the answer to hate — not in
the world of politics, at any rate. Color is indeed a political rather
than a human or a personal reality and if politics (which is to say
power) has made it into a human and personal reality, then only
politics (which is to say power) can unmake it once again. But the
way of politics is slow and bitter, and as impatience on the one side is
matched by a setting of the jaw on the other, we move closer and
closer to an explosion and blood may yet run in the streets.

Will this madness in which we are all caught never find a resting-
place? Is there never to be an end to it? In thinking about the Jews
I have often wondered whether their survival as a distinct group was
worth one hair on the head of a single infant. Did the Jews have to
survive so that six million innocent people should one day be burned
in the ovens of Auschwitz? It is a terrible question and no one, not
God himself, could ever answer it to my satisfaction. And when I
think about the Negroes in America and about the image of integration as a state in which the Negroes would take their rightful place
as another of the protected minorities in a pluralistic society, I wonder
whether they really believe in their hearts that such a state can actually
be attained, and if so *why* they should wish to survive as a distinct
group. I think I know why the Jews once wished to survive (though
I am less certain as to why we still do): they not only believed that
God had given them no choice, but they were tied to a memory of
past glory and a dream of imminent redemption. What does the
American Negro have that might correspond to this? His past is a
stigma, his color is a stigma, and his vision of the future is the hope
of erasing the stigma by making color irrelevant, by making it disappear as a fact of consciousness.

I share this hope, but I cannot see how it will ever be realized unless color does *in fact* disappear: and that means not integration, it
means assimilation, it means — let the brutal word come out — miscegenation. The Black Muslims, like their racist counterparts in the
white world, accuse the "so-called Negro leaders" of secretly pursuing
miscegenation as a goal. The racists are wrong, but I wish they were
right, for I believe that the wholesale merger of the two races is the
most desirable alternative for everyone concerned. I am not claiming
that this alternative can be pursued programmatically or that it is

immediately feasible as a solution; obviously there are even greater barriers to its achievement than to the achievement of integration. What I am saying, however, is that in my opinion the Negro problem can be solved in this country in no other way.

I have told the story of my own twisted feelings about Negroes here, and of how they conflict with the moral convictions I have since developed, in order to assert that such feelings must be acknowledged as honestly as possible so that they can be controlled and ultimately disregarded in favor of the convictions. It is *wrong* for a man to suffer because of the color of his skin. Beside that clichéd proposition of liberal thought, what argument can stand and be respected? If the arguments are the arguments of feeling, they must be made to yield; and one's own soul is not the worst place to begin working a huge social transformation. Not so long ago, it used to be asked of white liberals, "Would you like your sister to marry one?" When I was a boy and my sister was still unmarried I would certainly have said no to that question. But now I am a man, my sister is already married, and I have daughters. If I were to be asked today whether I would like a daughter of mine "to marry one," I would have to answer: "No, I wouldn't *like* it at all. I would rail and rave and rant and tear my hair. And then I hope I would have the courage to curse myself for raving and ranting, and to give her my blessing. How dare I withhold it at the behest of the child I once was and against the man I now have a duty to be?"

william faulkner

Jean Stein

this conversation took place in new york city, early in 1936

INTERVIEWER: Mr. Faulkner, you were saying a while ago that you don't like interviews.

FAULKNER: The reason I don't like interviews is that I seem to

Writers at Work edited by Malcolm Cowley. Interview by Jean Stein Vanden Heuvel. Copyright © 1958 by The Paris Review, Inc. Reprinted by permission of The Viking Press.

react violently to personal questions. If the questions are about the work, I try to answer them. When they are about me, I may answer or I may not, but even if I do, if the same question is asked tomorrow, the answer may be different.

INTERVIEWER: How about yourself as a writer?

FAULKNER: If I had not existed, someone else would have written me, Hemingway, Dostoevski, all of us. Proof of that is that there are about three candidates for the authorship of Shapespeare's plays. But what is important is *Hamlet* and *Midsummer Night's Dream,* not who wrote them, but that somebody did. The artist is of no importance. Only what he creates is important, since there is nothing new to be said. Shakespeare, Balzac, Homer have all written about the same things, and if they had lived one thousand or two thousand years longer, the publishers wouldn't have needed anyone since.

INTERVIEWER: But even if there seems nothing more to be said, isn't perhaps the individuality of the writer important?

FAULKNER: Very important to himself. Everybody else should be too busy with the work to care about the individuality.

INTERVIEWER: And your contemporaries?

FAULKNER: All of us failed to match our dream of perfection. So I rate us on the basis of our splendid failure to do the impossible. In my opinion, if I could write all my work again, I am convinced that I would do it better, which is the healthiest condition for an artist. That's why he keeps on working, trying again; he believes each time that this time he will do it, bring it off. Of course he won't, which is why this condition is healthy. Once he did it, once he matched the work to the image, the dream, nothing would remain but to cut his throat, jump off the other side of that pinnacle of perfection into suicide. I'm a failed poet. Maybe every novelist wants to write poetry first, finds he can't, and then tries the short story, which is the most demanding form after poetry. And, failing at that, only then does he take up novel writing.

INTERVIEWER: Is there any possible formula to follow in order to be a good novelist?

FAULKNER: Ninety-nine per cent talent . . . 99 per cent discipline . . . 99 per cent work. He must never be satisfied with what he does. It never is as good as it can be done. Always dream and shoot higher than you know you can do. Don't bother just to be better than your contemporaries or predecessors. Try to be better than yourself. An artist is a creature driven by demons. He don't know why they choose him and he's usually too busy to wonder why. He is completely amoral in that he will rob, borrow, beg, or steal from anybody and everybody to get the work done.

INTERVIEWER: Do you mean the writer should be completely ruthless?

FAULKNER: The writer's only responsibility is to his art. He will be completely ruthless if he is a good one. He has a dream. It anguishes him so much he must get rid of it. He has no peace until then. Everything goes by the board: honor, pride, decency, security, happiness, all, to get the book written. If a writer has to rob his mother, he will not hesitate; the "Ode on a Grecian Urn" is worth any number of old ladies.

INTERVIEWER: Then could the *lack* of security, happiness, honor, be an important factor in the artist's creativity?

FAULKNER: No. They are important only to his peace and contentment, and art has no concern with peace and contentment.

INTERVIEWER: Then what would be the best environment for a writer?

FAULKNER: Art is not concerned with environment either; it doesn't care where it is. If you mean me, the best job that was ever offered to me was to become a landlord in a brothel. In my opinion it's the perfect milieu for an artist to work in. It gives him perfect economic freedom; he's free of fear and hunger; he has a roof over his head and nothing whatever to do except keep a few simple accounts and to go once every month and pay off the local police. The place is quiet during the morning hours, which is the best time of the day to work. There's enough social life in the evening, if he wishes to participate, to keep him from being bored; it gives him a certain standing in his society; he has nothing to do because the madam keeps the books; all the inmates of the house are females and would defer to him and call him "sir." All the bootleggers in the neighborhood would call him "sir." And he could call the police by their first names.

So the only environment the artist needs is whatever peace, whatever solitude, and whatever pleasure he can get at not too high a cost. All the wrong environment will do is run his blood pressure up; he will spend more time being frustrated or outraged. My own experience has been that the tools I need for my trade are paper, tobacco, food, and a little whisky.

INTERVIEWER: Bourbon, you mean?

FAULKNER: No, I ain't that particular. Between scotch and nothing, I'll take scotch.

INTERVIEWER: You mentioned economic freedom. Does the writer need it?

FAULKNER: No. The writer doesn't need economic freedom. All he needs is a pencil and some paper. I've never known anything good in writing to come from having accepted any free gift of money. The good writer never applies to a foundation. He's too busy writing something. If he isn't first rate he fools himself by saying he hasn't got time or economic freedom. Good art can come out of thieves, bootleggers, or horse swipes. People really are afraid to find out just how much hardship and poverty they can stand. They are afraid to find out how tough they are. Nothing can destroy the good writer. The only thing that can alter the good writer is death. Good ones don't have time to bother with success or getting rich. Success is feminine and like a woman; if you cringe before her, she will override you. So the way to treat her is to show her the back of your hand. Then maybe she will do the crawling.

INTERVIEWER: Can working for the movies hurt your own writing?

FAULKNER: Nothing can injure a man's writing if he's a first-rate writer. If a man is not a first-rate writer, there's not anything can help it much. The problem does not apply if he is not first rate, because he has already sold his soul for a swimming pool.

INTERVIEWER: Does a writer compromise in writing for the movies?

FAULKNER: Always, because a moving picture is by its nature a collaboration, and any collaboration is compromise because that is what the word means — to give and to take.

INTERVIEWER: Which actors do you like to work with most?

FAULKNER: Humphrey Bogart is the one I've worked with best. He and I worked together in *To Have and Have Not* and *The Big Sleep.*

INTERVIEWER: Would you like to make another movie?

FAULKNER: Yes, I would like to make one of George Orwell's *1984.* I have an idea for an ending which would prove the thesis I'm always hammering at: that man is indestructible because of his simple will to freedom.

INTERVIEWER: How do you get the best results in working for the movies?

FAULKNER: The moving-picture work of my own which seemed best to me was done by the actors and the writer throwing the script away and inventing the scene in actual rehearsal just before the camera turned. If I didn't take, or feel I was capable of taking, motion-picture work seriously, out of simple honesty to motion pictures and myself too, I would not have tried. But I know now that I will never be a good motion-picture writer; so that work will never have the urgency for me which my own medium has.

INTERVIEWER: Would you comment on that legendary Hollywood experience you were involved in?

FAULKNER: I had just completed a contract at MGM and was about to return home. The director I had worked with said, "If you would like another job here, just let me know and I will speak to the studio about a new contract." I thanked him and came home. About six months later I wired my director friend that I would like another job. Shortly after that I received a letter from my Hollywood agent enclosing my first week's paycheck. I was surprised because I had expected first to get an official notice or recall and a contract from the studio. I thought to myself the contract is delayed and will arrive in the next mail. Instead, a week later I got another letter from the agent, enclosing my second week's paycheck. That began in November 1932 and continued until May 1933. Then I received a telegram from the studio. It said: *William Faulkner, Oxford, Miss. Where are you? MGM Studio.*

I wrote out a telegram: *MGM Studio, Culver City, California. William Faulkner.*

The young lady operator said, "Where is the message, Mr. Faulkner?" I said, "That's it." She said, "The rule book says that I can't send it without a message, you have to say something." So we went through her samples and selected I forget which one — one of the canned anniversary greeting messages. I sent that. Next was a long-distance telephone call from the studio directing me to get on the first airplane, go to New Orleans, and report to Director Browning. I could have got on a train in Oxford and been in New Orleans eight hours later. But I obeyed the studio and went to Memphis, where an airplane did occasionally go to New Orleans. Three days later one did.

I arrived at Mr. Browning's hotel about six P.M. and reported to him. A party was going on. He told me to get a good night's sleep and be ready for an early start in the morning. I asked him about the story. He said, "Oh, yes. Go to room so and so. That's the continuity writer. He'll tell you what the story is."

I went to the room as directed. The continuity writer was sitting in there alone. I told him who I was and asked him about the story. He said, "When you have written the dialogue I'll let you see the story." I went back to Browning's room and told him what had happened. "Go back," he said, "and tell that so and so — never mind, you get a good night's sleep so we can get an early start in the morning."

So the next morning in a very smart rented launch all of us except the continuity writer sailed down to Grand Isle, about a hundred miles away, where the picture was to be shot, reaching there just in time to eat lunch and have time to run the hundred miles back to New Orleans before dark.

That went on for three weeks. Now and then I would worry a little about the story, but Browning always said, "Stop worrying. Get a good night's sleep so we can get an early start tomorrow morning."

One evening on our return I had barely entered my room when the telephone rang. It was Browning. He told me to come to his room at once. I did so. He had a telegram. It said: *Faulkner is fired. MGM Studio.* "Don't worry," Browning said. "I'll call that so-and-so up this minute and not only make him put you back on the payroll but send you a written apology." There was a knock on the door. It was a page with another telegram. This one said: *Browning is fired. MGM Studio.* So I came back home. I presume Browning went somewhere too. I imagine that continuity writer is still sitting in a room somewhere with his weekly salary check clutched tightly in his hand. They never did finish the film. But they did build a shrimp village — a long platform on piles in the water with sheds built on it something like a wharf. The studio could have bought dozens of them for forty or fifty dollars apiece. Instead, they built one of their own, a false one. That is, a platform with a single wall on it, so that when you opened the door and stepped through it, you stepped right on off to the ocean itself. As they built it, on the first day, the Cajun fisherman paddled up in his narrow tricky pirogue made out of a hollow log. He would sit in it all day long in the broiling sun watching the strange white folks building this strange imitation platform. The next day he was back in the pirogue with his whole family, his wife nursing the baby, the other children, and the mother-in-law, all to sit all that day in the broiling sun to watch this foolish and incomprehensible activity. I was in New Orleans two or three years later and heard that the Cajun people were still coming in for miles to look at that imitation shrimp platform which a lot of white people had rushed in and built and then abandoned.

INTERVIEWER: You say that the writer must compromise in working for the motion pictures. How about his writing? Is he under any obligation to his reader?

FAULKNER: His obligation is to get the work done the best he can do it; whatever obligation he has left over after that he can spend any way he likes. I myself am too busy to care about the public. I have no time to wonder who is reading me. I don't care about John Doe's opinion on my or anyone else's work. Mine is the standard which has to be met, which is when the work makes me feel the way I do when I read *La Tentation de Saint Antoine,* or the Old Testament. They make me feel good. So does watching a bird make me feel good. You know that if I were reincarnated, I'd want to come back a buzzard. Nothing hates him or envies him or wants him or needs him. He is never bothered or in danger, and he can eat anything.

INTERVIEWER: What technique do you use to arrive at your standard?

FAULKNER: Let the writer take up surgery or bricklaying if he is interested in technique. There is no mechanical way to get the writing done, no short cut. The young writer would be a fool to follow a theory. Teach yourself by your own mistakes; people learn only by error. The good artist believes that nobody is good enough to give him advice. He has supreme vanity. No matter how much he admires the old writer, he wants to beat him.

INTERVIEWER: Then would you deny the validity of technique?

FAULKNER: By no means. Sometimes technique changes in and takes command of the dream before the writer himself can get his hands on it. That is *tour de force* and the finished work is simply a matter of fitting bricks neatly together, since the writer knows probably every single word right to the end before he puts the first one down. This happened with *As I Lay Dying.* It was not easy. No honest work is. It is simple in that all the material was already at hand. It took me just about six weeks in the spare time from a twelve-hour-a-day job at manual labor. I simply imagined a group of people and subjected them to the simple universal natural catastrophes, which are flood and fire, with a simple natural motive to give direction to their progress. But then, when technique does not intervene, in another sense writing is easier too. Because with me there is always a point in the book where the characters themselves rise up and take charge and finish the job — say somewhere about page 275. Of course I don't know what would happen if I finished the book on page 274. The quality an artist must have is objectivity in judging his work, plus the honesty and courage not to kid himself about it. Since none of my work has met my own standards, I must judge it on the basis of that one which caused me the most grief and anguish, as the mother loves the child who became the thief or murderer more than the one who became the priest.

INTERVIEWER: What work is that?

FAULKNER: *The Sound and the Fury.* I wrote it five separate times, trying to tell the story, to rid myself of the dream which would continue to anguish me until I did. It's a tragedy of two lost women: Caddy and her daughter. Dilsey is one of my own favorite characters, because she is brave, courageous, generous, gentle, and honest. She's much more brave and honest and generous than me.

INTERVIEWER: How did *The Sound and the Fury* begin?

FAULKNER: It began with a mental picture. I didn't realize at the time it was symbolical. The picture was of the muddy seat of a little girl's drawers in a pear tree, where she could see through a window where her grandmother's funeral was taking place and report what was happening to her brothers on the ground below. By the time I explained who they were and what they were doing and how her pants got muddy, I realized it would be impossible to get all of it into a short story and that it would have to be a book. And then I realized the symbolism of the soiled pants, and that image was replaced by the one of the fatherless and motherless girl climbing down the rainpipe to escape from the only home she had, where she had never been offered love or affection or understanding.

I had already begun to tell the story through the eyes of the idiot child, since I felt that it would be more effective as told by someone capable only of knowing what happened, but not why. I saw that I had not told the story that time. I tried to tell it again, the same story through the eyes of another brother. That was still not it. I told it for the third time through the eyes of the third brother. That was still not it. I tried to gather the pieces together and fill in the gaps by making myself the spokesman. It was still not complete, not until fifteen years after the book was published, when I wrote as an appendix to another book the final effort to get the story told and off my mind, so that I myself could have some peace from it. It's the book I feel tenderest towards. I couldn't leave it alone, and I never could tell it right, though I tried hard and would like to try again, though I'd probably fail again.

INTERVIEWER: What emotion does Benjy arouse in you?

FAULKNER: The only emotion I can have for Benjy is grief and pity for all mankind. You can't feel anything for Benjy because he doesn't feel anything. The only thing I can feel about him personally is concern as to whether he is believable as I created him. He was a prologue, like the gravedigger in the Elizabethan dramas. He serves his purpose and is gone. Benjy is incapable of good and evil because he had no knowledge of good and evil.

INTERVIEWER: Could Benjy feel love?

FAULKNER: Benjy wasn't rational enough even to be selfish. He was an animal. He recognized tenderness and love though he could not have named them, and it was the threat to tenderness and love that caused him to bellow when he felt the change in Caddy. He no longer had Caddy; being an idiot he was not even aware that Caddy was missing. He knew only that something was wrong, which left a vacuum in which he grieved. He tried to fill that vacuum. The only thing he had was one of Caddy's discarded slippers. The slipper was his tenderness and love which he could not have named, but he knew only that it was missing. He was dirty because he couldn't coordinate and because dirt meant nothing to him. He could no more distinguish between dirt and cleanliness than between good and evil. The slipper gave him comfort even though he no longer remembered the person to whom it had once belonged, any more than he could remember why he grieved. If Caddy had reappeared he probably would not have known her.

INTERVIEWER: Does the narcissus given to Benjy have some significance?

FAULKNER: The narcissus was given to Benjy to distract his attention. It was simply a flower which happened to be handy that fifth of April. It was not deliberate.

INTERVIEWER: Are there any artistic advantages in casting the novel in the form of an allegory, as the Christian allegory you used in *A Fable?*

FAULKNER: Same advantage the carpenter finds in building square corners in order to build a square house. In *A Fable* the Christian allegory was the right allegory to use in that particular story, like an oblong square corner is the right corner with which to build an oblong rectangular house.

INTERVIEWER: Does that mean an artist can use Christianity simply as just another tool, as a carpenter would borrow a hammer?

FAULKNER: The carpenter we are speaking of never lacks that hammer. No one is without Christianity, if we agree on what we mean by the word. It is every individual's individual code of behavior by means of which he makes himself a better human being than his nature wants to be, if he followed his nature only. Whatever its symbol — cross or crescent or whatever — that symbol is man's reminder of his duty inside the human race. Its various allegories are the charts against which he measures himself and learns to know what he is. It cannot teach man to be good as the textbook teaches him mathematics. It shows him how to discover himself, evolve for himself a moral code and standard within his capacities and aspirations, by giving him a matchless example of suffering and sacrifice and the promise of hope. Writers have always drawn, and always will draw, upon the allegories of moral consciousness, for the reason that the allegories are matchless — the three men in *Moby Dick,* who represent the trinity of conscience: knowing nothing, knowing but not caring, knowing and caring. The same trinity is represented in *A Fable* by the young Jewish pilot officer, who said, "This is terrible. I refuse to accept it, even if I must refuse life to do so"; the old French Quartermaster General, who said, "This is terrible, but we can weep and bear it"; and the English battalion runner, who said, "This is terrible, I'm going to do something about it."

INTERVIEWER: Are the two unrelated themes in *The Wild Palms* brought together in one book for any symbolic purpose? Is it as certain critics intimate a kind of esthetic counterpoint, or is it merely haphazard?

FAULKNER: No, no. That was one story — the story of Charlotte Rittenmeyer and Harry Wilbourne, who sacrificed everything for love, and then lost that. I did not know it would be two separate stories until after I had started the book. When I reached the end of what is now the first section of *The Wild Palms,* I realized suddenly that something was missing, it needed emphasis, something to lift it like counterpoint in music. So I wrote on the "Old Man" story until "The Wild Palms" story rose back to pitch. Then I stopped the "Old Man" story at what is now its first section, and took up "The Wild Palms" story until it began again to sag. Then I raised it to pitch again with another section of its antithesis, which is the story of a man who got his love and spent the rest of the book fleeing from it, even to the extent of voluntarily going back to jail where he would be safe. They are only two stories by chance, perhaps necessity. The story is that of Charlotte and Wilbourne.

INTERVIEWER: How much of your writing is based on personal experience?

FAULKNER: I can't say. I never counted up. Because "how much" is not important. A writer needs three things, experience, observation, and imagination, any two of which, at times any one of which, can supply the lack of the others. With me, a story usually begins with a single idea or memory or mental picture. The writing of the story is simply a matter of working up to that moment, to explain why it happened or what it caused to follow. A writer is trying to create believable people in credible moving situations in the most moving way he can. Obviously he must use as one of his tools the environment which he knows. I would say that music is the easiest means in which to express, since it came first in man's experience and history. But since words are my talent, I must try to express clumsily in words what the pure music would have done better. That is, music would express better and simpler, but I prefer to use words, as I prefer to read rather than listen. I prefer silence to sound, and the image produced by words occurs in silence. That is, the thunder and the music of the prose take place in silence.

INTERVIEWER: Some people say they can't understand your writing, even after they read it two or three times. What approach would you suggest for them?

FAULKNER: Read it four times.

INTERVIEWER: You mentioned experience, observation, and imagination as being important for the writer. Would you include inspiration?

FAULKNER: I don't know anything about inspiration, because I don't know what inspiration is — I've heard about it, but I never saw it.

INTERVIEWER: As a writer you are said to be obsessed with violence.

FAULKNER: That's like saying the carpenter is obsessed with his hammer. Violence is simply one of the carpenter's tools. The writer can no more build with one tool than the carpenter can.

INTERVIEWER: Can you say how you started as a writer?

FAULKNER: I was living in New Orleans, doing whatever kind of work was necessary to earn a little money now and then. I met Sherwood Anderson. We would walk about the city in the afternoon and talk to people. In the evenings we would meet again and sit over a bottle or two while he talked and I listened. In the forenoon I would never see him. He was secluded, working. The next day we would repeat. I decided that if that was the life of a writer, then becoming a writer was the thing for me. So I began to write my first book. At once I found that writing was fun. I even forgot that I hadn't seen Mr. Anderson for three weeks until he walked in my door, the first time he ever came to see me, and said, "What's wrong? Are you mad at me?" I told him I was writing a book. He said, "My God," and walked out. When I finished the book — it was *Soldier's Pay* — I met Mrs. Anderson on the street. She asked how the book was going, and I said I'd finished it. She said, "Sherwood says that he will make a trade with you. If he doesn't have to read your manuscript he will tell his publisher to accept it." I said, "Done," and that's how I became a writer.

INTERVIEWER: What were the kinds of work you were doing to earn that "little money now and then"?

FAULKNER: Whatever came up. I could do a little of almost anything — run boats, paint houses, fly airplanes. I never needed much money because living was cheap in New Orleans then, and all I wanted was a place to sleep, a little food, tobacco, and whisky. There were many things I could do for two or three days and earn enough money to live on for the rest of the month. By temperament I'm a vagabond and a tramp. I don't want money badly enough to work for it. In my opinion it's a shame that there is so much work in the world. One of the saddest things is that the only thing a man can do for eight hours a day, day after day, is work. You can't eat eight hours a day nor drink for eight hours a day nor make love for eight hours — all you can do for eight hours is work. Which is the reason why man makes himself and everybody else so miserable and unhappy.

INTERVIEWER: You must feel indebted to Sherwood Anderson, but how do you regard him as a writer?

FAULKNER: He was the father of my generation of American writers and the tradition of American writing which our successors will carry on. He has never received his proper evaluation. Dreiser is his older brother and Mark Twain the father of them both.

INTERVIEWER: What about the European writers of that period?

FAULKNER: The two great men in my time were Mann and Joyce. You should approach Joyce's *Ulysses* as the illiterate Baptist preacher approaches the Old Testament: with faith.

INTERVIEWER: How did you get your background in the Bible?

FAULKNER: My Great-Grandfather Murry was a kind and gentle man, to us children anyway. That is, although he was a Scot, he was (to us) neither especially pious nor stern either: he was simply a man of inflexible principles. One of them was, everybody, children on up through all adults present, had to have a verse from the Bible ready and glib at tongue-tip when we gathered at the table for breakfast each morning; if you didn't have your scripture verse ready, you didn't have any breakfast; you would be excused long enough to leave the room and swot one up (there was a maiden aunt, a kind of sergeant-major for this duty, who retired with the culprit and gave him a brisk breezing which carried him over the jump next time).

It had to be an authentic, correct verse. While we were little, it could be the same one, once you had it down good, morning after morning, until you got a little older and bigger, when one morning (by this time you would be pretty glib at it, galloping through without even listening to yourself since you were already five or ten minutes ahead, already among the ham and steak and fried chicken and grits and sweet potatoes and two or three kinds of hot bread) you would suddenly find his eyes on you — very blue, very kind and gentle, and even now not stern so much as inflexible; and next morning you had a new verse. In a way, that was when you discovered that your childhood was over; you had outgrown it and entered the world.

INTERVIEWER: Do you read your contemporaries?

FAULKNER: No, the books I read are the ones I knew and loved when I was a young man and to which I return as you do to old friends: the Old Testament, Dickens, Conrad, Cervantes — *Don Quixote*. I read that every year, as some do the Bible. Flaubert, Balzac — he created an intact world of his own, a bloodstream running through twenty books — Dostoevski, Tolstoi, Shakespeare. I read Melville occasionally, and of the poets Marlowe, Campion, Jonson, Herrick, Donne, Keats, and Shelley. I still read Housman. I've read these books so often that I don't always begin at page one and read on to the end. I just read one scene, or about one character, just as you'd meet and talk to a friend for a few minutes.

INTERVIEWER: And Freud?

FAULKNER: Everybody talked about Freud when I lived in New Orleans, but I have never read him. Neither did Shakespeare. I doubt if Melville did either, and I'm sure Moby Dick didn't.

INTERVIEWER: Do you ever read mystery stories?

FAULKNER: I read Simenon because he reminds me something of Chekhov.

INTERVIEWER: What about your favorite characters?

FAULKNER: My favorite characters are Sarah Gamp — a cruel, ruthless woman, a drunkard, opportunist, unreliable, most of her character was bad, but at least it was character; Mrs. Harris, Falstaff, Prince Hal, Don Quixote, and Sancho of course. Lady Macbeth I always admire. And Bottom, Ophelia, and Mercutio — both he and Mrs. Gamp coped with life, didn't ask any favors, never whined. Huck Finn, of course, and Jim. Tom Sawyer I never liked much — an awful prig. And then I like Sut Lovingood, from a book written by George Harris about 1840 or '50 in the Tennessee mountains. He had no illusions about himself, did the best he could; at certain times he was a coward and knew it and wasn't ashamed; he never blamed his misfortunes on anyone and never cursed God for them.

INTERVIEWER: Would you comment on the future of the novel?

FAULKNER: I imagine as long as people will continue to read novels, people will continue to write them, or vice versa; unless of course the pictorial magazines and comic strips finally atrophy man's capacity to read, and literature really is on its way back to the picture writing in the Neanderthal cave.

INTERVIEWER: And how about the function of the critics?

FAULKNER: The artist doesn't have time to listen to the critics. The ones who want to be writers read the reviews, the ones who want to write don't have the time to read reviews. The critic too is trying to say "Kilroy was here." His function is not directed toward the artist himself. The artist is a cut above the critic, for the artist is writing something which will move the critic. The critic is writing something which will move everybody but the artist.

INTERVIEWER: So you never feel the need to discuss your work with anyone?

FAULKNER: No, I am too busy writing it. It has got to please me and if it does I don't need to talk about it. If it doesn't please me, talking about it won't improve it, since the only thing to improve it is to work on it some more. I am not a literary man but only a writer. I don't get any pleasure from talking shop.

INTERVIEWER: Critics claim that blood relationships are central in your novels.

FAULKNER: That is an opinion and, as I have said, I don't read critics. I doubt that a man trying to write about people is any more interested in blood relationships than in the shape of their noses, unless they are necessary to help the story move. If the writer concentrates on what he does need to be interested in, which is the truth and the human heart, he won't have much time left for anything else, such as ideas and facts like the shape of noses or blood relationships, since in my opinion ideas and facts have very little connection with truth.

INTERVIEWER: Critics also suggest that your characters never consciously choose between good and evil.

FAULKNER: Life is not interested in good and evil. Don Quixote was constantly choosing between good and evil, but then he was choosing in his dream state. He was mad. He entered reality only when he was so busy trying to cope with people that he had no time to distinguish between good and evil. Since people exist only in life, they must devote their time simply to being alive. Life is motion, and motion is concerned with what makes man move — which is ambition, power, pleasure. What time a man can devote to morality, he must take by force from the motion of which he is a part. He is compelled to make choices between good and evil sooner or later, because moral conscience demands that from him in order that he can live with himself tomorrow. His moral conscience is the curse he had to accept from the gods in order to gain from them the right to dream.

INTERVIEWER: Could you explain more what you mean by motion in relation to the artist?

FAULKNER: The aim of every artist is to arrest motion, which is life, by artificial means and hold it fixed so that a hundred years later, when a stranger looks at it, it moves again since it is life. Since man is mortal, the only immortality possible for him is to leave something behind him that is immortal since it will always move. This is the artist's way of scribbling "Kilroy was here" on the wall of the final and irrevocable oblivion through which he must someday pass.

INTERVIEWER: It has been said by Malcolm Cowley that your characters carry a sense of submission to their fate.

FAULKNER: That is his opinion. I would say that some of them do and some of them don't, like everybody else's characters. I would say that Lena Grove in *Light in August* coped pretty well with hers. It didn't really matter to her in her destiny whether her man was Lucas Birch or not. It was her destiny to have a husband and children and she knew it, and so she went out and attended to it without asking help from anyone. She was the captain of her soul. One of the calmest, sanest speeches I ever heard was when she said to Byron Bunch at the very instant of repulsing his final desperate and despairing attempt at rape, "Ain't you ashamed? You might have woke the baby." She was never for one moment confused, frightened, alarmed. She did not even know that she didn't need pity. Her last speech for example: "Here I ain't been traveling but a month, and I'm already in Tennessee. My, my, a body does get around."

The Bundren family in *As I Lay Dying* pretty well coped with theirs. The father having lost his wife would naturally need another one, so he got one. At one blow he not only replaced the family cook, he acquired a gramophone to give them all pleasure while they were resting. The pregnant daughter failed this time to undo her condition, but she was not discouraged. She intended to try again, and even if they all failed right up to the last, it wasn't anything but just another baby.

INTERVIEWER: And Mr. Cowley says you find it hard to create characters between the ages of twenty and forty who are sympathetic.

FAULKNER: People between twenty and forty are not sympathetic. The child has the capacity to do but it can't know. It only knows when it is no longer able to do — after forty. Between twenty and forty the will of the child to do gets stronger, more dangerous, but it has not begun to learn to know yet. Since his capacity to do is forced into channels of evil through environment and pressures, man is strong before he is moral. The world's anguish is caused by people between twenty and forty. The people around my home who have caused all the interracial tension — the Milams and the Bryants (in the Emmet Till murder) and the gangs of Negroes who grab a white woman and rape her in revenge, the Hitlers, Napoleons, Lenins — all these people are symbols of human suffering and anguish, all of them between twenty and forty.

INTERVIEWER: You gave a statement to the papers at the time of the Emmet Till killing. Have you anything to add to it here?

FAULKNER: No, only to repeat what I said before: that if we Americans are to survive it will have to be because we choose and elect and defend to be first of all Americans; to present to the world one homogeneous and unbroken front, whether of white Americans or black ones or purple or blue or green. Maybe the purpose of this sorry and tragic error committed in my native Mississippi by two white adults on an afflicted Negro child is to prove to us whether or not we deserve to survive. Because if we in America have reached that point in our desperate culture when we must murder children, no matter for what reason or what color, we don't deserve to survive, and probably won't.

INTERVIEWER: What happened to you between *Soldier's Pay* and *Sartoris* — that is, what caused you to begin the Yoknapatawpha saga?

FAULKNER: With *Soldier's Pay* I found out writing was fun. But I found out afterward that not only each book had to have a design but the whole output or sum of an artist's work had to have a design. With *Soldier's Pay* and *Mosquitoes* I wrote for the sake of writing because it was fun. Beginning with *Sartoris* I discovered that my own little postage stamp of native soil was worth writing about and that I would never live long enough to exhaust it, and that by sublimating the actual into the apocryphal I would have complete liberty to use whatever talent I might have to its absolute top. It opened up a gold mine of other people, so I created a cosmos of my own. I can move these people around like God, not only in space but in time too. The fact that I have moved my characters around in time successfully, at least in my own estimation, proves to me my own theory that time is a fluid condition which has no existence except in the momentary avatars of individual people. There is no such thing as *was* — only *is*. If *was* existed, there would be no grief or sorrow. I like to think of the world I created as being a kind of keystone in the universe; that, small as that keystone is, if it were ever taken away the universe itself would collapse. My last book will be the Doomsday Book, the Golden Book, of Yoknapatawpha County. Then I shall break the pencil and I'll have to stop.

the actuality of god

Paul Tillich

god as being

GOD AS BEING AND FINITE BEING

The being of God is being-itself. The being of God cannot be understood as the existence of a being alongside others or above others. If God is *a* being, he is subject to the categories of finitude, especially to space and substance. Even if he is called the "highest being" in the sense of the "most perfect" and the "most powerful" being, this situation is not changed. When applied to God, superlatives become diminutives. They place him on the level of other beings while elevating him above all of them. Many theologians who have used the term "highest being" have known better. Actually they have described the highest as the absolute, as that which is on a level qualitatively different from the level of any being — even the highest being. Whenever infinite or unconditional power and meaning are

(From Paul Tillich, *Systematic Theology*, Vol. I [University of Chicago Press, 1951], Part II, Chap. II, section B, pp. 235–52.)

attributed to the highest being, it has ceased to be *a* being and has become being-itself. Many confusions in the doctrine of God and many apologetic weaknesses could be avoided if God were understood first of all as being-itself or as the ground of being. The power of being is another way of expressing the same thing in a circumscribing phrase. Ever since the time of Plato it has been known — although it often has been disregarded, especially by the nominalists and their modern followers — that the concept of being as being, or being-itself, points to the power inherent in everything, the power of resisting nonbeing. Therefore, instead of saying that God is first of all being-itself, it is possible to say that he is the power of being in everything and above everything, the infinite power of being. A theology which does not dare to identify God and the power of being as the first step toward a doctrine of God relapses into monarchic monotheism, for if God is not being-itself, he is subordinate to it, just as Zeus is subordinate to fate in Greek religion. The structure of being-itself is his fate, as it is the fate of all other beings. But God is his own fate; he is "by himself"; he possesses "aseity." This can be said of him only if he is the power of being, if he is being-itself.

As being-itself God is beyond the contrast of essential and existential being. We have spoken of the transition of being into existence, which involves the possibility that being will contradict and lose itself. This transition is excluded from being-itself (except in terms of the christological paradox), for being-itself does not participate in nonbeing. In this it stands in contrast to every being. As classical theology has emphasized, God is beyond essence and existence. Logically, being-itself is "before," "prior to," the split which characterizes finite being.

For this reason it is as wrong to speak of God as the universal essence as it is to speak of him as existing. If God is understood as universal essence, as the form of all forms, he is identified with the unity and totality of finite potentialities; but he has ceased to be the power of the ground in all of them, and therefore he has ceased to transcend them. He has poured all his creative power into a system of forms, and he is bound to these forms. This is what pantheism means.

On the other hand, grave difficulties attend the attempt to speak of God as existing. In order to maintain the truth that God is beyond essence and existence while simultaneously arguing for the existence of God, Thomas Aquinas is forced to distinguish between two kinds of divine existence: that which is identical with essence and that which is not. But an existence of God which is not united with its essence is a contradiction in terms. It makes God a being whose existence does not fulfil his essential potentialities; being and not-yet-being are "mixed" in him, as they are in everything finite. God ceases to be God, the ground of being and meaning. What really has happened is that Thomas has had to unite two different traditions: the Augustinian, in which the divine existence is included in his essence, and the Aristotelian, which derives the existence of God from the existence of the world and which then asserts, in a second step, that his existence is identical with his essence. Thus the question of the existence of God can be neither asked nor answered. If asked, it is a question about that which by its very nature is above existence, and therefore the answer — whether negative or affirmative — implicitly denies the nature of God. It is as atheistic to affirm the existence of God as it is to deny it. God is being-itself, not *a* being. On this basis a first step can be taken toward the solution of the problem which usually is discussed as the immanence and the transcendence of God. As the power of being, God transcends every being and also the totality of beings — the world. Being-itself is beyond finitude and infinity; otherwise it would be conditioned by something other than itself, and the real power of being would lie beyond both it and that which conditioned it. Being-itself infinitely transcends every finite being. There is no proportion or gradation between the finite and the infinite. There is an absolute break, an infinite "jump." On the other hand, everything finite participates in being-itself and in its infinity. Otherwise it would not have the power of being. It would be swallowed by nonbeing, or it never would have emerged out of nonbeing. This double relation of all beings to being-itself gives being-itself a double characteristic. In calling it creative, we point to the fact that everything participates in the infinite power of being. In calling it abysmal, we point to the fact that everything participates in the power of being in a finite way, that all beings are infinitely transcended by their creative ground.

Man is bound to the categories of finitude. He uses the two categories of relation — causality and substance — to express the relation of being-itself to finite beings. The "ground" can be interpreted in both ways, as the cause of finite beings and as their substance. The former has been elaborated by Leibniz in the line of the Thomistic tradition, and the latter has been elaborated by Spinoza in the line of the mystical tradition. Both ways are impossible. Spinoza establishes a naturalistic pantheism, in contrast to the idealistic type which identifies God with the universal essence of being, which denies finite freedom and in so doing denies the freedom of God. By necessity God is merged into the finite beings, and their being is his being. Here again it must be emphasized that pantheism does not say that God is everything. It says that God is the substance of everything and that there is no substantial independence and freedom in anything finite.

Therefore, Christianity, which asserts finite freedom in man and spontaneity in the nonhuman realm, has rejected the category of substance in favor of the category of causality in attempting to express the relation of the power of being to the beings who participate in it. Causality seems to make the world dependent on God, and, at the same time, to separate God from the world in the way a cause is separated from its effect. But the category of causality cannot "fill the bill," for cause and effect are not separate; they include each other and form a series which is endless in both directions. What is cause at one point in this series is effect at another point and conversely. God as cause is drawn into this series, which drives even him beyond himself. In order to disengage the divine cause from the series of causes and effects, it is called the first cause, the absolute beginning. What this means is that the category of causality is being denied while it is being used. In other words, causality is being used not as a category but as a symbol. And if this is done and is understood, the difference between substance and causality disappears, for if God is the cause of the entire series of causes and effects, he is the substance underlying the whole process of becoming. But this "underlying" does not have the character of a substance which underlies its accidents and which is completely expressed by them. It is an underlying in which substance and accidents preserve their freedom. In other words, it is substance not as a category but as a symbol. And, if taken symbolically, there is no difference between *prima causa* and *ultima substantia.* Both mean, what can be called in a more directly symbolic term, "the creative and abysmal ground of being." In this term both naturalistic pantheism, based on the category of substance, and rationalistic theism, based on the category of causality, are overcome.

Since God is the ground of being, he is the ground of the structure of being. He is not subject to this structure; the structure is grounded in him. He *is* this structure, and it is impossible to speak about him except in terms of this structure. God must be approached cognitively through the structural elements of being-itself. These elements make him a living God, a God who can be man's concrete concern. They enable us to use symbols which we are certain point to the ground of reality.

GOD AS BEING AND THE KNOWLEDGE OF GOD

The statement that God is being-itself is a nonsymbolic statement. It does not point beyond itself. It means what it says directly
and properly; if we speak of the actuality of God, we first assert that
he is not God if he is not being-itself. Other assertions about God can
be made theologically only on this basis. Of course, religious assertions
do not require such a foundation for what they say about God; the
foundation is implicit in every religious thought concerning God.
Theologians must make explicit what is implicit in religious thought
and expression; and, in order to do this, they must begin with the
most abstract and completely unsymbolic statement which is possible,
namely, that God is being-itself or the absolute.

However, after this has been said, nothing else can be said about
God as God which is not symbolic. As we already have seen, God as
being-itself is the ground of the ontological structure of being without
being subject to this structure himself. He *is* the structure; that is, he
has the power of determining the structure of everything that has
being. Therefore, if anything beyond this bare assertion is said about
God, it no longer is a direct and proper statement, no longer a concept. It *is* indirect, and it points to something beyond itself. In a word,
it is symbolic.

The general character of the symbol has been described. Special
emphasis must be laid on the insight that symbol and sign are different; that, while the sign bears no necessary relation to that to which
it points, the symbol participates in the reality of that for which it
stands. The sign can be changed arbitrarily according to the demands
of expediency, but the symbol grows and dies according to the correlation between that which is symbolized and the persons who receive it
as a symbol. Therefore, the religious symbol, the symbol which points
to the divine, can be a true symbol only if it participates in the power
of the divine to which it points.

There can be no doubt that any concrete assertion about God must
be symbolic, for a concrete assertion is one which uses a segment of
finite experience in order to say something about him. It transcends
the content of this segment, although it also includes it. The segment
of finite reality which becomes the vehicle of a concrete assertion about
God is affirmed and negated at the same time. It becomes a symbol,
for a symbolic expression is one whose proper meaning is negated by
that to which it points. And yet it also is affirmed by it, and this

affirmation gives the symbolic expression an adequate basis for pointing beyond itself.

The crucial question must now be faced. Can a segment of finite reality become the basis for an assertion about that which is infinite? The answer is that it can, because that which is infinite is being-itself and because everything participates in being-itself. The *analogia entis* is not the property of a questionable natural theology which attempts to gain knowledge of God by drawing conclusions about the infinite from the finite. The *analogia entis* gives us our only justification of speaking at all about God. It is based on the fact that God must be understood as being-itself.

The truth of a religious symbol has nothing to do with the truth of the empirical assertions involved in it, be they physical, psychological, or historical. A religious symbol possesses some truth if it adequately expresses the correlation of revelation in which some person stands. A religious symbol *is* true if it adequately expresses the correlation of some person with final revelation. A religious symbol can die only if the correlation of which it is an adequate expression dies. This occurs whenever the revelatory situation changes and former symbols become obsolete. The history of religion, right up to our own time, is full of dead symbols which have been killed not by a scientific criticism of assumed superstitions but by a religious criticism of religion. The judgment that a religious symbol *is* true is identical with the judgment that the revelation of which it is the adequate expression is true. This double meaning of the truth of a symbol must be kept in mind. A symbol *has* truth: it is adequate to the revelation it expresses. A symbol *is* true: it is the expression of a true revelation.

Theology as such has neither the duty nor the power to confirm or to negate religious symbols. Its task is to interpret them according to theological principles and methods. In the process of interpretation, however, two things may happen: theology may discover contradictions between symbols within the theological circle and theology may speak not only as theology but also as religion. In the first case, theology can point out the religious dangers and the theological errors which follow from the use of certain symbols; in the second case, theology can become prophecy, and in this role it may contribute to a change in the revelatory situation.

Religious symbols are double-edged. They are directed toward the infinite which they symbolize *and* toward the finite through which they symbolize it. They force the infinite down to finitude and the finite up to infinity. They open the divine for the human and the human for the divine. For instance, if God is symbolized as "Father," he is brought down to the human relationship of father and child. But at the same time this human relationship is consecrated into a pattern of the divine-human relationship. If "Father" is employed as a symbol for God, fatherhood is seen in its theonomous, sacramental depth. One cannot arbitrarily "make" a religious symbol out of a segment of secular reality. Not even the collective unconscious, the great symbol-creating source, can do this. If a segment of reality is used as a symbol for God, the realm of reality from which it is taken is, so to speak, elevated into the realm of the holy. It no longer is secular. It is theonomous. If God is called the "king," something is said not only about God but also about the holy character of king- hood. If God's work is called "making whole" or "healing," this not only says something about God but also emphasizes the theonomous character of all healing. If God's self-manifestation is called "the word," this not only symbolizes God's relation to man but also empha- sizes the holiness of all words as an expression of the spirit. The list could be continued. Therefore, it is not surprising that in a secular culture both the symbols for God and the theonomous character of the material from which the symbols are taken disappear.

A final word of warning must be added in view of the fact that for many people the very term "symbolic" carries the connotation of nonreal. This is partially the result of confusion between sign and symbol and partially due to the identification of reality with empirical reality, with the entire realm of objective things and events. Both reasons have been undercut explicitly and implicitly in the foregoing chapters. But one reason remains, namely, the fact that some theologi- cal movements, such as Protestant Hegelianism and Catholic mod- ernism, have interpreted religious language symbolically in order to dissolve its realistic meaning and to weaken its seriousness, its power, and its spiritual impact. This was not the purpose of the classical essays on the "divine names," in which the symbolic character of all affirmations about God was strongly emphasized and explained in re- ligious terms, nor was it a consequence of these essays. Their intention and their result was to give to God and to all his relations to man more reality and power than a nonsymbolic and therefore easily super- stitious interpretation could give them. In this sense symbolic interpreta- tion is proper and necessary; it enhances rather than diminishes the reality and power of religious language, and in so doing it performs an important function.

god as living

GOD AS BEING AND GOD AS LIVING

Life is the process in which potential being becomes actual being. It is the actualization of the structural elements of being in their unity and in their tension. These elements move divergently and convergently in every life-process; they separate and reunite simultaneously. Life ceases in the moment of separation without union or of union without separation. Both complete identity and complete separation negate life. If we call God the "living God," we deny that he is a pure identity of being as being; and we also deny that there is a definite separation of being from being in him. We assert that he is the eternal process in which separation is posited and is overcome by reunion. In this sense, God lives. Few things about God are more emphasized in the Bible, especially in the Old Testament, than the truth that God is a living God. Most of the so-called anthropomorphisms of the biblical picture of God are expressions of his character as living. His actions, his passions, his remembrances and anticipations, his suffering and joy, his personal relations and his plans — all these make him a living God and distinguish him from the pure absolute, from being-itself.

Life is the actuality of being, or, more exactly, it is the process in which potential being becomes actual being. But in God as God there is no distinction between potentiality and actuality. Therefore, we cannot speak of God as living in the proper or nonsymbolic sense of the word "life." We must speak of God as living in symbolic terms. Yet every true symbol participates in the reality which it symbolizes. God lives in so far as he is the ground of life. Anthropomorphic symbols are adequate for speaking of God religiously. Only in this way can he be the living God for man. But even in the most primitive intuition of the divine a feeling should be, and usually is, present that there is a mystery about divine names which makes them improper, self-transcending, symbolic. Religious instruction should deepen this feeling without depriving the divine names of their reality and power. One of the most surprising qualities of the prophetic utterances in the Old Testament is that, on the one hand, they always appear concrete and anthropomorphic and that, on the other hand, they preserve the mystery of the divine ground. They never deal with being as being or with the absolute as the absolute; nevertheless, they never make God a being alongside others, into something conditioned by something else which also is conditioned. Nothing is more inadequate and disgusting than the attempt to translate the concrete symbols of the Bible into less concrete and less powerful symbols. Theology should not weaken the concrete symbols, but it must analyze them and interpret them in abstract ontological terms. Nothing is more inadequate and confusing than the attempt to restrict theological work to half-abstract, half-concrete terms which do justice neither to existential intuition nor to cognitive analysis.

The ontological structure of being supplies the material for the symbols which point to the divine life. However, this does not mean that a doctrine of God can be derived from an ontological system. The character of the divine life is made manifest in revelation. Theology can only explain and systematize the existential knowledge of revelation in theoretical terms, interpreting the symbolic significance of the ontological elements and categories.

While the symbolic power of the categories appears in the relation of God to the creature, the elements give symbolic expression to the nature of the divine life itself. The polar character of the ontological elements is rooted in the divine life, but the divine life is not subject to this polarity. Within the divine life, every ontological element includes its polar element completely, without tension and without the threat of dissolution, for God is being-itself. However, there is a difference between the first and the second elements in each polarity with regard to their power of symbolizing the divine life. The elements of individualization, dynamics, and freedom represent the self or subject side of the basic ontological structure within the polarity to which they belong. The elements of participation, form, and destiny represent the world or object side of the basic ontological structure within the polarity to which they belong. Both sides are rooted in the divine life. But the first side determines the existential relationship between God and man, which is the source of all symbolization. Man is a self who has a world. As a self he is an individual person who participates universally, he is a dynamic self-transcending agent within a special and a general form, and he is freedom which has a special destiny and which participates in a general destiny. Therefore, man symbolizes that which is his ultimate concern in terms taken from his own being. From the subjective side of the polarities he takes — or more exactly, receives — the material with which he symbolizes the divine life. He sees the divine life as personal, dynamic, and free. He cannot see it in any other way, for God is man's ultimate concern, and therefore he stands in analogy to that which man himself is. But the religious mind

— theologically speaking, man in the correlation of revelation — always realizes implicitly, if not explicitly, that the other side of the polarities also is completely present in the side he uses as symbolic material. God is called a person, but he is a person not in finite separation but in an absolute and unconditional participation in everything. God is called dynamic, but he is dynamic not in tension with form but in an absolute and unconditional unity with form, so that his self-transcendence never is in tension with his self-preservation, so that he always remains God. God is called "free," but he is free not in arbitrariness but in an absolute and unconditional identity with his destiny, so that he himself is his destiny, so that the essential structures of being are not strange to his freedom but are the actuality of his freedom. In this way, although the symbols used for the divine life are taken from the concrete situation of man's relationship to God, they imply God's ultimacy, the ultimacy in which the polarities of being disappear in the ground of being, in being-itself.

The basic ontological structure of self and world is transcended in the divine life without providing symbolic material. God cannot be called a self, because the concept "self" implies separation from and contrast to everything which is not self. God cannot be called the world even by implication. Both self and world are rooted in the divine life, but they cannot become symbols for it. But the elements which constitute the basic ontological structure can become symbols because they do not speak of kinds of being (self and world) but of qualities of being which are valid in their proper sense when applied to all beings and which are valid in their symbolic sense when applied to being-itself.

THE DIVINE LIFE AND THE ONTOLOGICAL ELEMENTS

The symbols provided by the ontological elements present a great number of problems for the doctrine of God. In every special case it is necessary to distinguish between the proper sense of the concepts and their symbolic sense. And it is equally necessary to balance one side of the ontological polarity against the other without reducing the symbolic power of either of them. The history of theological thought is a continuous proof of the difficulty, the creativeness, and the danger of this situation. This is obvious if we consider the symbolic power of the polarity of individualization and participation. The symbol "personal God" is absolutely fundamental because an existential relation is a person-to-person relation. Man cannot be ultimately concerned about anything that is less than personal, but since personality (*persona, prosopon*) includes individuality, the question arises in what sense God can be called an individual. Is it meaningful to call him the "absolute individual"? The answer must be that it is meaningful only in the sense that he can be called the "absolute participant." The one term cannot be applied without the other. This can only mean that both individualization and participation are rooted in the ground of the divine life and that God is equally "near" to each of them while transcending them both.

The solution of the difficulties in the phrase "personal God" follows from this. "Personal God" does not mean that God is *a* person. It means that God is the ground of everything personal and that he carries within himself the ontological power of personality. He is not a person, but he is not less than personal. It should not be forgotten that classical theology employed the term *persona* for the trinitarian hypostases but not for God himself. God became "a person" only in the nineteenth century, in connection with the Kantian separation of nature ruled by physical law from personality ruled by moral law. Ordinary theism has made God a heavenly, completely perfect person who resides above the world and mankind. The protest of atheism against such a highest person is correct. There is no evidence for his existence, nor is he a matter of ultimate concern. God is not God without universal participation. "Personal God" is a confusing symbol.

God is the principle of participation as well as the principle of individualization. The divine life participates in every life as its ground and aim. God participates in everything that is; he has community with it; he shares in its destiny. Certainly such statements are highly symbolic. They can have the unfortunate logical implication that there is something alongside God in which he participates from the outside. But the divine participation creates that in which it participates. Plato uses the word *parousia* for the presence of the essences in temporal existence. This word later becomes the name for the preliminary and final presence of the transcendent Christ in the church and in the world. *Par-ousia* means "being by," "being with" — but on the basis of being absent, of being separated. In the same way God's participation is not a spatial or temporal presence. It is meant not categorically but symbolically. It is the parousia, the "being with" of that which is neither here nor there. If applied to God, participation and community are not less symbolic than individualization and personality. While active religious communication between God and man depends on the symbol of the personal God, the symbol of universal participation expresses the passive experience of the divine parousia in terms of the divine omnipresence.

The polarity of dynamics and form supplies the material basis for a group of symbols which are central for any present-day doctrine of God. Potentiality, vitality, and self-transcendence are indicated in the term "dynamics," while the term "form" embraces actuality, intentionality, and self-preservation.

Potentiality and actuality appear in classical theology in the famous formula that God is *actus purus,* the pure form in which everything potential is actual, and which is the eternal self-intuition of the divine fulness (*pleroma*). In this formula the dynamic side in the dynamics-form polarity is swallowed by the form side. Pure actuality, that is, actuality free from any element of potentiality, is a fixed result; it is not alive. Life includes the separation of potentiality and actuality. The nature of life is actualization, not actuality. The God who is *actus purus* is not the living God. It is interesting that even those theologians who have used the concept of *actus purus* normally speak of God in the dynamic symbols of the Old Testament and of Christian experience. This situation has induced some thinkers — partly under the influence of Luther's dynamic conception of God and partly under the impact of the problem of evil — to emphasize the dynamics in God and to depreciate the stabilization of dynamics in pure actuality. They try to distinguish between two elements in God, and they assert that, in so far as God is a living God, these two elements must remain in tension. Whether the first element is called the *Ungrund* or the "nature in God" (Böhme), or the first potency (Schelling), or the will (Schopenhauer), or the "given" in God (Brightman), or *me-onic* freedom (Berdyaev), or the contingent (Hartshorne) — in all these cases it is an expression of what we have called "dynamics," and it is an attempt to prevent the dynamics in God from being transformed into pure actuality.

Theological criticism of these attempts is easy if the concepts are taken in their proper sense, for then they make God finite, dependent on a fate or an accident which is not himself. The finite God, if taken literally, is a finite god, a polytheistic god. But this is not the way in which these concepts should be interpreted. They point symbolically to a quality of the divine life which is analogous to what appears as dynamics in the ontological structure. The divine creativity, God's participation in history, his outgoing character, are based on this dynamic element. It includes a "not yet" which is, however, always balanced by an "already" within the divine life. It is not an absolute "not yet," which would make it a divine-demonic power, nor is the "already" an absolute already. It also can be expressed as the negative element in the ground of being which is overcome as negative in the process of being-itself. As such it is the basis of the negative element in the creature, in which it is not overcome but is effective as a threat and a potential disruption.

These assertions include a rejection of a nonsymbolic, ontological doctrine of God as becoming. If we say that being is actual as life, the element of self-transcendence is obviously and emphatically included. But it is included as a symbolic element in balance with form. Being is not in balance with becoming. Being comprises becoming and rest, becoming as an implication of dynamics and rest as an implication of form. If we say that God is being-itself, this includes both rest and becoming, both the static and the dynamic elements. However, to speak of a "becoming" God disrupts the balance between dynamics and form and subjects God to a process which has the character of a fate or which is completely open to the future and has the character of an absolute accident. In both cases the divinity of God is undercut. The basic error of these doctrines is their metaphysical-constructive character. They apply the ontological elements to God in a nonsymbolic manner and are driven to religiously offensive and theologically untenable consequences.

If the element of form in the dynamics-form polarity is applied symbolically to the divine life, it expresses the actualization of its potentialities. The divine life inescapably unites possibility with fulfilment. Neither side threatens the other, nor is there a threat of disruption. In terms of self-preservation one could say that God cannot cease to be God. His going-out from himself does not diminish or destroy his divinity. It is united with the eternal "resting in himself."

The divine form must be conceived in analogy with what we have called "intentionality" on the human level. It is balanced with vitality, the dynamic side on the human level. The polarity in this formulation appears in classical theology as the polarity of will and intellect in God. It is consistent that Thomas Aquinas had to subordinate the will in God to the intellect when he accepted the Aristotelian *actus purus* as the basic character of God. And it must be remembered that the line of theological thought which tries to preserve the element of dynamics in God actually begins with Duns Scotus, who elevated the will in God over the intellect. Of course, both will and intellect in their application to God express infinitely more than the mental acts of willing and understanding as these appear in human experience.

They are symbols for dynamics in all its ramifications and for form as the meaningful structure of being-itself. Therefore, it is not a question of metaphysical psychology, whether Aquinas or Duns Scotus is right. It is a question of the way in which psychological concepts should be employed as symbols for the divine life. And with respect to this question it is obvious that for more than a century a decision has been made in favor of the dynamic element. The philosophy of life, existential philosophy, and process philosophy agree on this point. Protestantism has contributed strong motives for this decision, but theology must balance the new with the old (predominantly Catholic) emphasis on the form character of the divine life.

If we consider the polarity of freedom and destiny in its symbolic value, we find that there hardly is a word said about God in the Bible which does not point directly or indirectly to his freedom. In freedom he creates, in freedom he deals with the world and man, in freedom he saves and fulfils. His freedom is freedom from anything prior to him or alongside him. Chaos cannot prevent him from speaking the word which makes light out of darkness; the evil deeds of men cannot prevent him from carrying through his plans; the good deeds of men cannot force him to reward them; the structure of being cannot prevent him from revealing himself; etc. Classical theology has spoken in more abstract terms of the aseity of God, of his being *a se,* self-derived. There is no ground prior to him which could condition his freedom; neither chaos nor nonbeing has power to limit or resist him. But aseity also means that there is nothing given in God which is not at the same time affirmed by his freedom. If taken nonsymbolically, this naturally leads to an unanswerable question, whether the structure of freedom, because it constitutes his freedom, is not itself something given in relation to which God has no freedom. The answer can only be that freedom, like the other ontological concepts, must be understood symbolically and in terms of the existential correlation of man and God. If taken in this way, freedom means that that which is man's ultimate concern is in no way dependent on man or on any finite being or on any finite concern. Only that which is unconditional can be the expression of unconditional concern. A conditioned God is no God.

Can the term "destiny" be applied symbolically to the divine life? The gods of polytheism have a destiny — or, more correctly, a fate — because they are not ultimate. But can one say that he who is unconditional and absolute has a destiny in the same manner in which he has freedom? Is it possible to attribute destiny to being-itself? It is possible, provided the connotation of a destiny-determining power above God is avoided and provided one adds that God is his own destiny and that in God freedom and destiny are one. It may be argued that this truth is more adequately expressed if destiny is replaced by necessity, not mechanical necessity, but structural necessity, of course, or if God is spoken of as being his own law. Such phrases are important as interpretations, but they lack two elements of meaning which are present in the word "destiny." They lack the mystery of that which precedes any structure and law, being-itself; and they lack the relation to history which is included in the term "destiny." If we say that God is his own destiny, we point both to the infinite mystery of being and to the participation of God in becoming and in history.

GOD AS SPIRIT AND THE TRINITARIAN PRINCIPLES

Spirit is the unity of the ontological elements and the *telos* of life. Actualized as life, being-itself is fulfilled as spirit. The word *telos* expresses the relation of life and spirit more precisely than the words "aim" or "goal." It expresses the inner directedness of life toward spirit, the urge of life to become spirit, to fulfil itself as spirit. *Telos* stands for an inner, essential, necessary aim, for that in which a being fulfils its own nature. God as living is God fulfilled in himself and therefore spirit. God *is* spirit. This is the most embracing, direct, and unrestricted symbol for the divine life. It does not need to be balanced with another symbol, because it includes all the ontological elements.

Some anticipatory remarks about spirit must be made at this point, although the doctrine of the spirit is the subject of a separate part of systematic theology. The word "spirit" (with a lower-case *s*) has almost disappeared from the English language as a significant philosophical term, in contrast to German, French, and Italian, in which the words *Geist, esprit,* and *spirito* have preserved their philosophical standing. Probably this is a result of the radical separation of the cognitive function of the mind from emotion and will, as typified in English empiricism. In any case, the word "spirit" appears predominantly in a religious context, and here it is spelled with a capital *S*. But it is impossible to understand the meaning of Spirit unless the meaning of spirit is understood, for Spirit is the symbolic application of spirit to the divine life.

The meaning of spirit is built up through the meaning of the ontological elements and their union. In terms of both sides of the three polarities one can say that spirit is the unity of power and meaning. On the side of power it includes centered personality, self-transcending vitality, and freedom of self-determination. On the side of meaning it includes universal participation, forms and structures of reality, and limiting and directing destiny. Life fulfilled as spirit embraces passion as much as truth, libido as much as surrender, will to power as much as justice. If one of these sides is absorbed by its correlate, either abstract law or chaotic movement remains. Spirit does not stand in contrast to body. Life as spirit transcends the duality of body and mind. It also transcends the triplicity of body, soul, and mind, in which soul is actual life-power and mind and body are its functions. Life as spirit is the life of the soul, which includes mind and body, but not as realities alongside the soul. Spirit is not a "part," nor is it a special function. It is the all-embracing function in which all elements of the structure of being participate. Life as spirit can be found by man only in man, for only in him is the structure of being completely realized.

The statement that God is Spirit means that life as spirit is the inclusive symbol for the divine life. It contains all the ontological elements. God is not nearer to one "part" of being or to a special function of being than he is to another. As Spirit he is as near to the creative darkness of the unconscious as he is to the critical light of cognitive reason. Spirit is the power through which meaning lives, and it is the meaning which gives direction to power. God as Spirit is the ultimate unity of both power and meaning. In contrast to Nietzsche, who identified the two assertions that God is Spirit and that God is dead, we must say that God is the living God because he is Spirit.

Any discussion of the *Christian* doctrine of the Trinity must begin with the christological assertion that Jesus is the Christ. The Christian doctrine of the Trinity is a corroboration of the christological dogma. The situation is different if we do not ask the question of the Christian doctrines but rather the question of the *presuppositions* of these doctrines in an idea of God. Then we must speak about the trinitarian principles, and we must begin with the Spirit rather than with the Logos. God is Spirit, and any trinitarian statement must be derived from this basic assertion.

God's life is life as spirit, and the trinitarian principles are moments within the process of the divine life. Human intuition of the divine always has distinguished between the abyss of the divine (the element of power) and the fulness of its content (the element of meaning), between the divine depth and the divine *logos*. The first principle is the basis of Godhead, that which makes God God. It is the root of his majesty, the unapproachable intensity of his being, the inexhaustible ground of being in which everything has its origin. It is the power of being infinitely resisting nonbeing, giving the power of being to everything that is. During the past centuries theological and philosophical rationalism have deprived the idea of God of this first principle, and by doing so they have robbed God of his divinity. He has become a hypostasized moral ideal or another name for the structural unity of reality. The power of the Godhead has disappeared.

The classical term *logos* is most adequate for the second principle, that of meaning and structure. It unites meaningful structure with creativity. Long before the Christian Era — in a way already in Heraclitus — *logos* received connotations of ultimacy as well as the meaning of being as being. According to Parmenides, being and the *logos* of being cannot be separated. The *logos* opens the divine ground, its infinity and its darkness, and it makes its fulness distinguishable, definite, finite. The *logos* has been called the mirror of the divine depth, the principle of God's self-objectification. In the *logos* God speaks his "word," both in himself and beyond himself. Without the second principle the first principle would be chaos, burning fire, but it would not be the creative ground. Without the second principle God is demonic, is characterized by absolute seclusion, is the "naked absolute" (Luther).

As the actualization of the other two principles, the Spirit is the third principle. Both power and meaning are contained in it and united in it. It makes them creative. The third principle is in a way the whole (God *is* Spirit), and in a way it is a special principle (God *has* the Spirit as he has the *logos*). It is the Spirit in whom God "goes out from" himself, the Spirit proceeds from the divine ground. He gives actuality to that which is potential in the divine ground and "outspoken" in the divine *logos*. Through the Spirit the divine fulness is posited in the divine life as something definite, and at the same time it is reunited in the divine ground. The finite is posited as finite within the process of the divine life, but it is reunited with the infinite within the same process. It is distinguished from the infinite, but it is not separated from it. The divine life is infinite mystery, but it is not infinite emptiness. It is the ground of all abundance, and it is abundant itself.

The consideration of the trinitarian principles is not the Christian doctrine of the Trinity. It is a preparation for it, nothing more. The dogma of the Trinity can be discussed only after the christological dogma has been elaborated. But the trinitarian principles appear whenever one speaks meaningfully of the living God.

The divine life is infinite, but in such a way that the finite is posited

in it in a manner which transcends potentiality and actuality. Therefore, it is not precise to identify God with the infinite. This can be
done on some levels of analysis. If man and his world are described
as finite, God is infinite in contrast to them. But the analysis must go
beyond this level in both directions. Man is aware of his finitude because he has the power of transcending it and of looking at it. Without this awareness he could not call himself mortal. On the other
hand, that which is infinite would not be infinite if it were limited by
the finite. God is infinite because he has the finite (and with it that
element of non-being which belongs to finitude) within himself united
with his infinity. One of the functions of the symbol "divine life" is to
point to this situation.

poetry as a game of knowledge

W. H. Auden

A poet is, before anything else, a person who is passionately in love
with language. Whether this love is a sign of his poetic gift or the
gift itself — for falling in love is given not chosen — I don't know, but
it is certainly the sign by which one recognizes whether a young man
is potentially a poet or not.

"Why do you want to write poetry?" If the young man answers: "I
have important things I want to say," then he is not a poet. If he
answers: "I like hanging around words listening to what they say,"
then maybe he is going to be a poet.

As T. S. Eliot has said in one of his essays, the sign of promise in a
young writer is not originality of idea or emotion, but technical competence. The subject matter of promising juvenilia is as a rule slight
and unimportant, the style derivative, but this slight derivative thing
is completely said.

"Squares and Oblongs," from *Poets at Work*, ed. Charles D. Abbott, New York,
1948, pp. 171–81. Copyright 1948 by Harcourt, Brace & World, Inc.; reprinted
by permission of Harcourt, Brace & World, Inc.

In the first stages of his development, before he has found his distinctive style, the poet is, as it were, engaged to language and, like any young man who is courting, it is right and proper that he should play the chivalrous servant, carry parcels, submit to tests and humiliations, wait hours at street corners, and defer to his beloved's slightest whims, but once he has proved his love and been accepted, then it is another matter. Once he is married, he must be master in his own house and be responsible for their relationship.

The poet is the father who begets the poem which the language bears. At first sight this would seem to give the poet too little to do and the language too much till one remembers that, as the husband, it is he, not the language, who is responsible for the success of their marriage which differs from natural marriage in that in this relationship there is no loveless lovemaking, no accidental pregnancies.

Poets, like husbands, are good, bad and indifferent. Some are Victorian tyrants who treat language like a doormat, some are dreadfully henpecked, some bored, some unfaithful. For all of them, there are periods of tension, brawls, sulky silences, and, for many, divorce after a few passionate years.

In the course of many centuries a few labor-saving devices have been introduced into the mental kitchen — alcohol, coffee, tobacco, benzedrine — but these mechanisms are very crude, liable to injure the cook, and constantly breaking down. Writing poetry in the twentieth century A.D. is pretty much the same as it was in the twentieth century B.C.: nearly everything has still to be done by hand.

Rhymes, meters, stanza-forms, etc., are like servants. If the master is just enough to win their affection and firm enough to command their respect, the result is an orderly happy household. If he is too tyrannical, they give notice; if he lacks authority, they become slovenly, impertinent, drunken and dishonest.

The poet who writes "free" verse is like Robinson Crusoe on his desert island: he must do all his cooking, laundry, darning, etc., for himself. In a few exceptional cases this manly independence produces something original and impressive, but as a rule the result is squalor — empty bottles on the unswept floor and dirty sheets on the unmade bed.

Milton's intuition in his *Ode on the Nativity* gives the lie to his personal overestimation of the poet's importance. If the Fall made man conscious of the difference between good and evil, then the Incarnation made him conscious of the difference between seriousness and frivolity and exorcised the world. Before that, one might say that only children, i.e. those in whom the consciousness of good and evil was not yet fully developed, could play games. The adult had to take frivolity seriously, i.e., turn games into magic, and in consequence could never wholeheartedly enjoy them because necessarily he was always anxious as to whether the magic would work this time.

Two theories of poetry. Poetry as a magical means for inducing desirable emotions and repelling undesirable emotions in oneself and others, or Poetry as a game of knowledge, a bringing to consciousness, by naming them, of emotions and their hidden relationships.

The first view was held by the Greeks, and is now held by MGM, Agit-Prop, and the collective public of the world. They are wrong.

Being ignorant of the difference between seriousness and frivolity, the Greeks confused art with religion. In spite of this, they produced great works of art. This was possible because in reality, like all pagans, they were frivolous people who took nothing seriously. Their religion was just a camp.

But we, whether Christians or not, cannot escape our consciousness of what is serious and what is not. Consequently, if we try to treat art as magic, we produce, not great works of art, but only dishonest and insufferably earnest and boring Agit-Prop for Christianity, Communism, Free Enterprise or what have you.

How can I know what I think till I see what I say? A poet writes "The chestnut's comfortable root" and then changes this to "The chestnut's customary root." In this alteration there is no question of replacing one emotion by another, or of strengthening an emotion, but of discovering what the emotion is. The emotion is unchanged, but waiting to be identified like a telephone number one cannot remember. "8357. No. that's not it. 8557, 8457, no, it's on the tip of my tongue, wait a moment, I've got it, 8657. That's it."

There are events which arouse such simple and obvious emotions that an AP cable or a photograph in *Life* magazine are enough and poetic comment is impossible. If one reads through the mass of versified trash inspired, for instance, by the Lidice Massacre, one cannot avoid the conclusion that what was really bothering the versifiers was a feeling of guilt at not feeling horrorstruck enough. Could a good poem have been written on such a subject? Possibly. One that revealed this lack of feeling, that told how when he read the news, the poet, like you and I, dear reader, went on thinking about his fame or his lunch, and how glad he was that he was not one of the victims.

Christianity knows of only one predestined life like the lives of the mythical heroes of Greek tragedy and this life is (a) not a myth, (b) not a tragedy. Further, esthetic values have nothing to do with its ritual representation; whether the Mass is well or badly sung is irrelevant.

If I understand what Aristotle means when he speaks of catharsis, I can only say he is wrong. It is an effect produced, not by works of art, but by bull-fights, professional football matches, bad movies and, in those who can stand that sort of thing, monster rallies at which ten thousand girl guides form themselves into the national flag.

If art were magic, then love lyrics would be love charms which made the Cruel Fair give one her latch key. In that case a magnum of champagne would be more artistic than a sonnet.

The girl whose boy-friend starts writing her love poems should be on her guard. Perhaps he really does love her, but one thing is certain: while he was writing his poems he was not thinking of her but of his own feelings about her, and that is suspicious. Let her remember St. Augustine's confession of his feelings after the death of someone he loved very much: "I would rather have been deprived of my friend than of my grief."

Everyone in his heart of hearts agrees with Baudelaire: "To be a useful person has always seemed to me something particularly horrible," for, subjectively, to be useful means to be doing not what one wants to do, but what someone else insists on one's doing. But at the same time, everyone is ashamed to admit in public that he is useless. Thus if a poet gets into conversation with a stranger in a railway coach and the latter asks him: "What is your job?," he will think quickly and say: "A schoolteacher, a beekeeper, a bootlegger," because to tell the truth would cause an incredulous and embarrassing silence.

The day of the Master's study with its vast mahogany desk on which the blotting paper is changed every day, its busts of Daunty, Gouty and Shopkeeper, its walls lined with indexed bookshelves, one of which is reserved for calf-bound copies of the Master's own works, is over for ever. From now on the poet will be lucky if he can have the general living room to himself for a few hours or a corner of the kitchen table on which to keep his papers. The soft carpets, the big desks, will all be reserved by the Management for the whopping liars.

Over too, the day of the salon and the café, the select group of enthusiastic rebels. No more movements. No more manifestoes. Every poet stands alone. This does not mean that he sulks mysteriously in a corner by himself; on the contrary he may, perhaps, lead a more social life than before, but as a neighbor like his neighbors, not as a poet. Where his gift is concerned, he stands alone and joins nobody, least of all his contemporary brother poets.

The ideal audience the poet imagines consists of the beautiful who go to bed with him, the powerful who invite him to dinner and tell him secrets of state, and his fellow-poets. The actual audience he gets consists of myopic schoolteachers, pimply young men who eat in cafeterias, and his fellow-poets. This means that, in fact, he writes for his fellow-poets.

Happy the lot of the pure mathematician. He is judged solely by his peers and the standard is so high that no colleague can ever win a reputation he does not deserve. No cashier writes articles in the Sunday *Times* complaining about the incomprehensibility of Modern Mathematics and comparing it unfavorably with the good old days when mathematicians were content to paper irregularly shaped rooms or fill bath-tubs with the waste-pipe open. Better still, since engineers and physicists have occasionally been able to put his equations to destructive use, he is even given a chair in a State University.

The poet is capable of every form of conceit but that of the social worker: — "We are all here on earth to help others; what on earth the others are here for I don't know."

How glad I am that the silliest remark ever made about poets, "the unacknowledged legislators of the world," was made by a poet whose work I detest. Sounds more like the secret police to me.

The Prophet says to men: "Thus saith the Lord."

The Poet says firstly to God: "Lord, do I mean what I say?" and secondly to men: "Do you mean what I mean?"

Agit-Prop says to men: "You mean what I say and to hell with the Lord who, even if he exists, is rotten with liberalism anyway."

From now on the only popular art will be comic art, like Groucho Marx or Li'l Abner, and this will be unpopular with the Management. Whatever their differences, highbrows and lowbrows have a common enemy, The Law (the Divine as well as the secular), and it is the Law which it cannot alter which is the subject of all comic art. What is not comic will either be highbrow art, or popular or official magic.

It is a sobering experience for any poet to read the last page of the Book Section of the Sunday *Times* where correspondents seek to identify poems which have meant much to them. He is forced to realize that it is not his work, not even the work of Dante or Shakespeare, that most people treasure as magic talismans in times of trouble, but grotesquely bad verses written by maiden ladies in local newspapers, that millions in their bereavements, heartbreaks, agonies, depressions, have been comforted and perhaps saved from despair by appalling trash while poetry stood helplessly and incompetently by.

The frightful falsehood which obsessed the Greeks and Romans and for which mankind has suffered ever since, was that government is a similar activity to art, that human beings are a medium like language out of which the gifted politician creates a good society as the gifted poet creates a good poem.

A society which really was like a poem and embodied all the esthetic values of beauty, order, economy, subordination of detail to the whole effect, would be a nightmare of horror, based on selective breeding, extermination of the physically or mentally unfit, absolute obedience to its Director, and a large slave class kept out of sight in cellars.

The poet writes:
    The mast-high anchor dives through a cleft
changes it to
    The anchor dives through closing paths
then to

> The anchor dives among hayricks

finally to

> The anchor dives through the floors of a church.

The cleft and the closing paths have been liquidated and the hayricks deported to another stanza.

There's Creative Politics and Scientific Government for you.

All poets adore explosions, thunderstorms, tornadoes, conflagrations, ruins, scenes of spectacular carnage. The poetic imagination is therefore not at all a desirable quality in a chief of state.

The democratic idea that anyone should be able to become president is right. For to talk of the profession of politics or a gifted politician ought to be nonsense. A good politician ought to mean someone who loves his neighbor and, with God's help, anyone can do that if he choose.

If God were a poet or took poetry seriously (or science too for that matter), he would never have given man free will.

The old superstition that it is dangerous to love a poet is perhaps not without some foundation. Given the opportunity, a poet is perhaps more tempted than others to drop his old innocent game of playing God with words, and take up that much more exciting but forbidden game of creating a human being, that game which starts off with such terrific gusto but always ends sooner or later in white faces and a fatal accident.

His life was like a poem. If so, he was a very great scoundrel who said to himself early in life: "I will explore every possibility of sinning and then repent on my death-bed." Faust? Exactly. Marlowe was not as intelligent as Goethe but he had more common sense. At least he knew that Faust went to hell. Faust is damned, not because he has sinned, but because he made a pact with the Devil, that is, like a poet he planned a life of sin beforehand.

The low-brow says: "I don't like poetry. It requires too much effort to understand and I'm afraid that if I learnt exactly what I feel, it would make me most uncomfortable." He is in the wrong, of course, but not so much in the wrong as the highbrow whose gifts make the effort to understand very little and who, having learned what he feels, is not at all uncomfortable, only interested.

Orpheus who moved stones is the archetype, not of the poet, but of Goebbels. The archetype, not of the poet as such, but of the poet who loses his soul for poetry, is Narcissus.

Being esthetes, the Greeks were naïve psychologists. Narcissus does not fall in love with his reflection because it is beautiful but because it is like himself. In a later version of the myth, it is a hydrocephalic idiot who gazes entranced into the pool, saying: "On me it looks good." In another, still more sophisticated version, Narcissus is neither beautiful nor ugly but as completely average as a Thurber husband, and instead of addressing his image with the declarative "I love you," he puts to it over and over again the same question, "Haven't we met before someplace?"

The present state of the world is so miserable and degraded that if anyone were to say to the poet: "For God's sake, stop humming and put the kettle on or fetch bandages. The patient's dying," I do not know how he could justifiably refuse. (There is, of course, an inner voice which says exactly this to most of us, and our only reply is to pretend to be extremely hard of hearing.) But no one says this. The self-appointed unqualified Nurse says: "Stop humming this instant and sing the Patient a song which will make him fall in love with me. In return I'll give you extra ration-cards and a passport"; and the poor Patient in his delirium cries: "Please stop humming and sing me a song which will make me believe I am free from pain and perfectly well. In return I'll give you a penthouse apartment in New York and a ranch in Arizona."

To such requests and to the bribes that go with them, the poet can only pray that he will always have the courage to stick out his tongue, say, like Olaf the conscientious objector in Cummings' poem, — "There is some s. I will not eat," — and go on humming quietly to himself.

Younger than any child

8:00   10:00   12:30

Mon   Bact   Clinic
Tue
Wed   Photo   English
Thus.   Nut.   Rad.